The Georgia Open History Library has been made possible in part by a major grant from the National Endowment for the Humanities: Democracy demands wisdom. Any views, findings, conclusions, or recommendations expressed in this collection, do not necessarily represent those of the National Endowment for the Humanities.

"The roots of the present lie deep in the past, and nothing in the past is dead to the man who would learn how the present came to be what it is."

SIR PATRICK HOUSTOUN, FIFTH BARONET
1698-1862
From the miniature owned by Mr. James Patrick Houstoun, Jr., of Houston, Texas.

The
HOUSTOUNS
of
GEORGIA

Edith Duncan Johnston

The University of Georgia Press
Athens

Copyright 1950
The University of Georgia Press

Reissue published in 2021

Most University Press titles are available from popular e-book vendors.

Printed digitally

ISBN 9780820359359 (Hardcover)
ISBN 9780820359342 (Paperback)
ISBN 9780820359335 (Ebook)

To the Memory of
My Sister
Eugenia Marion Johnston

Foreword to the Reissue

AMERICANS' search for identity has been long and varied, illuminating along the way the story of America itself. This massive, mobile nation comprises immigrants who have a strong sense of national identity, pledging allegiance to the flag. Yet these same people may still personally be lacking firm roots, concerned about the loss of community and collective memory in a rapidly changing and often unfamiliar modern world. If we know where we come from, it is so much easier to find out where we are and where we are going. Edith Duncan Johnston's *The Houstouns of Georgia* (1950) is part of that journey, a rewarding mix of genealogy and history that takes us to the heart of early America and what it means to be American.

French historian François Weil identifies four "genealogical regimes" in American family history over the last three centuries.[1] The first started with the initial European migration, as a quest for social status in an outpost of the British empire. The second began around the War of Independence and saw genealogy in Enlightenment terms, as an egalitarian, moral, and familial concern. The third, from the mid-nineteenth to the mid-twentieth century, was characterized by a link between ancestral pride, a search for the origins of (white) racial purity, and the emergence of nationhood. Its expansion was fuelled by the advent of professional genealogy and a growing market for genealogical instruction, aids, and resources. Finally, present-day approaches come out of the questioning of authority and hierarchy (especially racial dominance) associated with the 1960s. Facilitated by the internet and developments in DNA science, modern American genealogy has become much more inclusive and varied, dealing with diverse ethnicities. It is the second most popular hobby in the United States and the second-most common reason for using the internet. In 2017 Ancestry.com generated more than $1 billion in revenue (growing at more than 30 percent per annum) and had three million paying subscribers.

Published three years before a British American team introduced the world to the double helix, *The Houstouns of Georgia* comes from a distinct era. It is about *people* and the society and culture that formed them and was in turn shaped by them. The problem with DNA ancestry is that it prioritizes genetic relationships over social and cultural history. It tells us our ultimate origins but not how we came to be who we are. We are our experiences and memories, formed by the material environment in which we live and the human relationships we make, regardless of where we acquired our chromosomes.

The founder of the Georgia dynasty that so fascinates Johnston was Patrick Houstoun of Paisley, who came from what was then a small but growing burgh (town) to the west of Glasgow, Scotland. One of several Scottish lairds (gentlemen) who settled in Georgia the year after its foundation in 1733, he inherited a baronetcy in 1751, giving him the title Sir Patrick. He held several important Crown offices. One-fifth of the book is devoted to him, the remainder to his five sons, who together straddled the American Revolution and its aftermath. The author unpacks the family's divided loyalties during the rebellion against George III, dealing with each of the sons in turn: Patrick Jr. and George were Loyalists; John and James were outstanding patriots; George McIntosh, the husband of the Houstouns' only daughter, Ann Priscilla, allegedly betrayed the colonists' cause. Following a range of occupations (medicine, law, planting, commerce, military) the menfolk were also prominent in public service (the women were there, too, but usually in the background). They held positions in all three branches of the government of Georgia as well as national posts, including in the legislative bodies of the colony and state, delegate to the Continental Congress and to the Constitutional Convention (William, the fifth son), and governor of Georgia during and after the Revolution. Descendants continued to be important, including Ann Priscilla's son John Houstoun McIntosh, who was involved in the annexation of East Florida. Born in 1878, Edith Duncan Johnston carried on the family tradition of civic duty in Savannah in the local and national Girl Scouts, Episcopal Diocese of Georgia, and in the cofounding of a Savannah historical organization. She died in 1963.

The Houstouns of Georgia is a book about a family in a specific time and place, but it illustrates many important elements within mid-twentieth-century history, genealogy, and society. One is the emergence of accurate, evidence-based genealogy. Donald Lines Jacobus established the first scholarly genealogy journal, the*American Genealogist*, in 1922. His aim was to set out how to use documentary evidence found in libraries and archives to cater to, but also to discipline, the emerging mass market for genealogy as both memory and identity. A prolific writer, he established rigorous methodologies, which are evident in Johnston's study. Johnston made exhaustive and meticulous use of a wide range of primary sources--mostly official records, family papers, and newspapers--all carefully and extensively footnoted and furnished with a full index.

Elements of cultural folkways such as kinship systems, originating in Ireland and Scotland, can be found in locations removed from areas more readily identified with Irish, Scottish, and Scots-Irish settlers, such as the Appalachians. Georgia is one. But the book is not just about Scots or Americans or Scots Americans. It is also about what the American political commentator Walter Lippmann termed, more than a century ago, an "Atlantic community"."[2] He meant that Britain and America shared aspects of common cultural engagement and exchange. His call was lost for a time in the isolationism of American politics in the 1920s and 1930s. Yet a recognition of the "profound web of interest" among North Atlantic nations grew strongly in the very different climate of the 1940s and beyond. While they began in Georgia during the 1920s, Johnston's later labors, in a swathe of archives and libraries, located in the United States, Britain, and Jamaica, exemplify the spirit of this era.

This substantial history also adds greatly to our understanding of the transition from colony to state, through a richly detailed biographical study of two generations of a family that played a significant part in the process. That does not mean it is an integrated history of political, business, and social life in eighteenth-century Georgia. The genealogical detail is sometimes minute, seemingly of family interest alone. Family history research is, after all, inherently personal in nature. Even when exploring a well-known historical event or actor as the catalyst for undertaking research, the perspective remains microhistorical because grand historical narratives of nationhood and belonging sit firmly within a familial context. The past is personal for most family historians, and this is especially true in Johnston's book. As a genealogical study, *The Houstouns of Georgia* is more engaging than most; as a family biography, it is best appreciated as a labor of love.

It does, nevertheless, afford many arresting glimpses into a period of monumental change and thus helps us to develop an imaginative understanding of people in place and time. Because it is human in scale and covers private as well as public life, it draws us into a very different material and mental world, where family ties and close-knit webs of sociability pervaded religion, business, and politics. The noted British historian G. M. Trevelyan wrote movingly in 1949: "The poetry of history lies in the quasi-miraculous fact, that once, on this earth, on this familiar spot of ground, walked other men and women, as actual as we are today, thinking their own thoughts, swayed by their own passions, but now all gone, one generation vanishing after another; gone as utterly as we ourselves shall shortly be gone, like ghosts at cockcrow."[3] It is this poetry that *The Houstouns of Georgia* captures so perfectly.

RAB (ROBERT) HOUSTON

http://www.st-andrews.ac.uk/history/staff/rabhouston.html

Twitter: *@ScotHistorian*

Notes

1. François Weil, Family Trees: A History of Genealogy in America (Cambridge, Mass.: Harvard University Press, 2013).

2. Walter Lippmann, Editorial, New Republic, February 17, 1917, 59–61.

3. G. M. Trevelyan, An Autobiography and Other Essays (London: Longmans, Green, 1949), 13.

Foreword

AMONG the biographies of the Colonial period the only accounts of the Houstoun men are two short narratives by C. C. Jones, Jr., in his *Biographical Sketches of the Delegates from Georgia to the Continental Congress,* which, in the light of research, give only a hint of what the men of the Houstoun family contributed to early Georgia. There is scarcely a volume of the *Colonial* and of the *Revolutionary Records of the State of Georgia,* the histories, some manuscripts, and other source material that do not contain items of the deeds and written words of the subjects of this history.

Within the span of fifty years there lived in Georgia a father and five sons, each of whom entered public life and rendered service, according to his talents, to the king, to the Revolutionary cause, or to the molding of the state. I believe this can be said of no other Colonial family in Georgia. In every period of the state's early history notable men, equally patriotic and gifted, served Georgia, meriting praise: friends and associates of the Houstouns, who had sons that succeeded them. No other father, however, except Sir Patrick Houstoun, Baronet, President of His Majesty's Council, gave five sons to follow in his footsteps, each of whom played important roles of leadership, and who were conspicuous in their devotion to the colony, to the province, and to the state. Some of them extended their influence and their energies to national affairs.

When my sister, the late Eugenia Marion Johnston, and I began our research on the Houstouns in the spring of 1928, we had no idea what lay ahead of us. We were inexperienced and not too well-informed on Georgia history. We had in mind a book totally unlike a historical biography. Our intention, then, was to put consecutively in short paragraphs facts on the lives of the Houstouns in Georgia. As we delved deeper into our examination of records we decided that we had to change the character of our plan. As the years passed we found that the men's lives were so involved in the economic, political, and civic life of Savannah and of the state that it was necessary to give, always, a historical background for each episode.

We started our research in the archives of Georgia, and from those records clues led us far afield, until by persistent research, and through correspondence both in this country and abroad, material was accumulated. By assembling facts concerning the Houstoun family of Georgia, we obtained valuable information from innumerable sources that helped to round out the story. I am confident that we have not exhausted all of the sources of information which might give the final record. While this is a history of a private family that lived in Savannah and on a near-by plantation, the background is Georgia history, necessarily so, but that has been made subservient to the life and work of the men of whom we have written.

It is not out of place, I think, to give the correct spelling and pronunciation of the name *Houstoun* as it is used in Georgia. We were informed, reliably, that in Scotland, it is pronounced "Hooseton"; in Georgia it has been, and is, pronounced "Houseton," and not "Huseton." The *Colonial* and the *Revolutionary Records of the State of Georgia* show the last syllable sometimes with the *u* and sometimes without it. Occasionally it was spelled "Howstown."

An evaluation of the Houstoun family is given here by quoting from one of Georgia's accredited historians, the Reverend George White, who, in his *Statistics of the State of Georgia*, wrote in 1849:

"The Houstouns are among the most ancient and reputable families in Georgia. The name often occurs in the history of our State, when under the direction of the Trustees, under Royal Government and after it had in connection with the other colonies declared itself independent. . . . Sir Patrick Houstoun was a prominent man under the Royal Government, being Register of Grants, and one of the Councillors when John Reynolds was Governor of Georgia."

Edith Duncan Johnston.

Savannah, Georgia

Acknowledgments

A BOOK of this character, dependent as it is on such varied and scattered sources of information, can be written only with the assistance of innumerable persons. Fortunately, the willingness to help of the many individuals, specialists, and others on whom I have called has made the writing not only possible but exceedingly pleasant.

First I wish to pay tribute to my sister, the late Eugenia Marion Johnston. We worked together for ten happy years, and her guiding spirit has been with me during the years I have worked alone. To her memory I have dedicated the book which originated with her.

Five persons, especially, I wish to mention for their generous help and encouragement, and to whom I render sincere and hearty thanks. But while expressing my gratitude I do not wish to suggest that they are in any way responsible for the book's shortcomings:

Mrs. Marmaduke H. Floyd of Savannah, authority on Georgia Colonial history and author of many monographs and articles on Georgia history.

Dr. Philip Davidson, dean of the Graduate School and of the Senior College of Vanderbilt University, Nashville, Tennessee.

Mr. Walter Charlton Hartridge of Savannah, student of history and editor of *The Letters of Don Juan McQueen to His Family* and of *The Letters of Robert Mackay to His Wife*.

Mr. Charles Francis Jenkins of Germantown, Pennsylvania, president of the Historical Society of Pennsylvania, author of *Button Gwinnett, Signer of the Declaration of Independence*, and of other works.

Dr. E. Merton Coulter, Head of the History Department at the University of Georgia and author of several books of history and biography on Georgia subjects.

It would have been impossible for my sister and me even to have begun writing without the guidance of Mrs. Floyd who taught us the technique of research, introduced us to some source material, and aided us repeatedly in special problems.

To Dr. Davidson, to whom we submitted part of the original draft of the manuscript, we owe the first words of encouragement. His many illuminating suggestions on planning and writing the book we tried to follow.

Mr. Hartridge has been an interested and an enthusiastic critic. Besides the many valuable suggestions he has offered, he has read the manuscript many times, he has contributed several important items from his research, and to his persistent "prodding" the completion of the book in its present form is largely due.

My correspondence with Mr. Jenkins through the years introduced me to a friendly and scholarly spirit whose advice, interest, and gifts of historical papers have heartened me many times.

Dr. Coulter has rendered me a service which I can repay only by these inadequate words. He read the entire manuscript, he made many suggestions for its improvement, he recommended it and he helped to further its publication. The assistance of so distinguished a historian has been a privilege and a most rewarding experience.

The many persons connected with the following organizations, offices, and libraries have given me assistance and have accorded me privileges for which I am grateful:

The Georgia Society of the Colonial Dames of America for the use of its library in Colonial Dames House, Savannah; the office of the Secretary of State, Atlanta; the Department of Archives and History of the State of Georgia, Atlanta; the Library of Congress; the Historical Society of Pennsylvania; the United States War Department, Adjutant General's Office; the United States Veterans Bureau; the General Land Office of the Department of the Interior; the New York Public Library; the New York Historical Society; the Savannah Public Library, especially the Reference Department; the Savannah Historical Research Association; the British Museum; the University of Edinburgh and St. Andrew's University, Scotland, and the Institute of Jamaica, B.W.I.

Last, but not least, there is a long list of individuals that I cannot omit because they have been gracious in assisting me in many ways which are impossible to specify:

Colonel F. W. Alstaetter (U.S.A., retired); Dr. Victor H. Bassett (deceased); Mr. Marmaduke H. Floyd; Miss Ola M. Wyeth; Miss Elizabeth Hodge; Miss Margaret Goodley; Mrs. Forman M.

Hawes; Mr. Thomas F. Walsh, attorney-at-law (deceased); Judge Raiford Falligant (deceased); Mr. William B. Clarke, A.I.A. (deceased); Mr. George H. Hoffmann; Mrs. Peter W. Meldrim (deceased); Mr. Raiford J. Wood; Miss Edith Inglesby; Mrs. S. Branch LaFar (deceased); Mr. James M. Holland, formerly superintendent of Fort Pulaski National Park, Cockspur Island; Judge Alexander R. MacDonell; Mr. G. Lloyd Roberts, former British Consul; Mr. Victor Schreck (deceased); Mr. W. Feay Shellman, of the City Engineer's Office; Mr. W. F. Shellman, Jr.; Lieutenant Smedley, formerly of the United States Engineer's Office; Mrs. J. C. Thompson; Mrs. Charles E. Waring; Miss Clermont Lee; Mr. Malcolm Maclean Young; Mr. G. Noble Jones; Colonel A. R. Lawton, attorney-at-law, all of Savannah.

Mrs. J. E. Hays, State Historian; Mrs. Perryman Little; Miss Ruth Blair; Mrs. Macartan Campbell Kollock (deceased); Miss Susan Marion Kollock; Dr. James Houstoun Johnston; Mrs. M. Hines Roberts; Mrs. George C. Griffin, Miss Elmira Boone, all of Atlanta. Mrs. Charles W. Rooney, of Decatur, Georgia.

Dr. Clarence S. Brigham, Director of the American Antiquarian Society, Worcester, Massachusetts; Mr. William Reitzell, Director of the Historical Society of Pennsylvania, Philadelphia; Miss Mary A. Givens of the staff of the Historical Society of Pennsylvania; Mr. James Marion Johnston of Chevy Chase, Maryland; Miss Mary A. Benjamin of New York City; Dr. James J. Waring of Denver, Colorado; Mr. J. Frederick Waring of Savannah and Hudson, Ohio; Miss Jessie L. Farnum, secretary to the Librarian, Library of Congress, Washington, D. C.; Mr. John Coddington, of Alexandria, Virginia; Mr. James Patrick Houstoun of Houston, Texas (deceased); Mrs. Isaac Read of Augusta, Georgia (deceased); Dr. Albert B. Saye, University of Georgia, Athens; Mr. Bayard Clinch Heyward of "Lamont," Habersham County, Georgia (deceased); Miss Fitsimmons, Librarian, Charleston Library, Charleston, South Carolina; Miss Bessie Lewis of Darien, Georgia; Miss Emma Bull of Charleston, South Carolina; Reverend George Muir of Renfrewshire, Scotland; Mr. J. J. Haggart-Spiers, Proprietor of Houston House, Renfrewshire, Scotland; Mrs. A. May Osler of Kent, England.

Finally, acknowledgement and my gratitude are due to the many lineal descendants of the Georgia Houstouns who have made possible the publication of this book. A list of the contributors will be found in the Appendix.

Contents

CHAPTER   PAGE

PART. I. *Sir Patrick and Lady Houstoun*

I.	The Heritage of the Georgia Houstouns	1
II.	Doctor William Houstoun, Botanist	9
III.	Patrick Houstoun in Georgia	21
IV.	Patrick Houstoun's Predicaments	35
V.	Marriage and Private Life	43
VI.	Patrick Houstoun's Public Life	61
VII.	Last Years and Death	94
VIII.	Lady Houstoun	99

PART II. *Georgia's Call to the Five Sons*

IX.	Sir Patrick Houstoun, Sixth Baronet	107
X.	Sir George Houstoun, Baronet, Man of Affairs	131
XI.	John Houstoun, "Rebell Governor"	193
XII.	James Houstoun, Surgeon in the Continental Army	291
XIII.	William Houstoun, Delegate to the Continental Congress	317
XIV.	Ann Priscilla, Wife of George McIntosh, and Their Son John Houstoun McIntosh	343
	Bibliography	391
	Appendix. Houstoun Descendants	403

Illustrations

Sir Patrick Houstoun, Baronet	Frontispiece
	FACING PAGE
Old Wing of Houstoun Castle	4
Sir Patrick and Lady Houstoun	50
Memorial to Sir Patrick Houstoun, Sixth Baronet	129
Sir George Houstoun, Seventh Baronet	131
Priscilla Houstoun	142
Robert James Mossman Houstoun	142
Colonel James Johnston, Jr.	163
Mrs. James Johnston, Jr.	163
Ann, Lady Houstoun	186
John Houstoun	193
Jonathan Bryan	225
Interior Views of John Houstoun's Residence	254
William Houstoun	317
Silver Watch, Gift of William Houstoun to his Brother, John	318
Six Houstoun Signatures	342
Colonel John Houstoun McIntosh	367
Mrs. John Houstoun McIntosh	367
The Refuge, Camden County, Georgia	382

MAPS

Plan of Rosdue Plantation	30
Plan of John Houstoun's White Bluff plantation	240
Portion of Henry Poppell's Map of North America, 1733	268

Title page design by Christopher Murphy, Jr.

Coat-of-arms from the original stone on the monument in Bonaventure Cemetery, Savannah, Georgia

Part I

SIR PATRICK AND LADY HOUSTOUN

Chapter I

THE HERITAGE OF THE GEORGIA HOUSTOUNS

SCOTTISH knights, earls, and lairds were the forebears of the Houstouns of Georgia. Patrick Houstoun, founder of the family in America, sailed for Savannah within a year of the establishment of the colony in 1733. He came from a long line of knights dating back to the twelfth century, and his inherited title, which he did not obtain until after twenty years' residence in Georgia, was conferred upon his grandfather, Sir Patrick Houstoun, Kt., by Charles II, when he was created first baronet in 1668.

The family of Houstoun in Scotland traces its name to Hugo de Padvinan, from Normandy, who obtained a grant of the barony of Kilpeter from "Baldwin de Bigres, Vice-comes de Lanark, i. e. Baldwin of Bigger, Sheriff of Lanark," in the reign of Malcolm IV (1153-65).[1] When names become fixed and hereditary "they are the most ancient which are derived from baronies and lands, and when these lands have only been enjoyed by the same family, it is manifest proof, that that name and family is of great antiquity."[2] The only other extant record of Hugo de Padvinan shows that he was one of the "witnesses" to Walter, high steward of Scotland's foundation charter of the Abbey of Paisley, about the year 1160.

Hugo's son, Sir Reginald, who succeeded him, obtained his lands of Kilpeter from Walden, the son of Baldwin of Bigar. From Walter, the high steward of Scotland, Sir Hugh, the son of Sir Reginald, received a confirmation of his grandfather's and father's lands. Sir Hugh was a benefactor to the monks of Paisley by bestowing upon them, in 1225, an annuity of "half a Merk" out of his lands of Achinhoss. The successor of Sir Hugh, his son

---

1. William Semple, *The History of the Shire of Renfrew. . . . Brought from the earliest accounts to the year MDCCX by Mr. George Crawfurd: And continued to the Present Period* (Paisley, MDCCLXXXII), 102.
2. *Ibid.*, 103.

Sir Finley de Houstoun, who lived in the reign of Alexander III, subscribed to the bond of submission to Edward I of England, commonly called Ragman Roll, in 1296.[3] Sir Finley was designated chevalier.

From those ancient Houstoun barons descended, in the reign of James II of Scotland, Sir Patrick Houstoun, Knight. He married Maria Colquhoun. He died in 1450 and his wife in 1456. He left a son and heir, Sir John, who died the same year as his father. By his wife, Ann Campbell, he left a son, Sir Peter Houstoun, who was with James IV at the battle of Flodden and who was killed September 9, 1513. Sir Peter married Helen Shaw "of an ancient family"; and their son, Sir Patrick, who obtained his knighthood from James IV, was associated with John, Earl of Lennox, in rescuing the Prince out of the custody of the Earls of Arran and Angus. Sir Patrick was slain at Avon near the town of Linlithgow in 1526, leaving a son by Janet Cunningham, "his lady." John, who was his son and heir, obtained a charter of Barons of Houstoun from James V in 1528. His wife was Agnes Hopepringle, a daughter of Hopepringle of Torsance, and he died in 1542, to be succeeded by his son Patrick, who was knighted by James VI. By his wife, another Janet Cunningham, Patrick had four sons and five daughters. Janet Cunningham was the daughter of Gabriel Cunningham of Craigsends. Sir Patrick Houstoun died in 1605, and his son John succeeded him. Sir John Houstoun, Kt., married Margaret, daughter of Sir James Stirling of Kier, and died in 1609. Their son, Sir Ludowick, Kt., married Margaret, daughter of Peter Maxwell of Newark by whom he had Patrick, his successor, and George, first of the Houstouns of Johnstone, and several daughters. Sir Ludowick died in 1662.

Sir Patrick, the son of Sir Ludowick, was a baron "of ample fortune" and was advanced by Charles II to the degree of baronet, his patent bearing date at Whitehall the last day of February, 1668. Before his father's death Patrick had married the Honourable Anna Hamilton, daughter of Sir John Hamilton who was created first Lord Bargany in the Peerage of Scotland, November 16, 1641.[4] Sir John matriculated at Glasgow University in 1624 as

---
3. *Ibid.*
4. Sir James Balfour Paul, *The Scots Peerage* (Edinburgh, 1904-1914), II, 28.

Sir John Hamilton of Bargame, and in 1635 he was commissioner to prevent the spread of plague and was served heir-general to his father April 23, 1642. Sympathetic to the Royalist cause during England's Civil War, Sir John, both a Horse and Foot Colonel, accompanied in 1649 the Duke of Hamilton on the "Expedition" into England. He was captured and upon his release from prison a year later went to the Netherlands. In 1651 he returned to Scotland with Prince Charlie. Captured a second time by the Cromwellian forces, Lord Bargany was imprisoned in the Tower. Released in 1652, he acquired during the next year the barony of Monktoun from James, Earl of Abercorn. Hardly a model subject in the eyes of the Lord Protector, Lord Bargany was excluded from the Act of Grace of April 12, 1654.[5] When the Stuart line was restored to the English throne in 1660, Sir John Hamilton was doubtless relieved. Two years after the Restoration he married Lady Jean Douglas, daughter of Sir William Douglas. In 1668 Lord Bargany died.

The Honourable Anna Hamilton's lineage was distinguished. She was the great-great-granddaughter of the second Earl of Arran; and was sixth in descent from the Princess Mary Stewart (daughter of James II, of Scotland) who married in 1469, under Papal dispensation, Sir James, first Lord Hamilton (1415-1479). He became one of the most trusted friends and counsellors of James III. By his marriage to "the king's sister, the house of Hamilton gained a great position, and became the nearest family to the throne."[6] The grandson of Lord Hamilton, James, second Earl of Arran and first Duke of Chatelberault, accompanied James V on his "matrimonial expedition" to France in 1536, and when the king died on December 14, 1542, a few days before the birth of his daughter Mary (1542-1579), Lord Hamilton was chosen governor of the realm during the minority of the infant queen. On "March 13, 1542/3, an act of State declared the Earl to be the second person in the kingdom and heir to the throne, failing the young Queen, to whom he was appointed tutor."[7]

Sir Patrick Houstoun, first baronet, and his wife, Anna Ham-

---

5. Lieutenant George Hamilton, *A History of the House of Hamilton* (Edinburgh, 1933), 104.
6. Leslie Stephen and Sidney Lee, eds., *Dictionary of National Biography* (New York, London, 1908), VIII, 1046.
7. *Ibid.*, 1042.

ilton, were the parents of five sons and four daughters: John, who succeeded to the title; Patrick; William; James; and Archibald; Margaret; Ann; Joan; and Henrietta.[8] Sir Patrick died in 1696. Lady Houston, it is said, was so frightened by the soldiers during the "convenanting troubles" that she "fell in a fever and died a few days later,"[9] May 3, 1678.

On the death of his father Sir Patrick Houstoun, first baronet, inherited the estate prior to receiving his title in 1668. The castle and barony of Houstoun on the river Guise was situated on an eminence which "afforded a very agreeable prospect of most of the shire." In 1710 the historian Crawfurd described the barony as "a large court which . . . has a most beautiful avenue fronting . . . the castle, regularly planted, and has orchards, gardens and a park equal to many in this part of the kingdom, with delectable woods surrounding almost the house."[10] It was a "real fortification," and formed a complete square, with an extensive area on the inside. "There was a large and very high tower on the north west corner which was the oldest part of the building with a lower house joined to the east end of the tower, having vaults below and a long and wide paved hall above, with antique windows in the front and without plaster on the roof. The timbers of the roof were arched and made of massive oak. On the front to the south were two turrets, between which was the grand entry into the area, arched above and secured by a portcullis. Over the door and entrance of one of the wings was inscribed:

Anno.   Dom.
16   25

The blessing of God rest upon this house
and familie, making us to do thy will, O Lord,—
For the just live by faith.—Heb. 10.[11]

---

8. Semple, 105.
9. Hamilton, *A History of the House of Hamilton*, 104.
10. *Ibid.*, 102.
11. Houstoun Family Papers owned by James Patrick Houstoun, Jr., of Houston, Texas. In the summer of 1934, through correspondence with the Reverend George Muir, minister of the old parish of Houston and Killellan, the author learned that Mr. A. A. Hagart Speirs was the owner of Houstoun house. Mr. Speirs kindly sent a photograph of the old wing, which, however, is not the oldest part, and also one of the new building attached to the wing.

OLD WING OF HOUSTOUN CASTLE, FACING AREA,
RENFREWSHIRE, SCOTLAND

Courtesy of Mr. A. A. Hagart-Spiers, of Houston, Scotland

Connected with the castle was the parish church of Houston where, as early as 1450, the Houstoun knights and their ladies were interred. A "fair monument" was erected to the memory of Sir Patrick Houstoun, who died in 1450, and to his wife. The inscription is in Latin:

> Hic jacet Patricius Houstoun de
> eodem, miles, qui obit anno
> MCCCCL
> Et D. Maria Colquhoun, spousa dicti
> domini Patricius quae obit
> MCCCCLVI[12]

Sir Patrick's son and successor was also entombed in the chapel "under a canopy of freestone with the effigies of himself and his lady as big as the life; about the verge of which tomb is the inscription in Saxon capitals:

> Here lies Patrick[13] Houstoun lord of that ilk, and
> Annes Campbell his Spouse, who died anno 1456."[14]

The effigy, representing Sir John Houstoun, "is dressed in a coat of mail, his head lying on a pillow and his feet on a lion, with wide mouth holding a lamb in his paws under him, the image of the lady is dressed in grave clothes neatly cut in stone, both hands elevated as in a praying or supplicating posture."[15]

Among the many Houstouns buried in the chapel was Lady Anna Houstoun, wife of Sir Patrick Houstoun, first baronet. On her tomb was inscribed:

> Hic Sita est Domina Hamilton dilectissma Patricii
> Houstoun deodem Baronetti Conjux suo quae obit
> tertio die idus Maias anno Salutis parta Milesimo
> Sexcentessimo et Septuagesimo octavo.[16]

---

12. Semple, 103.
13. Semple evidently made an error in copying, as the previous paragraph mentions Sir John who was the husband of Ann Campbell.
14. Semple, 104.
15. Houstoun Family Papers. In 1934, Mr. Muir wrote of the effigies, which have survived: "these have been mounted on a large slab, and are housed in a special chamber which was built to contain them. They are in excellent preservation, and have been much admired by several experts."
16. Mr. Muir wrote of the tomb: "There is also a mural tablet in this chamber, a memorial to Lady Anna Hamilton, the wife of Sir Patrick Houstoun. Some of the figures are unfortunately somewhat mutilated and the inscription is now difficult to read."

The Houstoun coat-of-arms is described by Crawfurd: "The coat armorial of this ancient family is *or*, a chevron checquie *azure* and *argent*, betwixt three martlets *sable*, supported by two hinds [rampart—a broken column] and for crest a sand-glass [inverted with the sands running out] and with this motto, 'In time'."[17] The story of the origin of the emblem is that at an early period in the history of the Houstouns, "John Houstoun [?] with a body of soldiers reinforced a broken column, and for his courage and unexampled energy was knighted on the field of battle. The grey hounds or hinds indicate the fleetness of his command in coming to the rescue; the last sands of the hour glass, the perilous extremity of the army; and the motto, 'In time', the victory."[18]

Sir Patrick Houstoun, first baronet, was succeeded by his son John, who married Lady Ann Drummond. Their son, John, who became the third baronet married Lady Mary Shaw, and their son, John, fourth baronet, married the Honourable Eleanor Cathcart, daughter of Charles, Lord Cathcart. When Sir John Houstoun, fourth baronet, died in 1751, without male issue, the title reverted to his cousin, Patrick (son of Patrick, the second son of the first baronet), who was then living in Georgia, in America.

Before the Georgia Houstoun received his title, the barony of Houstoun was sold, and finally became the property of James McRae, governor of Bombay, in the East Indies, who left the estate to James M'Guire, of Ayrshire; and his son "in 1780-81 demolished the manor or castle of Houstoun, and applied the stones thereto to the building of a new town . . . ."[19] In April, 1782, the barony of Houstoun was alienated to Alexander Speirs, Esq., of Elderslee.

When the parishes of Houstoun and Killellan were united in 1771, a larger church was needed, and in 1774 a new building was erected on the same site. It is thought some parts of the old chapel were incorporated in the new church. In 1874, however, the building, which had stood for a hundred years, was torn down,

---

17. Semple, 105.
18. Houstoun Family Papers.
19. Semple, *The History of the Shire of Renfrew*, 106.

and a new one was built as a memorial to Captain Speirs of Elderslee.[20]

---

20. Letter from the Reverend George Muir, of Scotland, July 14, 1934.

> General Sam Houston (1793-1863), of Texas, came from Scotch-Irish descent. In the *Houston Post*, April 24, 1916, the genealogy of General Houston is given as being of Scotch-Irish descent and shows that his line goes back only to 1450. The genealogy was compiled by F. M. Houston of Bourbon County, Kentucky. He gives Robert House Son of Ireland as the ancestor who *may* have been a second or third son of the knighted Houstouns. He was born in Dublin in 1450, and his lineal descendant, Alfred, who was born in 1752, came to Jamestown, Virginia, and changed his name to Houston. He was an ancestor of General Houston, who was born in Rockbridge County, Virginia, in 1793.

Chapter II[1]

DOCTOR WILLIAM HOUSTOUN, BOTANIST

DOCTOR William Houstoun, a kinsman of the Patrick Houstoun who went to Georgia, played an important part in the latter's venture to the new land because he presented to the Georgia Trustees Patrick's application for a grant in the youngest English colony. He was then negotiating with the Trustees for a position on his own account, and the results were to make him prominent among the savants of his time. It is a matter of conjecture whether or not Dr. Houstoun ever touched the shore of Georgia before Oglethorpe founded the first settlement, but the evidence seems likely. He was appointed botanist for the colony in the summer of 1732 and gave great assistance in the development of the Trustees' Garden in Savannah by sending specimens of tropical plants from the West Indies to be cultivated in the experimental garden laid out on the bank of the river. His connection with the Colony of Georgia reveals the standing of his branch of the family in Scotland and, also, the position he held as a scientist of his day.

One of the children of Sir Patrick Houstoun, first baronet, and his wife, Anna Hamilton, was William, who, if the date of his birth, 1695[2], is correct, was born one year before the first baronet died. He would thus have been the uncle of Patrick Houstoun of Georgia, with only three years' difference in their ages. While the conjecture could be true, the more likely surmise is that Dr. William Houstoun and the younger Patrick were cousins and therefore of the same generation.

The scientist, a native of Scotland, had already become well known in London before he brought his kinsman's name to the attention of the Georgia Trustees. Dr. Houstoun died in 1733, at the age of thirty-eight, but he had an interesting career, and

---

1. This chapter was printed first in *The Georgia Historical Quarterly*, XXV, No. 4 (December, 1941), 325-339. The first paragraph was re-written to conform to this narrative.
2. *Dictionary of National Biography* (1908), IX, 1319.

the results he attained have lived after him. No facts of his early life have been obtained. If the evidence previously mentioned can support the theory that he was the first baronet's son, he was born in the old Castle; if not, at least he grew up in its atmosphere as another branch of the family lived in the county of Renfrewshire at Johnstone Castle, approximately ten miles from Glasgow. In preparation for the profession of surgeon and botanist, Dr. Houstoun matriculated at some of the foremost universities in Europe. He was enrolled as a student of St. Salvators College of the University of St. Andrews, Scotland, on February 19, 1719.[3] In the eighteenth century the qualifications for entering a European university required a high standard of scholarship. Dr. Houstoun must have acquired that at the University of St. Andrews. Eight years later, October 6, 1727, he entered the University of Leyden, where he studied medicine under the great Herman Boerhaave (1668-1738), who had been connected with that university since the year 1705, when he became professor of botany and medicine. Princes and noblemen were sent to Leyden to be instructed by "the illustrious Boerhaave, physician of Europe," who was so styled by a Chinese mandarin. When Peter the Great (1672-1725), attended the university he elected that his studies should include a course under the tutelage of Professor Boerhaave, who was to his students "not only an indefatigable teacher, but an affectionate guardian."[4] While Dr. Houstoun was a student at the University of Leyden, "he performed in conjunction with Van Sweeten, the experiments in animal respiration in the 'Philosophical Transactions' under the title 'Experimenta de Perfontaine Thoracis ejusque in Respiratione Effectibus'."[5] In 1728 he was elected to the French Academy of Science. Dr. Houstoun was graduated a doctor of medicine, Leyden University, in 1722, and shortly afterward he arrived in England, where he was elected a Fellow of the Royal Society. Then it was that he seems to have turned his attention almost exclusively to botany. In 1732 he obtained the degree of doctor

---

3. Obtained from the Secretary of The University, St. Andrews, January 24, 1938.
4. *Encyclopaedia Britannica* (ninth edition), III, 855.
5. *Dictionary of National Biography*, IX, 1319-1320.

of medicine from the University of St. Andrews.[6] In the year 1730 he entered the service of the South Sea Company[7] and was given the position of surgeon on one of its ships that plied between the British Isles and South America. At the same time he was also in the employ of Sir Hans Sloane, to whom he wrote on the flora of the tropics and on the specimens he had collected while on shore. To be a protege of Sir Hans Sloane in the 1730's was a marked distinction. Sir Hans was a physician to the nobility and a botanist of eminence. He was born in Ireland in 1660, of Scottish ancestry, and in his youth he showed a decided taste for gathering objects of natural history. In time he became a collector and while studying medicine included botany in his studies. Sloane travelled extensively on the continent of Europe and was given his degree of doctor of medicine by the University of Orange. On his return to England, after some of his journeys, he was elected to membership in the Royal Society. When he became a member of the College of Surgeons he went to Jamaica in the suite of the Duke of Albermarle, and spent over a year collecting hundreds of specimens, the descriptions of which he embodied in a Latin catalogue. When he was again in London he was elected secretary of the Royal Society, and was appointed physician general to the army. In 1716, he was created a baronet and "was the first medical practitioner to receive an hereditary title."[8] When Dr. Houstoun came under his notice, Sir Hans was president of the Royal Society, having succeeded Sir Isaac Newton in 1727.

By 1730, Dr. Houstoun had reached Jamaica. From Kingston, in December of that year, he sent Sir Hans a report of his studies and of his collection of plants. Apologizing first for his not having written for sometime, giving as his reason he had "nothing worth troubleing" him about, Houstoun continued, "I cannot flatter my-

---

6. "It appears that 'William Houstoun' sometime student in this University, obtained the degree of Doctor of Medicine of the University in 1732." Letter to the author from Andrew Bennett, Secretary, The University, St. Andrews, January 24, 1938.
7. Although the collapse of that company occurred in 1721, it continued to exist without great prosperity until the nineteenth century. *Encyclopaedia Britannica* (1929-32), Vol. 21, p. 94.
8. *Ibid.* (ninth edition, 1894), XXII, 160. Sir Hans Sloane died in 1753, and he left to the British Museum, to be purchased, his collection of books, drawings, prints, etc., valued at considerably more than £20,000.

self so far as to think anything I am to communicate to you now deserves your notice yet I chuse rather to run the risk of beeing troublesome than negligent." With the letter, he wrote, he was sending a "Collection of Plants and other natural curiosities from Vera Cruz." Then followed a description of his work:

    ... The Drawing of the Manufactory of Cochoneel I did from an Indian Painting in the possession of one M^r· Knightsbridge an English Gentleman who has been long in the Kingdom of Mexico, the description too I copied from him, but there are some things in it which seem very incoherent, particularly touching the generation of the animal. Tho' all the Jallap is exported from Vera Cruz, yet I could learn nothing there concerning it; but when I go back, if I can have leave from my Superiors, I design to take a journey to that Province. The Contrayerva used in England is the root of the Dorstenia Pluvis N.G. There are two kinds of it, whose roots are used indifferently, and the Plants themselves are not very unlike to one another; tho' plainly distinct species; as you may see by the dryed specimens, and I can confirm who have seen them growing. The first kind has its leaves cut deep, and the calix (or rather Placenta) which sustains the flower, is oval and erect. This is the Dorstenia Sphondylu folio, Dentariae radice Pl. N.G. and probably the Juspatli of Herdnandez 147. it grows some few leagues from Vera Cruz where I purchased some plants of it in earth, and have brought the box to Jamaica, but in the Hurrican which we met with at Sea, I lost all that was above ground of it, and am afraid the roots are dead too. The second kind has its leaves sometimes shaped like those of violets, but more frequently angular, and sometimes divided, but never near so deep as in the other kind. Its calix is quadrangular oblong, and placed transversely upon the footstalk. The figure in Plumiers N.G. has been done from it, and it seems to be the Caapia of Piso. This I found growing plentifully about Campechy, on high stony ground, and always in the shade. I brought some plants of it in earth to Jamaica, but dare not send them home at this time of year. I met with a great many Plants on the Continent which I could not possibly reduce to any Genus yet described, and therefor have made bold to characterize some of them, giveing them the names of Botanists, which is a practice now authorized by custom. But as I have but few books here to consult, it's very possible that they may have been described already by some person or other; wherefor I desire to submit my Nova Genera, in that as in all other points to your better judgement. . . .⁹

The botanist concluded his letter to Sir Hans by assuring him that he was always ready to serve him to his utmost powers and begged his employer not to expect him "to do so much as if I lived ashore," because "of the many hindrances that one must necessarily meet with in a sea faring life and especially in a small vessel."¹⁰

Before Dr. Houstoun again wrote to his benefactor, the ship on which he was employed had suffered disaster on the coast of Mexico, and he was much perturbed over the possibility of his not being retained as a surgeon of the South Sea Company. In another communication he asked the assistance of Sir Hans in recommending him for his reappointment. It will be seen from the letter that Dr. Houstoun had planned a trip to Carolina and was to depart for England in two weeks' time. From that sentence in his letter the deduction is made that he carried out his intention of disembarking at Charles Town on his way home, and so may have touched on what was later to be Georgia soil, then part of the colony of South Carolina. If so, he became familiar with the climate, the tidewater and the flora of that region. The letter was written from "La Vera Cruz, March 5 O.S., 1731":

> The Honb.ᵗᵉ S.S. Company's Snow *Assiento* whereof I was Surgeon, was unfortunately drove ashoar here and lost the 6th of last month. I had indeed the good luck to save most of what belong'd to me, but the loss of my bussiness obliges me again to have recourse to you, begging that you'd use your interest a second time to put me in a way of liveing capable to serve you.
>
> It's highly probable that as soon as this news comes to England another Snow will be built in room of her that is lost; and as I have been already in the services, I think my pretensions to be Surgeon of her pretty well founded, but it being a place much sought after, I need to make all the interest I can to secure it; and my friend Dr. Houstoun [probably a distant relative] being absent, I have now but yourself to depend upon, wherefor I humbly beg that you'll take it to heart.
>
> I hope to have the honour of seeing you in a few months, being to sail in about a fortnight for Carolina; but I take the oppor-

---
9. Sloane MS, British Museum, 4051, fo. 141.
10. *Ibid.*

tunity of sending this in the mean time by the way of Campechy because it may probably come to England sooner, and so prevent my being supplanted.

I wrote to you about three months from Jamaica and sent you a collection of Plants from this place and Campechy among which was the Contrayerva. After the Vessel was cast away, I designed to have gone up to the Province of Jalappa, to enquire about the Plant of that name, but could not obtain leave of the Governour, tho' I made use of the Doctors interest. However I have sent up an Indian who has brought me down 4 small roots of it which I hope will grow, and I believe we shall find it a Plant quite different from the Marvel of Peru.

About ten days ago there was a Spanish Vessel put ashore here, and 40 of her people drowned. And it is said here that there have not blown so many and so hard Norths a great many years past as this winter.[11]

Dr. Houstoun must have reached London the end of the year 1731, or early in 1732, because in his March letter he expressed the hope of seeing his patron "in a few months."

Two years previously some distinguished men of London, in particular James Edward Oglethorpe, Member of Parliament, were planning the founding of another English colony in North America, which would form a barrier for the Carolinas against the Spaniards in Florida. Oglethorpe, the originator of the idea, saw his hope taking shape in June, 1732, when a company of twenty-one men organized under the title, Trustees for Establishing the Colony of Georgia in America, with a Common Council of eight members as a governing board, and received their charter from the Crown. Amid all of the arrangements required for the embarkation of the first settlers, the Common Council took under consideration, as one of the provisions of settlement, the employment of a botanist for an experiment in which they wished to engage. The Trustees' intention was to have a public garden "To aid in determining and effecting the economic destiny of Georgia . . . . While this institution would supplement the private gardens of the settlers in providing needed vegetables, its principal purpose was two-fold; to serve as an experiment station in testing out plants best adapted to the soil and climate of Georgia; and to constitute a nursery to furnish seeds, par-

---
11. Sloane MS., British Museum, 4052, fo. 82.

ticularly young mulberry trees and vine cuttings, for planting in the farms and gardens of the colonists in order to carry out the predetermined culture of silk and wine."[12] It was assuredly on the advice of Sir Hans Sloane that negotiations began with Dr. William Houstoun as early as August 23, 1732.[13] Six weeks before the Georgia colonists sailed for America, the agreement between the council and Dr. Houstoun was signed. The Trustees received sufficient financial assistance for the creation of their venture—a garden in the colony for raising herbs and tropical plants, etc.—and were relieved entirely from raising funds for the purpose. Seven titled men pledged annual contributions for six years. The largest donor was Lord Petre, who promised to give fifty pounds per annum if he lived the three-year period of Dr. Houstoun's services with the Trustees. The next largest patron was the "Rt. Hon. the Earle of Digby," whose contribution was also fifty pounds a year. In succession the other guarantors were: His Grace the Duke of Richmond and Lennox, thirty pounds; Sir Hans Sloane, Baronet, twenty pounds; the "Company of Apothecarys," twenty pounds; Sir Charles Du Bois, Esq., ten pounds; George Heathcote, Esq., five pounds; and James Oglethorpe, five pounds.[14]

Dr. Houstoun signed his agreement with the Trustees on October 4, 1732, in the presence of Thomas Richards and Andrew Balston. By its terms he was to receive an annual salary of £200 for a total of three years, unless shortened by the Trustees. He was to proceed at once to America and for a period of two years, unless otherwise ordered by the Trustees, he was to collect and deliver to Georgia such plants as the Trustees requested. At the termination of this period of preparation he was to take up his residence in the colony and supervise the preservation and propagation of his collection of plants.

---

12. James W. Holland, "The Beginning of Public Agricultural Experimentation in America. The Trustees' Garden in Georgia," in *Agricultural History*, XII, No. 3 (July, 1938), 274.
13. A. D. Candler, ed., *The Colonial Records of the State of Georgia* (Atlanta, 1904), I, 23. (Hereafter cited *Colonial Records of Georgia*.)
14. A. D. Candler, ed., *Colonial Records of Georgia*. Transcripts (16 unpublished volumes in the State Archives, Atlanta, Georgia. Typed copies in the Georgia Historical Library, Savannah), XXXII, 225-228. (Hereafter cited Unpublished Colonial Records of Georgia). In the above list the last two contributors were Trustees.

The day before he signed his contract with the Georgia Trustees, Dr. Houstoun drew up a letter of attorney, appointing Philip Miller[15] his representative in London during his absence. That he had received his reappointment with the South Sea Company is attested by the opening sentence of the letter of attorney. Following the introduction were directions for the transaction of any legal or business contingencies that might occur regarding his personal affairs, "saving only so far as relates to my claim and Interest in and to Ten Baggs of Havana Snuff in the custody of the South Sea Company for transacting which I have executed a peculiar power to M^r. Silvanus Bevan."[16]

Dr. Houstoun receipted for his one-half year's salary of seventy-five pounds on October 4, 1732. A week later his orders were ready. Ordered to Madeira and to Jamaica aboard the *Amelia*, lying in the Thames River, the botanist was instructed upon arrival at the former place to study that island's wine industry and to carry with him to Jamaica, or to send directly to Mr. St. Julian at Charles Town in South Carolina "Vines, & Seeds, Roots or Cuttings of any other useful plants . . . which are wanting in the British Colonies, but particularly the Cinnamon tree."[17] From Jamaica Houstoun was to go to several Spanish settlements at Carthagena, Puerto Bello, Campechy, and Vera Cruz, and if he could he was to cross to Panama. At all those places he was to use his "utmost diligence to procure Seeds & Roots of all usefull plants, such as Ipecacuana, Jallap, Contrayerva, Sarsaparilla, & Jesuites Bark; the Trees which yield the Peruvian, & Capivi Balsoms, the Gum Elemi, etc., the Cochineel Plant with the Animals upon it; and all other things that you shall judge may be of use to the Colony of Georgia."[18]

Upon his return to Jamaica he was directed to leave all of his collection with the person he found most capable and willing to care for them, while he went to other Spanish ports in search of more material. If, however, he found a ship going to Charles Town he was still to send "some of each kind" to Mr. St. Julian.

---

15. Philip Miller was a horticulturist, and was placed in charge of the Chelsea Garden, when in 1722 Sir Hans Sloane made the final grant of his gift to the "Company of Apothecarys."
16. Unpublished Colonial Records, XXXII, 144-146.
17. *Ibid.*, XXXIII, 3-5.
18. *Ibid.*

After he had visited all of the places and collected all that he could, further orders would be sent to him at Jamaica directing him how to "proceed in transporting yourself to Georgia where you are to spend the remaining part of three years, in taking care of the Culture of what you carry with you."¹⁹

In conclusion, Dr. Houstoun was particularly urged to study the nature and culture of the white mulberry tree "which is the most proper for the Nourishment of silkworms," and all "Sorts of Dogwood, & other Woods and Barks of use in Dyeing in order to the propagating of them in Georgia."

After the signing of the aforesaid papers, two objects in the Georgia Trustees' plans were realized in the next few weeks: the departure of the botanist for his horticultural undertaking, and the embarkation of the first colonists. Dr. Houstoun probably left toward the end of October, while the Trustees' ship *Anne* sailed from Gravesend, November 17, 1732, having on board one hundred and thirty-five persons, "all able-bodied and of good reputation."²⁰ As the galley cast off her moorings and slowly sailed toward the sea, some of the Trustees on shore waved good-bye to the men, women, and children who had responded to their call for settlers in an alien land.

When the Common Council was meeting on January 10, 1732/33, a letter directed to Mr. Oglethorpe from Dr. Houstoun dated Madeira, November 9, 1732, was opened and read, as the former was on his way to Georgia. Dr. Houstoun acquainted Mr. Oglethorpe that he had sent "two Tubs of the Cuttings of Malmsey and Other Vines on board a Ship, to be forwarded to Mʳ· Sᵗ· Julian at Charles Town for the Use of the Colony of Georgia"; and that he was to embark the next day for Jamaica.²¹ On March 31, Benjamin Martyn, the Trustees' secretary, wrote from London to Oglethorpe in Savannah that he had opened and read a letter addressed to Oglethorpe from "Mʳ· Houston," dated Kingston, Jamaica, December 21, 1732, advising him that he had "obtained of Mʳ· Prather, the South Sea Company's Agent, a Conveyance to Panama." Another entry in the minutes of June 27, 1733,

---

19. *Ibid.*
20. C. C. Jones, Jr., *The History of Georgia* (Boston, 1883), I, 117.
21. *Colonial Records of Georgia*, I, 96.

states: "Read a Letter from M^r. William Houston dated Carthagena, Jan^ry. the 25th 1732/33 directed to M^r. Oglethorpe."[22]

Dr. Houstoun fulfilled only in part the mission for which he was sent, and he was not able to see the fruit of his labors or to visit his kinsman, Patrick Houstoun. After his visit to Carthagena he traveled only as far as Jamaica, and became ill in Kingston. He had received from the Trustees a further remittance on his salary, but foreseeing that he would be unable to render future service, he wrote to his attorney, Philip Miller, and "Directed him to Reive [sic] no more of his Said Salary on Acc^t. of his ill State of health, whereby only Nine Months Salary of the said three years have been paid...."[23]

Dr. Houstoun died of heat in Jamaica on August 14, 1733, and was buried in Kingston the next day.[24] The Georgia Trustees were apprised of his death at their meeting of February 20, 1733/34, and entered in their minutes the brief mention of the decease of "Mr. William Houston." On the recommendation of Sir Hans Sloane, the Trustees appointed Robert Miller as Dr. Houstoun's successor. Miller left England on May 19, 1734, and on his arrival in Jamaica, July 25, he went "nixt [sic] morning to Dr. Cochran's and Demanded the Observations Made in Botany by Dr. William Houstoun together with the Collection of Dyed Plants which was left in his hands he told me he had Sent them all home already by one M^r. Houston, Surgeon a Relation of the Deceased Doctor William Houston and ther was now nothing in his Possession but a Parcel of Books w^c. he would only be accountable for to the heirs & Executors of his Deceased friend."[25]

The names of Karl von Linne, well-known as the Swedish botanist, Linnaeus (1707-1778), and Johann Friederich Gronovius (1690-1760), the eminent Dutch botanist of his day, are linked in some way with that of Dr. Houstoun's, but it has not been found that the two great botanists actually met the Scotsman. There was a

---

22. *Ibid.*, 128.
23. From instructions to Robert Miller. Unpublished Colonial Records of Georgia, XXXII, 225-228.
24. From certified copy of death certificate of Kingston Burials Copy Register, Vol. I, fo. 101, furnished by the General Register Office, Spanish Town, Jamaica, June 16, 1939.
25. Unpublished Colonial Records of Georgia, XX, pt. 2, p. 66. Letter from Robert Miller, supposed to be to the Trustees, dated Jamaica, December 20, 1734.

difference of twelve or more years between Linnaeus and Houstoun, and the two attended different universities. Gronovius lived in Leyden where he may have made the acquaintance of Dr. Houstoun. The two men were interested in the same science, and there was less disparity in their ages. Linnaeus visited Gronovius in 1735, subsequent to the death of Dr. Houstoun. It is probable that Linnaeus then met Houstoun's former professor, Boerhaave, because the latter recommended Linnaeus to a botanist in Amsterdam. It was Gronovius who dedicated the genus *Cinchonaceae Houstonia* (Order of Rubiaceae), to the memory of Dr. Houstoun, and Linnaeus, in publishing his botanical works, retained the name "which later merged into the genus Hedyotis."

In 1828, a Scottish poet published a book to which he gave the title, *The Columbian Lyre or Specimens of Transatlantic Poetry* . . ., and in the quite small volume is a poem with the title, "To the Houstonia Cerulea."[26] There is no reference to Dr. Houstoun in any of the stanzas. The name of the Scottish botanist has been attached to many species of Houstonia which grow both in Europe and in North America. On the latter continent there are about twenty-five species, the common names being "Bluets," "Quaker ladies," "Quaker bonnets," "Innocence," and "Venus's Pride."[27]

In the Institute of Jamaica for the Encouragement of Literature, Science and Art are Dr. Houstoun's manuscripts, drawings of plants of Jamaica, and "also the plants themselves which he

26. (Glasgow, 1828), 227. There is a difference in the spelling of the species. Stephen Elliott in *A Sketch Book of the Botany of South Carolina and Georgia* (Charleston, South Carolina, 1821), I, 192, spells it "Houstonia Coerulea"; and L. H. Bailey, *Standard Cyclopedia of Horticulture* (New York, 1915), III, 1611, uses the "a", caerulea. The Scottish poet above spells the species, cerulea.
27. Among the botanies that list the species Houstonia are: W. W. Chapman, *Flora of the Southern States* (New York, 1865), 173; Francis Peyre Porcher, *Resources of the Southern Fields and Forests* (Charleston, South Carolina, 1869), 445; F. Schuyler Mathews, *Field Book of American Wild Flowers* (New York, 1902), 440. Mathews, who spells the species, "coerulea," states: "Named for William Houston, an early English botanist." Frederic William Stack, in *Wild Flowers Every Child Should Know* (New York, 1909), 368, writes, "Linnaeus dedicated this genera to Dr. William Houston, an English botanist in tropical America, and who died in 1733." He spells the species, "caerulea"; and Homer D. House, *Wild Flowers* (New York, 1934), 265, 268, lists several species, and there is a colored plate of the delicate blue Houstonia coerulea.

sent to Philip Miller, and which Miller grew from the seeds he sent, in the Chelsea Garden. His letters to Banks[28] and other mss. are in the old Building."[29] Dr. Houstoun also "left a manuscript catalogue of the plants he had collected, with engravings on copper by himself. The manuscripts, as well as his specimens, now in the botanical department of the British Museum, after Philip Miller's death, came into the hands of Sir Joseph Banks by whom the catalogue was published in 1781 as 'Reliquiae Houstonianae' with the copper plates."[30] Philip Miller's numerous correspondents in "Siberia, at the Cape in North America, and especially Dr. Houstoun's collections led him to plan a series of all known genera."[31]

From the connections which he made with noted men of science, it is more than a matter of surmise that if Dr. Houstoun's life had not been terminated so abruptly by the effects of a tropical climate, he would have contributed even more than he did to the science of botany. It is to be regretted that efforts to find the burial place in Kingston, Jamaica, have been futile.[32]

---

28. Sir Joseph Banks (1743-1820) was an English patron of science, and at one time was president of the Royal Society.
29. Through a letter to the American Consul, Kingston, October 7, 1936, from the late Frank Cundall, Secretary of the Institute of Jamaica, a copy of the letter was sent to the author.
30. *Dictionary of National Biography*, IX, 1320.
31. *Ibid.*, XIII, 421.
32. Dr. Houstoun has received recognition in Savannah where Mr. and Mrs. Marmaduke H. Floyd in 1940 established a museum of the Trustees' Garden history and a small herb garden on a portion of the site of the Trustees' Garden. In commemoration of Dr. Houstoun they laid out a parterre flower bed in the pattern of a conventionalization of the Houstonia cerulea. In June, 1948, the property on which is the garden was purchased by the Trustees' Garden Village, Inc. (*Savannah Morning News*, June 26, 1948).

Chapter III

PATRICK HOUSTOUN IN GEORGIA

A timely topic in London in 1733 was the newest colony in America. It had been sixty years since Englishmen had discussed colonization in the plantations across the Atlantic, as the Carolina settlements were founded in the sixteen-seventies and by 1733 were well established. Titled men of England as well as commoners were among the Georgia Trustees, and that lent distinction to their plan. Church circles aspired to convert the Indians, and contributions poured into the Trustees' treasury to be devoted to the salary of a missionary and for the erection of a church building in the colony. Such organizations as the Associates of the Late Dr. Bray, the Society for the Propagation of the Gospel in Foreign Parts, and the Society for the Propagation of Christian Knowledge ably assisted James Oglethorpe by giving contributions through John Lord Viscount Percival, later the Earl of Egmont, the Trustees' president. The Associates of the Late Dr. Bray sent with the first shipload of settlers, the Reverend Henry Herbert, D.D., a priest of the Church of England.

It was not long before residents of North Britain were informed of the establishment of Georgia. Soon after the colony was settled two Scottish gentlemen with their thirty servants emigrated to Georgia where they received grants for plantations. Other Scotsmen heard of the new colony. Their native fondness for adventure led them to abandon their home occupations and strike out for the new land. Patrick Houstoun may have been the instigator of the venture, since his kinsman Dr. William Houstoun certainly had told him of Georgia, and had perhaps inspired him with the idea of founding a new home for himself. Patrick either interested some friends or they persuaded him, for plans took shape in the late spring of 1733. Learning of the Trustees' requirements for settlement for men of means: to pay their own expenses, to take ten or twelve servants and to plant and cultivate mulberry trees for the propagation of silkworms, Patrick Houstoun and possibly his brother James, both of Glasgow, were in the Scottish company of new settlers, as were the following: Dr. Patrick Tailfer, a physician of Edinburgh; Andrew Grant and John Bailie, merchants, also of Edinburgh; Thomas Bailey, of "Orkney in Scotland," Alexander and Robert Bailie, brothers; Hugh Stirling, and perhaps others.

The Houstoun cousins probably corresponded about Patrick's plan, as it was Dr. Houstoun who petitioned the Trustees at their meeting on July 11, 1733, for his kinsman, "Mr. Houston, of Glasgow," to go to Georgia and to carry twelve servants on his account, and two weeks later the Trustees at their meeting, August 1, received one pound one shilling from Dr. Houstoun, (then ill in Jamaica), "the Consideration money mention'd in the Grant of Patrick Houston."[1]

Patrick Houstoun was born in Scotland in 1698, the son of Patrick, the second son of the first baronet and his wife.[2] Although he is referred to officially as being from Glasgow, family tradition connects him with Paisley. The two places are about ten miles apart. The city of Glasgow lies in the counties of Lanark and Renfrewshire, and when Patrick Houstoun was living there the population was about 17,000. He grew up in what was then a large city. Paisley, which is in Renfrewshire, was an old burgh situated on rising ground on the west bank of the White Cart River, and had long, regular streets. Houstoun Castle was in the town of Houston in the same county, and whether his father

---

1. *Colonial Records of Georgia*, I, 132. The grant read:
    An indenture of Grant and Enfeofment dated the first of August 1722 to Patrick Houstoun of Glasgow merchant of 500d Acres of Land in Georgia to hold to him and the Heirs male of his Body under the yearly Rent of 5d the first payment of the 1st. day of the 11th. Year from 9 June 1732 Conditions are to go with ten men Servants in a year and abide 3 Years to clear 200d Acres in ten years & Plant 2000d White Mulberry Trees & 1000d White Mulberry Trees and Every 100d Acres of the other 300d Acres as clear'd which is to be in 18 Years from the date, or such part thereof of unclear'd to Revert, with Covenant from the Trustees to Grant 20 Acres to each of such men Servants when requested by the Grantees, as by a counterpart thereof remaining with the said Trustees more fully appears. Unpublished Colonial Records of Georgia, XXXII, 147.
2. The name of the wife of the first baronet's son Patrick has not been found.

lived in Glasgow or in Paisley, Patrick must have visited often the castle of his ancestors. Sir Patrick Houstoun, his grandfather, had died there in 1696; and John, his uncle, the second baronet, and his cousins, John, the third, and John, the fourth baronets, occupied the castle before the former emigated to Georgia.

At the age of fifteen Patrick Houstoun matriculated in Glasgow University for the class of humanity and literature, under Professor Ross.[3] No record can be found of his having registered in any other course of study, or that he graduated from the University.[4] From the position which Patrick Houstoun occupied later in Georgia, it is apparent that his classical education at the University of Glasgow was sufficient, and endowed him with attainments and a certain confidence that proved him to be a man of ability and made him eligible to command leadership in the affairs of his adopted country. It is not known how long his parents lived.

Patrick Houstoun prized highly a devotion to duty; he also practiced meticulous care in any trust imposed upon him, and he jealously guarded his integrity when circumstances made it open to question. When the occasion demanded he was firm and resolute; but on the other hand, he knew the fine distinctions of courtesy. Such is a brief picture of one of the several gentlemen from Scotland, who set out for the shores of Georgia. Love of adventure and colonization, inherent in men of Scotland, seemed incapable of suppression, for even the disastrous attempt of the Darien scheme thirty-five years previous failed to leave Scotsmen cool to bold enterprise abroad.

Georgia, as well as other English colonies, profited by the indomitable spirit of Scotsmen. Patrick Houstoun was motivated by the same verve and daring. Because his father was the second son of a titled parent, probably it never occurred to him that he would one day himself hold the title of baronet. Since he had a kinsman in the service of the Georgia founders, his attention was drawn to an opportunity embraced by many younger sons of the British gentry, who for years flocked to the American

---

3. From a letter to the author from the Secretary of the Glasgow University Court, Mr. John Spencer Muirhead., D.S.O., M.C., L.L.B., October 6, 1934.
4. *Ibid.* "In the eighteenth century, 15 or even earlier was a normal age for attending a Scottish University."

colonies. Patrick Houstoun at the age of thirty-six left for Georgia, where for twenty-eight years he lived as a landed proprietor, giving unstintingly of his time in the service of his king and province.

The other members of the Scottish expedition, having each received his grant of five hundred acres, and the necessary preparations having been made including the "freighting" of their own ship, sailed from "North Brittain" in the early part of March, 1734. As each one of the Scotsmen was obligated to carry ten servants with him, the ship's company at the beginning of the voyage amounted to over one hundred persons exclusive of the crew. The ship sailed from a port probably on the eastern shore of Scotland and cruised through the North Sea to the English Channel. An unexpected delay necessitated laying the ship aground at Portsmouth, "in order to refit her, being pretty much Damaged by an unlucky accident which happened there." While the repairs were being made twelve or more servants were "enticed on Board the King's Ship at Portsmouth (a warm Press being on foot)," and when the vessel was made seaworthy again, she set sail and finally reached her destination, the port of Charles Town, South Carolina.[5] The friends were "given a very discouraging Character" of Savannah, but on hearing the account several of the men went to the Georgia town to "view it." They were told by Thomas Causton, keeper of the public stores, that he had orders not to give them anything, but he could allow them credit for twelve months' provisions. Returning to Charles Town, the delegation made its report to the other colonists. Undeterred by the disparaging stories of the Carolinians, the Scotsmen pushed on with their remaining servants to claim their grants of land. Further disappointment awaited them. The number of servants who were young and able men, most of them trained laborers, and a few women, was reduced to fifty-two; and when they arrived in Savannah, it was with much difficulty that their employers procured from Causton credit for three months' pro-

---

5. A fruitless effort was made to identify the ship. In the issue of *The South Carolina Gazette*, May 11, 1734, there is a notice of the arrival of the Snow Hope, Co. ship, *Greig*, from Leith, Scotland, which might have been the Scotsmen's ship, but there was no mention of the passengers. There are no maritime records in South Carolina.

visions and a few other things and not even those without paying for them.

To their consternation, the Scotsmen found that their land was not adjacent to Savannah but was situated on the Great Ogeechee River, thirty miles from its mouth. On their arrival at the appointed place they began at once to clear their acreage and placed themselves "in some posture of Defence . . . in case of an attack from the Enemy." Their servants were put to work to build a fort. Their remoteness from Savannah made the Scotsmen dissatisfied as they were put to great inconvenience, they wrote, in obtaining food and other necessities. The settlement of the Houstoun brothers, the Bailies, the Stirlings, and Dr. Tailfer was known as Stirling Bluff.[6] While the settlers continued in residence there they enjoyed good health and were industrious agriculturists. During their first season two hundred acres were planted in corn, peas, and turnips.[7] In time Thomas Causton lent them "four small cannon and small arms for all their people." The colony being seventy miles distant by water from Savannah, it was necessary for some of the men to visit the town frequently, and the comment of one of the residents of Charles Town that Scotsmen were seen on the bluff in their native dress and "laced hatts," in all likelihood referred to the settlers from the Great Ogeechee.[8]

By the end of January, 1735, however, the Scotsmen had become more dissatisfied with their situation. They wrote to Peter Gordon, the first bailiff, on the twenty-fifth of that month that they found it a "very great inconvenience to procure from time to time such things as we stand in need of . . . and although it has been a considerable Hindrance to the Clearing of our Ground, yet we believe that proportionable to the time of our Settling there is as much ground Cleared as anywhere else in this Province."[9]

In March, Andrew Grant, Hugh Stirling, Patrick Tailfer, and Patrick Houstoun wrote a joint letter to the Trustees in which

---
6. The site is now (1948) one mile down the Ogeechee River from Richmond Hill Plantation, home of the late Henry Ford, in Bryan County, Ga.
7. Unpublished Colonial Records of Georgia, XX, Pt. 2, 576.
8. *Ibid.*, 241. Letter from Samuel Eveleigh of Charles Town to Colonel Oglethorpe.
9. Unpublished Colonial Records of Georgia, XX, 495, 496.

they gave particulars of their voyage and of their settlement, apprising the Trustees that when they obtained their grants, they never doubted in the least but that they should have the same privileges and encouragement given to other people. On their arrival in Georgia, they wrote, they had expected to receive "provisions for their servants for twelve months, tools for building & clearing the land, nails for their houses & other iron work, arms and ammunition," etc., but the results were contrary to their expectations. The distance of their settlement from Savannah obliged some of them to settle there in order to supply the others " . . . with provisions and other necessaries as well as upon the Account of our Business." It is evident that they had not received the full allotment of acres, because they asked that the remaining part of their land be given to them next to the town "of any not yet been taken up."

It would seem that Patrick Houstoun was one of the men who later took up his residence in Savannah, and that he desired to carry on the business in which he had been engaged in Glasgow. He had become identified with the life in Savannah and had made friends and acquaintances, among them Peter Gordon and Captain Dunbar. On the first of March, 1735, he wrote from Savannah a letter full of news and gossip to Peter Gordon who, with his wife, was in Charles Town preparatory to sailing for England. Expressing the opinion that Gordon would have been wiser to remain longer in America, Houstoun then passed on to his friend the latest gossip about the alleged relations between Mrs. Musgrove and Thomas Causton, keeper of the public stores. In Houstoun's opinion Mrs. Musgrove's husband was likely to kill Causton. Further, some settlers were so "disobliged at Mr. Causton they would run yet risk of sacrificing all to be avenged of him...."

Concluding his resume of the Musgrove-Causton affair with a pledge to exert his influence to pacify Musgrove, Patrick Houstoun then requested Peter Gordon to use his influence with the Trustees to procure a lot near the town, and asked particularly for one in the square where the public mill stood, saying if it were given to him he would build a home upon it to beautify the town "as much as a house would do." Enclosed in his letter to Peter Gordon, which he sent by Captain Dunbar, was a letter to "My Lord Percival . . . being I hear created ane Earl," also a letter to Doctor Houstoun (his death was still unknown to his kinsmen) "who procured your countrymen grants which please seal & deliver he will do you & all his countrymen service if it be in his power I have wrote him no complaints for I know he is very hott & would resent our treatment in a different manner I incline for."

Continuing his lengthy letter to Peter Gordon, Houstoun complained about the Trustees' treatment of the colony. Unless conditions improved he threatened to settle in Port Royal and even go to England "nixt harvest and prevent any more of my friends or countrymen being deceaved as I have been. . . ." Houstoun also offered a frank defense of his violation of the Trustees' ban on the sale of rum. Rum was the commodity which brought the "most ready money." Because they thought it had healing properties, many people wanted it and were willing to pay a high price for it.[10]

Patrick Houstoun was not alone in his violation of the Trustees' ban on the sale of rum. Peter Gordon, prior to his departure from Georgia, accused both Thomas Causton, the storekeeper, and Thomas Christie, one of the bailiffs, of infringement of the rule. Paul Amatis, the Swiss instructor in silk culture, divulged the names of others, and admitted that he was a lawbreaker himself. He wrote to the Trustees in June, 1735, that he had a small quantity of rum for "his own provisions," but finding it was more than he could "spend," he thought it was no crime to dispose of what he did not want, "Seeing it was publicly sold." He was fined, but he thought partiality was shown to others "since the fine goes to the benefit of the colony." He then mentioned those who were selling the liquor: "Mr. Edward Jenkins, Mr. John Fallowfield, Mr. Patrick Houstoun, Mr. James Gould, chief of the store, Mr. John Ambrose," giving as their reason for not paying a fine, "because they are Intimate to Mr. Causton. I do not say because they are Free Masons."[11] Although Patrick Houstoun may have escaped censure at that time, he was later to pay the penalty for his misdemeanor.

Patrick Houstoun then offered his services to Peter Gordon in endeavoring to sell his house but expressed the fear that he would

10. *Ibid.*, 592-598.
11. *Ibid.*, 472.

not be able to find a tenant until more people arrived in the town for there were nearly twenty empty houses. He advised: "if you had ordered the house to be partitioned & a floor above & a littell kitchen built it would have answered the expense." Peter Gordon's house was well situated for business and had a chimney, which was considered a convenience. He had evidently left his affairs in the hands of Patrick Houstoun, who asked in his letter the number of cattle Peter Gordon had, and what brand he wished put upon them.

Continuing, Houstoun set forth what was really his ambition: "Itt will be a great encouragement to the Collony if the Trustees give power to grant lisences here for the Ingiens if they send over any goods for to furnish the traders with I should wish to be store keeper for incline to turn myself entirely in merchant business...."

Patrick Houstoun concluded his long letter by offering "his Humble deuty" to Mrs. Gordon wishing them both "a good and prosperous voyage." He asked the favor of Peter Gordon in finding for him an "honest cliver young man who writes a good hand, a master of figures and book Keeping & knows something of Merchant business to engage him for some years for me to give him what wadges you think proper . . . I would be singularly obliged to you to send him over here I do not doubt abundance such are out of business about London & would be glade of this occasion."[12]

When Patrick Houstoun settled in Savannah the town " . . . was a buzzing community. It had its hopes and ambitions, fears and emotions, its likes and dislikes, its marriages, deaths, and births. A Mrs. Close bore the first child in Georgia, and thereby won 'A Silver Boat and Spoon' which a Mr. Hume of South Carolina gave her. A lad some sixteen years of age, signing himself P Thickness, and having lately arrived from England, wrote his mother in 1736 that Savannah had upwards of 300 houses not counting the huts. Although the climate was deadly to many, he seemed to thrive unusually well. He declared, 'The Country Seems to agree with me very well, for every Coat and Wast Coat I have is much too little for me, that it will not button within 4 inches, and I am grown tall and tan'd with ye Sun, so

---
12. *Ibid.*, 592-598.

yt nobody guesses me to be under 20 years of age.' There was plenty of game all around and he added "You would not fear Shooting of a Deer every day if you will; Turkeys, & Wild Ducks swimming 1000s of ym, in ye River all ye Winter.' In fact he was perfectly satisfied; Georgia was a great place in which to advance. 'Tell George,' he said, 'if He & I had come, when we first talk'd of it, He had been a Justice of the Peace at least by now.' "[13]

The custom of keeping holidays was started early in Georgia. The date the colony was founded[14] was a great time for celebration, and by 1736, the birthday of Oglethorpe, December 21, was likewise observed with festivity. The day "was begun by the principal inhabitants gathering at the fort where about noon, with some Bottles of Wine and some Biscuit they drank the health of the King and all his family, and then thirteen guns were fired. Then some more drinking to the health of the Trustees and of Oglethorpe; and in the evening all who could find partners brought them to the tavern where they danced and were merry."[15]

In February, 1734, before Patrick Houstoun arrived in Georgia, James Edward Oglethorpe, who was a member of a "military lodge" in England, had formed a lodge of Free Masons, but the lodge did not receive its charter from London until 1735.[16]

Houstoun joined Solomon's Lodge in October, 1734. A page in some recovered minutes shows that he was initiated and entered as an "apprentice" on the ninth of that month. The entries of his and other names were made in 1756, five years after Patrick fell heir to the Houstoun baronetcy. On the first page

---

13. E. Merton Coulter, "When John Wesley Preached in Georgia," in *The Georgia Historical Quarterly*, IX, No. 4 (December, 1925), 323. (Citations from *Colonial Records of Georgia*). (Hereafter cited "When John Wesley Preached in Georgia.")
14. February 1, Old Style; February 12, New Style Calendar.
15. Coulter, "When John Wesley Preached in Georgia," 324.
16. William Bordley Clarke, *Early and Historic Freemasonry in Georgia. 1733-34-1800* (Savannah, Georgia, 1925), 31, 32. Fragments of the minutes were discovered by Mr. Clarke, then Grand Master of Georgia, in the Library of Congress, and identified by him because of his familiarity with Georgia names. At the instigation of Mr. Clarke, and through the efforts of the late Charles G. Edwards, Congressman, and Senator Walter F. George of Georgia the papers were presented to Solomon's Lodge by an Act of Congress. A copy of the Act is in the files of Solomon's Lodge.

of the minutes recording those who had attained by 1756 the degree of master mason, his name appears sixth in the roster of members:

    Sir Pat Houstoun   in Geo^{ia} Octob. 9 .. 1734 E. P.[17]

Patrick Houstoun must have been granted the lot he wanted for a store, for he remained in Savannah to trade with the Indians. At the same time he became a planter. In 1736 he received a grant of five hundred acres from the Trustees, and it seems probable that he spent part of his time there engaging in the required pursuit of agriculture. His second grant was twelve miles from the town, on a neck of land between the Vernon and the Little Ogeechee Rivers. A creek connects the two streams, and facing that creek, where the sea breezes swept over the marsh land, Patrick Houstoun built his home and gave his plantation the name of Rosdue.[18] John Wesley mentioned in his Journal, on December 19, 1737, describing various places in the colony, that "Mr. Houstoun's" plantation was twelve miles from Savannah, and Stirling's farther up the Ogeechee.[19] That entry was made six months after the marriage of William Williamson to Sophy Hopkey, the great divine's first love, and just two months before the sorrowing clergyman left Georgia.

While conducting his business in Savannah, Patrick Houstoun

---

17. *Ibid.*, 30.
18. In old deeds in the Chatham County Court House the name is spelled Rose Dew and Rosedhu. The spelling of the name in this history is taken from a letter written by Sir Patrick Houstoun in 1754. Through the courtesy of the late Judge Raiford Falligant of Savannah,' I visited the site of Rosdue plantation, which was then owned by the estate of the late Louis A. Falligant. In 1849, when the place was owned by another Patrick Houstoun, grandson of the fifth baronet, George Jones Kollock wrote his wife: "Here I am luxuriating in the hospitable Halls of Sir Patrick of Rosedew...." The letter, owned by Miss Susan M. Kollock of Atlanta, a lineal descendant of Sir Patrick Houstoun, seems to verify the fact that the original house was standing in 1849. The property changed hands several times, and in 1874 was owned by Edward Houstoun (younger brother of the above Patrick) whose daughter Eliza McQueen Houstoun was married in the original house to Raymond McAllister Demeré in that year. All the buildings were burned after 1876.
19. Nehemiah Curnock, ed., *Journal of the Rev. John Wesley* (London, 1909), I, 406. The name "Mr. Houstoun" is included among those owning prominent plantations on the Little Ogeechee at an early date. Charles C. Jones, Jr. "Dead Towns of Georgia," (1878), *The Georgia Historical Collections*, IV, 250.

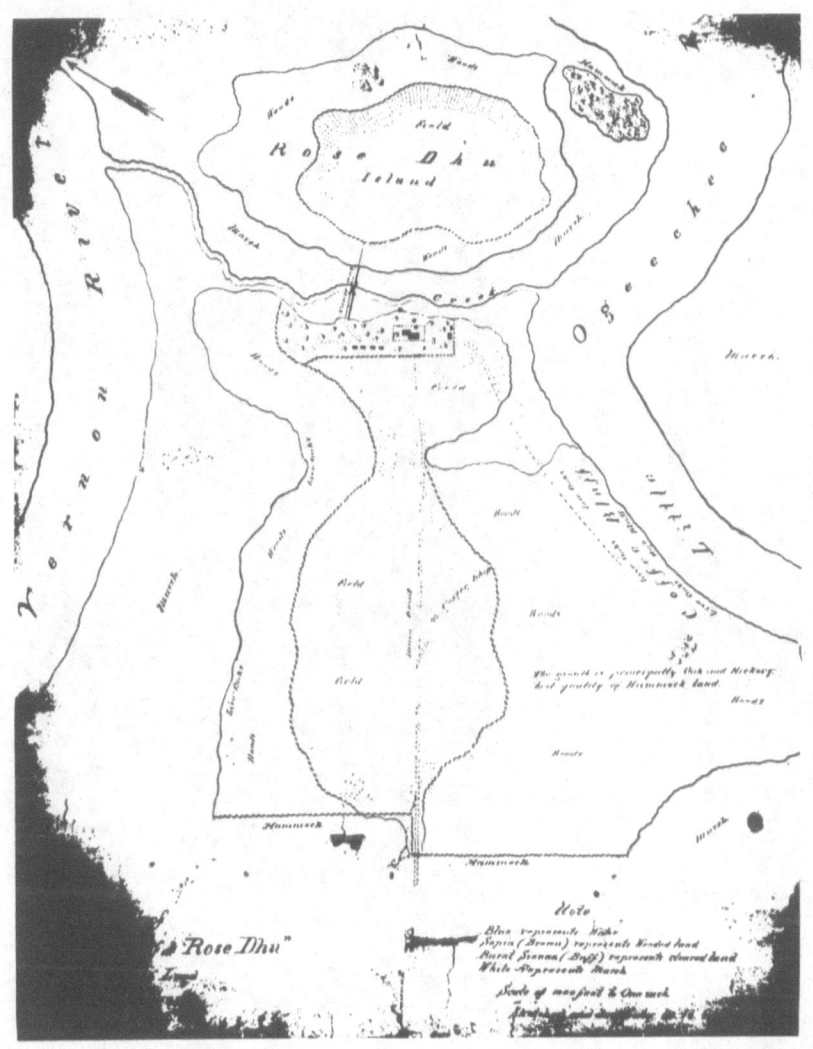

PLAN OF ROSDUE PLANTATION

Drawn by M. B. Grant in 1876.

Courtesy of the late Judge Raiford Falligant of Savannah, Georgia.

was much concerned because the Indian trade of Georgia was diverted to Charles Town. Savannah did not keep enough "goods"; that is, pots, pans, kettles, drygoods, etc., which were the articles the Indians wanted in exchange for their hides, furs, and pelts. Houstoun, nevertheless, was not unsuccessful in his enterprise, for in July, 1735, Elisha Dobre, a colonist, in writing to the Trustees mentioned that the traders "took to the value of ab^t 3000 currency of Goods from Mr. Houston here."[20] In the same month Houstoun himself wrote to the authorities in London, enclosing two petitions for lots in Savannah. One of the petitions had been drawn by a group of traders who were doing business with the Creek and Chickasaw Indians. Repeating the economic threat of Charles Town, a familiar theme with him, Houstoun urged favorable action on that petition. The other petition was that of Andrew Bell, a former servant, who had just completed his indenture. Described as a competent blacksmith who "has had very great offers made him to go to Port Royal," the writer continued by expressing the hope that the Trustees would give suitable encouragement to Bell.

Controversy regarding rules for the traders in the Provinces of Georgia and South Carolina continued for some time. The Savannah River was admitted to be the boundary line. Oglethorpe tried to be fair and just to his Indian neighbors, and Tomo-chi-chi, Mico of the Yamacraws, whose tribe had given the land for Savannah, was in London in 1734. While there Tomo-chi chi asked particularly that certain stipulations be made regarding the accuracy, quantity, quality, and prices of goods and the accuracy of weights and measures in determining the articles offered in purchase of the Indians' buffalo hides, deer skins, and pelts. The Trustees established regulations satisfactory to the Indians, but they involved the matter of licenses to those who did the trading. That was not agreeable to the Carolina traders, and because they would not apply to Oglethorpe for licenses, they were not allowed to traffic in Georgia. They carried their complaints to the Provincial Assembly of South Carolina, and a conference of committees from the two Provinces was held in Savannah, August 2, 1736. Oglethorpe answered the allegations of the South Carolina committee in regard to Georgia's regulations that he

---
20. Unpublished Colonial Records of Georgia, XX, 377-379.

had refused no trader who had agreed to comply with the rules and that he would instruct his Georgia traders to yield to those issued in the Province of South Carolina, stating that both provinces should communicate their regulations to each other. He asserted further that he would direct all of his traders to make no distinction between the two provinces but to speak in behalf of His Majesty's subjects. The commissioners were satisfield with the result of the meeting, although they still objected to the requirement of permits.

Patrick Houstoun, however, desired to remedy the situation in Savannah by procuring a loan from the Trustees and on July 3, 1736, he addressed his request to Oglethorpe who was then in Savannah. Informing Oglethorpe that Indian traders who had come to the Georgia town for their licenses had during "this Year" brought "Leather to the value of £14 or £15,000," Houstoun explained that the traders were compelled to carry their leather to Charles Town because Savannah lacked a sufficient supply of goods to take care of their needs. To prevent a recurrence of such an economic disaster the Savannah merchant had a plan. He would provide the goods for future traders' wants, if the Trustees "will be pleased to give me Credite for one year for £1,000 of the Public Money." Outlining a plan of security, Houstoun requested the loan be repaid in Savannah instead of London to save the expense of "Commission and Exchange" which would have to be paid for remitting money by way of the Carolina town. As a part of his program for enticing traders away from Carolina, Houstoun further suggested that the Trustees assist with a plan to provide "a number of Men and horses upon Call," explaining that once the traders were assured of goods and services in Savannah they would do business there. Concluding, the Georgia merchant requested Oglethorpe to instruct the Trustees, in case they granted him a loan, to pay the money to Peter Symonds, a London merchant, to whom Houstoun had sent "the Invoice & orders to buy the Goods."[21]

Oglethorpe thought well of most of Houstoun's proposition. In writing to the Trustees the day after he received the Georgia merchant's letter, Oglethorpe endorsed Houstoun's plan of re-

---

21. *Colonial Records of Georgia*, XXI, 186, Original Papers Correspondence . . . 1735-1737.

mitting money without losing the exchange. "I have," he wrote, "a good opinion of it, since it will save Commission and Exchanges, which I find very difficult now for they will not take the Georgia Bills in Carolina unless I give them below the Exchange. Wherefore I have rather chose to draw upon you."[22]

Two references are sufficient to show that the Trustees approved of the proposal to lend Patrick Houstoun the money and ordered it to be carried out. A resolution to that effect was passed at a meeting of the Common Council held on September 10, 1736: "A Bill of Exchange for forty Pounds drawn by Mr Oglethorpe July 3, 1736, to Patrick Houston or Order for Value received on Account of the Colony was presented Septr 10 by Mr Sheafe, Ordrd."[23] and a second resolution was read at a meeting of the same council held on November 10: "Bill of Exchange drawn by Mr Oglethorpe, July, payable to Patrick Houston or Order for Sixty Pounds Value received in Account for the use of the Colony, was presented Octr 26." At the end of a number of similar entries it was ordered that the secretary sign the said instructions.

There was no interchangeable currency between the Provinces of Georgia and South Carolina, and the Georgia Bills mentioned in Oglethorpe's letter referred to the sola bills issued solely for use in the colony. The only real currency in Georgia was a few copper coins and a Spanish milled dollar;[24] so for a medium of exchange for the colony the Trustees sent over, previous to the date of Oglethorpe's letter, one thousand six hundred and fifty pounds in what were called sola bills. They were "in themselves only Bills of Parcels for Goods sold and deliver'd to be paid for in England or Georgia as the Trustees shall think proper."[25] The bills were in denominations of from one to twenty pounds, and Oglethorpe was given the right to issue them in paying the debts of the Trustees. When Georgia became a Royal Province, all sola bills which had not been paid were recalled.[26]

Although Patrick Houstoun endeavored to comply with the

---

22. *Collections of the Georgia Historical Society*, III, "Letters from General Oglethorpe," 37, 38.
23. *Colonial Records of Georgia*, II, 169.
24. E. M. Coulter, *A Short History of Georgia* (Chapel Hill, North Carolina, 1933), 60 (Hereafter cited Coulter, *History of Georgia*).
25. *Colonial Records of Georgia*, II, 223.
26. Coulter, *History of Georgia*, 60.

requirements of the Trustees that those colonists who came to Georgia on their own account and with a grant for five hundred acres must bring ten servants with them, some of his servants must have been among those who deserted the Scotsmen when they were forced, in 1734, to put in at Portsmouth for repairs to their ship. Two years later Patrick Houstoun was in need of more hands on his plantation, and on August 3, 1736, he wrote to the Trustees requesting that they instruct Captain Dunbar or any other man who might be sent to North Britain to bring him ten men-servants and two women-servants. Upon their arrival he agreed to pay the prevailing market price. To Archibald Mackbane, who was paid by the Trustees to hire servants in North Britain, Houstoun had sent a note describing the sort of servants he wanted.[27]

From an extract of a letter of Thomas Hawkins, of Frederica, to Benjamin Martyn in London, secretary to the Trustees, the name of another of Patrick Houstoun's servants has come down in history. Hawkins wrote, November 28, 1737: "Of Building— I am sorry I cannot give a Better account than that one Sinclare, formerly a Servant of Mr Houston at Savannah has Built a small Timber house of Saw's work."[28]

---

27. *Colonial Records of Georgia*, II, 180; XXI, 201.
28. *Ibid.*, XXII, Pt. 1, 16.
    For an authentic account of the early settlers of Georgia, see Albert B. Saye, *New Viewpoints in Georgia History* (The University of Georgia Press, Athens, 1943), 3-50.

Chapter IV

PATRICK HOUSTOUN'S PREDICAMENTS

NOT far from Rosdue was Bewlie, the Vernon River plantation of Colonel William Stephens, the Trustees' secretary in Georgia. Stephens looked upon Patrick Houstoun as a "good neighbor." Bewlie was easily accessible to Rosdue by water, and by means of their plantation boats there must have been frequent exchange of visits between the two places. Colonel Stephens was twenty-seven years the senior, but in spite of the great difference in their ages, apparently there existed between the two men a congenial friendship.

On Thursday, August 31, 1738, Patrick Houstoun was invited to dine with Colonel Stephens at his home in Savannah, and that friendly gesture brought forth direful consequences to the former who paid dearly for what appeared to Thomas Causton, recorder and store-keeper, as the partiality of Stephens for Houstoun. Causton was concerned with his own evil deeds and had no connection with the "Nightly Club," often mentioned in Stephens's Journal.[1]

In August of that year Patrick Houstoun was in debt to Thomas Christie, a bailiff who owned a plantation "about two miles out of town." The incident that followed the dinner at Colonel Stephens's home was particularly distasteful to Patrick Houstoun, who probably had his own reasons for not having discharged sooner the debt to Christie. After he was taken into custody by Causton and released, Houstoun expressed himself in free and vitriolic language which undoubtedly relieved his pent-up anger.

Colonel Stephens's version of the affair which he sent to the Trustees tells them that on Saturday morning, September 6, Causton called on him taking "Bailiff Parker" with him, who Stephens thought from what followed, was there as an observer. Stephens related that on Thursday

... having a Bit of fresh Beef for my Dinner, I had engaged

---
1. *Colonial Records of Georgia*, IV, Pt. I, 257.

Mr. Pat Houston, and Mr. William Sterling, to take Part of it with me, in return to a Compliment of the like Nature made me by them: Mess. Causton and Christie chanced to come voluntarily, and take a share with us; which I esteemed a Favour, and bade them heartily welcome: After a little easy and agreeable Conversation when we had dined, the Recorder pulled out a pretty large Bundle of Warrants which had been served, and were supposed to be the Subject Matter of the Court which was intended per Adjournment to sit tomorrow. . . .

While Causton was "perusing" some of the papers, Stephens's son "accidentally looking" into one of the warrants noted that it ordered the "Body of the Party charged" brought before one of the magistrates. Stephens explained to his son that it was the usual form of warrants "where the Matter was of such Consequence to need it," but "he presumed it was not general, so as to make no Distinction between offences of high Nature and Trifles of Dangerous Debts and petty Controversies." To which Causton replied "with a little unexpected Warmth," that they made "no Distinction nor did he think any such ought to be made, let the Warrant be against the best Man in the Province." Stephens's answer was he supposed that it was a form prescribed by the Trustees, from which Causton "ought not to swerve," and if that were so he "humbly asked Pardon for the Freedom I have used." Causton's retort was plain. He said, "No, it is a Form of my own, which I have thought necessary upon finding an ordinary Summons often set at nought." Whereupon Stephens replied, "that wherever such Contempt appeared, undoubtedly they ought to vindicate their own Authority, and let such Persons feel their resentment." After a few more words of "little import," and finding that Causton "grew warm," Stephens thought it best to drop the "Discourse," diverting it to some other "Topick"; but after a short while Causton "fell into his usual Talk of late, complaining of the Magistrates Want of sufficient power &c," which Stephens wrote he did not understand, but said nothing, and that he was "not conscious of the least Offence which should occasion his parting so much out of Humor."

When Causton arrived at Stephens's home on Saturday morning he "no longer contained himself from giving Vent to his Passion of Thursday." In "plain Words" he told Stephens that he could not get over what had happened and that Stephens "had given the greatest Wound to his Honor that ever he felt in his life."

Nonplused and astonished, Stephens was undecided "whether it was most eligible to be serious or endeavor to bring him into better Temper by being a little more jocular." He tried both, he wrote, and then insisted that Causton should explain how he had been wounded. In response Causton unfolded his story:

A short while before the Thursday incident Christie had taken out a warrant against "Mr. Houston" for seven or eight pounds sterling, Causton granting the warrant; and the tything man who executed it, after taking Houstoun into custody, carried him as a prisoner to Parker, and on finding Parker out, then to Causton where the "Affair" was ended "to the Satisfaction of the Complainant." But not so to "Mr. Houston," who as related by him to Stephens

> ... took the Freedom to expostulate with them upon the severe Treatment (as he called it) which he had found; to be carried around the Town in the Custody of an Officer, Malefactor-like, for such a Sum, to his great Disgrace, as a Spectacle to all his Acquaintances; when it was well known from his large Plantation, and other visible Circumstances that he was not running away, &c. ...

It turned out that when Houstoun and Causton met at Stephens's home and began conversing, "Mr. Causton conceived a Jealousy," and thought that what Stephens said was in vindication of Houstoun, and "to throw a blot on him." Stephens was not aware that there was any "Difference" between the two men, and it was not until Causton left the house that Houstoun told him "the Whole." Houstoun informed him that his "Discourse" undoubtedly would be construed by Causton as a "Thing" concerted between them. And that is exactly what happened.

After hearing Causton's story when he called on Stephens on Saturday, the latter tried to convince him that he and Houstoun had had no "previous Talk." Colonel Stephens then asked Causton if he believed he had at any time conspired to "lessen his Character as a Magistrate," and whether or not he knew that on all occasions he had done all in his power to "espouse the Magistrates, and do what in me lay to support their Authority." The Recorder and Parker frankly acknowledged that Stephens was correct, whereupon they departed for Causton's plantation, thus ending an unpleasant incident.²

Causton's standing in the Colony, his farcical trial of the Reverend John Wesley, and the complaints against him are known to all familiar with the early history of Georgia, and Patrick Houstoun's indignation at the treatment accorded him by a man of such ill repute can be understood easily; likewise his "expostulations" when he regained his freedom. By October of that year, Colonel Stephens, by order of Oglethorpe, wrote a letter dismissing Causton from the office of keeper of the stores, at the same time requiring him to deliver all books, papers, and accounts to the inspector of the accounts. He was brought to justice and sent to England to appear before the Trustees. As he had failed to carry his vouchers with him, he was returned to Georgia to procure them, but he died on the voyage back and was buried at sea in the year 1746.³

Reference has already been made to Patrick Houstoun's disappointment after he reached Georgia, and in writing to one of the Trustees he said, in substance, that the accounts given of the colony did not come up to specifications. Other colonists had the same sentiments; a group of them banded together in what Colonel Stephens called the "Nightly Club," composed of the gentry of the town. The club met frequently to discuss the affairs of the colony generally, and Mr. Oglethorpe particularly. Its activities began as early as 1737, and the organization, which in Stephens's opinion was "the greatest remaining Root of Discontent," met at the Tavern, and its members were mostly Scotsmen, "but promiscuous also open to any that would come in the Manner of a Coffee-House, where every one called for what he liked; And usually once or twice a week I made it my Choice to go and sit an Hour among them: thinking it right to mix now and then with all sorts indifferently." The affairs of that club were evidently a live topic of conversation with the upper classes, and no doubt with the masses as well.

Colonel Stephens kept his eye on the malcontents and continued to inform the Trustees, by caustic comment, of their deeds. If

---

2. *Ibid.*, 193-196.
3. Coulter, *History of Georgia*, 71; also Jones, *History of Georgia*, I, 266, 274, 288, 300.

Patrick Houstoun had any association with the members it did him no lasting harm, and later he informed the Trustees he had no connection with them.[4] He was reported to the Trustees as "one of the best of the inhabitants," and "a quiet, modest landholder."[5] His standing in the colony twenty years later, when he held two Crown offices, certainly leaves no room for doubt as to the manner in which his conduct was construed in the early period.

The leader of the agitators, Dr. Patrick Tailfer, "was a thorn in the side of General Oglethorpe."[6] Histories and Colonial records recite the subsequent career of Dr. Tailfer, whose conduct became so notorious that he, with others, was forced in September, 1740, to leave the province and take refuge in South Carolina.

No evidence has been found to show that Patrick Houstoun belonged to the "Nightly Club," but if he did he must have dissociated himself from his fellow-countrymen when matters grew too hot, for he continued his quiet residence in Georgia while the leaders took up their abode in the neighboring colony. Certainly Patrick Houstoun was dissatisfied when he first came to Georgia. When the Trustees made grants of land to freeholders of the colony for a small money consideration, certain requirements were made by them which admitted of forfeiture of the land if the grantees were unable to fulfill them. One of the demands was that a certain number of acres must be cultivated and planted within a certain time.

In May, 1740, one of the colonists, Lieutenant Horton, visited London and on the twenty-first of that month dined with the Trustees and acquainted them with the affairs of the colony. The Earl of Egmont, President, recorded in his *Journal* of that date that Lieutenant Horton in commenting on the civil affairs of the colony remarked that the Trustees should abolish the use of forfeitures. It was, he continued, "impossible ... to fulfill them, and every one is now forfeited if the Trustees should rigorously insist upon it." All of this, concluded Lord Percival's informant, was discouraging

---

4. Historical Manuscripts Commission, ed., *Diary of the First Earl of Egmont, Viscount Percival* (London, 1923), III, 214. (Hereinafter cited *Earl of Egmont's Diary*).
5. *Colonial Records of Georgia*, VII, 500.
6. Jones, *History of Georgia*, I, 309.

to the people, "the best of them were determining to quit the Colony, Mr. Houston for one, who is now killing off his cattel."[7]

Lord Percival has recorded that the forfeitures of the landholders were forgiven with the result that Georgia landholders were given permission to lease and bequeath their property in whatever manner pleased them, except that a daughter could inherit no more than 2000 acres. Entries in Percival's diary warrant the inference that the Trustees, acting on data supplied by the magistrates, adopted a generous plan in dealing with the problem of forfeitures.[8]

Patrick Houstoun became involved to some extent in an intrigue—although apparently not to his detriment—a plot of Thomas Stephens, son of Colonel William Stephens, to redress the alleged wrongs of some of the malcontents by appealing to the King and Parliament in their behalf. Thomas Stephens was their self-appointed manager in England, and upon his return to Savannah, in 1742, (with much assiduity) stirred the inhabitants to great excitement. The whole story, related in a letter from Thomas Jones to Harmon Verelst dated Frederica, 26 April 1742,[9] in which the latter was asked to inform the Trustees what was happening in Savannah, is too long to narrate here. Briefly, Thomas Stephens began his intrigue by telling the inhabitants of Savannah that they had been unfairly treated by the Trustees who had kept them from their rights. The hardships to which they had been subjected consisted of the lack of rum, the prohibition of Negro slavery, free tenures of land, and the liability of repaying the Trustees the sums of money advanced to them. It was enough to incite any group of persons led and brought together by an unscrupulous man—"A Stephanian Scheme," Thomas Jones called it. The whole matter caused great sorrow to the young man's father, and it led to antagonism and their separation.

Henry Parker, later President of the Colony, played an important part in forming a "new alliance," and in some way, "acted in conspiracy," so says Thomas Jones, "wth the Baronet, Mr. Norris, Fallowfield & a constable and Associates." The baronet referred to was a gentleman from South Carolina.[10]

---

7. *Colonial Records of Georgia*, V, 356, Journal of the Earl of Egmont.
8. *Earl of Egmont's Diary*, III, 362.
9. *Colonial Records of Georgia*, XXIII, 288-304.
10. *Ibid.*, 322. Sir Richard Everard.

Patrick Houstoun's Predicaments 41

How far Patrick Houstoun was implicated it is impossible to say, but there is evidence in Jones's letter that "Henry Parker in July last (lodging one night at Tisdale's in the same room with Mr Patrick Houston) came in drunk (at which time he is usually very talkative and free) and related to Mr Houston the Substance of what is contain'd in his Affidavit. Mr Houston came (next morning) and acquainted me wth what Parker had said."[11] From that occurance it would seem that Patrick Houstoun was not in sympathy with the guilty inhabitants.

Stephens devotes considerable space to some information conveyed to him by Patrick Houstoun: On Wednesday, February 20, 1740, "Mr. Patrick Houston coming to Town from his Plantation near Vernon River, whom I look on as a good Neighbor there, and who made good Improvements, by cultivating a considerable Tract of Land, &c. called on me this Morning; and knowing that he had been lately at Frederica, we naturally fell into some Talk about what was doing there, and how great Things the General had in view; Among other Matters, telling him that I had heard from several, there was a Box directed to me from the honorouble Trustees, wherein were said to be many Papers, which I had no Advice of by any letter. . . . He readily told me, that there was such a Box directed to me which he saw lying in the Stores at Frederica . . . ."[12]

The narrative of the box, called by Stephens a "Dark Work," throws some light on what Patrick Houstoun was doing at that time. In March, Houstoun was again in Frederica because Stephens recorded that he had received a letter from him there telling Colonel Stephens he had inquired of Mr. Hawkins about the box. That appears to be the end of Patrick's connection with the mysterious package, but it also adds a little mystery to Houstoun's frequent visits to Frederica.

In July, 1740, the Common Council of the Trustees appointed "Patrick Houston in Georgia a conservator of the Peace within the Province" but on November 21, 1741, it was resolved in the session of the Council: "That the Order of the Common Council of July 21, 1740, appointing Patrick Houston a conservator of the Peace in the Province of Georgia be revoked the commission for

---

11. *Ibid.*, 298, 299.
12. *Ibid.*, IV, Pt. 1, 516, 517, 525, 533, 549, 611.

the same having never been made out."[13] The Earl of Egmont clears up the trouble when he writes in his *Journal* the above resolution and then puts at the bottom of the citation: "N.B. This was an error as to the Person for it should have been Patrick Grant."[14] No doubt Patrick Houstoun never even heard of that mistake of the Common Council.

Thomas Christie had his revenge on Patrick Houstoun, for when he was in London in July, 1740, he appeared before the Trustees to render a report on his accounts. Patrick Houstoun's peccadillo found him out then, as Christie acted the part of talebearer when he told the Trustees that Houstoun was a seller of rum and doubtless he was also one of the delinquents. The consequence for Houstoun was that he was fined forty shillings along with John Penrose for "selling spirituous liquors."[15] After paying for that offense Patrick Houstoun does not seem to have been guilty of any more misdemeanors.

---

13. *Ibid.*, V, 569.
14. *Ibid.*, 390.
15. *Ibid.*, II, 345.

Chapter V

MARRIAGE AND PRIVATE LIFE

WHEN Patrick Houstoun arrived in Georgia he was unmarried. Five years elapsed before he became the husband of Priscilla Dunbar, of Inverness, the sister of Captain George Dunbar. There was frequent communication by boat between Savannah and Frederica, and since Patrick Houstoun and Captain Dunbar were well acquainted, it is but natural to suppose that on some of his visits to the "Southward Settlements" Dunbar invited Houstoun to visit his home at Frederica, where he met the young Scotswoman.

George Dunbar preceded his sister to Georgia by three years, and he was one of the Scotsmen who settled the short-lived Joseph's Town in 1733. Captain Dunbar went back and forth between Great Britain and Savannah convoying settlers to the Georgia colony through the years 1734 to 1740. He was commissioned by the Trustees with Captain Hugh Mackay to recruit the colony of Scottish Highlanders, and in the ship *Prince of Wales* owned by Symonds and Company of London he brought the new colonists to Savannah to settle on the shores of the Altamaha River in the early part of 1736. Of the one hundred and ten men recruited by Mackay and Dunbar, the latter enlisted forty.[1] Priscilla Dunbar left her home and family in Iverness, and sailed October 18, 1735, under her brother's care, to endure the hardships of settlement life. She, too, showed the spirit of adventure which impelled chiefs and clansmen to leave their Highland homes in response to the call of the Founder of Georgia. C. C. Jones has said, "Besides this military band, others among the Mackays, the Dunbars, the Bailies, and the Cuthberts applied for large tracts of land in Georgia, which they occupied with their own servants.

---

1. Unpublished Colonial Records of Georgia, XXIX, 145; also J. P. Maclean, *An Historical Account of the Scottish Highlanders in America.* . . . (Glasgow, 1900), 149, 150.

Many of them went over in person and settled in the province."[2] George Dunbar obtained a grant of five hundred acres.

Priscilla Dunbar arrived with the Scottish Highlanders at a place near the mouth of the Altamaha River in February, 1736. The place previously had been named Darien by her brother George. This was related by the Earl of Egmont who wrote in his *Diary* under the date of December 11, 1736: "I received an account from Mr. McBane, a Highlander . . . that the first place settled by the embarkation this year to the Southward of Savannah is called Darien, so named by Captain Dunbar."[3] In a short time Priscilla Dunbar made a home at Frederica for her sea-roving brother who wrote to the Trustees in June, 1738, that he was building a house at Frederica on the "lott" the General had given his sister.[4]

Diligent effort was made to trace the ancestry of Priscilla Dunbar, and the results have been partially satisfactory.[5] In the parish registry of Inverness, Scotland, under date of October 31, 1711, is this entry: "James Dunbar, merchant of Inverness and Janet Dunbar his spouse had a child Priscilla, baptized by Mr. William Stewart."

In trying to ascertain the parentage of Priscilla some difficulty arose because there were other Dunbar families living in Inverness at the time of Priscilla's birth. Of three James Dunbars, two had wives named Janet. If there is a doubt that Priscilla was the daughter of a James and Janet Dunbar, it is slight, because the name Priscilla was unusual in Scotland; therefore, it seems conclusive that the above entry refers to Priscilla Dunbar, who became the wife of Patrick Houstoun. If October 31, 1711, *is* the record of Priscilla's baptismal date, then an error occurred in inscribing her age on her tombstone as sixty at the time of her death in 1775. Only one inference can be drawn from the tombstone record, and that is that Priscilla Houstoun's children were not informed of

---

2. Jones, *History of Georgia*, I, 200.
3. *Earl of Egmont's Diary*, II, 316. A few years later the town was called New Inverness in the District of Darien, but a short while afterward the settlers gave it the original name.
4. *Colonial Records of Georgia*, XXII, Pt. 1, 185.
5. On July 27, 1933, the author began a correspondence with the firm of Millar and Bryce, of Edinburgh, Scotland, professional Searchers of Records. On May 9, 1934, the firm sent the results of its search.

her exact age. In the above Dunbar family were three other daughters and one son named William, but no record could be found of George. It seems positive that George Dunbar's baptismal record must have been in another parish, because when in 1735 he was given a grant of five hundred acres, it was to "yourself and the Heirs Male of your Body and in failure thereof to William your Brother and Heirs Male of his Body all at the yearly Rent of Ten Shillings pr every 100d Acres."[6]

The official record of the union of Patrick Houstoun and Priscilla Dunbar is given in two colonial citations. The Earl of Egmont records in his *Journal* under date of January 26, 1740/41, that "the same day" Houstoun had written Harmon Verelst from Frederica that " he was settled on the lot of Capt. Dunbar's Sister whom he had married."[7] There must have been an error in copying or in the compilation of that volume, as the date of Houstoun's letter to Verelst seems clearer in a succeeding entry which the Earl of Egmont made on April 20, 1741. Noting that the letter was dated January 26, Egmont continues with: "he [Houstoun] was settled on the lot of Captain Dunbar's sister whom he had married."[8]

That Houstoun was still complaining of unfulfilled promises is evident from Egmont's entry of April 20, 1741. Further, he decried the encouragement given by the Trustees to other settlers "who had demerited." In spite of his protestations Egmont records that Houstoun claimed he "never joined the discontented party."

Six days later the Earl of Egmont mentioned in his *Diary*, "the Encouragement formerly given at 2 shillings bounty of corn sow'd in the Province had a good effect and Mr Patrick Houston a quiet landholder had received for his share of the bounty 75 pounds, others more or less in proportion, but some had gone without reward, the Trustees money not holding out."

Patrick Houstoun received an answer to his letter to Harmon Verelst. Its contents must have aroused in him not only a sense of satisfaction that the Trustees were pleased with him as a settler, but also that his efforts in agriculture to further the welfare of the colony received recognition and approval by the Trustees. Writ-

---

6. Unpublished Colonial Records of Georgia, XXIX, 161, 162, 183.
7. *Colonial Records of Georgia*, V, 442.
8. *Earl of Egmont's Diary*, III, 214.

ing under date of April 27, 1741, Verelst explained that Houstoun's letter of January 26 was "laid before the Trustees, who are much Pleased with the good Disposition you show of Promoting the Welfare of the Colony, and not joining with the Clamours of Unreasonable Men."[9] Houstoun in his letter, evidently had referred to promises made in his behalf by Doctor Houstoun, and in answering Verelst assured him "from my own Knowledge none such ever were, nor could be from the Nature of Your Tenure being a Landholder of 500^d Acres, and going at Your own expense; For the Trustees had no money granted them for any such Purposes; their Money appropriated for the Assisting only Persons sent upon Charity." Verelst closed by offering his "Service" to Houstoun and saying he would be glad to have it in his power to do him "any Friendship."

By the marriage of Patrick and Priscilla Houstoun the home at Frederica[10] was added to the plantation Rosdue in the Northern Division, as residences of the Houstoun family. A few years after the marriage an "Itinerant Observer"[11] from London visited Georgia in the beginning of the year 1745, and he left his impressions of his visit to St. Simon's:

> Frederica, . . . is the chief Town in the Southernmost Part of the Colony. . . . It stands on an Eminence, if considered with regard to the Marshes before it, upon a Branch of the famous River Altamaha. . . . It forms a kind of Bay before the Town, and is navigable for Vessels of the Largest Burden. . . . The Town is defended by a pretty strong Fort of Tappy . . . and commands the River both upwards and downwards. . . . The whole circumference of the Town is about a Mile and a Half. . . . The Town is situated on a large Indian Field: To the East it has a very extensive Savannah (wherein is the Burial Place) thro' which is cut a Road to the other Side of the Island which is bounded by Woods. . . . Down this Road are several very commodious Plantations, particularly

---

9. Unpublished Colonial Records of Georgia, XXX, 340.
10. In the library of the Georgia Historical Society, Savannah, is a blueprint traced from a map owned by Mrs. Agnes C. Hartridge, of St. Simon's Island, by Lydia A. Parrish, May 29, 1927, which shows "Houstoun's Lands" located on the east side of St. Simon's, east of Frederica. Under date of September 21, 1801, John McKinnon, surveyor, states he made a re-survey of tracts of several lands, in conformity with a re-survey made by Jacob Lewis, a surveyor, in the year, 1774.
11. *Collections of the Georgia Historical Society*, IV (Back of book, 1-7).

the very agreeable one of Capt. *Demery* and that of Mr. *Hawkins.* Pre-eminently appears Mr. Oglethorpe's Settlement, which, at a Distance, looks like a neat Country Village, where the Consequences of all the various Industries of an *European* Farm are seen. . . . On the South is a Wood, which is, however, so far clear'd, as to discover the Approach of an Enemy at a Distance; without to the Eastward, is the Plantation of Capt. *Dunbar.* . . . The Town is divided into several spacious Streets, along whose sides are planted Orange Trees. . . . Some houses are built entirely of Brick, some of Brick and Wood, some few of Tappy-Work, but most of the meaner sort, of Wood only. . . . They have a Market every Day: The Inhabitants of the Town may be divided into Officers, Merchants, Store-keepers, Artisans, and People in the Provincial Service, and there are often also, many Sojourners from the neighboring Settlements, and from *New York, Philadelphia,* and *Carolina,* on Account of Trade. . . . In short the whole Town, and Country adjacent, are quite rurally charming, and the Improvements every where around, are Footsteps of the greatest Skill and Industry imaginable.

One of the nearest neighbors of the Houstouns was Captain Raymond Demere of Oglethorpe's Regiment, whose place, Harrington Hall, was only about an eighth of a mile eastward; and Oglethorpe's Cottage was less than two miles to the northeast.[12]

Another description of St. Simon's Island in 1742 was recounted by one who was living at that time: "St. Simon's then . . . was peopled with a thousand men. There was civilization and the arts; and above, below and all around nature was fresh and free, and in her wildest mood. There was health too as well as enjoyment here, and the soldiers of General Oglethorpe, while at St. Simon's, were exempt from sickness."[13]

In 1741, the Earl of Egmont was visited in London by another Georgia colonial who informed him: "That Patrick Houston had laid much money out on his land but it answered not."[14] That appears to be the last time that Patrick Houstoun wrote or spoke

---
12. M. H. and D. B. Floyd, "Oglethorpe's Home at Frederica," in *The Georgia Historical Quarterly*, XX, No. 3 (September, 1936), 229-249.
13. Thomas Spalding, "A Sketch of the Late General James Oglethorpe," in the *Collections of the Georgia Historical Society*, I, 274. Thomas Spalding (1774-1851) was born at the Cottage, Oglethorpe's first home in Frederica. He gathered information from his grandfather, William McIntosh, who had served as a youth in the troops of Oglethorpe.
14. *Earl of Egmont's Diary*, III, 189.

of his disappointment. Later Mr. Carteret, a landowner in Georgia, attended a meeting of the Trustees in London and carried news of the colony. Of Patrick Houstoun he said: "He keeps his plantation of 500 acres in the Northern Division, but when he went down to Frederica the 2 servants he left to take care of it sold off his Cattel, hoggs & poultry unknown to him and contrary to his orders. That he is an honest man, and of tolerable Sense."[15]

During the years 1740 and 1741 Patrick Houstoun, when he was living at Frederica, was employed by Oglethorpe in a confidential capacity. William Stephens in writing to the Trustees reported on December 3, 1740, that "Mr. Houston (at present employed by the General at Frederica) sent a boat to his Plantation near Bewlie on the Vernon River for sundry Provisions . . . "[16] One of the men who made the trip, to Stephens's surprise, carried no letters to him from Frederica. Two months later Houstoun went to Savannah and he was the bearer of a letter to Stephens from Thomas Jones who gave to the recipient only a "short Hint that he found Mr. Houston had private Instructions, to make an Enquiry into the late Behavior of some People here, on Occasions of those different Representations of the State of the Colony, sent to the Trustees; which was so very extraordinary that the General was very unwilling to think some Persons, of whom he has entertained a good Opinion, could be guilty of what they are charged with he (Mr. Jones) thought to be the Reason why I had of late less frequent Advices from the General than heretofore . . . . "

Reflecting on that bit of information Stephens thought of all he had written to Oglethorpe and how it coincided with the reports he had sent to the Trustees, and he continued, " . . . knowing how careful I am to stick close to the Truth in all that goes out of my Hand, I have no Apprehensions of meeting with the contrary but if my Veracity must be estimated by the Report which Mr. Houston shall make to the General (a Person, whom I forbear to say more at present on this Occasion) I must bid Adieu to my Hopes of serving here with Honor or Comfort to myself, or Satisfaction to my Constituents: Wherefore I will not suffer any

---
15. *Colonial Records of Georgia*, V., 500.
16. *Ibid.*, IV, Supplement, 42.

Impressions to be made instantly, chusing rather to let these Mysteries unfold themselves, which I know must in a short Time be as open as the Noon-Day." A somewhat ambiguous statement, but it would seem to refer to his friend Patrick Houstoun. Stephens could not have had a guilty conscience, but he most certainly was hurt, as a week later he recorded on February 5, ". . . Mr. Houston left us, to return to Frederica; by him I wrote to the General . . . Whatever Mr. Houston's Negotiations might be here, I had very little Regard to; but I thought that upon his getting home I shall see whether Mr. Jones was right in his Opinion or not . . . ."[17]

The situation between the two friends clears somewhat by an entry in the Earl of Egmont's *Diary* for May 19, 1741, where he records that Stephens had written: " . . . Oglethorpe was suspicious that he [Stephens] did not send fair representations of the characters of the inhabitants and of proceedings at Savannah and had sent—Houston to Savannah to give him private accounts thereof."

Stephens's surmise that Houstoun might give an unfavorable report on him evidently was unfounded as further entries in his *Journal* reveal that correspondence between Oglethorpe and himself continued as before. Furthermore, on October 2, 1741, Stephens received a packet and letters from Oglethorpe together with a constitution from London and his appointment as president with four assistants of the "Jurisdiction of the County of Savannah."

Patrick Houstoun's plantation, Rosdue, was well under cultivation, for the reward of seventy-five pounds at two shillings per bushel of corn would indicate that he was the owner of hundreds of acres planted in that grain. Slavery still was prohibited in the colony, although the law was evaded by leasing Negroes from South Carolina for periods of ninety-nine years. Patrick Houstoun may or may not have been engaged in such subterfuge. In a letter dated in 1736, he wrote to Scotland for ten menservants. As his desire became urgent to farm more land, he may have found it necessary to acquire additional help. That is entirely possible as the winning of the bounty on corn was six years after he began the cultivation of his plantation.

---
17. *Ibid.*, 89.

Miniatures of Patrick and Priscilla Houstoun were taken, and from the appearance of both it would seem that they were done about the time of their marriage, or a few years later. For his likeness Patrick Houstoun wore a blue coat and ruffled shirt, and his back hair was dressed in curls. He had blue eyes and the broad, open countenance of the Scotsman. Priscilla Houstoun's miniature reveals her slight of frame, with sloping shoulders, round head and oval face. She wore a pink gown with square neck and a necklace of pearls. Her features were delicate and refined. She had brown eyes and a small mouth, with upper lips turned up at the corners. An air of primness is quite noticeable in the miniature.

Their first child was born in the year 1742. No Bible or other family record gives the birthplace of any of the Houstoun children, but from letters written by Patrick Houstoun throughout the 1740's, it appears that the family divided its time between Rosdue and Frederica. The older children probably were born in the latter place, and the younger ones at the plantation home in the Northern Division, for by 1751 their father's political duties kept him near Savannah.

Patrick Houstoun, Jr., was named for his father. In the year of his birth the Battle of Bloody Marsh was fought on St. Simon's Island, between a comparatively small contingent of Georgians and a large Spanish force. Young Patrick's uncle, Lieutenant George Dunbar, whose rank was changed when he relinquished his sea calling and was put in Colonel Oglethorpe's regiment, played a conspicuous part in that battle and throughout the whole of Oglethorpe's military campaign. Patrick Houstoun undoubtedly fought in the Battle of Bloody Marsh, as every man was needed to assist in preventing the Spanish invasion of 1742, and Houstoun, who was then a resident of Frederica, must surely have felt as keenly as any other man his obligation to participate in every effort to protect not only the town but the colony as well. Two weeks after the Battle of Bloody Marsh General Oglethorpe issued, on July 21, a proclamation ordering a Thanksgiving to be held to the praise of God and that He had put an end to the Spanish Invasion. The Reverend John Martin Bolzius, one of the ministers of the Salzburgers who came to Georgia in 1734, has given a report of the manner in which the inhabitants of Frederica

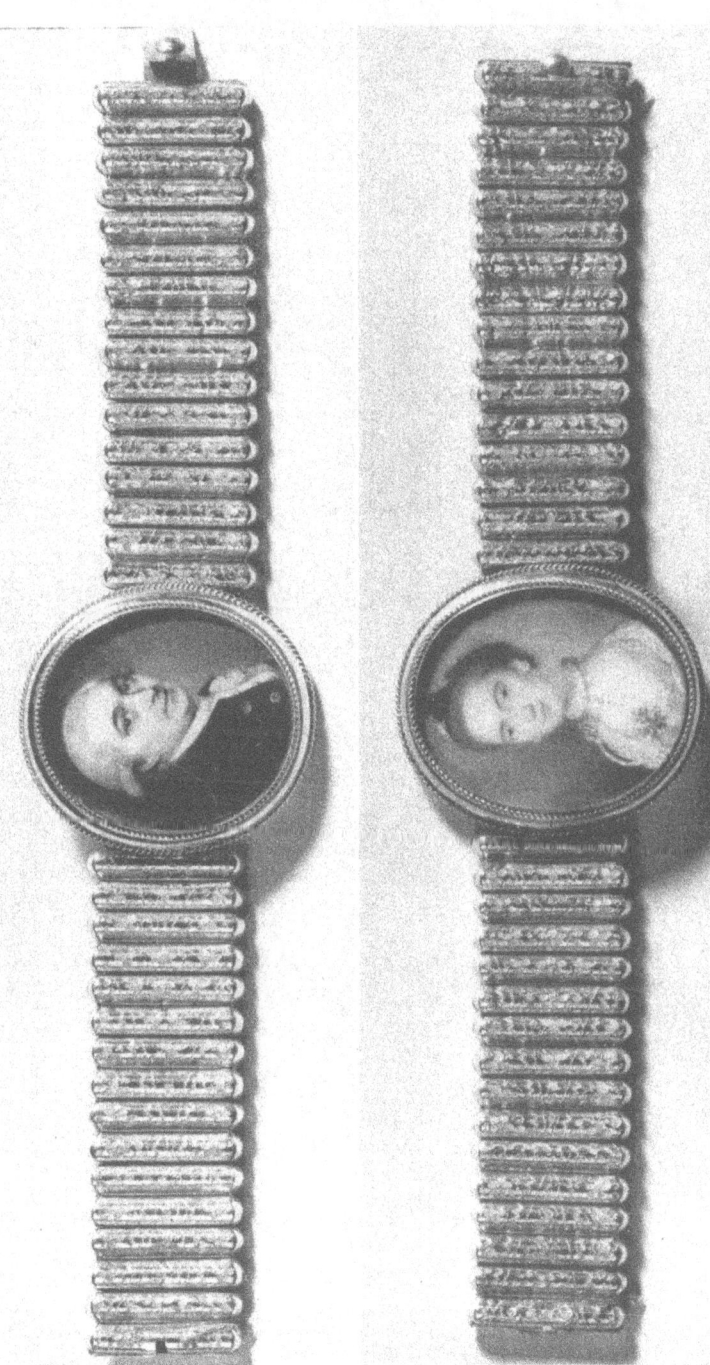

SIR PATRICK AND LADY HOUSTOUN
1698-1762   1711?-1775

From the miniatures owned by Mrs. Charles W. Rooney, of Decatur, Georgia. Upper attributed to Henry Benbridge

solemnly gave thanks for the victory. Under a September date, Mr. Bolzius entered in his diary: "Mr. Jones told me lately, that the people and soldiers at Frederica, on the day when the Thanksgiving was held [July 25] observed such a stillness and good order as he had never seen there. There was also a very pertinent and devout ascription of praise read which he (and Mr. Jones is a good judge of edifying things) pronounced to be very excellent: and moreover he maintained that it must have been prepared and composed by General Oglethorpe himself, for there was neither preacher nor schoolmaster at that time."[18]

The next year, 1743, Patrick Houstoun certainly was in active military service, and a few years later he held a royal commission in Oglethorpe's Regiment of Foot, which was formed August 25, 1737.[19] Patrick Houstoun was an officer in Oglethorpe's Expedition to St. Augustine in 1743, on the authority of Edward Kimber, who wrote in 1744 a narrative for his father, the Reverend Isaac Kimber. The younger Kimber accompanied the expedition, and his chronicle is in the form of a diary.[20] The troops left Frederica on February 28, 1743. In mentioning the officers under General Oglethorpe, Kimber lists, "Mr. Patrick Hourtein, Commissary."[21] There can be no doubt that he referred to Patrick Houstoun, as the name was often spelled incorrectly. Kimber describes the journey both by land and by sea, and tells of the difficulties and hardships endured by the men, in all of which General Oglethorpe shared with fortitude. There is only one reference to Patrick Houstoun in the diary, but the mention of the rations might cover information on part of the Commissary's duties during the campaign: "Every person carried his own Provisions, (in his Knap-sack or Haver-sack on his Back, Officers and Gentlemen not excepted) of which we had for seven days, at the Allowance

---

18. Thaddeus Mason Harris, D.D., *Biographical Memorials of James Oglethorpe, Founder of the Colony of Georgia in North America* (Boston 1841), 387-389. From the German translation of John Martin Bolzius.
19. W. R. Williams, ed., "British-American Officers, 1720-1763, Compiled from the Original Commission Register .... War Office Records .... Public Record Office, London," in the *South Carolina Historical and Genealogical Magazine*, XXXIII, No. 23 (1932), 194.
20. Edward Kimber, *A Relation or Journal of a late Expedition to the Gates of St. Augustine or Florida.* . . . Reprinted from the Original Edition (London, 1744; Boston, 1935).
21. *Ibid.*, "(Page 7, line 8, for Hourtein, read Houstein)", Corrections, 37.

of a Pound of Biscuit, and ten ounces of Cheese per Man; which, with Beef, if the Men chose it, was, and is the usual Allowance."[22] After two efforts to take the fort at St. Augustine, one by land and the other by water, General Oglethorpe determined to give up the venture. He gave orders to return to Frederica, where he arrived and disembarked on March 31, having been away fifty-nine days, "not having taken any Prisoner nor seen a Spaniard without the Walls, so much were they terrify'd with out late Attempts."

Whether Patrick Houstoun's visit to New York during the early summer of 1743 was for business or pleasure is beyond conjecture. That he was there was reported by a friend, John Provoso, who wrote from that city to Captain George Dunbar, then in London, begging that something be done to expedite the payment of General Oglethorpe's bills. Provoso was certain that failure to pay the General's bills was keeping needed supplies from the colony. There is no way of ascertaining whether or not Houstoun returned to Georgia in time to see General Oglethorpe before the latter made his final departure from Georgia, July 23, 1743; but even after he left his regiment remained intact, fully officered. On October 29, 1747, Patrick Houstoun was raised from the ranks to be commissioned adjutant in Oglethorpe's 42nd Regiment of Foot, and served until July 23, 1748, when he was shifted to quartermaster.[23] One year later the regiment was formed into Independent Companies of Foot with the same officers. Patrick Houstoun continued as quartermaster in Lieutenant Colonel Heron's regiment, certainly until the year 1750.

Two years after the Battle of Bloody Marsh, the Houstouns had a second son who was born on October 19, 1744, and whom they named George.[24] Family tradition claimed his birthplace as Frederica. Their third child was also a boy and was named John. History has confused the year of John Houstoun's birth with that

---

22. *Ibid.*, 22.
23. *South Carolina Historical and Genealogical Magazine*, XXXIII, 194.
24. Sir George Houstoun's tombstone in Bonaventure has inscribed on it under his name, "1744-1795": and recorded in his own Bible (owned by the heirs of Mrs. Macartan C. Kollock of Atlanta, Georgia, lineal descendants), in a different handwriting from the other entries is: "Sir George Houstoun, Bart., 9th, June, 1744 . . . aged 59 years, 7 months & 19 days."

of his brother George, for all historians who have recorded the date and place of John's birth have stated that he was born in "Burke County, Georgia, in 1744."[25] Rosdue and the home at Frederica were the only property owned by John's father in 1746, '47, '48, and St. George's Parish, later Burke County, then was forest land. In one of the above-mentioned years John Houstoun was born, and his birthplace, therefore, had to be either Rosdue or Frederica. There are no known records to disprove the inaccurate statement of historians, except George Houstoun's epitaph and the Bible record. On April 1, 1755, Patrick Houstoun made the public statement that he "had a wife and four children;"[26] so sometime after 1744 and before 1755 the two sons, John and James, the latter the fourth child, were born.

As the father spent his time during the seventeen-forties traveling back and forth between Frederica and Savannah, the question arises whether or not his family accompanied him. If so, it was no easy task for a mother and her small children to take such a tedious journey. In spite of the fact that Oglethorpe had had a fairly good road surveyed on the mainland, in a trip between Savannah and Frederica there were three rivers to cross by ferry; therefore it may be surmised that when the Houstoun family was occupying one of its homes and wished to take up its abode in the other, they went by water in a perriagua, or flat-bottomed boat. That trip in itself was a matter of two days or more and was made through the inland passage-way, the boat passing some of the beautiful coastal islands: Sapelo, St. Catherine's and Ossabaw. In February, 1745, Patrick Houstoun was back in the Northern Division, either in residence at Rosdue or in Savannah for attendance on duty. He occupied some position of trust under the President and Assistants,[27] then the governing body of the colony after Oglethorpe left Georgia. He wrote a "ship letter" from Savannah dated February 26, 1745, to Harmon Verelst in London, accountant for the Trustees. The frequent use of the pronouns "us and we" makes it obvious that Houstoun was an official.

---

25. James Grant Wilson and John Fiske, eds., Appleton's *Cyclopaedia of American Biography* (New York, 1888), III, 273.
26. *Colonial Records of Georgia*, VII, 142.
27. A search for Houstoun's official position at that time has been in vain.

From the contents of the "ship letter" some of Patrick Houstoun's traits of character are plainly recognizable. He began his communication with a minute acknowledgment of all letters he had received, then gave the news that "Mr. Gronau[28] had departed this life a few weeks since in Hope of a better elsewhere where notice is taken in my Journal."[29] Continuing, he expressed considerable anxiety with respect to earlier letters he had sent abroad. The prospect of their seizure by the enemy worried him. He then proceeded to list eight packets he had sent during 1744, mentioning the names of the eight ships that carried them, including the name of each vessel's master. "Two of my last," he wrote, "more especially are of the highest Concern to me: wherein we have endeavor'd with the utmost Exactness to fulfill the Trustees Commands in sending Coppies of Vouchers for all Payments made from Mich'mas 1739-Mich'mas 1743." Precise details then followed with exact information on "double vouchers" concerning accounts with individuals, which he said, "we have punctually observ'd."

The letter is a long one with details on the financial affairs of the colony, emphasizing the necessity of parcelling out a "few broken sums" where most needed and "the Demands most pressing." "That," he wrote, "has driven many People to seek Credit for Provisions to maintain their Families."

Assisting with the management of a youthful colony's affairs was an exacting work. That Patrick Houstoun diligently applied himself to this task would seem a reasonable assumption. Continuing his "ship letter," he referred to numerous "inconveniences." Supplies were short and in spite of careful management several public works had to be deferred. The prison, for example, was rotting away. Houstoun wrote " 'tis universally agreed by all, that Stone Work (however rough) is the most eligible as well for strength as Duration; tho' the greatest Expence therein will be Digging and Carting."

The most important intelligence in the letter was the report on the building of the church in Savannah. The Reverend George Whitefield, a missionary sent to Georgia from England in 1738 by the Society for the Propagation of the Gospel in

---

28. The Reverend Israel Christian Gronau, religious teacher at Ebenezer.
29. Nothing is known of that journal.

Foreign Parts, to care for the spiritual needs of the colony, had "£150 in his Hands" intended for the church. When the town was laid out, the lot for the church was set aside on Johnson Square. After a long delay the time seemed to have arrived to erect a place for divine worship. Patrick Houstoun's words indicate that he held some office of authority for superintending the construction. He explained to the Trustees that it was "Time to attempt what was so desirable;" and he gave as other reasons "it had been the subject of so much Talk for Years past especially among Strangers who are apt to scoff at it." Another reason he wrote was "some of the Artificers Apprehending" little prospect of their soon being employed were beginning to look for work in another province. "Wherefore," he continued, "taking the best Caution we could to inform ourselves rightly in the several Dimensions of a Church & fix upon what we thought was a due Proportion by divers Drafts of the particular Parts, & an entire Iconographical plan of the Whole; we next resolved to agree with the Workmen, Sawyers, Carpenters Masons, &c; at a certain rate . . . resolving to have as little to do as possible with Day Labour . . . & promised ourselves the little Fund we had, would sufficiently enable Us so farr to carry on the Building, as to see it well cover'd in and thereby safe from Damage." It was then to be left until another opportunity offered when the Trust should see fit to have the building completed inside and outside. Houstoun concluded, "I purposed to have herewith the Iconography of the church as it now stands; but the Drafts Man I employ'd has failed Me, & I must wait his time, to send it with my next."[30]

From Frederica Patrick Houstoun wrote again to Harmon Verelst on March 19, 1745, requesting him to have delivered to General Oglethorpe "a Small Cask with a Doz^n Bottles of Wine

---

30. *Colonial Records of Georgia*, XXIV, 363-370.

    The erection of the church continued under the Reverend Bartholomew Zouberbuhler, who, with the authorities, saw the completion of their task in 1750, when the building was dedicated, July 7. An effort was made through a research worker in London to procure a copy of the "Iconography," but with disappointing result. A copy, however, is in the state, but it is not procurable.

    For a description of the plans and of the specifications of the church see Unpublished Colonial Records of Georgia, XXIX, 106, 107; XXXI, 108, 109.

which is the pure juice of the Grape growing here without mixture whatsoever." Houstoun wrote that he had made about ten gallons the previous season, and "it was the first Wine made in the County of Frederica." Although the vines were young he believed "it Drinks a pretty Rhenish." "If," he added, "there were people Settled here that understood the Management of Vines I am positive Wine would be bro^t quickly to a great Perfection in this Colony, and repay the Government Sufficiently the charge of Settling and Maintaining the Country." Houstoun closed his letter by saying he "would be Singularly Oblig'd to you woul'd please let me know if the Wine comes Safe to You and if it be Drinkable in Britain."[31]

In the year 1745 the Georgia colonists were taking sides for and against the Reverend Thomas Bosomworth and his wife, Mary Musgrove. The long controversy and the end of the contention have a part in this narrative because Patrick Houstoun was one of twenty signers of a petition from the officers of General Oglethorpe and the principal inhabitants of the town and county of Frederica, to the effect that they had personal knowledge of Mrs. Mary Bosomworth from "their first arrival in the colony, and in justice to her character felt themselves obliged to make a public declaration." According to the residents of Frederica, the President and Assistants in Savannah allegedly were scheming to destroy the Bosomworths, and the Frederica townsmen, in their petition, testified to Mrs. Bosomworth's "loyalty as a British Subject in bringing her friends and relatives from the nation to fight against His Majesty's enemies . . . ." The petitioners in taking the part of the Reverend Mr. Bosomworth affirmed that they had had knowledge of him for five years, and "that he never behaved himself inconsistently with his duty and allegiance to his prince and had always conformed to the Liturgy of the Church of England. Their testimony they think will be sufficient to prove the wicked insinuations of her [Mary Bosomworth] Enemys False, Groundless and Malicious."[32] Patrick Houstoun was drawn further into the case by signing the Malatche paper, sometimes referred to as "the Bosomworth Papers." He acted as a witness to the signatures of fifteen lords

---
31. *Colonial Records of Georgia*, XXIV, 371, 372.
32. Unpublished Colonial Records of Georgia, XXVII, 26, 27, 381, 476.

on a document declaring Malatche as their Mico with full authority to transact all affairs relating to their Nation. Patrick Houstoun's attitude was undoubtedly cordial to the neighboring tribesmen. He had come into close relationship with them when they traded with him in his business in Savannah. His brother-in-law, George Dunbar, was intimately associated with them, and he had been sent on secret missions by Oglethorpe "up into the *Indian* Nations,"[33] to make friendly alliance with them, in preparation for the Spanish campaign. It is certain that Patrick Houstoun's witness of the signing of the Indian kings had no bearing on his later service in the colony. Had he been considered a disloyal subject, he would never have risen to appointment on the Royal Council and finally to the presidency of the same. The paper was sent to the Trustees in London, immediately after the signatures had been attached.

Some years later Patrick Houstoun was the bearer of a letter from the Reverend Mr. Bosomworth written to the speaker and to the members of the Assembly of the colony, and was dated March 16, 1752, asking that the writer be called upon to lay before the assembly his reasons for a true understanding of the state of Indian affairs for the justification of his character.[34]

It must have been about three years after the Bosomworth affair that the Houstoun family moved to the "Northern Division" to take up their permanent residency at their Rosdue plantation. In the year 1750 Patrick Houstoun then was included among the inhabitants of Savannah. In the summer of that year the principal citizens were so stirred over two circumstances that they resolved to refer their grievances to the Trustees whom they called their "Guardians." Patrick Houstoun joined his fellow-citizens, numbering nearly forty men, who, on July 7, signed the petitions. The first trouble which had aroused the ire of Savannahians was the chicanery of certain South Carolinians who were seeking to bring about the annexation of the Georgia colony to their own, perpetuating a feud which began when Oglethorpe was made Commander-in-Chief of the military forces of the

---

33. *Colonial Records of Georgia*, IV, 456; *Ibid.*, Supplement, 127.
34. Unpublished Colonial Records of Georgia, XXVII, 559. For Bosomworth's narrative, answering the charges against him and his wife by the President and Assistants, see *Ibid.*, 347-414.

South Carolina troops, as well as those of his regiment in Georgia. That inter-colony contention continued as a distinct irritation through many years to follow. The Georgia claimants set forth in their petition: "We should be not only greatly imprudent, but deficient in Point of Duty, if when alarmed with Schems artfully calculated for Purposes the most detrimental to this colony, we did not immediately apply to its Guardians."[35]

"We are sufficiently assured," concluded the petition, "that some Designing Men in our Neighboring Province are using their utmost efforts to get this Colony Annexed to those and insinuate that such a Junction would be agreeable to the Inhabitants of this. — That a Design of so bad Tendancy may not meet with Countenance, as our part of it is absolutely true." The signatures followed. The Trustees took cognizance of the complaint about a year and a half later when they issued a protest, entitled, "Objections to Annexing Georgia to South Carolina," which was sent to the Lords Commissioners of Trade and Plantations. What must have brought intense satisfaction to Houstoun and his fellow-colonists were the words in the text: ". . . The Jealousy which some Charles Town Merchants have of the Town of Savannah becoming from the superior fitness of its situation the great Mart for the Indian Trade to prevent which they will distress the present Inhabitants of Georgia by all the means in their power."[36]

Three weeks after signing the first petition most of the signatories, including Houstoun, gathered in the Council Room, on July 29, and signed a second one to be sent to the Trustees apprising them "concerning the great Inconveniences and Hardships the Inhabitants labour under from the Many Parties of Straggling Indians round our Settlements," asking for military protection.[37] The Indian question continued a vexing one for several years, until finally the officers governing the colony settled it.

There is little to relate of Sir Patrick's children, but with the knowledge that their parents owned property in two beautiful localities in the colony, one can easily imagine something of the life of four boys of that period, and some of their activities and recreations. Frederica had settled down to quiet and peace

---
35. *Ibid.*, XXXVI, 512, 515.
36. Jones, *History of Georgia*, I, 437, 438.
37. Unpublished Colonial Records of Georgia, XXXVI, 495-497.

during the years following the "Spanish Invasion." It is easy to picture the father and his boys standing on the ramparts of the fort at Frederica, while the parent recounted to his sons the story of that exciting day when Georgia troops drove the larger number of Spanish soldiers from the island.

A broad avenue lined with moss-draped live oak trees led from the Savannah road to the house on the Rosdue plantation. The view to the right and to the left showed the Little Ogeechee and the broad Vernon Rivers which converge into Green Island Sound five or six miles from the mainland. Ample grounds around the house furnished for children the best out-door recreation for building up fine physiques to encounter the strain that came later in their lives, although young Patrick appeared to have been the exception to the rule.

Some of the children of prominent colonists are mentioned in the earliest records, among them the Houstouns' two older sons who were given citations in the *Colonial Records of Georgia* in 1755 when their father petitioned the Royal Council for lot number sixty-seven and lot number sixty-nine in the proposed town of Hardwick for his sons Patrick and George, then thirteen and eleven years of age, respectively. The lots were never used, as the town did not materialize, and the project was abandoned. It would be of value, naturally, as a clue to their professions and interests later in life, to know something of the education of the Houstoun children. Although there were several private schools in Savannah, Southern colonists usually provided tutors for their children, and it is presumed that the Houstoun parents adhered to the custom. Young Patrick seems to have been the one selected for a foreign education. According to family tradition, Patrick, Jr., was a frail child. Therefore it is taken for granted that the condition of his health further influenced his father and mother to send him to Scotland for schooling in the hope that a vigorous climate might make of him a more healthy boy. It is not known when Patrick left Georgia, but he was in Glasgow at the age of twelve. On his arrival there, how wonderfully old and strange the foreign city must have seemed to his youthful eyes. Its streets were paved with cobblestones, its houses were built of stone, and there were also thatched cottages, so unlike the small houses of Frederica and Savannah. After young Patrick arrived in Glasgow his father wrote a letter from Rosdue, December 5, 1754, to his cousin, George Houstoun, of Paisley, in which he made reference to his son. It is disappointing that there is no family news in the letter and nothing about the affairs of the colony. "I suppose," wrote the Georgia Houstoun, "You see my son sometimes at Glasgow . . . ." Exhorting his kinsman in Scotland to give young Patrick good advice so that he would "turn out to be a prittie fellow," the elder Houstoun closed his letter with "Your Cousling & most Humble Sevtt."[38]

Without question Patrick's aunt took him to visit the ancient Castle of Houstoun, and the interest the boy showed in the home of his ancestors easily can be imagined. Perhaps before he left Scotland he even made the trip to Inverness to carry back to his mother the latest news of her family. It was an enlightening experience for the young lad, and the years he spent in the native country of his parents left their mark on the colony where he was born. As he was visiting relatives, he must have attended preparatory schools in Glasgow. It is known positively that he did not attend the University there, St. Andrews or the University of Edinburgh;[39] but in some manner Patrick was well prepared for the conspicuous part he played when he returned to the land of his birth before his father died.

Some time after April, 1755, Sir Patrick and Lady Houstoun's only daughter was born, and she was given the name of Ann Priscilla; and in the year 1757 the last child, William, was added to the family circle. Prior to 1755 the father had begun his public career, and even before he received his title. When the Colony of Georgia made a change in its governmental affairs, Patrick Houstoun was called into political service, from which he did not withdraw until death claimed him.

---

38. A photostatic copy of the letter was sent to the author by Mrs. Anne D. Houstoun of Johnstone Castle, Johnstone, Scotland, April 24, 1913. In her letter she mentioned a visit her husband had paid to "Rossdue," in 1874.
39. Verification in letters to the author from Mr. John Spencer Muirhead, D.S.O., M.C., LL.B., Secretary, Glasgow University Court (1934); Mr. John Millar, Assistant Clerk, University of Edinburgh (1936); and Mr. Andrew Bennett, Secretary, University of St. Andrews (1938).

Chapter VI

PATRICK HOUSTOUN'S PUBLIC LIFE

AT the time Patrick Houstoun made his entry into political life, the civil government of the colony was undergoing a period of transition.

In the year 1750 the President of the colony, William Stephens, was too infirm to continue the responsibility of managing its affairs, and realizing his feebleness, he retired to his plantation Bewlie and received a pension of eighty pounds per annum from the Trustees. He died in 1753. Henry Parker was appointed Vice President and with his assistants assumed charge of the province. His commission for president arrived in June of that year. "The same day provision was made for holding at Savannah between Michaelmas and Lady Day next, an assembly of the people of Georgia to propose, debate and represent to the Trustees, what shall appear to them to be for the benefit of the Province in general."[1] The Trustees thereupon adopted a resolution, and rules were issued for the "selecting of delegates to a provincial assembly to convene at Savannah on the 15th of the following January. Sixteen delegates were to compose that assembly, and they were proportioned to the population of the different parishes or districts."[2] The Assembly was to meet in Savannah once a year at such time as should be designated by the President of the colony and his assistants. It was to remain in session not longer than one month.

No law could be enacted by the Assembly as that privilege was vested solely in the Trustees, but the deputies were empowered to discuss and suggest to the latter "such measures as they might deem conducive to the welfare of particular communities and for the general good of the province." Every town, village, or district in the province containing a population of ten families was empowered to send one deputy. Any settlement

1. Jones, *History of Georgia*, I, 432.
2. *Ibid.*, 434.

embracing thirty families could send two delegates. Savannah was allowed four delegates. At first no qualifications were required of the representatives. By June, 1751, however, "no inhabitant could be elected a deputy who had not one hundred mulberry trees planted and properly fenced upon every tract of 50 acres he possessed." From and after June, 1753, no one was capable of being a delegate who had not conformed strictly to the prescribed limitation of the number of Negro slaves in proportion to his white servants, who had not in his family at least one female instructed in the art of reeling silk, and who did not produce annually fifteen pounds of silk for every fifty acres of land owned by him. "Such," writes a famous Georgia historian, "were the curious qualifications prescribed for membership of the first quasi-deliberative, quasi-legislative body which ever assembled in Georgia. They were evidently intended," he continues, "to stimulate the production of silk, that commodity which blinded the eyes of the Trustees and warped their judgment in directing the industrial pursuits of the colonists."[3]

Patrick Houstoun was elected to represent the Vernonburg District, and, presumably, he continued a member of the Provincial Assembly until it was succeeded by the Royal Council of which he was one of the charter members. The district which elected Patrick Houstoun as its representative had an interesting history. It was settled in 1742 by a colony of German-Swiss who had served as indentured soldiers of General Oglethorpe's Regiment. Patrick Houstoun's lands lay south of Vernonburg, but after Georgia became a Royal Province, an act was passed in 1755 which provided that the Southern District of Savannah should include certain villages and the lands beyond the settlement on the Vernon River.[4]

The first Provincial Assembly convened in Savannah on the day appointed, January 15, 1751, and continued in session for nearly three weeks. "After an exchange of courtesies with Vice President Parker, the assembly proceeded to business." Act-

---
3. *Ibid.*, 435.
4. Dolores Boisfeuillet Floyd, "Vernonburgh, Known as White Bluff, Originally Part of South Carolina Barony," in *Savannah Morning News*, June 26, 1932.

ing within the powers which had been given the Assembly it made a report under the "heads of grievances," which was considered necessary for the welfare of the colony. The eleven grievances which the deputies thought remediable were: a proper pilot boat; a building under the Bluff for the convenience of boat crews, Negroes, etc.; standard weights, scales, and measures; a survey of the river; a commissioner to regulate pilots and pilotage; an order to prevent masters of vessels from discharging ballast into the river; an inspector and sworn packer to examine the produce of the colony; a clerk of the market; suitable officers to command the militia; and repairs to the courthouse.[5] The board (the President and Assistants) answered the report by giving assurance that it would comply with the presentments as soon as possible, with the exception of those that had to be referred to the Trustees: the pilot boat and the standard weights and measures for which the board had already made application to the Trustees.

Before adjourning, the assemblymen submitted an address to be sent to the Trustees calling attention to important matters in the affairs of the colony, one of which was "Objections to annexing Georgia to South Carolina," which, if enacted, the deputies set forth, "would reduce it [Georgia] to the same desolate condition in which the Southern parts of South Carolina were before the Establishment of Georgia."[6]

In compliance with the request that suitable officers be commissioned to command the militia, President Parker and his assistants acted, on the following April, by organizing the militia of the province as Oglethorpe's Regiment had been disbanded. Male inhabitants possessing three hundred or more acres of land "were ordered to appear, well accoutred and with horses to be organized as cavalry." Those men who were possessed of a smaller number of acres were armed as infantry. A general muster in the lower districts was held at Savannah on June 13, 1751, "When about two hundred and twenty men, infantry and cavalry, armed and equipped, paraded under the command of Captain Noble Jones."[7] As Patrick Houstoun owned more than three

---
5. Jones, *History of Georgia*, I, 336.
6. *Ibid.*, 437.
7. *Ibid.*, 439.

hundred acres and as he had already held commissions in Oglethorpe's Regiment, it is hardly questionable that he responded to orders which seem to have been obligatory.

In the year 1751 Patrick Houstoun's position underwent a marked change. Then he rose from a landed proprietor to a titled gentleman in the realm of Great Britain. On the death in Scotland of his second cousin, Sir John Houstoun, fourth baronet, he succeeded to the baronetcy. The fourth baronet died without male issue on July 27, 1751. It was not necessary for the successor to a title to go to Scotland to make good his claim;[8] so it was through correspondence, presumably, that Patrick Houstoun received the title conferred first upon his grandfather.

The news of his elevation to a titled man must have reached Patrick Houstoun a few months after the death of his second cousin. He is mentioned next in the public records of the Royal Council as "Sir Patrick Houstoun, Baronet."

* * * *

After accepting his appointment as deputy to the Provincial Assembly from Vernonburg, Sir Patrick Houstoun never returned to private life. His next public duties took him into service for the Crown.

The charter granted by George II to the Trustees for Establishing the Colony of Georgia was for twenty-one years and was to expire on June 9, 1753. Because of the force of circumstances relating to the maintenance of the colony the Common Council of the Trustees memorialized the Lords of His Majesty's Privy Council.[9] Expressing the desire of the Trustees to surrender their charter and thereby to relinquish all responsibility, they asked that Georgia be made a separate and independent province of the Crown.

The proper formalities having been carried out, His Majesty agreed to accept the surrender upon the suggested conditions. The Trustees in London held their last meeting on June 23, 1752, and

---

8. Authority of the Lyon-King-at-Arms in Scotland. "A note in the printed *Complete Baronetage* states that Sir Patrick went to America taking with him portraits of his father and mother as also of his grandfather 1st. Baronet." Letter to the author from Millar and Bryce, May 9, 1934.
9. Percy Scott Flippin, "The Royal Government of Georgia," in *The Georgia Historical Quarterly*, VIII, No. 1 (March, 1924), 1.

on that day Georgia became a Royal Province. "By the terms of the surrender her integrity as an independent province, separate from South Carolina, was fully assured, and all grants of land hitherto made to the inhabitants were recognized and protected."[10] A proclamation was issued by the Privy Council that until the King should establish another form of government in the province, all those holding appointments, both civil and military, should continue in office. By March, 1754, the Board of Trade submitted a plan for a civil government in Georgia which was approved, and on August 6 of that year Captain John Reynolds of the British Navy was appointed the first Royal Governor of Georgia.

At the same time other officers received their warrants direct from the Crown, among them Sir Patrick Houstoun, Bart., who was selected as Register of Grants and Receiver of Quit Rents, with a salary of fifty pounds a year. Patrick Graham, the former President of the Colony, Sir Patrick Houston, Bart., James Habersham, Alexander Kellet, William Clifton, Noble Jones, Pickering Robinson, Francis Harris, Jonathan Bryan, and William Russell were all confirmed as members of the King's Council. Henry Yonge and William deBrahm[11] were commissioned as "Joint Surveyors of Land in Georgia." James Habersham was appointed secretary and register of records; William Clifton, Attorney General; Alexander Kellet, provost marshal; and William Russell, naval officer. Those men were the official associates of Sir Patrick Houstoun, and doubtless many of them were his personal friends.

Governor Reynolds arrived in Savannah on the man-of-war *Port Mahon* on October 29, 1754. He was welcomed and greeted with the usual demonstrations of the times. "Bonfires at night supplemented the general delight which was manifested during the day. After a formal introduction to the president and assistants in council assembled his commission was read. He was then conducted to the president's chair whence he announced the dissolution of the old board and the formation of a royal council under letters-patent from the Crown. The next morning, the members of the council took the oath of office and completed

---
10. Jones, *History of Georgia*, I, 459.
11. Some historians use the capital "D", but deBrahm's signature in his *History of the Province of Georgia* shows the small "d".

their organization. Other officers, named by His Majesty, were sworn faithfully to perform the duties devolving upon them. His commission as captain-general and vice admiral of the province was 'read and published at the head of the militia under arms before the council chamber. It was listened to with profound attention and saluted with several rounds of musketry and shouts of loyalty.' A public dinner, given by the members of council and the principal inhabitants of Savannah in honor of the governor, closed the public exercises of the occasion, and the province passed thus simply and joyously from the hands of the trustees into the direct keeping of the Crown."[12]

The Governor and Council held their first meeting in a house on the southern trust lot on Abercorn and Duke Streets facing west on the square, later named in honor of the first Royal Governor. That something of a catastrophe overtook the Crown dignitaries during one of the early meetings is gleaned from a letter written by Reynolds to the Board of Trade in December of that year, when he reported officially on Savannah and the Council. Part of the letter reads: " . . . . The town of Savannah is well situated and contains about a hundred and fifty houses, all wooden ones, very small and mostly very old. The biggest was used for the meeting of the President and Assistants, wherein I sat in Council for a few days, but one end fell down whilst we were all there, and obliged us to move to a kind of shed behind the Court House, which being quite unfit, I have given orders, with the advice of the Council, to fit up the shell of a house which was lately built for laying up the silk, but was never made use of, being very ill-calculated for the purpose as Mr. Ottolonghe informs me, wherefore he says he has no further use for it, but it will make a tolerable good house for the Council and Assembly to meet in, and for a few offices besides."[13] What a dire misfortune to occur after the auspicious inauguration of the first Royal Governor, and what an unexpected interruption to the proceedings of the Governor and Council suddenly to have a part of the room give way! It was no mean walk then from the Council House to the Court House which was several blocks away.

---

12. Jones, *History of Georgia*, I, 469.
13. *Ibid.*

Patrick Houstoun's Public Life

The legislative body of the province was to consist of three branches: the Governor and his Privy Council, or King's Council, which acted in an advisory capacity, and to which the Governor could refer his instructions or not as he pleased; the Upper House, and the Lower House, with the Royal Governor chief over all. He held the title "Captain-General and Governor in Chief of his Majesty's Province of Georgia and Vice-Admiral of the same," and was addressed as "Your Excellency."[14]

Sir Patrick, as required of the other members of the Council, took the prescribed oath swearing true and faithful allegiance to King George II, to his heirs, and to Governor Reynolds; to serve his King and promote the "Good of His Majesty's Affairs" with the best advice and counsel; to defend to the best of his ability the province from all "Foreign Invasions, and intestine Insurrections;" not to "Countenance or conceal any treasonable or seditious Speeches against His said Majesty;" not to reveal directly or indirectly the secret debates of the Council.[15]

As a member of His Majesty's Council, Houstoun served under the three Royal Governors and, for all save four months of the seven years of his membership in the Council, he was President of that body, and also of the Upper House of the Assembly. But for circumstances concerning the change of executives, he would have been, for a short period at least, acting Governor.

When George II appointed the members of the Council, the first name on the list was Patrick Graham. Precedence was given to him of course, as he was at that time President of the colony. According to the rules of the new government, the senior member of the Council became its President, and President of the Upper House of Assembly as well. If the Governor was absent, provision was made for the President of the Council to take his place, and act in the capacity of Governor. The second name on the list of Council members was that of Sir Patrick Houstoun, Baronet, and when Patrick Graham died in May, 1755, Patrick Houstoun, by virtue of his being the senior member, took his place. He held the office until his death in February, 1762. The name that appeared third on the list was that of James Habersham, and on the death of Sir Patrick Houstoun, he was advanced

---
14. *Ibid.*, 462.
15. *Colonial Records of Georgia*, VII, 13.

automatically to the presiding officer of the Council and ruler over the Upper House, serving those bodies as did his two predecessors. James Habersham, because of his office as President of the Council, became acting Governor from July, 1771, until February, 1773, during a visit of Governor Wright to England.

In November following his elevation to the office of President of His Majesty's Council, Sir Patrick was selected, with two of his associates, to accompany Governor Reynolds on a visit to the town of Augusta. It was frequently noted in the Proceedings of the Governor and Council that presents were sent from the King to pacify the Indians and keep them in a friendly attitude toward the colony. At a meeting of the Council held on November 7, 1755, Governor Reynolds requested three members of that body to accompany him to Augusta, where he was going to distribute "His Majesty's Presents" among the Indians. The Council responded by naming Patrick Houstoun, James Habersham, and James Powell.[16]

The delegation did not make the trip until the following month. Reynolds waited ten days in Augusta for the various chiefs to assemble and then he was called back suddenly to Savannah on an important business matter. The records do not state whether or not the three members of the Council returned with him or remained in Augusta, but the Governor did appoint his private secretary, William Little, a surgeon in the Royal Navy, whom he had made chairman and agent of Indian affairs, to represent him and make the addresses he had prepared. The Indians were placated with gifts and they renewed their pledge of allegiance to the Colony of Georgia.

It was Dr. Little who was the cause of Governor Reynolds's unpopularity in the province. When the latter was recalled after two years, on charges preferred against him by the colonists, he was relieved by Henry Ellis, sent to Georgia as Lieutenant Governor, but commissioned Governor a year later. As it happened, he reached Savannah on February 16, 1757, before Reynolds left. Had there been an interim between the departure of one and the

---

16. *Ibid.*, 294. Unpublished Colonial Records, XXXVIII, Pt. 1, 187-213.

arrival of the other, the governorship unquestionably would have devolved upon Sir Patrick Houstoun.

Governor Ellis found the climate of Georgia unsuited to his health, and asked the home government to relieve him of his duties. The Crown's next choice was James Wright, a resident of Charles Town, who was appointed Lieutenant Governor.[17] Wright arrived in Savannah November 2, 1760, and Ellis left the same day. Again but for the circumstance of the two governors exchanging office on the soil of Georgia, Sir Patrick would have been in full control of provincial affairs.

For a few days, however, Sir Patrick was the Governor's representative in Savannah. Two months after Governor Ellis assumed office, he found it necessary to visit the Southern District of the colony, and made his plans to depart April 20. Before leaving, he informed the Council that he had made provision against any matters needing attention during his absence, arranging for the senior councilor to call a meeting of the Council if he deemed it necessary. He then read a letter of detailed instructions addressed to Patrick Houstoun who was to act for the Governor in his absence.[18]

Since Ellis was present at the next meeting of the Council, the Governor was absent from Savannah not more than ten days. In that interval, however, Sir Patrick was authorized to act in his stead, if required. He was entrusted with the duty of opening important dispatches from the King, and of calling the Council together if the instructions needed the advice of the whole body.

A review of the Proceedings and Minutes of the Governor and Council shows that there were frequent meetings of that body, the Governor always being present. More often than otherwise, the business consisted of the reading of petitions from various colonists "praying" for new tracts of land. Members of the Council came in for their holdings, and Houstoun was no less a petitioner than most of his fellow-members of Council.

Many times the Council received delegations of Indians to air their grievances, sometimes against traders and sometimes to inform the Governor of the interference of the French who were

---
17. On March 20, 1761, James Wright was advanced to the full governorship. *Ibid.*, II, 26.
18. *Colonial Records of Georgia*, VII, 544.

endeavoring to sever the alliance between the English colonists and their red neighbors. At other times there would be communications from the Governor of South Carolina relating to similar questions.

Council met frequently, the Governor calling his advisors together fifty, sixty, or eighty times a year. The list of those present always preceded the record of the minutes, and Sir Patrick Houstoun's name invariably followed that of the Governor's, if present, as senior member of Council and as President.

Sir Patrick's attendance at the Council meetings appears, by reference to the records that are extant, about equal to the other members'. In his six years, his average was nearly fifty-nine per cent, if the secretary's records are held correct. That speaks fairly well for a country gentleman when it is realized he was the presiding officer of the Upper House which held separate meetings and met almost daily when the General Assembly was in session.

One interesting public event that occurred while Sir Patrick Houstoun was a member of the Council and for which he gave his vote was the issuing of a proclamation for the observance of a public day of Thanksgiving, twenty-six years after Oglethorpe landed on the soil of Georgia. On November 13, 1759, Council met as usual. The Governor presided and the Councilors present were: Sir Patrick Houstoun, Jonathan Bryan, James Mackay, James Edward Powell, William Clifton, and William Knox. It was unanimously agreed that "Wednesday the fifth day of December next, be observed as a publick Day of Thanksgiving throughout this Province for the late glorious Successes attending His Majesty's Arms both by sea and Land."[19] That was the time of the French and Indian War and the successes pertaining thereto, but before the fall of Quebec, which decided the issue. When the news of that victory reached Savannah some months after it occurred, Council ordered the observance of another day of Thanksgiving which was held on December 7, 1760. The first observance in 1759 may be styled the "first Thanksgiving Day" in Savannah.

---

19. Thomas Gamble, "Previous Peace Celebrations in which Savannah Took Part," in *Savannah Morning News*, November 18, 1924; also *Colonial Records of Georgia*, VIII, 189.

Under the government of the Royal Council all of the land grants from the Trustees had to be reconveyed to the original grantees. The usual form was the petitioning of the owner to the Council for possession. On November 7, 1755, the Royal Council reconveyed "To Sir Patrick Houstoun, Bart. Five Hundred Acres of Land situate on a point of land between Vernon River and a branch of the Little Ogeechee bounding East and West on the said Rivers and the Marshes of the same, South on a Creek leading from Vernon River and the Little Ogeechee and North on Lands granted to James Houstoun."[20]

Sir Patrick's duties as a member of the Royal Council did not interfere with the cultivation of his lands. An early venture of the colony, one on which the Trustees built great hope, was the promotion of silk culture. The experiment was not successful, and as late as the year of the surrender of their Charter, the Trustees "had succeeded in raising scarcely a thousand pounds of raw silk" while their expenditures reached the sum of nearly fifteen hundred pounds. Bounties and awards having been offered, many plantation owners expended a great deal of labor in the production of cocoons; and during the Crown's administration Patrick Houstoun was the recipient of the first prize given to the person who had planted and fenced the greatest number of mulberry trees. His award followed a report of the contest, dated May 20, 1756, and sent over the signatures of James Habersham and Joseph Ottolonghe to William Shipley, Secretary of the "Society for the encouragement of Arts Manufacture and Commerce" in Craigs Court, Charing Cross, London. After "mature consideration" Houstoun was adjudged the planter entitled to the premium of £10.[21]

While Sir Patrick was President of the Council there occurred many "Talks" with the war lords of the Indian Nation. Of much significance, was the "grand conference," which took place on November 3, 1757. Houstoun was present, and on the written contract entered into by the Council and the Indians, his signature appeared after that of Governor Ellis's, followed by that of

20. *Colonial Records of Georgia*, VII, 293.
21. *Georgia Historical Collections*, VI, 9, *Letters of James Habersham*.
   Joseph Ottolonghe was in charge of the silk culture. He had acquired a knowledge of the best method of conducting filatures. Jones, *History of Georgia*, I, 460.

James Habersham, Secretary. Next to sign were the "heads" of twenty-one different towns of the Upper and Lower Creeks. While the conference was in session the Council Chamber in Savannah was thronged with the townspeople "who attended with anxiety" to learn the outcome "upon which the tranquility of the Province depended." At the north the French and Indian War then in progress, and the activity of French spies in the "back country" among Georgia's Indian allies, kept the colonists constantly solicitous of their welfare. The agreements pledged that day resulted in the province's retaining the old alliance with her Indian neighbors.[22]

* * * *

When the Crown of England took over the direction of Georgia, a complete form of legislative government was laid out, similar to the one in use in the other provinces of the King. It was vested in three branches: an executive, who was the Royal Governor; his Advisory Council, also called His Majesty's Council; and the General Assembly, or the Royal Legislature. When the King's Council was sitting without the Governor, it was called the Upper House of the Assembly; and the Lower House, when it convened at the call of the Governor, was known as the Commons House of Assembly. The latter sometimes designated itself as the House of Representatives. The two houses together constituted the General Assembly.

The Governor and Council remained in charge from October 31, 1754, to January 7, 1755. There is no statement that has been found in the Proceedings of the Governor and Council to indicate that there was a resolution passed to organize the General Assembly; however, history shows that it did come into being on the latter day and year. From other references the supposition is that the Governor summoned the electors of the people to come to Savannah for the above purpose, and to take their place in the provincial government to enact laws for the betterment of the province.

On Tuesday morning, January 7, 1755, there were assembled in the Capital, to form the Lower House of the Legislature the eighteen newly elected legislators for the town and district of

---

22. For full account of the conference see *Colonial Records of Georgia*, VII, 644-648.

Savannah; the towns of Abercorn and Goshen; the islands of Skidaway, Wilmington, and Green; the town and district of Ebenezer; the district of Vernonburg; the district of the Great and Little Ogeechee; the town and district of Halifax; and the district of Midway.

It is interesting to read the names of those early electors, as many of them were prominent in the life of the colony. They included Dr. Noble Wimberly Jones, Esq., the son of Noble Jones, who was a member of the King's Council; James Houstoun, a younger brother of Sir Patrick, it is thought, who sat also in the Assembly; Lewis Johnston,[23] a noted physician of Savannah; Joseph Ottolonghe, who was in charge of the silk culture and the filature, having received his training in Italy; Henry Yonge, one of the surveyors with deBrahm; and there were three prominent citizens of Ebenezer, George Cuthbert, Clement Martin, later a member of the King's Council, and James DeVeaux.

Shortly after assembling, two of the legislators were sent to apprise the Governor in the Council Chamber that those who had been duly elected were present, and would be pleased to know when he would be attended by the said gentlemen, that they might take and subscribe the oath. Governor Reynolds was sitting with his Council and Sir Patrick Houstoun was present. The Governor, on receiving the message of the legislators, ordered them to the Council Chamber where they took the State Oaths appointed by law and declared and subscribed the Test. Following that he instructed the members to withdraw and elect their Speaker. Soon afterward the Governor received a second message that the Lower House had elected David Douglas, of Augusta, as their Speaker. The legislators returned to the Council Chamber accompanied by their Speaker. He was presented and approved by His Excellency. Douglas then requested the Governor, in the name of the House of Representatives, "That they might have free access to His Excellency's person, Liberty of Speech, Protection for their Persons and that the Imperfections of the Speaker might not be imputed to the House." The Governor replied all would be granted that would be consistent with His Majesty's instructions.

---

23. Dr. Lewis Johnston later was connected with the Houstoun family through the marriage of his nephew, Colonel James Johnston, Jr., to Ann Marion Houstoun, granddaughter of Sir Patrick Houstoun.

The Governor was sitting with his Council when the members of the Lower House joined them. "He made an inaugural address which was complimentary and conciliatory," addressing them as "Gentlemen of the Council and of the Assembly."[24] His speech is printed in the proceedings of both houses. At the conclusion of his address, the Governor withdrew, and the Lower House filed out to its own room. Each House then proceeded to organize for business. The Journal of the Upper House states that "Mr. President," Patrick Graham, took the chair. Both houses offered, by resolution, their thanks to the Governor for his address, and in the Upper House, Sir Patrick Houstoun, Alexander Kellett and Francis Harris were ordered to prepare the address for that body. Two days later all of the members of the Upper House, on receiving a message from the Governor that he was ready, repaired to the Governor's room and the address was read to him.

It was unfortunate that the duties of the two houses were not clearly defined at the time of the formation of the Assembly, as it would have averted some of the trouble that ensued. From the beginning the Commons House of Assembly denied the right of the Council to call itself the "Upper House of Assembly," but continued to speak of it as "the Council," claiming the members had been appointed to hold only advisory powers. It was not until a few years prior to the Revolution that the Lower House recognized the Upper House as such, with the right to inaugurate measures. At first the Lower House reserved to itself the prerogative of originating all bills, insisting that the Upper House endorse them, and gave it the right to *suggest* amendments, but *not* to pass them.

One of the first and most important acts passed by the General Assembly provided for the regulation of the militia for the security and defense of the province; and another was one "empowering surveyors to lay out public roads in Georgia to facilitate speedy communications between the inhabitants residing in distant parts of the province and providing for the establishment of ferries."[25]

Not only was Sir Patrick Houstoun interested in those pro-

---
24. Jones, *History of Georgia*, I, 474.
25. *Ibid.*, 479.

jects from a personal standpoint, as his plantation lay some distance from the town on one of the waterways leading to the sea, but his concern also was official, as he was selected one of a committee to act for the Assembly. But three years passed before that body carried into effect the preliminaries necessary for further fortifying the province.

In July, 1757, Sir Patrick was appointed one of the commissioners "for building such forts as shall be planned and designed for the respective commissioners," the rest of the act reading: "for the town and District of Savannah, and as far westward as Abercorn Creek, Southward as Great Ogeechee River and East the Sea, including the Islands as far South as Ossabaw Inlet." The name of "The Honorable Sir Patrick Houstoun, Baronet" as a commissioner for the town and district of Savannah was mentioned first and the others were James Habersham, Francis Harris, Jonathan Bryan, James Edward Powell, William Clifton, William Knox, Noble Jones, Esquires (all members of the Council), and others.[26]

In January of the previous year Governor Reynolds had sent a report to the Board of Trade in London, which showed the weak condition of the province for defenses; at the same time he submitted a detailed and comprehensive plan indicating where fortifications should be erected both for land and for sea protection, the former including forts on navigable rivers. The report included the descriptions of how certain forts should be built, the necessary repairs on those already in existence and how they had fallen into disrepair, and the required number of guns for each, with specifications amounting to an expenditure of twenty-eight thousand pounds.[27]

The matter of the roads seems to have attracted earlier attention, and some action was taken. In March, 1755, the Royal Legislature appointed Sir Patrick Houstoun and five other surveyors for the Southern District. The road to Vernonburg and the adjacent village, later known as White Bluff, came into consideration in an act that was passed by the Assembly late in 1756 and approved by the Council the following January. The act set forth that many of the inhabitants who were settled on the

---
26. *Colonial Records of Georgia*, XVIII, 204, 205.
27. Jones, *History of Georgia*, I, 505-510.

southern frontier, and who were obliged to attend the Assembly and the general courts in Savannah, were put to great inconvenience because there was no road to open communications from the town to the Ogeechee River. Complaining that the number of inhabitants who were obliged to work on the southwest road was too small, the legislators drafted the act for the purpose of making available for work on this road all who were liable for duty on the southeast and southern roads in addition to those who lived in several other places. The act specifically exempted from duty on the southwest road Patrick Houstoun, his servants and his slaves.[28]

* * * *

As already observed, the presidency of His Majesty's Council imposed no severe duties upon Sir Patrick Houstoun, because the Governor was always in the province while the former held office and presided at all meetings. Sir Patrick's duties as a member of the Council required of him mainly the obligation of attending the meetings, giving his advice and voting on the consideration of important matters brought before the Council by the Governor.

The above situation did not obtain, however, when Sir Patrick was sitting as President of the Upper House of the Assembly. There he was the executive, and his office as President automatically made him the presiding officer of the senior body of the Royal Legislature. Sir Patrick Houstoun did not become President of the Council until the first of June, 1755, on the death of Patrick Graham who held the office when the new government came into being, October, 1754, (Council) and January, 1755, (General Assembly).

The Upper House of Assembly held a somewhat anomalous position because of the refusal of the Lower House to recognize it as anything more than an advisory Council to the Governor, for which purpose the Lower House insisted it was formed. The latter house, however, granted to the higher body the right to "*suggest* such amendments as in their judgment would improve the proposed laws."

---

28. *Colonial Records of Georgia*, XVIII, 6, 182, 183. After a bill had passed both houses, it was sent to the Governor for his approval, following which it was sent to London to be passed upon by the King and his Council there.

Only one course could follow upon such a situation, and that was a feeling of antagonism on both sides. There was the Governor and Council which had governed Georgia for over two months on one side, and eighteen gentlemen elected by the people on the other side, to form the legislative body which was to govern Georgia for the future. There were in both houses friends sitting in different branches, and, in some instances, there were relatives; namely, Noble Jones on the Council and his son, Dr. Noble Wimberly Jones, in the Commons House, and Sir Patrick Houstoun in the Council and his brother, James, in the Lower House. At times the atmosphere must have been electrically charged; nevertheless, the enactments for bettering the condition of the province continued, and committees from each house met and worked, at least it is hoped, in harmony.

It is not the purpose here to give a synopsis of all the business transacted in the Upper House while Sir Patrick Houstoun was its president—that would belong to a history of the province— but to give glimpses of the part taken by him while he was the presiding officer of that body.

When the General Assembly was in session, the Upper House met daily, as did the Lower House, and the passing back and forth of bills and messages continued all through the meetings. In addition, joint conferences were requested from each House when the occasion demanded, and they were usually held.

At the third meeting after the General Assembly was organized, the Upper House asked the Lower House for a conference relating to the tenure of lands; and the President, Patrick Graham, appointed Sir Patrick Houstoun, Noble Jones, and Jonathan Bryan the committee to confer with the other house. The following day Sir Patrick reported to his house that the committee had met and had agreed on all resolutions save one. The report is not printed in the Journal.

Sir Patrick Houstoun's name appears on several of the committees for that session, and he was also appointed to deliver messages to the Lower House, and sometimes to the Governor.

That first session of the General Assembly adjourned in February and before it convened for the second time in November, 1755, Patrick Graham had died and Sir Patrick Houstoun became President of the Council, which had held many meetings in the interim. When the General Assembly was called to meet on the first day of December, the Upper House also assembled and the minutes note that "Mr. President" took the chair after the Governor had delivered his address before both houses. No mention is made of the death of Graham or the name of his successor, but by November 4 an address was sent to the Governor and Sir Patrick Houstoun signed his name as President. At no other time does the President's name appear in the minutes, but when there was a joint address written the Speaker of the Lower House signed his name below that of the President of the Upper House. By way of comment, the secretary's name was signed to the minutes only when the house adjourned. No names were listed of those present at the meetings. When messages from representatives of the King were received by the Governor, they were regarded as orders from the Crown and it was to his Advisory Council, sitting as the Upper House, that His Excellency sent the communication upon which action was taken.

An amusing touch was given to the dignified minutes of the Upper House when at its meetings on June 21, 1757, the committee for preparing rules and orders for regulating the proceedings of the house made its report. Acting on the recommendations of its committee, the house adopted fifteen rules of procedure. Three of them referred to the presiding officer, the first instructing him to uncover when addressing the house. The second rule required those members who arrived late to make "an Obeysance to the chair" before taking their seats, while the third aimed at preventing disorder by compelling those who would go from one side of the hall to the other to make "an Obeysance to the Chair."

Once the President was ordered by the house to reprimand absent members by the following resolution: "A motion was made and Agreed to—That letters be sent to Jonathan Bryan and James Mackay Esq^{rs} from the President requiring their attendance."[29] Those gentlemen were his personal friends, in all probability, and a formal reminder, signed officially, perhaps served to carry out the injunction. At any rate both of those gentlemen later served on important committees and their non-attendance was only a slight offense.

---

29. *Ibid.*, XVI, 117ff.

Whenever the Governor sent a message, "the President acquainted the House that he had a message from his Honour the Governor to this House signed by his Honour which he [the President] was directed to lay before this house." Sometimes it was a notice to adjourn the house; at others it was for the purpose of assembling his Council, and often it was to present official communications from England. When an address was made to the Governor, it was presented sometimes by the clerk of either house, by both houses in a body, or by the President of the Upper House in person; or, if in the Lower House, by the Speaker.

The duties assumed by Sir Patrick Houstoun on November 1, 1756, as President of the Upper House of Asembly, continued uninterruptedly for six years.

* * * *

It was in the second year of Sir Patrick Houstoun's presidency of His Majesty's Council and of the Upper House that an event occurred in his life which must have caused him embarrassment and extreme annoyance.[30] "One Mungo Graham" through a petition presented to the Lower House caused what Sir Patrick "apprehended" a reflection on his character. In the end Houstoun was entirely cleared, but the proceedings in the two houses covered a period of nearly three weeks, while the scene shifted from one house to the other. During that time Sir Patrick must have been in a state of continuous irritation over an assault on his character which undoubtedly came as a complete and unexpected surprise.

The troublesome business was first brought to light on January 18, 1757, when in the Lower House a petition from Mungo Graham was read charging that Houstoun had "possessed himself" of a commission addressed by the Trustees to Patrick Graham authorizing the latter to evict the Reverend Thomas Bosomworth from lands which Bosomworth claimed had been granted to him by the Lower Creeks. The petition requested that Houstoun be called on in the interest of the "Publick Good" to deliver to the House the commission he was charged with holding.

---
30. The story of the case will be found in *Colonial Records of Georgia*, XVI, 140-155.

When that piece of information fell upon the ears of the members of the house, it must have surprised them to hear such aspersions cast upon an officer of the Crown and a man long resident in the province. No mention is made of the reception given to the petition, but a resolution was passed immediately "That the said Mungo Graham attend this House to be examined Concerning the several matters alleged in his Petition."

Mungo[31] evidently was waiting patiently outside hoping to be summoned before the house, as the next item in the minutes states that "he attended accordingly and answer'd the Questions put to him by the House, and then he withdrew." Upon his departure the delegates spent much time considering the petition. They ended by dispatching a request to Governor Reynolds, "that he will be pleased to give Directions to the said Patrick Houstoun to lay the said Commission before this House." His Excellency returned the verbal message that he was "pleased to Answer that he would give directions accordingly." Immediately after the reading of the minutes in the Lower House the next morning, Sir Patrick Houstoun arose and denied having seen "such a Paper," explaining that he did not "believe any such Commission was in being."

Following Houstoun's refutation, Mungo Graham was called into the house. Upon examination he declared that he had seen the commission, read it and believed that it had been signed by Harmon Verelst, accountant for the Trustees. He was not certain whether it had been issued in 1752 or in 1753, but he explained that Patrick Mackay, a Mr. Cuthbert, and John Graham knew of Houstoun's receipt of the commission. Moreover, Mungo Graham declared he had asked Houstoun for a copy of the document to which statement the latter had replied that "it must never see the light more," a response which, it may be surmised, caused Graham to conclude that Houstoun had "possessed himself of the commission."

The next step in the proceedings was a message from the Upper

---

31. Who the said Mungo Graham was and whether or not he was any relation to the late President of the King's Council, Patrick Graham, research has failed to reveal. The only reference to him discovered is that in June, 1755, he petitioned His Majesty's Council for lot number 83 in the town of Hardwick, which later was granted. *Colonial Records of Georgia*, VII, 201, 686.

House asking that Patrick Mackay have leave to attend the Lower House to "give what intelligence he can in a matter now under inquiry." Mackay "informed the Assembly that the only two Papers he delivered to Sir Patrick Houstoun are now in the Secretary's Office."

It was ordered then that the papers be laid before the house for inspection. Somehow the papers were procured immediately and read. One revealed a commission directed to Henry Parker, Esq., President of the Province of Georgia, Patrick Graham, James Habersham, Noble Jones, Pickering Robinson, and Francis Harris, or any two of them to treat with the Indians on lands by purchase. The other was a title deed of lands from the Upper Creeks. Whereupon Mungo Graham announced that Mr. Thomas Burrington[32] could give some information "upon this affair." A messenger dispatched to summon Burrington returned with the information that the gentleman "was sick." Further consideration was then postponed. Immediately after the minutes were read the next morning Burrington testified that "he knew nothing of the Affair in dispute betwixt Sir Patrick Houstoun and Mungo Graham more than he had from Mungo Graham himself." Burrington then faded out of the picture and James Habersham, Secretary of the Province, came upon the scene to declare that he had given the Governor reasons why he would not deliver the letters [first mention of letters] applied for by the house and "by that resolution he would abide." He did "not hold those letters [he said] as Secretary of the Province but as Senior Surviving Member of the Board of the late President and Assistants, and that he had been ordered expressly by the other Surviving Members of that Board not to Deliver them."

32. Some light is thrown on the character of Thomas Burrington, when four years later he was clerk of the Lower House. On April 6, 1761, the Speaker of the House wrote to him: "Sir, the House having met this day and been obliged to adjourn on Account of your Non Attendance and being deprived of the use of their papers on the same account, have ordered me to acquaint you that they are fully determined not to suffer the like Neglect for the future, in which if you sho'd persist they will be under the necessity (however disagreeable to them) of applying to the Governor for Redress. By Order of the House, Elliott Grey, Speaker." *Colonial Records of Georgia*, XIII, 498. Previous to that date, however, Burrington had acted as Attorney General *pro tem*, when in 1758, William Clifton, the incumbent, was on leave of absence. *Colonial Records of Georgia*, VII, 826.

After that emphatic and somewhat mysterious statement Sir Patrick Houstoun entered the house, requested a copy of Graham's petition and promptly withdrew. The clerk of the house was ordered to deliver the petition to him. Later in the session a message was read from the Governor informing the house he had given direction to both the Secretary and Register of Records and likewise to Sir Patrick Houstoun, Bart., and had received answers from each of them which he sent to be laid before the house. Thus ended the third day of the case.

The scene shifted from the above to the Upper House at its meeting on Friday, January 21, when its President, Sir Patrick Houstoun, acquainted that body with Mungo Graham's petition to the Lower House. Expressing the opinion that the petition might reflect on his reputation, he requested the Upper House to "enquire into the same." Sir Patrick Houstoun's fellow-members responded by writing a message to the Lower House embodying the above allegation, and nothing more, as reported in the Journal of the Upper House. The Lower House received the message which when read, however, disclosed the information that the Upper House declared its intention of inquiring into the attack on its President, and asked that "the House of Representatives will lay before them the said petition."

The reading of the message from the Upper House occurred early after the convening of the Lower House on Friday, but no action was taken that day. Instead, the house took up the matter of the letters received from the Governor the preceding day. It was ordered that the reasons sent to the Governor by James Habersham and Sir Patrick Houstoun be entered into the Journal.

Habersham gave to the Governor a lengthier explanation than he gave to the Lower House of his reasons for refusing to deliver certain letters. He explained to the Governor that he had looked carefully over all the letters from the late Trustees to the late President and assistants (by them committed to his care), and could find none that related to the present state of affairs. Asserting that "those letters cannot be called Publick Letters," he branded the request of the Lower House as "unprecedented." Compliance therewith, he insisted, would amount to "the betraying [of] a Trust." The letters were not matters of record, he contended, but were intended for the guidance of the persons to whom sent. As well might the Lower House claim the right to inspect the "private" exchanges between the Governor and the Crown and thus open a door "which might invade an Essential Prerogative of the Crown." Such an "Innovation," concluded Habersham, "they think themselves bound to Guard against."

Sir Patrick Houstoun's reasons were that he never had seen and he believed there never was such a Commission in the beginning as mentioned in Mungo Graham's petition, but that the papers he received from "Mrs. Graham" were lodged in the secretary's office where he supposed they were still. It is impossible to account for the appearance into the story of *Mrs.* Graham. Whether she was the relict of the late Patrick Graham, President of the Province, or the wife of Mungo cannot be clarified.

Saturday morning the lower body took up the message sent the previous day from the Upper House, but first required Mungo to attend and "explain some Ambigious expressions in his Petition." When Mungo arrived he explained that the petition presented to the Upper House was intended for the "Assembly only"; and that while he might be mistaken in certain of his allegations, "he had no other View than to bring to Light a Paper he imagined would be Serviceable to the Publick and to his own interest [?] and not to hurt the Character or Reputation of Sir Patrick Houstoun or any other Persons whatsoever—And that he humbly desires leave to withdraw his said Petition." The records are silent in giving any intimation of Mungo's "interest" in the matter. By resolution Graham was allowed to withdraw his petition and a message communicating his desire was sent to the Upper House.

Why the members of the Lower House felt privileged to reprove James Habersham cannot be explained. But rebuke him they did when they passed a motion declaring his refusal "to lay before this House the Publick Letters from the late Trustees to the late President and Assistants is a contempt of the Governor's Orders, and a great disrespect to this House, and Impedes the inquiry into the State of the Province." Habersham's statement to the Governor that he had looked over the letters and had found nothing there that related to "the present state of the Province," should have been sufficient proof that he was making a true assertion of fact. But the then existing feeling of rivalry between the two bodies seems to be well illustrated in the above action. Having censured Habersham, the Lower House prepared another message for the Upper House, setting forth that it allowed Mungo Graham to withdraw his petition, repeating his words to the house.

Sir Patrick Houstoun's associates in the Upper House were by no means satisfied over the somewhat casual manner in which the affair ended in the Lower House when it received the latter's message the same morning. The communication was carried by a Mr. Elliott and after its reading, the Upper House adjourned, and no action was taken until the following Tuesday because an "affair of State" involving the possibility of an invasion of Georgia and South Carolina by the French and Indians required attention and the necessity of joining forces with Georgia's neighbor province for the mutual protection took pre-eminence in the matter of consideration.

On Tuesday, however, before adjournment, another message was prepared to be sent to the Lower House. Reminding its rival that Mungo Graham's petition was a reflection on one of its members, the Upper House explained by the Tuesday message that it expected the Lower House to reprimand Graham and, further, that he would be ordered by the body to which he had presented his petition to appear before the Upper House to acknowledge the injury he had done to its member. If the Lower House received that message the next day, its Journal makes no mention of it. It is possible when it was received it served as a firebrand and savoured too much of an order. The message was brought to the attention of the Lower House the next morning, but action was deferred.

By Friday, January 28, the case of "Sir Patrick Houstoun *vs* Mungo Graham" had been under consideration ten days, and the members of the Upper House had grown impatient over the dilatoriness of its rival body. Another message was dispatched which was probably read soon after delivery, as it appears in the minutes of that day's session, but no attention was paid to it until just before the close of the meeting when a curt reply was sent informing the Upper House that in the opinion of the Assembly Mungo Graham had made a satisfactory concession and that

Patrick Houstoun's Public Life

since his petition had been withdrawn the case was closed as far as the Lower House was concerned. Later in the day the Upper House received the above message. It would be exceedingly interesting to know how its members reacted to it. The Upper House had not, however, finished with Mungo, but the members let the matter drop for ten days and attended to various bills that had been sent to them from the Lower House for concurrence.

At the session of Tuesday, February 8, the Upper House asked the President to lay before it the petition of Mungo Graham. On the following morning Houstoun laid before the Upper Chamber a copy of the petition and Governor Reynolds's order thereon addressed to Houstoun on January 18, 1757, and then the President withdrew. The latter document reviewed the contents of the petition and ordered Sir Patrick to lay before the Assembly the alleged commission. After hearing the two papers Mungo Graham was again called before the Upper House to "Support the matter ascerted in his petition." Mungo promptly rejoined that he had "been grosly mistaken in regard to the Commission mentioned in my Petition which I am sorry for, and do therefore ask pardon of the Hon[ble] House." And then he was ordered to withdraw.

The Upper Chamber closed this unfortunate episode in Sir Patrick Houstoun's career with a series of resolutions denying the assertions of Graham's petition and, while exonerating the petitioner of malicious intent, nevertheless directing the "Presiding Member" of the House to "properly" reprimand the offender. Presumably the President had remained out of the room while the "Presiding Member" delivered the rebuke. Sir Patrick, upon returning to the chair, the hope may be vouchsafed, received the congratulations of his friends on the conclusion of a somewhat complicated performance on the part of an interfering, and, apparently, disgruntled person.

* * * *

As Register of Grants and Receiver of Quit Rents, for which position he received a salary of fifty pounds per annum, Sir Patrick Houstoun's office under the Crown was no sinecure. It was a difficult office to execute, and he fell heir to the complexities of the system from the proprietary period.[33]

The quit rent tax, which was enacted in all of the English colonies, dated in Georgia back to the distribution of the territory afterward known as the Georgia colony, and was involved in the part played by Sir George Carteret, Baron of Hawnes, in 1733, after the Royal Charter had been granted to the Trustees for Establishing the Colony of Georgia.

The Colony of South Carolina was founded in 1663 by eight English noblemen to whom Charles II had granted an immense tract of land south of Virginia, and they became the Lords Proprietors of the Colony of South Carolina. In the year 1715, the Lords Proprietors of Carolina found themselves in dire distress, and they became alarmed over their inability to protect their coast from the Spaniards and from pirates, and the interior of the colony from the Indians. Lord Carteret, one of the Lords Proprietors, addressed a communication to the Lords Commissioners of Trade and Plantation, asking that His Majesty graciously interpose in their behalf. Inquiry was made as to what would be required for the relief of the colony, and the government of South Carolina was asked if it ought not to surrender its "plantation," if the Crown was willing to bear the expense of its defense.

An act was passed in Parliament for the better regulation of the American colonies, and as conditions steadily grew worse in the Province of South Carolina, all of the Lords Proprietors of that colony with the exception of Lord Carteret, took advantage of the act and surrendered to the Crown "not only their rights and interest in the government of Carolina, but also their ownership of the soil." The indenture of purchase and sale was executed on the 25th of July, 1730, in the reign of George II, and the consideration paid amounted to £22,500.[34]

When, in 1732, the Georgia Trustees were granted their Charter by King George II and the land for settling their colony, the King ceded to them that part of the territory he had purchased from the Lords Proprietors of South Carolina which lies between the Savannah and Altamaha rivers, and a few months

---
33. For a more exhaustive study of this subject see James Ross McCain, *Georgia as a Proprietary Province* (Boston, 1917).
34. Jones, *History of Georgia*, I, 80, 81.

later Lord Carteret by deed conveyed to the Trustees his one-eighth share which he had retained.

In granting tracts of land to the colonists for settling Georgia, the Trustees included several regulations on the deeds, and one of them dealt with quit rents. That provision referred partly to reimbursing Lord Carteret for his portion of the land he had deeded to the Trustees. The regulation read—"that a quit rent of four shillings per hundred acres be paid annually after a lapse of ten years from the time of the grant."[35] Sixpence per hundred acres was the amount eventually to be paid to Lord Carteret, but it was never made clear whether that was to be in addition to the four shillings to be paid to the Crown or whether it was to be deducted from that amount.

As far back as 1735 a Register of Grants and Receiver of Quit Rents had been appointed by the Trustees.[36] At first he was only register of grants, and performed the duty of registering grants and keeping a record of all information concerning them. To the office soon was added that of receiver of quit rents. Difficulties and delays were numerous. The whole matter of quit rents had become very complicated. For example, there was the vexing problem of preparing a satisfactory rent roll. Actually nothing effective was done during the Trustee period. No money was ever collected for quit rents during the proprietary period either by the Trustees, by the King, or by Carteret. The most reasonable explanation for this failure was doubtless the general lack of prosperity and incompetent officials. During the last years of proprietary control economic conditions improved greatly and perhaps the Trustees could have collected quit rents had they remained in power a few years longer.[37]

The fact that a settler was allowed a period of years in which to pay the quit rent, in order that he might have sufficient time to cultivate his lands and receive some financial returns, also was probably accountable for the inability of the receiver of quit rents to collect the revenue. The quit rent problem, therefore, was an inherited one when Georgia became a Royal Colony, and

---

35. McCain, *Georgia as a Proprietary Province*, 228.
36. Flippin, "The Royal Government," in *The Georgia Historical Quarterly*, X, No. 1 (March, 1926), 20.
37. *Ibid.*, IX, No. 3 (September, 1925), 200. Quoted from McCain, *Georgia as a Proprietary Province*, 255, 256.

required the Crown appointment of an officer to continue to discharge the duties and attempt the collection of the revenue.

Although Sir Patrick Houstoun had received his appointment to that office at the same time that the Royal Governor and other officers received theirs in August, 1754, it was not until 1755 that he could produce his commission for the office. On September 30, 1755, at a meeting of the Council, he presented his royal warrant and "took the Oaths of Allegiance and Supremacy and declared and subscribed the Test, as also the Oath of Office."[38] The Test Act, "enforced upon all persons filling any office, civil or military, the obligation of taking the oaths of supremacy and allegiance and subscribing a declaration against transubstantiation, and also of receiving the sacrament within three months after admittance to office."[39] On February 17, 1757, Patrick Houstoun took the oath for his office as Register of Grants.[40]

Efforts were made by Sir Patrick Houstoun to collect quit rents, but it was made difficult by the lack of proper legislation to enforce the law pertaining to them. "There was on the part of the British government and also on the part of the Governor and legislature of Georgia recognition of the fact that the quit rent formed an important item in the revenues of the colony, but there were certain conditions which very decidedly interfered with the effectiveness of it. There seems to have been no general opposition to the quit rent on the ground that it was a royal revenue or tax imposed upon the colonists without their consent.

"There was considerable delay in securing action by the British government on the act of assembly passed in Georgia for the more effective collection of quit rents. The failure of the home government to adequately support the governor and the legislature in their efforts with reference to the quit-rents did undoubtedly greatly retard the securing of funds through this method."

There is evidence that Sir Patrick did make some collections of quit rents, and his attempts to fulfill his obligations bore result in the reports he made to the Council. When it came to perform-

---

38. *Colonial Records of Georgia*, VII, 265.
39. *Encyclopaedia Britannica* (ninth edition), XXIII, 199. (It was passed in 1672.)
40. *Colonial Records of Georgia*, VII, 489.

ing the duty of Register of Grants Sir Patrick Houstoun must have been kept fairly busy, although there were obstructions in his way even there.

The change in Georgia from a proprietary colony to that of a royal province affected the titles of land. In consequence, one of the early acts of Governor Reynolds was to issue a proclamation "that all landholders should surrender their grants for new ones which were to be issued in the name of the king and under seal of the colony. The new grants specified that a quit rent of two shillings on every hundred acres was to be paid to the King, and that at least five acres in every one hundred should annually be cleared and cultivated, and that the grant should be duly registered within six months from date."[41]

At nearly every meeting of the Council, petitions were read from colonists asking for grants of land and for town lots in Savannah, or the proposed new town of Hardwick, and the requests usually were granted. Sometimes they were granted conditionally, sometimes the warrants were prolonged, and sometimes they were refused. The petitions always were granted under a proviso.

The members of the Council themselves were frequently listed among the petitioners and many of them acquired additional territory adding hundreds of acres to their holdings. It was stated in the petitions that the land was needed for the grazing of cattle, or for the placing of their Negroes, but also it was for reasons of speculation, and many of the inhabitants improved their financial condition through the sale of newly acquired property. Thousands of acres ranging from allotments of ten to two thousand were granted, the most popular individual grant, however, being for five hundred acres, although one apportionment amounted to nine thousand two hundred and fifty acres on the island of Sapelo.[42]

In May, 1758, the Governor and Council authorized Houstoun to announce that those persons who had failed to register their grants would be given an additional six months to do so. Grants that were not registered within that period would be deemed invalid and liable to be granted to others.

---
41. Flippin, "The Royal Government," in *The Georgia Historical Quarterly*, IX, 202; X, 2, 3.
42. Flippin, "The Royal Government," in *The Georgia Historical Quarterly*, X, 11, n. 24.

Toward the close of his term of office Sir Patrick Houstoun, "in a memorial to the Governor and Council, register of grants and receiver of quit rents [October 6, 1761] commented upon the orders which he had received from the first two royal governors which prevented his having followed a consistent policy, and explained why grants had not been registered in due time, and requested instructions. It was ordered that he should be 'permitted to register all grants already signed, for six months to come, notwithstanding the time for registering the same may be elapsed.' "[43]

The whole matter of reconveying and claiming grants and the payment of the quit rents was so involved that it can be easily surmised from a critical review of Sir Patrick Houstoun's memorial that the sturdy, persistent, and methodical Scotsman, for such he undoubtedly was to have retained such an office for seven years, must have had his soul tried to the limit in dealing with procrastinating and unreliable inhabitants. The numbers who did comply with the requirements of the provincial government and claimed their grants proved the necessity of a faithful officer to attend to the important details and the legal side of land grants.

Sir Patrick Houstoun, in his office as Register of Grants and Receiver of Quit Rents, was able to render at least one financial report on the returns collected on registered grants. At a meeting of the Council, November 2, 1756, it was reported that he remitted to England a total of £6, 8s. 4d.[44]

---

43. *Ibid.*, 20; see also *Colonial Records of Georgia*, VIII, 577.
44. *Colonial Records of Georgia*, VII, 414.
   A copy of an application from one Owen O'Daniel to the Attorney-General for a tract of land, which application was referred to Sir Patrick Houstoun reads:
   GEORGIA
       This is to certify that_____Owen O'Daniel_____hath this Day entered a Memorial in the office of his Majesty's Auditor-General of_____One hundred & fifty_____Acres of Land situated and being in the Parish_____butting and bounding Easterly by Land of Joseph Perry & on_____every other side by Land vacant_____Originally granted by his Majesty King George the Third on the 5th Day of July—1760—unto the said Owen O'Daniel_____at the Quit-rent of Two Shillings per 100 Acres.
   Given under my hand at Savannah, this 4th Day of October 1760
                       William Handley for D. Auditor-Gen.
   To Sir Patrick Houstoun, Bart.
   His Majesty's Receiver-General
   Original owned by James Patrick Houstoun, Jr., of Houston, Texas.

While Sir Patrick Houstoun was working zealously to collect quit rents, with only partial success, his duties in connection with the registration of land grants demanded equal diligence and minute clerical labor. Thousands of acres were allocated during each year, and precise records were kept. First, after the Royal Council had conveyed the land, the register made an entry of the day the permit was authorized; next an abstract of the deed was registered, and then six months later the digest was examined and compared with the original entries; it was dated and signed, "Pat: Houstoun, register." Finally, a semi-annual report was sent to the authorities in London.

For instance: one year's work shows that on December 9, 1756, one hundred and fifty-two grants were delivered; and the abstracts made from January 27 to July, 1757, were examined and compared on July 29. During the next six months, one hundred and eighteen grants were conveyed, the same procedure was observed, and the examination was made on February 1, 1758. The total number of grants registered for the year 1757 was two hundred and seventy, and included acres in and near Savannah, Augusta, Newport, Medway, Halifax, Great Ogeechee territory, Ebenezer, Sapelo, Abercorn, and Darien.[45]

The preceding narrative shows plainly that for eight years Sir Patrick Houstoun, Bart., President of His Majesty's Council, President of the Upper House, Register of Grants and Receiver of Quit Rents, owner of a five-hundred-acre plantation under cultivation and many other grants, and the father of four children, later increased to six, was not an idle man. As the recipient of Crown grants he duly recorded his holdings in the above manner.

In 1751 Houstoun was anxious to obtain a lease on an island across from Rosdue, and on July 7 he addressed a request to the Secretary of the Trustees. Lying between the Vernon and Little Ogeechee rivers, opposite his house, the three-hundred-acre island and the adjoining marsh, he explained, were vital to his interests. If granted to one who "would not continue an Extreme good Neighbor I should be obliged to quit my present plantation...."[46] As Sir Patrick continued to reside at Rosdue, the inference is that

---
45. Unpublished Colonial Records of Georgia, XXVIII, Pt. 1, pp. 63, 88, 154, 169.
46. *Colonial Records of Georgia*, XXVI, 249.

the Trustees allowed him to lease the island for a number of years. Later it became the property of Henry Parker.

After the reconveyance by the Royal Council, in 1755, of his Rosdue acreage, Sir Patrick's holdings were increased by several thousand acres. His other grants included additional land on the Little Ogeechee and Vernon rivers, in Christ Church Parish, St. David's Parish, and in Darien, where he owned one thousand acres, and lots in Savannah and Hardwick.

On April 1, 1755, six months after the Royal Council was formed, Houstoun presented a petition for two land grants, one for five hundred acres on the south side of the Great Ogeechee River and the other for a vacant lot in Savannah.[47] He hoped, he said, to be favored with the addition as he had "a Wife, four children, two white Servants and twenty-four Negroes." Both requests were granted.[48]

Apparently the Council had thousands of vacant lots at its disposal, and some of the meetings of the Royal Council were extremely monotonous as the members were forced to listen to scores of petitions for land. It is quite possible petitioners were widely engaged in prospecting the southeastern portion of the province and there seems to have been no limit under the Crown's ownership to the amount of holdings a man might possess. Occasionally a petition was rejected, but there was always added to the granting of the request the usual stipulation, provided the grant was registered and the quit rent paid.

The next request for land that Sir Patrick made after the reconveyance of his second grant and the request for land on the Great Ogeechee was in June, 1755, when the Council heard his petition for a five-hundred-acre grant between the northern forks of the North Branch of the Newport River. Again on February 20, 1757, Houstoun had another petition before his fellow councilors, when he resigned one grant, the Newport River grant, which on survey he found to be three hundred acres short, and requested a thousand acres located on Cathead Creek, two miles above Darien. The surveying of that grant was completed and Sir Patrick complied with the rule of grantees, because in the

---
47. The lot assigned to him was part of the Trust lot in Anson Ward, sixty feet fronting Drayton Street, and ninety feet deep, known as the letter W.
48. *Colonial Records of Georgia*, VII, 142.

next generation, the Cathead Creek tract was owned by his oldest son.

Still Sir Patrick, like many other citizens of the province, was calling for more land. On November 1, 1757, the Council heard another petition from him. Explaining his desire to cultivate and improve additional lands, he asked for one hundred acres at a place known as Keelers Bluff on the Newport River, about four miles north of Alexander McDonald's plantation. The Council granted his request on the usual conditions, but in February of the ensuing year Sir Patrick reported to Council that the warrant to the said land had expired and he prayed that the surveyor-general "might be enabled and ordered to issue a new Precept on the same warrant granting further Time for surveying the said land."[49]

A list of some of Sir Patrick Houstoun's lots and acres the year in which they were granted, and where situated, shows some of his holdings to have been:

ACRES	LOCATION	YEAR
500	Between Vernon and Little Ogeechee Rivers	1736 and 1755
500	In District of Great Ogeechee River	1756
1000	On Cathead Creek, near Darien	1757
681	In Christ Church Parish	1759
481	"Ilay" Island	?
3162		

TOWN LOTS
1 — in Savannah		1756
1 — in Hardwick		1756[50]
1 — in Brunswick		

---

49. *Ibid.*, 886.
50. The above grants are only a partial list of Sir Patrick Houstoun's. Further research in the Colonial Records and in the office of the Secretary of State, Atlanta, should be made to obtain a complete list. The above was secured from the Secretary of State. Also, *Colonial Records of Georgia*, VII, 347, 590.

Chapter VII

LAST YEARS AND DEATH

EARLY in the year 1761 Sir Patrick Houstoun made his will. He and his wife were then the parents of six children. Their oldest, Patrick, Jr., was about twenty years old. George was a youth of nearly eighteen and the younger children were John, James, Ann Priscilla and William. With no birth dates available for any except Patrick and George, the ages of the remaining five cannot be given with exactitude, but from the will of Lady Houstoun, executed eleven years after her husband's death, she mentions William as a minor; so he was the youngest child. He and Ann Priscilla, then, were quite small children when their father died, the former about five and the latter six years old. As will be seen later in Lady Houstoun's will, James is not referred to as a minor; therefore the deduction is made that he was the fourth child.[1]

The commerce of Georgia had grown to such an extent in the few years previous to Sir Patrick Houstoun's death that by 1760, forty-two vessels plied between Savannah and other ports bringing besides their cargoes war news from the northern provinces. On November 19, 1760, the Council created a new Commission of Peace and appointed to that body the following members: Patrick Houstoun, James Habersham, Noble Jones, Francis Harris, Jonathan Bryan, James Mackay, James Edward Powell, William Knox, William Groover, William Clifton, and William Butler.[2]

Savannah, in 1760, was considered a healthful town, and rice

---
1. With no known tombstones to which to refer, and no Bibles having been found in which their births are entered, only a surmise of the ages of John and James can be made from the records of Sir Patrick Houstoun's statement made in April, 1755, of "his wife and four children." By reading Lady Houstoun's will, it can be seen that John was of age at that time, and it seems probable that James was fully grown. Therefore by means of calculation, it has been found that John and James were boys between eight and fifteen years old when their father died.
2. *Colonial Records of Georgia*, VIII, 425.

planters from the neighboring lowlands in South Carolina went thither during the "summer and autumn of the year that they might escape the fevers incident to the swamps. The dense forests growing upon Hutchinson's Island and the low grounds to the east and west of the town shielded it from the noxious vapors and malarial influences in the fields beyond which were cultivated in rice."³ Thirty-four hundred pounds of that staple were exported from Savannah in 1760. The population of Georgia at that time was barely 6000 whites and 3578 Negro slaves.⁴

In the month that Sir Patrick Houstoun made his will, the news arrived in Savannah of the death of George II. Governor Wright received the information by packet on the night of February 5, 1761, over three months after the occurrence, and acquainted his Council with the intelligence the following morning. After the letter from the Right Honourable the Lords of His Majesty's Privy Council had been read, with other official letters to His Excellency, Council immediately proposed that seventy minute guns be fired, "at the town of Savannah," on Monday the ninth between the hours of nine and twelve, and that Prince George of Wales, naming all of his titles, be proclaimed King George the Third, on Tuesday the tenth of February, and also at Sunbury, Frederica, and Augusta, in the said province under a triple discharge of the cannon and musketry. It was also decided that alterations be made in the Book of Common Prayer for the Royal Family to be duly observed in the several parish churches and other places of divine worship throughout the province.

Council met on the appointed day, February 10, and with them "numbers of the principal inhabitants and planters of the Province" who attended to hear read the Proclamation of the Lords of his Majesty's Privy Council, "having been prepared fair wrote on a large Sheet of Paper." It was signed by the Governor, seven members of the Council including Houstoun, and twenty-seven other inhabitants. "Then the Regulars and Militia, being under Arms, and drawn up by their respective Officers before the Council Chamber and the Windows thrown open the Clerk of the Council, by Order of His Honour, the Gov-

---
3. Jones, *History of Georgia*, II, 23.
4. *Ibid.*, 23, 24.

ernour, did publish the said Proclamation audibly and distinctly under a Discharge of twenty-one Pieces of Cannon; After which the said Proclamation being delivered to the Provost Marshall, His Honour and the Council accompanied by the principal Inhabitants and attended by the Regulars and Militia proceeded to the Market Place where the Provost Marshall published the said Proclamation under a like Discharge of Cannon; Then the Procession moved to the Fort in Savannah, called Hallifax Fort, where the Provost Marshall did again publish the same under a like Discharge of Cannon and a Triple Discharge of the Musketry: And his Majesty's Proclamation for continuing all Officers &c was then also published."[5]

The next day at the Council meeting the Governor and all of the Councilors had to take again, severally, the State Oaths, and subscribe the Test to the new King.

On Tuesday, October 6, 1761, Houstoun, apparently, attended his last meeting of Council. He was present at a meeting in August and one in September, only two having been held that month; so that his illness began, probably, some time after the October meeting. After hearing a resume of the sundry instructions issued by Governors Reynolds and Ellis to Houstoun as Register of Grants and Receiver of Quit Rents, the Council ordered on October 6 that he be instructed "to register all grants already signed for six months to come, notwithstanding the time for registering the same may be elapsed."[6]

Four months later, on February 5, 1762, Sir Patrick Houstoun died. In the minutes of the two Houses of which Sir Patrick Houstoun was the presiding officers, there is a strange omission, for neither of them makes any official mention of his death. The Royal Council met on February 3 and not again until the fifteenth, but if any resolution was passed on the death of their late president, the secretary omitted its record. The Upper House even met on the day that he died.[7]

---

5. *Colonial Records of Georgia*, VIII, 492, 493.
6. *Ibid.*, 578.
7. In the months that intervened between his attendance at the Council meeting on October 6 and his death on February 5, the Journal of the Upper House mentions in the minutes of various meetings that "the President shall sign the address etc.," or that "Mr. President reported that his Honor the Governor had made a speech to both Houses," or that "Mr. President informed the House" etc., with no clue whatever

Last Years and Death

Sir Patrick was interred in the old burying ground of Christ Church, and it can be presumed that the service of the Church of England was read by the Reverend Bartholomew Zouberbuhler, who, at that time was the minister of the parish church.

Cut into the tombstone is the Houstoun coat-of-arms, and the motto, "In Time." The epitaph of Sir Patrick Houstoun reads:

SIR PATRICK HOUSTOUN
Baronet, President of his
Majesty's Council of Georgia
died 5th Feb. 1762, Aged 64[8]

All that he owned, personal and real, he bequeathed to his beloved Priscilla. His wife and her brother, George Dunbar, were named executors of his will. Sir Patrick and his wife had lived happily together for twenty-two years and with the severing of the tie she was left to care for her six children, bringing up the younger ones and taking over the responsibility of their large plantation, as well as the other holdings of her late husband in the Province of Georgia.

---

as to whether it was the President, Sir Patrick Houstoun, or the next senior member, James Habersham, who would be acting president if Sir Patrick was too ill to be present.

8. Subsequent to 1871 the remains of Sir Patrick Houstoun and of his wife were removed to Bonaventure Cemetery, near Savannah, by "E. Houstoun," who had erected a large monument on which is cemented the original stone inscribed with the above epitaph. The "s" in the word Sir was cut off when the slab was removed. The "ir" is visible. For authority for the date, 1871, see *Savannah Morning News*, February 15, 1871, article entitled, "Sir Patrick Houstoun, Bart." The handsome brick vault of the Houstoun family probably was one of the oldest in the cemetery. It was razed after the removals.

9. "In the Name of God Amen. I Sir Patrick Houstoun Baronet in the district of Savannah in Georgia being weak in body but of sound and perfect mind and memory do this Eleventh Day of February One Tousand seven hundred and sixty one make ordain and publish this my last will and Testament, in manner following that is to say I give bequeath and devise to my well beloved wife, Priscilla Houstoun and to her Heirs for ever all my Estate both real and Personal of whatsoever Consists and I hereby ordain her my said wife and my beloved brother in Law Capt. George Dunbar Executrix and Executor of this my Last Will. In Witness whereof I have hereunto set my hand and seal the day and year above written:

Signed sealed Published and declared   Pat Houstoun LS
by the said Sir Patrick Houstoun the

Sir Patrick Houstoun's will was a brief document.[9] He had spent twenty-six years in Georgia and had done his part in the pioneer days in the promotion of agriculture. Three years he had been a representative of the people of his district in the Provincial Assembly, and six years he had served his King in the Royal Council. He had lived to witness his country engaged in a bloody struggle with the French, for the possession of Canada, and he lived to hear of the fall of Quebec.

Two weeks after his death Governor Wright wrote to the Lords Commissioners of Trade and Plantations in London, February 20, 1762:

> Sir Pat Houstown one of the Council here and Register of Grants and Receiver of quit rents dyed here the 5th Inst and I have appointed his son now Sir P. Houstown (I believe a very deserving young gentleman) for those offices.[10]

> Testator as and for his Last will and — Testament in the Presence of us who — subscribed our Names as Witnesses thereto and at his Desire
>
> Hugh Ross
> Ann Steuart
> John Ross
>
> Georgia by his Excellency James Wright Esquire Captain General and Governor in Chief of his Majesty's said Province And Ordinary of the same.
>
> Personally appeared before me Hugh Ross being one of the subscribing Witnesses to the last Will and Testament of Sir Patrick Houstoun Bart late of Savannah in the province aforesaid deceased and being duly sworn on the holy Evangelists made Oath that he was personally present and did see the testator, sign, seal, publish, pronounce and declare the same to be and .. [torn] .. his last Will and Testament and that he was of sound and disposing .. [torn] .. and Memory to the best of his knowledge and belief and that he with .. [torn] .. and John Ross, signed his Name as Witness to the said Will of the .. [torn] .. and in the Presence of the Testator and in each other's Presence.
>
> At the same time Dame Priscilla Houstoun Widow and Relict of the said deceased and Executrix — within Named Qualified as such before me.
> Given under my hand this 15 day of April 1762.
> Ja: Wright

Will Book A, 83-84. Original will in the Department of Archives and History, Atlanta.

10. Unpublished Colonial Records of Georgia, XXVIII, Pt. 1, 603.

Chapter VIII

LADY HOUSTOUN

WHEN Priscilla Dunbar arrived in Georgia her future husband had been a resident of the colony for nearly two years.

One likes to give full play to the imagination in wondering what could have been the emotional response of the young Scotswoman, Priscilla Dunbar, late of Inverness, to the tide-water country of Georgia as contrasted with her Highland home in Scotland. Throwing in her lot with her brother George when she came with him to Georgia, and then anchoring herself in the colony four years later by her marriage to a fellow countryman, Patrick Houstoun, of the Lowlands of Scotland, she showed herself a woman resolute and firm; and found contentment in a land so totally different from her old home—a country, too, that was only in the making. Dangers threatened everywhere, even though treaties with the native savages kept colonial affairs in Georgia peaceful on the whole. But it took courage to live then, especially for a woman, and the fact that Priscilla reared five useful sons for Georgia proved her worth as a woman of character and her ability to cope with colonial life.

Living on an isolated plantation could have been nothing but real hardship, and although her husband was able to supply her with servants, her need and longing for social contacts were probably seldom satisfied. There was much to do on a plantation. Her duties there, added to the constant care of her growing family, probably made the days pass quickly enough, especially before her husband was called into public life. His obligations no doubt kept him from her often and long. When their life together came to an end, with true Gaelic sturdiness she determined to win the battle of the succeeding years for the sake of her children. Her son Patrick had returned from Scotland before his father died, and was almost grown, and her next son, George, was old enough to be of great help to her. One likes to think that Lady Houstoun, among her other accomplishments, was a good horsewoman, and that when business required a trip to town she could take one easily on horseback, accompanied by one of her slaves. Now and then her name appears in the Colonial Records, or in advertisements in the *Georgia Gazette*.[1] Five months after the newspaper was established, Lady Houstoun decided to offer some of her property for sale. An advertisement appeared in the issue of September 15, 1763, offering one thousand acres described as "the greater part river swamp, well timbered with cypress, the remainder very good high land." This description warrants the inference that the land advertised for sale was the one thousand acres two miles above Darien granted to Sir Patrick by the Council in 1756. Apparently the advertisement did not produce a buyer. Since would-be purchasers were told to apply to Lady Houstoun in Savannah, she was probably then occupying her house on Broughton Street.[2] Lady Houstoun used the columns of the *Georgia Gazette* again on March 14, 1765, when she advertised a "sorrel Guelding with a small blaze on his forehead, about 14 hands high," which was found straying around Rosdue. The owner could have his horse by proving his property and paying the cost of the advertisement.

The next month Lady Houstoun applied to Council for some land. Her petition was presented at a meeting of the Council on April 1, 1765.[3] She asked for 500 acres on the Little Satilla, and further information stated it was lately ordered purchased by Sir Patrick Houstoun, her son. At a later meeting October 29, the grant was signed by Governor Wright to Dame Priscilla Houstoun of St. Patrick's Parish, the boundary of which was from the north branch of the Turtle River to the south branch of the Little "St. Illa."[4]

Some conjecture may be made of a few of the friends of Lady Houstoun, among whom were the Stuarts and the Rosses. The

---

1. The *Georgia Gazette* was the first newspaper in the colony and was founded by James Johnston, Sr., April 7, 1763, the year after Sir Patrick Houstoun's death. James Johnston was the uncle of Colonel James Johnston, Jr., who in 1797 married Lady Houstoun's granddaughter, Ann Marion Houstoun.
2. *Georgia Gazette*, August 17, 1774; January 3, 1776.
3. *Colonial Records of Georgia*, IX, 329, 434.
4. *Ibid.*, 434.

names appeared as witnesses on her will and that of her husband. Ann Stuart was left a legacy by Lady Houstoun, and a further proof of friendship was shown by Ann Stuart, probably a contemporary of Lady Houstoun's children, when she died, a "spinster" in 1812, by making one of Lady Houstoun's grandsons, John Houstoun McIntosh, an heir and one of her executors.[5] Thomas Ross and Hugh Ross were brothers, and John, a witness of Sir Patrick's will, was the son of Hugh. Hugh Ross's wife was Ann Stewart, daughter of Daniel Stewart, shipmaster from Inverness, Scotland; and Thomas Ross married the daughter of Mr. and Mrs. Henry Parker of Isle of Hope, near Savannah. It is not unlikely that the Stuarts were among the friends who voyaged across the Atlantic with the Highlanders of Scotland to Darien.

As the years passed Lady Houstoun acquired more land, and she then began deeding her property to her children. In May, 1773, she conveyed to her son George, five hundred acres of land in St. David's Parish, the boundary of that parish being all of the territory between the Altamaha River and the north branch of the Turtle River. The deed was witnessed by her two sons, John and William, and was signed by Thomas Moody, Deputy Secretary, later to be connected with the Houstoun family.[6]

In the year 1775, shortly before her death, Lady Houstoun disposed of Rosdue and Coffee Bluff, the latter on the Forest River (a branch of the Little Ogeechee) to Joseph Butler.[7] Broken health and the perilous times through which the colonies were passing may have made it necessary for her to relinquish all responsibility; and her sons, having property of their own, perhaps influenced her to sell her old plantation. It is possible to imagine the state of mind of the tired widow, and to realize the ache in her heart when she gave up the home to which she had been taken as a bride, where most of her life in Georgia was spent, and where some of her children were born. She did not long

---

5. Mabel Freeman LaFar and Caroline Price Wilson, *Abstracts of Wills Chatham County, Georgia, 1773-1817* (Washington, D. C., 1936), 117, 143.
6. Original deed in possession of the heirs of Mrs. Macartan C. Kollock, Atlanta, and Habersham County, Georgia. Deed recorded in Book D, Folio 94-95, Habersham County Courthouse, Clarkesville, Georgia.
7. From records of the late Victor Schreck, Savannah. At a later date part of the property was acquired by Sir George Houstoun, Bart., the son of Lady Houstoun.

survive the relinquishment of her home and its many acres. There are no facts that can be told that can give any idea of Lady Houston's last days.

Before she died dark clouds were appearing on the horizon of her adopted country, and she knew before she left this earth that war was inevitable. She knew, too, that her sons were eager partisans on both sides of the burning question of the day, and perhaps she was glad to leave it all to fate and join her beloved Patrick in the land beyond. Her heart may have been broken over what she saw was coming to Georgia, but three happy events took place before her death: namely, the marriage of her daughter, Ann Priscilla, to George McIntosh, which occurred in 1772; her son George's marriage to Ann Moodie in 1774; and the birth of her first grandchild, John Houstoun McIntosh, in 1773, the only child of her daughter.

The end came in February, 1775. When she died she was sixty-four years of age, although the tombstone gives her age as sixty. She was interred by the side of her husband, in the old cemetery on South Broad Street. The Reverend Haddon Smith, Rector of Christ Church, probably performed the burial service. To Sir Patrick's epitaph were added these words:

LADY HOUSTON HIS WIDOW
Died Feb. 26th, 1775. Aged 60.

Her will was made on June 10, 1772. The first bequest was to her daughter Ann, wife of George McIntosh. To her she left her "negro Girl named Chloe with her son George and any other Child or Children she may have at the time of my Decease, and also my rings and wearing apparel to be delivered to her immediately after my Decease." To her eldest son Patrick she bequeathed all of her "Silver Plate of whatsoever the same doth or shall consist in full of every claim otherwise than as a Creditor against my Estate he having been already much more proportionately provided for by me." The next item was the bequest to "Miss Ann Stuart," to whom she left a suit of mourning and a mourning ring to be purchased at the discretion of her executors. The next item related to her sons James and John. To James she left her Negro boy, Abraham, and to John her "negro wench called Hannah with her son Musan and any other Child or Children she may have at the time of my Decease." She directed that all of her Negroes then under lease or hire to her son, Sir Patrick, "be immediately upon my Decease or as soon thereafter as may be, delivered up to my Executors...." She next directed that her executors within four months after the receipt of the above should sell and dispose of the same and all the rest and residue of her estate not previously bequeathed, both real and personal, "for the most money that can be got for the same at Public Outcry," giving her executors full power and authority to make and execute conveyances and deeds. Of the debt of five hundred pounds lawful money of the province incurred by her son Sir Patrick, January 2, 1767, she directed that the principal and interest be paid into the hands of her executors to be looked upon as assets in their hands for payment of debts and legacies.

From the money arising from the sale of her estate she bequeathed the following legacies: to her fifteen-year-old son William, she left the sum of five hundred pounds "to be paid to him upon his attaining his age of twenty-one years or day of marriage which shall first happen"; until then she directed that within fifteen months after her death the five hundred pounds should be put at interest by her executors upon good security to be applied annually to the use and maintenance of her son William, until he should become entitled to the principal. In the event of his death before his marriage or before attaining his majority, the legacy was to be divided among her surviving children, share and share alike. Five hundred pounds she left, each to her son George and to her daughter Ann to be paid to them within sixteen months after her death. All the rest and residue of her estate and any money remaining in the hands of her executors she devised should be given to her sons "James and John beforenamed," to be equally divided between them share and share alike, and paid to them respectively within eighteen months after her death. She named her sons George and John[8] her executors and trustees or guardians of her son William.

Lady Houstoun concluded her will by ordering the payment of £100 to two Charles Town merchants, named Johnston and

---

8. Although twice she named her son James before John, in devising their legacies, the fact that she made John one of her executors seemed to point to the conclusion that John was the older of those two sons.

Simpson, for merchandise provided for her son John while he was in school at Charles Town. She further ordered that in case John should pay that sum that he should be reimbursed out of her estate. Again designating herself as Dame Priscilla Houstoun, she revoked all former wills and stated that she had set her "Hand at the Bottom of the three first of the said Pages." Her witnesses were Thomas Ross, James Simpson, William Ross, and James Beverley, who signed in the presence of His Excellency, Sir James Wright, Baronet. The will was probated on March 9, 1775, when Thomas Ross appeared as witness and at the same time George and John Houstoun qualified as the estate's executors.[9] Complying with their mother's request, her executors advertised in the *Georgia Gazette*, May 17, 1775, that on June 20 next the lands, Negroes, and other articles of the Lady Houstoun estate would be sold at the Vendue House in Savannah.

Lady Houstoun's estate, however, was not settled for sixteen years after her death at which time her executors applied for their discharge. In the *Georgia Gazette* of June 23, 1791, James Whitefield, register of grants for the County of Chatham, in the State of Georgia, advertised that Sir George Houstoun and John Houstoun, executors of Lady Houston's last will and testament, had appealed to him for "letters dimissory," and requested all creditors to appear before him July 24 to show cause why the executors should not be discharged.

[*End Part I*]

---

9. The original will is in the Department of Archives and History, Atlanta.

Part II

GEORGIA'S CALL TO THE FIVE SONS

Chapter IX

SIR PATRICK HOUSTOUN, SIXTH BARONET

WHILE it is certain that Patrick Houstoun, Jr., returned to Georgia before his father died, the date of his arrival home is unknown. Upon the death of his father he immediately fell heir to the title and, at twenty years of age, was recognized at once in the colony as the sixth Houstoun baronet. From that time the younger Patrick was always referred to in the Colonial Records as Sir Patrick Houstoun.[1]

As already cited, Governor Wright wrote to the authorities in London of the death of the elder baronet and of the appointment of the son to succeed to the offices the former had held. Governor Wright wrote that the salary was to be one hundred pounds a year with "perquisites about £37."[2] Sir Patrick's commission could not have reached him until late in the summer as it was dated London, May 15, 1762. Containing an expression of confidence in the ability and integrity of young Houstoun, the document commissioned him to serve, like his father, as Georgia's Register of Grants and Receiver of Quit Rents. Explicit directions followed for the manner and form of carrying out the duties of the office, for collecting quit rents, and what to do to those persons who were delinquent, and a requirement for making yearly reports.

Less than two weeks after his father's death the young Crown official was working at his predecessor's desk. On March 28, 1762, he signed his first report which was sent to London; it showed that in the last six months of his father's life, from July 27, 1761, to January 27, 1762, seventy-eight grants had been regis-

---
1. There has been confusion among historians, past and present, in writing of the Houstouns, especially of the two baronets in Georgia named Patrick. It is hoped this narrative will furnish the correct information necessary to distinguish father from son.
2. Unpublished Colonial Records of Georgia, XXVIII, Pt. 2, 427.

tered. On August 2 the first report of his own work of registering grants from January 27, 1762, to July 27, 1762, was sent abroad. In a year's time Sir Patrick was given an assistant, presumably his uncle, James Houstoun, who was made deputy register, and in the third issue of the recently-established *Georgia Gazette*, James Houstoun advertised that the office of Register of Grants and Receiver of Quit Rents had been removed to his house. He requested that all persons in arrears call and pay their quit rents and take out their grants that were "lying" in the Register's office. In the year 1763 the first semi-annual report from March 25 to September 25, recording sixty grants, and the second half-yearly one itemizing only fifteen grants, were both signed by James Houstoun, deputy register.[3] Sir Patrick Houstoun had not resigned his post, because in the following years reports were signed by him and in the same way his father wrote his signature, "Pat. Houstoun." On October 30, 1765, he registered a grant of five hundred acres in St. Patrick's Parish to his mother, "Dame Priscilla Houstoun"; the next year one to himself, a grant of three hundred acres of land in the Parish of St. Thomas,[4] and one to Ann Moodie, two hundred acres in St. Matthew's Parish.[5] The office of Register of Grants and Receiver of Quit Rents remained in the Houstoun family from 1754 to the beginning of the Revolution.

2

During the absence of young Patrick Houstoun, the province had been making strides in government under the first two Royal governors, John Reynolds and Henry Ellis, and when he came back, Governor Wright was in command of the colony. Returning to Georgia with a foreign viewpoint, as well as with a good education, Patrick kept his eyes wide open, no doubt, and learned much about the affairs of the legislative bodies of the colony before he entered the Assembly.

Since the change in the government from the Trustees to that of the Crown (1754) circumstances arose constantly which necessitated immediate action in the Assembly for solving the dilemmas that confronted the legislators. The Assembly was keenly alive

3. Unpublished Colonial Records of Georgia, XXXVIII, Pt. 2, 27-33; 75-77.
4. *Ibid.*, 455, 489.
5. *Ibid.*, XXXII, 580.

to the needs of Georgia, which in 1762 was twenty-nine years old, and the members framed many bills for the advancement and the good of the province. The membership of the Commons House at that time varied from eighteen to twenty-five members. The Assembly met both morning and afternoon, although the afternoon session was not always held. The morning session convened at eight, nine, or ten o'clock, with the Monday meeting usually beginning at ten o'clock. The afternoon sessions were held at two, three, or four o'clock.[6]

The Lower or Commons House of Assembly met downstairs in the same two-story house where the Council and the Upper House sat. That house fronted on an open square, later named Reynolds. It was a fairly large house, "presumably contained a fire place and certainly was provided with a bar, a table for the Speaker and another for the clerk." On what the members sat for the whole period cannot be said, but "red bay chairs costing £1, 5s were used in the latter part of the Assembly's existence. The mace was of silver and double gilt, cost about £100 and was purchased in England by Benjamin Franklin, Colonial agent for Georgia. At the same time that he bought the mace, he secured a gown for the Speaker and one for the Clerk of the House."[7]

The first session of the Sixth General Assembly of the province was convened at Savannah on Tuesday, November 20, 1764, by His Excellency James Wright, Esquire, Captain-General and Governor-in-Chief of the Province aforesaid, and Vice Admiral of the same. On that day young Patrick Houstoun, twenty-two years of age, entered the Lower House as an elected member representing the District of Vernonburg.[8] It is obvious in reading the records that he was a conspicuous figure in the Lower House. He was often called upon to serve on committees, frequently as chairman; he was singled out also many times to carry bills or messages to the Upper House, to the Governor, or to the President of the Council. From the week he entered the Assembly until his retirement (barring the time, of course, when

---

6. John Pitts Corry, "Procedure in the Commons House of Assembly in Georgia," in *The Georgia Historical Quarterly*, XIII, No. 2 (June, 1929), 112.
7. *Ibid.*, 111-112.
8. *Colonial Records of Georgia*, XIV, 136-137.

he was not a member) he was an active committeeman. He took his seat on a Tuesday, and on the following Friday he was appointed with John Milledge to present an engrossed address to the Governor in answer to the one the latter had made to a joint meeting of the two houses the previous Wednesday.

Young Houstoun's legislative career kept him in close touch with Georgia's problems. He participated in legislation for bettering the condition of Negro slaves and for improving the militia. When the Reverend George Whitefield applied for lands to endow a Georgia "Colledge," Sir Patrick was among those appointed to take under advisement the minister's application. He was chairman of a committee entrusted with the task of getting the Upper House to concur with a Lower House project to establish a ferry to South Carolina. He served on a committee to correspond with the colony's London agent, William Knox. In military matters Houstoun would seem to have been especially active, serving as chairman of a commission to provide £650 for building a fort in the Parish of St. Paul's, a guard house in Savannah, and for repairing the barracks in Frederica.[9] He also served on a committee appointed by the Governor to repair the barracks in Savannah.[10]

In March, 1765, the constituents of Vernonburg, Sir Patrick's district, were fearful of losing their property and homes. They were informed, to their surprise, that the lands were said to be claimed by Sir William Baker, Knight, under a grant from the proprietors of South Carolina prior to the division and settlement of the Georgia province. Farm lots and lots in Savannah, and the village of Vernonburg in particular, were all under the claim. A petition was sent to the Assembly requesting that the "Baker claim" be taken under advisement and put before the Colonial Agent.[11] The House resolved to instruct the Committee of Correspondence to direct the Colonial Agent "to solicit Relief in the Premesses." The "Baker claim" was never pushed and those

---

9. *Ibid.*, XVIII, 646. Other members of the commission were Noble Jones, Lewis Johnston, Alexander Wylly, and William Ewen.
10. *Ibid.*, 641. Other appointees were James Edward Powell, John Milledge, and John Simpson.
11. Among the signers of the petition were Patrick Houstoun, Noble Jones, Francis Harris, Noble Wimberly Jones, Charles Watson, William Ewen, William Spencer, and Henry Bourquin.

whose properties once seemed threatened were left in possession of their lands.[12]

It was necessary to enact laws for the regulation of the pilotage of vessels entering the province. Houstoun served on a committee to draft a bill for that purpose. The young baronet also served on a committee which recommended house action in cases involving statutes about to lapse because of time-limit clauses. The next important committee on which Sir Patrick Houstoun served was one "to examine the returns made to the treasurer by the several collectors of the general tax up to November 1765."[13] On that committee with Houstoun, who was chairman, was Dr. Andrew Johnston, a member of the Lower House who represented Halifax and the Parish of St. George.[14] Again Houstoun was selected as a committee member to inquire into the quantity of land proposed in a memorial from William Simpson who had purchased a lot on West Bay Street used as a thoroughfare to Yamacraw, which, if enclosed, would be entirely shut off, and the open view from the Bay to the westward would be obstructed. The memorialist desired to convey and make over to the public the lot, provided he received adequate compensation out of part of the Common which adjoined. Although not chairman of that committee Sir Patrick Houstoun two weeks later brought the prepared bill to the House.[15]

The above notations on the committee work of young Houstoun, which cover the first twelve months of his membership in the Assembly, illustrate the variety of subjects on which he was called upon to voice his opinion. Day after day he would be in the Assembly room, first reading a resolution "from his Place" then "walking to the table" to deliver it to be read again, which was a regular procedure for all bills or motions. Early in January, 1766, Sir Patrick Houstoun again was in demand. The previous months the Governor in his message had "encouraged

---

12. "The claim was pressed again in 1772 . . . but . . . was ordered postponed for a month, and it then disappears from available records. The Chaos of the Revolution . . . wiped out these claims. . . .", Floyd, "Vernonburgh, Known as White Bluff."
13. *Colonial Records of Georgia*, XIV, 298.
14. *Ibid.*, 259. Dr. Johnston later was connected with the Houstouns through the marriage of his son and Sir Patrick Houstoun's niece.
15. *Colonial Records of Georgia*, XIV, 309, 310, 325.

a Post for the Conveyance of Letters throughout the Province." It was ordered that Sir Patrick Houstoun and a Mr. Waters wait on His Excellency and give the Assembly's opinion that it could not make any provision for that service.

The Governor had recommended that a lazaretto be built at some convenient place near the entrance to the river where ships could lie in safety and the Negroes be "easily landed and Aired and where such as are distempered may remain for such time as shall be necessary." A committee was appointed to examine the land for that purpose. Sir Patrick Houstoun was a member of the committee which reported it had agreed to purchase a "spot" on Tybee Island where a house would be built for the reception of infected persons. A Mr. Simpson and Sir Patrick were appointed to wait on the Governor and carry him the address of the house. They returned with the Governor's answer that he was pleased with the report, and after consultation with the Council would send a reply.[16] The stream on which the house was finally built was named Lazaretto Creek.

The news of the enactment of the Stamp Act did not reach Georgia until April 15, 1765. The legislature was not in session at the time, but its Speaker, Alexander Wylly, during the recess received a letter from Samuel White, Speaker of the House of Representatives of Massachusetts, who informed Wylly that his house had unanimously agreed to a proposed meeting to be held in New York in October of committees from the several British colonies to discuss the action of Parliament in laying duties and taxes on the colonies. Upon receipt of White's letter Wylly dispatched "expresses" to the members of the Georgia legislature calling them to a meeting in Savannah on September 2. Sixteen out of the twenty-five members responded to the call, but on applying to the Governor, were advised by him that he did not think it expedient to call them together, and so no representatives were appointed to the New York meeting. Wylly, however, informed White that no representatives of any province espoused more warmly the common cause of the colonies than the people of Georgia. When the legislature convened in October, Speaker Wylly reported his correspondence with Samuel White, the

---

16. *Ibid.*, 384, 392, 424, 425. The act for empowering commissions to erect the lazaretto was not enacted until January, 1768. *Ibid.*, 502-503.

Massachusetts Speaker, and the Governor's refusal. The Lower House voted Speaker Wylly a resolution of thanks "for the extraordinary Care and Trouble he had been pleased to take on this very interesting and important Occasion."[17]

Governor Wright adjourned the Commons House of Assembly on June 10 to return to Savannah on November 10, but by proclamation he called the delegates in session again on July 16 to deliver an address before the two houses. He expressed his regret at having to summon them back at "an unseasonable and disagreeable Time of the Year." After congratulating the members on their proof of regard and affection for the King, he informed them he had to lay before them certain papers which he had received from one of His Majesty's principal secretaries of state. One of the documents was a printed copy of the repeal of the Stamp Act (March 18, 1766). When the Lower House had reassembled in its own room a motion was made that an address be presented to the Governor for his "affectionate speech." On the committee appointed to prepare the address were Thomas Burrington, Sir Patrick Houstoun, Colonel Mulryne and John Smith.[18] The engrossed report was read the next day by Burrington and, after expressing thanks, acknowledgment was made of the graciousness of the "best of kings" in condescending to "bend his Royal Ear" to the supplications of his faithful subjects by removing from them those "Evils they lamented Nor can we sufficiently venerate and admire the Magnanimity and Justice of the British parliament in so speedily redressing the Grievances by them complained of."[19] In years to come when he was to be faced with a vital decision Sir Patrick Houstoun's thoughts must have reverted to the part he took in the discussion required in drafting that address. The legislature adjourned on July 22, and reassembled on November 10. Sir Patrick Houstoun was present, and the next day he renewed his committee work, which continued day after day throughout the next two years. He was still attending in 1768 without re-election. In March, 1767, the members of the house requested the Governor to dissolve the Assembly

---

17. *Ibid.*, 270-274. "Georgia was represented at the meeting in the person of a messenger who was sent to obtain a copy of the proceedings." Jones, *History of Georgia*, II, 59.
18. *Ibid.*, 372.
19. *Ibid.*, 374.

because they had been in session three years and it "would be highly detrimental to many if they were obliged to give their attendance during any longer period."[20] In April, 1768, the house prepared an address to be sent to the Governor representing that there was no provision made in the law for limiting the duration of the sessions and again asking for dismissal. Sir Patrick Houstoun and John Simpson were ordered to deliver the address. The Governor replied that he had no objections to doing so, and had declined to act before because the members had not served three years. That was the last time Patrick Houstoun served for some years, because when the legislature met in November, 1768, Philip Box was returned for the Town of Vernonburg in the Parish of Christ Church.

3

Behind the simple statement that Philip Box was elected to fill the seat in the Lower House of the Assembly, was the fact that there must have been a hotly contested election and that Sir Patrick Houstoun was the defeated candidate. As far back as 1768 the "indirect vote" was being exercised in Georgia and probably long before then women had begun to "play politics." Sir Patrick Houstoun was the victim of a feud that began in May, 1768, before the election of delegates to the Lower House. The full story lies in oblivion, but the following items from the *Georgia Gazette* disclose that heated words were uttered and accusations were made to such an extent that the principals, unfortunately, resorted to the public press, hoping to vindicate their position, if not their honor. The members of some of Savannah's prominent families were involved in the unpleasant incident. The persons concerned were Mrs. Heriot Crooke, Mrs. James Mossman (her daughter), John Mulryne and Thomas Young. John Mulryne was a member of the Lower House representing the Islands of Wilmington, Tybee, Skidaway, and Green. He first took his seat, October, 1765, and was returned to the Assembly in November, 1768. The Mossmans, who lived on the Bay, were intimate friends of the Houstouns, and Thomas Young, a Scotsman, was presumably a friend also, as in 1804 some of the next generation of Houstouns were witnesses to his will.[21]

---

20. *Ibid.*, 465.
21. LaFar and Wilson, *Abstract of Wills, Chatham County* . . . ., 175.

The story can be told only as it appeared in the *Georgia Gazette*. On May 11, 1768, the *Gazette* published at the request of Mrs. Heriot Crooke, copies of two letters written by John Mulryne and a copy of an affidavit signed by Thomas Young. Attached to Mrs. Crooke's letter to the editor was a quotation from Shakespeare:

> Why let the stricken deer go weep
> The heart ungalled play;
> For some must watch, whilst some must sleep,
> So runs the world away.

John Mulryne's first letter was addressed to the editor:

> I propose to have ready for your next paper and the Carolina Gazettes, a curious Affidavit, with a short dissertation upon slander, the abuse of time, and the danger of envenomed tongues, as an introduction to a judicial investigation of facts that have been industriously and falsely spread to the prejudice of
> Your humble servant.

His second letter was written to Mrs. Crooke:

> I cannot consistent with the candor which I hope ever to maintain, send the above to the printer, until you had first seen it, and "if you think proper," shewed it to those to whom it may concern, that your objections to this and what must necessarily follow it (if you have any that should have weight with me) may be made this day by three o'clock or they will be too late.

The third communication was Young's affidavit:

> Thomas Young, of Vernonburg in the province of Georgia aforesaid, planter, being duly sworn, maketh oath, That on Wednesday last the fourth of this inst. May, Mrs. Heriot Crooke and Mrs. Elizabeth Mossman came in a chair to this deponent's house and asked his vote for Sir Patrick Houstoun to be Member of Assembly for Vernonburg, and upon his telling that he was pre-engaged having promised his vote to Mr. Tattnall[22] for Mr. Box, they told him that Mr. Tattnall was a captain now, but would not be so above one month or two months more, and that Mr. Mulryne, who busied himself in the matter had broke and sworn off once or twice in Carolina; that if the people did not vote for Sir

---

22. Mulryne's daughter, Mary, became the wife of Josiah Tattnall of Bonaventure Plantation.

Patrick they would pay thirteen and sixpence tax for negroes, and would be liable to pay the Governor's salary and all the Indian expenses.

(Signed) Thomas Young

I do certify that the above is a true copy of an affidavit this day made before me by Thomas Young.

John Green

Acton, 7th May, 1768

In the next week's issue of the newspaper Mulryne published an answer to Mrs. Crooke's communication. He also resorted to poetry and began:

> Truth, candid, decent, modest, easy, kind;
> Softens the high and sears the abject mind;
> Knows with just reins and gentle hand to guide,
> Betwixt vile flame, and arbitrary pride.
>
> Prior

As I was of opinion that the ladies whose names appeared in your last Gazette acted under the influence of a prompter or prompters, who *for reasons best known to themselves*, chose to wound me from behind a coverture, it occasioned my being at the trouble of writing the letters which were then published, and as that opinion is now, "by many probable circumstances," in some measure confirmed, I think myself under an absolute necessity of calling upon those ladies and their prompters to prove that I ever swore off as they were pleased to term it, which if true, may soon be done, from the records of the Court in Carolina, or by the deposition of some credible person who resided then in that province, and in either case I promise to pay any accessary expense that may attend such proof, which if they do not produce in a reasonable time, it will so exactly correspond with the *tax*, the *Governor's salary*, and *Indian expenses*, mentioned in Thomas Young's affidavit, that the publick will doubtless conclude the assertation to be groundless, and accordingly form a proper judgment of their conduct.

The footing and respect of intimacy which I thought myself upon with those ladies, and some gentlemen who are closely connected with them, (one of whom I have the sincerest friendship for) renders this subject extremely disagreeable to me, and necessarily shortens the inferences that I should otherwise have naturally drawn from it. But I am told one of the ladies declared she did not make the report; if she did not, it lay in her way, (as

Falstaff said of rebellion) and she found it. Though if propagating injurious reports be at all commendable, I have been, and shall be, all my life wrong, having ever discountenanced them; and it is with uncommon pleasure that I now reflect upon a time when I was at great pains to discredit and suppress some reports of others, which I would not have upon a just foundation believed of me, or my family, for all the wealth, and the grandeur, and "what may with some be still more tempting," all the pleasing gratification in murdering reputations that this world affords; nor would it have derogated from the characters of those ladies, or their prompters, had they acted towards me in the like friendly manner. I am, Your humble servant,[23]

Contrary to all tradition, man, upon that occasion had the last *printed* word. As far as publicity of the affray was concerned, no more letters appeared in the *Gazette* that year. Mulryne continued to sign his name to advertisements, and James Mossman's appeared an an executor of an estate. How far gossip was prolonged must remain in the forgotten past.

The defeated candidate, Sir Patrick Houstoun, then turned his attention from politics. For one interest he was occupied with the estate of Mark Fenton, as the executor, and there was much to do in connection with it because through the years 1769 and 1770 he was advertising for sale the testator's plantation at White Bluff, his farm produce, and household furniture.[24]

After just one year's absence from the legislature, Sir Patrick was elected, in 1769, with William Young to represent the Parish of St. Andrew's, and they took their seats on November 6.[25] Houstoun soon was active in serving on committees, one of which was to examine into the state of the colony's finances. He continued a member of the legislature through the year 1770, but he attended a session in April, 1771, appeared as a member of the house, and declined taking his seat, giving as his reason that his private affairs would not permit him to attend the meetings. On August 22, 1771, he was appointed a justice of the peace for St. Andrew's Parish and the other southern parishes, and the

---
23. *Georgia Gazette*, May 18, 1768.
24. *Ibid.*, January 4, 1769.
25. *Colonial Records of Georgia*, XV, 21.

next day he took the oath of allegiance and supremacy.[26] Apparently he was looking after his Cathead plantation near Darien. The urge for public life, however, was strong enough to induce him to reconsider, and accepting the election, he was back again in the Lower House at the fall session of 1772.[27] On December 15, Sir Patrick was made chairman of a committee to bring in a "bill to empower the several commissioners or surveyors to lay out and make such public roads in the Province and to improve the roads already laid out, and also to improve the rivers and creeks." On the same day he was placed on another committee to prepare and present a bill "for the preservation of deer by night." His name was presented with that of William Young, Esq., for Speaker of the House. He lost the election to his opponent.

So many of the committees on which Sir Patrick Houstoun served in the early part of 1773 were but repetitions of similar bills presented to the house during his previous membership there, that it is not necessary to mention them again. In 1772 and in the year following, his brother, Dr. James Houstoun, often served on the same committee with him.

The Governor's house had fallen into disrepair during Governor Wright's absence from the province, and in February, 1773, as he was soon to return from England, a committee was appointed, of which Sir Patrick was a member, to see that the house was put in order before His Excellency's return. Sir Patrick, with others, voted in the affirmative for the measure, while many voted against the motion. When the question was brought up in the house as to the personnel of the members who should meet the Governor, those who opposed the above motion were Dr. Noble Wimberly Jones, Jonathan Bryan, the Reverend John J. Zubly, a Mr. Bourquin and a Mr. LeConte; so presumably Sir Patrick Houstoun was among those who went down to "the landng" to greet Governor Wright on his return to Georgia.[28]

It is evident that at that time Sir Patrick was not certain in his own mind how he should conduct himself toward the new political attitude which was becoming increasingly perceptible,

---

26. *White's Historical Collections*, 40.
27. *Colonial Records of Georgia*, XV, 336.
28. *Ibid.*, 381.

Sir Patrick Houstoun, Sixth Baronet 119

and his frequent absences from his duties in the house were beginning to be noticed. There was a rule in the Lower House that a member absenting himself without a cause should be arrested. That happened to Sir Patrick more than once. On June 22, 1773, he was not present, and "the Clerk was ordered to write him immediately that the House required his attendance."[29]

On July 29, Sir Patrick again, with Jonathan Bryan and Button Gwinnett, was found guilty of the misdemeanor, and the three were arrested and put in custody.[30] On August 4 the House was informed that Sir Patrick Houstoun was at the door. He was called in and ordered to be discharged upon paying the required fee. That was his last appearance in the Lower House, and it furnishes a clue to his strong Tory leanings which he was later to show openly. However, the comment has no bearing on the other two who were his companions in "custody" as they were both ardent patriots in the war which came a few years later. It is a difficult matter to follow the working of Sir Patrick Houstoun's mind in those trying times with the approaching Revolution calling for adherents. His father had been a "faithful servant of the King"; his mother, of course, shared her husband's feeling of loyalty.

4

By the time war was declared, Sir Patrick no doubt was thankful that his father and mother both had passed away and could not witness his vacillation. For many Americans 1775 was a year of decision. On April 19 the Battle of Lexington took place. News in those days traveled so slowly that it was not until May 10 that accounts of the engagement reached Savannah. It caused great distress among the citizens, but it also opened the way for a definite decision among many of them. It was in 1775 that Sir Patrick Houstoun was appointed to the Royal Council. Governor Wright's correspondence with the Earl of Dartmouth[31] reveals that during that year frequent deaths made it necessary for

---

29. *Ibid.*, 433.
30. *Ibid.*, 471. The custom was not peculiar to the Georgia legislature. In 1782 Thomas Jefferson, Patrick Henry, and John Marshall were taken into custody for the same offense. See Albert J. Beveridge, *The Life of John Marshall*, I, 211, 213 (Boston and New York, 1916).
31. Secretary of State for the Colonies and President of the Board of Trade and Foreign Plantation.

the Governor to make numerous appointments to the Council. Before all of these appointments could be acknowledged by the London authorities the Governor was arrested and the King's authority was terminated abruptly. The Royal Governor broke his parole and fled to Bonaventure, the home of Colonel John Mulryne, whence he escaped to England. The Royal Government being no more, such Loyalists as were in Savannah slipped away. The Council of Safety and the Provincial Congress, composed of men who had espoused the Patriots' Cause, then were in command of Savannah.

"Glorious times that tried men's souls!" wrote Loyalist Lewis Johnston on his copy of the *Georgia Gazette*, late in 1774. That Sir Patrick Houstoun was tormented in 1775 by the necessity of making a decision would appear a logical surmise. He was residing at his plantation near Darien at the time of his appointment to the Council.[32] It would appear that he hoped to remain out of the controversy as long as he could. His position has been criticized as "equivocal."[33] It has been interpreted, also, as "neutral to the last degree."[34] Events of 1776 and 1777 would seem to prove the former opinion to be correct. During those years he was proscribed by both the Royal Legislature and the Colonial Assembly.

In 1776 Sir Patrick Houstoun became involved in an affair of his brother-in-law, George McIntosh, which brought great mortification and hardship to the latter. The accusation of treason against McIntosh came about through a partnership he had entered into with Sir Patrick Houstoun, when, with a third man, they united in putting into one consignment their rice crops which had been cultivated and harvested on their large plantations on the Altamaha River.[35]

Where Sir Patrick was during the trials and tribulations of George McIntosh is not known; but he was, probably, at first

---

32. Patrick Houstoun to Lachlan McIntosh, June 14, 1775, in Etting Collection, 1-72, Historical Society of Pennsylvania.
33. Charles Francis Jenkins, *Button Gwinnett: Signer of the Declaration of Independence* (Garden City, New York, 1926), 138.
34. William Bordley Clarke, *Early and Historic Freemasonry of Georgia* (Savannah, 1924), 38. Lorenzo Sabine, *Loyalists of the American Revolution* (Boston, 1864), Preface.
35. The whole story, which concerned McIntosh more than Houstoun, will be found in the chapter, "Ann Priscilla, Wife of George McIntosh."

in both Savannah and Darien, endeavoring to use his influence in helping to extricate his brother-in-law. However, he was not considered implicated in the charge fastened on McIntosh, and one hint of a possible journey north in April, 1777, is found in an item in a diary of Major Raymond Demeré, dated April 14. "Embarked in company with Sir Patrick Houstoun and Dr. Houstoun for Charlestown, on my way to Philadelphia, to join the Continental Army."[36] Charles Town was then in the hands of the Patriots. It seems likely that Sir Patrick continued on north with Major Demeré and his brother James. He evidently stopped in Philadelphia. General Washington's army had spent the winter at Morristown, New Jersey, the British had not captured Philadelphia, and it was the summer that General Lafayette reached the shores of North America. A friend of Houstoun in Philadelphia was Colonel Daniel Cunningham Clymer, who had been in the Philadelphia militia in 1776, but later was Commissioner of Claims of the Treasury.[37] After returning to Georgia, Sir Patrick wrote Colonel Clymer from Augusta, expressing the hope that the Philadelphian would pay him a visit. "Next fall," he wrote in June, 1778, "I hope you will do what you intended doing last and therefore I take this opportunity of introducing to your acquaintance the agreeable companions who will be returning about the time you would choose to travel Southwardly; Mr. McLean[38] & Mr. Cowper[39] who mean to pass the Summer visiting the Northern States, both my worthy and particular friends."[40]

36. Copy in the possession of his lineal descendant, Edward Houstoun Deméré, Jr., of San Francisco, California.
37. "Daniel Cunningham Clymer, the son of William and Ann (Roberdeau) Clymer was born in Philadelphia, April 6, 1748. Losing his father in early life he was brought up by his uncle, General Roberdeau. He graduated at Princeton in 1766, read law, and attained an enviable position in that profession. . . . He married Mary Weidner. . . . He died in 1819. His relationship to George Clymer the Signer is unknown." The Historical Society of Pennsylvania.
38. Andrew McLean, in 1776, was thought to further the Loyalist cause but was later cleared of that suspicion. Subsequently he was appointed to hold a treaty with the Creek and Cherokee Indians of Augusta. Allen D. Candler, ed., *The Revolutionary Records of the State of Georgia* (1908), I, 127-129; II, 218, 490, (Hereafter cited *Revolutionary Records of Georgia*).
39. Basil Cowper was a member of the Council of Safety, but later joined the Loyalists. *Collections of the Georgia Historical Society*, V, Pt. 1, 1, 18.
40. Patrick Houstoun to Daniel C. Clymer, June 11, 1778, Clymer Collection, 45. Historical Society of Pennsylvania.

5

The ensuing few years brought Sir Patrick Houstoun conspicuously to the forefront as a person of uncertain opinions. The Patriots on March 1, 1778, passed in their General Assembly the Georgia Act of Attainder whereby they accused of high treason one hundred and sixteen specified Loyalists whose names were included in the Act. The edict stated that estates, both real and personal, were to be confiscated to the use of the State. Sir Patrick Houstoun's name was *not* on the list of Loyalists at that time.[41]

Governor Wright returned to Georgia from England on July 14, 1779, and re-established for a time the Royal Government in the colonial capital. On May 1, 1780, the Royal Legislature passed a retaliatory measure called "The British Disqualifying Act" rendering "incapable the several persons hereinafter named from holding or exercising any office of trust, honour, or profit in the Province of Georgia for a certain time and for other purposes therein maintained." One hundred and fifty men by name were included in that act. Sir Patrick's name was on that list, a fact which would justify the inference that from 1778 to 1780 Houstoun was either acting with the Patriots, or his indecision had not yet brought him under the suspicion of the Provincials.

The publishing of those two acts, the one by the Patriots in 1778 when Sir Patrick Houstoun's name was *not* on the list of the accused Loyalists, and the other list issued by the Royal Legislature in 1780, two years later, when he *was* mentioned among those included in the British Disqualifying Act is conclusive evidence that he was considered a Patriot at that time, but no record has been found of his contributing to the republican cause. Sir Patrick was not on the Council of Safety, and he was not a member of the Provincial Congress, although two of his brothers, George and John, were members of both.

It is known that Sir Patrick Houstoun received a commission as Captain in the Light Infantry Company of Colonel Francis Harris's Regiment on August 18, 1767.[42] No further record has

---
41. Jones, *History of Georgia*, II, 421; *Revolutionary Records of Georgia*, I, 348-356.
42. State Officers Appointments 1754-1827, Department of Archives and History, Atlanta.

been found of his military service, so that it is impossible to say whether in the dramatic incident which follows he was acting in a military capacity or as a private citizen. It remains an enigma why the Royal Legislature disqualified Sir Patrick Houstoun in 1780, because in September of that year he played a conspicuous part on the side of the British when an attack was made on the "White House" near Augusta.

After the British had captured Savannah (December, 1778), some of the troops were sent up the Savannah River to seize Augusta, and by the end of January they had taken the town only to abandon it in less than a month. A year later the British were re-occupying Augusta. They were to hold it for several months. Lieutenant Colonel Thomas Brown with other British officers, had command of the "White House" about a mile and a half from the town. The house had been fortified and converted into a fort.[43] The Americans closed in on the little fort, and Colonel Brown, realizing the precarious situation he and his men were facing, dispatched messengers to Colonel John Harris Cruger stationed at Ninety-Six, South Carolina,[44] to come quickly to his aid. Sir Patrick Houstoun was the first of those messengers to reach Colonel Cruger who at once left his troops for Augusta.[45] A bloody conflict ensued which resulted in the retreat of the Americans. Colonel Brown wreaked terrible vengeance on the prisoners, and the fighting in and around that house has been considered some of the hardest in the Revolution on Georgia soil.

Sir Patrick in 1781 petitioned the Royal Council for restoration to good standing. It would appear that the Council took his petition under advisement sometime in 1781. The official minutes would convey the impression that not the least important consideration in producing the Council's favorable action was Houstoun's part in the "White House" engagement, a contribution to the Royal cause for which Colonel Cruger expressed his gratitude by assisting Patrick to win absolution. Yet it should

---
43. The historic "White House," known as No. 1822 Broad Street, is still standing (1949).
44. Edward McCrady, *The History of South Carolina in the Revolution 1780-1783* (New York, 1902), 139.
45. Jones, *History of Georgia*, II, 457; McGrady, *History of South Carolina . . . 1775-1780*, p. 736.

be noted that the Council was constrained to commend Houstoun for "the whole of his Conduct before. . . ." By unanimous opinion he was restored to the status of a loyal subject.[46]

6

Part of the conflict which Sir Patrick Houstoun was undergoing in the four years between 1775 and 1780 may have been due to unhappiness in his private life. A contemporary letter tells of his engagement to a Miss Nelly Graham. As it is known that Patrick never married, the conclusion is, of course, that something went amiss during the war to prevent the marriage. Nelly Graham's baptismal name was Elena. She was born in Savannah in 1759, and she was the daughter of Lieutenant Governor John Graham, whose wife was Frances Crooke, the sister of Mrs. James Mossman. Fourteen of the Grahams' seventeen children were born in Savannah, six of them dying in infancy. Among the coterie of friends of the Houstouns and the Grahams were Robert Mackay and his wife, who was Mary Malbone of Newport, Rhode Island. In Savannah on business, Mackay wrote his wife in February, 1775, that Houstoun and Miss Nelly Graham were soon to be married.[47]

John Graham was born in Scotland about 1718. He came to Georgia in 1753 expecting to inherit a large fortune from a relative, but on arrival he was disappointed; thereupon he engaged in business. In 1760 he met Governor Wright, who three years later appointed him commissary and clerk of the courts with a salary of sixty pounds a year.[48] Previously, Graham had abandoned business to engage in agriculture. He became a planter with large holdings, having developed three plantations, and he had accumulated two hundred and sixty-two slaves. In March, 1776, he received a commission as lieutenant governor without salary. During the next two months the Patriots became aroused and formed in

---

46. Original document on file in office of Department of Archives and History, Atlanta.
47. The original letter was given in February, 1943, to the Georgia Society of the Colonial Dames of America by the late Mrs. Franklin Buchanan Screven of Savannah, who was the great-granddaughter of Robert Mackay. The letter is in the Mackay-McQueen-Cowper Collection in Hodgson Hall, Savannah.
48. Saye, *New Viewpoints in Georgia History*, 117.

Savannah the Council of Safety. At its meeting on May 1, the Council ordered that "permission be granted to John Graham to depart the Province with his family with necessary servants and provisions for the voyage leaving his property behind him for security of his creditors and he has leave to return." The next day the Council ordered that John Graham be required to give bond of £10,000 as security to the public on his departure from the province.[49]

On May 13, Graham left Georgia with his family "being twelve in number (exclusive of servants)," but, "at great expense he was obliged to freight a vessel to take him to England."[50] Among the members of his family were Sir Patrick Houstoun's fiancee, Elena, and the following sisters and brothers: Frances, Susannah (named for her aunt, Mrs. Alexander Wylly), Elizabeth (named for another aunt, Mrs. James Mossman), Mary, Ann, Alexander, and Clement. When the Grahams arrived in England they went to live at St. Lawrence, near Canterbury, where Elena, or Nelly, died in 1808.[51]

Up to 1779, Sir Patrick was declared a Loyalist. The next year he was listed as a Patriot. Could his broken romance have had something to do with his vacillation? At any rate, after the "White House" incident in 1781, Sir Patrick Houstoun's position was no longer equivocal. He was an out-and-out Loyalist, but, unlike many others, he did not leave the country at once when the war was over because he wished to discharge his obligations to the state. As he was a large property owner it required some time to adjust his affairs. The Royal Council had restored him to

---

49. *Collections of the Georgia Historical Society*, V, Pt. 1, 47, 48.
50. "Memorial of Lieut.-Governor Graham to the Right Honorable Lord Germain His Majesty's Principal Secretary of State for America," in *Collections of the Georgia Historical Society*, III, 376, 377.
51. John Graham returned to Georgia in 1779 when Savannah was under British rule; and until the end of the year 1782, he engaged in Loyalist activities, when he returned to England. He died in Naples in 1795.
   NOTE: Information on the Graham family was obtained from a letter written to Dr. E. Merton Coulter of the University of Georgia (who gave permission to use it) by Miss Cecily Gertrude Papillon of Hawkley, near Liss, Hampshire, England, requesting information on her great-great-grandfather, Colonel John Graham, when he was in Georgia. Miss Papillon is descended from his daughter, Mary (born in Savannah, in 1772), who married Sir Henry Oxendon of Broome Park, Kent. A copy of an oil painting of Ann Graham (born in Savannah, in 1774, died at Torquay, England, in 1806) hangs in Colonial Dames House, Savannah.

British favor in 1781, as previously mentioned, and it will be noted presently that although having forfeited his property he was able to leave his home in Georgia with a clear conscience. The Georgia House of Assembly (Provincial) was dissolved on December 26, 1778, when news reached Savannah that the British troops were about to enter the town, and the members moved speedily to Augusta where, for the immediate future, all meetings were to be held.

Commissioners of the Confiscated Estates were elected by the Executive Council of the State Legislature on May 4, 1782. Thirteen members were named from eight counties, and on the thirteenth day of the following month they began their work. On July 24, when the Assembly was again meeting in Savannah, it was resolved in Council that it be recommended to the Commissioners of Forfeited Estates to postpone for one month the sales in the respective counties, and public notice thereof be given. On the same day a petition from Sir Patrick Houstoun was read, and it was re-read on July 26. The next day the Committee on Confiscated Estates reported that it was the unanimous opinion of the members, "that as some favorable circumstances appear in behalf of the Petitioner he ought to be taken off the Confiscation and Expulsion Act and Put on the Amercement Act and amerced agreeable to the rates which others in similar cases are, which was agreed to."[52] Again, at a meeting of the House of Assembly held on August 3, the committee reported that it had divided the list of those to be amerced into three classes. Members of the first class were to be fined twelve per cent, if paid in cash, on all property real and personal. They were permitted forty days to file under oath an appraisement of their property. Within three months they were expected to make a final settlement. The second class was to be amerced eight per cent. Members of the third class were to serve as soldiers, or to find substitutes. The report was adopted and Houstoun was placed in class number one. On March 20, 1783, the Council, declaring Houstoun in default of his amercement, ordered that his three-thousand-acre plantation near Cathead Creek, Darien, be sold at public auction at Savannah's Vendue House. Previous to the March 20 action

---

52. *Revolutionary Records of Georgia*, III, 154.

of the Council Patrick's brother William had purchased at £10 per acre 2500 acres of Cathead Creek plantation.⁵³

Besides the grants previously mentioned the Council had bestowed others upon Sir Patrick Houstoun and in the last years of his residence in Georgia, he was a wealthy landowner. Among other conveyances he was possessed of five hundred acres in St. Patrick's Parish, one hundred and fifty additional in St. Andrew's, three hundred and fifty in St. Philip's, one hundred in St. George's, one hundred in St. David's, three hundred and fifty in St. Paul's, four hundred in St. Thomas's, one hundred at Frederica,⁵⁴ and three thousand unlocated acres.

Having been placed in class number one of the Amercement Act, Sir Patrick Houstoun finally yielded to the mandate of the Assembly. On April 1, 1783, the Executive Council acknowledged receiving from Houstoun the sum of £100 in specie. It agreed to suspend proceedings against the delinquent Loyalist and, further, granted him until the meeting of the next Assembly to complete his amercement.⁵⁵

After that application of Sir Patrick Houstoun for deferment of his castigation for being a Loyalist, there appears to be no further mention of his name in the meetings of Council through 1784, although several times the reports of the commissioners are mentioned. His proclivity for acquiring more land assailed him again in April, 1784, but instead of asking for a grant his intention was to purchase land from a "governor" to whom he wrote from Savannah, April 13, 1784. It could not have been the Governor of Georgia, as his brother John was then serving his second term in that office. The implication is that this request for land was addressed to the Governor of South Carolina who, it would appear, had advertised certain of his holdings.⁵⁶

7

Sir Patrick had wished to leave Georgia even before peace was declared. It may have been that he wanted to follow the thousands of expatriated Loyalists who, not wishing to live in

---
53. *Ibid.*, I, 496.
54. Record in Secretary of State's office, Atlanta.
55. *Revolutionary Records of Georgia*, II, 485. The records of the transactions of the commission are imperfect. *Ibid.*, I, 413.
56. The Historical Society of Pennsylvania (Dreer Collection.)

the new nation, had established homes in other lands under the British flag; or he may have found it necessary to try to recover his health which was impaired by the mental strain of the war years. In 1781 it was evident to Council Members that Sir Patrick had "manifested a disposition to leave the country and detach himself from the party in rebellion." It is not unlikely that after the war was over he made his home with his brother George at White Bluff. As the summer of 1784 approached, he began making plans for his departure for England. He made his will in May and in mid-summer he sailed for London. He left three brothers at home, and the fourth, William, was at the Continental Congress in New York; his only sister, Mrs. George McIntosh, had died in 1777. He seems to have had a high regard for his brother George. If he had any bitter feeling toward his patriot brothers, it was for James, as the bare mention of the latter's name in his will, cutting him off with five shillings, implies there was animosity between them. It may have been personal and not political, but the bequest gives a hint of a sad leave-taking. Toward William, the youngest member of the family, who was fifteen years his junior, Sir Patrick exhibited a tender affection.

Sir Patrick's will was written less than ten months before his death. Prepared in Savannah, it was dated May 10, 1784.[57]

---

57. .... I, Sir Patrick Houstoun, Baronet, do make my last Will and Testament in manner and form following.
.... I give and bequeath unto my ever affectionate, dutiful and beloved Brother George Houstoun, his heirs and assigns forever all the Lands, Negroes, Bonds, notes goods and effects of every kind whereof I die possessed and all that shall remain after the payment of my just debts........... and the Legacies hereinafter mentioned.
I give unto my Brother James five shillings.
I give unto my Brother John one hundred pounds.
I give unto my Brother William five hundred pounds
The above to bear Interest at the expiration of six months after my decease and to be paid in twelve months after my death.
.... I give unto my Nephew John Houstoun McIntosh one hundred Pounds to bear interest from my death and to be paid to him when he arrives at the age of twenty one years, but if he should die before he arrives at that age then I direct that the said sum with the interest that may be due thereon be paid to the eldest surviving daughter of my Brother George, and Lastly I do hereby make and ordain my said Brother George sole Executor of this my last Will and Testament.
It was signed P. Houstoun, and the witnesses were John Irvine, John Moodie and Peter S. Lafitte. (Chatham County Court House, Will Book "B").

MEMORIAL TO SIR PATRICK HOUSTOUN, SIXTH BARONET, IN THE ABBEY CHURCH, BATH, ENGLAND

On his arrival in London, or soon thereafter, Sir Patrick went to Bath in hope of regaining his health. The cure failed; on March 24, 1785, he passed away in his forty-third year, alone and far away from home and family. He was buried outside of the walls of the Old Abbey Church at Bath. A black and white marble tablet is fastened to a side wall inside the church. On it his brother, Sir George Houstoun, had inscribed the date of his death, his age, his home and that he was "greatly Lamented by all his Relations and Friends." It is interesting that Sir George, appreciating his brother's loyalty to the Crown of England, ignored the Georgia home and had inscribed on the tablet the words "North Britain" as Patrick's residence instead of Georgia, his birthplace.[58]

The news of his death reached Savannah on Monday, August 8, and his obituary was published on Thursday:

> On Monday last arrived in this river from London, the ship planter, Capt. Grieve. By her we have an account of the death of Sir Patrick Houstoun, Bart. of this State, who about 12 months ago went to London. The many amiable qualities of this worthy gentleman having rendered him extremely dear in life, his death cannot but be an event of uncommon concern and regret to all his numerous connexions and acquaintances.[59]

---

58. A photograph of the tombstone at Bath is in the possession of the author, the gift of Mr. Wallace Houstoun, of Scotland, 1911. It is regrettable that the stone cutter of Bath misspelled the name Houstoun. He undoubtedly read carelessly the written instruction of Sir George, who inherited the title.
59. *Gazette of the State of Georgia*, August 11, 1785.

SIR GEORGE HOUSTOUN, SEVENTH BARONET

1744-1795

From the portrait formerly owned by the late Dr. William Patrick Johnston, of Washington, District of Columbia

Chapter X

SIR GEORGE HOUSTOUN, BARONET, MAN OF AFFAIRS

CHARACTERISTICS, interests, and talents dissimilar to those of his brothers made the life of George Houstoun diverge to entirely different pursuits. Early in life he chose business rather than politics, although the latter had been the particular interest of his father and elder brother, Patrick. Later in life George Houstoun had conferred upon him honors that proved him to be a man with a strong urge for leadership, and the ability to put that urge into effect. On reviewing his history one may conclude that George Houstoun led a well-balanced life. He was a likable person, as shown by his election to the highest office in nearly every enterprise in which he had membership. His versatility expressed itself in the spheres of commercial, philanthropic, fraternal, civic, and social occupations.

When the younger Patrick Houstoun returned to Georgia, he and George soon must have revived their brotherly friendship which had been interrupted in childhood, and when renewed, existed until the end of the former's life. In 1768 and 1769 Patrick Houstoun was taking a leading part in the Commons House of Assembly, and while living at the home plantation no doubt made his daily horseback ride to town to attend its sessions. One can picture the two brothers discussing the affairs of the colony, the political questions of the day, and private matters in regard to Rosdue. What was most important to the younger brother probably was the advice he received from the elder on his future career.

In the year 1773 George Houstoun acquired through a deed from his mother five hundred acres of land in St. David's Parish. The deed was witnessed and signed by his two brothers, John and William.[1] Through the years George Houstoun became the owner of considerably more property.

---

1. Copy of deed in possession of the heirs of the late Mrs. Macartan C. Kollock of Atlanta.

When quite a young man George Houstoun was interested in military affairs. On April 7, 1774, he received his commission as second lieutenant in Captain Thomas Netherclift's company of Foot Militia and on June 4 he took the oath of allegiance and supremacy. Savannah was a military colony from its inception; so it is natural to conclude that George Houstoun's connection with the militia of the province did not begin with the receipt of his commission, but that probably he was promoted from the ranks.

Before George Houstoun entered upon a business vocation, he had had some preparation for a profession. The first hint that has been found to his adult life reveals that when he was twenty-four years of age he was called in as an attorney by the members of the firm of Kelsall, Darling, and Munro, who advertised in the *Georgia Gazette* of March 16, 1768, that their efforts to collect funds due them had proved entirely futile and they had retained George Houstoun as their attorney to begin suit "without respect to persons, to collect bonds, notes and accounts due."

In the colonial period indigo became one of the staple commodities produced on many plantations in coastal Georgia, and its cultivation continued into the next century, before it became profitable to produce that article. In January, 1774, George Houstoun was sufficiently established financially to own a plantation; his advertisement appears in the *Georgia Gazette* for an overseer "who understands the management of an Indigo plantation; he must be well recommended for his honesty, sobriety and knowledge of his business; such a one will meet with encouragement by applying to Geo. Houstoun."[2]

Serving as attorney could not have sustained the interest of George Houstoun very long as he soon became one of "the leading merchants in Savannah." Just when he changed professions has not been ascertained.[3] By 1774 he was established in a business which prospered well over ten years. If he had not started his business partnership before 1769, he at least must have taken a lively interest in the attitude of the Savannah merchants, who,

---
2. January 15, 1774.
3. Through the courtesy of Dr. Clarence S. Brigham, Director of the American Antiquarian Society, Worcester, Massachusetts, it was learned that no library has a file of the *Georgia Gazette* for the year 1773.

on September 19, 1769[4], had a meeting at which they passed unanimously resolutions to "import no articles that could be manufactured or produced at home."

It is quite likely that George Houstoun had formed a business connection before 1774, for the partnership of George Houstoun and Company was one of several firms engaged in mercantile business in Savannah at the same time. There was, too, noticeable rivalry, judging from the advertisements of the various concerns. Houstoun's firm was a regular advertiser in the weekly newspaper announcing for sale early in 1774 a quantity of "Indico seed," Lisbon and Port Wines "by the dozen," and a "fresh supply of goods" to be sold on "reasonable terms." Later in the same year the *Georgia Gazette* carried the following announcement for George Houstoun and Company: "Have just imported from Boston by way of Charlestown white, blue, green and drab colored plains, striped duffels, white, scarlet and striped flannels; saddlery; window glass; white lead, Spanish, brown and yellow oker ground in oil; linseed oil and white wine, vinegar in jugs, an assortment of nails, iron pots, skillets, frying pots, grid irons, etc."[5]

One of the rival merchants, John Foullis, made an alluring appeal to the ladies of the town, offering "a neat and Genteel Assortment of European Goods, suitable for present and approaching season [spring]. Also an assortment of Glasgow goods." Later in the month, Foullis notified his customers that he could offer them "linens, dowals, checks, check handkershiefs, and check hollands, figured dimities, printed linens, and cotton."[6] As both firms advertised foreign goods for sale, it is evident an agreement had been reached among the Savannah merchants and the embargo on foreign goods had been lifted.

2

Sometime before or during 1774 George Houstoun and Ann Moodie became engaged, as their marriage occurred in that year. Both Ann Moodie's father and mother were from Scotland and were born in Fifeshire. Their marriage was a romantic one. "When about twenty-one years of age, Thomas Moodie who was of the

---

4. *Georgia Gazette*, September 20, 1769.
5 *Ibid.*, February 2, 9, 16; March 23, 1774.
6. *Ibid.*, March 2, 23; August 31, 1774.

Laird of Cocklaw, Parish of Beath, Fifeshire, ran away with a beautiful girl, Miss [Jean] McKenzie, and later they emigrated to America. Their daughter, Ann, was born in 1749 before they left Scotland. Miss McKenzie's mother was a Miss Crawford, of the Rhodes, an estate near New Berwick within twenty miles of Edinburgh."[7] Thomas Moodie was Deputy Secretary to Governor Wright, and on August 14, 1774, signed "By His Excellency's Command," a proclamation, prohibiting the people of Savannah "to assemble or hold meetings under colour of pretense of consulting together for the Redress of Grievances or imaginary Grievances."[8]

It is not difficult to imagine the preparations made by Ann Moodie for her wedding and to picture her purchasing the cloth for her trousseau from Houstoun and Company. One even gets a fairly intimate glimpse of Ann Moodie's trousseau. It is known where she may have bought some of her hats and gowns. A Mrs. Parker, a Savannah dressmaker, in the spring of 1774 notified her patrons through the columns of the *Georgia Gazette* that she had taken part of Miss Molly Bowley's house "opposite the church" for the purpose of making "Sacks and Coats, Brunswicks, Fiscuits, Corsican Hats and Bonnets." Her garments, she announced, were to be offered "at most reasonable prices."[9]

While the bride was busy with her wedding plans, the groom found himself in trouble with the Court, but he had company in his predicament, and good company, too. The trouble was caused by failure to answer a jury summons on October 11. As a result His Majesty's General Court notified Houstoun, George Brown, Archibald Bulloch, James Habersham, Jr., and John Martin that they had been fined a sum not to exceed four pounds. The fine was to be waived in case the defaulters "do shew good & sufficient cause" within thirty days.[10]

The Moodie-Houstoun wedding took place on December 14, and the Bible record indicates the ceremony was performed in

---

7. Family paper, unsigned and undated, in the possession of the heirs of Mrs. Macartan C. Kollock of Atlanta.
8. Jones, *History of Georgia*, II, 151.
9. *Georgia Gazette*, March 9, 1774.
10. *Ibid.*, October 19, 1774.

Christ Church by the Reverend Haddon Smith.[11] At the time of their marriage George Houstoun was thirty years old and Ann Moodie was twenty-six. The newspaper notice of their marriage was brief. "Thursday last," it read, "was married in this place Mr. George Houstoun, Merchant, son of the late Sir Patrick Houstoun, Baronet, to Miss Ann Moodie, daughter of Thomas Moodie, Esq."[12]

The partnership known as George Houstoun and Company had been a success, but Houstoun was anxious to go it "on his own." Consequently when the terms of partnership expired, they were not renewed. Instead Houstoun went into business by himself. Within a month after his marriage he had invited the customers of the late partnership to do business with him. That Houstoun was called on to assist with community affairs is shown by the files of the *Georgia Gazette*. For example, in April, 1775, he served with James Habersham and Dr. John Irvine as an assignee of the estate of Timothy Lowton. He carried on his thriving business, and he continued his advertisements in the newspaper announcing in one issue the arrival from London of "an assortment of goods . . . suitable to the season . . . on reasonable terms."[13]

3

While Houstoun was carrying on his business enterprise, he was drawn into the political arena. Resentment against Great Britain was waxing warmer and warmer everywhere, and Savannah, where the Provincial Council met, of course felt the reverberation. An association was formed in January, 1775, by forty-five of the deputies to choose delegates to the Continental Congress. George Houstoun was among those who signed the twelve provisions, the signers agreeing to associate themselves "under the sacred ties of virtue, honour and love of country."

11. The first item in George Houstoun's Bible is the record of his marriage. The missing words, impossible to decipher, were supplied by the newspaper: "George Houstoun was married to Ann Moodie, daughter of Thomas Moodie on Thursday [sic] 1774 in Savannah [sic] in [sic] by the rector of Christ Church." The Bible is in the possession of the heirs of his lineal descendants, the children of the late Mrs. Macartan C. Kollock of Atlanta. The Bible is hereafter cited Houstoun Family Bible.
12. *Georgia Gazette*, December 21, 1774.
13. *Ibid.*, January 11, April 19, May 17, 1775.

Amid his newfound happiness, business success, and the turbulence existing in Savannah, George Houstoun lost his mother. She died in February, 1775. Shortly afterward he was called upon to act with his brother John as executor of her estate. The month following her death, the executors, pursuant to her will, advertised for sale the house she had lately occupied, all the household furniture, and other effects.[14] The George Houstouns' first child was born the following September, and was named Jean, and in January, 1777, a son, whom they called Patrick, was born, both in their Savannah home.

For three years George Houstoun was allied with those who later were termed "rebels," and apparently he was carried along with the enthusiasts of the Patriot cause; but after the Revolution he suffered the experience of having his estates confiscated by the victors. George Houstoun's attitude resembled, in its uncertainty, that of his brother Patrick. Whether or not he was heart and soul for the Patriot cause at first, when many were declaring themselves in open rebellion, is difficult to determine. He certainly attended the meeting at Mrs. Cuyler's on Friday, June 13, 1775.[15] Men were present then who, in the ensuing years, were so divided that they were avowed enemies of each other. When the Council of Safety was formed later in the month, on June 22, George Houstoun was one of the fourteen members. By July a Provincial Congress had been formed. It held its first meeting on July 4th in the Long Room of Tondee's Tavern, and George Houstoun was one of the elected representatives from the town and district of Savannah. After the organization of the Congress, the members adjourned to the Presbyterian meeting house on Ellis Square, where the Reverend John Joachim Zubly preached a sermon on the "alarming state of American affairs." Upon the re-convening of the Congress at Tondee's Tavern, the members passed a resolution of thanks to Dr. Zubly for his excellent sermon and a committee composed of five members, two of whom were the brothers George and John Houstoun, was appointed to convey the message to the Reverend Mr. Zubly. The next day George Houstoun again served on a committee of the Congress

---

14. *Georgia Gazette*, March 22, 1775.
15. *Revolutionary Records of Georgia*, I, 232. Mrs. Jeremiah Cuyler's home was on the southeast corner of Broughton and Bull streets.

to act with seven other members to carry a message to Governor Wright requesting him to "appoint a day of Fasting and Prayer throughout the Province on account of the disputes subsisting between America and the parent state."[16]

A week later the Provincial Congress adopted the Association, which had resolved that the rights and liberties of America depended "under God, on the firm union of the inhabitants in preparing for their safety, expressing alarm at the design of the Ministry to raise revenue in America, and shocked by the bloody scene now acting in the Massachusetts Bay, and associating themselves to carry out the recommendations of the Continental Congress and the Provincial Convention until a reconciliation could be obtained between Great Britain and America." By resolution fourteen members, one of whom was George Houstoun, were appointed to present the Association to the inhabitants to be signed. The Congress imposed expediency on its committee, directing it to give an account to the general committee of all who declined to sign. George Houstoun continued a member of the Council of Safety at least through November, 1775, when his name is recorded in the minutes of the meeting on the third day of the month, affixed with an asterisk referring to a note which states, "afterwards joined the Royalists." Another member, however, Basil Cowper, who had frequently served on committees of the Provincial Congress with George Houstoun, was placed in the same category.[17] Later in the month, George Houstoun declined taking his seat in the Provincial Congress, although he had been formerly elected one of the Representatives of the Town and District of Savannah. Lachlan McGillivray was chosen the member "in his room." George Houstoun's political desertion did not come for some time. Following the Declaration of Independence his name appeared on the bills of credit in the form of certificates issued to raise funds to equip the province of Georgia with arms and ammunition.[18]

---

16. *Revolutionary Records of Georgia*, I, 231.
17. *Ibid.*, 72, 253.
18. Georgia—1776—No. 5991
   This certificate entitles the bearer to Four
   Spanish Milled Dollars, or the value thereof.
   according to Resolution of Congress.
   Jas Habersham   W^m. Ewen
   E. Telfair   W^m OBryan
   Geo Houstoun   Seal.
   Jones, *History of Georgia*, II, 215, 216.

On July 19, George Houstoun, his brother John, and three others, were chosen by the Council of Safety as commissioners for the White Bluff Road. If that appointment was not the motive for George Houstoun's acquiring a plantation at White Bluff, something else influenced him, for in less than two years he was possessed of five hundred acres there situated on a creek which empties into the Vernon River. The plantation was named Retreat. The house on high land, visible from the road, was built in the simple style of the period, a story and a half. A piazza on high brick pillars was across the front of the house and partly on the sides. The hall extended through the house with large rooms on each side. In the rear of the house was a flower garden with beds bordered in large sweet boxwood, and massive live oak trees grew back of the garden.[19] There on January 24, 1778, Ann Marion, the third child of the George Houstouns, was born.

In the early part of January, 1778, the Houstoun family had the distinction of having one of its members, John Houstoun, elected Governor of the newly formed state. His brother George was still associated with the rebel cause. On February 23, the executive council ordered a special watch for the protection of the town naming "twenty respectable inhabitants" to serve for that purpose and George Houstoun was listed with the score of citizens appointed to that trustworthy post of duty; "two of them were to meet and sit by rotation in some convenient house in Town every night from nine o'clock . . . until Day Break." After nine o'clock every person passing the street was to be led by the several sentinels in the town to the two specially appointed inhabitants if the countersign could not be given. If the person was not a soldier, he was to be discharged at the discretion of the committee, or committed to the guard until morning when a report was to be made to the Governor. Each morning the Town Major was required to inform the two men who were to be on duty that night of the countersign issued by the Governor.[20]

From what transpired later it seems to have been in 1779 that George Houstoun showed a leaning toward the views of the Loyalists. In that summer he was living with his family at White

---

19. Description from the late Mrs. Macartan C. Kollock of Atlanta, a lineal descendant, who lived there in her childhood.
20. *Revolutionary Records of Georgia*, I, 324; II, 42, 43.

Bluff, as his fourth child, George, was born at Retreat on July 8th. By the end of the year Savannah was in the hands of the British, and it must have been from that time on that George Houstoun was in favor with the Crown adherents. Many have tried to analyze that inexplicable situation, but one writer succeeded in arousing sympathy for those throughout the thirteen states who were guilty of vacillation. He expresses it most aptly: "To change from one side to the other, both during the controversy which preceded the shedding of blood and at various periods of the war was not uncommon. . . . There was the absence of fixed principles, not only among people in the common walks of life, but in many of the prominent personages of the day."[21]

The hour of retribution came to those who wavered in their loyalties. George Houstoun felt the power of the law when on May 4, 1782, the State Assembly, sitting in Augusta, passed the Confiscation and Banishment Act, listing two hundred and seventy-eight men and decreeing their banishment from the state forever. His name, with that of Patrick Houstoun, was found thereon. On June 13, his brother William bought one of George's confiscated estates of 500 acres on the Great Ogeechee River for seven hundred and fifty pounds. The White Bluff Plantation, fortunately for posterity's sake, escaped confiscation. A petition was sent by George Houstoun on July 24, 1782, to the House of Assembly. He asked to be restored to the rights of citizenship, and the Assembly appointed John Houstoun and John Wereat to prepare a bill for that provision. Apparently the bill was passed, since on August 3 George Houstoun was listed among those amerced eight per cent on all of their property.[22] With the war over rancor and hate gradually subsided, and "the children of the winners and the children of the expatriated losers . . . lived again in the newly formed state . . . and all helped in the up-building of the commonwealth."[23]

---

21. Lorenzo Sabine, *Biographical Sketches of Loyalists of the American Revolution* (Boston, 1864), Preface, v.
22. *Revolutionary Records of Georgia*, I, 375, 456; III, 141, 142, 178.
23. Sabine, *Biographical Sketches of Loyalists*, Preface, vii.

4

Life certainly began anew for George Houstoun. After his restoration to citizenship his interests extended, his business continued to flourish, and he showed himself once more a man of spirit. The psychological effect was decidedly marked, and his unusual gift for leadership is discernible in numerous activities for the development of Savannah.

In the years intervening between the birth of George and Ann Houstoun's fourth child and the day of George's freedom from the accusation of disloyalty to his state, two more children were added to the family circle. A son, Thomas, was born on January 15, 1781, but for the first time sorrow came to the household at Retreat, as the infant died five months later, on June 16. The birth, on October 12, 1782, of the sixth child, named John, is recorded as those above in the family Bible. He lived only three years.[24]

Besides his other accomplishments, George Houstoun had acquired the skill of horsemanship, as attested by his well-filled stable and membership in a hunt club. His advertisements in the weekly newspapers often referred to his horses. One advertisement concerned a dun-colored horse which had strayed from the "subscriber's pasture at White Bluff" and was described as being "13 hands high, white tail and mane, with brand," and for the return of which a reward of four dollars was offered. Later a reward of twenty guineas was offered by George Houstoun for the return of a "gray mare, a strawberry Roan, a Black Horse and a Sorrel Horse" which had been stolen from his stable at White Bluff.[25]

The little suburban resort "on the salts"[26] had a social life all its own. In 1783 it boasted a club house, frequented by surrounding plantation owners and by residents of Savannah, and used by both communities. Plans for a society were outlined in the newspaper of December 18, 1783, and the announcement offers

---

24. In a collection of mourning rings in the Baltimore Museum of Art is one that presumably belonged to Ann, Lady Houstoun. On the outside rim is inscribed: "Robert Moodie [her brother] ob. 9 March 1789, AE 36," and engraved underneath is "J. Houstoun ob. 6 Sepr 1785 AE 3 years."
25. *Gazette of the State of Georgia*, August 28, 1783; May 5, 1794.
26. A term used by Savannahians indicating residence on a salt river.

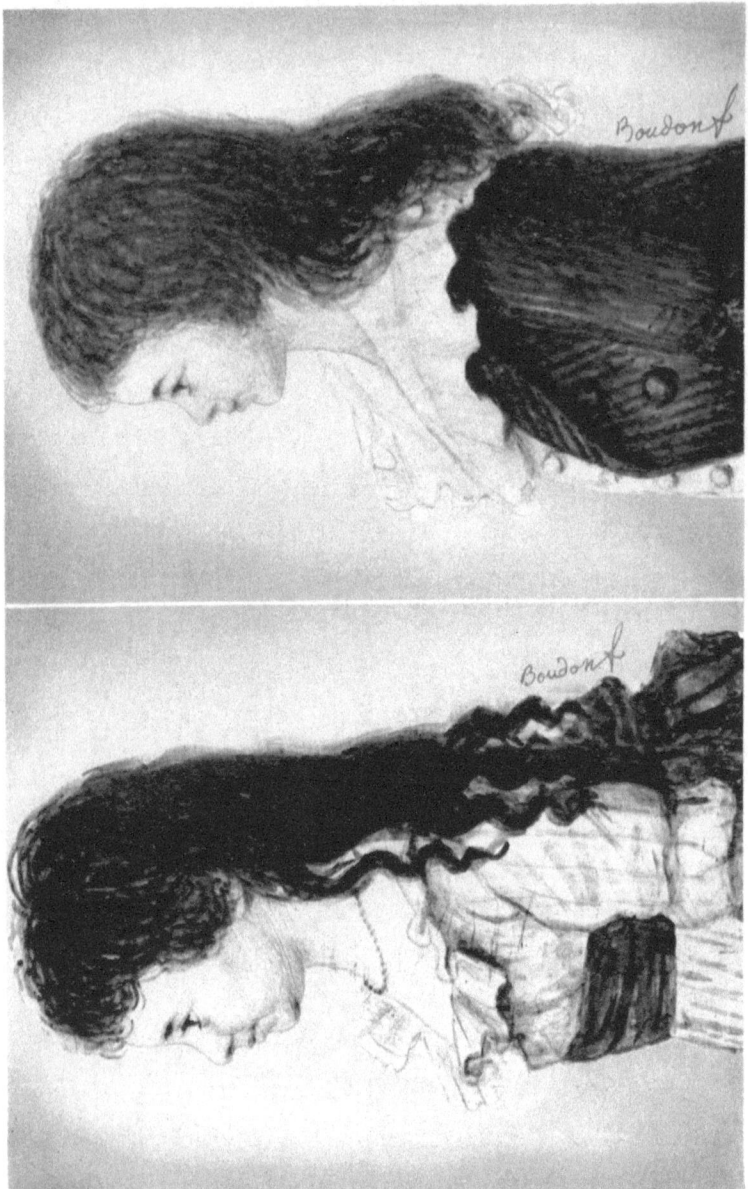

PRISCILLA HOUSTOUN ROBERT JAMES MOSSMAN HOUSTOUN
1784-1837 1785-1818

From the miniatures by David Boudon owned by Miss Edith Duncan Johnston, of Savannah, Georgia

a glimpse of men's social and recreational activities during the years following the Revolution. The members were to be "Men of Intelligence and good Character," and by meeting together and "joyously joining in the Sports of the Chase," they would "probably set an Example of Benevolence and improvement in society. The society," the notice continued, "would encourage an improvement in the breed of horses and beagles"; and those members "who from the Professions are compelled to a sedentary life" would "experience the greatest possible Advantages from the Exercise." Twenty-one sportsmen, including George Houstoun and his two brothers, James and William, "upon Principles of Honor and Benevolence" announced that they were forming themselves into a society to be "Styled the HUNTING CLUB," and they agreed on a set of rules which were: meetings to be held every second Saturday, beginning that week at the White Bluff Club House, when "a Place would be fixed for a House"; every member had to furnish a beagle for the use of the club; persons wishing to become members were to apply in writing, their names to be balloted for at the next meeting, "and admitted, if there shall be no negative." There would always be a president for the day to be taken in rotation, and refreshments would be "only Bread, a Round of Beef, Beefsteaks or a Ham and a Case of Liquors to consist of Rum Brandy and Geneva."[27]

In 1784 while still engaged in his mercantile business George Houstoun was again beginning to evince an interest in civic affairs.[28] The State Legislature's act of February, 1785, permitting the erection of a hospital for sick seamen, included George Houstoun in its appointment of commissioners, but the fulfillment of that enterprise was delayed for many years. In the year 1789, Sir George Houstoun resigned the office. It was only a few months after his hospital appointment that he received the news from abroad of the death of his dearly loved brother Patrick, in Bath, England.[29] After acting as the executor of his brother's estate, he lost no time in following the precedent of his father and older brother in notifying the Lyon-King-at-Arms of his

---

27. *Gazette of the State of Georgia*, December 18, 1783.
28. George Houstoun was a regular advertiser in the weekly newspaper. In *Gazette of the State of Georgia*, January 1, 1784, he announced he had for sale a general assortment of European and East India goods.
29. See *ante*, 129.

claim to the baronetcy, which was officially acknowledged. His name has been recorded thereafter in documents, newspapers, historical writings and some official papers, with the prefixed title. On one occasion his title disqualified him for a municipal appointment.[30]

In the years 1784 and 1785, the family circle of the George Houstouns increased by the addition of two more children. Priscilla, their seventh child, named for her paternal grandmother, was born on February 8, 1784, and her younger brother, Robert James Mossman, arrived on April 12, 1785. Both were born in Savannah, and both lived to maturity. When they were eleven and ten years old, respectively, their miniatures were painted by David Boudon, "Limner of Geneva Switzer-land."[31] Boudon, who lived a few years in Savannah, was a French refugee, and worked also in Charles Town in 1795 and 1796. The Houstoun miniatures were done in May and June, 1795. Boudon painted miniatures of the James River planters,[32] and later went to live in Pittsburgh.

At the age of forty-two, Sir George Houstoun decided to close his business house, the inference being that in addition to achieving success in the commercial field, he had inherited a large share of his brother Patrick's estate, and could retire and enjoy life in other forms of activity. In March, 1786, he was calling on his creditors to discharge their debts to him, as he intended to close out his business, but his desire in that regard did not become a reality until several years later.

It was the custom in that period of the state's history for the prominent men of the times to follow in the footsteps of their fathers in becoming owners of many plantations and Sir George Houstoun was no exception to the rule. Among his plantations

---

30. See *post*, 144.
31. The miniatures are owned by the author. They were preserved in the family of Mrs. George Jones Kollock, their great-niece. On the back of the frame of the girl's picture was written in a handwriting, other than Mrs. Kollock's, "Aunt R. Moodie Houstoun." As "little Moo" died in 1792 at the age of four, obviously the likeness was not hers. It seemed only reasonable to assume that the miniatures were of the brother and sister who were only fourteen months apart in age.
32. An exhibition of Boudon miniatures was held at the Virginia Museum of Art in Richmond, Virginia, in December, 1941, and among them were many eighteenth-century James River planters.

Sir George Houstoun, Baronet, Man of Affairs   143

was one on the eastern end of Hutchinson's Island,[33] on the Savannah River directly opposite the town. Although his father's slaves were exempted in 1755 from working on the roads, there was included in the presentments of the Grand Jury in October, 1786, a recommendation "to the court to order that, in the future, the Negroes belonging to Sir George Houstoun and James Mossman, Esq., on Hutchinson's Island, liable to work on the roads, be employed on the first division of the Southwest road."[34] Plantation life as well as business was still occupying the Baronet's attention in 1787. In April he was buying rice seed from Joseph Habersham, who wrote to his brother John on April 9: "Sir George Houstoun is to have 60 or 70 bushels of rice seed as soon as our accots. are settled, I suppose."[35] The same month, Sir George Houstoun was advertising the fact that eight Negro men had run away from his plantation on Hutchinson's Island. He gave descriptions as means of identification and offered a reward for their capture.

Sir George Houstoun numbered among his friends and associates the most prominent men of Savannah and of the state. In addition to those previously mentioned, he was frequently associated with William LeConte, elder brother of the two famous scientists, Doctor John LeConte and Doctor Joseph LeConte of Liberty County.

The year 1787 marked the time when Sir George Houstoun first received recognition in Savannah as a leader. Early in the year he was made Chairman of Commissioners of Pilotage. The position was no sinecure, for the commissioners were entrusted with the safeguarding of the shipping of the port of Savannah, with fixing the price of pilots' charge, and the matter of providing incoming vessels with pilots for their safe arrival at the docks. Shortly after mid-February Houstoun notified the members of his commission to meet at the Coffeehouse on February 24 to receive "proposals from those who are inclined to under-

---

33. A lot marked "Sir George Houstoun's" is shown on a map reproduced in facsimile for J. F. Minis of Savannah, for private circulation, by Stanford's Geographical Establishment, London. (In office of City Engineer, City Hall, Savannah).
34. *Gazette of the State of Georgia*, October 19, 1786.
35. Ulrich Phillips, "Some Letters of Joseph Habersham," in *The Georgia Historical Quarterly*, X, No. 2 (June 1926), 154.

take the pilotage of the port of Savannah" and "to contract with a proper person to repair the lighthouse on Tybee."[36] In 1790, when the Congress voted a sum to repair the Tybee lighthouse, Houstoun and his commissioners informed the public of that action. Sir George was still with the Commissioners of Pilotage in 1791, for early in that year he advertised for bids to undertake the removal of wreckage and other obstructions from the river.[37]

In the year 1787 the George Houstoun family was living in its town residence. On February 26 of that year the ninth child was born and was registered in the family Bible by the name William. The child's life was destined to be short, as he lived only until the age of five years.

The next year Sir George Houstoun found that his British title was a handicap in civic affairs. Savannah was placed under the authority of seven wardens elected by the proprietors of lots or houses, one warden for each ward, according to an act of the legislature which had met in Augusta the previous month. In March Sir George Houstoun was elected the representative from Derby Ward, but when his name was returned by the clerk with the title "baronet," he was not commissioned. However, Sir George turned the tables, because at the next annual election for town wardens when he was again chosen from the same ward, he "declined acting," and Robert Woodhouse was elected "in his room."

5

Steadily Sir George Houstoun rose to a position of high command in the town's activities. In April, 1788, he was elected vice-president of the Union Society, a charitable organization then nearly fifty years old. The Union Society had been incorporated by an act of the legislature in 1786. Its antecedent was the St. George, a club of Scotsmen formed in 1750, for the purpose of supporting orphans, and the Union Society continued as its own the object of the parent club. The election of Sir George Houstoun as an officer of that organization was announced in the *Gazette of the State of Georgia* on April 24, 1788. The members

---

36. *Gazette of the State of Georgia*, February 22, 1787.
37. *Ibid.*, April 15, 1790, March 31, 1791. The other members of the commission were Leonard Cecil, John Wallace, and Robert Bolton.

met at the Coffeehouse and "celebrated the day with harmony and sociability which has ever distinguished the Society."[38] When Sir George Houstoun was elevated in 1789 to the presidency of the society, the *Georgia Gazette*, having a few months previously resumed its original name, reported "the members of the UNION SOCIETY met at the Coffeehouse and celebrated their 39th Anniversary. After the business was dispatched the members (among them were several upwards of 60 years of age) enjoyed themselves with an excellent dinner and passed the day with their usual festivity. The following gentlemen were elected officers for the current year: Sir George Houstoun, Bart. President; Hon. Noble Wimberly Jones, Esq. Vice President; David Montaigut, Esq. Secretary; George Basil Spencer, Esq. Assistant Secretary; Mr. Lewden and Mr. Fahm, Stewards."[39]

Sir George continued his membership in the society after his term of office expired, thereafter serving on numerous committees. If a member absented himself from the "Anniversary Meeting," according to the rules he was required to pay a fine of one dollar. At the quarterly meeting of the society held at the Filature on June 3, 1793, Houstoun gave a satisfactory excuse for non-attendance at the previous anniversary meeting and "was admitted." The members also were required to make donations for "schooling the children and other Expenses of the Society." The record shows that on several occasions Sir George Houstoun adhered to the requirements.[40]

In 1789 Sir George Houstoun was made a Justice of the Peace for Chatham County. The *Georgia Gazette* of December 31, 1789, published his appointment for the White Bluff District with "Nathaniel Adams, James Houstoun, and Peter Henry Morel, Esqrs."

The principles and teachings of Freemasonry seem to have appealed more to Sir George Houstoun than to the other Houstoun men, for while his father and his four brothers were all members of Solomon's Lodge, Sir George was the only one who was selected to hold office, according to existing records. At the close

---
38. Adelaide Wilson, *Historic and Picturesque Savannah* (1889), 27, 82, 83.
39. *Georgia Gazette*, May 7, 1789.
40. *Minutes of the Union Society . . . From 1750-1858* . . . . (Savannah, Georgia, 1860), 1-31 *passim.*

of the year 1789, he was elected to the highest post in the Masonic order, that of Grand Master of the Grand Lodge in Georgia, an office which he held for three years. Mention has already been made of his father's entrance into the Lodge in October, 1734,[41] but it can be added here that the Lodge at one time almost passed out of existence, and was kept alive through the membership and efforts of seven members, one of whom was Sir George's father.[42] The early records were lost; so the time that the Houstoun brothers joined the Lodge is unknown, except that before the Revolution Sir Patrick, sixth baronet, George, John, and James Houstoun were all members, and later on William was initiated. In 1785 Solomon's Lodge was reorganized, the English order was abandoned and the Lodge was reconstituted, at which time Sir George Houstoun was one of the first officers to be installed when he was made Worshipful Master. In that period of its history, the meetings of the Lodge were held at Brown's Coffeehouse. Sir George Houstoun was next elected to the office of Senior Grand Warden of the Grand Lodge of Georgia, an office he held for two years.

Gradually Sir George Houstoun was being singled out as eligible for positions of higher trust in the Society of Masons in Georgia. He was elected Deputy Grand Master at a "Quarterly Communication of the Grand Lodge of Georgia" held in Savannah in 1788 and "on December 27 that being the day of the General Communication" he was invested with the insignia of his office at Brother Copp's Long Room in Savannah. "He and the other incoming officers were exhorted by the Grand Master in Warm and affectionate terms to a pointed discharge of their respective duties." At last Sir George Houstoun reached the top rung of the ladder in Masonry. On December 5, 1789, he was elected Grand Master of all the Lodges in Georgia, and was presented by the Lodge with the Grand Master's jewel. In December of the following year he was re-elected Grand Master,[43] and then

---
41. See *ante*, 29.
42. William Bordley Clarke, *Early and Historic Freemasonry in Georgia* (Savannah, 1924). (Hereafter cited *Freemasonry in Georgia*.)
Georgia Gazette, December 11, 1788; January 15, 1789; December 10, 1789; and December 9, 1790.
43. *Georgia Gazette*, December 11, 1788; January 15, 1789; December 10, 1789, and December 9, 1790.

came the great event in his life. In May, 1791, the first President of the United States made a tour of the Southern states, and during the few days General Washington spent in Savannah he was visited by a delegation of the Grand Lodge of Georgia, eight of whom belonged to Solomon's Lodge. On Saturday, May 14, the members gathered at Brown's Coffeehouse and then marched to the Tavern on the northwest corner of State and Barnard streets, which had been given to the President for his use while in the town.[44] It devolved upon Sir George Houstoun, Baronet, as Grand Master of Georgia to deliver the address of welcome to "Brother Washington":

> The Grand Master, Officers and Members of the Grand Lodge of Georgia, beg leave to congratulate you on your arrival to this city;
> Whilst your exalted character claims the respect and deference of all men, they, from the benevolence of Masonic principles, approach you with the familiar declaration of fraternal affection.
> Happy indeed that Society, renowned for its antiquity and pervading influence over the enlightened world, which, having ranked a Frederic at its head, can now boast of a Washington as a brother—a Brother who is justly hailed the Redeemer of his Country, and by his conduct in public and private life has evinced to Monarchs, that true majesty consists not in splendid royalty, but in intrinsic worth.
> With these sentiments, they rejoice at your presence in this state, and in common with their fellow citizens, greet you thrice welcome, flattering themselves that your stay will be made agreeable.
> May the Great Architect of the Universe preserve you, whilst engaged in the work allotted you on earth, and long continue you the brightest pillar of our temple; and, when the supreme fiat shall summon you hence, they pray the Mighty I am may take you into his holy keeping.

The President neatly "covered the ground" in his very brief reply.

The formal ceremonies being concluded, the Grand Master in-

---

44. Clarke, *Freemasonry in Georgia*, 101.

troduced to the President the Right Worshipful Past Grand Master, officers and members.[45]

In December, 1791, Sir George was re-elected Grand Master for the ensuing year. The next annual election was a memorable occasion. The *Georgia Gazette* gives an interesting report of the event. The meeting was held on Thursday, December 27, "in the great public room" (presumably the Filature) on the anniversary of St. John the Evangelist, and was attended "by all the Lodges of the City and the Free and accepted Ancient York Masons from all parts of the world, in business in town." The Right Worshipful William Stephens was instituted Grand Master of all the Lodges in Georgia as successor to Sir George Houstoun, "who was pleased to resign." All of the officers of the different Lodges were present and after the ceremonies all repaired to Christ Church, where a sermon was preached.[46] They finished the day with a dinner to which one hundred sat down.[47]

A tradition from the older members of Solomon's Lodge is that the Bible presented to the Lodge by General Oglethorpe in "1733/34" was preserved by the Houstoun family during the Revolution. Inasmuch as Sir George was considered an adherent of the Loyalist cause between 1779 and 1783, it seems safe to conjecture that it was at his home at White Bluff that the treasured relic was hidden during that perilous time.

Sir George Houstoun's efforts to retire from business were futile up to the year 1790 when he was still endeavoring to sell plantations. Among his debtors were some who had been under obligation to him since before the Revolutionary War. He was rather peremptory in calling on his creditors whom he notified through the *Georgia Gazette* that unless satisfactory settlement was made he would be "under the disagreeable necessity of placing their bonds or accounts in the hands of an attorney. . . ."[48] In the same issue of the *Georgia Gazette* Sir George urged those

---

45. Archibald Henderson, *Washington's Southern Tour* (Boston and New York, 1923), 224, 225.
    See also, Julius F. Sache, *Washington's Masonic Correspondence* (Philadelphia, 1915), 65, 66.
46. The Reverend Edward Ellington was rector. The Reverend John D. Wing, D. D., ed., *Year Book of Christ Church* (1918).
47. *Georgia Gazette*, January 10, 1793.
48. March 4, 1790.

who had not declared their claims against the estate of his late brother, Sir Patrick, to do so at once. The elder Houstoun had been dead five years and his executor was anxious to settle his estate.

In the year 1790, Savannah, which then had a population of 2,300 inhabitants, was a growing town. It had been incorporated the previous year, and in October the city fathers took under consideration a provision for future extension. They appointed commissioners to "lay off into lots certain parts of the Common appurtenant to the city, and for disposing of same." Included among the nine commissioners was "Sir George Houstoun Bart."[49] Part of the Common was the territory south of South Broad Street, which up to 1790 and later, was the town's limit. Another reason for laying off the Common was to relieve the property owners from taxes, and their consent had to be gained before there could be an enactment. It took some time to obtain permission of the lot holders, and an ordinance was not passed until September 23, 1791. The matter was then put into the hands of the nine commissioners who employed surveyors to establish and fix the wards and to draw a correct plan of the town. Sir George Houstoun's brother John was the mayor under whom he served as commissioner[50] for a short period.

6

After reviewing the active part which he took in civic matters, there can be a glimpse into the private life of Sir George Houstoun in the year 1791. He no doubt felt the need of recreation and the revivifying effects of an ocean voyage. He also had ties that drew him to the north. His brother, William, was married and living in New York, and his two sons, Patrick, nearly fifteen years of age, and George, twelve years old, were at school somewhere in the vicinity of that city. He was away from Savannah over two months, so that his vacation on land must have lasted at least five weeks. From the letter that follows it is seen that his journey carried him as far north as Boston. He must have taken the trip alone, for there were too many little children at home for their mother to leave behind and accompany

---
49. *Georgia Gazette*, October 7, 1790.
50. See *post*, 277.

him. The letter was written to his second daughter, then thirteen years old. Sir George's eldest child Jean, at that time, was sixteen; Ann, thirteen; Priscilla was seven and a half; Robert, six and a half; William, four and a half; and little "Moo" (Rachel Moodie), the baby of the family, three years and six months. The Miss Bayard referred to was the sister of Mrs. William Houstoun.

The Savannah paper announced the departure of Sir George Houstoun on August 15: "On Monday, sailed for New York, the brig *Eliza*, Capt. Burham, Sir George Houstoun Bart.,"[51] followed by a list of other passengers. After he had been north a week or so, the affectionate father wrote to his daughter Ann Marion:

New York 20th Sept. 1791

My Dear Daughter

I yesterday received your Letter which I assure you gave me great pleasure. I see you remember my orders, I shall by next opp'ty. expect a packet from Jane and also another from you. Tell my Dear pet that I do as she says. I have had several sweet kisses from Miss Bayard, and I shall give you all a good share of them when we meet. I saw a young Lady in Boston who I would have kissed for your sake, she has your exact face but full as tall as Miss Glen. Mrs Houstoun thinks that both you and Jane have made a mistake on your shoe measurements, she thinks them quite too large, yours in particular being as long as Jenny's, she therefore thinks it best to have but one pair of each, then if I can get them in time shall go by this opp'ty. and if they fit you must write to your Aunt & she will have more made for you, kiss my dear Priscilla Robert Will and Moo for me. I wrote a letter to you and Jane before I went to Boston which I hope you will receive. I expect your brothers over today I long much to see them, it being now three weeks since I saw them,

I am my dear Annie
Your affec. Father[52]

Sir George came home the latter part of October and the *Georgia Gazette* of October 27, 1791, announced "since its last issue," Sir George Houstoun had returned from the north.

---

51. *Georgia Gazette*, August 18, 1791.
52. Original owned by Miss Susan M. Kollock of Atlanta, Georgia.

7

Two months after his return to Savannah, Sir George Houstoun was called upon to assume new duties and responsibilities. Bethesda Orphan House had been under the care of the Reverend George Whitefield, its founder, until his death on September 30, 1770. His will disclosed that he left the estate of Bethesda to his great friend and helper, "that most elect Lady, that Mother in Israel, that mirror of true and undefiled Religion, the Right Honourable Selina Countess of Huntingdon."[53] On accepting the turst Lady Huntingdon placed in charge of the school several superintendents, some of whom were priests of the Church of England. Her selections were generally unfortunate. In 1778 the Georgia Assembly declared the Countess an alien by passing an act making her title legal in Georgia during her life, and at the same time appointed trustees to manage Bethesda. The death of the Countess in June, 1791, concluded the Trust, and a new act was passed by the Assembly in December, making the same trustees a corporate body to do all things "necessary and beneficial for carrying the original intention of the institution into full effect." The Reverend John Johnson[54] was the incumbent at Bethesda at the time of the Countess's death. The original trustees who were reappointed as the Body Corporate were Sir George Houstoun, President; William Stevens, William Gibbons, Sr., Joseph Habersham, Joseph Clay, Jr., William Gibbons, Jr., John Morel, Josiah Tattnall, Jr., John Milledge, James Whitefield, George Jones, Jacob Waldburger and James Jackson. There was considerable friction between the trustees and the last superintendent. The Reverend Mr. Johnson had received instructions from England to continue the work of managing the property, to which plan the trustees objected.

Johnson received a letter from the Speaker of the House of Assembly, William Gibbons, written on December 10, 1791,

---

53. The account of the Bethesda incident in Sir George Houstoun's life will be found in Bethesda MS. Letter Book, Letter Box, No. 6, in the Georgia Historical Society Library, Savannah. See also, "Bethesda's Crisis in 1791. Disaster to Whitefield's House of Mercy Averted," in *The Georgia Historical Quarterly*, I, No. 2 (June, 1917), 108-134.

54. [John I. Stoddard] *History of the Independent Presbyterian Church and Sunday School* (Savannah, 1882), 19. Mr. Johnson was pastor from 1790-1793.

informing him of the passage of the bill, making it plain to him that the Countess of Huntingdon had had only a life interest in the property and that on her death it was vested in certain trustees. The superintendent called on Gibbons and signified his purpose to refuse possession to the trustees, also his intention "of making it a Question of Congress." The minister had been living in Savannah, but, fearing the trustees would outwit him, he decided to "keep close possession by residing day and night and Sundies" at Bethesda to defend the Negroes on the place. For the remainder of December and up to January 9, 1792, matters remained *in statu quo.* On that date Johnson received a letter from Sir George Houstoun:

> We do ourselves the honor to enclose a copy of an act of the General Assembly respecting the Orphan House estate and Bethesda College. The Trustees will be at the Orphan House and Plantation on Tuesday next to take possession of the Estate.
> It will be necessary that an Inventory of the whole property should be delivered to them on that day.
> It will naturally strike you that no property ought to be removed from the plantation without instructions from the Trustees.[55]

Johnson replied to Houstoun the same day with a long, rude letter, still refusing to give up possession "without recourse to law." In the letter Johnson presented what he considered was the claim Lady Huntingdon's heirs had upon Bethesda, and stated he thought it was "both unrighteous and impolitic to the last degree" for the General Assembly of Georgia to claim the property for the State of Georgia. "Be on your guard Sir George," he continued, "the whole world will soon sit in judgment upon your character in particular as president of such a Commission." In further justifying the claim of the late Reverend Mr. Whitefield and the Countess of Huntingdon, he wrote: "We shall not ask leave of thirteen commissioners to promote our appeal to Congress for an explanation of your explanation itself. Till then despair of possession Sir George, but if you attempt it tomorrow I wish you to understand, I would much rather open my breast to your fatal steel than act unworthy of my present trust." Nevertheless, according to another letter written by Johnson

---

55. Bethesda MS. Letter Book.

Sir George Houstoun, Baronet, Man of Affairs 153

to Houstoun on January 13, he informed the latter that the sheriff's officer and two constables, armed by the authority of the Commissioners, had "violently dragged Mrs. Johnson and himself off the premises." The couple was taken to the house of "Mr. Scrimger opposite the burying ground"[56] where they remained prisoners of honor. The above letter was sent to the care of William Stevens, one of the Commissioners, because Johnson, in his letter to the latter wrote "the enclosed comes to your hand in mercy to Sir George's feelings who yesterday experienced a bereaving providence for which I am very sorry."[57]

In describing in his journal the situation in which he was placed, the minister naturally presented a prejudiced point of view, and one that would make his position appear to be the right one. Apparently the reason the Commissioners made no charges against him was that they considered the matter settled when the Act of 1791 was passed, placing them in charge of Bethesda. Johnson, by remaining on the property when he had been notified by Sir George Houstoun to leave the Orphan House, did so illegally. His persistency in doing so raised an issue from which he suffered the consequences. Had he submitted to the orders of the Commissioners and left the Home peaceably, "Bethesda's Crisis in 1791" would not have occurred.

Johnson was kept in custody until January 24, when he was released by Justices of the Peace, they "not finding any charge against him." On his release, he went to Charleston to inquire into some investments relating to the Home. After he returned to Savannah, conditions remained the same between himself and the Commissioners, and finding that a correspondence with certain interested persons in England availed nothing, Johnson and his wife went back to England, and so the matter ended.

---

56. Bethesda MS. Letter Book quoted from a copy of a note to the "Public Printer", January 16, 1792. The burying ground was then Christ Church cemetery (now Colonial Park). Mr. Scrimger's house was on South Broad Street, as that was the town's limit until 1815, and Abercorn Street was part of the Common. See Chandler's Historical Map, *Georgia Historical Quarterly*, I, No. 4 (December, 1917).
57. The reference was to the death of little Rachael Moodie Houstoun, the tenth child of Sir George and Lady Houstoun, who died on Thursday January 12, 1792. Houstoun Family Bible.

8

True to his Scottish heritage, Sir George Houstoun was a member of the St. Andrew's Society, as were his four brothers.[58] Complete records of the Society seem to be lacking, but from the beginning of the colony, at least as early as 1755, there were numbers of Scotsmen in Savannah and in other parts of the colony. Allusion has been made to the "Nightly Club," so disturbing to Colonel William Stephens,[59] when men who emigrated to Georgia from Scotland met together to discuss the affairs of the day. Out of that small association grew the St. Andrew's Society. On November 8, 1769, its president, H. Preston, announced in the *Georgia Gazette* that a meeting of the St. Andrew's Society would be held on Monday, November 20, at Alexander Creighton's Tavern. Rules and regulations governing the Society were passed in 1764, and its purpose, as explained in the preamble, was "to cherish the recollections of our homes and the birthplace of our fathers; to promote good fellowship among Scotchmen and their descendants in this adopted country; and to extend to unfortunate Scotchmen and their families assistance and counsel in case of necessity."[60] The Houstoun men joined the Society probably as soon as their ages permitted them to do so, that they might carry on the traditions of their forefathers; but again it was Sir George Houstoun who showed not only the inclination to do more than was required of him in the way of membership, but who demonstrated to his fellow-members that he was capable of becoming their leader. It was in 1792 that he reached his zenith in the St. Andrew's Society. Whether or not he held office before 1790 is not known, but in that year, at a meeting held in the Filature, General Lachlan McIntosh was elected president, and Sir George Houstoun was chosen vice-president.[61] The next year the same officers were re-elected at Brown's Coffeehouse, but the routine of election was a mere commonplace to what followed. The annual meet-

---

58. Information furnished by the President of St. Andrew's Society of Savannah, Judge Alexander R. MacDonnell (1936).
59. See *ante*, 37.
60. Adelaide Wilson, *Historic and Picturesque Savannah* (1889), 139.
61. *Ibid.*, 91.

Sir George Houstoun, Baronet, Man of Affairs   155

ings of the Society were always held on the birthday[62] of the patron saint of the Society, and in 1791 the newspaper account says the company consisted of upwards of seventy, "... who after the election sat down to a sumptuous and elegant dinner, after which they spent the remainder of the day with that harmony which has ever distinguished the meetings of the Sons of that Saint."[63]

It was in the following year that Sir George Houstoun was advanced to president,[64] and he continued in office for three years. The last year that he was re-elected president of the St. Andrew's Society, which was in 1794, the anniversary came on a Sunday; so according to custom the celebration was held the following day. A brief account of the meeting appeared in the *Georgia Gazette*. Following the elections the members "at 4 P.M. sat down to an elegant dinner . . . after which many applicable toasts were drank and the evening was spent in harmony and mirth."[65]

Not unmindful of his religious duties, Sir George Houstoun also took part in the activities of his parish life, and his election as senior warden of Christ Church in 1795 was the culmination of his apparent devotion to his church. It was but natural that he attended the church in which his father worshipped. The elder Houstoun had had some part in planning for its erection,[66] small as that first building was. After the completion of Christ Church in 1750, the Houstouns, of course, were regular attendants, and owned a pew as was the custom in those days. The first indication that has come down that Sir George Houstoun had any connection with Christ Church was in 1775 when he, James Habersham, Jr., and John Irvine advertised in the newspaper that they had been appointed assignees in the estate of the Reverend Timothy Lowton[67] who was the rector of Christ Church from 1771 to 1773. The elections for wardens and vestrymen were always held the Monday after Easter at the church.

---

62. November 30, and continue so to this day (1949).
63. *Georgia Gazette*, December 1, 1791.
64. According to the record furnished by Judge MacDonnell.
65. *Georgia Gazette*, December 4, 1794.
66. See *ante*, 54, 55.
67. *Georgia Gazette*, April 26, 1775.

On April 8, 1790, Sir George Houstoun's name first appeared in print as a member of the vestry. He was re-elected a vestryman on April 25, 1791, and on April 1, 1793, he was chosen the senior warden.[68]

9

Toward the close of his life, Sir George Houstoun was endeavoring to dispose of some of his numerous plantations, and for three years he was offering them for sale through newspaper advertisements. One plantation which was two miles from White Bluff, and contained five hundred acres, was placed before the public in 1790;[69] another nine miles from Savannah apparently was valuable land, but advertisements appeared three years in succession, and evidently it was finally taken off the market. The first year that particular plantation was offered for sale, it was described as a "Settled plantation containing by original survey in the year 1762, 500 acres, part of which is oak and hickory land."[70] The following year the advertisement specified that the situation was "high, healthy, and pleasant," that "one hundred and thirty-five acres were cleared about half of which under fence and in order for planting." Further, that it was "well adapted for either cotton, indigo or provisions," and that "on the premises are a small dwelling house, negro houses, corn and pea houses." The owner announced if "the said plantation was not disposed of before the 10th of next February, it will then be rented for the ensuing year." In January, 1794, an advertisement again carried the same information, and in January, 1795, Sir George Houstoun was still possessed of his plantation of "580 acres on Little Ogeechee River."[71]

Sir George's failing health began in August, 1794, when he made his will declaring "he was very unwell." The following April, at the anniversary meeting of the Union Society held in the Filature on the twenty-third of the month, "the President [Joseph Habersham] on behalf of Sir George Houstoun, stated that since August last he had been sick, and unable to attend the Society, wherefore his fines amounting to eight shillings were

---
68. *Ibid.*, April 8, 1790; April 28, 1791; April 4, 1793.
69. *Ibid.*, June 28, 1790.
70. *Ibid.*, February 9, 1792.
71. *Ibid.*, December 16, 1793; January 2, 1794; January 1, 1795.

remitted."[72] A few weeks later Sir George evidently decided that he would be benefited by a trip, as he advertised in the *Georgia Gazette* that he intended to be absent from the state for a few months, asking his creditors and those indebted to him to settle with John Houstoun, James Mossman, or James Johnston, Jr., all legally authorized to handle his business.[73]

But Sir George was destined never to take the trip he had planned. Less than two weeks later, Tuesday, June 9, the seventh Houstoun baronet died. He was buried the following Tuesday. Thirty-seven members of the Union Society by "order, assembled at the house of Mr. Carsans to attend the funeral..."[74] The same day his obituary appeared in the *Georgia Gazette*. It characterized Houstoun as "a gentleman whose virtues, both social and private, endeared him in life, and whose death is now a subject of sincere regret...."[75] In his own Bible, probably in the handwriting of Lady Houstoun, was this entry:

> Sir George Houstoun, Bart. died after a long illness on Tuesday the 9th of June 1795 about ten o'clock in the evening, aged 50 years, 7 months and 19 days. His remains were deposited in the family vault on Thursday 11 June.[76]

A man of considerable means, Sir George Houstoun made ample provision for his widow and children. His will, dated August 26, 1794, urged that "strictest economy" be observed in the conduct of his funeral. The first beneficiary named in his will was the Grand Lodge of Georgia, to which he bequeathed twenty-five pounds for the relief of distressed Masons or their families. To his wife, Ann, he bequeathed his post chaise, riding chair, carriage horses, stock of cattle, hogs and sheep, household furniture, plate, china, table and bed linen and kitchen furniture,

---

72. *Minutes of the Union Society*, 26, 27.
73. *Georgia Gazette*, May 28, 1795.
74. *Minutes of the Union Society*, 33.
75. *Georgia Gazette*, June 11, 1795. In Charleston, the *City Gazette*, June 22, 1795, carried in its marriage and death notices, this entry: "Died on Tuesday the 9th Inst. in Savannah, Sir John Houstoun, bart." (*South Carolina Historical and Genealogical Magazine*, XXIII, 33). The paper erred, of course, in the first name.
76. Houstoun Family Bible. The family vault was in Christ Church burying ground. When the remains of his father and mother were removed to Bonaventure Cemetery those of their son and his wife were interred also under the large monument. See *Ante*, 96.

and also the use of the following Negroes, during her life, viz: Garrick, Pollydore, Kate, Beck, Charlotte, Phillis and Die. The executors were ordered to pay an annuity to Lady Houstoun from the proceeds of the estate until the division took place, as much money as she deemed sufficient for the support of herself and his family, including all expenses for board, clothes, education, to be used at her discretion, adding, "having the highest confidence that she will apportion and apply the money, or as much as she may think necessary, among my children, as their situations may severally require."

After providing for his wife, the testator mentioned each of his children, naming the boys first. To his oldest son, Patrick, he left his plantation on Hutchinson's Island, containing about two hundred and five acres, "with all the Buildings and improvements thereon," also thirty-six Negroes employed there. George received the house and lot in Savannah where the family resided, a wharf lot with one hundred and fifty feet frontage together with all the buildings and improvements. Sir George's legacy to the ten year old Robert James Mossman was the plantation called Coffee Bluff, adjoining Rosdue, a tract of land containing two hundred and fifty acres together with ten Negroes, a four hundred and fifty acre tract of land "in Great Ogeechee," and a lot in Hardwick. To Jean was bequeathed four hundred and thirteen acres; and to Ann Marion, a five hundred acre plantation, "The Forrest," and land in Burke County; and to the youngest daughter, Priscilla, went six hundred acres in Burke County, "originally granted to Timothy Lowten," as well as a tract of land containing five hundred acres in Glynn County, "originally granted my late mother." Two lots in Brunswick were included in Priscilla's legacy.

Attached to all of the bequests to his children, Sir George Houstoun made the condition that two years after his death, his executors were to cause a just and true appraisement and valuation of all his property, real and personal, in order that each child might have an equal apportionment.

The valuation placed by Sir George upon his Mason's jewel was shown in the following item in his will:

> I Give and Bequeath, to either of my sons who shall first attain the Degree of a Master Mason, my Three Mason's Jewell,

marked Br. Houstoun 5751 also the past Grand Masters Jewell, presented me by the Grand Lodge of Georgia trusting, that he who wears them, will ever act to all mankind agreeably to the rules of 'Square and Compass' and it is my desire that those Jewels, shall not be included in any inventory of my Estate, but considered by my Executors as sacred deposits in their hands for the above mentioned purpose.

After his just debts were paid, the testator directed that the remainder of his property be divided among his six children, share and share alike, and from his brother Patrick's estate, which had not been settled, he provided that certain sums of money due from deeds and bonds should be paid to his beloved wife, Ann Houstoun. From his brother's estate, Sir George directed "in consideration of the great regard I have for Mr. James Johnston Junior, and of the faithful discharge of his duty to me during his apprenticeship, I give and Bequeath to him one hundred pounds Sterling."

His executors were his wife, his brother John and his friends, Joseph Habersham, Jr., and James Johnston, Jr. As each of his sons became of age, they were to replace the executors, with the exception of his wife. A codicil was added in May, 1795, to the effect that since making his will "some circumstances have happened that seem to make it proper" that his brother, John Houstoun, did not desire to continue as an executor. The latter's appointment was revoked and in his stead James Mossman and William Stephens were appointed.[77]

It is impossible to close the story of Sir George Houstoun with the account of his death and burial; for since he left a large family, necessarily many events of interest occurred after his career had ended. Allowing a brief period of mourning to elapse, Sir George's widow began informing his debtors of the necessity for a settlement of their obligations. A month after his death Lady Houstoun inserted in the Savannah newspaper an advertisement requesting all those who had any demands against her husband "in his private account or on account of his Mercantile transactions in Company to make payment as soon as

---

77. Original will in Department of Archives and History, Atlanta.

possible" and to render payment to Mr. James Johnston, Jr.[78] Advertisements for the sale of plantations, tracts of land in Chatham, Glynn, Burke, and other counties, city lots in Savannah, Brunswick, and Hardwick, other property, and sale of runaway Negroes,[79] continued to be printed in the local papers until the early part of 1798, but the estate was not entirely settled until after the opening of the new century. In the year 1815, Lady Houstoun made a gift of a piece of silver to one of the executors, James Johnston, Jr. The inscription reads: "Lady Houstoun presents this pitcher to Colonel Johnston with her grateful thanks for his attention in settling the estate of Sir Patrick and Sir George Houstoun."[80]

In March, following Sir George Houstoun's death, the first marriage occurred among the children when Jean was married to George Woodruff, attorney-at-law, on Wednesday evening, March 30, 1796. The notice of the marriage, published in the *Georgia Gazette* the next day, mentioned the bride as "the eldest daughter of Sir George Houstoun, Bart., deceased." George Whitefield Woodruff came from a distinguished New Jersey family and some of his ancestors were the founders of Elizabethtown in the middle of the seventeenth century. He was born there in 1765, and his parents were Elias and Mary Joline Woodruff. His brother, Aaron Dickerson Woodruff, was an eminent attorney general of the state for about twenty-eight years. After

---

78. *Georgia Gazette*, July 9, 1795.
79. *Columbian Museum & Savannah Advertiser*, January 2, February 16 and 23, 1798. *Georgia Gazette*, October 29, 1795; March 17, 1796; December 8, 1797.
80. The pitcher owned by the author until 1947 was presented by her to her nephew James Houstoun Johnston, III, of Atlanta, Georgia. The receipted bill for same from Fletcher and Gardner, Philadelphia, Nov. 15, 1815, is in the possession of the heirs of Mrs. Macartan C. Kollock of Atlanta, who also own a silver coffee pot engraved with the coat-of-arms, bought by Lady Houstoun at the same time. James Patrick Houstoun, Jr., of Houston, Texas, owns a small silver waiter with coat-of-arms, two salt cellars with crest, and a large seal with coat-of-arms, that originally belonged to Sir George and Lady Houstoun. A mourning ring engraved "Lady Houstoun, Priscilla Feb. 26, 1775," is owned by Miss Minna Alston Waring of Savannah, and a Houstoun tankard, engraved with crest and motto, is in the possession of James Marion Johnston, Jr., of Chevy Chase, Maryland. Mrs. George Pettus Raney (Claudia Bond Houstoun) and Patrick Houstoun Wall of Tampa, Florida, each owns a silver gravy ladle, marked "P.H." All of the present owners are lineal descendants of Sir George and Lady Houstoun.

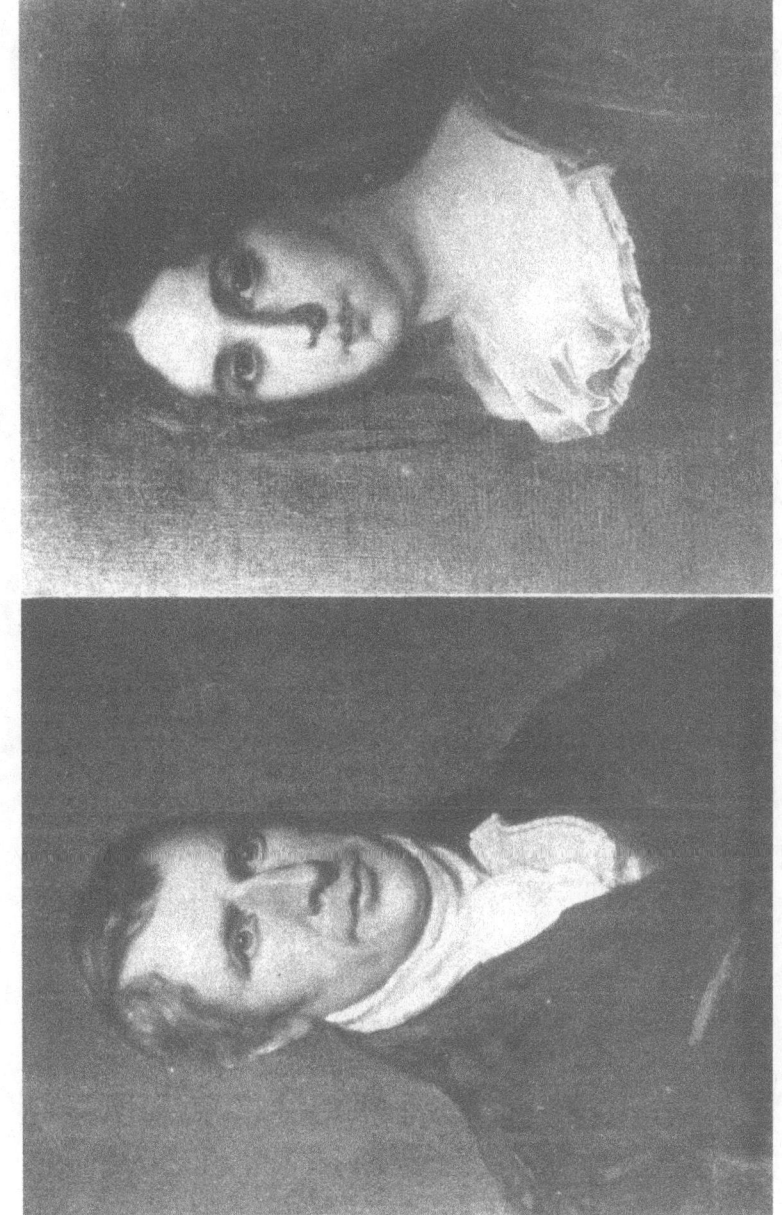

COLONEL JAMES JOHNSTON, JR.
1769-1822
From the portrait owned by Mrs. Sharon Farr, of
Chevy Chase, Maryland

MRS. JAMES JOHNSTON, JR.
1778-1817
From the portrait owned by Mr. James Marion
Johnston of Chevy Chase, Maryland

graduating from the College of New Jersey (Princeton University) George Woodruff studied law and was admitted to the bar in 1788. Soon afterward he was sent to Savannah by President John Adams who appointed him District Attorney for the State of Georgia. He was a man of retiring manner, but "was possessed of a well-cultivated" and a "well-stored mind."[81] In 1792 he was practising law in Savannah, and two years later he became a member of the Union Society. He was an alderman of the city in 1805. The Woodruffs were the parents of six sons and five daughters; two of the latter died in infancy.[82] All were born in Savannah except the youngest child.

Lady Houstoun's young son, George, a promising youth in his late 'teens, was paying a visit at Sullivan's Island, near Charleston, South Carolina, in the summer of 1796, when he contracted a malignant disease and died suddenly. His death record gives the brief comment, "play actor."[83] An interesting aspect might have been thrown on his short life if further information had been found.[84] His bereaved mother made a memorandum in her family Bible which is the last in the book following the entry of his father's death: "The fourth child George at Sullivan's Island after a few days illness of a contagious fever Monday 22 August 1796, aged 17 years, one month and fourteen days. His remains were interred on Tuesday 23 August in St. Philips Churchyard in Charleston where a stone is erected to his memory at the desire of a fond mother." The inscription on the tomb-

---

81. *New Jersey State Gazette*, September 11, 1846. (Obituary)
82. Houstoun Family Tree, and Woodruff Family Papers. A Sully portrait of the Reverend George Houstoun Woodruff, eldest child, is owned by the Atlanta Art Association, and hangs in the High Museum of Art. He was a deacon in the Episcopal Church and was unmarried. The other Woodruff children who married were: Patrick Houstoun, who married his first cousin, Louisa Caroline Johnston of Savannah; Robert James, who married Belle Swift; Thomas Moodie, who married Eliza Swift; Mary Priscilla, who married Charles Pearson. Aaron Dickerson, the youngest, lived to maturity, but did not marry.
83. From Cemetery Book, No. 2, p. 50. Entry: "Houston, Geo. Play Actor, Number 801 tombstone." Obtained through the late Reverend S. Carey Beckwith, rector of St. Philip's Church. A survey of the Western Cemetery of the churchyard was made in 1835, and a plat by Charles Parker dated June, 1844, shows where the tombstone is located.
84. For an account of Charleston's plays and players of that period see Eola Willis, *Charleston Stage in the XVIII Century* (State Company, Columbia, South Carolina, 1924).

stone, presumably written by his mother, is almost an analysis of her son's character: "Sacred to the memory of George Houstoun ... who died ... Aged 17 years," it begins. Then follows the characterization of the youth by a "disconsolate Mother" who perpetuated his memory with the tributes, "a most engaging manner," "a heart as warm as sincere," and one who "obtained many friends."

Saturday afternoon, November 26, 1796, was cold and frosty in Savannah, and a good breeze was blowing from the northwest. Some of the inhabitants, among them probably the Houstoun family, were comfortably warm indoors, when suddenly between six and seven o'clock the city was in flames. The fire had started in the market square. Citizens, officers, and crews from the vessels in port rushed to the scene. Failure to observe certain fire precautions[85] was responsible for the destruction of the greater part of the city that for twenty years had been undergoing material improvements although there were too many frame buildings. The season had been dry for two months, and that afternoon a strong wind came up. Burning shingles, boards, and other light substances were whirled into the air and added confusion to the other terrors of the conflagration which continued until after midnight, and only abated when the flames were stopped by the Common on the southern edge of the town. The inhabitants dragged their possessions into the streets, and some were forced to move their property several times to zones of safety. The Houstoun family evidently was among the latter, but it is not known whether or not their home was burned, although it was in the path of the fire. Sunday morning the devastated city presented a scene of desolation and distress. Two hundred and twenty-nine houses, besides private property, were destroyed, three hundred and seventy-five chimneys were left standing bare, and four hundred families were without homes. Donations of money and provisions poured into Savannah from all over the state.[86]

Two weeks after the fire Lady Houstoun had not found some of her valuable possessions. Hoping to regain them she adver-

---
85. Gamble, *History of the City Government*, 51, 52.
86. Wilson, *Historic and Picturesque Savannah*, 101.

Sir George Houstoun, Baronet, Man of Affairs 163

tised in the newspaper the loss of "7 old mahogany chairs, 1 new do. 1 mahogany desk with drawers 1 chest of drawers, 1 quarter cask madeira wine, 1 trunk of paper hangings containing 40 pieces." A liberal reward was offered for information about her lost possessions.[87]

II

Eleven months after the wedding of her sister Jean, Ann Marion Houstoun was married to James Johnston, Jr., who was born on July 27, 1769, the son of Dr. Andrew and Bellamy Roche Johnston, of Augusta, Georgia. The marriage took place at White Bluff on May 31, 1797, and the ceremony was performed by the Reverend Mr. Monteith.[88] At the time of his marriage, James Johnston was a member of the firm of Johnston and Robertson. His partners were his brother Matthew and his brother-in-law James Robertson. In the spring of 1791, the firm shipped to England, for the account of Francis and Lefett, "ten thousand pounds of black seed cotton grown on Skidaway Island by Major Barnard . . . which established the character of Georgia Sea Island Cotton, and was the first shipment of any consequence."[89]

From 1795 to 1797, Johnston was the secretary of the St. Andrew's Society; and in 1799 he was secretary of the Golf Club, which had been in existence in Savannah for several years. He was an alderman of the city, 1801-1802, and again in 1817-1818. In 1811 he was a vestryman of Christ Church, and was appointed chairman to receive subscriptions for the completion of the red brick building, the second erected on the original Trust lot set aside for a church in the beginning of the colony. In February, 1812, a campaign was begun for more funds to complete the construction of the new building. In May it was reported in the paper:

The roof of Christ Church is raised ready for covering. The

---

87. *Columbian Museum & Savannah Advertiser*, December 12, 1796. Further research could not be made in the above paper in the Georgia Historical Society Library. Because of misuse the volume has been withdrawn from the public.
88. Johnston Family Bible, owned by the heirs of Mrs. Macartan C. Kollock of Atlanta; and *Columbian Museum & Savannah Advertiser*, June 2, 1797.
89. Anon., "The Beginning of Cotton Culture in Georgia," in *The Georgia Historical Quarterly*, I, No. 1 (March, 1917, 39-45), 41.

progress in the rebuilding of this place of worship, so ornamental to the city, must give pleasure to all classes of citizens; we regret to learn the funds collected are expended. It is hoped the liberality of the citizens will not allow it to come to a stand. The subscription paper is in the hands of Col. Johnston; those who have not yet contributed their mite, will no doubt make a point of calling and paying up their contributions. It would be more than disgraceful to suffer the thing now to fall through than if nothing had been attempted."[90]

The next year James Johnston was senior warden of the parish, and with John Lawson advertised the sale of pews in Christ Church. Some had been sold, but more funds were needed, and the wardens and vestrymen announced that a public auction would be held for the sale of all of the pews on the ground floor "for the support of the minister and other expenses of the church."[91] In 1814, after undergoing storm, cyclone, and fire the church was finally completed.

James Johnston, with other business men of the city, urged the establishment of another bank, and in December, 1807, the legislature passed an act to incorporate the Planters Bank. Nothing, apparently, was done to forward the plan until December, 1810, when a second act was passed repealing the one of 1807. The following month James Johnston was appointed one of the commissioners to sell subscriptions for the new bank.[92] The charter, obtained the previous month, stipulated that the capital stock should be one million dollars divided into ten thousand shares of one hundred dollars each, of which one thousand were to be reserved until January 1, 1812, for purchase by the State of Georgia.[93] By February two thousand shares had been taken up, but the commissioners were not satisfied with the result. They advertised that the bank could not be opened for business until certain provisions of the law and of the charter were adjusted and complied with. An editorial in *The Republican; and Savannah Evening Ledger* of February 2, 1811, stated that "the necessity of a bank in this city must be obvious to everyone en-

---

90. *The American Patriot*, May 1, 1812.
91. *Ibid*.
92. *The Republican; and Savannah Evening Ledger*, January 17, 1811.
93. *Ibid.*, January 19, 1811.

gaged in business, and we sincerely hope the present institution under the existing charter, may go into operation as speedily as possible, particularly as the tenure of the charter of the branch of the U. States Bank in this city seems held under a very precarious tenure."

Toward the close of the year it was clear that the only way to obtain an acceptable charter was to elect a man to the state senate who could make it possible. A campaign ensued as three candidates were presented for election. During September, 1811, their friends wrote letters to the newspapers defining the qualifications of their favorites. A DEMOCRATIC REPUBLICAN was the signature at the end of a long letter urging the election of James Johnston: " . . . . Many important advantages might ensue from the appointment of at least one mercantile gentleman to represent our interests . . . . Charters have been twice granted . . . . The charter granted is partially so inadequate . . . arising from the political situation of our country as regards the belligerents in Europe . . . . A native Georgian, Col. James Johnston has been promised the support of many, judging from his high mercantile character and integrity, that he can promote by just explanation, the desired amendment to the Charter for incorporating the Planters Bank, and being himself a planter, he will be enabled to promote the planting and mercantile interest of his entire state."[94]

A few days later A GEORGIA REPUBLICAN, vehement in his opposition, declared in print that the other candidates, Proctor, Bryan, Telfair or Cuthbert, would receive better support than Johnston. In the same issue of the paper ALFRED, in his letter, urged the election of Isaac Minis on the grounds that he was better able to adjust the differences in amending the charter between the Legislature and the State Banking Department.[95] The next week, TRUE AMERICAN wrote urging the election of Johnston rather than Dr. Proctor, as he believed the former would have more influence; and in the same issue, NO MERELY NOMINAL DEMOCRAT violently opposed Johnston.[96] A third appeared in the same copy, signed, ANOTHER OF THE PEOPLE. The writer declared while he was opposed to some of

---

94. *The Republican; and Savannah Evening Ledger*, September 14, 1811.
95. *Ibid.*, September 19, 1811.
96. *Ibid.*, September 24, 1811.

James Johnston's creeds, he would urge his election to the State Senate because he believed in his integrity, and felt sure he would have more influence than any of the other candidates in adjusting the charter of the Planters Bank. The first column of *The Republican; and Savannah Evening Ledger* of November 12, 1811, carried the news of the election of James Johnston as senator for the ensuing year, and on December 13, the bill incorporating the Planters Bank passed both houses, awaiting the governor's signature. Early in January, Johnston became chairman of the board of commissioners. John Bolton was elected president of the bank which opened for business on January 24. James Johnston continued a member of the board of directors until he was elected president in 1817.[97] The bank was located on the northwestern Trust Lot on Reynolds Square. The building formerly housed the Bank of the State of Georgia and was bought by the Board of the Planters Bank in May, 1812. It remained the bank's property until May, 1820.[98] The release paper on the sale was signed by James Johnston, president, and James Marshall, secretary.[99]

Allusion has been made to James Johnston as a planter. One of his principal plantations was located on St. Catherine's Island. On April 12, 1812, he paid $10,300 for the southern moiety, reputed to contain four thousand acres.[100] The island was a grant from George II to Mary Bosomworth in 1760.[101] It contained six thousand two hundred acres. In 1765 the island was bought by Button Gwinnett.[102] The property passed through the ownership of several persons before it came into the possession of James Johnston who maintained a plantation for raising cotton and rice. There is no evidence that he ever lived on the island. Like other gentlemen planters, he believed it was not

---

97. *The Republican; and Savannah Evening Ledger*, December 3, 1811; January 2, 1912.
98. The building was first a residence. It was built for James Habersham in 1789, and in 1802 or 1803 it was bought by James Willing. In 1821, the Planters Bank was sold to William Scarbrough and others. The house is now known as "The Pink House." (1949)
99. Book *2k*, folio *62*, Chatham County Court House.
100. Book *C, 194*, Liberty County Records.
101. *Register Book B, 274*, Secretary of State's Office (Atlanta); Book *2, folio 92*, pp. 93, 94, Liberty County Records.
102. Book of Conveyances, C, Part 2 (1761-1766), 1081-1084, State Department of Archives and History, Atlanta.

necessary to have a residence on land where commodities were planted, as overseers were placed there to manage the business. The slave quarters of tabby on the Johnston plantation were built according to the Spalding pattern. Colonel Johnston still owned his part of St. Catherine's Island at the time of his death, and it remained the property of his heirs for thirty-five years thereafter.[103]

12

James Johnston was active in the War of 1812. Although Savannah at once began to make preparations for the protection of the city, no British attacks were made in Georgia for two years. Savannah's proximity to the sea made it liable to assault at any time, and the inhabitants were kept on the alert. Fort Wayne, which had been built at the eastern end of the city overlooking the river, held the magazine and it was fortified. Fort Oglethorpe[104] was two miles below the city on the Savannah River. On the south a line of defenses was constructed around the town. Johnston was an officer in the First Georgia Regiment, United States Militia. By 1811 he held the rank of lieutenant colonel, and was in command of the regiment.[105] He was put in charge of the troops in Savannah, and Council notified him, when, in 1814, British vessels were sighted off the Georgia coast. Governor Stephen Early sent him one thousand dollars for supplies and ammunition, and on February 18, 1814, Colonel Johnston replied to the Governor's letter written from the capital in Milledgeville:

> The supply of one thousand Dollars for defraying the expense of Watch Boats at Tybee & Wassaw, is reasonable and very acceptable. I have written to Gen¹ McIntosh on the subject of 150 Stand Arms design for my Regiment, as yet I am without a supply.
> With much pleasure I accept the agency for receiving the

---

103. Deeds, 3Q, 62, Chatham County Court House; Deeds O, 278, Liberty County Records.
104. Changed to Jackson by the Government, January 24, 1905. War Department, G. O. No. 10. See "War Department Furnishes Data," in *Savannah Morning News*, January 29, 1928.
105. Muster Roll of the Historical Department of the War Department, February 23, 1815. Photostatic copy owned by the Chatham Artillery Association, Savannah.

> Powder, Rifles and charge of the Magazine from City Council of this place. I addressed a note on the subject to the Mayor [Dr. George Jones] on the 8th Int.' on the same day they passed a Resolve appointing a Committee to deliver over to me the Powder, Rifles & Key to the Magazine. As yet I have not heard from the Committee, and it is probable it will be some time before I do, as large bodies move slowly. As soon as I am put in possession of the articles, I will do myself the honor of informing you . . . .[106]

Three weeks elapsed before the committee of council discharged its duty. On May 7, Colonel Johnston wrote to Governor Early:

> I duly received your letter of 6th. Ult., and have now the pleasure to inform you, that a Committee of the City Council have this moment put me in possession of the Keys of the Magazine and have delivered to me as Agent of the State fourteen Barrels eight half Barrels & thirteen Kegs Tennessee Gun Powder equal to 85^r. each. The Powder appears of a pretty good quality and the Kegs I opened were dry and in good order. I examined the exterior of the Corks, but did not open them all, as they appeared in such good order.
> The twenty one Rifles cost $420- as stated by the Mayor. Any further order you may be pleased to give in this, or any other matter will be promptly attended to with pleasure.[107]

In a few months' time the British had reached the Georgia coast, and on August 23, Colonel Johnston wrote again to the Governor:

> I am sorry to inform you that the British are committing depredations on our coasting Trade, between this and Amelia Island. Ten days ago they captured 6 or 8 vessels near St. Catherines, and on Saturday last 3 in Wassaw Sound, one they burnt, and took two off- the force then off Ossabaw was two ships and a Brig^r., our last certain accounts are down to Sunday noon when they were standing to the Northward, and as it blew very fresh yesterday from the N.E. they doubtless will stand off until the weather moderates or clears, when they may be expected to return. The Captain of the Lacedemonian informed a Prisoner, since liberated, that he expects a reinforcement of 3

---

106. Department of Archives and History, Atlanta.
107. *Ibid.*

Sir George Houstoun, Baronet, Man of Affairs   169

or 4 vessels; should they bring any Troops, we may calculate on an attack on this place, or they will sweep our Islands of the Negroes and stock.

Co^1. Manning arrived here on Saturday with 400 Troops. On Sunday he manned 5 barges and sent them for Wassaw & Ossabaw inlets, with the remainder of his force he marched to Beaulieu. Should the British send 1500 or 2000 on our Coast, they will be very apt to *scratch* us. The Rifles you were to send, will be very acceptable.[108]

Savannah was never attacked, but two captured vessels were brought into the harbor. Although the city escaped any encounter with the enemy, when peace came in 1815, the inhabitants celebrated the event with jubilation and their customary military parade. General John Floyd was in Savannah at the time, and in a letter to General David Blackshear,[109] he gave a description of the observance:

Savannah, February 25, 1815

The accounts of peace having been concluded between our country and Great Britain appear to have filled the hearts of the populace here with joy. The accounts were received on the evening of the day which the Mayor [Matthew McAllister] had proclaimed should be celebrated by illumination and music in commemoration of the illustrious Washington's birth, and in celebration of General Jackson's victory over our implacable enemy at Orleans.... Joy gleamed on every countenance. The night was gloomy and calm. The streets were crowded with people of all colors, sorts and denominations, who with lighted candles on foot and on horseback, enlivened the streets.

The crowd led by the military traversed the streets in procession, accompanied by all the music of a material kind the city afforded. The vessels in the harbor were illuminated, and the air resounded with loud huzzas and firing of small arms. The seamen had a small ship which they carried through the streets, decorated, exclaiming, "Don't give up the ship."[110]

Colonel Johnston held another office in 1814, when he was president of the Union Society.

---
108. *Ibid.*
109. See *post*, 382.
110. Stephen F. Miller, *Memoirs of Gen. Blackshear* (Philadelphia, 1858), 463.

13

Reverting to the period subsequent to the time of the marriage of James Johnston and Ann Marion Houstoun (1797), a sprightly letter written in the last year of the eighteenth century gives a glimpse of the amusements and gaiety of Savannah. Summer and permanent residents on the adjacent sea islands, as well as the families of mainland planters, participated in the city's social life. Lady Houstoun and her married daughters were in the circle of friends that formed the cultured set. The letter was written from The Cottage,[111] January 3, 1799, by Margaret Cowper, the daughter of Basil Cowper, a former member of the Council of Safety, but later a Loyalist, to her cousin, Eliza, the daughter of John McQueen,[112] who was visiting her father in Florida:

> ... I wrote by the last post to Mr. Seagroves care and then told you everything since y^r departure till that date In our still, circumscribed round.... John has not been to Mulberry G.[rove] or have we heard a word of the family there.... Tomorrow is the great review of all troops in this district by Colonel Tattnall Y^r. Brother to make his appearance for the first time among the Invincibles, alias Colonel Gordons troop of Horse, Mary intends to go in to witness their gallant exploits & dine with M^{rs}. Woodruff: Aunt Betsy with her to see some wax work now in Town — the figures as large as life & tolerably well executed.... we went also with Mama, D^r. Cuthbert & John to the play on Monday night. "Such things are" by M^{rs}. Inchbald & the entertainment of the Adopted Child a very pretty little piece, & the performance very well.... M^{rs}. Williamson is a very pretty woman sings well & would be a good actress anywhere — & *our* friend Jones in low comedy has a great deal of humor. the house is always crowded, tho we went before five could get places only in the back row, however saw very well & on the whole were very well entertained.... Friday is to be the last night of performing, for M^{rs}. Williamsons benefit "the Highland Reel".... Lady Houstoun & M^{rs}. Johnston drank Tea here this afternoon &, made kind enquiry after you. A subject that is *at least* very old with us & cannot be Surprising to you must now take its re-

---

111. The Cottage was the Cowper home on the bluff at Thunderbolt, near Savannah.
112. Walter Charlton Hartridge, ed., *The Letters of Don Juan McQueen to His Family* (Columbia, South Carolina, 1943), xxi-xxxiv.

Sir George Houstoun, Baronet, Man of Affairs 171

view . . . the man we once thought so highly of is no longer the same . . . his wedding was the 20th. of last month, John was there & what I can collect of all particulars as follows — the company consisted of the Brides own family, Mr. & Mrs. Owens, Mrs. Bourke, & Misses Elberts Tom Netherclift & James Houstoun . . . the guests all dispersed and gone home by ten o'clock. — from all accounts a most dull evening — the Bride sighing, and the *happy* man gloomy and downcast without opening his mouth the whole evening — a very elegant supper superintended and set out by Kate McCredie — but strange to relate this sumptuous table could find room only in the old Generals bedchamber, literally bedchamber and appearing as such for the Bed was not removed — and *so* it was even *so* — the same Company were invited also the following day & went but Mrs. ——— having the ague could not, did not make her appearance. Cake was sent round to most of her acquaintances and among others us. . . . Mrs Bourke had a dance at her house the monday following & graced by the presence of the new married Couple . . . the Hunters and Maris Campbell went, from them heard that Mr. ——— was extremely delighted with his new situation, as fond as fond may be, expressing it to his amiable . . . by a Kiss several times — which you may suppose how pleasing to the company in general. and the sweet creature herself all *refinement* — they have been spending some days at Skidaway — So far now from regretting when I find anything to his disadvantage I rather am gratified that disdain may heal the wound esteem has Received. — On Thursday in the middle of this letter I was interrupted by a note from Town on the back of a play bill Mary having gone in the morning & finding the Highland Reel was to be performed that night instead of the next, and the last time too. Buba was dispatched out on one of Lady Houstouns horses for Aunt Wright and myself. . . . So in a violent hurry and bustle we determined at, once and went. Aunt W. to my uncles, myself to Mr. Woodruffs when I found Mrs. A McQueen and Harriet & in the evening went to see the "Road to Ruin" & the H. Reel. with them Mr. & Mrs. W. Aunts Betsy and Wright, Uncle A. & Mary & at The Theatre were joined by bell Hunter, & tho we could not find room all to sit together our party was also added to by Betsy, & Maria C. Mr. & Mrs. Jackson Mrs. Miller & Nat. Greene[113] (who Mary met at Mrs. Steven's seeing the Review & was a constant attendant of hers all the evening, I like him better than I expected

---

113. Son of General Nathanael Greene.

he is the picture of M^rs. Nightingale) also James Houstoun,[114] John was not there for the troop was not dismissed till the House was full but J. H. & G Baillie contrived (& sacrificing their dinner) to get in over the stage. — so we spent a pleasant evening tho the Highland Reel did not by any means answer our expectations being much curtail'd and entirely deficient in Scenery & Music. the Cottage bustle on the occasion Revived with former eclat. the laughing and the talking, the *difficulties*, all so enchanting, going and coming out. — we were fully determined to leave Town the next morning but M^rs. Jackson would take no denial to our spending the evening with her and having a hint from bell of a dance to be knocked up quite in a family way without any need of *preparation extraordinary* Could not decline it, & M^rs. Hunter wanted us to dine there this evening we Should also have liked but could not make it out, on account of several little necessary preliminarys to the evenings engagement, she was almost affronted we did not go, when we met at M^rs. Jacksons. M^rs. Miller & Nat & Ray are at present spending a few days there. So [sic] of the party was there M^r. & M^rs. Hunter. M^rs. Glen. the girls Sally Morecock, M. Campbell & ourselves after Tea dropped in quite casually D^r., Kollock,[115] Robert Watts, George Bailie & James Houstoun. & we had Charming dancing till past two in the morning, a very pretty supper. everything just as it should be, and we really spent a most agreeable evening. M^rs. J. would not permit us to leave her House that night in spite of Lady Houstouns sending the Carriage for us, so we had a Room of Marias & Remained there to Breakfast next morning. — we dined with M^rs. W. next day and afternoon Returned to the Cottage escorted by y^r. Brother and George Baillie (James H. set out in the morning for Louis Ville with J. Bryan) it was a drizzling uncomfortable night but yet he would not accept Johns invitation to stay and left us after Tea, & extremely dark. but in less than half an hour after his departure we heard a hasty knock at the door, which y^r. Brother opened & Bailie reentered our little parlor as pale as death. and in an agitated manner. — his Horse (a new purchase & a very pretty creature) took fright going over the Causeway & threw him over the ditch and ran away. he was bruised, & for some minutes stunned with the fall. but providentially nothing more. had he been thrown against a tree he must

---

114. James Edmund Houstoun, son of Dr. James Houstoun.
115. Dr. Lemuel Kollock who married Maria Campbell, February 10, 1802 (Kollock Family Papers).

have been Kill'd. — A little after he went we heard a Horse tear round the House with great violence (so much as to Knock down a pretty large Lombardy Poplar which John has planted near the end of the piazza). & it proved to be his, for the boys were sent in search & found him. — so, as the agreeable unfortunate soon recovered. & was but little hurt the evening passed very pleasantly & he returned to Town next morning after Breakfast. — this is Monday & the Hunters engaged to spend this week with us. but Miss Wayne gives a dance tomorrow & I fancy they may be at it. — it is dreadful Cold weather & they will find it *as* pleasant here if they stay till it is warmer . . . . give my best love to Aunt McQueen & Elizabeth & William & to Uncle M^c· — from all the family too. and for my dearest Eliza all that I can feel of the warmest and most Constant Affection, and excuse this horrid writing, inditing, &^{c} &^{c}· of y^r· Margaret Cowper, in great hurry for the alarm is given — Buba is going to Town be sure & burn this, do not suffer the monuments of my *Slovenliness* to exist, which is in y^r· power to Conceal by demolishness.[116]

15

Two of the sons of Sir George and Lady Houstoun grew to maturity and married; and each one, following the example of his father, his grandfather, and his uncles, used his talents in the interest of his native city for civic betterment.[117] Patrick, who was only eighteen when his father died, claimed the title, and he was recognized in Savannah as a baronet. He was eight years the senior of his brother, Robert James Mossman Houstoun, but he outlived him twenty-one years.

When the third Patrick Houstoun was twenty-five years old and a lawyer, he was married to Eliza Fuller McQueen, who was the daughter of Alexander and Elizabeth (Fuller) McQueen. Alexander McQueen (1755-1805) was the son of John McQueen and his wife, Ann Dalton, of Charles Town, South Carolina, where Alexander was born. His father was from London, and after becoming a resident of Charles Town he entered upon a

---

116. The letter is in the Cowper Collection of Letters in Colonial Dames House. It was presented in 1937 to the Georgia Society of the Colonial Dames of America by the late Mrs. Franklin Buchanan Screven and the late Miss Phoebe Herbert Elliott, who were lineal descendants of Mrs. Eliza McQueen Mackay. In 1949 the Mackay-McQueen-Cowper Collection was deposited in the Georgia Historical Society.
117. The only available source material in Savannah on the public life of the two Houstoun men is in the Savannah newspapers in Hodgson Hall.

mercantile business. Later he was a member of the Commons House of Assembly. His wife was born in Kilkenny, Ireland. After the death of her husband in 1762 his widow took her children abroad to have them educated. Later her two sons, John and Alexander, were put under the guardianship of James Parsons, an attorney of Charles Town. Alexander became a merchant, and John a landowner, both eventually living in Savannah; John some time after his marriage made his home in Florida.

In 1733 Alexander married Elizabeth Fuller, the daughter of Thomas Fuller, of Beaufort, South Carolina. The McQueens had a summer home at Montgomery, near Savannah. Mrs. McQueen died the latter part of 1797.[118]

Mrs. Houstoun was the first cousin of Eliza McQueen, the recipient of Margaret Cowper's letter. The McQueen-Houstoun marriage was announced in the *Georgia Gazette* of February 12, 1801. There were nine children from their union.

The activities of young Patrick Houstoun the first few years after his marriage are not known. The death of his wife occurred twenty-three years later. An invitation to her funeral was given in the *Georgia Gazette* of January 6, 1824:

> The friends and acquaintances of Mr. Patrick Houstoun are requested to attend the funeral of Mrs. Houstoun from his residence in the District of White Bluff at 11 o'clock this day where the funeral service will be performed. The interment will take place in the Old Cemetery at 2 o'clock.

In later years following his wife's death Patrick Houstoun was identified prominently in some of the city's organizations. As he was a planter he joined the "Agricultural Society of Georgia in Savannah" which was in existence as early as 1825. In that year on April 20 the society announced the program of premiums to be awarded at the anniversary meeting which was to be held the following February. Three silver cups valued at twenty-five

---

118. Walter Charlton Hartridge, *The Letters of Don Juan McQueen To His Family* (Columbia, South Carolina, 1943), xxi, xxii; 38, 42n., 83.

The Houstoun children were: Patrick, unmarried; three children married and two had issue: George Ann Moodie Houstoun married Alexander McDonald; Edward Houstoun married Claudia Wilhelmina Bond; and George Houstoun married Sarah Hazelhurst. The others were James Johnston, Robert James, Jane Harriet, and Moodie, who died either young or without issue.

dollars each were offered in three classes to planters: one cup to the owner who produced by the most approved mode of cultivation from not less than nine acres, an average of not less than 80 bushels of rough rice per acre, weighing not less than 46 pounds per bushel; one to the owner who raised an average of not less than one thousand pounds in the seed of black seed cotton per acre from four acres; and one to the planter who raised the greatest quantity of flint corn and blades from not less than four acres, and averaging not less than 50 bushels an acre.

The land had to be cultivated, the rules stipulated, within Chatham County, or if the planter's estate was in an adjoining county, or was in South Carolina, he had to be a member of the society. Further regulations for the contest were that the ground had to be "laid off by Planter's measurement of 5 poles of 21 feet to a quarter acre, and be rectangular, equilateral and regularly staked. All ditches and chains within the stakes to be included." Every candidate had to furnish the secretary with a detailed statement of the mode of cultivation specifying how the main ground was prepared, distance of rows, time of planting, flowing, hoeing, thinning, number of hoeings and ploughing, and the period of laying the crop, the quantity and kind of manure used, a description of the land and any other information that he thought necessary.

There were a general chairman and four special committees: premiums, rice, seed cotton, and flint corn. Patrick Houstoun was on the latter committee and the men associated with him on all of the committees were Alexander Telfair, James Proctor Screven, B. M. Morel, W. P. Marshall, "Bulloch, Daniel, Wallace, Jackson, Stiles, Habersham, Tim Barnard and S. M. Bond."[119]

Two years later, in 1827, Patrick Houstoun entered politics by offering himself as a candidate for the office of clerk of the Superior and of the Inferior Courts of Chatham County. The election returns were printed in the January 8 issue of *The Columbian Museum & Savannah Advertiser*. Houstoun lost in the election for clerk, but he was elected receiver of tax returns. The next office he held was a justice of the Inferior Court of the

---

119. *The Georgians* [Savannah] April 20, 1825. See also Duncan Clinch Heyward, *Seed from Madagascar* (Chapel Hill, North Carolina, 1937), 29, 30.

county, which he held from 1826 to 1831, but he resigned in November of the latter year. As city treasurer, a position to which he was re-elected in 1832,[120] and which he held for several years, he would announce the assize of bread; and in 1833 his report to city council showed that real estate and other assets owned by the city were valued at $412,748.[121] It was also within his province to publish in the local press when tax returns were due, and to publish a list of delinquent tax payers.[122]

Patrick Houstoun was on active duty during the War of 1812-1814, as following that event when the "Savannah Fencibles" was formed he was a member as a private. In 1832, James Hunter, who was the commanding officer, advertised that those men he listed in the newspaper, and who had been discharged at the close of the war by William R. Boote, Inspector General of the Army of the United States, were entitled to "draw one each in the contemplated Land Lottery."[123]

For several years Patrick Houstoun was a director of the Marine and Fire Insurance Bank, at least from 1832 to 1834, and in the latter year he was one of the stockholders owning fifty shares at thirty-five dollars a share. In 1825 the legislature granted banking privileges to the Marine and Fire Insurance Company, and it occupied the handsome building on St. Julian Street which was designed by the architect William Jay for the Branch of the United States Bank.[124]

Savannah, of course, was drawn into the political strife that harassed the nation during the two administrations of President Andrew Jackson, and later. Patrick Houstoun identified himself with the Union and States Rights Party of Chatham County. On Independence Day, 1834, the members of the party announced in the local press to "their fellow-citizens, who, with them cherish

---

120. *Columbian Museum & Savannah Advertiser*, November 13, 1827; November 1, 1831; January 13, 1832.
121. Gamble, *History of the City Government*, 171.
122. *Columbian Museum & Savannah Advertiser*, January 28, 1834; March 6, 1834; April 4, 1834.
123. *Columbian Museum & Savannah Advertiser*, April 27, 1832; *The Georgian*, April 27, 1832.
124. Thomas Gamble Scrap Book, "Savannah Banks, Money and Commerce, 1733-1865." In the main Public Library, Savannah. Later the bank was called the Marine Bank, and in 1866 the building housed the Merchants National Bank. The present Realty Building occupies the site.

an equally ardent attachment to the Union and the Rights of the States that a procession would be formed on this day at 11 A.M. in front of the Exchange thence to the Baptist Church on Chippewa Square where the Declaration of Independence would be read by Robert Pooler, Esq. followed by an address to be pronounced by M. Hall McAllister." The clergy, the officers, civil and military, the different societies of the city and the citizens generally were invited to join in the procession. The pews on the south side of the church were "reserved for the ladies."

Following the parade a luncheon was to be served at the Exchange at which William B. Bulloch, the president of the society, and the six vice presidents were to preside. The committee on arrangements requested all who joined in the procession to wear the usual badge of mourning on the left arm as a mark of respect to the memory of Lafayette. The Marquis de Lafayette had died on May 20, 1834. Soon after the news of his death was received in Savannah, council called a special meeting of citizens on July 1 when a memorial service was held, and a eulogy was pronounced by the Reverend Dr. Capers, the son of a Revolutionary officer.

The July 7 issue of *The Georgian* carries three columns on the parade and on the dinner on the "Natal Day of the Republic," and on July 10 the same paper reported:

"That the procession of the 4th. inst. of the Union and States Rights Party exceeded that of the Nullification Party by a *large number* is a fact as well known here as that the day we celebrated, and *no one* except one who has no character for veracity to lose would venture to deny it."

An important organization in which Patrick Houstoun took a part and one that had far-reaching results, was the Savannah Anti-duelling Association. The frequency of duels in the city had aroused to action a number of representative men, who, on the day after Christmas, 1826, held a preliminary meeting in the Long Room of the City Exchange; and four days later a second largely attended meeting was held and a constitution was adopted. It was brought out in the meeting that the association was formed for the purpose of restraining and, if possible, suppressing the practice of duelling. As set forth in the constitution the members "considered the practise of duelling as a violation of the law," and as "destructive to domestic life." In 1834 Patrick Houstoun became chairman of the standing committee,[125] and he presided at the "anniversary" meeting.[126] The standing committee reported that in 1834 there was but one duel "without injuries to the parties." "It was so silently conducted that the Standing Committee had not an opportunity to take the customary measures."[127] In time the vigorous and persistent efforts of the members of the association bore fruit, and after many years "affairs of honor" were a thing of the past in Savannah.

About the same time that the foregoing association was formed prominent men were agitated over the excessive use of intoxicating drinks, and they formed what the members styled the Savannah Temperance Society. In 1833 monthly meetings were held, and one in October took place at the new First Presbyterian Church which was located on the north side of Broughton Street, between Jefferson and Barnard streets. Eighteen months later the members felt the urge to make their organization more effective, and through the newspapers they issued an invitation saying that all persons who "feel a desire to aid in a good cause, and are willing to unite in the formation of a Society on true temperance principles, are invited to attend a meeting to be held at 9 o'clock this morning in the Sabbath School Room of the Independent Presbyterian Church."[128] The meeting was held on Sunday morning, July 8, 1835, and a constitution was adopted. Patrick Houstoun was elected president, and the name selected for the organization was the "Chatham County Temperance Society." The object, the constitution read, was to

> Discountenance and suppress Intemperance in all things particularly the use of ardent spirits- a pledge of entire abstinence from the use of wine not required- yet use of any intoxicating drink shall be declared a violation . . . .

Any person could become a member by subscribing to the constitution, an act tantamount to a pledge to "abstain from the use, manufacture, importing and vending of ardent spirits." The

---
125. Gamble, *Savannah Duels and Duellists 1733-1877* (Savannah, 1923), 185, 190.
126. *Columbian Museum & Savannah Advertiser*, January 1, 1835.
127. Gamble, *Savannah Duels and Duellists*, 198.
128. *The Georgian*, July 8, 1835.

meetings were to be held four times a year, and the executive committee was to be elected annually. The other officers who were associated with Patrick Houstoun were James Smith, Noble W. J. Bulloch, John Gardner, first, second, and third vice presidents, respectively; Joseph W. Robarts, recording secretary; J. Y. Chapman, corresponding secretary; and the Reverend Willard Preston, the Reverend Joseph S. Law, and James Smith forming the executive committee.[129] The society no doubt filled a much needed reform in its day, but the question might be asked, Did it succeed any better than the finally repealed Eighteenth Amendment? Perhaps it did, for a time at least, since the prohibition was voluntary as compared with the much abused law of the nation in 1919.

The next episode in Patrick Houstoun's life shows him again as one of the outstanding men of the community, but, also, it typifies that he was a person with interests and activities that were varied in character.

Through the will of Thomas F. Williams, probated in Savannah in December, 1816, a legacy was left to be held in trust for twelve and a half years to be paid to "the first incorporated Body for the Relief and Protection of afflicted and aged Africans." The testator died the same year, but his brother in time carried out the bequest when certain men in Savannah and in the coastal counties of Georgia resolved to found just such an institution. A memorial was presented to the Georgia General Assembly which, on December 24, 1832, passed an act incorporating "the Georgia Infirmary for the relief and protection of aged and afflicted Negroes." Patrick Houstoun was among the first trustees, who were from Chatham, Bryan, Liberty, McIntosh, and Camden counties. It has been alleged, substantiated by accurate sources, that the Georgia Infirmary of Savannah was "the first asylum and hospital founded in the United States solely by whites and solely for Africans."

Quoting from an historical sketch:

> To that gracious sentiment that makes men mindful of the suffering and impediment of the aged and afflicted, and prompts them to exert their energies and their resources in relief and protection, may the conception of the Georgia Infirmary be ascribed.

---
129. *Ibid.*, July 14, 1835.

> Far greater becomes the degree of sentiment when men of one race tender relief to those of another, who because of their inabilities which poverty or disease or neglect may have produced are helpless to cope with circumstances to which they have been reduced.
>
> It is not strange in a State where the importation of slaves had been prohibited in its Constitution of 1789 that men of Caucasian blood should interest themselves in the relief and protection of aged and afflicted Africans, for Georgia was a pioneer State in this. . . .[130]

The trustees held their first meeting on January 15, 1833, at the Exchange. Richard F. Williams, brother of the testator, was elected president, and Patrick Houstoun was chosen vice president. He later became president, and he held the office until his death.

Included in the legacy of 1816 was a city lot near the Filature, a tract of land on Crooked River near Bethesda Orphanage, and ten thousand dollars. When the act of incorporation was passed the legislature allocated four thousand nine hundred and eighty-five dollars and sixty-two cents. In a few years two buildings were erected in the Bethesda location, which housed the hospital with some additional buildings until 1838 when, because of the distance from the city, the Infirmary was moved near the town, and a building was erected on its present site on Thirty-fifth and Abercorn streets.[131]

A few glimpses can be given of the personal life of Patrick Houstoun. One is that he did some traveling. On April 6, 1806, and on April 3, 1807, *Columbian Museum & Savannah Advertiser* listed his name as having unclaimed letters in the post office; and in the autumn of 1833 he arrived by boat from New York. Three times news was carried in the paper that he had freight arriving by ship from New York. As a property owner he had land in Glynn County, and a house on the corner of Bull and Bay streets which he offered for sale in 1829. A brick house which

---

130. *Georgia Infirmary*, a centennial pamphlet published in Savannah in January, 1933, p. 7.
131. *Ibid.*, 18, 19.
 Thirty-two years after the charter had been granted General Sherman took possession of Savannah. His army wiped out the existence of the Infirmary and stripped it of everything but the land it owned. *Ibid.*, 23. It was rebuilt in 1871, and today (1949) is a modern hospital.

Sir George Houstoun, Baronet, Man of Affairs 181

he occupied in 1833 was offered for sale having been owned by "the late Major John Screven."[132] The house was located on St. James Square.[133]

Robert Houstoun was but twenty-four years old when he was brought before the public eye through an endorsement by a number of citizens who nominated members of the aldermanic board. The election was to be held on the first Monday in September, 1809. In was the custom then, previous to elections, for suggested names to be published in the local press. In July of that year "Republican Citizens" held a meeting and appointed a committee to nominate candidates for the coming election. Accordingly the committee members, who were Peter Deveaux, Alfred Cuthbert, Moses Sheftall, Thomas Burke, Thomas Mendenhall, Philip Box, William Gaston, and John J. Evans published this notice:

> Fellow-Citizens- In compliance with your request we have proceeded to nominate and now recommend to your support the following candidates to serve as aldermen for the ensuing twelve months. [Fourteen names followed, among them Robert Houstoun].
>
> We have endeavored [the committee concluded] to chuse from among our fellow citizens men of integrity, who have an interest in the prosperity of our city, and we believe them capable of fulfilling the duties required.[134]

All but two of those nominated were elected at the September polls. The highest number of votes cast was for John Eppinger who received 265, and Robert Houstoun was given 183.[135] The new council members took office on September 14, with William B. Bulloch as mayor.

132. *Columbian Museum & Savannah Advertiser*, November 2, 1833; November 23, 1833; April 8, 1834; November 3, 1834; March 19, 1812; February 20, 1829; January 22, 1833.
133. *The Georgian*, November 23, 1830. In the funeral notice of Major Screven, the location of his house was given. Major Screven was buried in the old cemetery on South Broad Street. See Georgia Society of the Colonial Dames of America, comp., *Some Early Epitaphs in Georgia* (Durham, North Carolina, 1924), 79.
134. *The Republican; and Savannah Evening Ledger*, July 7, 1809.
135. *Columbian Museum & Savannah Advertiser*, September 7, 1809.

When the young Robert Houstoun became one of the city fathers he found he was to be under certain rules in the observance of his duties. Aldermen were fined for non-attendance at meetings, and if they were late there was a fine also of four cents a minute not to exceed two dollars. The fines were given to the hospital.

According to the first official census taken the previous February, Savannah in 1809 had a population of five thousand three hundred and forty-two inhabitants; and of that number there were two thousand seven hundred and two white persons; the balance were Negroes.[136]

One of the matters that came before the new board was that of caring for the city's trees. The favorite one in Savannah at that time was the Pride of India which had been planted on the Bay as early as 1795. In the storm of 1804 the public trees on the Bay were blown down, but they were replaced, and others were planted in front of the Court House and the Filature. Fines were imposed on the public for riding under the trees because the branches were broken and the symmetry of the trees was marred. In December, 1809, council ordered all dead Pride of India trees on the Bay replaced, and the next year the same trees were ordered planted in Johnson and in Columbia squares.[137]

The Pride of India, colloquially styled "China-berry tree," is a "native of Syria, Persia, and the north of India, and is cultivated in many parts of the world as an ornamental tree. It was highly estimated in Savannah on this account, and also as a shade tree, for it was one of the first trees to put out its leaves in the spring."[138] In a few years a double row of the trees was planted down the center of South Broad Street[139] which came to be known as "Under the Trees." Some of them grew to a height of thirty or forty feet.[140]

A strange ordinance that was in effect when Robert Houstoun

---

136. Gamble, *History of the City Government*, 64, 73, 88.
137. *Ibid.*, 83.
138. Charles Seton Henry Hardee, *Reminiscences and Recollections of Old Savannah* (Privately printed, 1929), 65.
139. Now Oglethorpe Avenue.
140. About fifty years ago the Park and Tree Commission abandoned the planting of Pride of India trees on the streets of Savannah because the wood is brittle, and because "small boys" climbed them and broke the branches. (From William H. Robertson, superintendent, 1948.)

was an alderman was one prohibiting smoking in the streets, in lanes, in the squares, on the wharves, and in other public places![141]

"Alderman" Houstoun for some reason did not serve out his term of office, as he resigned on February 8, 1810, after having been on the board only five months. It may have been because of his interest in a personal matter. However, one "Voter" wished him back again in council. When the time came in July to prepare names for the September election a voter who "took the liberty of proposing the following list of names gentlemen as worthy the suffrages of the people of the city," thought "they were all Americans who are generally known to the inhabitants," and he included that of Robert Houstoun,[142] who was not elected.

The motive that may have actuated young Houstoun's resignation was his interest in his approaching marriage which took place on July 26, 1810. His bride was Sarah McQueen, the sister of his brother Patrick's wife.[143] Their union lasted only five years. She died at Kensington, near Savannah, on December 29, 1815, and she was buried in the family vault, presumably in the Old Burial Ground. There was only one child, a daughter, Sarah Ann Moodie Houstoun.

The newspapers of that day give only one piece of information about Robert Houstoun's activities during the next two years of his life. On the evening of February 7, 1817, a number of Savannah citizens met at the Exchange to discuss the feasibility of establishing a hospital and infirmary for Negroes. Robert Houstoun was secretary of the meeting, and he was appointed with John Bolton and Thomas Young a committee to consider the advantages of meeting with the "Savannah Poor House and Hospital Society." Two weeks later the committee published a notice to "the citizens of Savannah & Planters of the neighborhood" advising them of the intended institution, and begging for subscriptions. Undoubtedly the action of the committee was motivated by the will of Thomas M. Williams in which was a legacy for a hospital for Negroes, news of which must have been published about two months previously.[144]

---

141. Gamble, *History of the City Government*, 76.
142. *The Republican; and Savannah Evening Ledger*, July 7, 1810.
143. Mabel Freeman LaFar, Compiler, Marriage Book No. 1, 1805-1852. Date of license, July 26, 1810.
144. See *ante*, 179.

The mention in the resolution of the Savannah Poor House and Hospital referred to the hospital for white persons which was in existence in 1809. It was situated on the northwest corner of Broughton and East Broad streets, and in 1817 a plan for a new hospital was projected by those in charge. It came into being in 1835 when a charter was obtained.[145]

Whether or not the proposed Negro hospital came into being before the one on the Bethesda tract it does not concern Robert Houstoun, as he died the following year. His death occurred on February 21, 1818, "at his residence in St. Julian street one door from Lincoln." He was thirty-three years old. His brother Patrick was the administrator of his estate. As late as 1822 the latter offered through the newspapers various properties for sale: three hundred and fifty-four and a quarter acres of land in Bryan County; one undivided fourth part of fourteen hundred and fifty acres in McIntosh County situated on the Altamaha River; twelve lots in the town of Brunswick; Cedar Grove plantation of twelve hundred acres near White Bluff; a tract of fifty acres near the latter; one hundred acres on May Island on the marshes of the Little Ogeechee River; also between sixty-five and seventy slaves.[146]

16

When Lady Houstoun was fifty-two years of age she was asked to become a member of the board of directors of a girls' orphanage. The Union Society was formed "for the care and education of orphan and destitute children who without distinction of sex enjoyed the benefits of its charitable appropriations." In 1801, the Reverend Henry Holcombe,[147] pastor of the Baptist Church, conceived the idea of segregating the girls and the boys, and to carry out his purpose, presumably with the consent of the Union Society, suggested to "several ladies of piety and benev-

---

145. From the annual report of William Duncan, president, January 26, 1870, in the author's book of clippings. The work of the present building, the Warren A. Candler Hospital (formerly Savannah), was begun in 1836.
146. *The Georgian*, May 13, 1822; November 25, 1822.
147. For a sketch of Dr. Holcombe's life in Savannah see Mabel Freeman LaFar, *Henry Holcombe, D. D. (1762-1824), Minister, Humanitarian, and Man of Letters*, reprint from *The Georgia Historical Quarterly*, XXVIII, No. 3 (September, 1944).

ANN, LADY HOUSTOUN

1749-1821

From the portrait by Thomas Sully owned by Mr. James Marion Johnston, Jr., of Chevy Chase, Maryland

olence the propriety of a separation." He invited fourteen of the prominent women of the town to meet at his residence on September 17, 1801, to form a board of directors to govern the newly founded institution, the Female Orphan Asylum. The name of Lady Ann Houstoun was numbered among the members. The memory of her husband's work for the Union Society was kept alive in Lady Houstoun's mind as she continued in his footsteps, in helping with others to guide the indigent girls of Savannah.

Lady Houstoun was remembered in the will of Dr. Andrew Johnston, the father of her son-in-law, who died November 30, 1801. Dr. Johnston, of limited means, left "small memorials," and one item in his will read: "Of my friend Lady Ann Houstoun I request the acceptance of my Buchans Domestic Medicine as a small token of my sincere respect."[148]

In 1808 Mr. and Mrs. George Woodruff gave up their home in Savannah and left later for New Jersey to occupy the house George Woodruff had built in 1793, near Trenton. Their farm was called Oaklands,[149] and was occupied as a summer home until they decided to make it their permanent residence. The many Savannah relatives always found a welcome at Oaklands, and Lady Houstoun, with some of her family, visited her daughter nearly every summer.

It was through the influence of Lady Houstoun and her sons-in law that Savannahians in 1811 were offered an opportunity for further cultivation of the arts. Lawrence Smith of Trenton, New Jersey, was induced by his patrons to come to Savannah. Smith was an artist and offered to come to Savannah to teach drawing and to give instruction to those interested in "ornamenting ladies dressing boxes, tables, etc." He also announced that he would do portraits at from five to twenty-five dollars. The Trenton artist listed George Woodruff, Colonel Johnston, and Lady Houstoun as qualified to give information with respect to his training and background. He advertised for a room, suitably

---
148. Chatham County Court House, Will Book "D."
149. Shortly after the death in 1808 of the last owner, Colonel Aaron Dickerson Woodruff, United States Army, the place was sold and became the Trenton Country Club. When the membership outgrew the club house the place was sold again. Family papers owned by Miss Susan M. Kollock of Atlanta.

situated, for his drawing school. Those ladies, however, who wished private lessons would be instructed in their own "apartments."[150]

On one of her visits north Lady Houstoun had her portrait painted by Thomas Sully,[151] who settled in Philadelphia in 1810. His beautiful likeness of Lady Houstoun bears full witness to the comment made by Henry Tuckerman, a contemporary man of letters, who wrote with "just appreciation" of art and the artist's life: "His organism fits him to sympathize with the fair and lovely rather than the grand or comic . . . . Sully's forte is the graceful." It was written of Sully that he was "perhaps most successful in his portraits of women.[152]

The year 1817 brought another bereavement to the Houstoun family when Lady Houstoun's daughter, Mrs. James Johnston, died on August 29 at the age of thirty-nine years and seven months. She was survived by her husband and eleven children, all of whom grew to maturity, and nine of whom married. The care of her brothers and sisters devolved upon the oldest child, Ann Moodie, who had just passed her nineteenth birthday.

Seven weeks after her mother's death Ann Johnston wrote to her grandmother, Lady Houstoun, who was visiting her daughter Mrs. Woodruff, in Trenton. The letter was dated Savannah, October 7, 1817:

> In addressing you my dear Grand Mother so many tender feelings are awakened that my hardened heart in vain endeavors to find words to express what I do so much wish to say. I have so much to tell you - the weeks appear so long before I can look for your return. Oh! when will you come back. I so much need your council and advice to instruct me in my path of duty to my God. It is true the Almighty has been pleased to visit us with Affliction and Oh! how severe it is — to be deprived of such a blessing but forbid Heaven that I should raise a murmuring voice at thy gentle chastisements and fatherly corrections . . . .
>
> I wrote my dear Aunt [Priscilla Houstoun] a week ago and am very impatient for an answer to know your plans. I hope your health has been improved. Augusta [six year old sister] too I hope has improved from her voyage. My dear Brothers [George,

---

150. *The Republican; and Savannah Evening Ledger*, November 28, 1811.
151. The portrait is owned by James Marion Johnston, Jr., of Chevy Chase, Maryland.
152. *Appleton's Cyclopaedia of American Biography* (1888), V, 743.

aged fifteen and James, fourteen, evidently off at school] I trust continue in good health. Papa will be much obliged to you if you or Aunt Priscilla will see that they have their flannel stockings, warm clothes etc. before you leave Trenton. Aunt Priscilla was kind enough to offer to get us some Canton Crepe and I wrote for two pieces, it is so difficult to get here I wish she would get 2 & ½ pieces - I will also trouble her to get 2 pr of shoes for Mary [three year old sister] and two pr for Susan [the eleven months old baby] - Mary's black Morocco, and Susan's soft black kid, the sol^s very soft. I will enclose their measures . . . .

We expect Uncle Houstoun[153] and family to spend a little time with us as a change to his children. They are better. Poor uncle has also been visited with afflictions as you have heard by the death of his little son James -

Oh! my dear Grand-Mother were I to write all I have to say and all that my heart dictates - but no: paper cannot contain it. I am so anxious to see you. We are all as well as usual. I hope Aunt Woodruff has recovered - will she not pay us a visit this winter? Papa, Bell [sister, seventeen years old] and all the family unite in love to yourself and all our dear relatives - particularly our dear brothers and Augusta

Your affct. afflicted Grand daughter
Ann M. Johnston

Bell desires me to say to Aunt Priscilla
that she does not want the shoes.[154]

17

The next summer Colonel Johnston and his two daughters, Ann and Bellamy, went abroad. On July 18, 1818, Ann wrote from Glasgow, Scotland, to her aunt Priscilla, who was then in Trenton, "We have left our good Aunts [Lady Houstoun's sisters, Rachael Moodie and Mrs. Storr] quite well," she explained. Aunt Storr was her favorite—"there certainly is something about her which reminds me of my dear Grand Mother." Ann thought Scotland was a "charming country."

---
153. Sir Patrick Houstoun, eighth baronet.
154. Original letter owned by Miss Susan M. Kollock of Atlanta, lineal descendant of Lady Houstoun. Ann Johnston married Dr. William R. Waring of Savannah.

In describing her visit she wrote:

> We saw most of the public buildings in Liverpool, the Mansion House is an elegant suite of rooms. We spent three days with Mr. Gray at Craig's near Dumfries - it is a pretty spot. I could have spent a week there - the country round Dumfries is very beautiful and well cultivated .... We arrived at Glasgow on Thursday to dinner - it is a beautiful town. Mr. Graham (a *Bachelor*) took us all over the town yesterday. We saw a fair, in the evening we drank tea with him where he had invited friends to meet us and then walked to the Botanic Garden. It is a beautiful extensive garden, but quite in infancy - a military band was in the garden and played while the company walked. The music was delightful, the finest I have ever heard, I could have staid till morning I was so enchanted. We had a sight of Glasgow beauties and Belles. The Scotch ladies are really what they are represented to be - frank, hospitable and fascinating, though we were not introduced. (it is the fashion not to introduce) they are as familiar as old acquaintants. The lady we met at Mr. Grahams told us she would call this morning, we expect her every moment, she is a real Scotch character. The gentlemen were here this morning and wished us to walk out, but we preferred writing our dear friends - Papa continues much the same as when we landed. - I do not think we will extend our travels to London as the journey is too long for him in his weak state; he will determine before we leave Glasgow and if he does not go to London, we shall travel to the Highlands which I shall like a great deal better.
>
> We shall go to Edinburg and then pay Mr. Hume a visit at Carolside. We often wish for you dear Aunt to enjoy this delightful country with us. Certainly it is a charming country even with the little I have seen of it I may judge, but you would be astonished to see what an American I am. I am as tennasious of my country as ever an English man was - and nothing offends me more than the observation "Why, are you American." We are taken for either Scotch or English. I have so many anecdotes to relate it will take over a year to get through them.
>
> .... My poor sisters I suppose they are now at Bethlehem[155] (I

---

155. William Harden, "The Moravians of Georgia and Pennsylvania as Educators," in *The Georgia Historical Quarterly*, II, No. 1 (March, 1918), 47-56. In a list of Georgia girls who attended the Moravian Seminary in 1818 are Eliza Johnston, Jane P. Johnston, and Louisa Johnston.

Sir George Houstoun, Baronet, Man of Affairs 189

wish I was there too) How do they like it. Tell Louisa[156] Papa says he leaves it entirely to her Aunts whether she had best have her hair cut. I hope Eliza[157] and Augusta[158] have recovered from the sea sickness. I am uneasy about Jane[159], she looked so bad when we parted. Do when you write again tell me particularly how she is . . . . We have been expecting a letter from my Brothers.[160] I hope their health is good . . . .[161]

Returning from abroad, Colonel Johnston and his daughters went directly to the Woodruffs, where Lady Houstoun awaited them. Shortly after Christmas the Johnstons, the Woodruffs, and Lady Houstoun began the two weeks' voyage to Savannah.[162]

The Woodruffs returned home before summer, and, although nearing the end of her life, Lady Houstoun still braved sea voyages to visit her daughter in New Jersey. In the summer of 1820 the Houstouns and Johnstons again left for Oaklands, and that was Lady Houstoun's last visit to her oldest child. While in Trenton Lady Houstoun bought George Woodruff's share of a pew in Christ Church, Savannah. She agreed to pay Woodruff two hundred and fifteen dollars for his moiety.[163] The Savannah family returned from the north in mid-December, making the voyage in nine days.

Ann Moodie Houstoun had only a few more weeks to live. Her life came to a close at Retreat early in February when she

---

156. Louisa Caroline Johnston married Patrick Houstoun, her first cousin, of Oaklands.
157. Eliza Herriot Johnston married Edmund Molyneux, British Consul in Savannah, 1831-1859.
158. Priscilla Augusta Johnston married George Jones Kollock, son of Dr. Lemuel Kollock of Savannah.
159. Jane Priscilla Johnston married Dr. Phineas Miller Kollock, brother of George.
160. George Houstoun Johnston married Emily Greene Turner, granddaughter of General Nathanael Green; James Robertson married Elizabeth Catherine Dowers, daughter of John Dowers, II, of Philadelphia, and Elizabeth Vergerean Woodruff Dowers (sister of George W. Woodruff); William Patrick Johnston, the youngest son, married Mary Elizabeth Hooe of Alexandria, Virginia, and Susan Marion Johnston, the youngest child, was the second wife of George Jones Kollock. Bellamy Roche and Mary Helen Johnston remained unmarried.
161. Original letter owned by Miss Susan M. Kollock of Atlanta.
162. *Columbian Museum & Savannah Daily Gazette*, January 19, 1819.
163. Receipt in possession of the heirs of Mrs. Macartan C. Kollock, Atlanta. Another receipt shows that in 1812 Lady Houstoun owned a pew with James Johnston, Jr.

was seventy-two years of age. She was buried on February 10,[164] and, presumably, the burial service was read by the Reverend Walter Cranston, rector of Christ Church and friend of the family. She was interred in the Houstoun vault in the burying ground on South Broad Street.[165] Three children survived her, Mrs. George Woodruff, Sir Patrick (eighth baronet), and Priscilla Houstoun, who outlived her mother fifteen years. Lady Houstoun's will was not probated until January, 1822. Her estate was a large one, and she bequeathed legacies not only to her son and daughters, but to her many grandchildren as well.

Her son-in-law, Colonel James Johnston, died five months after Lady Houstoun. The family was paying its annual visit to the Woodruffs at Oaklands when he died on July 2, 1822, in his fifty-third year. His obituary in *The Georgian* declared him "a most respectable inhabitant of this city." His friendship, continued the account, was "never failing and disinterested." Eleven children survived Colonel Johnston. He was buried in a vault in the old burying ground on South Broad Street, where lay the remains of his wife.[166] Legacies amounting to nearly ninety-five thousand dollars, besides real estate and Negroes, were left to his children.

Priscilla Houstoun continued to live at Retreat where the garden was one of her chief pleasures. Large stone jars kept filled with rain water furnished the only means of watering her garden.[167] She died of scarlet fever on February 19, 1837, at the home of her nieces, the Johnston sisters, on Reynolds Square, in the house built by her uncle, Governor John Houstoun. She was fifty-three years old. Her will was probated on February 20,

---

164. Register of Deaths, September 1818 — December 1832, Vital Statistics, Health Department, Savannah: "Lady A. Houstoun, buried Feb. 10, 1821, native of Scotland, died at White Bluff, Ga., Dr. [Lemuel] Kollock."
165. On the Houstoun monument in Bonaventure Cemetery is inscribed:
 SIR GEORGE HOUSTOUN
 1744-1796
 LADY ANN HOUSTOUN
 1749-1821
166. Some years later the remains of both were removed to Bonaventure Cemetery and were reinterred in the Kollock Lot where a monument stands to their memory. See *Some Early Epitaphs in Georgia*, 28.
167. One of the jars is at Woodlands, the summer home of the Kollock family.

JOHN HOUSTOUN
17[?]-1796
From the portrait owned by Miss Edith Duncan Johnston, of Savannah, Georgia

1837. A few months before her death she deeded Retreat to her little grandniece, Augusta Johnston Kollock, who was born on November 23, 1836, the only child of her niece Priscilla Augusta Johnston Kollock, who had died at the baby's birth. Legacies were left to the following: her sister, Jean Woodruff, and her brother Patrick; her nieces, eight daughters of her sister, Mrs. James Johnston, Jr.; two daughters of her brother Patrick, one daughter of her sister Jean, and the daughter of her brother, Robert James Mossman Houstoun; ten nephews; two aunts, sisters of her mother; one grandniece, two grandnephews; six friends; Doctor William R. Waring, "Friend"; the Episcopal Missionary Society; the wardens and vestry of Christ Church, Savannah, and the Female Orphan Asylum. Priscilla Houstoun mentioned also in her will her farm and plantations in White Bluff District and Coffee Bluff; lands on Green Creek, Glynn County, "now in possession of my nephews James R. and George H. Johnston"; her stock in the Marine and Fire Insurance Bank, the Bank of the State of Georgia, the Planters Bank, and the Bank of The United States. Three years after the death of his sister, Priscilla, Sir Patrick Houstoun, planter, died at his residence in Broughton Street, Reynolds Ward, on November 30, 1839, at the age of sixty-three. His will was probated January 11, 1840. The heirs were his two daughters and his three sons.[168]

Strangely, the oldest child of Sir Patrick and Lady Houstoun, Jean, was the last to survive her father and mother. Her husband, George Whitefield Woodruff, died in New Jersey in 1846.[169] At his death he owned property in Chatham County, Georgia, known as "Monteith"; lands in Bulloch and McIntosh counties; and the "farm" on which he resided, Oaklands, in Ewing Township, Mercer County, New Jersey. His heirs were his wife, his three sons, one daughter, and his sister, Mrs. Susan V. Dowers,[170] who outlived him twenty-eight years. His obituary, published in the *New Jersey State Gazette*, paid high tribute to him as "an estimable citizen" who had been a member of the community where he had "been living a blameless life." Notwithstanding "his retiring manner, the influence which wealth and intelligence con-

---

168. Will Book "H", Chatham County Court House, Savannah. The title was left unclaimed after the eighth baronet's death.
169. From a family letter owned by Miss Susan M. Kollock of Atlanta.
170. Chatham County Court House, Will Book "H".

fer," he exercised his influence "on the side of right and usefulness." At the time of his death he was the oldest member of the New Jersey bar. The Mercer (county) Courts and Bar passed a resolution in which they expressed appreciation of his "virtues and acts of charity and kindness," and "his abiding interest in everything that pertained to the honor of his profession." His funeral was held on Saturday morning, September 5, at Oaklands. His wife, who survived him only two years, also died at Oaklands, in 1848, at the age of seventy-three. Her will was probated both in Trenton and in Savannah. Her heirs were her four sons, her daughter, a daughter-in-law, a son-in-law, and her niece, Eliza McQueen Houstoun, daughter of her brother Patrick. Mentioned in her will were her "images of Milton and Shakespeare," miniature paintings of her father and mother, and the "Houstoun coat-of-arms."[171]

---

[171]. From the four married children of Sir George and Lady Houstoun there are many descendants living today (1949).

Chapter XI

JOHN HOUSTOUN, "REBELL GOVERNOR"

JOHN HOUSTOUN, twice governor of Georgia, distinguished patriot, first mayor of Savannah, delegate to the Continental Congress, the chosen chief justice of the state, third judge of the Superior Court of Georgia, and an eminent lawyer, lies in an unmarked grave. Even the place of his interment is unknown. In early manhood momentous events forced him into activities that called forth native ability and prepared him for the several dramatic episodes in which he played leading roles. From the conspicuous part he took in pre-Revolutionary days to the end of his life, he easily displayed the qualities of a statesman. He was a man of "commanding influence," brave and zealous. Impetuous, enthusiastic, and full of energy, he was reputed to be an agreeable and a sociable person. He was so staunch in his loyalty to his native state that on one occasion he did not hesitate to isolate himself because of a conviction. Some called him stubborn, but if he thought of himself at all in that regard he must have felt that his birthright gave him strength of will. To have held the many offices that were thrust upon him in a career that lasted but a score of years, John Houstoun exhibited a mental capacity that deserved the comment, "He was a gentleman of liberal education, culture and refinement," and " . . . an ornament to his profession."[1] When his life is reviewed one may picture him as a man of fine bearing, quick of stride and always ready for action. John Houstoun was born to lead.

From the beginning of hostilities with the mother country there was no hesitation on the part of John Houstoun in choosing the side with which he would throw his lot. In 1775 he was one of the hot-headed rebels of the colony; unlike his brothers Patrick and George, John remained true to the cause of American liberty until the close of the Revolution. It does not require much imagi-

---

1. C. C. Jones, Jr., *Biographical Sketches of the Georgia Delegates to the Continental Congress* (Boston and New York, 1891), 106, 117.

nation to visualize the four Houstoun men discussing and arguing the vital question of the day—England's attitude and the reaction of her subject provinces—while the distressed mother sat nearby viewing with anguish the divided opinions and sentiments of her sons. Patrick and George, in their early thirties, with more mature judgment, thought in terms of empire and loyalty to their king; and the younger John and James, having only recently attained their majority, exhibiting an entirely different point of view, expressed their intention of joining their comrades.

Residence for a few years in a sister colony gave John Houstoun the opportunity of associating with able leaders who were inflamed over England's treatment of her American colonies. John Houstoun read law in Charles Town under a prominent attorney. There he also became acquainted with a conspicuous citizen, Henry Laurens, with whom he later formed a firm friendship. Henry Laurens, at least twenty years Houstoun's senior, was an importer and a commission merchant, who in the late 1760's assumed an active part in politics. The Province of South Carolina was seething with anti-British feeling, and although Henry Laurens was manifestly a loyal British subject before hostilities began, "he was not a worse patriot than his fellows, he was a better prophet." Early in 1771 he left Charles Town for England where he proposed to educate his three sons. His stay there lasted three years. Before his departure his attitude toward the Crown underwent a decided change. By 1771, after he had witnessed many of the outrages imposed upon his own province by the Royal Council, his sympathies then were specifically for the acts passed by the South Carolina Assembly.[2]

It was in an atmosphere fomenting with political animosities at first more pronounced and more hostile than in Georgia, that John Houstoun lived for awhile. Having reached man's estate, he received impressions and ideas that were to guide him when he returned home. His legal education finished, John Houstoun left Charles Town, probably in 1771, and on his arrival in Savannah opened an office for the practice of law. As a solicitor in the Court of Chancery he took the oath of allegiance and supremacy on July 2, 1771. He found in Savannah a strong anti-

---

2. David Duncan Wallace, *The Life of Henry Laurens* . . . (New York and London, 1915), 122, 170.

British sentiment, and one of its chief proponents was Dr. Noble Wimberly Jones. John Houstoun worked constantly with Dr. Jones, although the latter was a much older man. Their acquaintance had been a long one, as their fathers had been closely associated in colonial affairs.

On November 15, 1769, John Houstoun acquired three lots at White Bluff, of approximately one hundred and fifty acres, which were sold to him under execution against Martin Fenton, and conveyed by title from the provost marshal. On November 5, 1771, he petitioned the Royal Council for five acres in St. Philip's Parish, stating that he "had been born and bred in the Province that he was at present possessed of three slaves but purposed as soon as he conveniently could to purchase more."[3] The grant was given to him on April 7, 1772. By the next year he had built up his plantation at White Bluff, he had there several houses for his Negroes, and he purchased more slaves. On Wednesday, April 7, 1773, at a meeting of the Governor and council, Sir James Wright informed the members that "the Small Pox had broke out on the Plantation of John Houstoun Esqr at White Bluff." That announcement was not the first intimation that the pestilence had entered the port of Savannah, as in the previous March the brig *Ann* from the island of Antigua had arrived at Tybee with cases of smallpox on board among the Negro passengers.[4] John Houstoun appeared before the members of council, accompanied by Dr. David Brydie and Dr. Hayes, who explained that one Negro had died twenty days previously, although the diagnosis was uncertain, but it appeared that another slave was actually infected. Thereupon the Governor issued his proclamation: the infected Negro was to be kept in a separate house, the others to be segregated; no slave or any other person on the plantation was to leave the place, "nor that any Communication whatever be had with the same, on any pretense . . . except to deliver provisions, Medicines or other Necessities" to the person who was to be stationed at the outer gate of the plantation. The clothes of all of the slaves were to be cleansed and washed, and the garments of the sick Negroes

---

3. *Colonial Records of Georgia*, XIII, 117.
4. *Ibid.*, 312, 356.

were to be burned after the death or recovery of the patients. Proper "Centrys" were to be placed under the strictest orders to enforce the directions. Every doctor who was permitted to attend the sick was ordered to change his clothes before visiting the plantation. The order read besides, there must be a duration of thirty days after the recovery of any infected person before the embargo could be lifted. Three months later the treasurer was directed by the council to pay eighteen pounds to the Governor "for the pay of two men keeping Guard at the Plantation of Mr Jno. Houstoun to prevent the spreading the Small Pox from said Plantation."[5] Since the Royal Council apparently took no further notice of the trouble on John Houstoun's plantation, it may be assumed that the alarming situation was terminated soon after the payment made to the guards.

Before his twenty-fifth birthday, probably, John Houstoun was well established in his profession, and could boast of many clients, as evidenced by the number of legal citations published in the *Georgia Gazette* which name him as counsel. In early manhood, John Houstoun's mind matured rapidly, and his talent for the legal profession provided him with the power to fulfill his ambition as he advanced steadily to high offices. Comments on his legal sagacity during various periods of his life range from: he "was by profession a lawyer comparable to any in his day";[6] "an able lawyer";[7] "one of the leaders among Georgia Lawyers of the day";[8] to Jenkins's statement that he was "the important lawyer in Savannah."[9] Behind John Houstoun's career as an attorney-at-law lay thirty-eight years of legal history in Georgia.[10]

5. *Ibid.*, XIX, Part 1, 503.
6. Stephen F. Miller, *The Bench and Bar of Georgia* . . . (Philadelphia, 1858), II, 97.
7. *Appleton's Cyclopaedia of American Biography* (1888), III, 274.
8. Jenkins, *Button Gwinnett*, 50.
9. *Ibid.*, 135.
10. The first public event in the colony was a "judicial function," when on July 7, 1733, five months after the founding of Georgia, Oglethorpe opened court on the Bluff in Savannah, magistrates were inducted into office, the first jury was impaneled, and the first case was tried. Thereafter, for some time, July 7 was observed in the colony as "Anniversary of Court Day." For a long period there were no practicing lawyers in Georgia because the Trustees permitted none in the colony, but there were many law suits tried in the local courts. After the inauguration of the Royal Governor and Council in Georgia, provision was made for erecting courts of judicature, and at that time, 1754, the Georgia

John Houstoun, "Rebell Governor"   197

A partial list of the clients who employed John Houstoun as their counsel in the years 1773 and 1774 will suffice to show that he had a creditable law practice for so young a man. He was attorney for James Bruce v. Samuel Carney; for James Black v. Edward Seyburn; for John Simpson v. Robert Bremer; for Andrew M'Corrie v. James Moore; for David Johnston v. Joseph Jones; for Philip Minis v. Benjamin Condon;[11] for Archibald Bulloch;[12] for Stephen Drayton v. Button Gwinnett;[13] and for several others. In 1777 John Houstoun was paid £7 10s. for legal advice concerning the will of Button Gwinnett.[14] Much later, when he was judge of the superior court, he licensed Thomas Spalding, of Sapelo Island, to practice law although the latter never made the law a profession. Houstoun was the attorney for Edward Telfair and Captain Telamon Cuyler, and he drew the latter's will; his death occurred in 1772.[15]

2

When the winter of 1774 had passed, John Houstoun found time outside of his law practice to do his part as a citizen in giving heed to the discussion of the grave situations then pending throughout the English colonies. He was alive to the political outlook, so much so that he either took the lead himself or was pressed into service by his associates to assist in arousing timorous Georgians. News had reached Savannah of the events in Massachusetts, and four prominent citizens, Dr. Noble Wimberly

---

courts admitted attorneys to the practice of law. History has failed to identify the first lawyer in Georgia, but the Georgia Bar Association puts the name of William Clifton at the top of its list of attorneys. Clifton, who came to Georgia in 1754, was the first attorney general, and he arranged a plan for erecting courts of judicature. At that time there was *"one other in the Profession in the Province."* Joseph R. Lamar, *The Bench and Bar of Georgia in the Eighteenth Century* (Reprinted from the Thirtieth Annual Report of the Georgia Bar Association, 1913), 5, 14, 15, 16. (References from *Colonial Records of Georgia*, IV, Pt. 1, 167*ff*; VII, 591, 592.)

11. *Georgia Gazette*, February 16, 1774; March 2, 1774.
12. Historical Society of Pennsylvania, Gratz Collection, Case 1, Box 4, MS. letter Archibald Bulloch to John Houstoun, Aug. 24, 1774.
13. Jenkins, *Button Gwinnett*, 50-53, From Emmett Collection in the New York Public Library, Emmett Catalogue, p. 266, No. 4128.
14. *Ibid.*, 176.
15. From Telamon Cruger Cuyler of New York City, August, 1948.

Jones, Archibald Bulloch, John Houstoun, and George Walton, decided to act. A comparison of their ages shows one of the many instances where John Houstoun was associated with men several years his senior.[16] He evidently had great admiration for older men, and that tendency may have been one of the contributing causes of the early development of his mind. Georgia had an intense Loyalist element, and the Royal Governor and his Council were keeping an eye to windward by watching every move of the Patriots. Mature judgment and enthusiastic youth brought forth a decision that was potent in its outcome, for suddenly on July 20, 1774, there appeared in the *Georgia Gazette* a call signed by the above four men:[17] "All persons within the limits of this Province do attend . . . at Tondee's Tavern on Wednesday, the 27th. instant, in order that the said matters [the acts of the British Parliament respecting the town of Boston] may be taken under consideration . . . ."[18] Pursuant to the call "a respectable number of the freeholders and inhabitants of the province assembled at the Watch Tower in Savannah on the day appointed."[19] By his open conduct, with his name appearing in the public press, John Houstoun proclaimed his sentiments, and "at a crisis so momentous," it has been written of him, "it was fortunate for

---

16. In 1774, Dr. Jones was fifty-five years old, Archibald Bulloch was forty-four, George Walton had reached thirty-five, and John Houstoun was in his late twenties.
17. An inexcusable error occurs in Candler's *Revolutionary Records*, where in writing of the above incident he states the call of the four patriots was published in the issue of July 14, 1774, whereas the date is July 20, 1774. There was no issue of July 14, but there was one of the 13th.
18. Jones, *History of Georgia*, II, 149. Colonel Jones, in his history, has made a curious conflict in telling of the 1774 meeting at Tondee's Tavern, when, on page 149, he states the meeting was held *at the Liberty Pole*. Twenty-seven pages further on (p. 176) he writes: "The first liberty pole erected in Georgia was elevated in Savannah on the 5th of June 1775." It is obvious that his statements do not agree. Unfortunately it is impossible to arrive at the truth, for on the authority of Dr. Clarence S. Brigham, Director of the American Antiquarian Society, Worcester, Massachusetts, it can be stated that the only issues of the *Georgia Gazette* for the month of July, 1774, are in Hodgson Hall, Savannah, except that of July 20, where Jones states the call was printed. That is a damaged copy, only one sheet of that issue being in the files at Hodgson Hall, and the call is *not* printed on that sheet. Nor is it in the issue of July 13.
19. *Ibid.*, 149.

Georgia that there were men like Mr. Houstoun, willing and able to serve her."[20]

The Tondee Tavern meeting was presided over by John Glen and resolutions and correspondence were read from some of the other colonies. A committee composed of John Houstoun and thirty others was appointed to draft resolutions similar to those read. The second public session was held at the Exchange on August 10, in direct opposition to the command of the Royal Governor. John Houstoun was appointed one of a committee of nine to solicit subscriptions to be sent to sufferers in Boston. A donation from the Province of Georgia of five hundred and seventy-nine barrels of rice was shipped from Savannah. At a session held at the market place on December 7 John Houstoun and his brother George, with others, were elected to the first Provincial Congress to meet in the beginning of the new year. When the meeting took place on January 18, 1775, Dr. Noble Wimberly Jones, Archibald Bulloch, and John Houstoun were chosen as delegates to the Continental Congress, but they declined to consider their election valid, as only five out of the twelve parishes of the colony were represented. Although Governor Wright was striving frantically to hold Georgia loyal to the Crown, the province was in the hands of republican leadership. The three delegates had been elected to the Congress, but their consciences guided them to remain in Savannah until they were supported by a stronger representation. They decided, however, that the new Congress which had been called to meet on May 10, should be apprised of the absence of the Georgia contingent. Accordingly they wrote to the President, John Hancock, on April 8, 1775.

"Sir," the letter began, "The unworthy part which the Province of Georgia has acted in the great and general contest leaves room to expect little less than the censure or even indignation of every virtuous man in America." The delegates explained at some length the divided sympathies among the people of Georgia, and the plight in which they, the delegates, found themselves. "Thus situated," the writers continued, "there appeared nothing before us but the alternative of either immediately commencing a civil war among ourselves, or else of patiently waiting for the

---

20. George White, *Statistics of the State of Georgia* . . . (Savannah, 1849), 30.

measures to be recommended by the General Congress . . . . Party disputes and animosities have occasionally prevailed, and show that the spirit of freedom is not extinguished, but only restrained for a time, till an opportunity shall offer for calling it forth . . . . We were sensible of the honor and weight of the appointment, and would gladly have rendered our country any services our poor abilities would have admitted of; but alas! with what face could we have appeared for a Province whose inhabitants had refused to sacrifice the most trifling advantages to the public cause, and in whose behalf we did not think we could safely pledge ourselves for the execution of any one measure whatso ever? . . . .

"We do not mean to insinuate that those who appointed us would prove apostates or desert their opinions; but that the tide of opposition was great: that all the strength and virtue of these our friends might be sufficient for the purpose. We very clearly saw the difficulties that would occur, and therefore repeatedly and constantly requested the people to proceed to the choice of other delegates in our stead; but this they refused to do. We beg, sir, you will view our reasons for not attending in a liberal point of light. Be pleased to make the most favorable representation of them to the Honorable members of the Congress. We believe we may take upon ourselves to say, notwithstanding all that has passed, there are still men in Georgia who, when an occasion shall require, will be ready to evince a steady, religious and manly attachment to the liberties of America. For the consolation of these, they find themselves in the neighborhood of a Province whose virtue and magnanimity must and will do lasting honor to the cause, and in whose fate they seem disposed freely to envolve their own."[21]

Those three loyal Georgians proved themselves to be prophets, and gradually the rising tide of indignation, patriotism and enthusiasm culminated on June 5, 1775, in a great demonstration. That day the first Liberty Pole in the colony was erected in front of Tondee's Tavern. The four leaders did not relax their activities, and on June 21 they issued another call to the inhabitants of Savannah, asking them to meet at the Liberty Pole on

---

21. *Revolutionary Records of Georgia*, I, 63, 66.

the following day at 10 o'clock in the morning. The response to their meeting called to incite the people to action and to bring Georgia in line with the other colonies, brought about the formation of a Council of Safety. At a meeting of the Provincial Congress on July 4 every parish and district was represented. John Houstoun was one of the twenty-five members from the Town and District of Savannah. The congress sat from Tuesday until Friday, July 7, and on that day, five delegates were elected to the second session of the Continental Congress then sitting in Philadelphia. They were John Houstoun, Archibald Bulloch, Noble Wimberly Jones, the Reverend Dr. Zubly, and Lyman Hall.[22]

Three of the delegates were to form a quorum. Dr. Zubly expressed much surprise at his election and informed the Georgia Congress that he could not accept the honor without the consent of his congregation, whereupon Jones and Houstoun were appointed a committee to obtain the permission of the members of the Presbyterian Church for their pastor to leave, which was granted. Of the five delegates two could not avail themselves of the privileges bestowed upon them by their fellow-Georgians. Jones, ardent patriot, son of a Loyalist parent, yielded to the express desire of his father to remain at home. Lyman Hall had already attended the first session of the Second Continental Congress which opened on May 10, arriving in Philadelphia three days after the opening as a delegate from St. John's Parish, whose inhabitants had early espoused the cause of the colonies. He presented his credentials and was permitted to take his seat "subject to such regulations as the Congress shall determine relative to voting." He remained in Congress until it recessed August 2, and presumably returned home.

The three remaining delegates decided to make the trip north by sea and they left from Savannah on August 1 aboard the brigantine *Georgia Packett*.

Upon their arrival in Philadelphia on August 11, they learned that Congress had taken a recess; so they found themselves with a wait of many weeks. Time could hardly have dragged, however, in that atmosphere of tense excitement. Signs of impending war

---

22. *Georgia Gazette*, July 12, 1775; *Revolutionary Records of Georgia*, I, 240, 241.

were prevalent everywhere. "Down High Street to Front, across 2nd, up Chestnut to Walnut, there were the quick rattle of drums and shrill whirling of fifes as sons of whigs and sons of liberal-minded Tories marched in military company. There were even Quaker youths parading soldierwise."[23] Not one, but many times, such scenes were re-enacted, and the sons of liberty made the air ring with their patriotic cheers as they marched up and down the streets of William Penn's city. Undoubtedly the three Savannahians met numbers of Philadelphians with whom they exchanged views on the events of the day and the hour.

At last, toward the end of August, word reached the city of the date for the return of the members of Congress which was to re-convene on September 2. The arrival of the delegates from Georgia, the last colony to send representatives, created some little stir. Two members, John Adams of Massachusetts and Richard Smith of New Jersey, were interested enough to mention the newcomers in some of their letters. Richard Smith reported that two of them "were dressed in Homespun suits of Cloathes;"[24] while the notable John Adams added that one of them was Archibald Bulloch. Adams paid tribute to John Houstoun by describing him as "A Young Gentleman by profession a lawyer, educated under a gentleman of eminence in South Carolina. He seems to be sensible and spirited, but rather inexperienced."[25] Considering Houstoun's age and the lack of opportunity he had had to engage in affairs of large import, the Bostonian's comment seems just. On September 17 in writing to his wife about the Georgia delegates he said that "Mr. Houston is the third, a young lawyer of modesty as well as sense and spirit, which you will say is uncommon."[26]

It was not long before John Houstoun and Archibald Bulloch were on friendly terms with John Adams. In his diary Adams wrote on Sunday, September 24: "In the evening Mr. Bulloch and Mr. Houston, two gentlemen from Georgia, came in to our room and smoked and chatted the whole evening. Houston and [Samuel] Adams disputed and chatted the whole time

---

23. Thomas Boyd, *Mad Anthony Wayne* (New York, London, 1929), 10.
24. Jenkins, *Button Gwinnett*, 65, 66.
25. *Ibid.*
26. Charles Francis Adams, *The Works of John Adams* (Boston, 1850-1856), I, 183.

in good humor. They are both dabs at disputation, I think. Houston, a lawyer by trade, is one of course, and Adams is not a whit less addicted to it than the lawyer. The question was, whether all America was not in a state of error, and whether we ought to confine ourselves to act upon the defensive only? He was for acting offensively next spring or fall, if the petition was recited or neglected. If it was not answered favorably, he would be for acting against Great Britain and Britons, as in open war, against French and Frenchmen; fit privateers and take their ships any where. These gentlemen give a melancholy account of the State of Georgia and South Carolina. They say that if one thousand regular troops should land in Georgia, and their commander be provided with arms and clothes enough, and proclaim freedom to all negroes who would join his camp, twenty thousand negroes would join it from the two provinces in a fortnight. The negroes have a wonderful art of communicating intelligence among themselves, it will run several hundreds of miles in a week or fortnight. They say, their only security is this; that all the king's friends and tools of government, have large plantations, and property in negroes; so that the slaves of the tories would be lost, as well as those of the Whigs."[27] The next week Bulloch and Houstoun were hosts to the Adamses. In his entry of Wednesday, September 27, John Adams wrote: "Mr. Bulloch and Mr. Houston, the gentlemen from Georgia, invited S. A. and me to spend the evening with them in their chamber, which we did very agreeably and sociably. Mr. Langdon, of New Hampshire, was with us."[28]

Not long after the Georgia delegates had taken their seats and presented their credentials, the spotlight was thrown on Dr. Zubly and the province of Georgia through a debate between the minister and Samuel Chase, a delegate from Maryland. John Houstoun came to the rescue, but his effort was a feeble one. Chase and Zubly began their battle of words, and the latter spoke several times so heatedly that he betrayed his Loyalist tendencies. On October 12 when the Congress was considering the proposed Confederation of the States, Dr. Zubly made the imprudent remark, "A Republican government is little better

---

27. *Ibid.*, 428.
28. *Ibid.*, II, 429.

than a government of devils. I look upon it the Association altogether will be the ruin of our cause."[29] It would have been natural if Dr. Zubly's speech had thrown the house into an uproar, but Chase took up the cudgels for the congress, and quickly gave this stinging rebuke: "I shall undertake to prove if the reverend gentleman's advice is followed we shall all be made slaves. If he speaks the opinion of Georgia, I shall sincerely lament they ever appeared in Congress. They can not, they will not comply! Why did they come here? Sir, we are deceived! Sir, we are abused Why do they come here? I want to know why their Provincial Congress came to such resolutions. Do they come here to ruin America? The gentleman's advice will bring destruction upon all of North America." John Houstoun's Scottish blood boiled to white heat, and he made his first speech in the Continental Congress, but so inflamed was the immature statesman that he was unable to express himself coherently, although his implication was not concealed: "Where the protection of this room did not extend, I would not sit tamely." To which Chase replied: "I think the gentleman ought not to take offence at his brother delegate." The state house and Philadelphia then became too warm for Zubly, and at the end of October he made a hasty departure, saying in a note to Archibald Bulloch and John Houstoun that he was "setting off for Georgia greatly indisposed . . . ."[30]

The prevalent myth that Dr. Zubly's defection prevented John Houstoun from signing the Declaration of Independence because the Congress asked him to follow Zubly to Georgia and watch his activities, can be exploded in a few sentences. The Zubly affair took place at the Second Continental Congress which opened May 10, 1775, while the Declaration was drafted and signed in the Congress of 1776, when neither Houstoun nor Zubly was present. Furthermore, Houstoun remained in Philadelphia long after Zubly's departure in 1775.[31]

---
29. Jenkins, *Button Gwinnett*, 55, 56.
30. *Ibid.* Note 1 says: Quoted from *Journal of Continental Congress.* "John Adams Debates," 494, 481.
31. Jenkins, *Button Gwinnett*, 67. Note 2 says: Zubly's letter is in the Emmett Collection, No. 1314, New York Public Library. Archibald Bulloch followed Dr. Zubly on or after November 10, 1775. Both attended

It is thought that Dr. Zubly's Loyalist disclosure struck terror among congressmen, especially when Chase accused Zubly of carrying on a correspondence with Governor Wright of Georgia. Their alarm took the form of an "Agreement of the Members to Secrecy," completed on November 9, 1775. John Hancock, as president of the Congress, was the first to sign, and thirty-eight others followed suit that day. On the following day Joseph Hewes of North Carolina was the first to sign the "Agreement." He was followed by the South Carolina delegates, Thomas Lynch, Christopher Gadsden, and Edward Rutledge, with the signatures of the two Georgia delegates, Archibald Bulloch and John Houstoun, below. There are a total of eighty-seven signatures on the document:

> IN CONGRESS November 9th., 1775
>
> Resolved That every member of this Congress considers himself under the ties of virtue, honor & love of his country not to divulge directly or indirectly any matter or thing agitated or debated in Congress before the same has & shall have been determined, without leave of the Congress: nor any matter or thing determined in Congress which a majority of the Congress shall order to be kept a secret, and that if any member shall violate this agreement he shall be expelled this Congress & deemed an enemy to the liberties of America & to be treated as such & that every member signify his consent to this agreement by signing the same.[32]

After signing the "Agreement of Secrecy," Archibald Bulloch returned to Georgia, but *John Houstoun remained in Philadelphia.* On December 11 the house appointed a committee of one delegate from each colony to "devise ways and means for furnishing these colonies with a naval armament, and report with all con-

---

the meeting of the Council of Safety in Savannah, December 19, 1775. The following day Bulloch was present, but Zubly was not.
(*Revolutionary Records of Georgia,* I, 77, 79). Zubly's Loyalists sympathies made him so unpopular that the Patriots banished him from Georgia in 1777. He went to South Carolina, but returned to Georgia in 1779. He died July 23, 1781. Marjorie Daniel, "John Joachim Zubly, Georgia Pamphleteer of the Revolution," *Georgia Historical Quarterly,* XIX, No. 1 (March, 1935), 1-16.

32. Reproduced through the courtesy and permission of the Chief of the Division of Manuscripts, Library of Congress, Washington, D. C., where the original is carefully preserved.

venience." Houstoun was not on that committee.[33] Three days later, December 14, Congress appointed a committee to carry into execution the resolutions for fitting out a naval armament, the choice to be by ballot. The second committee was composed of the men elected to the first, with two substitutions, and the name of "Mr. Houstoun" appears on the second list of names. The latter committee reported on December 22.[34] Houstoun was in Savannah three weeks after the report was read. He seems to have made the journey south by land; so he could have tarried in Philadelphia until December 22, left the next day, and still have made a stop-over on the way home, as a trip from Philadelphia to Savannah by stage-coach or on horseback consumed, at that time, about two weeks. What appears to have happened is that Joseph Hewes, delegate from North Carolina, hearing that John Houstoun was preparing to return home, requested him to carry a letter to Samuel Johnston, of Edenton, North Carolina. The letter was dated November 26, 1775.[35] Both Hewes and Johnston were prominent in their province. They came from Edenton, a town on the northern side of Albemarle Sound, and it was on the post road from the north. Coach and horse travelers from the north boarded a ferry there to cross the sound. If John Houstoun was unacquainted with Samuel Johnston, a letter of introduction from a mutual friend would have put them at once on a friendly basis. Only a few months previous to the probable visit of John Houstoun to Edenton, Samuel Johnston had been elected chairman of the Provincial Congress and virtually became governor. North Carolina's legislature was not in session during November and December, 1775; so it is likely that Samuel Johnston was residing at one of his several plantations, perhaps The Hermitage, near Williamston, thirty miles or more from Edenton across the Sound.[36] A land journey was fatiguing, and a hospitable plantation owner would hardly have allowed a delegate from the Continental Congress, bearer of a letter from a friend, to go on to his destination without inviting him to become his

---

33. Worthington Chauncey Ford, ed., *Journal of the Continental Congress*, I, 204.
34. *Ibid.*, 207.
35. Edmund C. Burnett, ed., *Letters of Members of Congress* . . . . I, xliv.
36. Information on Edenton furnished by Mrs. Henry A. Bond, genealogist, of Edenton, North Carolina.

guest. News from the center of the country's activities was not quickly obtained, and Samuel Johnston was no doubt eager to learn the latest information from an important visitor. John Houstoun's stay was necessarily short and he reached Savannah on January 14. The *Georgia Gazette* of Wednesday, January 17, 1776, announced that "Sunday last John Houstoun Esqr. one of the delegates from this province to the Continental Congress, arrived here from Philadelphia." Houstoun evidently made a land journey home, for had he returned by sea, the newspaper would have mentioned the vessel on which he was a passenger.

The moment John Houstoun reached Savannah he listened avidly to the political news of the day, and there was much to be retailed. On the previous Thursday voting began for the election of members to the Provincial Congress, called to meet on the nineteenth. When the polls closed on Friday afternoon at 5 o'clock, it was found that many prominent Savannahians had been elected, among them John Houstoun, and his friends Archibald Bulloch, Dr. Noble Wimberly Jones, Joseph Habersham, and Jonathan Bryan.[37] Three days after his return Houstoun attended his first meeting of the Council of Safety and "took his seat."

But something more important than the approaching Provincial Congress was soon to happen. In the early afternoon or evening of January 18, the Council of Safety met in special session and the members made their decision that Governor Wright and some of his associates "be forthwith arrested and secured." The commanding officer was ordered to carry out the decree. At a second session of January 18, held at mid-night, the council received the information that "a small band of patriots" had made the arrest. John Houstoun was present at the three meetings. The following morning at the Governor's house further orders were issued for the custody of Sir James Wright and his council. The Crown officers were given their parole, and Wright's included the edict that he could not leave the town or communicate with any officers on the ships of war then off Tybee. Four weeks later Governor Wright escaped "through a back door of his house, fled in the night time and made his way, under cover of

---

37. *Georgia Gazette, January* 17, 1776.

darkness, to an armed British ship anchored in the Harbor,"[38] and soon he was on his way to England.

The Provincial Congress did not meet on January 19 as originally planned, but convened in Savannah on the following Monday, and after organization proceedings the members elected Archibald Bulloch President of Georgia, and Jonathan Bryan, Vice President and Commander-in-Chief of the State.[39] It was not until Friday, February 1, that the congress transacted its principal business, which was to hold another election for delegates to the next Continental Congress, and the choice again fell on Bulloch and Houstoun with three additional members, Lyman Hall, Button Gwinnett, and George Walton.[40] Archibald Bulloch's duties as President of Georgia prevented his return to Philadelphia, but John Houstoun's reason for remaining behind cannot be ascertained. On May 10, 1776, when Hall and Gwinnett presented their credentials to the congress, "as fit persons to represent the province in the Grand Continental Congress" the names of Bulloch and Houstoun appeared on the document. The first of July, Adams wrote to President Bulloch expressing his regret that the latter was not returning to Philadelphia, and the reason for his not doing so: "I have been informed that your countrymen have done themselves the justice to place you at the head of affairs, a station in which you may perhaps render more essential service to them & to America than you could here . . . . " In a postscript he added: "Present my compliments to Mr. Houston. Tell him the colonies will have republics for their government, let us lawyers and your divine say what they will."[41]

Although no reason has ever been found for John Houstoun's absence from the Continental Congress of 1776, one theory seems plausible, which is the one John Adams expressed in his letter to Bulloch on the latter's position: he "could render better service to America" by remaining in Georgia. Who can tell but that Bulloch may have exerted his influence in guiding Houstoun in his choice between two obligations? He and John Houstoun

---

38. *Revolutionary Records of Georgia*, I, 101, 102, 269.
39. A legal paper signed by Jonathan Bryan, having that title, a private manuscript, a gift to the author from Mr. Charles Francis Jenkins.
40. *Georgia Gazette*, February 7, 1776. The last three named were the only signers from Georgia of the Declaration of Independence.
41. *Journal of the Continental Congress*, I, 348.

John Houstoun, "Rebell Governor" 209

were the only men in Georgia, except Dr. Zubly, then an avowed Loyalist,[42] who knew the mind and thoughts of the national leaders. Bulloch needed counsel in the administration of his new office. From whom could he seek it better than from his colleague, John Houstoun, who, as a member of the Council of Safety, was in close association with him? It is conceivable that Bulloch convinced Houstoun that he could serve Georgia better by remaining at home than by going to Philadephia. Following an address by the Council of Safety to its new president, Bulloch made a fitting reply in which he said: "I have the advice and assistance of gentlemen of known integrity and abilities."[43] At any rate, John Houstoun stayed and Archibald Bulloch used him.

3

It becomes necessary here to interrupt the narration of John Houstoun's political career to recount one of the most important episodes in his private life—his marriage to Hannah, daughter of Jonathan Bryan, which seemingly occurred in May, 1775, just before his departure for the Continental Congress. Continuous search for an authentic record of the event has proved futile, and the only clues on which to base the date are two deeds signed in 1782 by Hannah Bryan's brothers, James and William, where reference is made of her father's gift to her of six Negroes on May 28, 1775.[44] To substantiate the deduction, John Houstoun in his will, making his wife one of his residuary legatees, used the word "dower" in referring to those Negroes. Jonathan Bryan and his wife, Mary Williamson Bryan, were residents of South Carolina, and on the first day of June, 1751, he began to develop his new plantation in Georgia where he removed with his family on December 27, 1752. The Bryans then had eight children, and one had died. Hannah Bryan was born in October, 1759, and was baptized by the Rev. J. J. Zubly.[45] In none of the accounts

---

42. Marjorie Daniel, "John Joachim Zubly—Georgia Pamphleteer of the Revolution," 6.
43. Jones, *History of Georgia*, II, 221.
44. Copies of deeds in possession of Mrs. S. C. Lawrence of Charleston, West Virginia, a lineal descendant of Jonathan Bryan. Recorded Chatham County Court House, Savannah, January 7, 1787, Book D, fo. 75-78.
45. From Jonathan Bryan's Bible. Entries copied by the late Mrs. Franklin B. Screven of Savannah.

of John Houstoun's life is the merest mention of his marriage, except by implication in the deeds previously noted. Allusion is made to Hannah in 1782 as "the wife of John Houstoun."

4

In June, 1776, following his elevation to the presidency Archibald Bulloch laid a most important matter before the Council of Safety: a letter from the President of South Carolina, transmitting the request of General Charles Lee, Commander of the Continental Army's Southern Department, to send two representatives from Georgia to Charles Town to confer with him about the state's defense. The council complied and dispatched Jonathan Bryan and Houstoun along with Colonel Lachlan McIntosh, who the previous January was commissioned to command the Georgia Battalion. The delegation went to Charles Town, met with General Lee, and on July 5 handed their report to the Council of Safety. Their findings covered every possible phase of Georgia's inability to defend herself "against all enemies external and internal." It brought these salient facts to the attention of the council members: Georgia was the weakest of all colonies within and was much exposed from without; she needed assistance from the general Congress; there were plenty of provisions, numerous stocks of cattle, excellent inlets, harbors, and rivers; the inhabitants suffered on the east from ravages of British cruisers; Negroes were carried away from plantations; British fleets could be supplied with beef from well-stocked islands; to the south of her there was the menace of the Loyalist province of East Florida; to the west there were numerous tribes of Indians who could be supplied with ammunition from Florida; there was the danger of Negro uprising; and the conquest of Georgia would be a great acquisition by Great Britain, as it was a most excellent country, abounding with ship timber and lumber of all kinds, and was a convenient rendezvous for shipping. To ameliorate Georgia's situation three propositions were offered in the report: first, that General Lee be asked to state to the general Congress the peculiar situation of the Province of Georgia, and to obtain directions to raise and take into Continental pay, six battalions of men to defend Georgia; second, that a sufficient sum be granted by the Congress for building fortifications and gunboats; and

John Houstoun, "Rebell Governor" 211

third, to ask the Congress to provide presents of ammunition, clothing, and cattle for the Indians to keep them neutral and peaceful.[46]

While giving attention to public matters, John Houstoun continued his law practice. On July 25, 1776, he appeared before the Council of Safety, not as a member, but as an attorney-at-law to represent Shem and James Butler. The case concerned a Mrs. Croker, who was living at Rosdue, but "was tampering with the negroes and the plantation business." James Butler was forbidden to go to the plantation, while Dr. Charles Young, as physician to the family, was permitted to visit there professionally, provided he did "not intermeddle with the affairs of the plantation." No further explanation of the case appeared on the minutes of the council.

Savannah did not receive the news of the Declaration of Independence until August 8, 1776,[47] when President Bulloch received a copy of the document, with a letter from John Hancock. The council agreed that a public celebration should take place on Saturday morning at eleven o'clock. As one of the leading public men of Georgia, John Houstoun naturally took part in the exercises. In the procession, following the military, the secretary of the council bearing the Declaration, and "His Excellency the President, marched the honorable Council, and the gentlemen attending," to the Liberty Pole where they were met by the Georgia Battalion, commanded by Colonel McIntosh. A volley of thirteen guns was fired. The procession marched to the battery at the Trustees' Garden, where for the fourth and last time the Declaration was read and a salute fired from the siege guns planted at that point. After the military exercises were over, the officials and many others dined "under the cedar trees," where the assembled company drank toasts to the "prosperity and

46. *Revolutionary Records of Georgia*, I, 291-303.
47. *Ibid.*, 162, 163, 166, 168, 171, 174. John Houstoun was present at a meeting of the Council of Safety, July 5, 1776, the day after the Declaration of Independence was adopted (*Ibid.*, 150). The Declaration was signed by many of the delegates to Congress on August 2, after it had been engrossed, and later the others attached their signatures to the document on their return to Congress. (James Truslow Adams, editor-in-chief, *Dictionary of American History* (New York, 1940), VI, 121). John Houstoun attended a meeting of the Council of Safety on August 1, which is another proof that he did not attend the Congress of 1776 (*Revolutionary Records of the State of Georgia*, I, 170).

perpetuity of the United, Free, and Independent States of America." The whole town was illuminated in the evening and the inhabitants took part in paying their last respects to their former king by interring him in effigy in front of the court house and a prepared burial service was read.[48] It is disappointing that the committee which arranged the burial service has remained anonymous.

President Bulloch, realizing the necessity of establishing Georgia on a firmer basis, declared that the proper course was to have a state constitution based on a recommendation of the Congress. Therefore, he issued a proclamation to the inhabitants of parishes and districts calling for an election of delegates to meet in Savannah the first Tuesday in October. Furthermore, he circularized the province, admonishing the inhabitants of the necessity of making choice of upright and good men to represent them in the ensuing convention. Men of proven worth, loyal and prominent in their communities, were elected in response to their president's advice, men who were qualified to undertake the difficult task that confronted them. The legislature convened as appointed, and remained in session five months. Since the full proceedings of that first Georgia constitutional convention have been lost, there is no record of the whole list of elected deputies. Considering the position the Houstoun men occupied in other legislative assemblies, it is conceivable that one or more of them was a deputy. From his own letters, Joseph Clay, of Christ Church Parish, certified to the fact that he was a member.[49] While it is known

---

48. Jones, *History of Georgia*, II, 242-244.
49. Jenkins, *Button Gwinnett*, Note 2, "Letters of Joseph Clay," 13. Jenkins, page 108, quotes Allen Candler, editor of Georgia's *Revolutionary Records*, as stating in his introduction: "not a vestige of the minutes of the 1777 convention was to be found." Jenkins then continues: "It is a pleasure, therefore, to have discovered a fragment of these minutes, and the names of the committee selected by the Convention to prepare the Constitution." He then reproduces on pages 108-110, the exact copy of the discovered fragment. Through the author's correspondence with Mr. Jenkins asking where the minutes were found, he answered, November 2, 1937: ". . . . It prefaces the Constitution itself in the little pamphlet which was printed in Savannah in 1777 by William Lancaster, and to which I refer in the foot-note on page 109 of *Button Gwinnett*. There may be other copies of this little pamphlet in existence. This one may have belonged to Gwinnett himself or to some other prominent man, for some one has cut out the signature. . . ." The reference on page 109, to which Mr. Jenkins refers, shows that the pamphlet may be found in the Library Company of Philadelphia, Ridgeway Branch.

that Button Gwinnett was the Speaker of the House of Assembly as late as December 18, 1776, it is also on record that on January 22, 1777, the speaker was Dr. Noble Wimberly Jones.[50] On the committee, which on January 24 was elected by ballot to "revise the form of a Constitution" were, besides Button Gwinnett, William Belcher, of St. Philip's Parish, Joseph Wood, of Christ Church Parish, Josiah Lewis, of St. George's Parish, and George Wells, of St. Paul's Parish. Those seven men worked for five days before they brought in their report. It has been said that Button Gwinnett, chairman, did the bulk of the work of drafting "the document reflecting his political philosophy" and also the influence of a pamphlet by John Adams, *Thoughts on Government Applicable to the Present State of the American Colonies in a Letter from a Gentleman to his Friend.*[51] From January 29 to February 4, the house heard the draft read three times; then it was read paragraph by paragraph; amendments were then offered and the whole was read a fourth time. On February 5, the revised constitution was given the final reading. It was adopted unanimously the next day. Five hundred copies were ordered to "be immediately struck off."[52] Without any question John Houstoun took part in the debates and discussions. His election the next year to govern Georgia is an indication of his having had a voice in drafting and framing the first constitution.

Three weeks after that important convention, John Houstoun was called upon to mourn the untimely death of his friend and colleague, Archibald Bulloch. On February 22, the latter attended a meeting of the Council of Safety for the last time. Houstoun was not present at that meeting. The whole state deplored the death of its commander-in-chief, a zealous patriot and a true leader of the cause of freedom. Evil consequences followed his death which it is thought occurred on February 23, because on the following day Button Gwinnett was elected by the Council of Safety to fill the office of the late president.

---

50. Jenkins, *Button Gwinnett*, 102.
51. *Ibid.* Note 2 says White's *Historical Collections*, 203, prints a letter in which Dr. Jones is mentioned as speaker. . . . Letter from William H. Drayton to Humphrey Wells . . . given in Gibbs's *Revolutionary Documents*, II, 74.
52. *Ibid.*, 110. At the end of the fragment are these words: "'A true copy of the Minutes'—Edward Langworthy, Secretary."

On that day he commissioned two officers of the First Regiment of foot militia—John Martin as lieutenant colonel and Richard Wylly as major. The commissions were countersigned by Edward Langworthy, secretary, under the privy seal of Georgia. There was a meeting of the Council of Safety on March 4, and the legislature convened on May 8, called to elect a governor under the new constitution. John Adam Treutlen was elected to that office, and Dr. Noble Wimberly Jones was elected speaker. Of the twelve names on the first executive council, John Houstoun's appears second on the list. Eight days afterward occurred the duel between Button Gwinnett and General Lachlan McIntosh, fought because of political animosity. On the nineteenth Gwinnett died.

Governor Treutlen's term was cut short after nine months by his strange death. It has been alleged that he was murdered by Tories in South Carolina.[53] By Treutlen's death Georgia was left without a governing head, and the executive council functioned in directing its affairs until the legislature met in Savannah early in January. On the tenth of the month the members elected John Houstoun. Under the constitution the Governor was selected from the executive council, and his title was to be that of *Honorable*. At least one member of the executive council from each county was required to be in constant attendance at the residence of the governor. The House of Assembly, or legislature, was given the power to frame and enact laws which had to be signed by the governor and the speaker of the house.[54]

The year 1778 was an important one in Georgia from a military standpoint. Under Governor Houstoun's administration the state battalion was organized, and the military was active in preparing defenses. A resolution of the executive council required the commanding officers of the several battalions to make weekly returns to "his honor the Governor," who was commander-in-chief of the state's forces. General Robert Howe, who succeeded General Charles Lee as commander of the Southern Department, was kept informed of the military operations in Geor-

---

53. Jones, *History of Georgia*, II, 278. Note 1.
54. *Revolutionary Records of Georgia*, I, 286. Of Governor Houstoun's legislature there is in existence no journal, but there are in the State Archives one of his proclamations and a number of enrolled acts. *Ibid.*, 324.

John Houstoun, "Rebell Governor" 215

gia by the Governor and his council.[55] Commodore Oliver Bowen, in command of the state's naval forces, was ordered by the executive council to make a monthly return to Governor Houstoun, because "the gallies were originally undertaken and intended to be kept up . . . for the express purpose of protecting the River inlets and Plantations within the same. . . ."[56]

After any legislation by the council, Houstoun always conveyed the same by measure to the House of Assembly, which took it under consideration and acted. All acts and regulations of the house were sent as information to Governor Houstoun and his council and were duly recorded in their minutes. As an illustration, one piece of information thus received concerned the court martial of Captain Harding of Colonel Jack's regiment. Colonel Habersham appeared before the executive council and made affidavit that Steven Philips had apprehended a Florida scout and a Georgia deserter, and instead of commending Philips for his deed, Captain Harding drew his sword and "threatened the said Philips to make Sun and Moon Shine thro' him or words to that Effect."[57] A court martial ordered by the council sentenced Captain Harding, "of the minute men," to be discharged from the service. The episode was but one of many petty military details that had to receive the attention of the Governor and his council.

On Sunday evening, March 22, 1778, Governor Houstoun and his council witnessed a fire in Savannah which threatened the destruction of the whole town. Savannah's inhabitants went to the conflagration with "most Surprising Efforts and undaunted Conduct . . . stopping the progress of the flames." The following Tuesday, when the council met, the members passed a resolution of thanks "on behalf of the State to make their warmest acknowledgements to all the Citizens and Soldiers who were drawn together . . . by their ready and great exertions in extinguishing the fire which seemed for a time to threaten the whole town with ruin. . . . To the unparalleled activity [certain persons named] these Gentlemen may, under God, be ascribed the Salvation of the Court House, and consequently of a great part of the Town."[58]

---

55. *Ibid.*, III, 27, 31, 33, 35, 36, 48, *et al.*
56. *Ibid.*, II, 68-70.
57. *Ibid.*, 8.
58. *Ibid.*, 60, 61.

Less than three weeks after the fire, the executive council, on April 16, 1778, made an extraordinary move. It conferred upon Governor Houstoun practically the powers of a dictator because the members felt that the situation in the state was truly alarming, and that "without the most spirited and vigorous exertions the machinations of our Enemies threaten to Succeed."[59] If certain eventualities occurred that required "instantaneous measures," and there was no time for the Governor to call his council together, that body deemed it constitutional for the executive power to be vested in a single person to exercise the prerogatives of government pertaining to the militia or to the defense of the state. By the supreme power assigned to him Governor Houstoun was given the pledge of the council to uphold him. After considering the action of the board, Houstoun expressed himself as unwilling to take any action without the sanction of the council. He had found by experience, he said, that it would be difficult to gather the members together hurriedly, "when much depended upon a minute," but he agreed to act, as the council requested, during the crisis, or until the House of Assembly gave a contrary order.[60] The latter concurred in the emergency law by empowering the Governor to draft two hundred slaves from confiscated estates for the use of the Continental Army, or for the expedition against East Florida, to do fatigue duty. It was plainly evident that the state's authoritative powers sustained Governor Houstoun and his expedition against St. Augustine.

5

One of Houstoun's chief correspondents was his old friend in Charles Town, Henry Laurens, to whom he wrote from Savannah, June 9, 1778, referring to some of the acts of Congress, about which its president had informed him. He mentioned that South Carolina had aided Georgia by sending eight hundred men and a great number of volunteers to join the Georgia militia at the Altamaha River, adding that "no business was being done in matters of Civil Government."[61] Shortly afterward Governor Houstoun set forth on his Florida campaign to be joined by

---
59. *Ibid.*, 75-77.
60. *Ibid.*, 76.
61. *Henry Laurens*, Letter Book, V, 16, 139. MS. owned by the South Carolina Historical Society, Charleston.

Colonel Micajah Williamson of South Carolina. During the Governor's absence, the executive council was presided over by the president of the House of Assembly.

Two previous expeditions to East Florida were unsuccessful. One in 1776 led by General Charles Lee whose troops marched no farther than Sunbury, and the other, in the spring of 1777, commanded by Colonel Samuel Elbert, went only thirty miles below the mouth of the Altamaha River, when the discouraged commander ordered the expedition to return to the Satilla River.[62] Undaunted by those failures, Houstoun prepared for a march into the enemy's territory, with the capture of St. Augustine as the objective. His dream of subduing the British in Florida and thus preventing an invasion of Georgia, was doomed to disaster, for three commanders disagreed on the question of the right to direct maneuvers: General Robert Howe, in command of Continental troops; Commodore Bowen, commissioned by the House of Assembly, commander of Georgia's naval forces; and Governor Houstoun, leader of the state militia. When, on July 1, 1778, the three contingents joined forces at Fort Tonyn on the Florida side of the St. Mary's River, heated arguments began. Governor Houstoun held the position that with the authority granted to him he could not yield his right to command; Commodore Bowen refused to subordinate himself to anyone, contending that he was supreme in his naval department; and General Howe maintained that as an officer under the Continental Congress his authority was not to be disputed. In addition, there was Colonel Williamson who said his men refused to be subservient to a Continental general and would take orders only from him.

Governor Houstoun's attitude toward his military position in the Florida campaign was criticized severely by contemporaries and has been condemned by historians. The campaign was a tragic failure, but the type of army regulations exhibited at Fort Tonyn was characteristic of what was occurring throughout the colonies. It exemplified the resistance to authority, and resembled an adolescent emerging into maturity without proper training to assume responsibility. Georgia had hardly reached the adolescent stage. From pioneer days to the year 1778, the state was only forty-five years old. Preparation in that brief period of col-

---

62. Jones, *History of Georgia*, II, 248, 249, 269, 297.

onization, compared to that of some of the other colonies which had been in existence from six or seven decades to one hundred and seventy years, made Georgia incapable of conducting a military campaign. Governor Houstoun's refusal to bow the knee to anyone was entirely wrong in the light of modern warfare. As a military proposition the whole plan could not have succeeded without one commander. But it must be remembered, too, there was at that time only a vague amalgamation of the Thirteen States trying to hold together under a loosely framed document designated "Articles of Confederation and Perpetual Union Between the States," and a Continental Congress presided over by a president. What historians have omitted in their reports is a view of the campaign from the side of Georgia's Governor. He was not more than thirty years of age; he had been given dictatorial power by those who had the right to confer it, and he may have felt that he would not have been justified in shifting his responsibility. With that aegis to hold before him, the Governor of Georgia, with his state militia, numbering about three hundred and fifty men,[63] felt he must hold his ground. And John Houstoun was steadfast to what he believed his duty.

It has been said, "had a masterly mind been present, quickly would those discordant elements have been consolidated; rapidly by stern orders and enforced discipline, would the army, in all its parts have been unified and brought into efficient subjection. But there was no potent voice to evoke order out of confusion—no iron will to dominate over the emergency."[64] John Houstoun, apparently, endeavored to manifest both a mind and a will, but he was out-generaled.

General Howe, a native of North Carolina, was Governor Houstoun's senior by fifteen years; he had had two years active training in actual engagements on the battlefield, and had risen to the rank of major-general in 1777. Houstoun had practically no military training; he was young, spirited and a born leader. The aim of the expedition was to "destroy the British power in Florida."[65] The troops were transported through Georgia roads and through her waterways to the enemy's territory, with the

---
63. *Ibid.*, 289.
64. *Ibid.*, 298.
65. Coulter, *History of Georgia*, 126.

object of protecting the state from British invasion. It would seem that a solution of the problem might have been reached among the wrangling commanders if Howe had handled the Governor of Georgia more tactfully.[66] Perhaps he did try to do so and found the Governor obdurate. The general of the Continental Army was a man of wider experience and knowledge, not only in military tactics but matters in general. This criticism of the Continental officer seems justified from the fact that he called a council of war composed entirely of military leaders, excluding the Governor and Colonel Williamson. That might be called tactless; it was certainly discourteous and bordering on insult, from a layman's point of view. General Howe's officers upheld him on every detail that he submitted to them. One important point which he gave them was that he had accomplished the aim in delaying enemy troops from entering Georgia. Following the council meeting, General Howe left the Continental troops under the command of Colonel Elbert, and withdrew his headquarters to Savannah. It was not long afterward that Colonel Elbert followed with his troops, leaving Governor Houstoun and Colonel Williamson at Fort Tonyn. Those two officers, bereft of the assistance upon which they depended, planned an advance on St. Augustine, "conceived in a spirit of pride and vainglory"[67](!), but they soon abandoned it, and the officers and men returned to their homes. However, it had been conceded that the campaign, although foolish, had delayed the advance of the British troops into Georgia, and, astonishing as it may seem, in the month of November Georgians cherished another undertaking with a larger force; but the tide of events which flowed at that time turned their attention from the proposed campaign.

It is interesting to compare the later life of the three men whose antagonism caused a military campaign begun in a spirit of patriotic fervor to result in collapse. The conduct of General Howe cost him his good name in Georgia, because, although the House of Assembly held a court of inquiry and he was acquitted,

---

66. The supposedly angry combat of words between General Howe and Governor Houstoun was not the first time the former's authority had been questioned. In 1777 General Christopher Gadsden of Charles Town disputed with General Howe the right to command, the altercation resulting in a duel. Jones, *History of Georgia*, II, 324, 325.
67. *Ibid.*, 302.

he never recovered from the disgrace of losing the capital of Georgia to the hated British. He did not lose standing, however, in his native state.[68] He was replaced by General Benjamin Lincoln, who remained in charge of the Southern Department until the coming of General Greene, the year following the fall of Charles Town. Commodore Bowen did not fare so well. In August, shortly after the Governor's return to Savannah, news reached the executive council at their meeting on August 25, that the naval officer had circularized the Navy Board of his intention to leave the state, whereupon it was ordered that before the Commodore's departure, the Navy Board must require him to make a full settlement of all his public accounts of the galleys under his command.[69] In November, Commodore Bowen wrote such an insulting letter to Governor Houstoun that the House of Assembly, by resolution, requested the latter to suspend Oliver Bowen from a "command within the State." The executive council on November 15 ordered that the same be carried out. The house passed a further resolution which was sent to the council requesting that Bowen be referred to a proper tribunal for trial. At its meeting of December 2, the council decided that the only proper and competent board before which the Commodore could appear was the House of Assembly, because the latter had commissioned him under the State constitution.[70] He eventually went north and died in Rhode Island in 1800. As will be shown by the ensuing narrative, John Houstoun's reputation in Georgia was not impaired by the unfortunate episode in Florida nor was his career blighted. If the affair was discussed among the members of his council, no record was made either of censure or of commendation on the Governor's conduct in the campaign. Houstoun was present at the council meeting on August 5 when the Florida campaign was not mentioned.

At the council meeting of September 18, consideration was given to the information of the brutal acts of the Creek Indians

---

68. Alfred Moore Waddell, *A History of New Hanover County*, Privately printed (Wilmington, North Carolina, 1909), 41.
69. *Revolutionary Records of Georgia*, II, 87, 119.
70. *Ibid.*, 122. As there are no records extant of the Assembly of Governor Houstoun's first administration, no further information on the trial is obtainable from that source. In the year 1784, the executive council refused Bowen's petition for bounty land. *Ibid.*, 587.

within the state, and it was deemed "prudent and necessary" to make provision against further depredations. Accordingly, detailed instructions were planned for the militia of the counties of Wilkes and Richmond to give the alarm for calling out the regiment if the intelligence should require such action. Scouting parties were to be kept for that purpose on the county frontiers. Acting on instructions from his council, Governor Houstoun wrote on September 20, 1778, to Governor Richard Caswell, of North Carolina, apprising him of the situation in Georgia:

> I am sorry to inform your Excellency that Indian Affairs in this Part of the Continent at present wear the most serious aspect. The Creek Nation have actually begun a war and within this Fortnight passed have killed and cruelly butchered upwards of thirty of the Inhabitants of this State. Every Appearance seems to indicate that the Arts of our Enemies have at length prevailed and brought the Savages to espouse their Cause. The Tragedy of the Susquehana Settlement suggests that it is our Duty to catch the Alarm and be prepared against Contingencies.
>
> We have in Concert with South Carolina set on Foot a negociation, and in peremptory Terms demanded Satisfaction. What the result of this will be, a little time will inform Us, but for my Part I expect no answer but the *Hatchet*. their insolence and daring Conduct in driving off Cattle and Horses before the face of the owners for some Months past, have given Us to understand what progress the Enemy were making in their Friendship. and to accomplish their Points these more Savage Investigators have not been wanting in the most Profuse Presents.
>
> Under Circumstances like these, lie, we persuade ourselves your State will, if the negotiation now afoot should prove abortive, afford the most ready and generous Assistance, and that it will with the four Southern States be deemed a Common cause to subdue an Enemy whose indescriminate Attacks would of themselves produce such a Confederation.
>
> I shall take the earliest Opportunity of informing your Excellency of the Fate and Consequences of our requisition of the Creeks, and in my opinion if they hesitate we ought to be decisive. a powerful Army marching against them would have more weight than all the Treaties and Talks that could be in-

vented. and should they prove obstinate their country will pay us as we conquer it.[71]

On October 1 Governor Houstoun wrote to his friend, the President of the Continental Congress, conveying to Henry Laurens the news that war had commenced between Georgia and East Florida, and that persons from Florida in armed boats had carried off forty-four Negroes from the island of Sapelo. "The Creek Indians," he continued, "have broke with us and cruelly butchered upwards of thirty of our Inhabitants. . . . The enemy have adapted themselves to the Genius of the Indians, and have paid them for scalps taken indiscriminately from men, women and children." Again on November 25 the Governor wrote to President Laurens about the war: "The Enemy from East Florida entered the State of Georgia by land. Their savage warfare beggars description. The Parrish of St. John now presents one continued scene of horror, ruin and devastation."[72] Early in December the House of Assembly adjourned, but the executive council continued to hold its meeting through December 26.

The change in events referred to above was due either to the stupidity of General Howe, or to his unwarranted lack of military acumen. Slowly but surely the British troops were advancing upon Savannah, employing, as Governor Houstoun had written, cruel measures as they proceeded. General Howe was in command of Savannah in December, 1778, with six hundred and seventy men comprising his Continental troops, and a small detachment of the militia. Had Howe remained there and kept the town in a state of siege, the consequences would have been reversed. Surrounded on the east by tidal rivers and marshes, on the north by a navigable river, and having on the south a road fairly well protected, Savannah might have resisted capture. Because General Howe failed to heed the advice of his officers, certain strategic creeks were left undefended, and because of betrayal by a Negro, Colonel Augustin Prevost with his forces entered Savannah on December 29, 1778. The little town was in a panic. So was General Howe. He and his army retreated into South Carolina by way of one of the ferries, leaving Savannah to its fate.

---

71. The Historical Society of Pennsylvania.
72. Henry Laurens, Letter Book, V, 16, pp. 142, 144.

JONATHAN BRYAN

Silhouette from the collection of the late Charles Spalding Wylly, of Brunswick, Georgia

Courtesy of Mrs. M. Hines Roberts, of Atlanta, Georgia

6

According to tradition, Governor Houstoun was in hiding at Retreat, the home of his brother George. Naturally, the British were searching the town and the outlying territory for the "Rebell Governor," and on hearing of his probable hiding place they sent a boat and crew up the Vernon River through the creek on which Retreat was situated, to capture him. But a messenger carried the news to the Governor, and he had just time enough to run through the garden into the woods behind the house and climb a live oak tree where he remained until the raiding party took its departure.[73] If that incident really occurred, John Houstoun lost no time in leaving a place of danger for one of safety, since he made his escape to Augusta where he had ordered the seat of government to be removed. When John Houstoun left Savannah at the first sound of British troops, his departure was so hasty that he had no time to gather up and take with him his own important papers. His inability to do so, while unavoidable, was most unfortunate, as it later brought evil consequences upon a valued friend.[74]

John Houstoun's term of office ended the first Tuesday in January, 1779, and later in the month when he was at Purrysburg, South Carolina, Colonel Campbell, then in command of

---

73. The account of the incident was found in the papers of the late James Houstoun Johnston.
74. See *post*, 228. In explaining the loss of some of the records of Georgia in the year 1778, Allen D. Candler, editor of the *Colonial and Revolutionary Records*, makes conflicting statements in the prefaces of the two series regarding Governor Houstoun's orders for the preservation of state records. In the preface to Volume I, page 3 (1904) of the *Colonial Records*, he states: ". . . . When Savannah fell into the hands of the British in December, 1778, the Secretary of State, Captain John Milledge, by order of Governor Houstoun, conveyed the most important records of his office and those of the Governor to Charleston to prevent their capture by the enemy. . . ." In the preface to Volume I, pages 3, 4, of the *Revolutionary Records* (1908) he contradicts his previous statement: ". . . when in December, 1778, Savannah, the seat of government, was captured by the British, all the records of the state prior to that time were also captured and either carried away or destroyed except a few relating to the office of the Secretary of State which were saved only by the vigilence of the encumbent of the office, John Milton, who disregarding the orders of Governor Houstoun, conveyed his records . . . to Charleston." Candler gives no documentary proof for either statement.

Savannah, was still searching for the notorious and elusive rebel, John Houstoun. As soon as Savannah was captured, British vessels, under the command of Sir Hyde Parker, moved on to the town and one of the galleys continued up the river as far as the tide would allow. The object of Sir Hyde Parker's next move was to locate Governor Houstoun[75] after the failure of the raiding party to White Bluff. Suspicion rested on Union, at Purrysburg, the plantation of Jonathan Bryan, the friend and father-in-law of John Houstoun. The party of soldiers dispatched to Union did not find the man they were seeking, but found instead an elderly patriot and his son, James Bryan, who were immediately taken captive and put on board a prison ship.[76] Jonathan Bryan's wife and daughter, Mary Morel, widow of John Morel, with her little son Bryan and undoubtedly Mrs. John Houstoun, were at the plantation when the two Bryans were arrested. One of the daughters importuned for her parent and brother, beseeching Commodore Parker "to soften the suffering of her father, but with no avail, for she was treated with vulgar rudeness and contempt."[77] Jonathan Bryan and his son James, then twenty-six years old, were taken to Charles Town, and finally reached Long Island, where for over two years they were imprisoned and suffered extreme hardships. One of the Bryans' oldest children, William, thirty-five years of age, was not arrested when the father and younger brother were captured; so it is inferred he was in the troops of the Patriots.

In mid-January Colonel Campbell was detached with British forces numbering one thousand men to capture Augusta and thus complete the subjugation of Georgia. Advance information undoubtedly reached Governor Houstoun which made it necessary

---

75. From a letter addressed to Lord George Germain written by Major General Prevost dated January 18, 1779: "On the first of January, Lieutenant Clarke of the *Phoenix* was dispatched with row boats about seventeen miles up the Savannah River. . . . Upon information that the late Rebel Governor was at a plantation on the South Carolina Shore. . . ." White's *Historical Collections*, 605.

76. Information on the Bryan family was obtained from entries in the Jonathan Bryan Family Bible and were furnished by the late Mrs. Franklin Buchanan Screven of Savannah, who copied them from the original Bible, now in the possession of the family of the late Mrs. Willoughby Sharp of New York City, lineal descendant of Jonathan Bryan.

77. Hugh M'Call, *History of Georgia*, II, 176.

for him to leave the state before the House of Assembly met in Augusta to elect a new executive council on January 8. John Houstoun went to Purrysburg, South Carolina, where soon after the capture of Savannah, General Benjamin Lincoln, on January 3, 1779, arrived to assume charge of the Southern Department of the Continental troops, and established his headquarters.

A month after his arrival in Purrysburg, John Houstoun received a letter from his friend, George Walton, a war prisoner in Savannah, who begged the ex-governor to obtain his release. He wrote to John Houstoun on February 8, 1779, and the letter was addressed to the "Honorable John Houstoun in South Carolina":

> I received your very friendly and welcome favor a few days after my captivity, late at night and just before the return of the flag by which it came: so that had I have had strength, I had not had time to acknowledge it.
>
> Although my wound was generally thought mortal at first by all the surgeons, yet, by their skill, and some other fortunate circumstances, I hope I am now out of danger. I am, however, still confined to my bed, and expect to be so for some time, the cure of such wounds being very tedious.
>
> I must particularly request that your attention be directed towards an Exchange or liberation of the Militia taken with me. I have wrote to General Lincoln upon this subject, but I cannot say that his was explicit and satisfactory—I would have you look into it. The men are confined on Board Prison ships: and must suffer much in the course of the hot season. I trust that my liberty will be provided for against the recovery of my health. We were taken during your Administration, and therefore expect your assistance upon this occasion.
>
> I must request also that you will use your endeavors to procure me some hard money: for altho, by the bounty of those to whom I am Prisoner I have hitherto had everything either necessary, convenient or comfortable, yet it will soon be especially necessary that I should have some coin to keep me current. My situation rank and relation to this country, will, I hope, excite the necessary executions, somewhere, to supply me: but I wish to depend upon you.
>
> Upon these several subjects, be pleased to let me hear from you. I am with compliments to Mrs. Hounstoun . . . .[78]

---

78. Historical Society of Pennsylvania, MSS. Department.

George Walton was not liberated until September, 1779, which fact would seem to indicate that John Houstoun was unable to procure an exchange for his friend.

Upon reaching Purrysburg, John Houstoun learned of the plight of his wife's father and brother, and soon afterward took up their cause by using his influence with the former president of the Continental Congress, then a delegate from South Carolina, to whom he appealed in seeking to have Jonathan Bryan and his son exchanged and returned to their home. The president of the Continental Congress from 1777 to 1778 was John Houstoun's friend, Henry Laurens. After the latter's sojourn in England he returned to Charles Town and entered vigorously into the patriots' cause in his native state, especially in the provincial Congress "where he continued one of the most prominent leaders in South Carolina affairs until his departure for Congress."[79] He took his seat there on July 22, 1777, succeeding John Hancock as president on November 1st of the same year. Evidence of existing letters shows that a regular correspondence continued between the two friends, Laurens and Houstoun, and sometimes the communications were of a most confidential nature. In a previous letter John Houstoun had written to Henry Laurens, January 2, dating his letter, "Georgia," (John Houstoun was undoubtedly in Augusta then) when he informed him that Savannah was in the hands of the enemy and described the capture.[80] Because of their close affiliation John Houstoun felt free to appeal to Henry Laurens in Philadelphia in behalf of the Bryans. The letter was written from Purrysburg, January 22, 1779:

> I had forgot to mention in my letter the case of Old Mr. Bryan and his Son James. They were, three nights after the action at Savannah formally taken by a small Party of the Enemy from the Plantation in South Carolina called The Union and immediately put on Board a Prison ship called the Whitby. Mr. Bryan two days ago by some means got a letter to his Wife wherein he says he was just then ordered on Board the man of War and was immediately to be sent to New York—if an Exchange can be effected for him I dare say his age and your former Acquaintance with him will be sufficient Advocates in

---

79. Wallace, *Life of Henry Laurens*, 199. Laurens resigned the presidency December 8, 1778. *Ibid.*, 235.
80. Laurens, Letter Book, V. 16, p. 145.

his Favor to induce you to cause particular attention to be paid to his Case.[81]

But the wretched situation of the Bryan prisoners could not be altered so easily. On June 5, John Houstoun again wrote to Laurens from "South Carolina," saying: "In my former letters I took the Liberty of stating to you the Capture and Treatment of your Acquaintance Mr. Jonathan Bryan since which I find that Gentleman has been sent to N. York and is now a Prisoner on Board a Prison Ship at that place. I rest satisfied as do his Wife and family that nothing in your Power will be omitted to get him exchanged and restored to his Country as soon as such a Measure can be effected Since the Enemy make an Object of Resentment of him we ought in my Opinion for the same Reason make him an object of particular attention, and so far as relates to those who know him, I am persuaded this will be the case. Major Rice being just setting off I must conclude."[82]

That Henry Laurens was doing his utmost to arrange with British authorities for an exchange of prisoners is shown by a letter which he wrote to Jonathan Bryan from Philadelphia July 14, 1779:

> I received but a few days since your Letter of the 20th June. Almost in the same moment in which your favor by Genl Thomson reached me, I was informed that yourself & Mr. Bryan your Son were gone from New York under a flag for Georgia, this false intelligence restrained my pen & stopped the progress of a Letter from Mrs. Bryan which will now accompany this. I have cut the paper from the seal, knowing the impropriety of attempting to send sealed packets to a prisoner of War without special permission, but I am totally ignorant of the contents, the signature only excepted. I have before me a Letter from Mr. Houstoun dated the 5th June Mrs. Bryan and your family were then well.
>
> Congress will not consent to exchange Citizens in the manner you were captured, all solicitation on that head would be fruitless.
>
> If the Commander in Chief of his Britanic Majesties forces at New York will permit you to return to Georgia on parole &

---

81. Burnet, *Letters of Members of the Continental Congress*, IV, 321. Quoted from Laurens Letter Book, 1778-1782 (South Carolina Historical Society, Charleston), V. 16, p. 147.
82. *Ibid.*

your son also, I will pledge my honor that a suitable exchange shall be made or that both shall be forthcoming whenever a demand shall be made, when I reflect on the many instances of similar consideration which on our part have been extended to British Officers who have been in peculiar circumstances, I cannot help concluding that an application to Sir Henry Clinton will meet with success.

I am persuaded if Sir Henry knew of the many acts of kindness which as an individual I have shown to British prisoners he would not hesitate a moment, even upon my request for your enlargement on the terms above mentioned....

You Sir, who have been schooled in the doctrine of Christian fortitude will not suffer your spirits to sink under a light weight, reflect that you are on Long Island, where you enjoy wholesome air & have a proper scope for exercise, the contracted sphere of a ships hold occupied by 100 inmates might from an old man, extort a groan. In your present situation be thankful a little practice will make you cheerful.[83]

Two days after he had sent his letter to Jonathan Bryan, Laurens wrote to John Houstoun:

In answer to your favor of the 5th June permit me to assure you I have done everything in my power to assist our worthy friend Jonathan Bryan Esq. to whom I writ a Letter Yesterday, Copy of which you will receive herein and to which I beg leave to refer.

While I remain in Philadelphia my attention shall be continued and I trust I shall find means of obtaining his enlargement and you will observe that in my plan I include his Son....[84]

Mrs. Bryan and her daughters were safe at Purrysburg as long as General Lincoln's troops were occupying the town, and that was up to April, 1779, at which time Lieutenant Colonel Prevost began his march into South Carolina. General Lincoln had set out for Augusta on April 20, with two thousand light infantry, and General William Moultrie was left at Purrysburg with one thousand men, but on the approach of Colonel Prevost he retired toward Charles Town. Colonel Prevost crossed the Savannah River at Purrysburg and advanced as far as Port Royal,

---

83. Courtesy of Mr. Charles Francis Jenkins. Original in his private collection.
84. Burnett, *Letters of the Members of the Continental Congress*, IV, 321.

South Carolina, where he established a post, leaving a detachment there while he returned to Savannah.

It seems likely that when the above happened, Mrs. Bryan and Mrs. Morel, with the latter's little son, succeeded in slipping over to Georgia to their Brampton plantation, while John Houstoun and his wife hastened toward Charles Town, as the former was later referred to as "a refugee in South Carolina."

As late as December 27, 1779, John Houstoun again wrote to Henry Laurens about the Bryan men. Henry Laurens did not succeed in obtaining the release of Jonathan and James Bryan, as they remained prisoners at Long Island until the end of the war. To maintain his health and vigor, Jonathan Bryan was allowed to exercise while in captivity: "He swum around the prison ship in New York Harbor for exercise while British grenadiers watched him from the decks with muskets ready."[85]

7

In the spring of 1779 John Houstoun's friend, Henry Laurens, was placed in an embarrassing position before the members of the Continental Congress through the unintentional negligence of the former Governor of Georgia. Among the papers which John Houstoun was forced to leave behind him when he made his hurried exit from Savannah in late December, 1778, was a confidential letter from Laurens, President of the Continental Congress. The letter, in which Laurens severely criticised some of the delegates to Congress, was most indiscreet, considering the dangerous times, for it was written on August 27, 1778. While Congress was in session in May, 1779, the communication, purporting to be one from former President Laurens to Governor Houstoun of Georgia, appeared in Revington's *New York Gazette*. Its aftermath was the creation of several turbulent scenes in the United States Congress. On May 14, a Virginia delegate, Meriwether Smith, moved that the letter which he asserted "contained matter derogatory to the Congress," be read and that Laurens be called on to state whether or not he had written it.[86] The motion was defeated, and the next day Laurens, who was a mem-

---
85. John Stewart Bryan, *Joseph Bryan: His Times. His Family. His Friends. A Memoir*. (Privately Printed in Richmond, Virginia), 20.
86. Wallace, *The Life of Henry Laurens*, 347.

ber of the South Carolina delegation, and no longer in the chair, spoke in his own defense, first stating his opinion of the manner in which the delegate from Virgina had brought the matter before the House. Congress, and especially Henry Laurens, had had a long siege debating the Deane-Lee feud. Partisan politics over the two foreign representatives was seething, tempers were high and nerves were taut. On May 15 Laurens defended himself on the floor of the Continental Congress explaining that " . . . if I have been guilty of aught criminal or have inadvertently expressed anything amiss in my correspondence as a private citizen with Mr. Houston, I would rather receive a censure or a reproof from Congress than be charged with a want of candour, or commit my conduct to the whispers of malice, I take the liberty of informing Congress that I did on the 27 of August, write a private letter to Governor Houston."[87] The South Carolinian offered to submit the letter to Congress if requested to do so, but his offer was not accepted. The following day Smith, the Virginia delegate, presented his side in a written statement, asking that, as Laurens' paper, was, by vote, entered in the journal, he be granted a like privilege, but a negative vote denied the Virginian's request.[88] A contemporaneous writer put it that in the letter to "Governor Huiston [sic]," Laurens "had unbosomed himself with the unsuspecting confidence of a person communicating to a friend the inmost operations of his mind. In a gloomy moment he had expressed himself with a degree of severity."[89] The debate in Congress reached the ears of General Washington, then at his "own headquarters in the Jerseys in the neighborhood of Middlebrook."[90] It " . . . added much to the alarm with which [he] viewed that security which had insinuated itself with the public mind."[91] How damaging the Laurens letter in question was, can be seen:

> I am constrained to say that unless the several states will keep their representation in Congress filled by men of competent

---

87. *Journal of the Continental Congress*, XV, 293, 592, 593.
88. *Ibid.*, 610-613.
89. John Marshall, *The Life of George Washington* . . ., (Fredericksburg edition, New York, 1925), III, 88, 89.
90. Worthington Chauncy Ford, *The Writings of George Washington*, (New York and London, 1890), VII, 454.
91. Marshall, *The Life of George Washington*. (Fredericksburg edition), 89.

ability, unshaken integrity and unremitting diligence; a plan which I very much fear is laid for the subduction of our Confederate Independence will, by the operation of masked enemies, be completely executed; so, I mean, as relates to all the seacoast, and possibly to the present generation. Were I to unfold to you, sir, scenes of venality, peculation and fraud which I have discovered, the disclosure would astonish you; nor would you sir, be less astonished were I, by a detail which the occasion would require, prove to you that he would be a pitiful rogue indeed, who, when detected or suspected, meets not with powerful advocates among those who, in the present corrupt time, ought to exert all their powers in the support of these much injured . . . states. Don't apprehend, sir, that I color too highly or that in any part of these intimations are the effect of rash judgment or despondency. I am warranted to say they are not. My opinion, my sentiments, are supported every day by the declarations of individuals; the difficulty lies in bringing them collectively to attack with vigor a proper object. I have said so much to you, sir, as Governor of a State, not intended for public conversation, which sound policy forbids; and at the time, commands deep thinking from every man appointed a guardian of the fortunes and honor of these orphan States.[92]

But what about John Houstoun? How did he feel when he learned that through him his good friend Henry Laurens had been placed in a most unhappy position before the United States Congress? In time the information was conveyed to him, and it will be seen that his contrition was not lessened because the fortunes of war made those in whom he had confidence betray his trust. Writing from Round O, South Carolina, December 27, 1779, he gave a partial explanation of the publication of the ill-fated letter:

> It would take a long time to unfold to you Sir the manner in which your Letter to me published in the *New York Gazette* and which the Enemy mistakenly thought to draw an advantage from fell into the hands of Col. Campbell. Suffice it at this time, and until I have the pleasure of seeing you, to say and I assure you I was in no fault, the Enemy got it with many others of my papers thro' the unkindness of Forgetfulness of some — and the treachery of others from whom I expected things, how-

---

92. Wallace, *Life of Henry Laurens*, 289. Also, Henry Laurens, Letter Book, V, 17, No. 44, marked "Copy."

ever I was fully compensated in my feelings to find that it was intended by those desponding Agents of Injustice as a deadly Blow to your Reputation, terminated so much to your credit and advantage with every upright man in America.[93]

Before John Houstoun's letter reached him, Henry Laurens had resigned the presidency of the Congress because of the Deane-Lee feud, and was succeeded by John Jay of New York. He was appointed on a commission to Holland, but he returned to Charles Town before he could leave for The Netherlands. It was probably then that he and John Houstoun met and talked over the whole incident. It was not until after the first part of 1780 that Laurens set out on his mission abroad. The ship on which he sailed was captured off the coast of Newfoundland, and he was taken to London where he was imprisoned in the Tower for over a year. On his release December 31, 1781, he remained abroad serving with the Peace Commissioners in Paris, and engaging in diplomatic negotiations in London, trying to hasten the end of the war. He did not return to the United States until August, 1784.

Besides his correspondence with Henry Laurens, John Houstoun found consolation in communicating with another friend, Edward Langworthy, who was educated at Bethesda Orphanage, near Savannah, where later he became a teacher. Langworthy was a former secretary of Georgia's Council of Safety in 1775, Secretary of the Georgia Constitutional Convention in 1777, and at the time of his writing the letter to John Houstoun on April 5, 1779, he was an elected delegate to the Continental Congress. Langworthy understood John Houstoun's motive, and praised, rather than censured him, for his conduct in the campaign to East Florida. The primary object in writing to Houstoun was to introduce two officers, Major Mathew Clarkson and Major David S. Franks, who were then proceeding to join General Lincoln in the south. The letter was written from Philadelphia, April 5, 1779.

> ... I cannot express to you my distress for the misfortunes that have attended the inhabitants of my Country. It was always my Opinion, that something of this kind would happen, unless decisive measures were adopted against East Florida and I was highly

---

93. Henry Laurens, Letter Book, V, 16, pp. 335-337.

John Houstoun, "Rebell Governor" 233

pleased when I perceived that you were convinced of this point. I am conscious of what Efforts you have made to save an unhappy People, the difficulties you have encountered and what Chagrin you must have felt on being disappointed in your expectations, however, I would not have you despair, for I have abundant reason to assert that I make no doubt of your being again restored to your Country.[94]

Wherever John Houstoun was located at that time, at least the Georgia executive council and President, John Wereat, had been apprised. The seat of the government had been set up again in Augusta, and at a meeting held on August 31, 1779, the council balloted for delegates to represent Georgia in the Continental Congress. For the third time John Houstoun was chosen a delegate with Edward Telfair and Edward Langworthy. Three days later, September 3, the Council "ordered That Mr. President do write to Mr. Houston and Mr. Telfair acquainting them of being elected Delegates."[95] Again John Houstoun did not go to Philadelphia.

Since Edward Langworthy was advising John Houstoun of the addition to General Lincoln's troops of two northern officers, it seems an indication that Houstoun was already an integral part of the army that was fighting for the country's independence. He saw service in the Continental troops, as he joined the staff of General Lachlan McIntosh, who, after serving with distinction under General Washington, was ordered by the Commander-in-Chief of the American Army to join General Lincoln in Charles Town in the spring of 1779. The time when John Houstoun began his volunteer service in the Continental Army has not been ascertained, but he was definitely there in September, 1779. In the order book of Colonel John Faucheraud Grimké, of South Carolina, lieutenant colonel of artillery, is an entry to the effect that John Houstoun and several others, all "Volunteers in the Army are appointed Confidential Officers attendant on Gen'l McIntosh, & are to be obeyed & respected accordingly."[96]

---

94. Historical Society of Pennsylvania, Gratz Collection, Case 1, Box 21.
95. *Revolutionary Records of Georgia*, II, 175, 180. John Houstoun's second election as a Continental delegate took place on February 2, 1776. Jones, *History of Georgia*, II, 215; *Georgia Gazette*, February 7, 1776.
96. *South Carolina Historical and Genealogical Magazine*, XVII, No. 1 (January, 1917), 28.

John Houstoun's lines fell in pleasant places as General McIntosh was both a friend and a family connection. He was the brother-in-law of John Houstoun's sister. Since the ill-fated Florida expedition, Houstoun was a wiser man, having learned by bitter experience the first law of military discipline. Occupying no state office in 1779, it was then an easy matter to follow a superior officer, with no responsibility on his own shoulders. Since, in September, 1779, the American troops were planning the capture of Savannah, still in the hands of the British, and General McIntosh took part in the ensuing engagement, there is more than the barest possibility that Houstoun was with him in that fierce battle. It was on the afternoon of October 13 that McIntosh "formed a junction with the advance guard of Lincoln's army; and on the night of the 15th the two commands now wholly united, encamped at Cherokee Hill." John Houstoun, however, was not officially in the Continental Army.[97]

After the failure of the American and French forces to wrest Savannah from the British, John Houstoun probably joined his wife at Round O, as it was from there that he wrote to Henry Laurens in December of that year.[98] Round O was a settlement situated between a swamp or river of that name and the Ashepoo River, and about forty or fifty miles southwest of Charles Town. It was in the vicinity of Jacksonboro,[99] near which place it is likely that John Houstoun's plantation was situated. His wife was there the following summer. On June 11, 1780, Mrs. Bryan wrote from Brampton to her husband still on a prison ship off Long Island: "I heard from Hannah a month ago, at which time she was at Jacksonboro."[100]

While in South Carolina John Houstoun was attainted of high treason. When the Royal Legislature convened in Savannah in May, 1780, and passed the British Disqualifying Act, John Houstoun's name headed the list of persons "incapable from holding

---

97. Statement from the Veterans' Bureau, Washington, D. C., June, 1939.
98. See *ante*, 231.
99. Jacksonboro was a small village on the southwest bank of the Edisto, where the river is known by the name of Pon Pon. It consisted of the courthouse, jail, and two or three small houses, and was thirty-five miles from Charles Town.
100. Mrs. J. H. Redding, *Life and Times of Jonathan Bryan, 1708-1788* (Savannah, 1901), 84.

John Houstoun, "Rebell Governor" 235

or exercising any office of trust honour or Profit in the Province of Georgia . . . " as "late of this province Rebell Governor."[101] Although he had relinquished his office sixteen months previously, the opprobrium cast upon his brother disturbed George Houstoun with the result that he sent a memorial to the Commons House of Assembly which was read at its meeting in Savannah, June 8, setting forth "that having heard a Bill is now pending in this House for attainting and banishing, amongst which number is John Houstoun he begs leave to produce some Evidence on behalf of the said John Houstoun, touching his late conduct in the Province, which was granted him, several Gentlemen were called and examined accordingly." It was then ordered that "the said Memorial do lie on the Table for the perusal of the members."[102] By drawing on the imagination the scene in the Assembly easily can be pictured. No doubt silence greeted the last words of the reader as well as the evidence of the "several Gentlemen" who offered testimony on the late conduct of the former state governor. The delegates of the Royal Assembly in all likelihood listened with contempt or amusement while the memorial of George Houstoun, a Loyalist by that time, expressed the feelings of a devoted brother, defending one who was guilty of fighting against his king. With extreme care the secretary of the house omitted to give even a hint, as was often the case, of the content of the memorial or any of the testimony of the men who offered their opinion adversely or in favor of the former resident of the colonial capital. Some of the delegates of the Assembly may have had curiosity enough to scrutinize the document which did "lie on the table." At any rate there it rested, probably, until the secretary removed it with other papers, because the Crown legislators took no further notice of it in their proceedings. George Houstoun had his trouble for nothing, and the information was recorded as written.

8

While her father and brother still were held captives in New York state, Hannah Houstoun heard of the death of her mother in Augusta, March 21, 1781. Mr. and Mrs. Bryan had been married a little over forty-three years, and they had, in letters,

---
101. *Revolutionary Records of Georgia*, I, 348-363.
102. *Colonial Records of Georgia*, XV, 590, 591.

expressed their fear that they would never see each other again. The unhappy prisoner on Long Island wrote to his wife on June 3, 1780: "expect to see you no more on this side of time, as I decline fast, but shall meet you in heaven."[103] Before his letter reached her, Mary Bryan had written to her husband in her June 11 letter from Brampton: "We are far advanced in years [he was seventy-two] and according to the course of nature cannot live long."[104] In less than a year the husband's prophecy was fulfilled and his life companion had passed away.

Just five months after his wife's death Jonathan Bryan and his son James were back in Georgia. From the day of Jonathan Bryan's recorded reappearance at a meeting of the executive council, in Augusta on August 26, 1781, that body held fifty-four meetings through December 28. During that time Jonathan Bryan attended thirty-eight of them. In the month of November when the Council met fifteen times, Jonathan Bryan was absent once. That was an extraordinary record for a man who had endured the hardships and confinement of a prison ship and inferior rations for at least a year and a half. When his son James took the oath of office as treasurer on August 30, Jonathan Bryan was not present at the meeting of the executive council, although he did attend the next day. Even in the year, 1782, Bryan lived up to his reputation for regular attendance at the meetings of the council, as he was present twenty-two times out of twenty-six through January and February.[105] Thereafter it would appear that he returned to his plantation near Savannah, as his name was absent from the roll until July 14, after which time his regularity was obvious.

John Houstoun was recalled to Georgia in January, 1782, at the meeting of the House of Assembly of the state, held in Augusta on January 3. Letters were read to the members from the delegates in the Continental Congress enclosing an account of money drawn by the State of Georgia from the Continental Treasury. A committee was appointed to whom the matter was referred, and the next day William McIntosh from the committee re-

---
103. Redding, *The Life and Times of Jonathan Bryan*, 82.
104. *Ibid.*, 84.
105. *Revolutionary Records of Georgia*, II, 256-399.

ported "that John Houstoun Esq., be cited to appear in this state to render an acount of all money he has had in his hands on Account of the same and in case he refuses to comply, that application be made to the Executive Authority of South Carolina for sending him into the same agreeable to the Articles of the Confederation." Nothing in John Houstoun's previous mode of conduct could make the committee suspect that he would be unwilling to return to Georgia, or that he was incapable of accounting for all the money that had passed through his hands during his term as governor. No doubt he was most happy to be called back to his native state, but it must have been to Ebenezer that he first returned, since the British were still confined in Savannah by General Anthony Wayne.

The former Governor's financial report must have proved satisfactory in showing his disbursements of Continental funds, as on April 20 John Houstoun's name was read with three others as a delegate from Chatham County. He did not appear in the assembly, however, until July 3, when the legislature met in Ebenezer,[106] having adjourned there from Augusta, as the evacuation of Savannah seemed imminent. Houstoun was present then as an accredited delegate, and he continued his membership throughout the year.

July 11, 1782, was a happy day for expatriated Savannahians. In the morning the British troops evacuated Savannah, and in the afternoon General Anthony Wayne marched in with his troops and took possession of the town. He accorded to General James Jackson the honor of receiving at the principal gate the keys of the city as a symbol of the surrender. Governor Wright was conveyed by ship to Charles Town, other military officers were sent to New York, and Loyalists, women, children, Indians, and Negroes, left for Florida and the West Indies. After three and a half years of Crown rule, Savannah was again in the hands of republican leaders. The members of the legislature followed upon the heels of the departing Loyalists, and on Saturday, July 13, the assembly reconvened in Christ Church. John Houstoun was again present. When the assembly met on Monday, a committee on "privileges" and elections was appointed which later in the day reported "that they refer the right of John Houstoun and Thomas

---
106. *Ibid.*, II, 38, 44, 109, 118.

Maxwell Esquires, taking their Seats in this Assembly to the determination of the House." The house ordered that the report be considered the following day, when it was unanimously of the opinion "that the two delegates had a right to their seats in this House."[107]

On the day the Georgia assembly reconvened in Savannah, provision was made immediately to have some meeting place other than the church. A committee was appointed to request Governor Martin to order the public filature to be fitted up and put in order for the use of the assembly. Apparently the plan did not carry, for, soon after, the house met in a room at the home of Lucy Tondee and continued to sit there throughout the year 1782.[108] Back in harness once more, after four years absence from the routine of legislative activities, the ex-governor of Georgia was immediately drafted for committee work. The speaker of the house, James Habersham, waited until Wednesday before naming John Houstoun a committee member. His first assignment with William O'Bryan,[109] another delegate from Chatham, was to "Provide Accommodations Diet and other necessarys for the Members of this House during this Session and any engagements they may make or moneys they may advance; this House will comply with or reimburse them before the rising thereof."[110] There were forty-one members of the assembly at that session, seven of them from Chatham County. During the months of July and August, John Houstoun served on ten other committees: to bring in bills for opening the courts of justice; to establish churches and schools in the state; to report on the business necessary to be done before the house adjourned; to consider a letter from Daniel Murphey, superintendent of Indian

---

107. *Revolutionary Records of Georgia*, III, 122, 127.
108. *Ibid.*, 187, 544.
109. While governor of Georgia John Houstoun had occasion to write to Benjamin Franklin in London, March 17, 1778, "That the son of a Georgian, Mr. O'Brian, who was sent to school at Smith's Academy near London, the report prevails that he has been trepanned on board a British man-of-war in the Thames and detained as a prisoner; begs Franklin to enquire into this matter and if it is true, effect an exchange." From Calendar of the Franklin Papers, v. 1, p. 377. Letter found in v. 8, no. 175 of the Franklin Papers in the Library of the American Philosophical Society, Philadelphia.
110. *Revolutionary Records of Georgia*, III, 132.

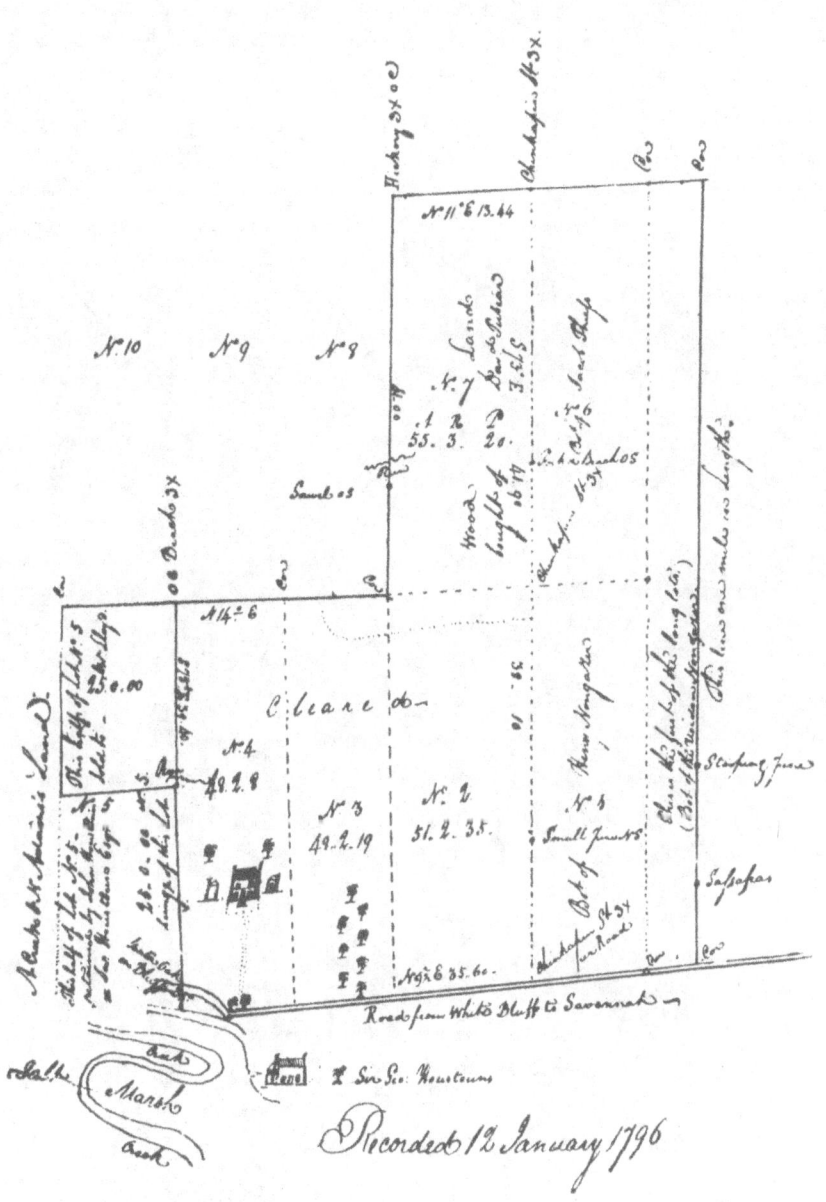

PLAN OF JOHN HOUSTOUN'S WHITE BLUFF PROPERTY
Chatham County Court House, Book P, [17]95, [17]96, p. 128.

John Houstoun, "Rebell Governor" 239

affairs, setting forth the desire of a number of Indians who wished shortly to pay a friendly visit; to inquire into the abuses that had been committed to the public boats, and the "quantity of Salt ordered to be sent up to Augusta for the use of the Inhabitants of the Back Country." He was also put on special committees: one to consider a letter from Brigadier General Wayne, enclosing a "Talk" to the Creek Indians; one to consider a proclamation to the inhabitants of East Florida; and another to take into consideration sundry recommendations from the governor. As chairman of the committee to consider the letter from General Wayne, John Houstoun brought in the report the day after appointment, which was Sunday, August 4, recommending that a committee be appointed to wait on the general and express to him the "high sense the house entertained of his important services already rendered to the state, giving him assurance that all of his plans and operations will have for their object the welfare of this and the other confederated states. . . . "[111] LeConte and Houstoun were continued on the committee to carry out the recommendations of their report. The last committee appointment received by John Houstoun at that session was to be one of the members to revise the minutes of the house and "to see that the Speaker sign the same." The date of adjournment was Monday, August 5, and the time set for the house to meet again was the third Tuesday in October. When that day arrived, October 15, "a number of the House of Assembly met but not being a Sufficiency to compose a House they were Adjourned till tomorrow morning at 10 o'clock." The same thing happened on Wednesday, Thursday, Friday, Saturday, and Sunday, and on Monday John Houstoun's name was listed for the first time as being present, but still there was no quorum, and on that day, October 21, "there being no likelihood of making a House,"[112] the legislature adjourned until the opening of the new assembly.

The time allotted for attendance and committee work at the July and August meetings was exactly twenty days and included some Sundays. The Chatham County delegates who were associated with John Houstoun, besides the speaker, James Haber-

---
111. *Ibid.*, II, 386; III, 147, 157, 163, 176, 177, 179, 180.
112. *Ibid.*, 188-191.

sham, were Joseph Clay, John Gibbons, Joseph Woodruff,[113] Frederick Rehm, and William O'Bryan. While the assembly was in session, John Houstoun's father-in-law, Jonathan Bryan, was attending regularly the meetings of the executive council.

While John Houstoun was a refugee in South Carolina, and the British were occupying Savannah, Dr. Lewis Johnston, provost marshal, advertised for sale "a lot in Savannah and one hundred and fifty acres in the township of Vernonburg . . . with dwelling house, buildings, hereditaments, members and appurtenances,"[114] all the property of John Houstoun. Neither sale was consummated, and it is evident that the Houstouns went to White Bluff to live when they returned to Georgia after the evacuation of the British from Savannah. On June 13, 1782, John Houstoun bought, through the board of commissioners appointed the previous month to take possession of confiscated estates, fifty acres at White Bluff, formerly owned by Robert McCormick, and for which he paid one hundred and twenty-seven pounds ten shillings. The tract was across the road from Houstoun's plantation on the one leading to Coffee Bluff. The frontage faced the creek, and gave a view of the Vernon River and the woods beyond. Two of the Houstoun brothers were neighbors, as Retreat, the plantation of George Houstoun, was across the road leading to Savannah.

With the opening of the year 1783, the Georgia House of Assembly was in session the first Tuesday in January. John Houstoun was returned as a member from Chatham County, and with him in the delegation was his brother William Houstoun. After the delegates had qualified, the temporary chairman, Benjamin Andrew, was chosen and a few committees were appointed, followed by the balloting for governor. Lyman Hall was elected. The next morning at 9 o'clock the house met, selected the executive council, and "the house then Proceeded to the Choice of a speaker When John Houstoun Esqr was elected."[115] After appointing the committee to draw up an address to the

---

113. Joseph Woodruff's relationship to George Woodruff, if any, has not been ascertained.
114. *Royal Georgia Gazette*, September 13, 1781.
115. *Revolutionary Records of Georgia*, III, 193. Also *The Gazette of the State of Georgia*, January 30, 1783.

John Houstoun, "Rebell Governor" 241

governor-elect, the new speaker's first official act was to sign the document on which the address was written, "John Houstoun, Speaker," as soon as the committee brought it in.[116] Houstoun presided Wednesday, Thursday, Friday, and Saturday, and he opened the house on Monday morning. The previous Friday Dr. Noble Wimberly Jones had taken the oath of a delegate as prescribed in the constitution. Monday morning John Houstoun made an unusual gesture in favor of an older man. If there was any motive to be put on his forthcoming act the minutes of the legislature fail to assign it, but simply state: "Mr Houstoun expressing a desire to decline The Chair in favor of Mr Wimberly Jones who arrivd [sic] since the choosing of a speaker the same was agreed to by the House and Mr Jones Accordingly took the Chair as Speaker."[117] Consideration for one with whom he had been associated closely on many occasions may have influenced John Houstoun in his resolution to waive his election as presiding officer of the house which had chosen him. But that may have been the understanding when he was elected. As presiding officer of the Georgia legislature, Dr. Jones was by no means a novice, and he was certainly popular with its members. As far back as 1768 he was elected to the office and served. He was chosen again in 1770, but the Royal Governor, Sir James Wright, refused to sanction the election because of Dr. Jones's views on the oppressive acts of Parliament. When the house was informed of Governor Wright's decree the members declared "it was a high breach of its privileges." For its incendiary attack on the governor, he immediately dissolved the assembly. When James Habersham was president of the Royal Council and acting governor in 1772, the house again chose its popular member, Dr. Jones, for its presiding officer, and so notified Habersham, who responded: "I have His Majesty's commands to put a negative on the Speaker now elected . . . ." Nothing daunted, the delegates' choice again fell on Dr. Jones, but naturally their vote for the second time received Habersham's disapproval. Dr. Jones was thus left to take his place as one of the leaders in the cause of liberty, and at the momentous convention of 1777, called to frame

---
116. *Revolutionary Records of Georgia*, III, 194.
117. *Ibid.*, 211. Also, *The Gazette of the State of Georgia*, February 2, 1783.

the first constitution of the state, he was at last in the chair of the presiding officer.

When John Houstoun stepped down from the rostrum in January, 1783, and Dr. Jones replaced him, the first act of the latter was to appoint John Houstoun one of a committee of three to consider the cession of lands from the Indians. Immediately afterward the chair appointed William Houstoun on an important committee. During the remainder of January and until February 18, the house met continuously, and of the numerous committees appointed, both standing and special, John Houstoun was assigned to serve on twenty. On February 18, the house adjourned to meet again in Augusta on May 15, but when that day arrived, once more there was no quorum, and the members who attended adjourned until the following day. William Houstoun's name appeared among the eight listed, but John's was missing. The few members who met from day to day endeavoring to "compose a House" finally decided to suspend business until July 1, when by proclamation of Governor Hall they re-convened in Augusta to be met with the same discouraging situation. John Houstoun attended on Monday, July 7, with his brother William, and the next day a sufficient number of delegates was present and the house proceeded to business. Petitions of those wishing to be taken off the amercement act or to be restored to citizenship, and reports from committees occupied the time of the members; and a record of the yea and nay votes shows that John Houstoun attended the meetings with regularity as did his brother. One special matter that was usually referred to "Mr Telfair, Mr Clay and John Houstoun,"[118] pertained to messages or papers presented from the governor. Such routine business came to a close the first of August when the assembly's work was finished for the year. The executive council, meeting concurrently, also adjourned on August 1 to Savannah where it held its sessions at the governor's house, and continued to meet periodically until the end of December.

The legislature met in Savannah the first Tuesday in January, 1784, but again lacked the required quorum of delegates for the transaction of business; so adjournment was in order until the

---

118. *Revolutionary Records of Georgia*, III, 355.

John Houstoun, "Rebell Governor" 243

next day, January 7, when nineteen "Gentlemen attended," among them John Houstoun returned from Chatham; the gentlemen qualified and took their seats, "But not being a Number Sufficient to Compose a House & Proceed on Publick Business they were Adjourned to Tomorrow Morning 9 OClock."[119] The next day, Thursday, January 8, brought better results, for ten more delegates arrived and the house proceeded to business by electing James Habersham speaker. The usual routine business continued until the special committee appointed to procure a place for the accommodation of the house reported that the "House in the temporary Possession of Hezekiah Wade was a fit Place for the Purpose," whereupon the meeting adjourned to Wade's residence. Other delegates arrived in the meantime, the number in attendance totalling forty, and with the arrival of eight additional members from Richmond County who were qualified and took their seats, "the House then Proceeded to the Choice of a Governor and on casting up the ballots John Houstoun Esqr was elected.[120] Next in order was the election of the executive council to serve with the governor, and the appointing of the committee to draw up the address to be delivered to him. That committee consisted of James Jackson and William Gibbons from Chatham and William Few from Richmond. Adjournment until the next day followed. In the morning the committee reported; the address was read, and then signed by the speaker. The same committee had been assigned to wait on the governor-elect to apprise him of his election. The members reported that John Houstoun had signified his acceptance, and that he would attend the afternoon session to qualify and give an address to the house. True to the arrangement the new Governor was present at four o'clock. Addressing the members, he pledged himself to carry out his full duties:

> Mr Speaker and Gentlemen of the Honorable House of Assembly. This Repeated and Unsolicited Mark of Approbation from My Country, cannot but excite in my breast sentiments of the Warmest Gratitude and Affection, And whilst on the one hand I feel some Reluctance at departing from a Resolution I had formed of confining myself in future to Private life on the other I am free to confess that the Present deranged State of

---
119. *Ibid.*, 418-420.
120. *Ibid.*, 422, 424.

our Publick concerns both as they respect our Federal Connexion & our internal Police—seems to Require that every Man should contribute his Part in the Sphere Assigned him by the Suffrage of his Fellow Citizens, towards the Accomplishment of a Respectable and Permanent System under the influence of this Impression, I shall not hesitate to Sacrifice all Considerations of a domestic nature to the superior duties of My Relative Station—and therefore agree to Accept of the Honor of your Appointment.

The toils and Dangers of War being now done away, by a Peace as Glorious as beneficial to our Country, Permit me to Assure you it shall be the Chief end and Pride of my Administration to improve the event into the most lasting Security for all the Rights and Privileges of Freemen—And Convinced as I am of the Necessity of Law and Government in order to Render Society a blession [sic] no Exertions on My part shall be wanting to reduce Refractory Individuals to a sense of what they owe the Community and on yours I shall trust for that Support which so desirable subject demands.[121]

John Houstoun was not destined to see the fulfillment of his desire to live as a private citizen for there lay before him ten years more of public service. Having delivered his address to the legislature, Governor Houstoun left the house to meet with his executive council with whom for the next twelve months he was to carry on the executive branch of the government of Georgia. The men who were associated with him, two from each of the six counties, Liberty, Burke, Wilkes, Richmond, Chatham, and Effingham, with John Habersham, the president,[122] were acquaintances of long standing. They had worked and served together for several years on committees and in the legislature, and that fact gave to the Governor the assurance of sympathy and understanding from his board. John Houstoun's regularity in meeting with his council was marked. The only times he failed to be present were the meeting after he took office on January 16, and the one on March 4; thereafter throughout his term, "His Honor the Governor" headed the list of those present at each meeting. One of the first tasks that confronted him on taking office was that of signing grants to applicants for two hundred or more

---
121. *Ibid.*, 427.
122. *Ibid.*, II, 576.

acres in the new counties Franklin and Wilkes, created out of the lands which had been added recently by cessions from the Indians. During the year Governor Houstoun signed over thirteen hundred and seventy-five grants of land covering hundreds of thousands of acres.

The Governor and council were constantly called upon to hear petitions from individuals desiring restoration to citizenship and from others who wished to be taken from the banishment act and put on the amercement list. It was not unusual for the Governor to take to his council certain queries on which he wished advice. Routine matters continued through January and February, and on the twenty-sixth of the latter month the House of Assembly adjourned its sessions.[123]

Although peace was signed in Paris, September 3, 1783, the official notification did not reach Savannah until six months later. At the council meeting held on Monday, March 1, 1784, the Governor laid before the Board some official dispatches sent through Governor Guerard, of South Carolina, by an express, for which the Governor of Georgia gave a draft to the treasury for ten guineas. Among the official papers was the ratification of the Definitive Treaty of Peace by, and a proclamation from, the Congress of the United States. The document received immediate consideration from the council which made plans for celebrating the event on the ensuing Wednesday. It was ordered that the "Printer" be furnished with a copy of the proclamation, and that he be directed to publish it in the two succeeding issues of his newspaper.[124]

The day was notable for Savannah. It was spent in gaiety and festivity and "with perfect decorum"! The proclamation was read and published through the town by the "Sheriff," and the men of Savannah feasted and drank toasts. What the women were doing the reporter failed to note, but from the town's unfailing custom on such occasions, they can be pictured with children of all ages and sizes and their Negro nurses, lining the streets as the parade marched by. The following day the *Georgia Gazette* gave a graphic account of the proceedings:

> ... The Militia of Savannah and its vicinity were paraded on

---
123. *Ibid.*, III, 574.
124. *Ibid.*, II, 601, 602.

the occasion, and after being reviewed by his Honor the Governor, Attended with the members of Council, and a number of Gentlemen, were marched to the East Green, where a barbecue being prepared for the militia, they spent the day with that mirth and felicity which so joyous an event naturally inspired. The Governor and Council, the Speaker and Members of Assembly, the Chief Justice, and Assistant Justices, the Honorable the Delegates to Congress; the Civil officers of the State, the Officers of the Military and Navy, Several Gentlemen of the Clergy, Law and Physick a number of Citizens, Captains of Vessels, and Strangers dined together at the Savannah Tavern, where the following toasts (with a number of others suitable to the occasion) were drunk: May the definitive Treaty of Peace be perpetual and Productive of liberty and universal benevolence; The United States in Congress Assembled; The State of Georgia; Our magnanimous and illustrious friend Louis XVI; The States of Europe which have demonstrated their Friendship to our Sovereignty and Independence; General Washington; The American Ministers at Foreign Courts; Integrity and firmness to the Governors and Magistrates of the respective states; The immortal remembrance of the great and heroick [sic] characters who have sacrificed their lives for the liberties of their country; Relief to all our friends who have suffered by the calamities of war; May the efforts and suffering of the brave defenders of their country never be forgotten; The friends of virtue and freedom throughout the globe; Uninterrupted Commerce and a truly respectable Navy. Each toast was accompanied with a discharge of cannon. The evening concluded with illuminations and bonfires, and the whole of the rejoicings were remarkably distinguished with decorum and propriety of conduct.[125]

In the latter part of April, the Governor informed his board that he had received a letter from Count d'Estaing, dated December 20, 1783, claiming twenty thousand acres in Georgia which had been promised to him; also one from Sieur Antoine Reiré Charles de la Foresté, informing him of his appointment as Vice Consul of France in Georgia, and that he had arrived in Charles Town where he had received orders to remain and perform the duty of consul until someone was appointed to take his place. Accompanying the letter was one from Congress, vouch-

---

125. *Georgia Gazette*, March 4, 1784.

ing for the character of Sieur de la Foresté asking the Government of Georgia to recognize him and to publish his appointment in the *Gazette*. Congress further advised Georgia's governor that the French agent was furnished with the powers from Count d'Estaing to take possession of his acres. The council decided that as the acres had been promised to the count a warrant should be issued to the land court in Augusta directing the surveyor general to "admeasure" and lay out the number of acres in one of the new counties, but reservation was made to wait until the assembly met in July before acting. In September, Governor Houstoun signed the grant, donating 20,000 acres in Franklin County to the French nobleman. The council disposed of the request of the Sieur de la Foresté by deciding that the executive authority could not furnish him with an "Exequatur or Notification of his quality" until his arrival in the state. The council requested the Governor to communicate the "substance of these resolves" to the French agent as early as possible.[126]

9

The ever perplexing, as well as vexing, question of the Indians cropped up again in Governor Houstoun's second administration. "Talks" with the Indians, present-giving, and arguments on the land cessions continued over the years, but the problem came up for the first time in Governor Houstoun's second regime when at a council meeting held on June 1, a copy of a letter from Alexander McGillivray was read "respecting the temper of the Indians, and their dislike to settlements [by whites] on the Oconee lands."[127] The subject was not new to Governor Houstoun. In January of the previous year, it had been discussed in the assembly, which appointed a special commissioner to hold a conference the following year with "the Kings and Beloved men" of the Creek and Cherokee nations.[128] While not a member of the commission, Governor Houstoun was familiar with the object for calling the congress, namely to demand a cession of land from the two nations as an atonement for many injuries perpetrated on some of the inhabitants of

---
126. *Revolutionary Records of Georgia*, II, 640, 717.
127. *Ibid.*, 655.
128. *Ibid.*, III, 207.

Georgia, and to renew the treaty of peace and friendship with the Indians. In 1783 the congress was held, and in February, 1784, the House of Assembly was informed by Edward Telfair, one of the commissioners, that he had promised presents to the "Tallise and the Fat Kings" in consequence of their fidelity . . . during the late war and for their support in the acquired cession." The assembly authorized the expenditure of fifty pounds to be applied for buying the presents.

Alexander McGillivray was the "aristocrat of the Creeks." The blood of four nations flowed in his veins; his father was Lachlan McGillivray, who emigrated to America from Scotland and settled in the back country of Georgia in the early colonial period. He married a Creek princess whose father was a French officer of Spanish descent. Alexander was educated by his father's relative, a Presbyterian minister of Charles Town, but later returned to his mother's people where he was accorded the pomp and deference of royalty. His influence was so great among the Creeeks and their allies that he was able to call 10,000 warriors to his side if he wished. He aided the British during the Revolution and for so doing Georgia confiscated his lands within what was claimed were the state's borders. Following the congress of 1783, McGillivray entered into negotiations with the Spanish governor of Pensacola. The story back of the time when Alexander McGillivray entered into correspondence with Governor Houstoun can be told briefly. After the original treaty with the Indians was signed in the time of Oglethorpe, more and more land was required from the Lower Creeks, although the territory was claimed by the several governments in Georgia as being in the original grant of the colony which extended west to the Mississippi River. When Alexander McGillivray established himself in the Creek Nation in 1783, he began what may be called his career, and he was then in his late twenties. The time was propitious for the Indians of that nation, as they had been abandoned by the English at the close of the Revolutionary War, and their trade interests likewise were neglected. Furthermore, the Creeks resented the encroachment on their lands by people from Georgia, who had settled on what the Creeks claimed was *their* territory. McGillivray took upon himself the leadership of his mother's tribe and began negotiations immediately with the Spanish governor of Florida to whom he wrote that the Creeks desired to be under the protection of Spain. The intrusion of the Georgia settlers incensed the Creeks. They protested that when the British were forced to desert them, they were not relinquishing a country that had never belonged to them because they were a free nation. They were allies, they said, and not dependents of England. The problem in 1784 was one of trade. McGillivray was carrying on a secret campaign with the Spanish authorities in Florida, and on May 31 and again on June 1, 1784, a congress was held at Pensacola where a treaty or "articles of agreement trade and peace," was drawn up and signed by McGillivray and three Spanish Officials.[129] On July 14 a head man and several others of the Creek Nation attended Georgia's executive council and delivered a talk from their nation, which was answered by the Governor in council. One week later a letter from McGillivray was laid before the executive council, and it was directed that a copy be sent to Lieutenant Colonel Elijah Clark, who had been ordered to take the necessary steps for "protecting the inhabitants of the several districts within his batalion," but he was "to take the utmost care not to do any act which may hastily bring on a rupture with the Indians if the same can be avoided." At the same meeting of the council, July 23, 1784, the Governor was authorized to sign a draft for £52, 16s, 11d to pay for the presents purchased for the "Tallasee and the Fat Kings."[130]

What occurred later can best be told by McGillivray himself, who wrote from his plantation, Little Tallassee on the Coosa River, September 18, 1784, to Charles McLatchey, William Panton's store keeper at St. Mark's, of Apalachee, Florida:

> Yesterday I received letters from St. Augustine from Governor Zespedes and another from Mr. Panton, urging me to come to that place at once, which is absolutely impossible for me in my present circumstances. One of my reasons is that a negotiation is pending between Governor Houston of Savannah and me. When Mr. Panton was here I wrote him a strong talk, which he has received. It was argued in the council, and was not a reproduction of mine. Nevertheless, in his reply, he says to me

---

129. John Walton Caughey, *McGillivray of the Creeks* (Norman, Oklahoma, 1938), 76. Also *Revolutionary Records of Georgia*, II, 666-670.
130. Caughey, *McGillivray of the Creeks*, 72.

> that the matter of my talk is of such importance and magnitude that he will take the occasion very soon to submit it to the consideration of the legislature, which is certain to be convened this month. I have returned him an appropriate reply and have submitted to his future consideration that he recommend to them that they determine upon Indian affairs, if not upon the principles of equity and justice, at least upon those of same politics, attending to the demands of the Indians, for only thus could there be honor and security for both parties. Enough of politics! . . . [131]

Governor Houstoun's official connection with McGillivray and the Creeks seems to have been terminated in the autumn. Again McGillivray supplies the information when he wrote from Little Tallassee to the Governor of Pensacola, Arturo O'Neill, November 20, 1784:

> I have taken this opporty. to Acquaint Your Excellency that I have been detained at home so long in expectation of receiving some dispatches from the American Governor of Georgia in answer to what I wrote him about our Lands on the Oconee river. The other day the tame King[132] arrived from Augusta & I have the Satisfaction to inform Your Excellency that the Americans have given a very Satisfactory answer. The Governor & assembly have forbid the Settling of those lands in the Strongest Manner so that the apprehensions I had that we Should be obliged to go to war with them to defend our lands is now at an end. But I must observe to Your Excellency that the americans are very uneasy that this Nation has entered into an alliance with the Spanish Nation, & that they have granted leave to English Merchants to Supply this Nation with a trade from the Floridas, because such Measures have made the Indians Independent, & not beholden to the americans for trade, so that they cant have the Sway of the Indians but have lost it, by this stroke of Policy in the King of Spains officers, who held the Congress with this nation in Pensacola. These are the true reasons that makes the americans pretend to be so moderate to us, tis out of their jealousy to Spain & I do not Thank Them for it . . . .[133]

---

131. *Ibid.*, 80, 81. From Spanish Translation, Library of Congress, East Florida Papers, 166L9.
132. A chief of the Creeks at Little Tallassee.
133. Caughey, *McGillivray of the Creeks*, 89. Quoted from Archivo General de Indias, Papeles de Cuba, Seville, Co., 197.

The Creek question, however, was not to be settled in Governor Houstoun's administration.[134]

An important matter came up in 1784 which affected Georgia's territorial rights, and five years later John Houstoun was to react to it by taking a significant stand in the interest of the state he loved so well. At a council meeting held in Savannah on June 18, 1784, the members noted that "certain persons in the State of South Carolina, have attempted to run the lands lying in the forks of the Tugaloo and Kiowee branches of Savannah River, and certain other persons have attempted to form settlements on the Western Territory of this state as is represented to this Board by the Governors of Virginia, and North Carolina—all which acts are manifestly encroachments upon *the property of this state*."[135]

The board reached the decision that it was "necessary and expedient that the Governor publish a proclamation[136] of the State as defined by the original Charter and late Treaty of Peace." Houstoun was directed to answer the letters of the governors of the above mentioned states, and to send a commission under the Great Seal to Dr. Noble Wimberly Jones in Charles Town requesting him to enter a caveat in behalf of Georgia against any grants of lands in the aforesaid district, to be signed by the Governor of South Carolina.[137]

Like Governor Houstoun, North Carolina's Governor Caswell was serving a second term. On June 20 Houstoun wrote the North Carolina executive describing as "unwarrantable" the "Encroachments attempted or intended." Continuing, the Georgian explained that he had issued a proclamation, a copy of which he was sending Governor Caswell.[138] In his proclamation Houstoun made it clear that not only Georgia's Charter to the Trus-

---

134. The United States Government and McGillivray signed a treaty of peace in 1790. He was paid $100,000, and given a commission as major general in the United States Army. See *Appleton's Cyclopaedia of American Biography* (1888), IV, 119. It was not until 1827 that the last vestige of Creek lands was ceded to Georgia by President John Quincy Adams. Coulter, *History of Georgia*, 215.
135. The italics are the author's.
136. *The Gazette of the State of Georgia*, June 24, 1784.
137. *Revolutionary Records of Georgia*, II, 661, 662.
138. The Historical Society of Pennsylvania.

tees, but the Treaty of Peace of 1763 and the Definitive Treaty of Peace of 1781 substantiated his understanding of Georgia's boundary which he defined on the north as extending from the mouth of the Savannah River along the north side to the most northern stream or fork which he stated included the land lying between the Tugaloo (being the southern) and the Keowee (being the northern) streams or branches of the Savannah River, "which plainly and manifestly belong to Georgia."[139]

A month later the board heard from Dr. Jones concerning the caveat. Governor Houstoun replied that he was authorized to do nothing further than to enter it "and then let the matter rest for a decision agreeable to the articles of consideration."[140] The minutes of the executive council record nothing further on the subject during the rest of the year 1784, but the irritating dispute of the boundary line between northeast Georgia and western South Carolina was to remain an unsettled question for many years.

Just before he went out of office, Governor Houstoun received a letter from John Hill who lived in Houstonborough, a town that was evidently named for him.[141] Dated December 2, 1784, the Hill letter opened on an apologetic note and quickly turned to praising "our town Houstonborough, on the Long Bluff, on the Oconey River." "I am sartin [sic]," boasted the writer, "[Houstonborough] will be one of the best Places of trade of any upland town in Georgia." What Hill wanted was "about twenty publick muskits" to prevent "any sudden attack by a credulous Indian who has forfeited there [sic] word so often." Excusing himself for his "tedouse way" of expression, Hill concluded his communication to the Governor.[142] What Houstoun did about Hill's request is unknown.

In the closing months of 1784, the date arrived for the election of representatives to serve in the General Assembly for the coming year, and again John Houstoun was one of the fourteen

---
139. *The Gazette of the State of Georgia*, June 24, 1784.
140. *Revolutionary Records of Georgia*, II, 675, 676.
141. Houstonborough apparently can be classed among the dead towns of Georgia, as no reference to it can be found.
142. Miscellaneous Papers, 1784-1799, Box No. 3, Georgia Historical Society Library, Savannah. No references to the letter could be found in the *Revolutionary Records of Georgia*.

INTERIOR VIEWS OF THE RESIDENCE OF JOHN HOUSTOUN ON REYNOLDS SQUARE, SAVANNAH, GEORGIA

The house was demolished in 1920

men to be elected from the county of Chatham. But that act was to bring more trouble on the head of Governor Houstoun, who several times had the misfortune of becoming the victim of circumstance or intrigue. He had the happy faculty, however, of extricating himself with honor. As the constitutional date for the election was set for the first Tuesday in January, Governor Houstoun and his council, like their predecessors, remained in office over the beginning of the new year. In the last weeks of December, and for a few days in January, the Governor's pen was kept busy signing furiously grants of land in the new counties and drawing drafts upon the treasury for individuals for various purposes, among them being one in favor of James Jackson, attorney-at-law, one to David Rees for his year's salary of twenty-five pounds as secretary of the council, and one to James Powell for twenty-eight pounds eighteen shillings eight pence for "being two months attendance in council."[143]

The council met on January 3, 4, 5, and 6. On the last date the minutes record: "This day the Honorable House of Assembly having proceeded to the choice of a Governor for the current year, the present Governor and council considered their Term as expired, and therefore did not meet again."[144] Thus John Houstoun's gubernatorial career came to an end, but on retiring he did not escape the toil or pleasurable duty of serving public interests. Innumerable bills brought before the House of Assembly during his administration were resolved into progressive measures for the betterment of the state, and passed on into acts of law, signed by Governor Houstoun.

Retiring from office, John Houstoun, on June 6, 1785, repaired to the House of Assembly to take his seat as a representative from Chatham County, but his right thereto was declared illegal because at the time of his election he held the office of governor. Technicalities of the house were overcome out of court, and a few days later Houstoun presented himself with others to the assembled body of delegates and "qualified." There-

---

143. Marbury and Crawford, *Digest*, 227. The Governor's fees 1784 for signing grants of land were: for 500 acres or more, 5 shillings 8 pence; over 500 to 1,000 or more, 4 pence; ordering the Great Seal to any paper of a private nature, 4 shillings 8 pence, the sums to be paid into the treasury for public use.
144. *Revolutionary Records of Georgia*, II, 786.

after, his committee work continued throughout the year as in the previous sessions of the legislature when he was a delegate.

10

Two years after their return to White Bluff, John and Hannah Houstoun began preparations for their residence in Savannah, which, when completed, probably in 1784, was the most pretentious in the city.[145] As early as 1773 Houstoun selected the site for his future town residence, although there is no evidence that at that time he contemplated building there. On January 8 of that year he bought from the estate of David Murray five lots containing one hundred and fifty feet front, and ninety feet deep, on what was then Duke Street, between Abercorn and Lincoln streets; but three days later he sold the western half to James Chapman. Perhaps John Houstoun had an eye to increasing his earnings, and made a profit by the transaction. While he was a fugitive in South Carolina, his half of the Duke Street property was advertised for sale, along with other lots, in the *Royal Georgia Gazette* of February 1, 1781. Evidently there was no purchaser and Houstoun claimed the lots after Savannah was evacuated by the British, as, on April 3, 1784, Chapman reconveyed his half to John Houstoun. It seems proper to assume that shortly after that date he began the building of his spacious two-story dwelling. "The simplicity of its exterior probably expressed his republican principles; the elaborate and beautiful interior bespoke the aristocrat."[146] The foundation of the house was of brick, traditionally reputed to have been imported from Holland, and the exterior walls were of wood. The Georgian doorway was supported by delicate columns, and the short flight of steps leading up from both sides to a stoop held a wrought-iron railing. The wide entrance hall with groined ceiling led through a beautiful mahogany archway to a graceful, winding stairway surmounted by a Palladian window. The stairway, the paneled wainscoting of the hallway, and the woodwork in the rooms on the first floor were of Santo Domingan mahogany. The

---

145. From Walter C. Hartridge in a forthcoming book on Savannah homes and architecture.
146. Florence Marye, "An Eighteenth Century Georgia Mansion," in *Atlanta Journal*, October 13, 1936.

house was built under the "immediate inspection" of the owner.[147] The stories were high. On the first floor were three large rooms and two small rooms, one of which was John Houstoun's library; and on the second floor were three large bedrooms and one small one. "The library was a room of great charm and dignity.... Lovely mantels in all the first floor rooms were imported from Italy, and the plaster work was as delicate and elaborate as any nineteenth century examples in America."[148] Underneath the house were good cellars, and the outhouses were of stone and brick. They consisted of a wash house, servants' rooms, carriage house and stable, and there was also a well. A three-sided brick wall east of the house concealed a formal garden, and on a bricked back yard was the long line of service buildings.

During their twenty years' occupancy, John Houstoun and his wife furnished their home with period furniture of mahogany. There were a "sweep" sideboard, table and chairs of the same wood in the dining room; card and tea tables, sofa, chairs, a "Pride of India" table, "window" chairs upholstered in blue, mirrors framed in mahogany and gilt, probably in the drawing rooms; fenders, fire dogs, shovels and tongs, apparently for every room; mahogany chests of drawers; bedsteads with "feathered mattresses pavilions and quilts"; and for the owner's personal use, a mahogany arm chair and a "mahogany table and dressing glass"; there was "one crib a pair of blankets & quilt." Was there once a baby of their own? Of the smaller furnishings the Houstouns possessed the usual silver and glass found in other homes of wealth, among the pieces being silver castors "with glasses compleat," silver decanter stands, with glass decanters; long jelly glasses, chafing-dishes, and other appurtenances. During the years of his law practice, John Houstoun increased his law library to one hundred and thirty volumes, and there were dozens of books in his house library. The Houstouns had several equipages, among them a chair, a chair-box, a four-wheeled carriage, and a sulky. They had a bay chair horse, a "cream" cart horse, and at least four others, and they kept a cow.[149]

---

147. Hartridge, manuscript on Savannah homes and architecture. See also *Georgia Gazette*, August 6, 1801.
148. Marye, "An Eighteenth Century Mansion."
149. Ordinary's Office, Chatham County Court House. From an inventory and appraisement of John Houstoun's estate made August 20, 1796. Box H, 1-47, No. 22. Conforming to the "march of commerce," the

II

The year 1786 was one of intense political excitement in Georgia, and since it affected John Houstoun the man, it is necessary to recount the story in detail. In February the House of Assembly sat in Augusta, with Governor Telfair and his executive council meeting concurrently in the same town. The incident that started the imbroglio might be characterized as the beginning of the bitter and long-lasting feud between the "up counties" and the "low counties" for the balance of power in state government. It is rather surprising to find that the part played by John Houstoun in the fray has been slurred over and decidedly misrepresented, until one writer unearthed the whole story from original sources and presented the true and enlightening facts.[150] The long-drawn-out controversy began calmly enough on February 9 when the House of Assembly elected its state officers. One week later it chose other officials, among them John Houstoun as chief justice. The legislature was meeting in Augusta to conform to a rule that its sessions be held there alternately to appease the representatives from the up counties. Since it had been decided the previous month that there should be a fixed seat of government, a place to be named, Louisville was selected by ordinance which further provided that the governor, the secretary, the treasurer, and surveyor-general, and the auditor

---

Houstoun-Johnston-Screven house was razed to make way for a moving picture theater. When the property was bought by the late Arthur Lucas, in 1920, he offered the house to the late Miss Eugenia Marion Johnston, who endeavored to interest the patriotic societies of Savannah to have it moved to a suitable site, to be used for their headquarters. Meetings were held to discuss the plan, estimates were obtained, and public interest aroused; but without avail, as the conclusion was reached that the cost (about $15,000) was prohibitive. (Correspondence and records on same in possession of the author.) The house was torn down, and when the theater was completed a bronze tablet was erected on the west wall, but it is unfortunate that the inscription thereon contains so many errors:

UPON THIS SITE
Where Arthur Lucas Built This Theatre
Which opened December 26, 1921
There stood the home of Sir [sic] John Houston [sic]
The First [sic] Governor of Georgia

150. The Editor, "A Neglected Period of Georgia History," in *The Georgia Historical Quarterly*, II, No. 4 (December, 1918), 198-224, from which the entire story was taken.

should reside in Augusta until provision was made for the officials to live at the new capital.[151] At the same time, the legislature took under consideration ways and means of transporting the public records to Augusta, until the anticipated buildings were built to house them. James Pearre, Jr., was approved by the executive council as a "fit person" to undertake the task. It was directed that the documents be packed in trunks and carried from Savannah in "good covered wagons, with four horses each, two drivers, and three able-bodied men well armed and accoutred," who, with James Pearre, were to act as a guard to remain with the convoy until it reached Augusta.

On March 4 John Houstoun received for the first time the official notice of his appointment as chief justice, his commission being presented to him by Joseph Clay and William O'Bryan, assistant justices, who informed Houstoun that they had been delegated by the Governor to qualify him. John Houstoun replied that he was fixed in his determination to decline the appointment, and asked them to transmit his answer to Governor Telfair. That night Houstoun wrote to the Governor declining the appointment.[152] John Houstoun's consternation may be imagined when he read in the *Georgia Gazette* of March 17, that "John Houstoun, Esquire, appointed to the office of Chief Justice be, and he is hereby suspended from exercising the duties of the aforesaid office." Suspended at the same time were William O'Bryan, Joseph Clay, and William Gibbons, assistant justices for Chatham County, and several justices of the peace. In a preamble to the suspension order, council expressed itself as follows: "When the events of human affairs are progressing to anarchy, and the leading principles of the Constitution are infringed, the laws and ordinances violated, and when conductors of the opposition to the known order of government are chiefly persons whose peculiar situation render the guardianship of the laws the object of their care, the crime is peculiarly aggravated.

"The Board, from the urgent necessity occasioned by such unwarrantable proceedings, and in order therefore that the fountain of justice may run pure, and the laws and ordinances

---
151. *Ibid.*, 199. Quoted from Watkins' *Digest*, 320, 321.
152. *Ibid.*, 210. Quoted from the *Georgia Gazette*, April 13, 1786.

may be fully executed in the County of Chatham, have and do solemnly . . . resolve . . . ."

In replying to the published act of the Governor and council, former Governor Houstoun wrote an open letter to the editor of the paper in which he expressed his sentiments in scathing language. The letter is an unduly long one, but it is quoted almost in its entirety because it is indicative of John Houstoun's mental growth in the eleven years since his maiden speech in the Continental Congress, because it brings forth his judicial knowledge, and because it shows his ability to write in the style of the day:

> There is in the affairs of life, a point at which absurdity itself disarms resentment, and assuming a coarser appellation, excites no emotion but that of pity or contempt. Had Solomon lived in our day and witnessed some late proceedings in our State, he would, in all probability, have retracted his opinion and confessed he saw in the political world, at least one new thing— a dismission from, preceding the acceptance, nay following the absolute refusal of, an office. Other countries for the advancement of justice in certain cases admit of fictions in law, but I believe it is essential to our land, and has been reserved for the ingenuity of a modern administration to invent fictions in government for the ends of private vengeance. Permit me to enquire what grounds of dismission from the place of Chief Justice could be applied to me? So preposterous an act must, in point of view, recoil, with disgrace, upon its author, and will forever remain a satire on record against both his head and his heart. Had I really been in possession, I make no scruple to say the edict of suspension would have made no more impression on me than a bull wrapt in all its terrors, and accompanied with all its thunders from the Pope. However malignant in its nature, I should have felt it extremely harmless in its effects. Dignities and honors, the children of sovereignty, flow from the people; and as, under our form of government, we ascribe neither majesty nor infallibility, and but a very moderate title of pre-eminence, to a Governor, it would be highly rediculous and inconsistent to sacrifice at his shrine the independence of a Judge, so essentially necessary, in the opinion of all writers, to national freedom and private happiness. Originally the only body in a free state entitled to question a judge for his conduct or opinion is the people. By the 49th article of our Constitution that power is delegated to the House of Assembly, but how or where the Governor

obtained by prerogative as it were a concurrent jurisdiction with
them is hard to discover. If his claim is founded it evidently
proves by direct inference the servant to be greater than the
master, or in other words, the Governor superior to the House
of Assembly; for the latter, however, impliedly powerful in
other respects, hold their controlling authority in this in consequence of a special grant from the people; whereas the former,
the being of the year, and politically speaking but secondary to
the people's choice his election being by the legislature, finds
a title to it comprehended, though till now concealed, in his
very appointment itself. Armed with such a weapon, and to
which may easily be added, as in the days of the Star-Chamber
of England, restraints upon the press, with an abolition of trial
by jury . . . what might not an ambitious man, with very
limited talents, accomplish? But there is no occasion to reason
on the general principles of government, or argue by analogy,
when we have a guide so directly in point. If the very first
section of the Constitution of this State does not make the
Judges as independent of the Governor as the Governor is of
them, I know not what form of words could be employed to
express such an intention. It is a misfortune incident to shallow
politics to be deceived by habit. Without recurring to reason
and principle we are apt to be misled by use, and conclude,
because of a King's Government formerly claimed the right of
suspending a King's Judge, therefore a State's Governor has the
same power over a State's Judge. But surely no man of common
intellect and who barely knows the difference between a mon-
archy and a democracy, will maintain such a position, or insist
on the comparison or inference being just. Besides, we are to
recollect that this political stride of Britain was, ever after
the Revolution of 1689, altogether confined to her American
governments, and is really one of the very acts of tyrany and
distinction assigned by Congress, in their Declaration of Independence, as causes of our separation; for in England, although
the twelve Judges hold their appointments from, and are, in
legal contemplation, servants of the Crown; yet the King has it
not in his power to suspend, much less to dismiss, one of them
from his office, or even to withhold or reduce his salary, unless
in consequence of a former address from both Houses of Parliament. So materially do the notions of our Cabinet on the scale
of liberty and politics differ from those of the world.

But, as I waved all pretensions to the office of Chief Justice,
it was not my intention, when I began, to enter into a discussion

in this place of the tenure by which it is held. All I mean, or am in anyway solicitous about, is to prevent, as far as I am concerned, any imposition on the public. To this end I shall lay before them a plain state of the case, and leave each one to his own remarks, as in truth the proceedings themselves will, to the most ordinary capacity, furnish a very sufficient comment.

The writer then recounted the interview with Clay and O'Bryan, and quoted verbatim his letter of declination to Governor Telfair. After his letter had reached the Governor, he received an order from the Council, bearing the date of March 13, empowering the Secretary of State to prepare a writ, or as the minutes record it a *dedimus potestatem*, empowering the three justices (Clay, O'Bryan, and Gibbons) to qualify him as Chief Justice of the State. Houstoun then continued to the editor:

> ... I took no further notice of the affair, until I was, on the third instant, again surprised by a receipt of another account that the Governor had suspended me from, and appointed a successor to the Office of Chief Justice. Whether it is not a perversion of language, under the circumstances before stated, to call the proceedings a suspension, is a point deserving a more serious enquiry than that by a newspaper. For my part I choose to call it by its right name—if it has any name—a dictatorial dismission unencumbered by the previous forms of charge, hearing, or trial .... but of one thing I can assure him, if he took into his calculation to give me any uneasiness, he has missed of his aim, for I can incur no reproach on this score, from any good citizen, I shall secure in conscious rectitude, most heartily despite the opinion or attempts, however, signified, of every bad one, whether in or out of office.

Following Houstoun's letter was an affidavit signed by Joseph Clay and William O'Bryan, certifying that all of the proceedings described were correct, and that Houstoun's missive had been forwarded to the Governor by Colonel Samuel Jack. Also, that at the last Superior Court[153] held in Savannah after the receipt and return of the commission, they had sat as judges, but that

---

153. "Prior to the election of a judge of the Superior Court the justices of the peace [designated assistant and associate judges] were authorized to sit with the chief justice, and in his absence to hold Superior Court." (Lamar, *The Bench and Bar of Georgia*, 26.)

John Houstoun did not appear as chief justice, or "in other character than as a private practitioner."

What actuated the order for the suspension of the judges was the refusal of prominent citizens of Chatham County to hand over the records and other public papers to James Pearre when he appeared in Savannah in March. John Houstoun, certain in his own mind that he was not an official of the state, joined with nine other Savannahians to protect the county's claim to its own property. They "did repair, without tumult or disorder, to the house where the papers of the secretary's office were kept, and having sorted out the records of grants for all the lots in five and forty-five acre lots adjoining the town of Savannah, and other books containing documents altogether of a private nature, and belonging ... to the inhabitants of the lower counties, delivered the same into the custody of James Bulloch, clerk of the court." The men who acted thus were accused of withholding what they said "in strictness of language be called 'public' in any other view than as being in a public office." So careful were they to avoid taking any books or papers that could be decreed state records that they requested the clerk in the secretary's office to examine all of the books in Bulloch's possession to point out any that were, "properly" speaking, public. "After completing their work, the secretary, Pearre proceeded with all the other papers of his office; amounting to no inconsiderable number," and arrived safely in Augusta. "No sooner was the affair reported there than that Body [the Governor and council] (with all the solemnity and dread of the Senate of Rome on discovering the conspiracy of Catiline) met in their Chamber and commenced a shower of political vengeance," meaning, of course, the suspension of the several justices.

The culprits, if so they may be called, published in the *Georgia Gazette*, April 27, 1785, a lengthy letter to the editor which related a history of the whole proceedings. It was signed by John Houstoun, Joseph Clay, William O'Bryan, William Gibbons, William Stephens, Richard Wylly, Peter Deveaux, Samuel Stirk, James Jackson, and George Walton. In explaining their position, the signatories were careful to assert that they were voicing the sentiment of the inhabitants of the county. They explained that Pearre's arrival in Savannah with the wagons "resolved itself into two opinions—the one, that as the officers and offices were directed by law to be removed to Augusta, therefore all the records and papers belonging to them respectfully must be comprehended as so many appendages, and that even if the law had not been full on this head, yet the vote of the house of Assembly, and order from the executive authority places the matter in a light indisputably clear." The other opinion was that "the Constitution upon this occasion was to be the polar star for our guide . . . ."

The constitutional right under which protection was claimed was the fiftieth article of the constitution: "Every county should keep the public records belonging to the same, and authenticated copies of the several records now in the possession of this State shall be made out and deposited in that county to which they belong."[154] Continuing their communication, the signers explained that "as the general voice required something to be done, it seemed more eligible to do that which appeared legal and constitutional by a few who would take care, both from public and private motives, that none of the papers should be lost or injured, than run the risk of having it done in a manner less moderate, and with more danger of damages to the papers by a concourse of people agitated with the idea that an attack was meditated against one of their chartered rights." Further, the signatories insisted they were motivated by a desire for "peace, order and good government." "And we disclaim," they concluded, "all distinction of interest between upper and lower counties, and hold those as enemies to both who shall by such pretended difference endeavor to sow the seeds of jealousy between us."

Amazing to the writers was "why the blow was aimed at the Judiciary department." "Several of us," they wrote, "have the honor to be Members of the Legislature; why not then as well suspend from our seats there as on the bench. The one department is not more distinct from and independent of the Executive than the other, and the history of the reign of Charles 1st, of England, and some of his predecessors, would have furnished precedence of the proceedings more perhaps in favor of vacating seats than suspending Judges."

---

154. Walter M. McElreath, *A Treatise on the Constitution of Georgia* . . . (Atlanta, 1912).

John Houstoun, "Rebell Governor" 263

In March the vacancies in the judiciary were filled, William Stith, Sr., receiving the appointment of chief justice, and Nathanael Greene and Joseph Habersham, assistant justices. General Greene, it was said, upon hearing the facts declined to serve, and Habersham resigned on April 16.

The result of the political calamity was that by November 20, the secretary of the council informed the Governor that he had received the records under fire.[155] Governor Telfair was severely arraigned in the *Georgia Gazette*, first by "Georgiensis" who declared he was happy to perceive that most persons agreed in declaring "the Executive have not the power to suspend Judges"; and next by "Legion," who wrote to the Governor: "*You* have suspended a solemn law of the state by refusing credentials to a gentleman who is, by that law, appointed an agent in the controversy now subsisting between this state and the state of South Carolina, in whose acknowledged abilities and long experience as a lawyer and a statesman the citizens of this state most immediately interested, principally depended . . . ."[156]

Telfair has been credited with having transferred the public records "so promptly and decisively that both the dignity and the majesty of the law were maintained."[157]

In the midst of the heated combat between Governor Telfair and the citizens of Chatham County, John Houstoun continued his membership in the state legislature. An advertisement appeared in *The Gazette of the State of Georgia*, April 27, 1786, calling for an election to be held the following month for a representative from Chatham County in place of John Houstoun, already chosen a delegate to the Continental Congress. Houstoun, however, did not assume that obligation, for reasons unexplained.

He was called to service in another direction. On Easter Monday the annual election was held for the wardens and vestry of

---

155. *The Georgia Historical Quarterly*, II, 223. There seems to be no authentic account extant relating how the records were finally released, but the above story explains the reason why the early original wills, deeds, and other records of Chatham County are filed in the Department of Archives and History in Atlanta. The records that date from 1773 are in a good state of preservation in Chatham County Court House.
156. *Georgia Gazette*, May 4, 1786. Quoted in *The Georgia Historical Quarterly*, II, 220.
157. Jones, *Biographical Sketches of Delegates to the Continental Congress*, 163.

Christ Church, and William Stephens and John Habersham were named wardens, and "Sir George Houstoun, Bart., John Houstoun, Joseph Clay, Sen., William O'Bryan, James Mossman, James Habersham, Joseph Habersham, Samuel Stirk, Richard Wylly and Leonard Cecil, Esqrs.", were elected vestrymen.[158] The structure in which the Houstouns worshiped, it will be recalled, was begun in 1745 under the supervision of Sir Patrick Houstoun, the fifth baronet, and was completed in 1750.

12

When in June, 1784, the executive council of Governor Houstoun's second administration was apprised of the granting of land to South Carolinians in the area between the Tugalo and Keowee rivers, and a caveat was served on Governor Guerard of South Carolina, it was not the first time that Georgia had proclaimed jurisdiction over that section. It seems to have been an annual occurrence. The old matter of boundary lines has always caused friction until agreement is reached to the mutual satisfaction of those vitally interested. In 1787 the final solution of Georgia and South Carolina's boundary dispute was far in the future by over three score years, but before that time that part of the border was a jarring note in the legislative halls of the two neighbor states.

In February, 1783, the House of Assembly appointed General Lachlan McIntosh, John Houstoun, and Edward Telfair as Georgia's agents to settle and adjust the northern boundary. The executive council was notified, and Governor Hall was requested to communicate the resolution to the Governor of South Carolina that his legislature might cooperate "in the measure." Two days later, February 15, Hall signed the commission under the Great Seal, and the three agents were given full power to conclude "the said business" with the representatives of South Carolina "in such way and manner as shall be comfortable to the rights of the inhabitants of this State as declared and secured to them as well by charter . . . ."[159] By 1785 the wrath of South Carolina had been aroused over the disputed territory, and she applied to the old Confederation Congress for a court of arbitration. But

---

158. *The Gazette of the State of Georgia*, April 20, 1786.
159. *Revolutionary Records of Georgia*, II, 454, 456, 457.

before a court could convene, the states came to an agreement which it was thought settled the trouble. A treaty was signed with the Indians on November 28, 1785, when they made relinquishment of land upon the Keowee River.

Georgians and South Carolinians no doubt wearied of the boundary question which arose constantly in the two governmental bodies. Before the summer session of the Georgia legislature of 1786 adjourned commissioners were appointed again to settle the dispute. John Houstoun was named first, and with him were appointed General Lachlan McIntosh and Joseph Clay. Relief was in sight but not before eight months had elapsed. Houstoun was to prove himself a valiant defender of Georgia's rights, by arguing strenuously to keep faith with the authorities who trusted him.

South Carolina was still so incensed in 1786 that she acted on the right given to the states under the Articles of Confederation and Perpetual Union Between the States, and carried her claim to the Continental Congress for decision. She was dissatisfied, however, with the handling of her demand by that body. It became necessary to bring the quarrel to an issue by holding a conference of representatives from the two commonwealths. The altercation reached its peak in April, 1787, when commissioners were appointed to meet and end the long struggle. General McIntosh and John Houstoun were selected again, and Major John Habersham was substituted for Joseph Clay. South Carolina's appointees were Charles Cotesworthy Pinckney, General Andrew Pickens and Pierce Butler. The delegations were composed of men who already had distinguished themselves, not only in the recent conflict with England, but also in the affairs of their states. Colonel Pinckney, a barrister by profession, was formerly attorney general of the Province of South Carolina. An aide-de-camp to General Washington, he was one of the officers who took part in the 1778 expedition against Florida, at which time he came in contact with John Houstoun. He had criticized severely the latter's conduct there. General Pickens, of Huguenot descent, was a brave fighter in the Revolution, and in 1781 was in command of the Georgia troops in the Southern Department under General Nathanael Greene. In an expedition against the Cherokee Indians, General Pickens obtained a large territory from them, and settled in Hopewell, Georgia, on the Keowee River, in the heart of the disputed territory. Pierce Butler, a native of Ireland, was an officer in the British army. He was stationed in Boston, but resigned in 1766, to settle in Charles Town. If at first a Tory sympathizer, he turned eventually to the Patriotic side, as he served his adopted state in the Continental Congress. The commissioners of Georgia were as important and eminent as their contemporaries on the other side of the Savannah River. General McIntosh, born in the Highlands of Scotland, was a notable figure in the Revolutionary War. After his tragic duel with Button Gwinnett, he was repudiated by a group of Gwinnett sympathizers, but subsequently went north and was assigned in the Continental Army under General Washington. A member of the Continental Congress in 1784, he was made a commissioner to trade with the southern Indians. Major John Habersham served during the Revolution in the First Georgia Continental Regiment. Later he was a member of the Continental Congress, and he too was appointed by General Washington an Indian agent, and was greatly trusted by the tribesmen of the South. John Houstoun's career up to 1787 is a matter of record in the previous pages of this history. Five of the commissioners, therefore, were men who had fought brilliantly in the late war. They were all men in middle life with the exception of General McIntosh, who in 1787 was sixty-two years of age.

The conference met in the colonial town of Beaufort, South Carolina, and was called the Beaufort Convention. Several days ahead of time the Georgia delegation left Savannah in John Houstoun's boat manned by five Negroes. On April 24, the two groups met and debated the momentous question for four days. From a study of the majority and minority reports one can almost conceive the trend of the parley. The six men knew that the purpose of the gathering was to determine the disputed line between their states, and they had accepted the delicate mission with the promise from both legislatures that their decision would be ratified in each assembly.

From the preamble to the majority report, it seems probable that the subject was opened by a South Carolinian. He reviewed for his hearers the charter of the older colony which was a grant from King Charles II in 1663 to eight Lords Proprietors. In it

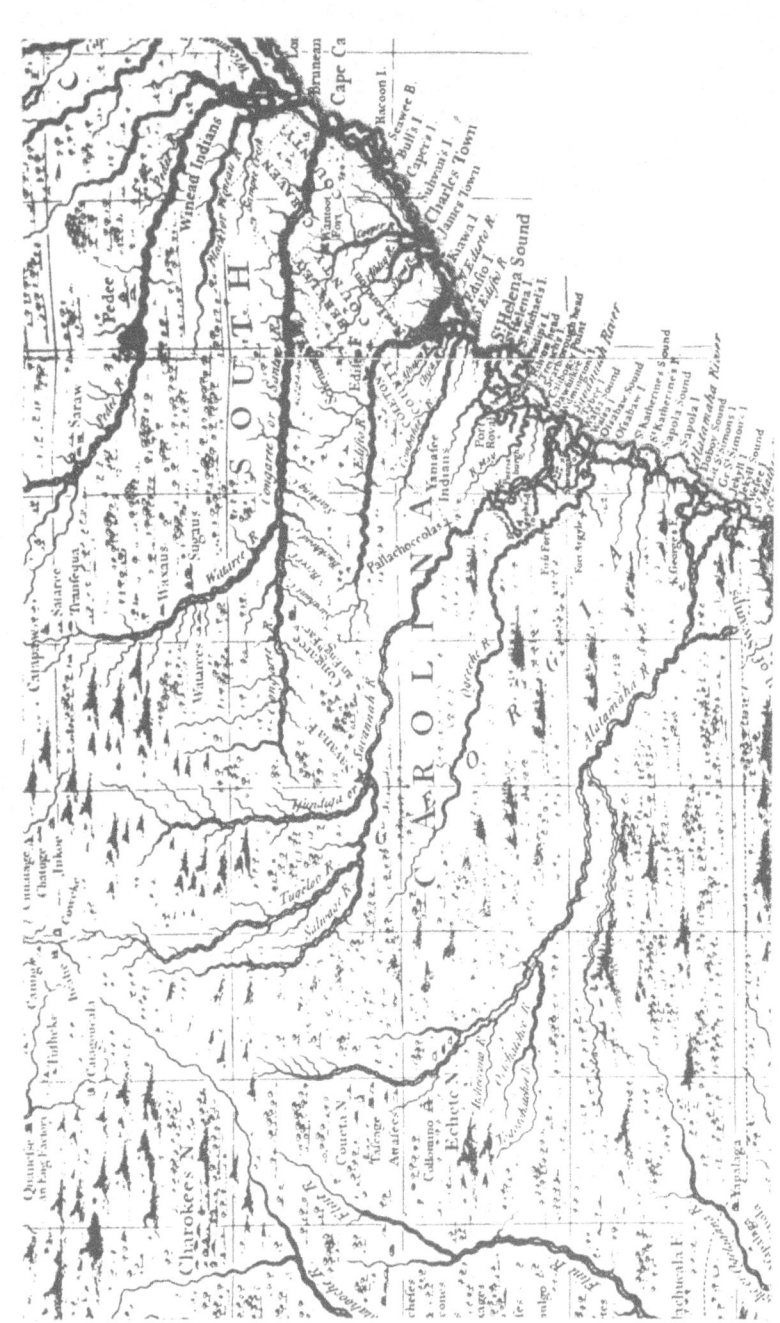

PORTION OF HENRY POPPELL'S MAP OF NORTH AMERICA, 1733, SHOWING ISUNDIGA (KIOWEE), THE SOURCE OF THE SAVANNAH RIVER.
Courtesy of the Library of Congress.

was defined by latitude and longitude the vast region of their holdings. When the Lords Proprietors were repudiated by the Carolina settlers who sought Crown government (the speaker must have pointed out) all but one of the grantees sold their colonial possessions to George II. Lord Carteret declined to surrender his acreage in the grant later made to the Trustees for Establishing the Colony of Georgia. When the leader from Georgia was given opportunity to put his side of the question, he would naturally have referred to the charter of *his* colony, formerly a part of the territory of the Carolina proprietors. In Georgia's charter (the speaker must have recalled to the assembled group) the northern portion of Georgia was distinctly described as the "most northerly part of the stream up to its headwaters," and that last word became the crux of the whole matter. Tempers may have been held in check, but a heated argument was obliged to be forthcoming when the root of the trouble was to determine the source of the Savannah River. So the first point of attack was the Keowee River. The South Carolina deputation claimed *that* river was a separate stream, while Georgia's representative (or, according to the facts, at least one of them was adamant on the subject) protested that the Keowee was a *branch* of the Savannah River. The South Carolina claimants insisted that the source of the Savannah was at the confluence of the Tugalo and Chatooga rivers, which was about forty miles farther up the river and contended that the Savannah changed its name where the Keowee flowed into it. The argument must have continued for hours.

John Houstoun, convinced that he was doing his duty in protecting Georgia's rights by taking care that the land in question was not wrested from her, held out until the last minute. His fellow-commissioners yielded to the suavity of the astute South Carolinians. How far were McIntosh and Habersham motivated by an outside influence in reaching their conclusion to submit to the persuasions of the South Carolina deputies? And how long, if at all, did they stand with John Houstoun? All of the members were in close association with the Indians. Did they know whether the Keowee River was named after or before the town Keowee? Did the Indians consider it a separate stream, or did the Cherokees hold that it was a branch of the Savannah? Was the situation a stalemate, or did McIntosh and Habersham possess information on the Savannah-Keowee debate that clinched the argument, or did they have a personal ulterior motive by finally casting their votes with the Carolinians? What did John Houstoun know of the headwaters of the Savannah that made him hold out against the other five commissioners? Was his alleged Scottish stubbornness coming to the front? Courage is required to stand alone for one's convictions. It is certain that he had not forgotten the explicit, or, to be more exact, the positive orders that he, McIntosh, and Telfair received when they were commissioned in 1783. Unquestionably John Houstoun was familiar with Henry Poppell's Map of North America of 1733, which was known to Georgians in the colonial period. He knew that on that map was shown the branch, Isundigo, or Savannah River (later named the Keowee), from its source to its mouth, and therefore he held to his argument on Georgia's charter-designation defining her colony grant through geographical knowledge which was contemporaneous with Georgia's founding. It should be borne in mind, too, when considering South Carolina's contention, that General Pickens, whose plantation was at Hopewell, Georgia, on the Keowee, was a South Carolinian! John Houstoun may also have recalled that fourteen years previously the noted botanist William Bartram, of Philadelphia, visited Savannah, where he met many residents of the town. Bartram traveled through the Keowee River valley and he wrote in his journal May 15, 1773: "In the course of this day's journey I crossed several rivers and brooks, all branches of the Savannah, now called Keowe, above its confluence with Tugilo, the West main branch."[160]

The Carolinians won their point on the decision of the headwaters of the river. Whether or not in the final analysis its source was determined upon arbitrarily, or by one member's correct knowledge from Indian neighbors, both McIntosh and Habersham signed their names to the document below the signatures of the three South Carolina commissioners. Once the boundary matter was settled there came up for discussion the subject of navigation, and the agreement reached there was to make the

---

160. Mark Van Doren, ed., *The Travels of William Bartram* (Reprint, 1928), 268. "I became acquainted with many of the worthy families . . . of Carolina and Georgia." *Ibid.*, 31.

Savannah River free from "all duties tolls, hindrance, interruption and molestation whatsoever, attempted to be enforced by one state on the citizens of another, and all the rest of the river Savannah to the southward of the foregoing description is acknowledged to be the exclusive right of the State of Georgia."[161] The last clause referred to the islands in the Savannah River to the upper end of Hutchinson's Island. South Carolina's one concession was to waive her right to the islands south of the Altamaha River. John Houstoun's comments on that compromise shown in his report are illuminating, and even the other Georgia delegates declined entering into any negotiations relative to the lands mentioned in that article of the treaty, because, they stated, they were not authorized to do so by the powers that were delegated to them. The net result of the convention was that the State of Georgia found herself gouged[162] of approximately 1,575 square miles, or about 1,008,000 acres. Houstoun's clear and temperate protest followed the signed Beaufort Treaty. His attempt to frustrate the efforts of a sister state to deprive Georgia of some of her rightful acreage has been preserved to history. His minority report of one against the three South Carolina commissioners and the two Georgians was dated April 28, 1787. His dissent had two divisions:

"1st. I conceive, from the words of the charter of Georgia, *all the lands which lie* south and southwest of the most northern part of the stream of the river Savannah, up to its head or source; from thence within a direct line running due west to the river Mississippi, and extending southwardly as far as the boundaries of East and West Florida, are the right of Georgia. This stream here described I take to be that branch of the river Savannah by the name of Keowee; if so, all the lands which lie in the fork of the two branches of Savannah River called Tugalo and Keowee, ought to fall into Georgia, whereas by this convention they are yielded to South-Carolina. As to the relinquishment on the part of South-Carolina of all her claims in the southern district of Georgia, I do not conceive this by any means an equivalent; for although the two territories in question may be

---
161. Marbury and Crawford, *Digest*, 662-666.
162. The word is used advisedly, and will be understood by a glance at any modern map of Georgia showing the extreme northeastern portion.

equally fertile, or perhaps the difference in point of extent and value even in favor of the Southern, yet I apprehend the title of Georgia to the lands now ceded to South-Carolina was good and valid, whereas the pretensions of South-Carolina to the southern country appear to me to be so slender, that the right of Georgia to those lands is neither strengthened or weakened by the present convention; and therefore as, in my opinion, the nature of the claims ought to be considered in the negocaition [*sic*] as well as the value and extent of the soils, I cannot admit the exchange to be equal.

"2dly. As to the free navigation of the river Savannah, now given up to South-Carolina, I conceive this point is, in the first place, not an object of our commission; but if it was, however disposed I might be always to wish an indulgence to a sister state on this head (which I believe has hitherto been the case) yet I am not inclined to give that *indulgence* the color of a *right*. Where settling commercial regulations with South-Carolina, to permit the free navigation of the river might be just and proper, the title then would depend on and be derived from such agreement; but to yield this point *as a claim*, in the present instance implies that the *right* has been aborigine in South-Carolina. Such a position would be inconsistent with my idea of our boundary; for if we hold the sovereignty 'from the most northern part of the stream,' it seems to me the exclusive right of navigation follows of course: This is neither a forced or new construction of our charter, but has uniformly been the opinion for a series of years past of most people in Georgia; and all the documents produced tend only to show the point has been contested but never decided on. On the whole, although I should be amongst the foremost to concede to this neighborly privilege in return for some other perhaps less valuable to the citizens of South-Carolina, yet I should wish to see it held by them, under some restrictions, from Georgia, and not a right proved and established at the present meeting."[163]

---

163. Marbury and Crawford, *Digest*, 666, 667. The following information furnished by the Library of Congress, November 30, 1937, would seem to substantiate the claim of John Houstoun that the Keowee River was the source of the Savannah: "Henry Poppell's map of North America, 1733, names the Savannah and its tributaries. . . . From it one might infer that during the Colonial period the source of the Savannah River

John Houstoun, "Rebell Governor" 271

When Houstoun set down his conclusions on paper, he felt himself absolved of all responsibility. He could at least leave Beaufort with a clear conscience. Immediately on his arrival in Savannah, John Houstoun sent in his bill for his service to the state of Georgia. He itemized his expenses as, twelve days attendance at the convention, £11.4; cash paid to hire of five hands £10.10; provisions and house for the hands £2.10, total £23.19. The bill showed Houstoun had received £20, and that a balance of £3.19 was owing him. On the bill was a notation, "The Boat being my own I do not charge for her."[164]

In August the South Carolina delegates had the report ratified in Congress. Houstoun's name was included in the list of the six commissioners, but no mention was made of his dissent. What became of the minority report? The Georgia Assembly met in Augusta in February, 1788, and, true to its promise, ratified by act the arduous work of the conferees in Beaufort, "as binding upon the citizens of this state, any law to the contrary notwithstanding." It was signed by Nathan Brownson, speaker of the house. And thus the difference of the two states supposedly was settled.[165]

---

may have been considered to be the same as the source of the first large tributary of the main stream. This is probably the tributary now designated as the Seneca River." And on March 17, 1939: "After 1818 the name Seneca River seems to have been applied to the stream."

164. Department of Archives and History, Atlanta.
165. Edward M. Douglas, *Boundaries, Areas, Geographic Centers and Altitudes of the United States and Several States*. . . . (Washington, 1930), 817: "In 1917 the Legislature of Georgia authorized the bringing of a suit in the Supreme Court of the United States in order to settle a long-standing dispute between that State and the State of South Carolina regarding their common boundary." *Ibid.*, 153. The act (257 U. S. and 259 U. S. 572) decided where the state line was located midway in the river, giving the islands in the Chatooga to Georgia. *Ibid.*, 2. Disputes between states regarding boundaries must be settled by the United States Supreme Court, whose decisions are final." Further proof of John Houstoun's claim is found in John Gerar William deBrahm, *History of the Province of Georgia with Original Maps of Surveys 1751-1771*, 54: "The Cherokee Towns comprehended in this Province are Tugelo, Keowee . . . all on the west side of Savannah River." Also in White's *Historical Collections*, 604: In 1774, after the meeting in Tondee's Tavern a protest was made and resolutions passed beginning with the words: "We the inhabitants of Keowee and Broad River Settlements . . . ." Dated "Georgia Parish of St. Paul's, August 24, 1774." Also, Lamar, *The Bench and Bar of Georgia*, 25: ". . . left to the voters to determine whether the court house of Richmond County should be located at Kiokee, Brownsville or Augusta. . . ." (c. 1776). Quoted from *Revolutionary Records of Georgia*, III, 565.

13

In January, 1788, Houstoun was occupied with a case to be tried in the Court of Common Pleas in Charleston, in which Philip Hart was the plaintiff. Houstoun's counsel was Edward Rutledge, a distinguished attorney of South Carolina, and a signer of the Declaration of Independence. He was one of the delegates appointed by the Continental Congress in 1776 to confer with Lord Howe on his proposals for a reconciliation. In 1780, Rutledge was sent on an important mission by General Benjamin Lincoln but was captured by the British and sent to St. Augustine where he was confined for a year before his exchange. When the British evacuated Charles Town, he returned home and engaged in legislative duties.

On receiving a letter from Rutledge early in January informing Houstoun that the "cause would be held in the ensuing court" on January 12, and desiring him to acquaint the writer if his witness, Philip Minis, could swear that he might send a commission to examine him, Houstoun learned that he had erred in reading the court's calendar. Meanwhile he had been preparing his case for the third Tuesday in February. He had concluded that there was time enough to have Minis make his affidavit before one of the assistant judges, as the chief justice was away, and he was "alarmed" because he could not get the commission from Charles Town and return it in nine days. "The weather coming on rainy and unusually severe there was no opportunity to get the papers to Charleston." He concluded, "As I have just come to Town and find the vessel on the point of sailing I have not time to get my affid^{t} put under the Seal of the Court; however I hope it will answer, as it is, the Purpose for which it is intended under the 4th. Art of the Confederation." Both the letter and the deposition were dated January 7.[166]

---

[166] MS. letter in the Historical Society of Pennsylvania. The last paragraph would seem to refer to the concluding section of the fourth article of the Articles of Confederation and Perpetual Union Between the States: "Full faith and credit shall be given in each of the States to the records, acts and judicial proceedings of the courts and magistrates of every other State." Benson Johnson Lossing, *Harper's Encyclopaedia of United States History*, New Edition, (New York and London, 1901), II; (Alphabetical: Confederation, Articles of).

On Sunday, March 9, 1788, Hannah Houstoun lost by death her aged father, Jonathan Bryan, in his eightieth year. His end closed the notable career of that fine patriot, who, during fifty years' residence in Georgia, filled many government positions, and served loyally his adopted state. He was interred in the family vault on Brampton plantation. John Houstoun was one of his executors.

Notwithstanding his desire to retire from public life, which he expressed in 1784, John Houstoun continued to be the people's choice for service in their behalf. He was selected again for a special convention in 1788, following Georgia's unanimous ratification in January of the Federal Constitution. New Hampshire's ratification on June 21, 1788, completed the requisite quota of nine states. Georgia needed a new constitution, and, as the time was propitious, Governor George Handley ordered an election for delegates to attend a convention to meet in the autumn to consider the alterations and amendments necessary to change the state's constitution. John Houstoun, John Habersham, and General Lachlan McIntosh were named to represent Chatham County. In October two of Chatham's delegates, Houstoun and Habersham, declined to serve, and their refusal necessitated the calling of a special meeting to elect their successors. It required two conventions to make the necessary changes in the new state constitution, and a third one to ratify it in May, 1789.

In the early autumn John Houstoun and other constituents of Chatham County were concerned over the fall elections which was one of the chief topics of conversation among politicians. Some anxiety was felt over the vote of the "northern merchants," and General Anthony Wayne, it was hoped, would use his influence with them. Since 1782 General Wayne had lived part of the time at his plantation west of Savannah, which that year was given to him by the legislature in recognition of his military service in the South during the War of the Revolution. On September 30, 1789, his friend Richard Wayne wrote that a spirited contest was under way. "I had yesterday," continued Richard Wayne, "a Serious chat with our Mutual Friend Mr. J. Houstoun, he expresses a wish for your being In Town for the

Election . . . . Your influence with the Northern merchants may have much weight."[167]

One aspiration of John Houstoun remained unfulfilled. In the summer of 1789 he made application for the appointment of a Federal judgeship, but President Washington gave the office to Nathaniel Pendleton (1756-1821). On July 17 a bill passed the Senate of the United States organizing the Judiciary, and thirteen district courts were created. In the interim between the passage of the Judiciary Act and the appointment of judges, it is thought that the President had the Georgia applicants' names under consideration, because he approved the measure on September 24, and two days later his nomination commissioning Nathaniel Pendleton as the first United States judge in Georgia was confirmed by the Senate. Pendleton was known personally to the President who held him in high regard.[168] There may have been other Georgia applicants besides the two mentioned, but at least John Houstoun's was accompanied by "very respectable recommendations."[169]

Several changes pertaining to the governorship were made in the 1789 Georgia constitution, the chief one providing that the tenure of office should be two years instead of one. The status of the Georgia Assembly, likewise, was altered. A senate body was added to the house of representatives, thus causing a revision in the rules for electing the governor. Under the new arrangement the house was to choose three names to be sent to the senate, which was given the power to elect. When the two branches assembled in Augusta on Tuesday, November 7, 1789, a new situation was before the members. On the first day the senate elected its president and secretary, and the house its speaker and clerk. The next day the first order of business was the election of a governor, and when the ballots were counted in the

---

167. From photostat copy loaned by Alexander A. Lawrence, Jr., of Savannah. Original in the Anthony Wayne Collection in the Historical Society of Pennsylvania.
168. Warren Grice, "Nathaniel Pendleton, Georgia's First United States Judge," in *Report of the Fortieth Annual Session of the Georgia Bar Association* (1923), 119-137. Pendleton was Alexander Hamilton's second in his duel with Aaron Burr.
169. Warren Grice, "Joseph Clay, Junior," in *Report of the Forty-Second Annual Session of the Georgia Bar Association* (1925), 336.

house, the vote stood as follows for the three names: Edward Telfair, twenty-five; John Houstoun, twenty-five; and William Pierce, nineteen. The names were sent to the senate, and when the votes were counted there, Telfair and Houstoun received the same number. The second ballot was not held until Friday, when the votes again were equal. On Monday a third ballot was cast when Edward Telfair was unanimously chosen to that important office. Although in the end he was defeated, Houstoun had the satisfaction of finding himself a candidate in a contested election for governor for the third time. Before the assembly adjourned near the end of the year, John Houstoun was elected one of ten justices of the peace for Chatham County. The next high position to which he was called brought him distinction as well as honor, for no other had ever held the office.

Steadily through the years the little colonial settlement, Savannah, had grown. In the year 1789, with the population exceeding two thousand, the town was determined to change its status from a town to a municipality. By act of the legislature Savannah was incorporated a city December 23, 1789, the style of the act designating it as, "The Mayor and Aldermen of the City of Savannah and the Hamlets thereof."[170] The day after the passage of the act, Governor Telfair issued a proclamation directing Joseph Clay, Richard Wylly, and William Gibbons to attend as judges for the election of aldermen, requiring all who were entitled to vote to meet at the market place on the first Monday in March of the ensuing year between the hours of ten in the morning and twelve noon for the purpose of electing aldermen. When elected, the latter were directed to convene the following Monday to elect a mayor "out of their own body." "Savannah was a very important little city .... Enjoying an extensive and lucrative trade, it was proud of its past, confident of its future, and eager to put on the style of a full-fledged municipality. Its citizenship embraced men of national note; its merchants were in touch with the great world of commerce, and in all it had the attributes of an intelligent, wealthy and progressive community . . . ."[171]

---
170. Gamble, *History of the City Government*, 47.
171. Thomas Gamble, "Municipality 125 Years Old Today," in *Savannah Morning News*, March 8, 1915: Only two other Southern cities had preceded Savannah in having incorporated municipalities: Richmond, Vir-

On Monday, March 1, 1790, the electorate of the newly incorporated municipality walked to the market place on Ellis Square to ballot for the first city fathers. With what eagerness the entire citizenry, women as well as men, must have waited for the election returns, which, when the announcement was made, gave the election to Joseph Habersham, John Houstoun, Matthew McAllister, Samuel Stirk, Edward Lloyd, Joseph Clay, and Justus H. Sheuber, chosen aldermen for one year. Those seven well-selected men were true and tried patriots of Georgia, and their constituents were fully aware of their calibre and ability when the choice was made. But there was yet the climax to come when the new aldermen were to discharge their orders from the Governor to select one of their number to be the chief magistrate of the city. Accordingly, one week later the aldermen gathered in the council room in the court house for that purpose, and "on counting the ballot it appeared that John Houstoun, Esq., was elected, who having taken the chair the board proceeded to business, having first taken an oath . . . ."[172]

For the next few days the mayor and aldermen devoted much time to working out details; providing for the several city officers, fixing salaries, drafting rules for transacting their business, devising a seal for the city, arranging the time for their regular meetings, which they decreed should be held every Tuesday morning at 10 o'clock, and setting fines for late attendance. Thereafter Savannahians were notified of the approaching meeting of council by the ringing of the church bell, a ceremony which continued for many years.

Considerable improvements were undertaken and accomplished during John Houstoun's year as mayor. Bids were called for public wells to be sunk in the squares to give the city an adequate water supply; fire-engines were purchased; fire ladders and hooks were stored in the market and in the vendue house on the Bay; and better police protection was provided.[173] But there were public nuisances which the mayor and aldermen found necessary

---
ginia, which was incorporated in 1782, and Charleston, South Carolina, in 1783. Thomas Gamble, "Savannah's Incorporated Government is Third Oldest in the South," in *Savannah Morning News*, February 21, 1932.
172. Gamble, *History of the City Government*, 48. Quoted from the minutes of the meeting, *Georgia Gazette*, March 11, 1790.
173. *Ibid.*, 48, 49, 50.

to correct by ordinances. One was "to prevent as much as may be the dreadful Effects of Canine Madness." The ordinance was passed on April 30, 1790, and it was made lawful for any person for the space of twenty days afterward "to kill and destroy all or any dogs found or discovered in any square, street, lane or any other open place within the limits of Savannah."

Another ordinance regulated and restricted the retailing of spirituous liquors, and "the Use of Billiard Tables, Shuffle & Skittle Alleys within the limits of the City of Savannah and the Hamlets thereof," stipulating that in order to use the above, "every person must have a license within his house or out of it."[174] Toward the latter part of the year, council made provision for the several bodies by passing an ordinance for laying off into lots particular parts of the Common to be appropriated for purposes announced to the public through the columns of the newspaper. Four lots were "reserved and vested forever in the Wardens and Vestry of the Episcopal Church called Christ Church and their successors in office." Three were reserved for the Presbyterian meeting house, two for the German Lutherans and for the Hebrews, eight for the academy, and two for the hospital.

When the seventh of March, 1791, arrived, John Houstoun again was elected to the aldermanic board, his name heading the list published in the *Georgia Gazette*. Three members of his old board were returned with him. To his amazement, no doubt, he was re-elected mayor. Then he voiced an emphatic *no*, as the newspaper the following Thursday announced that, "Monday last Thomas Gibbons, Sen., Esq., was chosen one of the aldermen and next mayor of this city in the room of John Houstoun, Esq., who resigned."[175] A day intervened between the election of Houstoun and Gibbons; so it is possible that John Houstoun's objections were overruled by his board before he had time to give serious reflection whether or not he should consider serving a second term. When he made his decision, it was in the negative.

It is interesting to conjecture if Houstoun knew of the approaching visit of the President of the United States to the city of Savannah, and if so whether or not he would have declined the

---
174. *Georgia Gazette*, April 29 and May 6, 1790.
175. *Ibid.*, September 30, 1790; March 10, and March 17, 1791.

mayoralty just a few weeks before the event. General Washington left Mount Vernon for his tour of the South in April, 1791, and arrived in Savannah in the early afternoon of Thursday, May 12. He left the South Carolina plantation of Thomas Heyward at five o'clock in the morning for Purrysburg, where he breakfasted and was met and greeted by five eminent patriots from Savannah, who composed the official committee: Dr. Noble Wimberly Jones, Colonel Joseph Habersham, John Houstoun, General Lachlan McIntosh, and Joseph Clay. The committee presented him with "an address of welcome in behalf of Savannah and its Vicinity, convened for the reception of the President," and "conducted him in a boat which had been equipped and neatly ornamented for the occasion."[176] The President was greeted on the bluff by a concourse of persons, and was handsomely entertained during his four days' visit to the city.

John Houstoun's last important office was conferred upon him at the close of the year 1791 when he was elected a judge of the superior court of Georgia. There was no supreme court in the state until a much later time, and the superior courts were supreme in their respective circuits. In the period between the close of the Revolution and the organization of the new government, a number of men were designated chief justices. The new constitution provided that the superior court judges should have a competent salary which was not to be diminished during their continuance in office, and they were to hold their commission for a term of three years.[177]

Nominated by the house of representatives of the state of Georgia, John Houstoun's name was one of three sent to the senate for appointment as a judge of the superior court. The senate concurred with the house on December 22, while the assembly was sitting in the state house in Augusta. The procedure was for the newly appointed judge to go to Augusta to qualify before the governor. Upon receiving notification of his

---
176. *Georgia Gazette*, May 19, 1791.
177. Marbury and Crawford, *Digest*, 17. The first judge of the superior court in Georgia was Henry Osborne, who was elected by the senate in December, 1789. He served for one year when he was suspended. He was impeached, and deprived of the right to hold office in Georgia for thirty years. Executive Minutes 1789-1790, 65; Senate Journal of 1791, p. 31. (Department of Archives and History, Atlanta).

election, Houstoun wrote Governor Telfair that he could not attend him "without manifest inconvenience to his concerns."[178] In consideration of Houstoun the Governor sent a *dedimus potestatem* appointing William Gibbons, senior, Joseph Clay, senior, and Dr. George Jones, three of the judges of the inferior court of Chatham County, or any two of them, to administer the oath, which was done in Savannah, January 5, 1792.[179]

When the *dedimus* was returned to the Governor, qualifying John Houstoun as judge, and signed by the three appointed judges of the inferior court, the secretary of state was ordered to prepare the commission which was signed by Edward Telfair, Governor, and John Milton, Secretary of State, January 17, 1792.[180]

Shortly after receiving his commission, Judge Houstoun was formally complimented by the mayor and aldermen of Savannah on February 7, 1792. On that occasion the newly appointed judge was presented with an honorarium of £150 which had been voted by the council as a "mark of the esteem and regard of the citizens of Savannah." Judge Houstoun's response to the liberality of Savannah was simple and brief. He said:

Gentlemen

I feel myself happy in being able to add to the honor of my appointment the approbation of your honorable Body.

Sensibly impressed with gratitude for the liberality and attention of my friends, it is not more my duty than it shall be my endeavor to justify, by every means in my power, the very favorable opinion you are pleased to entertain of me.[181]

In spite of pressure from affairs of state, John Houstoun found time to look after his plantation interests in McIntosh County. On April 7, 1791, he wrote his friend William Stevens (or Steven)

---

178. Senate Journal of 1791, 52; Executive Minutes, 1791-1792, 64, 110; Department of Archives and History, Atlanta.
179. Minutes of the Superior Court of Chatham County, February 14, 1792; Clerk's Office, Savannah, Georgia, Book 2, pp. 267-269.
180. Miller, *The Bench and Bar of Georgia*, II, 98-100. Lamar, *The Bench and Bar in the Eighteenth Century*, 25, "... and John Houstoun—whose commission is interesting in itself and by comparison with the brevity of those now used, when the State has two hundred times as many inhabitants." (1913).
181. *Georgia Gazette*, February 9, 1792. Also Gamble, *History of the City Government*, 130.

at Windy Hill on the Altamaha River apprising him of a shipment by boat of seed potatoes, rice, and seven hands.[182] Houstoun called Stevens's attention to one of the hands, an old driver, who, while "not very active . . . has many good Qualities," and his wife, a wench for whom he could not "say much." Apologizing for his failure to obtain an "Iron Crank," he suggested that Stevens try to have one made in Frederica. "I don't think," he concluded, "you can venture to plant for above fifty hands this year, and even that not a large crop."

Plantation annoyances pursued John Houstoun, and in the spring of 1792 he was apprised of the fact that his overseer, a Mr. Gervy, on the McIntosh County plantation, had left his services abruptly. Again he wrote to William Stevens of Windy Hill. Gervy had left the McIntosh County plantation to become overseer on the plantation of Alexander Bissett. Houstoun learned of Gervy's move from Thomas Spalding. That Stevens had not kept him informed about such an important matter as the loss of his overseer at the beginning of the planting season irritated the former governor. He rejected Gervy's alleged plea of ill health and warned that "such pretences will not authorize him to trifle with my Interest." Convinced that his former overseer had violated an agreement, he complained that "I cannot think myself well used by him or those who tempted him out of my service by the offer of a larger salary."[183]

While he held the office of judge, John Houstoun's portrait was painted. Unfortunately the artist has not been identified, but undoubtedly he was one of distinction, because his work on the portrait "represents the fine style of the period. It is simply handled with all the emphasis on the head and face, and has dignity and quality."[184] In the portrait Judge Houstoun is shown wear-

---

182. Autograph letter signed. A gift to the author from Charles Francis Jenkins.
183. Autograph letter signed. Owned by the author.
184. *Savannah Morning News*, April 2, 1941. The portrait was purchased by the author on March 31, 1941, from Mrs. Marie Bayard Collins of New York City. Up to that date there was no known portrait of John Houstoun in existence. C. C. Jones, Jr., in *Biographical Sketches of the Delegates from Georgia to the Continental Congress*, 119, wrote in the sketch on William Houstoun, ". . . his portrait as well as that of Governor Houstoun with the family plate and many papers of historical value were unfortunately consumed by fire in Southwest Georgia,

ing his judicial robe, which dates it in 1792 or 1793. In December, 1792, Judge Houstoun resigned his office to the senate whose secretary relayed the information to the House of Representatives. In nominating three men the names of Matthew McAllister, John Houstoun and William Stephens were sent to the senate for election. When the ballots were counted John Houstoun was the choice of that body.[185]

14

In the year 1792 a new honor and more work came to John Houstoun. His capabilities were called upon for one more executive office when he was made president of the board of trustees of the Chatham Academy. In 1788 when the legislature met in Augusta, an act was passed establishing an academy in Chatham County. For its maintenance one thousand pounds specie from confiscated property in the county was ordered placed in the hands of a board of trustees, composed of John Houstoun, John Habersham, William Gibbons, Sr., James Habersham, Samuel Elbert, Seth John Cuthbert, and Joseph Clay, Jr. Apparently the board was not able to fulfill the trust until 1792. Houstoun was

---

whither, during the late war between the states, they had been conveyed in the hope of promoting their safety." The recently purchased portrait is in the original frame, and on the back is a brief biographical account, but unfortunately it has obvious errors. Evidently, it was written by someone a long time after John Houstoun's death, and not by the original owner who would have known the date of his birth:

> John Houstoun Governor
> of Ga. 1778-1784 son of Sir
> Patrick Houstoun died
> 1796. The painting was
> done in 1791, age 49 years
> Given to Dr. Nicholas Bayard
> & wife Cath. Livingston Bayard
> & later their son [in-law]
> Nicholas [Serle] Bayard & his
> son Nicholas James Bayard
> & later to Nicholas R. Bayard
> N. Y. C.

The portrait was restored in November, 1941, by Edward J. McMullin of Philadelphia.

185. Senate Journal 1791, 1793, pp. 253, 255. Department of Archives and History, Atlanta. In Receipt Book 47, also in the Department, it is shown that Judge Houstoun's salary for one quarter, November 4, 1793, was £87.10s.

president of the board. In May of that year John Houstoun wrote to city council applying for the use of the filature. On the twenty-second of the month the board met at the home of the president who read a letter from Mayor Joseph Habersham apprising him that council had agreed to the trustees' request by allowing part of the filature for the use desired. The board immediately began to organize the academy by deciding on the salary of the first tutors, which was to be twenty-five dollars annually, beginning from the second Tuesday in June; and other tutors were to be added, one "at the rate of three poor children to be educated gratis." The "rates of schooling" were for those who were to study reading, writing, and arithmetic [no figure] dollars a quarter; for those who were to be taught languages and other branches of learning, six and a half dollars a quarter. The Reverend Benjamin Lindsay, rector of Christ Church, who had also been the classical tutor at Bethesda, and Joseph Turner were appointed first and second tutors. They were to collect all the money from the pupils and give credit to the board which at the end of the year would make up any deficiency that might be necessary to raise the tutors' salaries to the amount of twenty-five dollars. The board further decided to notify all persons who desired to place their children or wards in the academy to give in the names of the prospective pupils to the secretary, John Habersham, before the second Monday in June. Dr. Donald McLeod and Joseph Clay were appointed the committee to draft by-laws and regulations to lay before the board at its next meeting. Nine months later the academy was in full running order. The trustees took their guardianship seriously, as they attended an examination of the pupils, and expressed themselves satisfied with the progress made. At the board meeting held on March 20, 1793, the members decided it was "their duty to recommend to parents and guardians to place their children" in the academy. The decision was reached also that when the next examination was held the trustees should distribute premiums to those pupils who excelled in their studies.[186] The pupils of the academy had six months in which to prepare for the event, which took place on September 12. That day five boys and one girl awaited the arrival of the board of trustees who were to present the awards. When John Houstoun, president,

---

186. *Georgia Gazette*, June 8, 1788, May 24, 1792, and March 21, 1793.

with John Habersham, William Stephens, William Gibbons, Richard Wylly, and Joseph Clay, Jr., arrived at the filature, they superintended the examinations, and then the prizes were awarded. Isaac Minis, as the best Latin scholar, was presented two volumes of *Telemachus;* Archibald Clarke, "the best writer, and in other respects, a good scholar," was given two volumes of *Telemachus;* George Haupt received two volumes of *Beauties of Shakespeare,* as the best speaker; Samuel Elbert, the best reader in the first class, was awarded Goldsmith's *Rome;* George Glen, the next best reader, was also given Goldsmith's *Rome;* and Sarah Brown, as "the best female reader," was presented with a copy of Goldsmith's *England.*[187] When the next issue of the newspaper appeared, the trustees announced that they highly approved of the situation in which they found the academy, and of the advancement made by its pupils. It was requested that any persons wishing to accept appointments of first and second tutors might lodge their names with the secretary.

At last the time arrived when John Houstoun was in a position to keep his determination to retire to private life. He did not complete his three-year appointment, but resigned his judicial office in December, 1793, although his term of office did not expire until January, 1795. When the General Assembly met on December 19, his resignation was accepted, and George Walton was elected to succeed him.

The previous September John Houstoun's younger brother, Dr. James Houstoun, had died, leaving his brothers George and John his executors.[188] John Houstoun and his wife adopted one of the daughters of Dr. James Houstoun, Harriet Thompson Houstoun,[189] who was probably a young girl at the time of her father's death. For lack of evidence to the contrary, the year 1794 may have been a quiet one for John and Hannah Houstoun, providing an opportunity for the former to give his time and attention exclusively to family matters as well as to a neglected law practice. The next year, however, he was again in prominence, following the death of his brother George in June, 1795.

187. *Ibid.*, September 19, 1793.
188. See *post*, 309-10.
189. See *post*, 311.

During that summer Savannah felt a repercussion from a question over which the whole country was aroused. John Jay, Chief Justice of the United States, had been sent by President George Washington to England to obtain a new treaty with Great Britain, which, when ratified by Congress, raised a storm of abuse from Republicans, and caused dismay even among Federalist party members. Leading men in Savannah called a meeting of citizens at the court house on Saturday, July 25. General Lachlan McIntosh presided and the conclusion was reached by resolution that notice be sent throughout the county requesting persons to meet at the courthouse the following Wednesday morning at 10 o'clock to consider the proper measures to adopt respecting the treaty. When the men of the city and county assembled it was found that the courthouse would not hold the crowd; so the assemblage adjourned to Christ Church. General McIntosh begged permission to resign the chair whereupon Dr. Noble Wimberly Jones, who was nearing seventy years of age, was called upon to preside. By resolution a committee of fifteen was appointed, among whom was John Houstoun, to consider the treaty and to bring in a report the following Saturday. On motion it was resolved "that it is the opinion of this meeting that the impending Treaty of Amity, Commerce and Navigation between his Brittanic Majesty and the United States of America, is an infraction of the sovereignty of the said United States, and derogatory to the honor, interests, and happiness, of the citizens thereof." During the intervening three days, the committee worked assiduously, and when the adjourned meeting opened it was ready with a lengthy report which was read by the chairman, John Y. Noel. Taking their cue from the sentiment expressed by those who had attended the former meeting, the committee members expressed their opinions in an exhaustive report covering the twenty-eight sections of the treaty. On its conclusion, Noel and James Habersham were appointed a committee to prepare an address to be sent to the President of the United States. Two copies were ordered engrossed to be signed by the chairman in behalf of those present, and it was directed that the report and the account of the proceedings be "transmitted by land and water to the President of the United States with all possible expedition." Then followed a vote of thanks to the chairman and gentlemen comprising the committee for their attention and faithful discharge of the trust to which they were appointed.[190]

15

Early in January, 1796, John Houstoun sold his White Bluff plantation. The indenture was made on January 6 between John and Hannah Houstoun and Edward Lloyd, Esquire, of Savannah, who paid four thousand seven hundred and fourteen dollars and twenty-eight cents "and one half Cent" for three hundred and seventy-five acres. Thereafter it was known as "Lloyd's Tract."[191] The Houstouns retained one-half of the lot overlooking the Vernon River, all of which John Houstoun had bought in 1772. It seems likely they had a summer residence there.

It can be assumed that in the spring John Houstoun's health began to fail as his was not a sudden death. In May a distinguished French émigré, the Duc de la Rochefoucauld-Liancourt, spent eight days in Savannah, and recorded that there were only a few lawyers in the city. The nobleman, commenting further on the legal profession in Savannah, wrote: " . . . the business of a lawyer is one of the most lucrative professions."[192] It is possible that he met John Houstoun, and included him among those to whom he made reference in general terms.

In the early summer, John Houstoun lay ill of bilious fever at White Bluff, and passed away in July. Although he died in a small suburban community only eight miles from the city, the newspapers, being weeklies, could not publish his death notice until their next issue. The news appeared first in the *Columbian Museum & Savannah Advertiser* of July 22:

> Died at White Bluff on the 20th. inst. the Hon John Houstoun Esquire.

Six days later the *Georgia Gazette* carried this obituary:

> July 20, 1796, died at White Bluff, of bilious fever, John Houstoun, former governor and first Mayor of Savannah, a

---

190. *Georgia Gazette*, August 6, 1795. Savannah.
191. County Records 1795, 1796, p. 124*ff*. Chatham County Court House, Savannah.
192. Duc de la Rouchefoucauld-Liancourt, *Travels Through the United States of America* . . . (English Translation. London, 1799), II, 460.

gentleman no less conspicuous for the amenity of his manners than eminent for his talents as a lawyer and a statesman.

From a friend's letter a few more details can be added. Mary Anne Cowper, the daughter of Basil Cowper, was in July, 1796, residing with her family at New Hope, South Carolina, only a few miles down the river from Savannah. In answer to a letter from her cousin, Eliza McQueen, she wrote: " . . . it makes us very happy to hear of you all being well by James & who brought me your very acceptable letter—tho some of the accounts are far from being so—& M^r· John Houstoun's death gives us real concern, we pity M$^{rs.}$ H. extremely, and those so nearly interested, his two nephews & Harriet—poor Man, death has been long making its Appearance & I hope found him prepared . . . ."[193]

Since John Houstoun died at White Bluff it would seem that his remains would have been interred on his own property as was customary at that time, but to date (1949) his burial place has not been identified.[194] Another mystery is added to John Houstoun's life. The birthplace and year, the marriage date, and the grave of one of Georgia's distinguished sons seem destined to remain in obscurity.

In his will written on May 2, 1796, and probated on July 22, 1796,[195] he left legacies to his brother William and his wife; to his nieces and god-daughters, Ann and Priscilla Houstoun, daughters of his brother George; to Johanna Houstoun, a god-daughter, daughter of his brother Dr. James Houstoun; to Harriet Louisa Baillie, a connection of the Houstouns; who with Johanna was in Scotland, and to other relatives. Ratifying and confirming the manumission of a "black woman named Doll," he "made free" also his Negro woman Venus and devised that fifty dollars be paid to her within one year after his death. To all of Doll's children he left six hundred dollars each to be paid to them within two years after his death. The rest and residue of his estate, real and personal, he bequeathed to his wife, his god-

---

193. From the Mackay-McQueen-Cowper Collection owned by the Georgia Society of the Colonial Dames of America deposited in the Georgia Historical Society, Savannah. Typed copy is in the collection, but the original letter is lost; so the date cannot be checked (1949).
194. The property is now (1949) owned by Mr. Raiford J. Wood, the Director of the Telfair Academy of Arts and Sciences, Savannah.
195. LaFar and Wilson, *Abstracts of Wills, Chatham County, Georgia*, 57.

daughter, Harriet Louisa Baillie, his "adopted daughter, (being my niece) who now lives with me Harriet Thomson Houstoun," to be divided among them share and share alike.

On receiving her share, his wife had to consent and agree to "throw in all and every the negroes which she may claim under or which are contained or comprehended in a certain Deed executed by her Father . . . into common stock . . . and also this further consideration that my said Wife set up no claim against my Estate for Dower . . . But if my said Wife shall set up any such Claim of Dower or make other Demand than under this will or refuse to throw in the said negroes . . . then it is my will . . . that my said Wife shall receive nothing further out of my Estate than the said negroes . . . which . . . I do . . . hereby ratify and confirm to her and a reasonable sum to be settled (by my Executors if that can be done, and if not in Court of Law) for her Dower." Following that clause was the provision that the remainder of his estate was to be divided among the other two residuary legatees. His executors were his three nephews Patrick Houstoun, James Edmund Houstoun, and John Houstoun McIntosh.[196]

Although the appraisers mentioned the "negroes subject to Mrs. Houstoun's claim," it would appear that Hannah Houstoun accepted her husband's decree, as the Reynolds Square house remained in her possession several years longer. Two years after his death John Houstoun's estate was still unsettled. From a study of the advertisements of his executors no conclusion can be reached as to the solvency of John Houstoun at the time of his death. It is almost certain that much of his property had to be sold to pay his debts and legacies. The first notice appeared in one of the newspapers in October following his death, and offered for sale a small stock of cattle and hogs and some household furniture at the "thicket," near Darien, in McIntosh County.[197] The next announced a sale, to be held at the courthouse on December 6, 1796, of a plantation or tract of land in Liberty County, in the district of Sapelo, 35,000 acres, under cultivation, with a new barn and Negro houses. Also, in the first part of December, a notice stated that on January 23 of the next year all of the

---

196. Ordinary's Office, Chatham County Court House, Box H, 1-47, No. 22.
197. *Georgia Gazette*, October 13, 1796.

household property would be on sale at the house of the late John Houstoun, conditions cash.[198] In the year 1798 more property was sold. In April a public auction took place at Cathead plantation of a moiety of slaves belonging to the estate of John Houstoun. Cathead, it will be recalled, was the plantation of his brother Patrick. All of the Negroes, also two valuable, improved, rice plantations, one of 2500 acres, on Cathead Creek, and one of 3500 acres within a few miles of the latter, called Turkey Camp, were to be sold on February 5 of the following year.[199] Of the Negroes, the notice read: "the gang consists of sawyers, jobbing carpenters, and prime field hands, amounting in all to upwards of an hundred. Persons inclined," it was advised, "to purchase seasonal Negroes had better avail themselves of this opportunity, as perhaps so good a one may not occur for some time . . . ."[200]

As one of the heirs of her father Hannah Houstoun held property in her own right. She owned a lot in Yamacraw, which once belonged to the Reverend Mr. Zubly, left to her by her mother, and the six Negroes given to her by her father in his lifetime, presumably her dower. She had plantations on Wilmington and Skidaway islands, and the unsold half-lot at White Bluff. On June 5, 1799, the hammer fell on her beautiful home on Reynolds Square, when the property was sold to George Woodruff and James Johnston, Jr., sons-in-law of Sir George Houstoun, Baronet, in trust for the heirs of the latter.[201] Two years later Hannah Houstoun gave a quit claim of the property to the above-named trustees.[202] Later in the month she requested her nephew, Joseph

---

198. *Columbian Museum & Savannah Advertiser*, November 29, 1796, December 9, 1796.
199. *Ibid.*, December 7, 1798. Turkey Camp plantation was not sold until many years later. The proceeds were divided among the grandchildren of James Johnston, Jr.
200. *Ibid.*, December 13, 1798.
201. Office of the Clerk of the Superior Court of Chatham County. Book V, 408.
202. *Ibid.*, Book V-469. Later in the month the trustees, who were the husbands of Jean Houstoun Woodruff and Ann Marion Houstoun Johnston, conveyed one undivided interest to their wives and their children. (Books Y-317 and X-384). In June, 1808, the Woodruffs deeded their half to Colonel and Mrs. Johnston, (Book 2B-214), who on their deaths left the house, known in the family as "The Mansion," to their children, the youngest of whom was Susan (Book 2Z-507). In 1840, a marriage

Bryan, by letter, to pay her brother-in-law, Richard Wylly, the sum of $1000, "which is my due for my Proportion of the Union."[203]

Mrs. John Houstoun lacked three months of being thirty-seven years old when her husband died, and during the eleven years of her widowhood she turned her energies to farming. From an inventory of her estate made some years after her death, it seems that she planted cotton on her main plantation on Wilmington Island, where she had seven Negroes valued at seventeen hundred dollars, two cotton gins, and twelve "head of cattle."[204]

Ten months before her death, Mrs. Houstoun, her sister Mary Wylly, and their nephew Joseph Bryan, paid to the former wife of their deceased brother James, Mrs. Ann Middleton and her husband, David Middleton, of South Carolina, the sum of three thousand dollars, who in turn released all claim whatsoever to the estate of Jonathan Bryan, with the exception of a tract of land on the Great Ogeechee River near a place known as Bryan's Cowpen, relinquished by the above named heirs.[205]

In August, 1807, Hannah Houstoun's health began to decline. She lingered until the latter part of November when she returned to the city "from the country,"[206] and died at her residence in Savannah, of fever, a few days later on November 23, 1807, at the age of forty-eight. She was buried the next day. In December, Mrs. Wylly and Joseph Bryan, her nearest relatives, applied for letters of administration on her estate. Like that of her husband, her last resting place is unknown.

Thirty-five years after John Houstoun's death the legislature of the State of Georgia passed an act on May 15, 1821, setting

---

settlement was entered into between Susan Marion Johnston and George Jones Kollock, who became the owners of the house (Book 2Z-79) until August 14, 1849, when the property was sold to Dr. James Proctor Screven. (Book 3G-58).

203. Copied from original order and receipt, with signature of Hannah Houstoun, owned by Mrs. Samuel C. Lawrence of Charleston, West Virginia.
204. Chatham County Court House, Ordinary's Office. File No. 61.
205. Copy of deed owned by Mrs. S. C. Lawrence.
206. Mortuary Records of the City of Savannah, Vol. 2, p. 19. It is recorded she was by "profession a planter."

aside Houston County;[207] and by a strange coincidence, the new county was formed within the territory of the Creek Nation which had been acquired by the United States for the use of Georgia through a treaty concluded at the Indian Spring in the previous January. Houston County is a part of "the territory lying between a line commencing on the Ocmulgee River opposite Fort Hawkins and running due west on the Flint River...."[208] In naming the county those who wrote the text of the act did not even pay the former governor the compliment of mentioning the reason why the county was thus named, but left it to other state records to preserve the fact that it was designated Houston County for a man who had served the state faithfully.[209] A street in Savannah, in the old part of the town, is named for John Houstoun, but it is spelled "Houston"; and one in Augusta likewise in the old section, is named for the former governor, and is also spelled "Houston."

Two estimates of the character of John Houstoun have been selected to close the story of the "Rebell Governor": "The name of John Houstoun is entitled to the highest respect; for he was indeed a man of strong abilities, of purest patriotism, and of the most determined courage;"[210] and Charles C. Jones's tribute. "John Houstoun," he wrote, "was amongst the most zealous advocates of the rights of the colonists. Of honorable descent and liberal education, of acknowledged bravery and commanding influence, his memory is indissolubly associated with some of the best traditions of the epoch and community in which he dwelt."[211]

---

207. The honor would have been greater if the legislators who framed the act had seen to it that his last name was spelled correctly. There is little excuse for the error, as contemporaneous official records, more frequently than not, carry the name spelled correctly. No doubt an indifferent and inattentive clerk is responsible for the blunder.
208. Certified copy of the act furnished the author by the late John B. Wilson, Secretary of State of Georgia, October 7, 1937.
209. Ruth Blair, State Archivist, compiler, *Georgia Official and Statistical Register*, 1929 (Atlanta): "Houston County . . . named for Governor John Houstoun." See also White, *Statistics of the State of Georgia*, 332, where the name is spelled Houstoun.
210. Miller, *Bench and Bar of Georgia*, 96.
211. Jones, *History of Georgia*, II, 203.

Chapter XII

JAMES HOUSTOUN, SURGEON IN THE CONTINENTAL ARMY

JAMES HOUSTOUN'S second appearance in this history presents him as a young man of property. On October 2, 1770, he was one of the petitioners praying the Royal Council for one hundred and fifty acres of land in St. Matthew's Parish, explaining he had long been in the province and had one slave. The tract of land he desired had been granted formerly to Michael Joyce, but James Houstoun stated it had lapsed in the surveyor general's office. His petition was granted. However, he could not have acquired the land he coveted, because one year later, November 5, 1771, he again sent a petition to the Governor and council "setting forth that he was bred up in this Province had had no land granted him, that he was possessed of five slaves and intended soon to purchase an additional number, and being desirous of obtaining land for cultivation, therefore praying for 500 acres of land on Finhalloway Swamp."[1] That application was also granted. Finhalloway Swamp was a desirable tract in the northern part of St. Andrew's Parish, about ten miles from the coast, but again James Houstoun was disappointed in his choice of land. He had not reckoned on the fact that a large portion of cultivable land in that parish had been taken up by the Scottish settlers of Darien, particularly all available acres around Finhalloway Swamp.[2] He obtained the rights from the council, but during the month that followed he evidently discovered that the tract had been surveyed and granted to other persons, as on December 3 he "prayed in lieu thereof five hundred Acres of Land ordered to James Lucena on the Altamaha."[3] James Houstoun had reached that age when a man should support himself, and he decided, for the time being at least, to be a

1. *Colonial Records of Georgia*, XI, 138; XII, 118.
2. Information from Marmaduke H. Floyd of Savannah.
3. *Colonial Records of Georgia*, XII, 130.

planter. The particular land which he at last succeeded in owning was in a district especially adapted to the cultivation of rice, a commodity then popular for trading with the merchants in foreign ports south of the colonies as well as in the colonies themselves. By the next year lot number 63 in the newly surveyed town of Brunswick had been added to James Houstoun's holdings.

The next event in James Houstoun's career demonstrates the predilection for political life that seems to have been the bent of all the Houstoun men of that generation, with the exception of George, since on December 9, 1772, James entered the Lower House of Assembly as an elector from St. James's Parish, although he was a resident of Christ Church Parish. The qualifications for membership in the Commons House of Assembly were determined by an act passed on June 9, 1761. It was decreed that any person elected or returned to serve must be "a free born Subject of Great Britain or of the dominion thereunto belonging or a fforeign [sic] person Naturalized professing the Christian Religion and no other and that hath arrived at the Age of Twenty One Years and hath been a Resident of this Province for twelve Months before the date of the said Writ and being legally possessed in his own Right in this Province of a Tract of Land containing at least ffive [sic] hundred acres."[4]

On the day he became a member of the house he pledged the oath of abjuration and took his seat, and his brother Patrick returned to the Royal Legislature as a delegate from St. Andrew's Parish. Sir Patrick Houstoun, sixth baronet, was then living on his plantation near Darien. James Houstoun was frequently assigned to committees and often served with his brother Patrick. He continued a member of the assembly through the years 1773 and 1774.

As he was always referred to on those committees as "Dr. Houstoun," it is evident he had already prepared himself for a later contribution to his state, that of surgeon in the Continental Army. In Georgia's colonial period there was but one way for a man to obtain training as a physician, and that was under the instruction of a recognized doctor who acted as preceptor. "For reputable physicians the training period was a minimum of two years, and frequently, three to five years from European schools,

---

4. *Ibid.*, XVIII, 467.

or licenses from licensing bodies in England, Scotland, or Continental Europe. Not many physicians had attended the few medical schools then existing in America, and not all who did had medical degrees. The courses of lectures in the American medical schools were only four months long, and extended over two years. Physicians who took the regular courses of four months each for two years received degrees; those who attended only one course, did not. Often, for those physicians who took medical degrees from American schools, it was necessary that a period of preparation be spent with a preceptor."[5] When those who had been trained by a preceptor entered the Continental Army, they received a wider experience under the guidance of, for that day, more highly trained men, and those assistants were called "surgeons' mates."

There were several physicians living in Savannah in the 1770's who might have been the preceptors of James Houstoun. Among them was Colonel Noble Jones, one of the earliest colonists and an associate of James Houstoun's father. Colonel Jones was "bred to the profession of physic, which he practiced in England until he removed to Georgia."[6] Dr. Noble Wimberly Jones, son and pupil of the former, was by the year 1756 practicing medicine in Savannah. There were also Dr. Lewis Johnston, formerly a surgeon in the Royal Navy, and his brother Dr. Andrew Johnston, both trained in Scotland, who came to Georgia in the 1750's. Among the medical contemporaries of Dr. Houstoun were Dr. William Martin Johnston, Dr. James Cuthbert, Dr. Charles Young, Dr. David Brydie, "Dr. Hazes," Dr. George Fraser, and others. Dr. Houstoun entered into partnership with the latter, and was associated with him until Dr. Fraser's death. The partnership of Houstoun and Fraser indicates that James Houstoun received his medical training before 1775.

James Houstoun was married on February 4, 1775, to Eliza

---

5. Information contributed by the late Dr. Victor H. Bassett, Health Officer of Savannah, (1936), Librarian and Past President of the Georgia Medical Society (Savannah).
6. Victor H. Bassett, *A Medical Biography*, (Extracts from *Bulletin of the Georgia Medical Society*, Savannah, 1936), 3.

Crooke Tannant,[7] the daughter of Mrs. James Mossman by her husband Edmund Tannant, a Savannah merchant. Mrs. Mossman, the former Elizabeth Crooke was descended from distinguished families of St. Christopher's, B.W.I. and South Carolina. She was born at St. Kitt's, and her mother, Heriot, the daughter of Robert Cunningham, of South Carolina, was a widow when she married Clement Crooke in 1771.

The Crookes owned a house on Bay Street "adjoining the Honorable Noble Jones."[8] Their daughters intermarried with some of Savannah's most prominent families. Frances became the wife of Lieutenant Governor John Graham; Susannah married Alexander Wylly, at one time speaker of the House of Assembly; Jane married Philip Young, Sr.; Elizabeth was Mrs. Tannant (later Mossman); and Jourdina was the wife of George Baillie. Their sons were Robert, who apparently died young, and Richard, who at the time of his death was a clerk of the Commons House of Assembly. Mrs. Tannant was left a widow with four children, three daughters and a son. The daughters were Mary, who married James Hume, Attorney General of Georgia; Eliza Crooke, who married Dr. James Houstoun, and Heriot Crooke Tannant. Edmund Tannant in his will, probated January 10, 1763, left a legacy to his daughter Eliza Crooke.[9] A little over a

---

7. The author is indebted to Mrs. Maxfield Parrish of St. Simon's Island, Georgia, for clearing up the maiden name of Mrs. James Houstoun. In a family Bible examined some years ago by the author was an entry, "Dr. James and Eliza Crooke Houstoun." It was natural to assume that the latter's family name was Crooke. Mrs. Parrish's research proved it to be Tannant. That, coupled with a reference in a letter of Robert Mackay written on February 5, 1775, indicating that the marriage took place the day before, was further evidence of the correct surname. The aforesaid Bible is not now (1949) available. Several issues of the *Georgia Gazette* for 1775 are lost, and it is possible that the marriage notices of both John and James Houstoun may have been in some of the missing issues.
8. The house was on the south side of Bay near Lincoln streets, and was offered for sale in the *Georgia Gazette*, June 8, 1768, and often thereafter. It happened in many instances that property offered for sale in the colony's newspapers was not always disposed of, as in the instance of the Crooke residence, but remained in the family, at least until the year 1845, when it was owned by Miss Jane Young (died, 1883). The number was 33.
9. Georgia Colonial Wills, Telamon Cuyler Collection, numbers 57 and 63, in the State Department of Archives and History, Atlanta. Transcripts in Hodgson Hall, Savannah.

year later, on April 7, 1764, Mrs. Tannant married James Mossman,[10] a Savannah merchant, and later an ardent Loyalist.

By 1775, the town of Sunbury, beautifully situated in St. John's Parish between the Midway and Newport rivers, had come into prominence as the rival port of Savannah. James Houstoun obtained a choice lot on King's Square, known as number 70, and probably held it as an investment as later he offered it for sale.

Early in the following year Dr. Fraser died, and in January, 1776, his executors, one of whom was James Houstoun, advertised in the *Georgia Gazette* asking all persons indebted to Dr. Fraser to discharge their obligations immediately. In the same issue appeared another advertisement announcing the expiration of the Houstoun-Fraser partnership and urging both debtors and creditors to arrange for prompt settlements. Further, the same issue advertised the sale of the property of the late partnership, including the shop, medicines, utensils, and three Negro men.[11]

The sale of the shop probably temporarily interrupted Dr. Houstoun's practice, since war clouds were gathering and he must have felt he would soon be needed for hospital duty whereever he might be called. At any rate, a year later he was making his plans for active service. Like his brother, John, there was no hesitation on the part of James Houstoun on which side he should throw his lot, and he made a prompt decision to espouse the cause of the Patriots.

2

In the spring of 1776, Dr. Houstoun played the part of intermediary for a Loyalist friend, James Hume, his wife's brother-in-law, and a nephew of Governor Wright, who had gone to London in January.[12] The Council of Safety at its session on May 29, 1776, sitting in Savannah, decided that it was necessary to have the courthouse repaired and cleaned. It was thereupon ordered that the guard be moved from that building to the house of Hume, who had formerly held the office of attorney general under the Royal Council, but it was added to the reso-

---

10. *Georgia Gazette*, June 14, 1764. Data on the Crookes supplied by Mrs. Maxfield Parrish and Walter Charlton Hartridge.
11. *Georgia Gazette*, January 10, 1776.
12. "Letters of Governor Sir James Wright," in *Collections of the Georgia Historical Society*, III, 229. Governor Wright spoke of him as "a young man of Great Veracity."

lution, "or any other house that may be agreeable to the gentlemen of the Batallion."[13] The news having reached the ears of Dr. Houstoun that same day, he immediately wrote to Archibald Bulloch, President of the Council of Safety, endeavoring to prevent the action against his friend. Bulloch presented the letter to the council at once. Dr. Houstoun, in his letter, informed Bulloch he understood from Mr. Langworthy, secretary of the council, that it was the desire of the latter to obtain the keys of Hume's house as the president had ordered that it be used for a guard house during the session of the council. Dr. Houstoun commented: "The house has received very great damage from the companies that have been in it (during the alarm) such as ripping the whole of the paper, burning the chimney piece in the best room, etc."[14] Dr. Houstoun concluded by saying the attorneys were just preparing to renovate the house for "the reception of a family," and courteously requested council to find another house for the purpose desired. The council, however, was not to be deterred from its first selection, and was of the unanimous opinion that Hume's house should be commandeered for a temporary guard house. Bulloch thereupon wrote to the commanding officer of the guard, apprising him of the course decided upon by the council, stating that when application was made to Dr. Houstoun for the keys, none could be procured. He then issued the following order: "You will, therefore, endeavor by the best means in your power to enter the house and make use of it accordingly." At five o'clock in the afternoon, President Bulloch answered the letter of Dr. Houstoun informing the latter he could not depart from the decision of the council, but expressing his regret for any loss that individuals might sustain, ending his letter with this terse sentence, "but the public good must be considered."[15]

---

13. *Revolutionary Records of Georgia*, I, 133.
14. The "alarm" to which Dr. Houstoun refers occurred in the month of March, previously, when eleven merchant vessels laden with rice were lying at the wharves of Savannah, and British warships entering the harbor sailed up the river and succeeded in burning three ships. The patriots of the town, reinforced by troops from South Carolina, threw up breastworks on Yamacraw Bluff, a skirmish followed, and the British were frustrated in their attempt, but many Loyalists were forced to leave town. Jones, *History of Georgia*, II, 222-30.
15. *Revolutionary Records of Georgia*, I, 133, 134, 135.

The letter to the commanding officer and the one to Dr. Houstoun evidently closed the matter, and James Houstoun's efforts in behalf of his friend proved futile. James Hume was a member of the Royal Council in 1772, and for that reason was unpopular with the Patriots in control of Savannah. The rebels showed no mercy when they desired to heap indignities upon the King's loyal subjects, but the tables were turned when the British reigned supreme in Savannah, because the Loyalists wreaked vengeance upon those Patriots who remained in the captured town.

Dr. Houstoun was in Savannah in March, 1777. He and his wife acted as sponsors at the baptism of Patrick, the oldest son of James's brother George, but on April 14 Dr. Houstoun left Savannah with his brother Patrick and Major Raymond Demere for Charles Town. Major Demere recorded in his diary that he embarked with the above mentioned men "on his way to Philadelphia to join the Continental troops." Unquestionably James Houstoun accompanied him to the northern city to make his own arrangements for entering the Continental Army, because in October he returned to Savannah bearing a letter from Henry Laurens, delegate to the Continental Congress (later in the year president), to Joseph Clay, who in August of that year had been recognized by the congress as deputy paymaster general in Georgia with the rank of colonel. The letter in which Joseph Clay referred to Dr. Houstoun was dated Savannah, October 16, 1777,[16] and began: "Since my last to you I have received your several favours of the 20th August and 2d Ulto, the latter per Dr. Houstoun who arrived here last Saturday Evening, who gives us a very pleasing and Interesting Account of our Affairs Northerly —he mentions a very considerable detachment of Howe's Army[17] I think 2000 being killed or taken. . . . " Colonel Clay continued by elaborating on his high expectations. Indeed he had a hopeful view of the times, because, in a succeeding letter, he expressed

16. Joseph Clay, *Joseph Clay's Letters, Merchant of Savannah, 1776-1793* . . . in *Collections of the Georgia Historical Society*, VIII, 10, 46. (Hereafter cited as *Clay's Letters*.)
17. Sir William Howe, British General under General Gage. Because of his indolence in Philadelphia, in 1777, 1778 when General Washington was at Valley Forge, he was superseded by Sir Henry Clinton. *Appleton's Cyclopaedia of American Biography* (1888), III, 280.

himself to his friend Laurens thus: "I thank God I see a Dawn of Hope arising amidst all our distresses."[18] His concept of the situation was sadly premature; the disaster that was to overtake Savannah was not many months away.

In the spring of 1778, General Robert Howe, Governor Houstoun, and Colonel Elbert were making their plans for the fatal expedition to Florida, and by April the latter with his troops was on the march to Fort Howe. Dr. Houstoun was attached to the hospital department as a surgeon's mate. By the time the troops reached Sunbury the army had many sick on its hands, and sometime in June Dr. Houstoun wrote to Colonel Clay "that twelve of the sick soldiers had died before he reached there, 117 were in a very poor way, and that there were 120 at Sapelo who were in a fair way of recovery."[19] Captain Morris, Commissary Coddington, and Dr. Houstoun were in charge of the sick at Sunbury, and the latter part of June Dr. Houstoun made a requisition upon Colonel Clay for money to purchase the many "necessarys the soldiers were in want of," telling him that supplies could not be procured without cash and that the commissary of hospitals had no money to provide for the needs of the "Poor Unhappy People." Colonel Clay reported the situation to General Robert Howe who was then with his Continental troops at Reid's Bluff on the Altamaha River. In his reply to Dr. Houstoun, Colonel Clay informed him he was exceedingly sorry to learn of the situation of the soldiers, and, although it was entirely out of his province to send money in the manner proposed, "Nevertheless," he wrote, "it must not on this occasion be wanted, Humanity & every other obligation forbid it . . . however I shall not hesitate to pay it in that way that will the most speedily & effectually relieve these poor people from their Distressed condition."[20] General Howe evidently approved of Colonel Clay's action, as the deputy paymaster wrote on July 3 to Deputy Commissary Purchaser Coddington that he had paid Dr. Houstoun one thousand pounds and had his receipt for "the same."[21] While Dr. Houstoun was at Sunbury his brother John, the Governor of Georgia, passed through the camp on his way to join General

---
18. *Clay's Letters*, 55.
19. *Ibid.*, 94.
20. *Ibid.*, 87, 88.
21. *Ibid.*, 95.

Howe at Fort Tonyn, and of course the two brothers met and exchanged news both of a family and of a general nature.

Neither the date of Dr. Houstoun's commission as a surgeon's mate in the Continental Army nor his separation from it has been located. His name first appears on the pay roll of the Continental Army covering the period from July 1 to November 1, 1779, which shows that his pay commenced May 1, and his name is last borne on the pay roll from November 1, 1779, to February 1, 1780, which indicates that he was paid to that date. He was a surgeon in the First Georgia Continental Battalion commanded successively by Colonel Robert Rae and by Major John Habersham.[22] The date of Colonel Rae's commission has not been recorded, only the fact that he was a colonel in the Georgia troops, but Major Habersham was mustered into the Continental service first as a lieutenant, January 7, 1776, then advanced to captain and finally was promoted to brigade major of the Georgia forces in the Continental establishment of which Lachlan McIntosh was the ranking officer and Samuel Elbert the second in command.[23]

After Dr. Houstoun's medical work at Sunbury his hospital duties continued. In August, 1779, he and General Lachlan McIntosh were in Augusta, conferring on a place to set up a hospital for the army's sick soldiers. Their problem was solved when they appealed to the executive council of the state at its meeting in Augusta held on August 17. They requested the "use of the Church in Augusta as a hospital." The council promptly granted the request, and appointed a committee to " . . . see that the proper care is taken of the pews and other matters belonging to the Church . . ."[24] The church referred to was St. Paul's (Church of England Mission) which was built opposite to Fort Augusta about 1750. The town of Augusta was captured by the British

---

22. Information received through the courtesy of Brigadier General Frank C. Burnett, Acting The Adjutant General, War Department, August 28, 1936.
23. Francis B. Heitman, *Historical Register of Officers of the Continental Army During the War of the Revolution* (Washington, D. C., 1893), 203. See also, C. C. Jones, Jr., *Biographical Sketch of the Honorable John Habersham of Georgia* (Cambridge, 1886), 14, 15. Privately printed. Also Jones, *Biographical Sketches of the Delegates to the Continental Congress.*
24. *Revolutionary Records of Georgia*, II, 160.

in February, 1779, but it was evacuated by them in two weeks, when the American forces re-occupied it. Dr. Houstoun, of course, remained with the hospital corps. When General McIntosh united with Brigadier General Pulaski and was directed to move from Augusta to join General Benjamin Lincoln for the attempted but unsuccessful siege of Savannah, Dr. Houstoun was behind the lines engaged in his work of attending and relieving the wounded. Following that engagement Dr. Houstoun found his way to Charles Town and when General Lincoln, who was defending that city, was forced to capitulate to Sir Henry Clinton on May 12, 1780, Dr. Houstoun was taken prisoner. Not long after that disaster occurred he evinced a desire to visit his family in Savannah. He gave his parole to General Alexander Leslie, who was in command of Charles Town and obtained permission from Sir Henry Clinton to go to Savannah. To Dr. Houstoun's surprise and chagrin, when he arrived in Savannah he was arrested by order of the chief justice and was kept in custody at the home of his wife's step-father, James Mossman, where he was detained in close confinement. Houstoun was fortunate in the selection of his place of captivity. James Mossman owned a large brick house on the Bay, with eight rooms neatly furnished, six of them having fireplaces. There were several outbuildings built of brick, a kitchen, a stable for three horses, and a carriage house.[25]

But in a few weeks Dr. Houstoun could contain his anger no longer. On June 21 he wrote to Lieutenant Colonel Sir Alured Clarke, commanding at Savannah, stating his position and asking for redress. Dr. Houstoun's main grievance, according to his letter to Colonel Clarke, was that while he was a prisoner in the service of the United States and held a "commission as Physician and Surgeon to the Hospitals of the United States,"[26] he was being kept under guard by civil authorities for high treason because he had worked in the American hospitals during the time of the siege of Savannah. This, he said, "must appear to every unprejudiced Person Cruel and unprecedented." If, he wrote, he had been arrested for any information of a private nature against him he would not expect to be protected by his parole. Dr. Houstoun had tried every expedient

---
25. *Royal Georgia Gazette*, October 18, 1781.
26. Unpublished Colonial Records of Georgia, XXXVIII, 392.

known to him, but without success. He had made application, without avail, to appear before a general court which had been held during his incarceration, and to appear and answer any charges *if* they were of a private nature, but his request had been refused. He was under the impression that another court would be held in December, and he had "offered security to appear at that time," and again he was denied his request. As a prisoner of war he had, as a last resort, approached Colonel Clarke, adding, "In this situation I hold it my Duty to apply to You for Redress, and flatter my self you will not permit Your Prisoner to be insulted and confined without Cause contrary to the Articles of Capitulation entered into and ratified by the Commanding Officers of the two Armies before the Surrender of Charles Town."

3

The arrest and letter of Dr. Houstoun commanded the attention of high officials in both Georgia and South Carolina, and his letter to Colonel Clarke even reached the hands of Lord Cornwallis. Readers of the correspondence may be quite puzzled to find where the truth really lies; and the insinuation in the letter which Attorney General Robertson wrote to Governor Wright the day following Dr. Houstoun's to Colonel Clarke, might even appear that "the lie was passed" between the two men. All of the accusations on both sides merely show the temper of the times, and the sad but true tale of bitterness that existed between friends, Loyalist on one side and Patriot on the other. Attorney General Robertson wrote Governor Wright he had "been favored with the perusal of Mr. Houstoun's letter to Colonel Clarke," stating that his office gave him opportunity of being well acquainted with the case and also "privy to many of the Circumstances he alludes to." He went fully into the details of the arrest of Dr. Houstoun and others, saying they were carried before the chief justice, adding that to the best of his knowledge "six or seven Informations were read charging Mr. Houstoun with being Active in Rebellion expressly which charges he made light of." Both attitudes were perfectly natural in the light of the times. Dr. Houstoun, Attorney General Robertson alleged, was ready to give bail but the chief justice acquainted him with the fact that offences were not bailable, and called on the attorney general for an opinion. The latter, it seems, felt himself not at liberty to give his consent for the accused to take bail, but thought there would be no impropriety in committing the prisoners to a private house under the care of "special gaolers" if they would suggest an abode agreeable to themselves. Thus it was that Dr. Houstoun was committed to the home of Mr. Mossman, the former residence of Dr. Houstoun's wife, and according to the attorney general a "Place of Resort for his most particular Friends." Then followed what may be termed a conflict of statements. Attorney General Robertson assured Governor Wright that he did not recollect "to have exchanged one word with him [Dr. Houstoun] on the cause of his confinement, neither did he in person, inform *me* that he was desirous to be brought to trial," adding that even if he had done so, he, the attorney general, believed it out of his power to comply with his request because several of the witnesses of "his Conduct during the Siege" lived too far from town to attend court. The next part of Attorney General Robertson's letter contained information that redounds to the credit of Dr. Houstoun and shows his intention to be true and faithful to the cause of the American patriots. The other prisoners wished to solicit a pardon from the commander-in-chief. Two resolved to return to their former allegiance and requested that the state oaths might be tendered them. One had already taken the oath, and the other intended doing so the next day; "but," wrote the attorney general, "Mr. Houstoun shows no such Disposition, on the Contrary I am informed is sullen and obstinate in his Aversion to the British Government. Yet he expects the same Favor with the others." Three friends of Dr. Houstoun intervened for him and received the same answer from the attorney general, "let him do as the others had done and he was entitled to the same Indulgence." Attorney General Robertson concluded his letter thus:

> I leave Your Excellency therefore to judge, how far the Treatment of this Man, is either Cruel or Unprecedented, how far, he can be said to be insulted and confined without cause, and how far I have shown any intention to detain him longer in Confinement, than the Duty of my Office and Respect for his Majesty's Government requires.[27]

---
27. *Ibid.*, 480-483.

The next communication was from the attorney general of South Carolina, James Simpson, written to Governor Wright, dated Charles Town, July 6, 1780, in which the South Carolina official wrote that "Lord Cornwallis hath been pleased to refer to me a Letter from Doctor James Houstoun to Colonel Clarke," and repeated the facts as stated in the previous letters. Simpson's view of the case of Dr. Houstoun was that since it was of a military nature it could not be prosecuted in a court of justice. His charge of high treason antedated his capture in Charles Town and he held his parole under the terms of the capitulation. The attorney general informed Governor Wright that Lord Cornwallis and General Patterson were "both of Opinion that as long as Dr Houstoun remains a Prisoner under the Terms of Capitulation, he ought not to be called to answer for the Treasons he may have committed before that time." He concluded with the assumption that the Georgia governor would give the necessary directions to restore Dr. Houstoun to the "relative Situation in which he was placed by the military commanders." It would be much easier to explain if the matter had ended there, because the sequence is not so pleasant to relate.[28]

In the interim between Attorney General Simpson's letter and the answer communicated to him by Georgia's attorney general, something happened to Dr. Houstoun which, if true, is not illuminating in the light of his professed allegiance to the Patriot cause. Attorney General Robertson answered for Governor Wright, under the date of August 8, when he informed Attorney General Simpson that "Dr. James Houstoun, who was before Your letter came to hand, admitted to Bail in consequences of Assurances that he means to return to his former Allegiance and obedience." "Had he done that sooner," Attorney General Robertson adds, in what would appear petulance or impatience, "he would have merited with the others the same Indulgence and saved us all much trouble. It is His Excellency's Desire that I write You on this Subject, and he desires it may be made known to Lord Cornwallis and General Patterson, that he has a high Esteem for, and shall always shew every Respect and Attention to the opinions of these Gentlemen, and every Person employed in

---

28. *Ibid.*, 484-485.

His Majesty's Service in every other matter that may come properly under his Direction and lye within his Sphere."

The Georgia attorney general went on to explain to South Carolina's official that it was not in the power of the governor to order any person charged of high treason to be discharged when once apprehended, and explained Governor Wright's inability to comply with Simpson's request.

"It is to me a Matter of very serious concern," he concluded, "and in my Opinion of a dangerous Tendency to see Notorious Offenders at large in this Province, under Military Passports.... In Regard of the particular Case of Mr Houstoun, I am of opinion the Commissioners' Pardon will avail him much more in a Court of Law than the Articles of Capitulation on the Surrender at Charles Town. You acknowledge circumstanced as he is, at a future Day, that he may be amenable to Justice, for prior Offences I think so too, and that he is equally amenable at present.

"Yet granting that it be not improper to put the Law in force against him, I presume You will agree with me that it is both proper and expedient, to teach such Persons, that no Reasons of State can control the Decress of Law, when a civil Government prevails. And that for their own security they should at least, keep without Reach of the Influence of a Power, which pays no respect to Persons.... I am inclined to think General Leslie did not consider the Consequences when he enlarged Mr Houstoun's Passport to Georgia before he had given full Assurance of his Intentions."[29]

While Dr. Houstoun was being kept a prisoner in Savannah, Governor Wright's council passed the British Disqualifying Act on July 1, 1780, and James Houstoun was numbered among the "cream" of Savannah's patriotic citizens as being incapable of holding any office of trust, but it affected him as little as it did the other "Rebels" who continued their activity in the Revolution. In spite of the fact that Dr. Houstoun was "admitted to bail" he apparently was still worrying the authorities in Savannah, because in August, 1780, he, together with the Patriot Chief Justice John Glen and John Sutcliffe, "Noted rebels," were "boldly appearing in Savannah and defying the royal authorities."[30]

---
29. *Ibid.*, 485-487.
30. Jones, *History of Georgia*, II, 426.

4

After that incident Dr. James Houstoun is lost sight of in records until the War of the Revolution was over. On February 17, 1783, he was listed among the applicants for the land bounty which was due them for their services in what was called the Georgia Continental Establishment. In 1785, under United States warrants but granted by the State of Georgia, he was awarded nine hundred and twenty acres in Washington County, for service in the Revolution.

When the war was over, the officers of the Revolutionary Army under the leadership of their commander-in-chief, General George Washington, established "The Society of the Cincinnati." Dr. James Houstoun was one of the original members, and one of the founders of the Georgia society. The object of the society was to perpetuate the friendship of the officers and to raise a fund for relieving the widows and orphans of the men who had died during the war.

The "Institution Society" was formed at Newburgh, New York, on May 13, 1783, and in the months following societies were formed in each of the thirteen states. The Society of the Cincinnati in the State of Georgia was organized in Savannah on August 13, 1783, and the members then adjourned to meet the next day to elect their officers: President, Major General Lachlan McIntosh; vice president, Brigadier General Samuel Elbert; secretary, Captain Milton; treasurer, Lieutenant Colonel McIntosh; and assistant treasurer, Major Habersham.

On September 1, the society met again and Dr. Houstoun was appointed on a committee to draw up rules and regulations for the internal government of the society. The same day he was appointed on a committee to draft an address to be sent to the governor of the state, Lyman Hall, to inform him of the organization of the society. On January 12, 1784, a meeting was held in Savannah for the purpose of electing delegates to represent Georgia at a meeting of the general society. Dr. Houstoun was one of those chosen for that honor.[31]

---

31. Information received through the courtesy of Mrs. Marmaduke H. Floyd, formerly Librarian at the Georgia Historical Society Library, Savannah, who derived it from her research work in the Manuscripts Division of the Library of Congress. Also from G. Noble Jones, president of the Society in the State of Georgia.

On January 19, 1784, Dr. Houstoun was in the Georgia House of Assembly, re-elected from Chatham County with James Green, and they took the oath prescribed in the Constitution and took their seats immediately. At that session of the assembly three Houstoun brothers were simultaneously members of the body. At the time of James's arrival, his brother John had been elected governor of the state just ten days previously. William Houstoun on the same day was elected for the second time a delegate to the Continental Congress, and was sitting in the house as such. From then on through the years 1784-1786 Dr. Houstoun was active in legislative work. The month following his admission to the state assembly, Dr. Houstoun's name was added, with seven other members, to the list of justices of the peace for Chatham County. Dr. Houstoun held that office until the year 1790. Soon after he resumed his seat in 1784, the assembly "Resolved that James Houstoun, Joseph Habersham, Peter Bard and William Stephens Esquires, be commissioners to contract for building a market in the Town of Savannah, and the said Commissioners are hereby empowered to give the rent of the same as a compensation for the expense of erecting the Building, for such time as they may agree upon."[32] Three years elapsed before the market was built on the public slip of ground at the end of Bull Street below the bluff, and opposite the vendue house.

Another appointment which the legislature made to Dr. Houstoun in February, 1784, was that of commissioner of roads for the northwest road in Chatham County, with seven other members assigned to the commission. Dr. Houstoun held that office also through the year 1790. During that session of the legislature which lasted from January 9 to February 26, 1784, Dr. Houstoun was paid seventeen pounds, fourteen shillings, eight pence for his services as an assemblyman.

The northwest road was the highway to Augusta and had been so designated even earlier than 1775.[33] There was a definite reason for Dr. James Houstoun's appointment as a commissioner of the "North-west Road," because the road passed through the district

---
32. *Revolutionary Records of Georgia*, III, 571.
33. Marie E. Reddy, "Some Notes About Cherokee Hill," (Savannah, 1936), unpublished manuscript in files of the Savannah Historical Research Association, 11. Quoted from *Georgia Gazette*, July 12, 1775. (Hereafter cited Reddy, "History of Cherokee Hill".)

known as Cherokee Hill where Dr. Houstoun was the owner of Colerain, his plantation eight miles up the Savannah River. It was "conveniently located for the residence of a gentleman owning tide lands," contained pine sufficient for plantation use, that is, for building purposes such as barns and fences, and some part of the tract was "good provision land." On the premises were a commodious dwelling house, kitchen, stable, and other buildings.[34] Other property owned by Dr. Houstoun was a tract of land containing nine hundred acres, part of the plantation known as "Nineteenth," twelve miles from Savannah. In February, 1784, Dr. Houstoun memorialized the legislature for permission to sell his property there, but his memorial was referred to a special committee, which recommended that the sale be postponed until the next session of the legislature. The delay in granting Dr. Houstoun's request was due to the fact that "Nineteenth" plantation was involved in the old subject of confiscated estates. General James Jackson had been one of the purchasers of lands under that category and owned part of "Nineteenth."

Nine years after the death of Dr. Fraser, his estate and the estate of the firm of Houstoun and Fraser still remained unsettled. Dr. Houstoun, as executor of the former, and "surviving co-partner" of the latter, advertised in *The Gazette of the State of Georgia*, March 24, 1785, that since he had moved into the country, he was placing his books, the books of the Fraser estate, and those of the Houstoun-Fraser partnership in the hands of Joseph Welsher, who had been authorized to "settle the same." All persons concerned were urged to make a "speedy and final settlement." It was in September of the same year, that James Houstoun offered his Colerain plantation for sale, "on credit," but no purchaser appeared up to the time of his death.[35]

5

When his brother George was Worshipful Master of Solomon's Lodge, James Houstoun was an active member. In December, 1785, the various lodges in the city were notified through the newspaper that the Festival of St. John the Evangelist would be

---
34. *The Gazette of the State of Georgia*, September 15, 1785.
35. Colerain later was merged in the large Potter tract on the Savannah River. Reddy, "History of Cherokee Hill." (See map attached to paper.)

celebrated at Brown's Coffee-house on Tuesday the twenty-seventh, "where the Masters, Wardens and Brethren of the different Constituted Lodges within this State, and all transient Masons, were invited and expected to join the Grand Lodge in due order at nine o'clock in the morning." Tickets at two dollars each, it was stated, could be had "of Brothers James Houstoun and Joseph Habersham." The notice was signed by "Ja⁸ Habersham, G. S. By order of the Grand Master."[36]

By an act of the Legislature of the State of Georgia, assembled in Augusta, February 13, 1786, provision was made for a health officer of the port of Savannah and surgeon of the Seamen's Hospital, to be under the direction of James Houstoun and others, previously appointed commissioners, who were to have the hospital erected. The health officer was entitled to receive the sum of three shillings sixpence for "every Topsail Vessel and two shillings and four pence for every other Vessel, Coasters and Vessels in distress only excepted."[37] The act further stipulated that of the money received on account of tonnage the sum of three pence for every ton was to be appropriated and set apart towards erecting a hospital for the reception of sick and disabled seamen in the town of Savannah. The commissioners had been appointed in February two years previously, and consisted of Dr. James Houstoun's brother George, Joseph Habersham, Joseph Clay, William O'Bryan and Leonard Cecil. Civic movements of that nature progressed slowly in those days, and the intention of the legislature, although planned so carefully, did not come to fruition until the year 1809.

Dr. Houstoun was instrumental in promoting educational as well as medical and civic interests. When in 1788, the Georgia Legislature passed the Act appointing trustees for an academy of learning, he was one of the seven men named to establish the Chatham Academy.

On April 16, 1791, Dr. Houstoun's wife died. They had been married only sixteen years. Her obituary appeared in the *Georgia Gazette* of April 21:

> On Saturday last departed this life, Mrs. Houstoun, wife of

---

36. *The Gazette of the State of Georgia*, December 8, 1785. For description of a celebration of that festival see *ante*, 198.
37. *Colonial Records of Georgia*, XIX, Pt. 2, 513, 514.

James Houstoun, Esq. a lady of exemplary merit. Happily tempered by nature for her several stations of daughter, wife, mother and friend, she dignified the whole with the character of a good Christian.

A few months after his wife's death Dr. Houstoun went to Scotland, the home country of his father and mother. He visited his old Loyalist friend from Savannah, James Hume, at his place, Carolside, near Edinburgh. It seems likely that Dr. Houstoun took some of his children with him. The deduction is made from a letter written by his daughter Harriet to her first cousin Priscilla Houstoun, although there is no mention of her father. Undated, it was written from Carolside:

> My dearest Cousin
> How happy did it make us to see my Dear Brother James we had not the smallest Idea of his coming till he came to Carolside it was an agreeable surprise to us all and we are very happy with him but look forward with sorrow to the time that we are to part with him again I wish my dear Priscilla that would never come
> Mossman is at present with Mr Balfour who is married Mr Meins eldest sister and they live near us which gives us an opportunity of seeing him often he says that you must tell Robert he will write him soon
> I am happy to hear that I have got too little cousins how I would like to see you all again
> My Uncle Aunt Miss Searls and Eliza join me in best love to my Aunt and your self and Cousins.[38]

The Houstouns probably remained abroad nearly two years, but Dr. Houstoun was back at home in September, 1793. He was absent from the meeting of the Trustees of the Chatham Academy on September 12, "because of illness," and died five days later, on September 17:

> "On Tuesday last departed this life, James Houstoun, Esq., a gentleman much respected while living and now universally regretted by all who had the pleasure of his acquaintance."[39]

---

38. Original letter owned by Miss Susan M. Kollock of Atlanta. On the back of the letter was scrawled "Housto Robert," who in 1793 was five years old.
39. *Georgia Gazette*, September 19, 1793.

Besides his three brothers, he left four children, James Edmund, Mossman, Harriet Thompson, and Johanna.

His will, made on June 25, 1791, wherein he stated he was "About to depart for Great Britain," was probated September 27, 1793, and his executors were his brothers, Sir George and John Houstoun; James Hume of Great Britain; and James Mossman. Legacies were left to his sons and to "each of his dear daughters." He mentions his plantations, Greenwich on Argyle Island, and Colerain; land on Hog Island; and "lands purchased from Mary Warnack."[40] Two years after his death his executors advertised for an experienced rice planter to "take over the management of James Houstoun's plantation in Savannah River."[41]

The saddest note in the life of Dr. James Houstoun was the item in the will of his brother Patrick which reads, "I give unto my brother James five shillings."[42] What animosity existed between those two brothers that caused Patrick, when making his will shortly before leaving his native land for the last time, to bequeath a mere pittance to his younger brother James? After a study of the life of Dr. James Houstoun the only conclusion that can be reached is that there existed a bitter personal feud between Patrick and James; the older brother at the end of his life was still strong in his allegiance to the King of England, and the younger one allied to the cause of freedom from British rule. It was a situation that existed in many families throughout the original thirteen states. No better illustration can be used to show how those were "the times that tried men's souls" and caused brother to revolt against brother.

James, the oldest child, was only fifteen years old men his father died, and the three others were correspondingly younger. When he was twenty-eight years old James married Mary Ann Williamson and had six children. Two died in infancy and were buried in the Brampton cemetery,[43] on the plantation of Jonathan Bryan, later owned by the Williamson family. Four children

---
40. LaFar and Wilson, *Abstract of Wills*, 57.
41. *Georgia Gazette*, January 1, 1795.
42. See *ante*, 173 ff.
43. Jane, 1805-1806; James Edmund, 1809-1817 (From tombstone in Brampton cemetery, and the James Houstoun Bible formerly owned by the late Miss Nina Anderson Pape of Savannah, not now available).

lived to maturity: Eliza, Mary Williamson, John, and James Edmund, Jr.⁴⁴ The father died at Marengo, in McIntosh County, on September 15, 1819. His obituary described him as "possessing fine talents, great energy of mind and unshaken integrity—he represented Chatham County and M'Intosh in the Legislature, and was elected by that Body some years ago, as elector for President and Vice-president—he filled several honorary offices civil and military, and justly acquired the confidence of the state and of all who knew him. His political principles were those of a firm, liberal and decided republican . . ."⁴⁵ His widow married Major Jonathan Thomas, and they lived at the McIntosh County plantation. Harriet Thompson, adopted daughter of John and Hannah Houstoun, married first a Mr. Proctor, and after his death she was married again, on January 17, 1821, to Andrew Brown, by the Reverend Walter Cranston. The second daughter, Johanna, married George Baillie, and died prior to 1827. Their children were Harriet and Eliza.

6

Only the birth date of Dr. James Houstoun's oldest child, James Edmund, is known. The second son, Mossman, never married. He followed a military career. On March 12, 1807, he was commissioned an ensign in the second company of militia of Chatham County. He was a young man, presumably in his late twenties, when he was made one of the managers of the Savannah assemblies. A short notice appeared in the *Columbian Museum & Savannah Advertiser* on Tuesday, March 24, 1807, announcing an assembly which was to be given at the Exchange. Mossman Houstoun's name appeared as one of the three managers.

The next year Houstoun was elected recorder of Savannah on the death of Thomas W. Whitefield, and in a few months he was an officer in the United States Army, although he was never admitted to the United States Military Academy as a cadet.⁴⁶ The

---

44. Eliza (1810-1836) married, in 1834, Charles Spalding, son of Thomas Spalding; Mary (1815-1870) died unmarried at Bath, England; John (1817-1861) died unmarried, and was buried at Brampton; and James (1819-1852) died unmarried, and was buried at Darien.
45. *The Georgian*, September 21, 1819.
46. Certified in a letter from Lieutenant Colonel Arthur Purvis, Adjutant General United States Military Academy, West Point, New York, October 3, 1941.

record of his advance to the rank of captain has not been found, but in May, 1808, when he was in Savannah he was captain in the Third United States Infantry. In July he received instructions from the Secretary of War, Henry Dearborn, "to open a rendezvous [in the city] for the purpose of recruiting a part of the army ordered to be raised by Congress." Captain Houstoun's advertisement, which had the caption "TO ARMS! TO ARMS!," notified "those desirous of serving their country as regulars, or who prefer the glorious enterprises of the tented fields to the plodding cares of domestic life," had the "excellent opportunity of indulging themselves." Prospective recruits were admonished that they "must be sensible that advantages ever result in such cases from early application."[47] By October Captain Houstoun was offering a reward of thirty dollars and expenses paid for information of one Stephen Lofetin, alias John Brown, who had deserted.[48]

On Christmas Day, 1808, which fell on Sunday, Captain Houstoun was on duty with Captain Armistead, who was in command of the corps of "artillerists" stationed in Savannah, in pursuit of some British naval officers. The night before, the brig *Sandwich*, Lieutenant Foley commanding, coming from Nassau anchored off Tybee, and the lieutenant, with a mid-shipman, went up to the city. That was a violation of a proclamation of President Thomas Jefferson ordering that no British ships should enter the waters and harbors of the United States. When the infraction was reported to Captain Armistead, he dispatched Captain Houstoun in quest of the officers with a note ordering them to depart from the city. James Wallace, the British vice consul, got wind of the order and wrote to Captain Armistead that the *Sandwich* had brought official dispatches to him on His Majesty's service. In the meantime Captains Armistead and Houstoun called on the collector of the port who informed them that the consul and a naval officer had been to see him that morning to apprise him of the arrival of the *Sandwich*, whose object in going to Savannah, they said, was to make inquiry concerning a Spanish felucca, which was a prize of the British brig *Fire-fly*, and which had put into the port in distress the previous August. The cargo, the collector informed the Savannah officers, had been forfeited

---

47. *The Republican; and Savannah Evening Ledger*, July 7, 1808.
48. *Ibid.*, October 28, 1808.

for a breach of the revenue laws, and the felucca libeled for the seamen's wages.

When Captain Armistead thought enough time had elapsed for Lieutenant Foley to conclude his business, he decided to enforce the law; so about three o'clock in the afternoon he sent a second note by Captain Houstoun, who was given a detachment order authorizing him to see the British officer on board his "barge." The order commanded Foley to "leave the city without one moment's delay," and on arrival at his ship to "leave the river with all expedition." Captain Houstoun was told to see that the officers "did not reland."

After searching for Foley, Houstoun finally found him at George Anderson's residence and requested an interview with him. Foley left the dinner table in response to the message and confronted Houstoun; he was informed of the nature of the mission and given Captain Armistead's note. After reading it, Foley asked permission to finish his dinner, whereupon Houstoun told him that "the order was peremptory" and he "would not admit of it." Before departing, Houstoun asked Foley if he had an answer for Captain Armistead. The Britisher replied he had no time to write, but he "wished Captain Armistead to be informed that his orders would be strictly complied with, and he would proceed to sea with all possible dispatch."

Captain Houstoun saw to it that the British officers left town about half-past three o'clock, but a little after dusk he was informed that instead of going to his ship as he had promised, Lieutenant Foley had boarded a vessel which was at anchor at Five Fathoms. At midnight, Ensign McIntosh was dispatched down the river, where he found the two recreant officers preparing to "turn in" on the vessel at Five Fathoms. McIntosh "shipped them off a second time," and supposed they went to their own ship. Although the wind was favorable, on Monday evening it was learned that the *Sandwich* was still at the mouth of the river, and "adding insult to injury" Lieutenant Foley committed an outrage on the pilot boat *Malaparte*, one of the vessels belonging to the port of Savannah. According to five of its seamen, who made an affidavit before John Pettibone, justice of the peace, their boat was proceeding to sea on Monday night when a British vessel lying off Tybee lighthouse fired on them with "a shot from a musket," and they were ordered to come to anchor or be sunk." When the seamen refused, their boat was "fired on from a cannon charged with a ball." The men on the pilot boat, refusing a third order to stop, after a second charge from the *Sandwich's* cannon, changed their minds, and they accordingly put about for Savannah, deeming it unsafe to go to sea.[49] The newspaper's story ended there, and, presumably, the *Sandwich* left Georgia waters soon after the encounter with the *Malaparte.*

From Savannah, Captain Houstoun was ordered to New Orleans, to take charge of a recruiting office there. In April he was advertising in the newspaper of that city offering rewards for deserters.[50] In a year's time he was back in Savannah where he remained for two years. In 1810 he made a map of the city. In the next two years he engaged in the city's activities although he had not lost his commission in the army. He had previously studied law, and in January, 1811, he announced to prospective clients that he was returning to the practice of law.

In January, 1812, Mossman Houstoun was elected Captain of the Chatham Hussars, a corps, as published at the time, "recently to be raised in the County." The other officers elected at the same time were Richard F. Williamson, first lieutenant; George W. McAllister, second lieutenant; George L. Cope, cornet. Another troop of cavalry was already in existence in Savannah, the Chatham Light Dragoons, and in 1823 the two united and formed the Georgia Hussars. Houstoun gave up his captaincy in the Chatham Hussars after a month to accept a majority in the new army for Georgia.

Major Houstoun was assigned to the Eighth Infantry as aide to Governor Mitchell, and in May he was dispatched to Augusta to be commandant in place of the Governor's former aide, Colonel John A. Cuthbert. The garrison at Augusta was "supplied with Salt provisions, but much in want of bread."[51] Major Houstoun was soon raised to the rank of lieutenant colonel of the Eighth United States Infantry, and served in that capacity until August 15, 1813. He was deputy adjutant general of the Southern Department when that office was discontinued.

---

49. *The Republican; and Savannah Evening Ledger,* December 28, 1808.
50. *Louisiana Courier,* April 7, 1809.
51. *The Republican; and Savannah Evening Ledger,* May 26, 1812.

WILLIAM HOUSTOUN

1757-1812

From the portrait by Archibald Robertson owned by Miss Edith Duncan Johnston, of Savannah, Georgia

Colonel Houstoun's next place of residence, it was found, was in Philadelphia, in 1827. In February of that year he and his sister, Harriet Houstoun Brown, and the children of James Edmund Houstoun, and of Johanna Houstoun Baillie applied to the United States Government for bounty lands of Dr. James Houstoun for his services in the Revolution. The records of the Veterans Administration show that Warrant No. 1231, for four hundred and fifty acres was issued to them on March 14, 1827, but the files of the General Land Office fail to show that a warrant of that number issued by the United States was ever surrendered for location on the public lands.

Harriet Brown died in Savannah in 1833 and in her will, which was probated on March 4 of that year, she left legacies to her brother, Mossman Houstoun, of Philadelphia, Pennsylvania, and to her nieces Eliza and Mary Houstoun.

In 1829, Patrick and Priscilla Houstoun, first cousins of Mossman Houstoun, and John Houstoun McIntosh were paying the expenses of their relative who was in a mental hospital in Philadelphia. Mossman Houstoun was quite old when he died, and he survived his sister by many years, but the year of his death has not been found. On November 4, 1882, Clifford Wayne Anderson, the grandson of Mossman Houstoun's first cousin, Robert James Mossman Houstoun, applied for letters of administration for the estate of Colonel Houstoun "who died intestate in 1832"; but on December 27 he made a second application, stating that his cousin's death occurred in 1876. Both dates are unquestionably wrong. The estate amounted to two hundred dollars, and land in Cherokee County, Georgia.

An unhappy episode in Mossman Houstoun's life seems to have been the cause of his confinement in a mental hospital when he was in middle life. A broken engagement to Susannah Cunningham Wylly, of St. Simon's Island, must have occurred some years prior to 1827. Susannah Wylly never married, and to the day of her death, it was said, she had never loved anyone but Mossman Houstoun. Circumstances point to his exhibiting the same loyalty. Susannah Wylly was the daughter of Alexander Campbell Wylly (1759-1833) and his wife, Margaret Armstrong Wylly (1769-1850), and she was the granddaughter of Alexander Wylly and his wife Susannah Crooke Wylly, the latter the great-aunt of Mossman Houstoun. Before coming to Georgia the Wyllys lived in the Bahamas, and their daughter Susannah was born at Nanan, New Providence, on August 29, 1788. Following the birth of three of their children, Alexander Wylly and his wife moved to St. Simon's Island, and resided in what was then known as The Village. Susannah in her young ladyhood visited Boston and boarded in the same house with Gilbert Stuart and his family. While there a beautiful portrait of her was painted by Stuart, according to family tradition.[52] Susannah Wylly often visited Savannah as the guest of "the Frasers" and it can be assumed it was there that the romance began between the young girl and the military officer Mossman Houstoun. No clue has been found to the reason for their broken engagement, but whatever may have been the cause, the breach was never healed. Susannah Wylly lived to be forty-one years old. She died on October 19, 1829, at the plantation of her brother-in-law, James Hamilton Couper, in Wayne County. He was the husband of her sister, Caroline. Susannah Wylly was buried in the cemetery of Christ Church, Frederica, St. Simon's Island, not far from her home.

With the death of Mossman Houstoun and of the children of his brother James, the line of Dr. James Houstoun became extinct in this country. The two Baillie daughters, Eliza and Harriet, lived in England which they considered their home. There were no descendants of James Edmund Houstoun after the third generation. Three of the five Houstoun brothers, Sir Patrick, John and James, left no continuing line.

---

52. The portrait is owned by Miss Margaret Couper Stiles of Savannah, the great-niece of Susannah Wylly. It is thought now by experts that if Gilbert Stuart was not the artist, the portrait may have been painted by one of his daughters who were portrait painters also.

Now owned by Miss Edith Duncan Johnston, of Savannah, Georgia

SILVER WATCH, GIFT OF WILLIAM HOUSTOUN TO JOHN HOUSTOUN

Chapter XIII

WILLIAM HOUSTOUN, DELEGATE TO THE CONTINENAL CONGRESS

PRIOR to his mother's death in 1775, William Houstoun, if he did not have a tutor, probably received his adolescent education in the Savannah schools, as it seems likely that Lady Houstoun was living then in her Broughton Street house. There were several good private schools which William might have attended. Among them was one that was constantly being advertised in the *Georgia Gazette*, the principal of which was John Holmes, who from 1766 to 1772 offered "a most ambitious curriculum, including classic languages."[1] In the year following his mother's death William must have made his home with one of his brothers, as his sister was married and had gone away to live. He studied law in his brother John's office and became his clerk. On October 2, 1775, he made a deposition before Attorney General Anthony Stokes for John Houstoun, who had a case in the General Court: James Pritchard v. James Butler. The deponent swore he had "duly posted on the Door of the Court House ordering the defendent to appear within ten days, . . . and that he had searched the record and had found no appearances asked or plea filed."[2] On January 7, 1776, William Houstoun again acted for his brother in making a deposition on another case of the same character. Before the summer came William Houstoun must have expressed a desire to go abroad for further study. His guardians, who were his brothers George and John, from the interest on the legacy left to William by their mother, made arrangements for him to go to London. Bidding farewell to his brothers and other relatives, he sailed from Savannah in June to enter the Inner Temple for a course in law when he was nine-

---

1. Martha Gallaudet Waring, "Savannah's Earliest Private Schools," in *The Georgia Historical Quarterly*, XIV, No. 4 (December, 1930), 326.
2. Autograph deposition signed, Historical Society of Pennsylvania, Etting Collection, M.O.C.

teen years of age. Houstoun remained abroad at least four years and perhaps longer. Besides his stay in London he visited his Scottish relatives and also went to Paris. He was fond of social life, and indications show that he was a dressy young man and liked handsome and colorful suits of clothes. When he returned home he must have brought presents to all of his family. His gift to his brother John was a handsome silver watch which he had inscribed on the back of the case, "To my Brother John Houstoun, William Houstoun 1780."[3] The earliest reference to William after the war was in 1782. Governor Wright, in a letter to Under Secretary William Knox, dated Savannah, February 23, 1782, makes allusion to ". . . Sir Patrick Houstoun & his Brother William, Lately come from England . . ."[4] William Houstoun's name did not appear among those on the Banishment and Amercement Act, and when he came home he "espoused the cause of the Revolution,"[5] and received a commission. On January 27, 1785, he received a bounty grant from the state of Georgia of two hundred and eighty-seven and a half acres of land in Washington County. When the confiscated estates were offered for sale, William Houstoun, on June 13, 1782, purchased, for seven hundred and fifty pounds, five hundred acres on the Great Ogeechee River that had belonged to his brother George; and on June 19, he helped his brother Patrick when he bought in two thousand five hundred condemned acres for twenty-five thousand pounds. The young man twenty-four years old could not possibly have had such a large amount of money to invest; so his brothers, unquestionably, supplied the cash to buy back their own property.

2

Having prepared himself for the legal profession, William Houstoun applied to the Georgia Assembly, on August 3, 1782, for permission to practice law in the state, and his petition was granted.[6] One of his clients was his brother, Dr. James Hous-

---

3. The watch was bought by the author from Mrs. Marie Bayard Collins in March, 1941. The hallmark shows the silversmith's date, 1769.
4. "Letters from Governor Sir James Wright . . ." in *Collections of the Georgia Historical Society*, III, 373.
5. Jones, *Biographical Sketches*, 118.
6. *Revolutionary Records of Georgia*, III, 175. That procedure for admission to the bar was changed some years later.

toun, who engaged William to collect an unpaid medical bill. It was necessary for Dr. Houstoun's attorney to apply to the court to have a process issued. The court reviewed the application and granted his attorney's request.[7]

In December, 1782, Houstoun was elected to the State Legislature as a representative from Chatham County. On Tuesday, January 7, 1783, he qualified as a member and took his seat in the assembly which was meeting in Savannah. The first order of the day for the house was to proceed to the appointment of a committee on privileges and elections. Later the committee reported and it was ordered "that the House do Take the Same into Consideration on thursday next." The eligibility of William Houstoun as a member of the house was questioned immediately at that meeting, because a special committee was appointed, composed of "Mr. Andrew" and "Mr. West" of Liberty County and "Mr. Deveaux" of Chatham County to investigate the matter. The following morning the special committee reported that it begged leave to refer the question back to a committee of the whole house, because the members did not feel competent to determine how far the British lines extended at the time William Houstoun retired from them. From what followed, it is evident that the house understood the situation: "It is unanimously agreed that the Reconsideration of the eligibility of William Houstoun, Esquire, and the Report of the Special Committee be adjourned sine die." And shortly afterward William Houstoun was appointed on a committee with "Mr. Telfair" and "Mr. Gibbons."[8] That cleared William Houstoun of all doubt of his right to his seat in the assembly.

But the explanation of the incertitude of the committee was brought out when the regular committee on privileges and elections reported that William Maxwell, William Bryan, Thomas Netherclift, and William Horsby were not eligible to sit in the house, "for not having resided Twelve Months in this state since their being British Subjects, and the same being debated in the House." It was agreed on motion that their seats be declared

---

7. The Historical Society of Pennsylvania. Autograph deposition signature. Old Congress Convention, Case 1, Box 7, under William Houstoun. There is no date on the document to show when the process was issued.
8. *Revolutionary Records of Georgia*, III, 198, 200, 201.

vacant.[9] That ruling was conformable with the Constitution of 1777, which required that no one could serve as a member of the legislature who had not resided in the state twelve months and in his county three months.[10]

A side light on the commotion created in the assembly on the day of the above debate is gleaned from a contemporaneous letter of the Honorable Joseph Clay of Savannah to Cornelius Coppinger of Havana, written February 8, 1783, and describing the situation: "We had very violent struggles in the present House of Assembly, but they have all preponderated as we would wish so far as our circumstances permitted. The seats of 4 or 5 men who had taken protection under the British Govt were declared vacant from their not having been long enough under the American Govt. to make them eligible to so important a trust."[11]

Major General Nathanael Greene and Mrs. Greene were visiting in South Carolina and an invitation was extended to them to come to Savannah for a special purpose. They arrived on January 12, 1783, and the morning after their arrival the legislature met and appointed a committee to prepare an address of welcome to the illustrious general. It was ordered that Mr. William Houstoun, Mr. Telfair, and Mr. Jackson be that committee.

Before the session closed that day the committee presented its address, in part as follows: "The Legislature of the State of Georgia wish to assure you of the real happiness your Presence in their Capital has given them . . . They congratulate you on the signal success wherewith the arms of the United States under your Command . . . has been Crowned by the total expulsion of the Enemy from the Southern States." The report was received and the address ordered to be delivered. Two days later General Greene's reply was received and read before the house. In his letter he said, "Your Polite and Obliging address To welcome me to the State afford me the most Singular Satisfaction. . . . I beg the Legislature to believe I am highly sensible of the Honor they have done me. . . ."[12] General Greene had received from Georgia, in appreciation of his service to the state during the Revolution, the planta-

---
9. *Ibid.*, 206.
10. *Clay's Letters*, 172.
11. *Ibid.*
12. *Revolutionary Records of Georgia*, III, 215, 217, 218.

tion Mulberry Grove, valued at fifty thousand pounds, and the confiscated estate of the former Lieutenant Governor John Graham.

One month after William Houstoun had become a member of the House of Assembly an honor was conferred upon him when he was elected, by ballot, with Joseph Habersham, William Few, and Joseph Clay, a delegate to represent the state in the Congress of the United States for one year. But it happened, for reasons hereafter explained, that not one of the above-named delegates ever attended the Continental Congress in 1783. However, William Houstoun continued to serve through that session of the Georgia assembly on various committees, until July 8 when "Mr Seth John Cuthbert was returned Elected for the County of Chatham in the room of William Houstoun, Esquire who is elected a Continental Delegate, appeared and took the Oath Prescribed in the Constitution."[13] From that time on William Houstoun sat in the Georgia House of Assembly as a delegate to the Continental Congress with the power to vote and the privilege of serving on committees and taking part in debates, which was his Constitutional right.

The 1784 session of the assembly opened on January 6 in Savannah. The fact that none of the four elected delegates to represent Georgia in the Continental Congress for the previous year had ever attended the congress during that time, puzzled and disturbed the assembly. On January 9, 1784, a committee was appointed to inquire why the state was "unrepresented" at the Continental Congress in 1783. The committee was composed of Stephen Heard "of Wilks," William Gibbons and James Jackson, of Chatham County.[14]

Shortly afterward on the same day, the house chose four delegates to represent Georgia in the national congress. They were William Houstoun, Samuel Elbert, Edward Telfair, and Joseph Habersham. Houstoun was thus chosen a second time and was re-elected in 1785 and 1786.

On January 20, the committee to report on those who were absent from the Continental Congress in 1783 was ready. A motion was made that the report of the committee be postponed, which

---
13. *Ibid.*, 320.
14. *Ibid.*, I, 425.

being debated was carried in the negative by a close vote, twenty-two to twenty-one. Gibbons and Jackson of the committee voted in the negative and Heard did not vote. Two of the Continental delegates, Habersham and Houstoun, voted in the negative, and Few, elected the previous year, voted in the affirmative. The other two delegates were not present.

The report was then called for and read: "It Appears to the committee as well from the letter of the late Governor Mr. [Lyman] Hall as from the Information that the Proper Credentials were never sent on to one of the Delegates at the time of his Appointment then in Virginia or Official information of Such Appointment given him till the month of August, when his Affairs did not Permit him to Proceed to Congress; it further Appears to the Committee that another Gentleman held himself in Readiness to go to Congress till the month of September and declared the same by letter to the late Governor Mr. Hall through William Houstoun Esquire another of the Delegates but Never Received either Credentials or Supplies and that the said Mr. Houstoun was Prepared from the time of the Election offering to bear his own expenses, but was Refused his Credentials whereby this State has been unrepresented in Congress for the last year to the Manifest injury of the same."[15]

The salary paid to the Continental delegates was four dollars a day each to be estimated during their attendance there and the time in going and returning to Congress. In those days a journey to New York meant thirty days by sailing vessel, or from two to three weeks in a vehicle. That probably prevented some of the Georgia delegates from a continuous attendance. The congress required two delegates from each state to be present at a session, a hard matter to regulate where the Southern states were concerned.

On February 24, 1784, the house proceeded to the choice of Trustees for a College, when the following "Gentlemen" were elected: "John Houstoun, James Habersham, William Few, Joseph Clay, Abraham Baldwin, William Houstoun and Nathan Brownson, Esquires." The next day it was resolved that His Honor the Governor be requested to grant eight land warrents for five thousand acres each in the names of the trustees or their successors

---
15. *Ibid.*, III, 449, 450.

in office, in trust for the college to be established in the state.[16] But it was not until 1801 that arrangements had been completed for the first building of Franklin College. There had been months and months of preparation and meetings before it was decided, definitely, to erect the university building on a small plateau above the Oconee River. Later a part of the tract became the town of Athens. William Houstoun's part in the college's affairs was small. During the first years of the organization, 1784-1787, he was in attendance at the Continental Congress and it was impossible for him to attend the meetings. Finally he resigned in 1797, as he was then living in the North.

3

About six weeks after the election of January 9, 1784, the house, on February 23, elected other Continental delegates in addition to those already chosen: William Few, William Gibbons, Esquires, and General Lachlan McIntosh.

A notable fact is that William Houstoun and Joseph Habersham were the only two of the original delegates who were re-elected each time. At a May meeting of the executive council, the records specify, "William Houstoun Esquire, having by letter, signified his being ready to proceed to Congress, and there to remain for six months; and William Gibbons, Esqr also, his intention of proceeding with him, thereto remain for four months; it was ordered that the Delegates have drafts on the Treasury for the amount of their allowance for the said respective terms, agreeable to the resolve of the Assembly in such cases made."[17]

The following day, May 13, the grant was signed, and on receiving the draft, William Houstoun made his preparations to leave. By May 15, he and William Gibbons were off for Philadelphia. They arrived June 12 after the congress had adjourned. On June 30, William Houstoun attended his first meeting and at once presented his credentials under the Great Seal of the State of Georgia signed by Governor Houstoun, his brother, and John Wilkinson, the Clerk of the Georgia Assembly. On July 5, the credentials of the Georgia members were re-read and the

---
16. Augustus Longstreet Hull, *Historical Sketches of the University of Georgia* (1894). Also, *Revolutionary Records of Georgia*, III, 557, 563.
17. *Revolutionary Records of Georgia*, II, 649, 650; III, 540.

members were presented to the congress as representatives of the state of Georgia. A few days later, July 8, William Houstoun was placed on a committee with five others to prepare a talk in answer to one received from the Chickasaw Nation.

Late in the summer of his first year as a member of the Continental Congress, William Houstoun heard of the death of his brother Patrick in Bath, England. The news had reached Savannah in August. That was the first break in the life of the five Houstoun brothers.

From November 2 until the day before Christmas congress sat in Trenton, and William Houstoun and William Gibbons represented Georgia. In the middle of December congress received a note from M. Francois, Marquis de Barbe-Marbois, Charge d' Affaires, of France, with a letter from Don Francis Rendon, agent of the Court of Madrid, and an extract of a letter from Don. J. Galvez, Minister of his Catholic Majesty, touching the boundaries of Louisiana and the Mississippi River. The letter and enclosures were referred to a committee on December 15. William Houstoun was a member of that committee, which reported two days later that it was necessary for the United States to have a commission at the Court of Madrid for the purpose of adjusting the claims of the two nations. Following the acceptance of the report, William Houstoun offered a resolution, which was carried, that the next Wednesday be assigned for the election of a minister to Spain. The same committee served to draw up instructions for the prospective minister. William Houstoun was appointed to serve on another interesting committee, composed of one delegate from each state, to receive the Marquis de Lafayette. The committee was instructed to assure the Marquis that congress "continued to hold the same high sense of his ability and zeal to promote the welfare of America both here and in Europe, which they have frequently expressed on former occasions."[18] On the committee with Houstoun were, among others, John Jay and William Guerry. Lafayette had returned to the United States earlier in 1784 on the invitation of General Washington whom he visited at Mount Vernon, and then made an extended tour in Virginia and Massachusetts. Congress adjourned on December 24,

---

18. Hunt, *Journals of the Continental Congress*, XXVII, 673.

and returned to New York in time for the committee to receive the Marquis before he sailed on Christmas Day for France.

Some of the other committees of congress on which William Houstoun was appointed during his first year as a delegate there, were to serve with Francis Dana and Edward Hand to consider another committee's report on the necessity of having a commercial agent to represent the United States at Havana; one on rules for committees for the states, Indian affairs in the Southern Department, superintendent of finances, and several others.

Before continuing the narration of William Houstoun's official life, there are some descriptions of his appearance and character that throw light on his personality. In the opinion of one Georgian, "he was a thorough gentleman, an accomplished lawyer, and a citizen of high repute."[19] He has been described by another writer as sturdy, and he has been written of as "the fiery young Georgian."[20] William Pierce, who was later to be a fellow deputy to the Constitutional Convention, however, was not so complimentary in his remarks about Houstoun. He wrote: "Nature seems to have done more for his corporeal than his mental powers."[21] In referring to his speeches in Congress, Pierce commented that he had "none of the talents requisite for the orator."[22] However harsh Pierce's criticism was, credit has to be given to Houstoun for trying out his powers, and for working as assiduously as he seems to have done. One anecdote of William Houstoun has been preserved which gives a picture of him in the hall of the convention. "Mr. Houstoun was a lawyer of note in his day. Loyal to his native state and section, he was quick to avenge any insinuation that reflected against either. On one occasion the Reverend James Manning, delegate from Rhode Island, made some remarks which he [Houstoun] construed as reflecting on the people of the South, and the next morning he appeared in Congress with a sword. His friends intervened and the fiery young

---

19. Jones, *Biographical Sketches of the Delegates from Georgia*, 119.
20. White, *Abraham Baldwin*, 106.
21. Max Farrand, *Records of the Federal Convention* (New Haven, 1927), III, 97.
22. William Pierce, *Sketches of Characters in the Convention*, 108.

Georgian was persuaded to send his sword to his rooms by his servant, thus closing the incident."[23]

Congress convened again in New York on January 11, 1785. The Indian controversy still was disquieting to the members of congress, and complications and up-risings continued to that year when relations with the Indians were acute both in Georgia and in congress. Georgia was not represented on the Congressional Indian Commission, and William Houstoun, who took umbrage at that slight to his state, wrote to Governor Samuel Elbert on April 2, 1785:

> As we were much connected with the So. Indians, I took the liberty to mention that I thought a Commissioner ought to be appointed from our State, but I was very severely replyed to for suggesting that the least countenance ought to be given to so unworthy a State, and one that had not taken a single federal measure. . . . The whole body of Congress are become so clamorous against our State, that I shudder for the consequences. . . . It is very seriously talked of either to make a tryal of voting Georgia out of the Union or to fall upon some means of taking coercive measures against her. . . . The most infamous motives are imputed to her.

In expressing his attitude toward his own state he wrote bitterly:

> I, Sir, as well from a disinterested Zeal, God knows, of serving my country, as from the warm persuasions of those who paid more attention to public Matters than to my private Interest, I agreed to leave a comfortable place in the midst of relations and friends, when if I was not amassing wealth I was however making more than my daily expenses . . . to come to a strange land amongst Strangers, under the full confidence that my country would not abandon me and make the ungrateful return of giving me up as a Victim. . . . I was induced to remain in Congress thinking I should at least have my Expenses remitted to me and I have been borrowing money . . . for which I am exceedingly pressed . . . and it is impossible for me to think of moving till I receive necessary relief sufficient to extricate me.[24]

---

23. From the Library of Congress; quotation from W. Berrien Burroughs, "Sketch of William Houstoun," in William J. Northern, *Men of Mark in Georgia* (Atlanta, 1907), I, 173, 174.
24. Burnett, ed., *Letters of Members of the Continental Congress*, VIII, 81, 82.

He then besought the Governor to send him at least enough money to enable him to return home.

Congress finally decided Georgia should have a commissioner, and the appointment was given to General Lachlan McIntosh.

It seems fitting to explain the cause of the clamor of congress against Georgia alluded to in Houstoun's letter. There are three reasons why Georgia was in such bad repute in the Continental Congress: one, she had had no delegates there for three years; two, she had not made any provision for paying her quota on the import measure; and three, she had made treaties with Indians in violation of one of the clauses of the Articles of Confederation and Perpetual Union Between the States.

As previously shown, the Georgia Legislature in 1783 had elected delegates to the Continental Congress, but none had attended, and the fact had been noted in the first session of 1784. In the preceding years Georgia's representatives attended from 1775 through 1779; but in 1780 and 1781, as well as 1783, there was none present from Georgia. In 1782, William Few and Joseph Habersham took their seats in May, and the next year, as noted above, Few, Gibbons, and Houstoun failed to attend because no funds had been provided for their expenses. Georgia was not the only state that merited disapproval. On December 23, 1783, Congress passed a resolution that letters be sent to the executives of the unrepresented states, New Hampshire, New Jersey, Connecticut, New York, South Carolina, and Georgia, informing them that "the safety, honor and good faith of the United States require the immediate attendance of their delegates in Congress."[25] Georgia at least acted even though she took five months to do so.

At the time William Houstoun wrote to Governor Elbert in April, 1785, New York and Georgia were the only states that had not adopted the right to levy taxes.

Under the suggestion of punishment to which Houstoun referred, chastisement had been considered by one member of congress for those states to which quotas had been assigned, and Georgia was but one to fall under the ban. Some light is thrown on the feeling in congress through a letter written in April, 1783,

---

25. Edmund Cody Burnett, *The Continental Congress* (New York, 1943), 591, 592.

by Stephen Higgenson, of Massachusetts, to Theophilus Parsons, of Boston:

> If quotas assigned to the several States . . . and a majority of the States should make provision for the discharge of their quotas, will they not find means to coerce those that are delinquent? Will not two or three frigates in time of peace be sufficient for the purpose?[26]

The proposal was made on the assumption that only a minority of the states would be guilty of negligence. Happily such severe measures were never taken, and Georgia was spared punishment on that account.[27]

In considering Georgia's attitude toward treaties with Indians, it is well to keep in mind that under the Articles of Confederation all states felt free to act independently when they saw fit. Georgia was no exception, and she regarded the Indian problem as her own affair. Even before, after, and during Governor Houstoun's administration, as noted above, Indian matters were the concern of the state's executive committee. Clashes and terrorism in South Carolina and Georgia caused the latter to take action. In 1782, a treaty was made with the Cherokees; and in May, 1783, a meeting with the Indians was held in Augusta when a treaty was signed by Governor Hall and five commissioners appointed by the legislature, and a number of Indian chiefs and warriors. In the following November a treaty was made with the Creeks, and in 1785 another treaty was made with the same tribe, all having to do with boundaries and cessions of lands. The section in the Articles of Confederation upon which Georgia appears to have been infringing was somewhat vague. It declared:

> No state without the consent of the United States in Congress assembled, shall send any embassy from, or either enter into any conference, agreement, alliance or treaty with any king, prince or state. . . .[28]

The loophole through which Georgia may have thought she could slip was her interpretation that Indian chiefs and warriors

---
26. *Ibid.*, 569, 570.
27. *Ibid.*, 570. Georgia adopted the measure in March, 1786 (*Ibid.*, 643).
28. Watkins, *Digest of the Laws of the State of Georgia*, 798. Article VII.

could not be regarded as "kings or princes." Or, perhaps her leaders gave it no thought at all!

Governor Elbert answered Houstoun's letter, and on June 26, the latter wrote again to Elbert from New York representing the Georgia delegation:

> Your letter of the 5th May I have had the honor to receive and no oppy. having offered since that time and for some time before for Savannah, makes it now necessary to send a number of dispatches together — as they are all large, together with the Journals, and newspapers I have delivered Mr. Gibbons the bearer of this letter for you, they will give you every public information the Delegates therefore at present have no occasion for making any observations in their official capacity — but have requested me I should answer your private Letter to assure your Honor of their being here in N. Y. that every means in our power is to be used to keep them supplied — and the necessity of the Delegation of the State being kept up is apparent from the advantage we already attained in Congress — they have been disapp. in not receiving the one hundred and fifty Pounds from [?] & Thomson. The delegation will write by Doctor Vicars who goes in a few days — As Mr. Gibbons is now just going off in haste and can give any acct. of matters here. I hope I shall experience in future the advantages of a salary more forcibly than I have hitherto received.

He added in a postscript:

> I wish it was in the power of the State to pay my arrears of salary.[29]

William Houstoun and William Few were elected by the Georgia legislature on February 10, 1786, to represent Georgia again in the Continental Congress and to serve until the first Monday in November. They went to New York and appeared in congress the first Monday in June, producing their credentials. On August 7 a "Grand Committee" was appointed "to report such amendments to the Articles of the Confederation and such resolutions as may be necessary." The members of the committee were Samuel Livermore, of New Hampshire; the Reverend James Manning, of Rhode Island; Nathan Dane, of Massachusetts; Melancton

---
29. Historical Society of Pennsylvania. Autograph letter signed, Gratz Collection, Case 1, Box 25.

Smith, of New York; William Samuel Johnson, of Connecticut; John Cleves Symmes, of Delaware; Charles Pettitt, of Pennsylvania; William Henry, of Pennsylvania; Richard Henry Lee, of Virginia; Timothy Bloodworth, of North Carolina; Charles Pinckney, of South Carolina; and William Houstoun. Committees on changes in the articles met from January to October, and during that period about sixty reports were submitted to congress, covering alterations and revisions.[30] The Annapolis Convention held in September attracted delegates from only five states. Congress met in February, 1787, to consider the report of Alexander Hamilton, and then resolved to call a convention in May for the sole purpose of revising the Articles of Confederation.

4

The experience gained by attending the many sessions of the Continental Congress from 1784 through 1786 prepared Houstoun for his next office: a deputy to the Federal or Constitutional Convention. The Georgia legislature in February, 1787, appointed six deputies to the Philadelphia convention: Abraham Baldwin, William Few, William Houstoun, William Pierce, George Walton, and Nathaniel Pendleton. Few was present on the opening day, May 14. Although still an elected delegate to the Continental Congress, Houstoun did not attend any sessions in New York that year. He arrived in Philadelphia on May 31, and presented his credentials and took his seat the next day. The president of the convention made a note in his diary under date of May 31: "Another representative increased by the coming in of the State of Georgia by the arrival of Major Pierce and Mr. Houston."[31] Baldwin followed Houstoun and Pierce in ten days and remained in constant attendance. Pierce grew weary and returned to New York. Houstoun and Few attended the convention intermittently, but they were not both absent at the same time.[32] "Houstoun on four occasions [spoke in open convention] suggested minor amend-

---

30. Fitzpatrick, ed., *Journals of the Continental Congress*, XXXI, 965.
31. *Washington's Diary*, containing seventy-eight pages of which four cover his sojourn in Philadelphia, May to September, 1787. Original in the Library of Congress.
32. White, *Abraham Baldwin*, 93-96. "No roll call was kept; so attendance of individual deputies cannot be stated positively."

ments which were sometimes adopted and sometimes not."[33] On a vote taken on June 29 on the representation of the senate in the legislature, Georgia's vote was a tie, Baldwin and Houstoun differing in their opinion. Baldwin voted with the small and Houstoun with the large states. William Houstoun attended the convention regularly throughout the month of June and three weeks in July, and served on the committee on state representation in congress. He offered one resolution affecting the election of the President of the United States: "that he be appointed by the national legislature." Six states supported the Georgia delegation at first. " . . . in Houstoun's opinion it was impossible that capable men from the more distant states would undertake the service of electors appointed by state legislatures." The final vote including Georgia's was carried for the latter procedure, and George Washington was elected the first President of the nation.[34] Seven of Houstoun's speeches have been recorded briefly; the longest one, delivered on July 18, contains fifty-one words.

Houstoun entered a debate on a resolution proposing "that Congress guarantee to each state a Republican Constitution and its existing laws." There was strong protest against the measure, and in expressing his views Houstoun said he feared the perpetuation of the existing state constitutions. "That of Georgia," he stated, "is a very bad one," and he hoped it would be revised and amended. He explained how hard it would be for the national government to decide between contending political parties in the state each of which claimed the sanction of its Constitution.[35]

Few had returned to Congress in New York, but went back to Philadelphia the end of July knowing that only two deputies were needed at the Federal Convention. It is thought that after Few joined Baldwin William Houstoun left the Convention on July 26. It is recorded that "imperative business called Houstoun from the Constitutional Convention to which he gave such hearty

---

33. *Ibid.*, 101.
34. Thomas Gamble, "Georgia's Part in the Making of the American Constitution," in *Savannah Morning News*, October 17, 1937. On Houstoun's speeches see Albert B. Saye's quotations from Madison, *Debates in Formation of the Union*, in his thesis "Georgia Delegates. . . ." (University of Georgia, 1934).
35. Gamble, "Georgia's Part in the Making of the American Constitution." Georgia's Constitution was revised in 1789.

support."³⁶ Baldwin and Few remained in Philadelphia and signed the document and then joined Pierce in New York. Pierce carried a copy of the constitution to Georgia, where a convention, called for the purpose of reviewing it, met in Augusta from December 2, 1787, to January 2, 1788. The constitution was adopted on the latter date, Georgia being the fourth state to give its official approval. Although four of the deputies were present at the Augusta convention, Houstoun was not, which conveys the impression that he had returned to New York where personal business awaited him.

Attending the Continental Congress at the same time as William Houstoun was William Churchill Houston, of New Jersey. Ten years the senior of the Georgia representative, William Churchill Houston was a native of South Carolina, the son of Archibald and Margaret Houston. The parents moved to North Carolina, and their son, after receiving his education at the College of New Jersey (Princeton University), was made professor of mathematics and natural philosophy at the college; and later he was a member of the New Jersey legislature. In March, 1777, he was elected deputy secretary of the Continental Congress, Charles Thomson being secretary. To the deputy secretary fell a large part of the correspondence of the congress, and other secretarial tasks. Houston was elected a delegate to the congress, 1779, and in 1787 he was a deputy to the Constitutional Convention. He died August 12, 1788.³⁷

---

36. Nannie McCormick Coleman, *The Constitution and its Framers* (Chicago, 1910), "Sketch of William Houstoun," 471 *ff.*, (Courtesy of the Library of Congress). Among the other nineteen deputies who, for various reasons, left the convention without signing the Constitution were: Eldridge Gerry, Thomas Russell Gerry, and Caleb Strong, of Massachusetts; George Mason, Edmund Randolph, and James McClurg, of Virginia; Luther Martin and John Francis Mercer, of Maryland; and William Richardson Davie, of North Carolina (United States Constitution Sesquicentennial Commission, *Loan Exhibition of Portraits* . . . Washington, D. C., 1938).

37. Thomas Allen Glenn, *William Churchill Houston, 1746-1788* (Privately printed, Norristown, Pa., MDCCCCIII). In the appendix the author has written: ". . . his family derived its name from the Parish of Houston in Renfrewshire," and he then gives quotations on the early lineage of the Houstoun family found in Semple's *The History of the Shire of Renfrew*, quoted in the first chapter of this book. Glenn *assumes* that Sir Patrick Houstoun, first baronet, was the ancestor of the South

5

When William Houstoun was a delegate to Congress in New York he met Mary Bayard whom he married. Her father and mother were Nicholas Bayard III and Catherine Livingston Bayard. The Bayards trace their ancestry back to the French knight who was styled "Sans peur et sans reproche." An early Nicholas Bayard (1644-1707), a Huguenot minister, fled from France to The Netherlands after the massacre of St. Bartholomew.[38] His son Samuel married Ann, a sister of Peter Stuyvesant (1602-1682), the last Dutch governor of New York, who married Judith, the sister of Samuel Bayard. After the death of her husband, Mrs. Samuel Bayard with her three sons and one daughter in 1647 emigrated to America with the Stuyvesants. The eldest Bayard son, Nicholas, who was born in The Netherlands in 1644, was known in this country as Nicholas Bayard I. The old Bayard mansion was on the west side of the Bowery, and was near the Stuyvesant estate. Nicholas Bayard became secretary of the province of New York, was mayor of New York under the English regime, was a member of the Royal Council and held other important offices. In 1666 he married Judith Verlet. Their son Samuel (1669-1745), who was a member of the Colonial Assembly of New York and Judge of the Court of Common Pleas, Bergen County, New Jersey (1711), married Margaret, the daughter of Oloff Stevense Van Cortlandt (1600-1684), who came from Utrecht, Holland, to the New Netherlands as an officer in the West India Company. After resigning from military service he held some of the highest offices in the colony, among them burgomaster in 1685. He was one of the richest men in New Amsterdam. He married Annetje Loockermans in 1642. Samuel Bayard's son, Nicholas Bayard II, married Elizabeth Reinders, and their son, Nicholas Bayard III, married Catherine, one of the twelve children of Peter Van Brugh Livingston. The Bayards were well-known officials in Colonial and federal New York, and they were equally prominent

---

Carolina family without giving the exact lineage. He adds: "Another branch of the family settled in Georgia."

While doing research on William Houstoun in the *Journals* of the Continental Congress, I found the work was simplified because the two names were spelled correctly when members of committees were listed: "Mr. Houston" and "Mr. Houstoun."

38. Lucien J. Fosdick, *The French Blood in America* (New York, 1906), 308.

in the social life of the city. As a family "their unique record of distinguished public service is all the more notable in that it has been conspicuous for dignity and a scrupulous sense of official proprieties, coupled with ability of an unusually high type."[39]

Mrs. William Houstoun's ancestry on her mother's side was also distinguished. Her great-great-great-grandfather, Robert Livingston, was born in Scotland in 1654, and died in Albany, New York, in 1725. A member of his family, Mary Livingston, went to France with Queen Mary Stuart (1548-1558) as one of her maids of honor. Robert Livingston came to America in 1673, and settled in Albany, New York, where he became secretary of the commissaries. He was a member of the colonial assembly in 1711, and in 1718 he was made speaker. He was appointed secretary of Indian affairs, which office he held over a period of years. He was called first lord of the manor. His Crown grant from George I was situated in Dutchess and Columbia counties. He first married Mary Tong, by whom he had eleven children, and his second wife was the daughter of Killian Van Rensselaer, the widow of Adomiah Schuyler.

Robert Livingston's eldest son, Philip (1686-1749), second lord of the manor, succeeded his father as secretary of Indian affairs, and was a member of the Provincial Council. He married Catherine Van Brugh, of Albany, New York, a lineal descendant of Johannes Pieterse Van Brugh (1624-1697), Burgomaster of New York in 1673.

During the latter part of his life Philip Livingston entertained lavishly at his three residences in New York, Albany, and at the manor. His namesake, Philip, his fifth child (1716-1778), was a signer of the Declaration of Independence, and held numerous important offices. The second son, Peter Van Brugh Livingston (1710-1792), was President of the first Provincial Congress of New York, was one of the committee of one hundred, and was one of the founders of the College of New Jersey. He engaged in shipping business with William Alexander, "Lord Stirling," whose sister Mary he married in 1739. He furnished supplies to Governor Stirling in his expedition to Acadia in 1755. Peter Livingston's

---

39. *The Encyclopedia Americana* (New York and Chicago, 1940), III, 363. On the Livingston family, see George Norbury MacKenzie, *Colonial Families in the United States* (New York and Chicago, 1940), VI, 336.

mansion was on the east side of New York, and his property extended to the East River. One of the daughters of the Peter Livingstons, Catherine, the widow of Mr. Provost, married Nicholas Bayard III, on April 20, 1762.

The residence of the Nicholas Bayards was on Canal Street, near Broadway, and they were members of the Reformed Dutch Church. The baptisms of two of their daughters, Mary and Eliza, have been preserved in the "Record of Baptisms."

	Ouders	Kinders	Getuygen
"Å 1766 Jan	5 Nicholas Bayard Catharina Livinston	Mary, or Maria	Judit Bayard, Wed^e Van Jeremia Van Rinselaar
Å 1769 Maart	26 Nicholas Bayard Catharina Livinston	Elizabet Reinders"[40]	

Sometime in the year 1788 Mary Bayard was married to William Houstoun, and they made their home in New York City. Nicholas Bayard owned a large tract in the lower part of New York, and through a section of his land he opened a street which he named Houstoun in honor of his son-in-law.[41] Mary Hous-

---

40. Information received through the courtesy of H. P. Miller, Assistant Clerk of the (Collegiate) Reformed Protestant Dutch Church, of the City of New York, August, 1936. The translation of the Dutch words is: "Ouders", parents; "Kinders", children; "Getuygen", witnesses or god-parents.
41. Broadway crosses Houston Street, which runs east and west. The eastern end connects with Houston Ferry, East River. (Information from Major Morrison V. R. Weynant of Brooklyn, New York. Early maps show that the street was spelled "Houstoun".) Some historians, in searching for the origins of names, come to queer deductions. Alvin F. Harlow, in his *Old Bowery Days: The Chronicles of a Famous Street* (New York and London, 1931), on page 158, writes:

> A street system, such as it was, had been established as far up as North Street, the dividing line between the DeLancy and Stuyvesant properties at the East River, a street whose name enthusiastic New York Democrats changed in 1830 to Houston in honor of Sam Houston, though the old General would turn over in his grave if he could hear the New Yorker of today pronouncing it Howston.

When a letter was written to the New York Historical Society in April,

toun's sister Eliza married John Houstoun McIntosh, the nephew of William Houstoun; another sister, Margaret, married Robert C. Johnson, of Connecticut, and Ann married her first cousin, Dr. Nicholas Serle Bayard.[42]

1942, for an explanation of the above, the reply from the librarian was illuminating. Miss Barck wrote:
> The source of New York street names is often difficult to ascertain unless the reason for the name is stated in the minutes of the Common Council of the City. I do not find in those minutes any record of the naming of Houston Street.

An unidentified newspaper of August 8, 1897, Miss Barck continued:
> "gave the course as named to commemorate some notable Knickerbocker."

To substantiate that claim Miss Barck gave a quotation from *De Halve Maen*, a quarterly published by the Holland Society of New York, Vol. XI, No. 11, January 7, 1936, from a note initialed, "L. B. S., Jr."
> .... We discovered that the street [Houston] name comes from the Dutch huijs and *tuijn*, the former meaning "house", and the latter "garden". Literally translated, therefore, the street marks the "Gardens of the houses (in the village)". The pronunciation of the Dutch words also bears out the present day New York pronunciation of Houston.

It would seem that the conclusion of "L.B.S. Jr." is decidedly far-fetched, considering further information given by Miss Barck:
> What is now East Houston Street was originally known as North Street. On the Bridges map or Randel Survey of 1811 a street running west from Broadway to Hancock Street is clearly designated Houstoun.... The map in Blount's *Stranger's Guide* for 1817 shows *Houstoun* Street running from Broadway west to Hancock. On Goodrich's Map of the City of New York, post 1836, the street running west from the Bowery to Hancock is spelled Houstoun, and east of the Bowery it is designated as "Houston ante North."

In the Minutes of the Common Council, according to Miss Barck, the street is spelled both ways: In October 1808 it is spelled Houstoun; in 1806 it is spelled Houstoun, and in 1813, it is Houston.

Since the official records of New York show that Houstoun Street was named before General Sam Houston came into prominence, it is useless to fear that his "last sleep" will be disturbed by the New York pronunciation.

42. After the death of his wife, Dr. Bayard went to live in Savannah. He served in the yellow fever epidemics in Savannah and St. Mary's, Georgia, in 1808. He survived the disease, and died in Savannah of "malignant fever" in 1821 (from the notes of the late Doctor Victor H. Bassett of Savannah). On September 5, 1804, he married, on Cumberland Island,

6

After their marriage, William Houstoun and his wife, accompanied by the latter's sister, Eliza Bayard, visited Savannah. The event that called them to William Houstoun's old home was the baptism of the tenth child of his brother, Sir George Houstoun, baronet, which took place in Christ Church on Sunday, June 29, 1788. The two Houstouns and Eliza Bayard were godparents for the baby who was named Rachael Moodie. During his visit to Savannah William Houstoun had been notified that he had a letter in the Dead Letter Post Office in Savannah and was given until June 20th to collect.[43] It is presumed he claimed his letter.

Barely a week after the christening of the baby the Houstouns and Eliza Bayard left for their northern home. The weekly newspaper of Savannah, *The Gazette of the State of Georgia*, announced in its issue of Thursday, July 11, that "On Friday last, sailed for New York, the sloop *Jenny*, Capt. Schemerhorn, in which William Houstoun Esq., Mrs. Houstoun, Miss Bayard, Major Webb, Mr. John Fisher and Mr. Richard Randolph were passengers." After an absence of a year and a half William Houstoun returned to Savannah.

Early in December, 1789, William Pierce, friend of William Houstoun and fellow delegate to the Constitutional Convention, became ill and on the seventeenth of the month, *The Gazette of the State of Georgia* published the notice of his death: "Last Thursday night [December 10] died at his plantation, Major Pierce. On Saturday evening his remains were attended from the house of James Seagrove Esq., at Yamacraw to the place of interment." In the same issue appeared the following notice: "The sloop, *Jenny*, Capt. Schemerhorn [arrived] from New York. William Houstoun Esquire (et al) December 13." By a strange coincidence Wil-

---

Georgia, Mrs. Esther Ward, widow of John Peter Ward (*Columbian Museum & Savannah Advertiser*, October 7, 1804), and they made their home on Cumberland Island. He was buried in Colonial Cemetery in the family vault of General Lachlan McIntosh (*Some Early Epitaphs in Georgia*, compiled by the Georgia Society of the Colonial Dames of America, Durham, North Carolina, 1924, page 67). His will is filed in Chatham County Court House, probated 1822, File 164. Dr. Bayard was one of the founders of the Georgia Medical Society (Lee and Agnew, *Historical Record of Savannah* [Savannah, 1869], 186).

43. *The Gazette of the State of Georgia*, April 24, 1788.

liam Houstoun arrived in Savannah the day after his friend's funeral. Could he have heard several weeks before that Pierce was ill and hoped to reach Savannah before he died? Or was he just coming to Savannah for another visit and happened to arrive at that time? Two of William Pierce's friends must have attended his funeral because an item in the same paper announced that Abraham Baldwin and Colonel William Few had sailed for New York on the sixteenth of the month.

In the spring of 1789, the United States had its first President when General George Washington was inaugurated in New York on March 4. Mrs. Washington did not accompany her husband for the ceremony, but tarried at Mount Vernon for a month before joining him. New York in 1789 is described as a "squalid, insignificant, eccentric little town of 29,000 inhabitants whose narrow crooked streets were cluttered with filth in which hogs rooted in contented defiance of municipal regulation, and suffering from the effects of seven paralyzing years of British occupation during the War of Independence and two disastrous fires."[44]

Mrs. Washington left Mount Vernon the latter part of May, and on her way stopped overnight in Elizabethtown, New Jersey, where she was entertained at Liberty Hall, the country seat of Governor William Livingston (1723-1789), the uncle of Mrs. William Houstoun. Prominent guests were entertained by Governor Livingston, who was the father of four daughters, one of whom married John Jay. For the reception of Mrs. Washington, the house was beautifully decorated with flowers, and distinguished guests attended to do her honor. In the morning the President went from New York to escort her to the city, where she arrived on May 27.[45] Within a month after her arrival the ladies of the city called on her to pay their respects. The executive mansion on Cherry Street at Hanover Square was "large and comfortable, and the furnishings were augmented by additional furniture and pictures sent by sailing vessel from Mount Vernon."[46]

---

44. *The New York Times*, October 1, 1939, "State Historians Close Convention."
45. *Appleton's Cyclopaedia of American Biography* (1888), III, 742.
46. George Bothwell Brown, "World Pays Honor to George Washington Today, 150 Anniversary of His First Inauguration," in the *Sunday American*, Atlanta, April 30, 1939.

The Savannah paper published a list of those who called on Mrs. Washington, among whom were Mrs. William Houstoun and her sisters.[47]

7

The Supreme Court of the United States held its first session under the Constitution on February 3, 1790. Two days later, five practitioners appeared before its bar and were admitted as counselors. Following the English custom of the practice of counselors and attorneys one of them stipulated that "it shall be requisite to the admission of Attorneys and Counselors to practice in this court that they shall have been such for three years past in the Supreme Court of the State to which they respectively belong, and that their private and professional character shall appear to be fair." During the next three days, six more men were admitted as counselors from various states and seven attorneys [among the latter William Houstoun], "all of New York."[48] The admission of William Houstoun to practice as an attorney in the Supreme Court of the United States, under the aforesaid rule, establishes the fact that he had been an attorney-at-law in New York City for three years, and that he had been trying cases in the Supreme Court of that state. The Georgia newspaper took cognizance of the action of the Supreme Court by announcing the incident in its columns: "The Supreme Court of the United States was adjourned on the 10th of last month till the first Monday in August next. The following is the roll of the Gentlemen admitted to practice in said Court."[49] Eighteen counselors and nine attorneys were listed with, of course, the name of William Houstoun included. Thus were his Georgia friends apprised of his latest achievement.

While he was abroad William Houstoun evidently formed a friendship with Archibald Robertson, who went to New York in 1791. Robertson, who was a painter, designer, and etcher, was born in Monymusk, near Aberdeen, Scotland, in 1765. He studied art in Edinburgh and in London from 1782-1791. When he came to the United States he brought with him "from his patron the

---
47. *Georgia Gazette*, July 9, 1789.
48. Charles Warren, *The Supreme Court in the United States* (Boston, 1923), I, 48, 49.
49. *Georgia Gazette*, March 18, 1790.

Earl of Buchan, for presentation to General Washington, a box made of the oak that sheltered Sir William Wallace after the Battle of Falkirk. At the request of the Earl of Buchan, Washington sat for his portrait to Robertson."[50] William Houstoun also sat for his portrait which Robertson painted soon after he came to this country. The subject wore a brown coat with a waistcoat of yellow, red, and blue stripes, a lace ruffled shirt and neckerchief. In his portrait he shows a marked resemblance to his mother, Priscilla, Lady Houstoun. In the left hand corner of the portrait is inscribed in red letters, "A. R. 1791."[51] The portrait was later owned by Nicholas Bayard III, father-in-law of William Houstoun.

The first child of William and Mary Houstoun of whom there is a record was born in 1795. According to the will of William's brother John Houstoun, written on May 2, 1796, a legacy was left to his brother, "William and wife now in New Jersey."[52] Since Mrs. Houstoun had Livingston relatives in Elizabethtown, she and her husband may have been living there at that time. A child was born to them on November 7, 1795, was baptized in the Dutch Church, New York City, March 28, 1796, and was named Catherine Priscilla Ann. She died in infancy. Their second child, Maria Church Houstoun, was born November 28, 1798, and was baptized on Christmas Day; while their third child was

---

50. Mantle Fielding, *The Dictionary of American Painters*. Robertson was one of the founders of the American Academy of Art. (Courtesy of The Historical Society of Pennsylvania.) Constitution Sesquicentennial Commission, *Loan Exhibition of Portraits of the Signers and Deputies to the Convention of 1787* (Washington, D. C., 1938), 8, ". . . the Columbian Academy of Painting was opened in New York City in 1792 by Archibald Robertson and his brother, . . ."

51. The portrait, owned by the author, was bought in March, 1941, from Mrs. Marie Bayard Collins of New York. On the back is written:
    Likeness Hon. Wᵐ
    Houstoun Admitted
    Inner Temple London
    1776. Delegate of Congress
    1784-1787.
    Done in N. Y. C. 1791 by his friend.
    Archibald Robertson.
    The portrait, with that of his brother, Governor Houstoun, was at the Bayard homestead at Westerly, Long Island, but was removed before the fire of 1937.

52. LaFar and Wilson, *Abstracts of Wills, Chatham County, Georgia*, 57.

Will: Houstoun

Pat Houstoun

Rosdue 5th Decr 1754

Pryscilla Houstoun

P Houstoun

John Houstoun

M Houstoun

SIX HOUSTOUN SIGNATURES

born on April 29, 1801, and was baptized Elizabeth Bayard, May 26.[53]

In the year 1808, Mrs. William Houstoun paid a visit to her sister, Mrs. John Houstoun McIntosh, whose husband owned a plantation on Fort George Island, at the mouth of the St. John's River, Florida, and there she died and was buried.[54]

William Houstoun outlived his wife only four years. He was taken ill suddenly and was beyond relief when a physician arrived. He died the next day at the home of his father-in-law, Nicholas Bayard, in Canal Street. His death occurred in the year 1812 when he was fifty-five years old. He was interred in the Bayard family vault, and his remains were removed the next year and were re-interred in the churchyard of St. Paul's Chapel in lower Broadway March 17, 1813. He was the last of the children of Sir Patrick and Lady Houstoun to pass away.[55]

---

53. Record from Baptisms in (Collegiate) Reformed Protestant Dutch Church of the City of New York, furnished by H. P. Miller, August, 1936.
54. The inscription on a slab of a vault on the east side of Fort George Island on a point near the mouth of the river is: "Mrs. Ann Bayard Houstoun, daughter of Nicholas Bayard of New York, sister of Mrs. Eliza Bayard McIntosh." The omission of her husband's name and the error in Mary Houstoun's own name is explained in Carita Doggett Corse, *The Key to the Golden Isles* (Chapel Hill, North Carolina, 1931, pages 111, 133-144), from papers owned by Mrs. Millar Wilson of Fort George Island, the daughter of the late Mr. John F. Rollins of New Hampshire, who bought the island in 1868. Mr. Rollins found the McIntosh burying ground screened by a thick hedge of bittersweet oranges in which grew narcissi, jonquils, moss-roses, and snow drops. "Mr. Rollins felt obliged to use this space for part of his orange grove and carefully buried the headstones in their proper places . . . he afterwards regretted the act because a little later a certain Mr. McIntosh arrived with two headstones to place on the graves of his relatives. The old gentleman was rather non plussed when Mr. Rollins explained what he had done, but happening on some ancient brick graves of Oglethorpe's day, he tied the names of his ancestors to these tombs. He seemed so relieved at this solution of his dilemma that Mr. Rollins did not have the heart to forbid it, but the inquiries which have multiplied in regard to those graves caused him much annoyance in after years." The author is indebted to Marmaduke H. Floyd for the inscription on Mrs. Houstoun's tablet.
55. Correspondence with the Surrogate Court of New York reveals no record of William Houstoun's will ever having been probated in New York. Georgia and New York newspapers have been searched without success for mention of his obituary. In September, 1937, when the United States Constitution Sesquicentennial Commission, of which the late Sol Bloom, M. C., was Director General, placed wreaths on the graves of the deputies to the Federal Convention, an effort was made to locate that of William Houstoun. Unable to find it, the commission had a wreath put in St. Paul's churchyard to commemorate Houstoun.

The William Houstouns had no sons and their two daughters survived them. The elder, Maria Church Houstoun, married Lieutenant Commander John Ripley Madison, United States Navy, in 1818. Mrs. Madison's grave is in the small family burying ground of John Houstoun McIntosh's plantation, Marianna, in Camden County, Georgia. She died November 22, 1822, in the twenty-fourth year of her age, leaving an infant son. Inscribed in her epitaph is information on her husband: "Captain Madison sailed from St. Mary's, Georgia, in command of the U. S. Schooner Lynx, bound for Jamaica in February, 1821. No intelligence has since been received from him or the unfortunate vessel."[56]

The second daughter of William and Mary Houstoun, Elizabeth, married Duncan Lamont Clinch.[57] There were two children who died in infancy.

---

56. The son lived to grow up and marry Sarah Jane Dummett. He died at Federal Point, his plantation on the St. John's River. He and his infant son are buried in the Protestant Cemetery, just outside the gates of St. Augustine. Their epitaphs are:
   In Memory of
   John Houstoun M J [McI] Madison
   Born May 5th. 1820
   Died Dec. 20th. 1853
   and of his Son
   John Ripley Madison
   Born March 26th 1851
   Died May 6th. 1852
   There are many descendants from three other children of the Dummett-Madison union.
57. Houstoun Family Tree. After her death Lieutenant Clinch (afterward General), married the daughter of John Houstoun McIntosh.

Chapter XIV

ANN PRISCILLA, WIFE OF GEORGE McINTOSH, AND THEIR SON JOHN HOUSTOUN McINTOSH

THERE is little factual information concerning the short life of Ann Priscilla, the only daughter of Sir Patrick and Lady Houstoun. It stands to reason she was the pet of the four older brothers and special guardian of the younger one so near her own age. Lady Houstoun, the mother, had the moral support of her stalwart sons following her husband's death; but, surely, it was to the little daughter that she turned for feminine companionship and sympathy when she needed surcease and recreation from her manifold duties of plantation life. There was evidently a home in Savannah by 1763 which made life more interesting for a growing girl than the far-away plantation. The mother, no doubt with the help of teachers, guided her daughter's education, but one likes to bring forth the picture of the mother and daughter sitting on the piazza at Rosdue, sewing together and discussing the news from town, or one reading while the other was engaged in needlepoint or cross-stitch work.

When the family took up its residence in town, probably for the winter months, Nancy Houstoun of course attended the "best schools."[1] There were many from which Lady Houstoun could select for her young daughter's education. During the time that Nancy was of school age, that is from 1763 to 1772, those who advertised in the *Georgia Gazette* were: John Portrees, who in 1763 taught school at Gibbons's plantation near Savannah; Timothy Cronin, who had his school in the town in the house where the late Mr. Heleventine had his school, and "in addition to writing and mathematics he promised Dancing twice a week"; John Holmes, who included classical languages in his curriculum; Peter Gandy, who taught in a part of Mrs. Cunningham's house adjoining that of the Honorable James Read, Esq.; John Franklin, who taught

---

1. Johnston, *Recollections of a Georgia Loyalist*, 43.

"reading, writing and arithmetick after a new and most concise method at 12 s. 6 d. Sterling per quarter at his school next door to Mr. Robert Boltons' "; Alexander Findlay and James Seymour, whose school was located "in the lower end of Broughton St., next door to Mr. Andersons the Surveyor"; James Cosgrove, who could boast of a classical education at seminaries and academies in the British Isles and in America, opened a school in 1768 for "the education of young Gentlemen and Ladies in reading English with propriety and emphasis; writing accurately all the different hands in use . . . Mathematics . . . the English and French tongues Gramatically." His wife taught young ladies to "sew and read." There was also a boarding school kept by Elizabeth Bedon, who included all kinds of needle work with her reading, writing and arithmetic courses.[2] If Lady Houstoun was not satisfied with the practical and cultural advantages offered in the several schools in Savannah, she may have employed Edward Langworthy, "who taught young ladies English, Grammar, writing, etc., privately."[3]

Life changed only slightly in the colony, and customs that prevailed in one decade can well describe the social conventions of the previous one or the one following it. By the time Nancy was approaching young womanhood transportation consisted of coaches for the rough roads to the outlying plantations, carriages for city life, and the use of the "chair," carried by Negro slaves when ladies attended church. One of the chief interests of the social class was church worship, and the established religion of the colony was that of the Church of England. Christ Church, for which Ann Priscilla's father had had the "iconography" made in 1745, was the church the Houstoun family attended, and it was only two blocks from the Houstoun residence in Broughton Street.

When Ann Priscilla was fifteen years old, word reached Savannah that the Reverend George Whitefield, the minister of the church from 1738-1746, had died in Newburyport, Massachusetts. Although he was buried there, the people of Savannah mourned

---

2. Martha Gallaudet Waring, "Savannah's Earliest Private Schools," in *The Georgia Historical Quarterly*, XIV, No. 4 (December, 1930), 324-334. Prize essay in the contest of the Georgia Society of the Colonial Dames of America, March, 1930.
3. *Georgia Gazette*, November 8, 1769.

his death, and it must have made a deep impression on the young girl when she attended divine service following the news of his death, to find the "pulpit and desks of the church, the benches, the organ loft and the pews of the Governor covered with black."[4] The Reverend Samuel Frink was the rector at that time.

One of the delightful ways of entertaining in Savannah in the seventeen-seventies was the giving of formal dinners. That meant lavishness in all kinds of viands, and manifested the Southern custom for setting a well-laden table. Game from the nearby woods and fresh fish from the tide waters were added to other delicacies. Served with each course was the wine that was especially appropriate, for every "gentleman" has his wine cellar always well stocked with madeira, port, and sherry, imported from abroad.

Ann Priscilla, having four young brothers active in the town's political, commercial, social, military, and professional life, naturally gave the Houstouns a large circle of friends. Dinners at the Houstoun home must have been frequent affairs.

"Dancing Assemblies" held at the several taverns, Creighton's, Liberty, or Tondee's, had come into vogue by the time Ann Priscilla was a young woman. It is easy to surmise that she and her four brothers were active in community social life during the early seventeen-seventies. There were the three Habersham boys, sons of her father's friend, James Habersham: James, Jr., Joseph and John, the latter almost the same age as herself; the three Johnston youths, sons of Dr. Lewis Johnston: William Martin, Andrew, and James. There were John Milledge and Richard Crooke; Josiah Bryan, the last son of Jonathan Bryan; and the sons of Sir James Wright, the Royal Governor, another friend of her father. All of them probably were frequent callers at the home of the Houstouns. Among her girl friends, no doubt, were her future sisters-in-law, Ann Moodie, Hannah Bryan, and Eliza Crooke Tannant, and many others.

But it was after two or three years of the gaities of Savannah's social life that the thought of marriage surely began to take shape in Nancy Houstoun's mind and the man who became her husband was not selected from among her Savannah friends, but was George McIntosh of St. Andrew's Parish. He was the young-

---

4. Elfrida De Renne Barrow and Lalla Palmer Bell, *Anchored Yesterdays* (Savannah, 1923), 58.

est of the four sons of John McIntosh Mohr, the leader of the Scottish clansmen of Darien. George's brothers were William, Lachlan, and John, and they were known as the Borlam McIntoshes. George McIntosh was born in 1735 or 1736, and when he was eleven years old he was taken to Charles Town, South Carolina, by his brother Lachlan and put in a grammar school. When he had finished what education he could obtain there he was bound for four years to an architect, and after his apprenticeship he returned to Georgia and was appointed commissary of supplies for the troops in the garrison at Frederica and adjacent parts. His brother Lachlan had him instructed in geometry and surveying, and under his direction George learned to acquire valuable property, bought slaves, studied planting, and soon became a landed proprietor. As early as 1759 he built a house and made improvements on a tract of five hundred acres on the south side of the "Sapala" River in St. Andrew's Parish, and later added to it by two hundred acres. That plantation was probably Rice Hope. George McIntosh became one of the most thriving planters in the colony. He was made the official surveyor of St. Andrew's Parish in 1768. In 1764 he was elected to the Commons House of Assembly from St. Andrew's Parish, and was returned in 1768 and in 1772. His membership in the house required his attendance in Savannah, and he fell in love with Nancy Houstoun probably during that time. He must have known her from childhood, as he was a friend of her brother Patrick. At the time of his marriage he was thirty-five or thirty-six years old, and his bride was sixteen or seventeen. Neither the date of the marriage nor the place where the ceremony took place is known. When Ann Priscilla's mother made her will in June, 1772, she mentioned her daughter, Mrs. George McIntosh; so it is likely that the wedding took place in the spring of that year. It must have been to Rice Hope that George McIntosh took his bride. The young wife found many friends and acquaintances when she arrived in St. Andrew's Parish to make her new home. Her brother Patrick was already living there on his Cathead plantation, not many miles from her house, and in the year of her marriage he was one of the elected delegates in the Lower House of Assembly from St. Andrew's Parish. Other neighbors were Button Gwinnett, who lived on St. Catherine's Island, and Raymond Demere, and Robert Baillie, both of whom lived on the mainland. On the first day of May, 1773, a son was born to the George McIntoshes. He was named John Houstoun in honor of his mother's favorite brother. The year after his son's birth, George McIntosh was elected again to the Commons House of Assembly to represent St. David's Parish, and the year following, when the Provincial Congress assembled in Savannah on July 4, 1775, George McIntosh, with his brothers Lachlan and William and eleven others attended as representatives of St. Andrew's Parish. Before George McIntosh left for the provincial Congress he received a letter dated June 10, 1775, from John Houstoun which gave him news of the political activities that were stirring in Savannah:

We have had the devil to pay in Town – the great Mr. [—] himself has found that Pride must shrink when Fear gives the alarm. Our neighbors it seems have erected dog-Houses at Camden for the Reception of such whose Demerits call for Justice in either Province. Our Govr [Sir James Wright] either convinced or informed that he was one of these worthies has discovered the most evident tracks of apprehension.

He was willing to have who would risk *or at best promised to risk* their lives for him and therefore called a meeting of a number of People – principally those of the opposition – and acquainted them with the Scheme meditated against him in Carolina. After expatiating largely upon the Reflexion it would be to the Province to have their Governor stole away, perhaps by night, he at last beg'd their Protection for his *own proper Person*. Some promised – others refused the favor – for my Part I have very little to say about him, but think he has little room to claim any Assistance from others when he has insulted in the manner he has done us by his letters to Lord Dartmouth. They think of raising a highland company as his Life-Guard. I am much mistaken if this is not a political Manuvou and perhaps is intended as a Bait for St. Andrew's. I wd. have you be on your Guard and be ready to counteract Emissaries who I dare say will be amongst you.– In short, George, I believe from all accounts the last appeal will soon be made. I have begun to think very seriously and mean to go to the No wards very soon – however I shall see you first. A Civil war was very near commencing last Monday – the account of this you'l see in the Newspaper. . . . Remember me to Nancy and Jack. I mean to see you soon at Sapela[5]

The next month George McIntosh went to Savannah to attend the provincial congress at Tondee's Tavern, and he was one of the first to sign the *Article of Association*, adopted on July 18. The following December he shipped one hundred and eleven tierces of rice from his Sapelo River plantation to his brother-in-law, George Houstoun, merchant, in Savannah, a circumstance that was referred to eighteen months later. In May, 1776, George McIntosh was a member of the Council of Safety and was present at four or five meetings, after which he returned, apparently, to his plantation for a few weeks.

2

The year 1776 brought disaster upon the McIntosh family, but the circumstance which created it was harmless enough in its inception. Reference to Sir Patrick Houstoun's (sixth baronet) part in the rice episode has been made, but as George McIntosh was so involved it became necessary for him to vindicate himself. The whole episode is here explained:[6] In June, 1776, George McIntosh joined with his two neighbors, Robert Baillie and Sir Patrick Houstoun, Baronet, in purchasing a small brigantine, *Betsy and Nancy*, of "240 barrels of burthen," at the freight of ten shillings a barrel, Captain Vallence master, then lying in the Sapelo River near McIntosh's plantation, and had her loaded with rice to go to Surinam and return with the value in Dutch goods. Unfortunately for George McIntosh, William Panton, keeper of an Indian store on the St. John's River in East Florida, happened to go to Sapelo at that time. He plead with the three partners to be allowed to have a fourth part in the shipment, saying that he had no "respondents in Surinam that he was acquainted with trade (which none of the others were) and would take all the trouble off their hands, and continue the business from Surinam to Geor-

---

5. The Historical Society of Pennsylvania. Etting Collection.
6. The events narrated hereafter are taken from *The Case of George M'Intosh, Esquire, a member of the late council and convention of the State of Georgia with the Proceedings thereon in the Hon. the assembly and council of the State*. Printed in the year MDCCLXXVII. A copy is in the Library of Congress. A photostatic copy is in Hodgson Hall, Savannah, presented by the author to the Georgia Historical Society.

gia." Although McIntosh and Panton "differed widely in political sentiments," McIntosh agreed reluctantly to Panton's proposal, and then never "troubled or concerned himself afterward about the brig and cargo, except to get a clearance for the brig at Savannah for Surinam and gave bond in one thousand pounds sterling for the performance of the voyage." McIntosh remained in Savannah through the remainder of the month of June, in attendance at meetings of the Council of Safety. The previous month he had taken oath before the council as a justice of the peace for St. Andrew's Parish and swore to "maintain the Constitutional Authority of this country as established by Congress." It is presumed McIntosh spent most of July and August at Rice Hope. He attended one meeting in September, six in October, and two toward the end of November.[7] He was to hear evil tidings in August. The *Betsy and Nancy*, in the meantime, had begun her historic voyage down the Sapelo River, her bow pointing south, heading obstensibly for Surinam, Dutch Guiana. When the brigantine had "dropped down as far as Mr. Roderick McIntosh's Bluff," a Captain Stewart, owner of the ship, boarded her and said he intended to sell her, which he did, and with Captain Vallence went to Savannah. George McIntosh, who had just returned from the provincial capital for a short visit, approached the mate, James Johnston,[8] and asked him to take charge of the vessel, saying that Panton would give him directions and letters to some Surinam merchants. Johnston agreed, and when he reached Sapelo Sound took Panton and his brother Thomas aboard the ship. The new captain was told by the Pantons that Thomas Panton was to direct the vessel and cargo, by the express desire of Mr. George McIntosh and Sir Patrick Houstoun. The captain asked if they had any orders from "those Gentlemen's hands" to give him, and was told there were none. The captain wished to consult McIntosh as he was "displeased to have Thomas Panton put on board and the direction of the vessel given him," but being informed that McIntosh had returned to Savannah, he "proceeded over the bar." Once the boat had reached the sea Thomas Panton told Johnston to make for the St. John's River. The captain objected and maintained that his clearance was for

---

7. *Revolutionary Records of Georgia*, I, 128, 129, 136-143, 203-210, 216, 217.
8. Not Colonel James Johnston, Jr., who, in 1776 was a little boy.

Surinam. In reply Panton said he was to get a clearance from Florida also, "to secure the vessel and cargo from the Men of War." The captain then went up the St. John's. His ship was boarded by "sixteen armed men belonging to Osborne," a pirate. Panton then destroyed the Georgia clearance.

Before leaving the St. John's River the brigantine's name was changed to the *St. Andrew*, and on August 3, the governor of Florida, Patrick Tonyn, sent from St. Augustine a signed permit to Captain Johnston authorizing him to sail from the St. John's River to the British island of Tobago and thence to the port of St. Augustine. The permit was addressed to "all Flag officers, Captains, Commanders, and other Commissioned Officers, in his Majesty's Pay; and also to all others, to whom these presents shall or may concern."

The ship then went to St. Augustine where Panton took out a new register and clearance papers for Tobago, in the Lesser Antilles, and "got the vessel clear from Osborne." During the five weeks' stay in the St. John's the hatchway was not opened and only about ten barrels were taken out of the brig, which William Panton ordered out of the cabin to supply his Indian store up the river. No lumber was taken on board, only wood and water. On August 9, with Thomas Panton still on board, the vessel set sail for Tobago, but the sails were found to be in "bad order," and being in need of water, the ship could not reach the island; so she ran down to Antigua and got a supply. Panton tried to sell the cargo there but failed; he went to Jamaica where he disposed of it, consisting of 230 barrels of rice. He then proceeded to purchase rum, sugar, and coffee, to the amount of the whole cargo. That business concluded, the ship left Jamaica and arrived back at St. Augustine, January 6, 1777.

Although the minutes of the Council of Safety do not record the name of George McIntosh as being present during the month of August, 1776, from his own account he did attend at least one session that month. He heard the report in August that the brigantine had discharged her cargo of rice at St. Augustine, and was then loading with skins and lumber for Europe, and it was that report which "raised the first clamor against him." McIntosh declared in council, "that Mr. Panton must have deceived him, with the intent to make the whole his own property; that everyone must be convinced, that any person of common sense, for the profit that could be made upon sixty barrels of rice, which was his share of the cargo, would not forfeit a bond of £1000 sterling, which was only *promised before*." McIntosh then delivered his statement to the President, Archibald Bulloch, who desired to have it ready "to put in force" if ever McIntosh was found to be privy to the vessels going to East Florida, "which fully satisfied the President, Council, and every other person at that time."

Not long after the incident in the Council meeting, McIntosh's neighbor, Button Gwinnett, who had returned from Philadelphia in August after signing the Declaration of Independence, "unravelled the whole mystery to him" which "gave him great satisfaction." Besides giving McIntosh a full account of the alleged proceedings in the St. John's River, including the intention of the pirate Osborne to take the brigantine as a prize, Gwinnett disclosed to McIntosh the rumor that "he would never see a farthing for his share of her," to which McIntosh replied "he was indifferent about [that] and happy that his reputation was cleared." The whole story soon became known and no more was said or thought of it for the time being, to the prejudice of George McIntosh.

For the next six months George McIntosh and his wife continued to live their "easy, domestic life," while their evil genius, Governor Tonyn, for some unaccountable reason, had executed the deed that brought about the ruin of George McIntosh. On the evening of February 22, 1777, or sometime on the following day, Georgia was stunned by the news of the mysterious death of its revered president, Archibald Bulloch. Mrs. George McIntosh in her twenty-first year died, "the same day that Button Gwinnett was chosen president."

It is not known whether Nancy Houstoun McIntosh died in Savannah or at Rice Hope, nor is it known where she was buried. She was survived, besides her husband, by her little son, John Houstoun McIntosh, who was not quite four years of age, and another child. Nancy was spared the sorrow of witnessing the humiliation and the indignities that were heaped upon her husband during the following months.

The day Button Gwinnett was elected president neither Nancy McIntosh's husband nor her brother John Houstoun was present at the council meeting, but both attended on March 4 when Gwinnett's commission was to be signed. The feud between Button Gwinnett and Lachlan McIntosh began when the latter received, the previous September, the command of the First Continental Battalion, an office which Gwinnett coveted and expected to receive. General McIntosh and Gwinnett were also rivals for the command of the Georgia brigade over which Lachlan McIntosh was made a brigadier general instead of Button Gwinnett. Bitter animosity existed thereafter between Gwinnett and the McIntosh family, and George McIntosh was the sufferer. And he suffered intensely. When at the March council meeting George McIntosh was handed the President's commission to sign, he refused to do so, and told President Gwinnett he was not present when the latter "was elected and if he had, he would be the last person in the world he would choose; to which Mr. Gwinnett replied 'By G—d this will be the last day you and I will ever sit together in Council.'" His words were a prophecy as the next day McIntosh, who was then sick, became extremely ill and was confined to bed.

In the latter part of March, Button Gwinnett received a letter from John Hancock, President of the Continental Congress, which was intended for Archibald Bulloch since he was president of Georgia at the time the letter was written.

President Hancock wrote from Baltimore, January 8, 1777, to the Honourable the President and Council of the State of Georgia:

> I have the honor to enclose you a copy of an intercepted letter from the Governor of East Florida to Lord George Germaine, containing among other things, the most convincing proof of the treasonable conduct of Mr. George M'Intosh of your state. This Gentleman, it seems, is a member of the Congress in Georgia, and under that character is secretly supporting, by every act in his power, the designs of the British King and parliament against us.
>
> The United States of America have hitherto suffered extremely from the misrepresentations of their enemies, but much more from the baseness and perfidy of their pretended friends. I have it, therefore, in command from Congress, to request, that you will

cause the said George McIntosh to be immediately apprehended, and take every other step in this matter which shall appear to you to be necessary for the Safety of the United States of America.

The portion of the letter of the perfidious Governor Tonyn, intercepted at sea, referred to by President Hancock, was written from St. Augustine on July 19, 1776, while the brigantine was still in Florida waters. The Florida governor declared:

> I had also the honour to write your Lordship that I expected from sundry places supplies of provisions, but I have not so effectually succeeded in any of them, as I have in those taken up by Mr. Panton. He has now brought four hundred barrels of rice into St. John's River, a thousand more are shipped, and expected to arrive every hour. Mr. Panton executed this business with great hazard to life and fortune. He has been greatly assisted by Mr. George M'Intosh, who is compelled to a tacit acquiescence with the distempered times, and is one of the Rebel Congress of Georgia, intentionally to mollify and temporize, and to be of all the service in his power. I am informed his principles are a loyal attachment to the King and Constitution. He would, my Lord, be in a dangerous situation was this known.

Also enclosed in Hancock's letter was a copy of the resolution of congress instructing its president to recommend to the Georgia authorities the apprehension of George McIntosh.

After reading the above communications Gwinnett endeavored to hold a meeting of the council which had adjourned a short time previously, but being unable to secure a quorum, he took the responsibility of ordering the arrest of McIntosh and no doubt enjoyed his revenge. On the order of the President, the provost marshal with a party of men, called on George McIntosh at his home, arrested him and took him in a "harsh and cruel manner." They carried him to "a dirty and offensive gaol," occupied by felons, and he was fettered in irons. Savannah, already torn into factions, was in an uproar. No one knew why one of its prominent citizens and a member of the council was submitted to such indignity or with what crime he was charged. The unhappy prisoner himself was not apprised of the reason for his seizure; his friends, the chief justice, other magistrates, and the members of the council were likewise ignorant of the reason for the seizure.

The secrecy of the proceeding naturally led to the suspicion that McIntosh was guilty of a gross violation of the law, "which removed all their pity and compassion." A few days after the incarceration of McIntosh, Gwinnett left for the "southward" to make preparations for his Florida expedition. During his absence, the council met on March 19 with the Honorable Jonathan Bryan as chairman, and sat upon the affair of George McIntosh "who was brought before them." By that time McIntosh had knowledge of Tonyn's intercepted letter and William Panton's duplicity as he declared upon oath that:

> ... he never shipped, or was concerned with shipping, any rice to any part of the world, out of the State of Georgia, except his concern in the brigantine *Betsy and Nancy* ... intended for Surinam last June ... that he never had any kind of correspondence with any person, either East or West Florida, by writing, message, or otherwise; that he was at a loss to guess or conceive the motive or view Governor Tonyn could have in asserting such falsities in his letter to Lord Germain, respecting the examinent, or William Panton, who he thinks must have informed the Governor, unless it was vanity to recommend themselves to each of their respective patrons, officiousness, or which is worse, designed villainy.

Following McIntosh's declaration of his innocence, council passed a resolution:

> George M'Intosh, Esq., being brought up agreeable to order, and being heard upon oath ... as to the charge preferred against him; it was unanimously resolved, that the said George M'Intosh be enlarged, upon giving sufficient security, in the penalty of twenty thousand pounds, Georgia currency, for his appearing; and being forthcoming, to answer the said charge whenever further proof and evidence shall be brought against him, and he shall be duly summoned to answer the same; and that, in the meantime, he shall not depart the State, or remove, or cause to be removed, any part of his property out of the State ... without leave first had and obtained for that purpose ... that the said George M'Intosh have leave to write a letter to be perused by this board, to any person in St. Augustine, and to endeavor to procure ... any affidavit tending to exculpate and acquit him of said charge; and that he ... have leave to send a person with such letter, at his own expense, under the inspection of this board. ... That upon the above mentioned security being given, the

guards being placed upon the plantation be withdrawn, and no steps be taken further in regards to his estate until after trial. . . . That in case [he] shall, at any time, between this and October next, desire to repair to the Continental Congress, there to answer this charge, he shall be at liberty to do so, upon giving security for that purpose, in the same penalty as before mentioned, and defraying the expense of any evidence which this State shall think necessary to send to the Congress against him.

As a result of the council's resolution, "a bond was immediately given in the enormous and excessive sum of £2000, sterling, in which most of the members of council, and many other respectable characters joined, and many more crowded in, who had not room, but not a single Tory as has been asserted." McIntosh was suffered to "go at large," under the belief that he had been cleared of the charge against him. He wrote a letter to William Panton which was approved by the Council, but he was requested to defer sending it until the Florida expedition was concluded for fear of giving intelligence to the British. McIntosh acquiesced, and, expecting no further trouble, was satisfied.

3

In March, 1777, affidavits, allegedly proving the innocence of George McIntosh, were taken before the magistrates in St. Andrew's Parish and the Chief Justice in Savannah. On the twenty-fifth, Andrew Cook, his former overseer, appeared before Raymond Demere, one of the justices of St. Andrew's Parish, and swore that he had lived with McIntosh since November, 1775, in the capacity of overseer or manager of his plantation to the time of making his affidavit. Cook made solemn oath that no rice or any other provision was sent or shipped from McIntosh's plantation, except about one hundred barrels of rice which had been sold to George Houstoun on board his schooner for Savannah, in the month of December, 1775; that which was shipped in the brig, *Betsy and Nancy* in June, 1776; a few barrels of old rice, sent at different times to his indigo plantation for his Negroes' provisions, and small quantities sold to neighbors in the parish for their consumption, the latter not exceeding twenty barrels.

Of considerable importance was the affidavit of Robert Baillie, "a professed Tory, or advocate for the old British Government, but deemed a very honest man." His deposition was made before Raymond Demere, at "Sappello" on March 27, and was sworn to before Chief Justice Glen. In a long statement Baillie rehearsed the circumstance of the beginning of the transaction which he, George McIntosh, and Sir Patrick Houstoun had had with William Panton; of the negotiations Baillie had with the captain of the brig *Betsy and Nancy* in trying to induce Panton to have his vessel remove Baillie and his family and effects to some other country, and how the negotiations failed because the captain "apprehended great danger from the men of war"; of the visit of William Panton to his house where he told Panton he desired to "leave the province on account of the unhappy disturbances which he thought would greatly distress it, and in all probability would be involved in an Italian War"; and of his asking Panton if it would be possible to procure in East Florida a "new register and clearances in order to screen her from the men of war," to which Panton had declared he did not think it possible, but that he would try. Panton left, the deponent said, and "after a considerable time" the contract was made with the captain of the *Betsy and Nancy* to ship the rice to Surinam.

On Panton's return he informed Baillie he could not procure the register from East Florida as the brig was not in those waters. On being informed by Baillie that he, McIntosh, and Houstoun were about to charter the brig to go to a foreign market with a load of rice, Panton, who had with him "a few goods," asked to "be concerned in the cargo of the brig," and after disposing of his goods, upon receiving permission from the committee of St. Andrew's Parish, he conferred with McIntosh, and it was decided to allow Panton to join the "charter party" in shipping the cargo of rice to a house in Surinam. Soon afterward McIntosh sent a clearance from Savannah. In a strange confession Baillie incriminated himself by declaring that it was privately agreed between Panton and himself that the brig should touch at St. Mary's, Georgia, or St. John's, Florida, for a register and clearance which was to be concealed from the knowledge of McIntosh, as it was known he would not concur in it. Then it was that the owner of the vessel, Captain Vallence, appeared in Darien, sold the boat to Baillie and Panton, and the mate James Johnston was appointed master. Baillie stated in his affidavit that he firmly believed the mate was unacquainted with the plan of the vessel's touching at any other place than at the port of Surinam. He then declared that since the sailing of the brigantine from the Sapelo River he had never heard from Panton by letter, message, or otherwise. Baillie admitted that at the time the report prevailed that the *Betsy and Nancy* was in the St. John's River, McIntosh frequently had expressed to him his great uneasiness, saying he was afraid they had been deceived. Baillie, having seen a letter from Governor Tonyn to Lord George Germaine respecting McIntosh, was induced to declare upon oath what he knew of that gentleman's sentiments. In every conversation the deponent said he had had with McIntosh, he ever found him to be a warm friend of the American cause. He declared further that during Panton's short stay at his house in June, 1776, political disputes arose frequently between Panton and McIntosh, when the latter always warmly supported the "Measures of the Continent." Panton mentioned privately to the deponent his concern for McIntosh, saying that, on account of the active part the latter had taken in the disputes, he was apprehensive McIntosh would be a sufferer. Panton expressed himself as convinced that South Carolina would shortly be reduced by the British fleet and army then before it, and that the Province of Georgia would inevitably follow its fate. Baillie declared those sentiments induced him to believe Panton "urged by motives of friendship and regard for McIntosh, was the reason for representing to Governor Tonyn what he thought would prove favorable to McIntosh, in case matters terminated as he had suggested." A strange deduction considering the outcome.

On April 12, Raymond Demere, a strong supporter of the Patriot cause, appeared before Chief Justice Glen in Savannah and declared his belief in the loyalty of George McIntosh. He asserted he "had frequently the honor, with Mr. George McIntosh, to represent the parish of St. Andrew's in Convention, and has ever had the strongest reason to believe him to be a warm friend to the American cause . . . Mr. George McIntosh was among the first of those advocates in this State who early stood forth at the hazard of life and fortune, to support the measures of the Continent . . . and uniformly conducted himself in avowing his attachment to the cause and supporting its interests." Demere further declared that owing to McIntosh's indefatigable pains most of the residents of St. Andrew's Parish signed the association as early as they did, and was the means of keeping up the public meetings and committees. He knew of no action or circumstance of McIntosh's conduct, he affirmed, that gave him reason to think otherwise than that he was a true and just friend to the American cause in which he so early engaged. Demere maintained that, as one of the principal charges against McIntosh was his having supplied the enemy in East Florida with provisions, he knew of "no one instance that has the least tendency towards the support of such an accusation," and thought it "scarce possible that such a communication could have been carried on without his knowledge."

Affidavits from those two men "widely different in political sentiments, and who had every means of knowledge and information," proved according to George McIntosh's statement, that his conduct, conversation, and practice were always uniform in his attitude toward the American cause, and also gave further confirmation that he had not sent any provisions to the enemy in East Florida or was concerned with supplying them.

More affidavits in McIntosh's favor followed in the ensuing two months. On June 19, George Houstoun declared before the chief justice, that in December, 1775, he had sent his schooner to the plantation of George McIntosh at "Sappelo"; that the ship had returned to Savannah the following month with one hundred and eleven barrels of rice; and that since that time he had not purchased or received any rice from McIntosh. The master of the *Betsy and Nancy*, James Johnston, was examined on June 23, and gave his testimony. He recounted the history of the transaction of McIntosh and Houstoun with Panton, as far as he knew of it, and of the voyage of the *Betsy and Nancy;* but he gave it as his sincere opinion that had the boat not been boarded by Osborne and his pirates, a circumstance which caused Panton to destroy his Georgia clearances, the boat would have been taken to Surinam and thence returned to Georgia. He believed, he said, that the unexpected visit of the pirates caused the alteration in the voyage, but he did state that Panton had made the change without the knowledge of McIntosh and Houstoun, who, in his opinion, "intended the vessel and cargo for Surinam and were much surprised and offended with Panton for doing otherwise. He was also convinced, he said, that Panton had never accounted for or remitted any part of the proceeds of the voyage to the shippers but had "kept the whole in his own hands, and applied the whole to his own life." As part of his evidence he produced the original permit signed by Governor Tonyn and sent from St. Augustine to the brig's master before he left the St. John's River. The permit authorized Johnston to proceed with his ship and the cargo of two hundred and sixty barrels of rice and five thousand staves for dunnage from the River St. John's to His Majesty's Island of Tobago, there to unload and return to St. Augustine. The text of the license, as Johnston pointed out, was in contradiction to the wording of the Governor's letter wherein he falsely asserted that the brig's cargo was landed in East Florida, as stated by Johnston, but the wording of the aforesaid letter read "Panton had brought four hundred barrels of rice into the St. John's River . . . and had been greatly assisted by Mr. George McIntosh."

The third and last deposition given on July 1, also before Chief Justice Glen, was from Samuel Stiles whose plantation was on the Ogeechee River near Savannah. He was a seafaring man, he said, and he had gone to East Florida to try to recover his schooner, the *Race-Horse*, which had been captured by Osborne. He stated that while there he was informed that the brig *Betsy and Nancy*, afterwards called the *St. Andrew*, had sailed out of the River St. John's for Tobago without unloading her cargo.

In spite of all the evidence produced by McIntosh to prove his innocence, he was not cleared of guilt in the minds of the members of Georgia's House of Assembly. Button Gwinnett, the enemy of the McIntosh family, had died in May from bullet wounds inflicted in a duel between himself and General Lachlan McIntosh. The first state constitution had been adopted, and the assembly had approved the proceedings of the late Council of Safety in putting George McIntosh in custody. At the same time it censured the council for letting him out on bail, and ordered that he be sent to the Continental Congress as soon as possible under a strong guard. The argument in favor of such a move was that the Continental Congress had ordered McIntosh imprisoned, and "no power inferior to them could release, try or acquit him, however innocent," as Tonyn's letter contained convincing proof of McIntosh's treasonable conduct. George McIntosh, however, while showing deference to the president of the congress, felt the latter went too far in condemning him before obtaining firsthand information, and asserted that congress could not act as a judicial court. "These matters," he contended, "they leave to the local laws of the particular states . . . having things of higher importance, fully to employ their time; and would be falling into the same error with the British Parliament, whereof we so much complained, in carrying persons for their trial, where they have neither friends, acquaintance, or money."

In putting his defense in writing, McIntosh argued that the council had ordered that the suspected person be apprehended and secured, taking such effectual measures as judged necessary for the safety of the United States, not to put him in custody. McIntosh felt that as an innocent man, a great injustice had been done to him, who was entitled to the protection of the state, and that a dangerous precedent had been established which had proved alarming to the inhabitants of the state of Georgia.

Governor Treutlen and his council on June 10 ordered General McIntosh as one of his "securities," to produce George McIntosh that morning. The summons was not complied with, and days later, John Martin, secretary of the council, applied to John Houstoun, one of the other bondsmen, requesting him to produce George McIntosh, and informed him that General McIntosh had apprised the secretary he had written to his brother to his plantation, but he had learned George was not there. The General, Martin wrote to Houstoun, would try to locate his brother and would write and acquaint him of the summons. Both bondsmen were notified that unless George McIntosh was produced, "agreeable to the tenor of the bond, the same would be forfeited." On June 14, a second notice was issued to General McIntosh. On Monday June 16, George McIntosh returned to Savannah and "delivered himself," whereby his bond, he thought, became void, and his bondsmen ceased to have charge of him. He asked to have a hearing before the Governor and council, but was refused although he used every possible argument to have his trial in Georgia, where, according to the constitution, he was entitled to have it held. When his arguments failed, McIntosh asked permission to send for William Panton because he was the only person who could throw light on the case and disprove the charges against him by giving his reasons for what he had written to Governor Tonyn. But the members of council said they would hang Panton if they saw him. McIntosh then asked permission to write to Panton requesting an affidavit of him, also that he might be treated "as a Gentleman" on his journey to Philadelphia whither the Governor and council had ordered him to go under guard, to appear before the Continental Congress. Both requests were allowed and entered on the minutes, with the stipulation that he could give the answer from Panton in three weeks' time. The next morning, while council was in session, George McIntosh appeared at the door still in the custody of the provost marshal, "who followed him from nine in the morning till past one in the afternoon." McIntosh sent in the letter he had written to Panton, but he was not called into the meeting, nor did he receive any answer from council. The accused man was surprised and uneasy when he was not called, fearing something had happened to change the opinion of council, and that he would not be allowed to send his letter to Panton as promised. He continued to make preparations for his journey, while "everything was kept in profound secrecy, (except out of door remour) although there were councils held almost continually." After a period of suspense, before he was allowed to finish his examination, "and while a Taylor was taking his measure for a suit of clothes," he received word from his brother Lachlan that John Martin had acquainted him that a fresh order had been issued by the council to produce the body of George McIntosh, calling on the general as one of the securities, expecting an immediate compliance with the order.

4

George McIntosh was startled at the turn of events, especially as he had heard a report that he was to be sent on to the congress under a guard of twenty military officers who were going there upon recruiting service. He was the more perplexed because he had not broken his parole. Having considered the "whole matter maturely," he decided it was "prudent to retire out of the way for a while, until he saw how matters went on," or until his fellow citizens "took the alarm at the precedent, and interfere in his behalf." Naturally his conduct caused gossip and censure. A certain "Delegate of Congress and prime instrument in getting the resolve passed at the Assembly, declared publicly that Mr. George McIntosh should be sent to Congress and that he would take care that he [McIntosh] would never return." Another person "high in office" went around in June "with a grave face and far more industry than he ever served the publick, declaring with his hand upon his heart, and a deep sigh, that he always thought Mr. McIntosh *perfectly* innocent till *now*, but his absconding *fully convinces* him of his guilt." He accused McIntosh of having gone to St. Augustine, although he had seen a letter from McIntosh proving the contrary to be true, and "yet his worthy personage goes fervently," McIntosh wrote, "to his prayers morning, noon and night."

George McIntosh did not go to St. Augustine, but to St. Andrew's Parish where he found that his property had been "squandered, neglected and dispersed." On July 4, 1777, he wrote to an unnamed person from St. Andrew's:

> Since I wrote you last, the Parish of St. John's men (they say by the Governor's orders) have taken possession of my estate, destroyed all my crops on the ground by turning their horses into it, killed and drove off all my stock of every kind, broke open my house barn and cellar, plundered and carried off everything of value they could find, and still continue there committing every waste in their power.
>
> I would only ask any honest man, by what law, or shadow of justice, they do all this? They have not proved one single crime against me with all their art and malice, and they are afraid to give me a fair hearing, either before the Legislative, Executive or Judicial Departments; well knowing and convinced, that I can clear myself of everything they lay to my charge. . . . I am now without house or home, in my native country, and what property I have been collecting in an honest way, these twenty years past, arbitrarily and unjustly taken from me, without any form of trial; my poor unfortunate and helpless children made beggars, and myself wandering from place to place through the woods like a vagabond and an outlaw. . . . I am resolved to stand it awhile longer and see what lengths my enemies will go. I find few of my friends dare speak their minds or say a word in my behalf,

though conscious of my innocence. They are afraid to lose their popularity or their property.

The gallant St. John's men have drove my faithful and trusty over-seer off my plantation. Excuse the writing, as it is upon my knee, and under a tree.

Two days later he wrote again from St. Andrew's Parish, and the further accusations he made against the liberty-loving inhabitants of St. John's Parish included whipping one of McIntosh's trusty Negroes on his indigo plantation, because he would not tell where his master was; taking into custody the slaves and overseers of William McIntosh and James Spalding, when a fine crop of indigo was about to be harvested, almost ruining the population of the county and threatening to join them to their own; and driving off many of the inhabitants to the oyster banks where they could find sustenance. Concluding his letter, George McIntosh wrote, "Deplorable as my own situation is, not knowing yet what I shall be drove to, my heart bleeds for the distresses of some of the poor people the oldest settlers and natives of my country."

As might be expected George McIntosh's health had suffered after five months of harsh physical treatment, anxiety, anguish, and humiliation. He described his condition as "a mere skeleton, worn off his legs and hardly able to stand, and is grown indifferent to his family, property, and everything else."

In August McIntosh's pamphlet was issued and in the opening paragraph he wrote what he considered was necessary for the enlightenment of the public:

> The case of George M'Intosh, Esq., having engrossed much of the publick attention in Georgia, and as it may probably have been the subject of conversation in the neighboring States, it may not be improper to lay before the candid impartial publick, a full and true state of the matter; in order to prevent their being imposed on by misrepresentations, to enable them to judge, whether Mr. M'Intosh is guilty or innocent, and whether or not in the proceedings against him that attention has been paid to the Liberty, Safety and Security of the Subject, which is consistent with the principles on which the present Struggle for Freedom is founded. If in the subsequent pages the Reader should observe any inaccuracies in the stile, he will readily excuse them, as Truth, not Elegance of Language, is the object of the Author.

Governor Treutlen was furious; and it can be understood why, as McIntosh did not spare him or his council by vituperation and invective. George McIntosh left for Philadelphia to plead his own case before congress, after having failed in his effort to be given a hearing before his state's legislative body. He arrived there on August 20. Through John Wereat, a friend of the McIntoshes, and the Continental agent, the executive council of Georgia learned of George McIntosh's departure and in a letter to President Hancock Treutlen wrote: "He has skulked off like a guilty thing."[9] In telling of McIntosh's pamphlet, which he described as "replete with falsehoods and misrepresentations," he wrote:

> George M'Intosh's thought in stealing away was that he would be spared the humiliation of being carried as a prisoner, perhaps in irons and possibly riding in a cart on the long trip through the states. He made a quick trip, reaching Philadelphia on August 20.[10]

Strengthened with letters from influential friends, including Jonathan Bryan, John Wereat, Henry Laurens, and other prominent men who believed in his innocence and who considered that his persecution was animated by the enemies of General McIntosh, George McIntosh presented his memorial to congress.

On taking a vote as to the legality of that body trying the case the vote was eight to two that congress had the power, and a committee composed of John Adams of Massachusetts, James Duane of New York, and William Williams of Connecticut, was appointed to examine all documents and papers. The committee reported the next day that there was no adequate reason for detaining McIntosh, and he was forthwith discharged.

McIntosh returned to Georgia a heartbroken man, but with the satisfaction that the highest body in the land had cleared him of guilt and his honor was saved. What became of him during the next three years can only be a matter of conjecture. From his own statement there were children, his son John Houstoun

---

9. Jenkins, *Button Gwinnett*, 162. Quoted from MS. letter in the Library of Congress, dated August 6, 1777.
10. *Ibid.*, 162. Quoted from South Carolina and American *General Gazette*, October 2, 1777.

COLONEL AND MRS. JOHN HOUSTOUN McINTOSH
1772-1836   1769-1847
From the miniatures owned by Miss Katherine Bayard Heyward, of Columbia, South Carolina.

McIntosh, four years of age, and a baby, probably only a few months old. The McIntoshes and Houstouns, in all likelihood, gave shelter and care to the three stricken members of their family. The baby died, and later John was spoken of as the only child. George McIntosh died intestate in 1780, before Charles Town fell to the British, but he was possessed of considerable real estate amounting to thirteen thousand and eighty acres divided into forty-five tracts situated in the different counties of Liberty, Glynn and Camden, a lot in Savannah, Negroes appraised at three thousand seven hundred and sixty-two pounds, and seventeen pieces of silver consisting of spoons and other old plate.[11]

General McIntosh was in Augusta when he learned of his brother's death, and although he left immediately, he did not arrive until several days after the funeral,[12] which took place in St. Andrew's Parish. General McIntosh remained a few days at the "habitation" of his late brother, and examined the effects and papers which were "scattered about" and "huddled" into unlocked broken trunks, but found nothing of consequence except a grant and titles of land, which were all put into a small portmanteau trunk and secured by the General's family when the British were approaching Georgia and while General McIntosh was a prisoner in Charles Town. Before he left Sapelo, the General engaged a "Waggoner" to carry to Charles Town to the care of Mr. Philip Minis, a "parcel of Indigo" belonging to his brother, to keep it out of reach of the enemy. When the inhabitants of St. Andrew's Parish were fleeing from the enemy, all of the personal effects of the deceased were left at the Plantation on Sapelo River in the care of an overseer.[13]

Sir Patrick and George Houstoun and Robert Baillie were appointed administrators of the estate of George McIntosh, and in January, 1781, they advertised requesting all debtors of the deceased to make immediate payment, and others who had made demands upon him to apply to the administrators.

---

11. Editor, "The Case of George McIntosh," in *The Georgia Historical Quarterly*, III, No. 3 (September, 1919), 137.
12. *Ibid*. In his statement General McIntosh does not say where the funeral took place.
13. *Ibid.*, III, 138.

5
JOHN HOUSTOUN MCINTOSH

The son of George and Ann Priscilla McIntosh, John Houstoun McIntosh, became one of the significant figures in East Florida during the second Spanish occupation, and later an influential and wealthy planter in southern Georgia. On the death of John's father, two of his Houstoun uncles, Sir Patrick and George, undertook the guardianship of the seven-year-old boy and the infant, if it was still alive. It can be assumed they lived in Savannah with their relatives. In 1784, John's paternal uncle, William McIntosh, petitioned the chief justice for a revocation of the letters of administration to the Houstouns, and asked that the management of the estate of George McIntosh be granted to him as the eldest brother. His request was granted, whereupon he added his brother Lachlan's name without his consent. General McIntosh later accepted the appointment, and the two brothers took over the administration of the estate, and continued to manage it for several years.

As John Houstoun McIntosh grew older, he inquired concerning the status of his late father's estate, and, prior to 1793, through his guardian, Sir George Houstoun, Baronet, filed with the court a bill of complaint against his McIntosh uncles.[14] On September 11, 1793, as one of the defendants, General McIntosh filed his answer in the superior court, sworn to before Judge John Houstoun. In it he recited the history of his brother George's life, and some of the actions of the former administrators, the Houstoun brothers. Sir George had filed writs to recover a debt to him from the estate, but the litigants appeared to have had a difference of opinion. The judgment of the court found Houstoun to be in error. He was required to pay certain sums to the estate. That, however, was not the conclusion of John Houstoun McIntosh's proceedings in equity against the McIntosh uncles. It was not until 1795 that the suit was settled. The previous year impartial arbiters were selected by the two "parties" to whom the several allegations of each could be submitted for examination. The men

---

14. Chatham County Court House, Savannah, Judgments, Box 7, No. 1085. The document was missing from the box when searched (1942). It was issued before the period of recording judgments; therefore the date could not be ascertained nor the text examined.

chosen were James Mossman, Joseph Habersham, and Richard Wylly. Evidently a thorough investigation was made and both sides must have consented to the decision of the referees, because it was as late as August 11, 1795, that the suit was ended. On that day John Young Noel, solicitor for the defendants, William and Lachlan McIntosh, appeared in court and produced the "award" of the arbiters, which was "filed agreeably to the Rule made, and moved that the same be entered up as a judgment of the court." After hearing "Mr. Gibbons," counsel for the complainant, John Houstoun McIntosh, the court ordered the award made. The defendants were to deliver to the complainant sundry funding certificates totaling approximately $3,500. John Houstoun McIntosh in his part of the award was to "indemnify and save harmless" the defendants from all "claims and demands to which they may be liable by Elizabeth Moore, late widow of Philip Moore for the use and acceptation of the Farm called Constitution Hill near Savannah or the furniture left in the House on the Said Farm."[15] The document was dated May 11, 1794, and was witnessed by George Woodruff and McCradie & Co. Thus ended the McIntosh vs. McIntosh controversy. In the meantime John Houstoun McIntosh had married.

When William Houstoun and his wife went to Savannah in June, 1788, to stand as sponsors at the baptism of their niece Rachael Moodie Houstoun, they were accompanied by Mrs. Houstoun's sister Eliza (or Elizabeth) Bayard, the daughter of Nicholas and Catherine (Livingston) Bayard of New York. Eliza Bayard was also a godmother of the infant, and she may have met John Houstoun McIntosh at that time. She was nineteen years old, and he was fifteen. In spite of the four years' difference in their ages, they were married in the Dutch Reformed Church in New York, April 20, 1792. It is conjectured that McIntosh took his bride to his plantation, Refuge, in Camden County, Georgia, on the Satilla River. The property of five hundred acres had been a Crown grant to George McIntosh in 1765.[16] His son planted

---
15. Superior Court Minutes, Book G, No. 3, p. 363, Chatham County Court House, Savannah.
16. The original document was owned by the late Duncan Clinch Heyward of Columbia, South Carolina, a lineal descendant. The plantation was later owned by John Houstoun McIntosh Clinch of Savannah, the grandson of John Houstoun McIntosh. It became one of the largest rice plantations in the South, and remained in the family until the death of Mr. Clinch in 1905.

both cotton and rice. Eleven years after his marriage, John Houstoun McIntosh bought from John McQueen Fort George Island, Florida, at the mouth of the St. John's River. The island bore the Indian name Alamacani originally, but Oglethorpe, who made it an outpost for his Georgia colony, renamed it for his British sovereign. McIntosh lived at Fort George for ten years. His house, which overlooked Nassau Sound, was built by McQueen in 1798. It was a large and substantial building on a tabby foundation. It had slender columns in front and a steeply sloping roof. In 1808, McIntosh's young daughter Mary died on the island, and was buried near her aunt Mary, Mrs. William Houstoun.

6

During the period when the United States was incensed over the British seizure of American seamen, the Washington government feared that Florida might be a probable base of naval operations for the British, should war break out. After the Revolution, the Loyalists and many others of English descent, flocked to East Florida, particularly into that section which comprised the territory lying between the St. Mary's River and St. Augustine. In 1763 Spain ceded Florida to Great Britain in exchange for Havana, and in 1783, Great Britain retroceded it to Spain, at which time a large proportion of the English population left Florida, but a number continued to live there under Spanish rule. Subsequently, not only the government of the United States, but the border-land Georgians, and the inhabitants of East Florida as well, desired annexation to the United States. Among the latter was John Houstoun McIntosh, who by 1811 had become the leader of the Scottish and American residents of East Florida. McIntosh had acquired property in Negroes, horses, and boats, and held profitable contracts for cutting pine timber. The President of the United States, James Madison, who had secret designs on East Florida, sent George Mathews (Governor of Georgia, 1787), there to represent him. Mathews had served successfully as one of the commissioners of West Florida, which was under the jurisdiction of the American government. He was vested with full authority to act for the President, and, as it was revealed later, to aid and abet the residents of East Florida. The task was easy since the inhabitants were ready to revolt. **They** were anxious to free themselves from the sovereignty of Spain, and to wrest their land for cession to the United States. And that, too, was what Madison wished to accomplish. In the early spring of 1812, two hundred or more planters of East Florida, and some of their Georgia neighbors, met at a plantation on the St. John's River to form an independent republic.[17] They elected John Houstoun McIntosh director of the Territory of East Florida.

Soon after his appointment Mathews went to St. Mary's, Georgia. There he learned that Amelia Island, off the coast of Fernandina, Florida, had become a rendezvous for smugglers, and captains of British ships were violating the non-intercourse act of 1810. Secure in the confidence and support of Mathews, and through him, of the President, the first move of the revolutionists, or patriots, as they styled themselves, was to attack the Spanish fort on Amelia Island. Mathews, exercising his prerogative, had communicated with Commodore Hugh George Campbell, who had carried United States gunboats to the harbor of Fernandina. The patriots demanded surrender from the Spanish officer of the fort, Don Jose Lopez. The commander obeyed, and John Houstoun McIntosh hoisted the flag of the United States over the fort. A company of United States troops was then garrisoned there.

The patriots had bigger plans ahead should their initial venture succeed. On March 12, 1812, McIntosh wrote a confidential letter to George McIntosh Troup, of Darien (elected governor of Georgia in 1823), a member of the United States House of Representatives, telling him that the province of East Florida "would be in the quiet possession of the officers of the U. States." He continued:

> .... Our plan is all arranged to take the Fort at St. Augustine and the governor on Monday night next by surprise and in a half hour I set off to lead a few chosen Friends to execute this commission. The thing has been for some time in agitation between General Mathews & myself, but I am afraid never would have been accomplished had not the general been governed by the spirit of his instruction and the declared wishes of the country.

---

17. Corse, *The Key to the Golden Isles*, 109-13. In chapter IX, "The Rickety Gate is Unhinged," Dr. Corse has confused John Houstoun McIntosh with a relative, Major General John McIntosh, a hero of the American Revolution.

> My horses are at the Door and my wife & children are all around me in tears. Advise my Dear Sir, and let me assure you, that my last breath would declare, I have ever valued the rights and Privileges of a Citizen of the U. States as the greatest blessing on Earth, and that I would rather leave my children in the enjoyment of them than the mines of Peru.[18]

Flush with the victory of Amelia Island, the patriots, led by a detachment of United States regulars, began their march on St. Augustine. They were attacked by Indians and a company of free Negroes led by a free black, and were forced to retreat. Undeterred by failure to take St. Augustine, and incidentally the governor, the revolutionists adopted a constitution on July 17. The constitution was signed by John Houstoun McIntosh and others, who were fully convinced that they had the backing of the American government. All were anxious to have their republic a component part of the United States.

President Madison, in the meantime, found himself in an embarrassing situation. On one side the Spanish minister was remonstrating against the actions of Mathews, and on the other the British minister was protesting against a "flagrant violation of neutral territory."[19] Madison slipped out of the predicament by repudiating his accredited representative and declared that Mathews had overstepped his authority. He recalled Mathews and in his place appointed David B. Mitchell, Governor of Georgia. Mitchell's instructions were to withdraw the American troops from Amelia Island, and to protect the patriots of East Florida.

When McIntosh and his followers learned of Mitchell's assignment to Mathews's post, they became alarmed, and soon were cognizant of the fact that they were the dupes of a timorous President. On July 30, McIntosh, as the elected head of the Republic, wrote an official letter to James Monroe, Secretary of State. After apprising the Secretary of his election "to the office of Director of East Florida who engaged in the Revolution,"

---
18. Territorial Papers, Florida, January 1812 - December 1812, Vol. 2. Records of the Department of State in the National Archives, Washington, D. C.
19. Fuller, *The Purchase of Florida*, 196.

McIntosh rehearsed all that led up to it. He wrote that it was the desire of "the whole planting interest, in declaring themselves free" after suffering for a long time "under a Government, corrupt in itself," to take possession of the country and hold it until they surrendered it by cession. He declared that the revolutionists had believed in the protection of the United States, under the assurance of Mathews. He described the signing of a deed of cession between Mathews and the commissioners appointed by "our constituted authority," a copy of which deed the patriots were told had been sent to the President. McIntosh then continued:

> With surprise and concern, we heard shortly after, that the President refused to ratify any of the acts of his commissioner: but having every reliance, and confidence, in the justice and humanity of the U. States, we never despaired of being protected. We could not believe, that Men whose Error had been an unbounded confidence in an authorized agent, of the U. States, and whose crime was an ardent love for your government, would be left to the revenge of an arbitrary jealous, and vindictive power. Indeed we were told through official and semi-official channels that *"not a hair of our heads would be touched."* Latterly we have heard with inexpressible anguish, that the Troops and Gun boats of the U. States, which constitute our only security, are to be withdrawn — our slaves are excited to rebel, and we have an array of negroes raked up in this country, and brought from Cuba, to contend with. Let us ask, if we are abandoned, what will be the situation of the Southern States, with this body of Men in the neighborhood? St. Augustine, the whole province will be the refuge of fugitive slaves, and from thence emissaries, can and no doubt will be detached, to bring about a revolt of the black population in the U. States. A Nation that can stir up the savages round your western frontiers to murder, will hesitate but little to introduce the horrors of St Domingo into your Southern country. In addition to this, the Creek Indians have been provoked to hostility against us, and have already committed murder and robbery on our frontiers. This we believe to have been caused by the war between the U. States and G. Britain — for before that event, the savages professed friendship for us, or at least a neutrality, tho instigated to war by the corrupt government in St Augustine.

> Deplorable as is our situation, it is made worse from the im-

possibility of carrying into the U. States, what slaves may remain faithful, without violating your Laws, and thereby making them liable to seizure. A great Many of us have been accustomed to the sweets of affluence, and most of us to the enjoyment of plenty. We in common with other citizens would willingly have sacrificed all we have, had it been in defense of the U. States, but to be beggared and branded as Traitors, is wretchedness, indeed, to Men, who thought they were acting as some of their forefathers had done in 76. We have heard of the disposition of the efforts of the President, the House of Representatives and a respectable minority in the Senate to benefit our situation. Allow me, Sir, of the Repb. of E. Florida to interest the President and his cabinets council, to take into consideration our unhappy, unexpected and unmerited situation; and that it will be determined that a sufficient number of troops and Gun boats be ordered to remain for our protection, until a cession of the country shall be accepted by the U. States; or a reinforcement thrown by the British into St Augustine when, offensive operations might be resorted to.

Upon the principle of justice and humanity we call for the protection of the U. States. with it we become free and happy, without it we must become wanderers upon the face of the Earth, or tenants of loathsome dungeons, the sport of cruel and inexorable tyrants.

Our state of anxiety will be our apology for begging you to send me an answer as speedily as possible.[20]

Humiliation and ruin faced McIntosh. After waiting two months for a reply from the Secretary of State, and receiving none, he wrote again on October 3:

Should I feel any mortification on not hearing from a Gentleman to whose honor and humanity I had appealed, such is my confidence in the justice and intentions of your Government, that I am willing to believe that my letter of 30 July has been unanswered for reasons undoubtedly good. I had addressed you as the Director of East Florida and in this impression you perhaps have not felt yourself disposed? to make a reply Under this impression, I now take the liberty of addressing you as a private individual.

The writer, under the supposition that his letter had mis-

---
20. Territorial Papers, Florida, January 1812 - December 1812, Vol. 2.

carried, said that he enclosed a copy of his former communication, also that he had written to Commodore Campbell. McIntosh explained further:

> I know there are many men, who are enemies to liberty, to the administration, & the prosperity of the U. States; and the measure of their possessing E. Florida, as it would deprive them of principle of smuggling, who are in the habit of publishing many falsehoods respecting us. However, whatever may be the sufferings of the unfortunate people of Florida, I believe they have generally refrained, from saying anything, which would gratify a malignant [blurred]. They have looked up for succour to your Government, they believed that when this succour could be properly afforded, it would not be withheld, and confident that no Tribunal would judge more humanely and impartially of their case than that over which Mr Madison presided they determined to appeal to no other.
>
> If one who had been instrumental in bringing about the revolution in E. Florida and who had greatly involved and every day was further involving his private property in this cause, and had been assured by Commissioner Mathews, that the funds arising from the customs at Fernandina should be appropriated for the support of this revolution, and reimbursement of the advances he had made; will he not be pardoned for a little warmth, when he sees these customs collected, and the monies arising from them, denied him, at an hour too perhaps, when he feels pecuniary distress, a distress to which he has ever been a stranger before? And when in common with the other unhappy people of Florida, he has heard the Anglo-Spaniards at Amelia, exulting at our misfortunes, boasting that the U. States give protection to their property only, and that they yet expect to possess our Estates under a confiscation, can we be blamed for wishing to lay them under some constitution? I do however solemnly assure you, that no order for this purpose has ever been issued from the Patriots, but for the one for Horses.
>
> Allow me to mention, that I told Capt Massias, a day or two ago, that I should write to Governor Kinderland of St Augustine, and inform him, that if he permitted his motley mercenaries to have any more of our Horses, I would retaliate, by ordering to be burnt, as many Horses of his friends on Amelia. These friends have a constant and regular correspondence with him, and under such a threat, might prevail upon him, to desist in his barbarous

mode of warfare. This threat (for it was only a threat) was not impressed. I may have said something more to Capt Massias, but it all related to the same object.

The inhabitants of our country are much dispersed, and many of them have left it altogether. Those however who have had most faith in the justice of the U. S. have never desponded. Having placed their families generally in a place of safety, on Tuesday next, I hope to be able to carry on a company of about fifty of them, to the South side of the St. John's. But we can act only as Guirillas.

Col. Smith one of the bravest. and most discerning of officers, has been obliged to retreat to St. John's. as you however will have no doubt an official information of the situation of the Troops of the U. States, I will be silent on the subject. I will only observe, that our own situation becomes every day more and more critical; and that whatever we may hope, we have had no certain information, to cheer our spirits.[21]

After performing his duties to the satisfaction of the President, Governor Mitchell was recalled late in the year 1812. He was replaced by General Thomas Pinckney, commander of the United States troops who were still in East Florida. About March 27, 1813, "Mr. Morris," General Pinckney's aide de camp, arrived at St. Mary's, and in a day or two proceeded to St. Augustine. The unsuspecting patriots, among them John Houstoun McIntosh, gained the impression that Morris's mission was to be favorable to them. Their assumption was confirmed by his assurance that "he himself, was ignorant of the purport of his message and on his return a week later he repeatedly made the same declaration."

Still intact, the government of the Republic of East Florida met on March 20, 1813, and wrote a proclamation which was issued to its constituents:

> Resolved unanimously, that the Legislative Council view with disdain & Abhorrence the proffer of pardon by the corrupt Government of St. Augustine that they will & do pledge their reputation & property, to support the glorious cause in which they are engaged, & persist, until they secure the safety, independence, & liberty of themselves & constituents.

---

21. Territorial Papers, Florida, February 1813 - December 1817, Vol. 3, John Houstoun McIntosh to James Monroe.

Patriots of East Florida.

At last the corrupt Government of St Augustine has come forward with a proclamation offering "amnesty to the Insurgents who have cooperated in the invasion, (literally so called), of East Florida." Weak must be the mind, that can have the least dependence upon a promise so hollow & deceitful. Can any one believe that such a corrupt, jealous, & arbitrary Government will adhere to promises however sacredly made? Will they not screw every tittle of your property from you under the pretext of making retribution for damages done to Individuals who have adhered to their oppressors? Aided by a venal Judge, supported by a cruel Government your enemies will harrass you as long as a cent remain with you. But it is needless to dwell upon the subject: the pardon no doubt has been manufactured in St Augustine — the Government of Spain knows nothing of it — it is designed to entrap the unwary, thinking that you are depressed by the rumor (however false), that the troops are to be removed. . . .

Can You! Will You! in poverty become the sport of slaves & the abhorred army in St Augustine?

It has been unanimously resolved by the Legislative Council, that they in their representative & individual capacity will not receive the pardon so treacherously offered; but will proceed & act to the utmost of their power until liberty & independence are secured. We call upon you all to write, & by our joint exertions secure our safety, property, liberty, & independence. There can be but two parties: friends & enemies, those that are not with us will be treated as foes. Measures are now, & will be taken to punish vigorously those who basely desert. Spies & emissaries will meet their just punishment.

Done in Council, 30th March, 1813 . . .
[signed.]
B. Harris
Presid^{t.} of the Legislative Council
Daniel F [?] Delaney
Secretary of State
John H. McIntosh
Director Terr^y East Florida[22]

General Pinckney arrived at St. Mary's on April 12, and was waited on that day by McIntosh, who was told by the general that through the instrumentality of an agent of the United States

---
22. Territorial Papers, Florida, February 1813 - December 1817, Vol. 3.

government a general pardon had been obtained from the Spanish governor for the insurgents. President Madison, Pinckney informed McIntosh, was satisfied when the Spanish authorities acknowledged and published the pardon, and felt that his government had been exonerated, and was no longer committed to protecting the inhabitants of the Republic of East Florida.

Shocked at what he felt was ruin for him and for his compatriots, McIntosh told Pinckney: "few of us would be willing to depend on a mere pardon. We have planned our crops and the season is too late to plant elsewhere." McIntosh presented Pinckney with a memorial from the people of the Republic, and begged him to delay ordering the troops out of the province until he could represent the situation to the President. Pinckney replied: "I have no discretionary power, my orders are positive, and I have already arranged matters with the Governor of St. Augustine."

McIntosh then asked to have the troops remain in his country until the people could take out their "movable property." Pinckney agreed, reluctantly, to postpone the march for a short period.

Not satisfied with his personal interview with General Pinckney and wishing to reiterate what he had said and to make his position stronger, McIntosh sent a letter to him the next day:

> When the Governor of the U: States instructed you to withdraw their troops from E. Florida: When you corresponded with the Governor of St Augustine a fortnight before the Revolutionists had any intimation of the determination of the U. States Government: it would appear that both you & your Government acted under the impression that the pardon as exhibited by Mr Onis would be unanimously accepted by them. On your arrival at this place, we have taken the first opportunity to assure you, & through you, the Government of the U. States that we believe this promise of pardon, fallacious & treacherous. That our objections to accept it might not appear captious, or as trifling with you, or your Government, we beg to appeal as to the propriety of them, to a Gentleman, whose knowledge of human nature & whose acquaintance with Spanish Governments & whose candour & liberality justly entitle him to our confidence; We repeat it Sir, We appeal to yourself to declare from the observations you have & will be able to make while you are at this place, whether you believe that our persons & property would be secured against the

St Augustine Government, from the pardon issued by the Cortez of Spain. Allow us to remind you of the Spanish character generally, but particularly against a few of us of the impunity with which they may violate any obligations they may make to us, & of the triumphant wrath, which a party composed of ignorance, venality & bigotry will feel at victory.

If Sir you are aware of our situation, & feel for our distress, we beg that you would allow the troops under your command to protect us until you can represent us to your Government. We would not wish to believe that a Government for whom we have risked our all would surrender us to our former Tyrants merely on the declaration of the impotent Cortez of Spain (evidently suggested by their Minister at Washington) & we trust Sir that your high standing in society, & that confidence which your Country has so frequently placed in you, would authorize you at our earnest solicitation to wait but for a few weeks, & not to deliver us up to an enraged & vindictive Government for safety & protection. We are sensible that it requires the consent of the Legislative as well as of the Executive branches of your Government to afford us perpetual protection; but we have reason to believe that the President has particularly commiserated our unhappy situation, that he would on your representation, require some pledge or guarantee from Chevalier Onis for the protection of the lives & property of those among us who might be obliged or willing again to bend their neck to the Spanish yoke. To those among us who are determined never to be others than Citizens of the U. States, whatever may be the sacrifices they shall be obliged to make, it might be permitted to them to reap their present crops & then to sell their lands. This might be done by extending the time for the acceptance of the pardon. Mr. Onis might particularly stipulate that we should have the liberty when we pleased, of going in & out of the Country until a certain period, & that we might remove our property at any time across the St Mary's without its being subject under any pretences whatever to any other demands than such as existed previous to the late contentions. If such conditions were made & secured to us, though they are far, very far short of our expectations when we took up arms against the Government of St. Augustine, we should presume they were the best that could be procured under our unhappy circumstances. Were you authorized in behalf of the U. States to guarantee these conditions to us, we should be satisfied that we had the best assurance of the fulfillment of them.[23]

The following day General Pinckney replied in writing to McIntosh that his orders were to withdraw the troops of the United States from East Florida. McIntosh's communication he promised to forward to the Secretary of State.

Not to be daunted, the indefatigable McIntosh wrote to the Secretary of State, on April 16 from St. Mary's. He rehearsed in a long letter all that had transpired since his letter of March 30, and dwelt in detail on the matter of the Spanish promise of pardon. McIntosh was sensible of the responsibility he bore to his constituents in acting as their intermediary and he knew that, moreover, his own affairs and property were in jeopardy if they were abandoned to the Spaniards. For his own part he wrote:

> . . . with all my exertions, and they are already commenced in the removal of my effects, I shall be necessarily obliged to desert not only my crop but a great deal of seed cotton now in the Barn, with all my livestock etc. Indeed if I can save my plantation Tools, negroes and provisions enough to support them this year I shall be fortunate. No one in the Country has the means of moving which I have, and the Insurgents as they have been called by Gen¹ Pinckney, must either throw themselves on the mercy of these Tyrants, or give them up all they possess. This dreadful alternative will I am persuaded drive many of them to the necessity of bending their necks to the foot of the Spaniard or the negro. General Pinckney has promised to request Govr Kinderlen to allow us to secure our crops & effects without taking the pardon, but it is very improbable that Govr Kinderlen will grant us any favors and indeed, as General Pinckney declares that he will at any rate withdraw the Troops on the 2d, the few of us who can move, dare not risk what we wish to save on an uncertainty. If he prevents a confiscation of our land, he will do more than we expect. It is said that the Anglo-Spaniards on and about Amelia whose arrogance rises in proportion to our distress and despondency, threaten to rob me of my property on its way to this place under the pretense of Losses they have sustained in our contest. All the property that I will be able to move, lies between the U. States Troops on Amelia and St. Johns—and these people who reside within

---

23. *Ibid.*

the same district of Country have uniformly been protected by the Troops of the U. States and have suffered comparatively nothing. Should any of my property or that of others, be thus stolen, and Gen¹ Pinckney not think it within his instructions, to have such property restored, I beg Sir, that you would request the President to grant an order to the Commanding officer at this station, for its restoration . . . .

I have now Sir to apologize for having troubled you with so long a letter—and will only observe, that Gen¹ Mathews found me with a numerous family, possessed of affluence to give them the best education and to carry them in the most fashionable circles in America, but I owe it to the memory of Gen¹ Mathews to declare, that I was warmed by his honest Zest. I revered his virtue and shall ever respect his memory. Gen¹ Pinckney will have me poor and without the means of living anywhere but in retirement. My Children—Tis happy for them that they are generally too young to be sensible of their change of fortune.[24]

7

The evacuation of the United States troops from Amelia Island occurred on May 16 and peace and quiet were restored.[25] The promise of pardon was redeemed by the Governor of St. Augustine, but John Houstoun McIntosh was a marked man. His cause had been repudiated by the government under which he held citizenship and to which he felt he had displayed great loyalty, and he was regarded as a traitor by the government under which he had lived for several years. Because he and his companions were revolutionists, he might have lost his life, but the Spanish governor, recognizing the fact that he was a personage in Georgia, allowed him to leave Florida unmolested.

During the height of the revolution McIntosh was challenged by Don Manuel Solana, one of the Spanish leaders, who was incensed over the rebellion against his government. Solana wrote he would "fight him by day or night, on foot or on horseback,

---
24. *Ibid.*
25. The end of the ill-fated Republic of Florida took place in 1816 when Governor Coppinger had three districts laid off in East Florida where the revolutionists could reside if they would return to Spanish rule. They were allowed a magistrate's court and a company of militia elected by the people, and on their acceptance they were promised "all the past should be buried in oblivion." Caroline Mays Brevard, *A History of Florida* (Deland, Florida, 1924), 30.

with any weapon." With strong hatred of the Spaniards, a legacy from his Georgia ancestors who fought against them in the early Colonial days, McIntosh's reply was sarcastic:

> Was he a private man and Don Manuel Solana (whom he did not even know) a decent character, he would meet him by day, with any weapon but a knife or stilletto, but as Mr. McIntosh had lived among the Spaniards long enough to know that those among them who have any honor left are great sticklers for etiquette, and as he is the Director of East Florida and is extremely solicitous to retain the love of his dear and honorable friends in St. Augustine, he could not condescend to accept a challenge from any individual in that place but Colonel Kinderland (Kintelan), Governor of all the town and castle of St. Augustine.[26]

Apparently no challenge was sent from the governor and no duel took place.

In midsummer of 1813, McIntosh went to Washington to try to obtain some remuneration for the heavy losses he had sustained in the attempt to make East Florida a territory of the United States. He had friends, among them, George M. Troup, member of the House of Representatives, and William H. Crawford, Secretary of the Treasury, who were political friends of the administration. They advised McIntosh that, although they regretted his circumstances, they felt it necessary to oppose his application. However, he was "assured that the highest members of the government felt much for his distress, and that of others in the same situation," and "that he could tell his friends in East Florida that every honorable exertion would be made to have their country annexed to the United States."[27] McIntosh waited until his patience was exhausted. With no intimation that his pleas would be answered, he sent his appeal on August 14, 1813, in writing, to the Secretary of State, James Monroe. Explaining that the people of East Florida had surrendered the town and port of Fernandina to General Mathews, the United States commissioner, with the understanding that those who might make "pecuniary advances"

---

26. Thomas Gamble, *Savannah Duels and Duellists 1733-1877* (Savannah, 1923), 101, 102.
27. John Houstoun McIntosh to John Quincy Adams, Camden County, 5th May, 1818. Miscellaneous Letters relating to John Houstoun McIntosh. National Archives.

THE REFUGE, CAMDEN COUNTY, GEORGIA

Courtesy of the late Mr. Bayard Clinch Heyward, of Habersham County, Georgia

in support of the "cause" would be reimbursed from the custom duties received at the port, McIntosh declared that he had borne "all the expenses which were incurred by the revolt of the people of Florida, . . . and which were very considerably beyond the sum of four Thousand Dollars." Further, he understood that from three to four thousand dollars in custom duties had been collected under Commissioner Mitchell. He had been duly authorized, he continued, by the people of East Florida to receive such money. Mitchell had explained that it would be paid when ordered by the government of the United States. McIntosh requested Secretary Monroe that such an order be given.[28]

By September McIntosh was back in Camden County, where he was endeavoring to retrieve some of his Florida property. While in St. Mary's he wrote to the collector of the port asking to be relieved of the import tax on a large shipment of cotton from his Florida plantation. Referring to his change of residence and his loyalty to the United States, he wrote he was "a man . . . who has lost a very large possession and is now almost ruined from his attachment to that Government."[29] Four years later he deeded Fort George to Captain Kingsley, a Scotsman, who obtained it by foreclosure of a mortgage.

McIntosh had already bought from James Seagrove in 1811, a tract of six hundred and fifty acres, called Marianna. It was situated on King's Bay, across from Cumberland Island. When he went to live in Camden County he built at Marianna a large rectangular house "on brick pillars a few feet off the ground, with an octagonal wing of one story at each end of the rectangle, with octagonal roofs, so high in proportion to the rest of the building that they were suggestive of towers. The octagonal wings were about thirty feet in diameter."[30] In 1819, McIntosh purchased two thousand nine hundred more acres adjacent to

---

28. Territorial Papers, Florida, February 1813 - December 1817, Vol. 3.
29. Coulter, ed., *Georgia's Disputed Ruins*: Floyd, "Certain Tabby Ruins," 143. The letter is in the possession of Marmaduke H. Floyd of Savannah.
30. *Ibid.*, 144, 145. The house remained standing until after the War Between the States. The author visited the site in July, 1928, with Mr. and Mrs. Floyd, and the octagonal foundations of the wings were plainly noticeable. There is an illustration on a MS. map at Hodgson Hall, Library of the Georgia Historical Society.

Marianna, formerly owned by John Boog, including "the Dark Entry" swamp, and in 1821, he acquired one thousand and forty acres, the remainder of the Seagrove grant, which he named New Canaan.

One of McIntosh's friends was General David Blackshear (1763-1837), an early settler of Laurens County, Georgia. During the War of 1812, General Blackshear served under Major General John McIntosh, the first cousin of John Houstoun McIntosh. When General Floyd was wounded at the battle of Antossee, Alabama, in 1813, General Blackshear took his place in the Camden County district until General Floyd could resume command of his troops. The John Houstoun McIntosh family, presumably, visited the Blackshears in Laurens County soon after the war was over and evidently they made the return trip of one hundred and seventy odd miles by carriage. McIntosh wrote to General Blackshear soon after he arrived home:

The Refuge, April 2, 1815

Dear Sir:—A day or two after we left you, one of our carriage horses took sick on the road and died. This accident, together with the badness of the roads, prevented us from reaching here until the latter part of last week. The bearer (Mr. Saltonstall,) who, I believe is a good man, tells me he intends living in your neighborhood, and being now on his way up, I embrace the opportunity of dropping you a line—which I do more readily as our mails, since the war have been extremely irregular.

The conduct of the British (particularly of the officers), both at St. Simon's and at St. Mary's excels even what you and I believe of them in flagitiousness. Nothing was of too little value to tempt them; and everything was grasped, let it belong to friend or foe, widow or orphan. Mrs. Shaw, however, is an exception to this general rule. Cockburn, [Admiral] though her negroes were the first to join him, had them all returned to her, together with a quantity of cotton, some of which belonged to other persons . . . .

The account of the Patriots having killed a great many of them is correct. The officers found it necessary, after they were fired upon from two bluffs, to douse their epaulettes and all the marks of an officer. Cockburn was so enraged when his six boats returned, with two-thirds of their crews killed and wounded, that he made a signal for all the boats and marines to come from the vessels, and swore that he would burn St.

Marys and every house between the Altamaha and St. Mary's; but I am confident that nothing would have prevented him from trusting his men any distance out of their boats . . . . Pray remember me to the major, and tell him I never think of him without gratitude for his hospitality and attention, and that I have taught all my children to play "Maurice," which I call, after him "Blackshear," a name certainly as pretty as that of "Maurice" . . . .

Our seasons have in this part of the country been uncommonly wet . . . . We had a night or two ago, cold almost enough for frost.

Mrs. McIntosh and my daughters are well, and join with me in kind and best remembrance to your amiable lady, Mrs. Bryan, Miss Bush[31] and yourself. We all expect that Miss Bush will shortly lose her name, though not her verdure. That she and you may never change your situation but for the better, is the wish, my dear Sir, of your sincere and obedient servant.[32]

In 1817 McIntosh was troubled again about his friends in East Florida. After the situation cleared, and the Spanish governor had taken back the territory on the withdrawal of the United States troops, undesirable persons began to congregate there. While Colonel Morales, the Spanish officer, was in command, Gregor McGregor, who claimed to be the brother-in-law of Simon Bolivar, the South American liberator, arrived in Fernandina and on July 14, 1817, captured the fort. In September, McGregor departed for the Bahamas for supplies and reinforcements, and left in charge one Hubbert, a former sheriff in New York. About the first of October, Louis de Aury, a Spanish naval officer, who was governor of Texas the year before, entered the harbor of Fernandina with a small fleet. The inhabitants appealed to him for assistance. He consented to help them if they would haul down McGregor's emblem from the fort and replace it with the flag of Mexico. His request was granted and Amelia Island was declared part of the Republic of Mexico. Aury's rule was brief. When the President of the United States learned of the invasion, he sent his troops to suppress what was called "the Liberation movement," and Aury, without protest surrendered Fernandina

---
31. Relatives of General Blackshear.
32. Stephen F. Miller, *Memoir of David Blackshear* (Philadelphia, 1858), 465, 466.

to the United States navy and sailed out of the harbor. Fernandina was "held in trust for Spain," but the occupation of Monroe's troops was of short duration as yellow fever soon depopulated the town and also caused the evacuation of the marines.[33]

The above account of the Florida situation was given in part in a letter to William H. Crawford, Secretary of the Treasury, from John H. McIntosh written from The Refuge on October 30, 1817, but he added interesting information:

> The present chief, Commodore Aury, got the command, very much against the inclinations of Sheriff Hubbert, and Coll Irwin.[34] When he arrived at Fernandina with his squadron of privateers and prizes, they were entirely without money. He disclosed "that if he gave them any aid, it must be on the conditions of being made Commander in Chief; and that as Genl McGregor never had any commission whatever, the flag of the Florida Republic must be struck, and that, of the Mexican Republic hoisted, and that Fernandina should be considered, as a conquest of the Mexican Republic, (under which he was commissioned) without its being necessary, that any other part of the Province of E. Florida should be conquered. Hubbert and Irwin reluctantly agreed to the mortifying condition of resigning the command. They were never friendly with the Commodore and endeavored, but in vain, to gain over by intrigue, a part of his men. Their own party considerably increasing shortly after, they were several times on the point of comming to open war with Aury and his followers; and under the pretense that Aury's forces were composed chiefly of Brigand negroes. A few days before Mr Hubbers death (who was called Governor, without having any power) Aury marched to his quarters with a body of armed men, and obliged him to make such concessions as drove him to an act of intemperance, which soon after terminated his existence. Since the death of this Gentleman there has been little or no disturbance among them. But it would appear, as if the suspicions of the Frenchman, did not die with Hubbert, as none of his Privateers have yet left Fernandina.
>
> The Parties are designated as the American and French, and I have been assured from Individuals belonging to them both, that each are anxiously looking for reinforcements. Aury has

---

33. Fuller, *The Purchase of Florida*, 234.
34. Not to be confused with Jared Irwin (1750-1818), Governor of Georgia in 1796.

a number of Frenchmen, who are as it is said, Officers of Boneparts. They find it their interest, as well as their inclination to support their Countrymen. His great dependence however is, on about a hundred and thirty Brigand negroes—a set of desperate bloody Dogs.

The American Party, which are rather more numerous than the other, consist generally of American English and Irish sailors, but now have no declared leader. Irwin wants either spirit or popularity to assume that character. For my own part, I believe that in point of morals, patriotism and intentions, they are exactly on a par. Aury's Blacks however make the neighborhood extremely dangerous, to a population like ours; and I fear, that if they are not expelled from that place, some unhappy consequences may fall on our Country. It is said, that they have declared, that if they are in danger of being overpowered they will call to their aid, every negro within their reach. Indeed I am told that the language of the Slaves in Florida, is already such, as is extremely alarming.

The patriots of Fernandina had about ten days ago, an unexpected strange reinforcement. Twenty half pay British officers by the way of Turks Island, arrived at St John's River, and mistaking it for Amelia, a Colonel and a couple of others, were made prisoners by the Spaniards. The others got safe to Fernandina; but finding that General Gregor McGregor had abandoned it, they determined immediately on doing so too.

In a few days I intend bringing my family here from St Mary's and perhaps may not see that place again for several months thereafter as I will not have it in my power to give you any information that can be interesting, this letter will close my communications. If any information that I have given shall have been of such importance, as in your opinion, was necessary that you should be acquainted with, I will think myself well rewarded for the frequent letters I have had the pleasure to write to you.

Was it not incompatible with your relations to the Government, I should be glad to have from you, what prospects there are of the U. States possessing E. Florida. Had the wishes of our old and worthy friend Genl Mathews been carried in to effect, nay had your advice & that of the President been followed a few years ago, that unhappy Province, would now have been a flourishing Country, under the Government of the U. States—and probably his Catholic Majesty, his ministers and allies, perfectly reconciled to the measure. The immense losses which I sustained directly and indirectly, have put me out of humour, while I was suffering under privations I had ever been a stranger to, and when my person and property were threatened both by the Marshall and Sheriff and particularly when I reflected on the unfortunate policy of the U. States on the subject of possessing the Floridas—I however never doubted but that the President, the Administration generally, and the good old General, acted from the finest and most patriotic motives in their endeavors to make these Provinces territories of the U. States.

The kindness of my friends aided me in my distress—which with economy and industry on my part, and the sale of a part of my property, have again placed me in independent circumstances. Could I live in St Augustine under the Government of the U. States, I believe that some years would be added to my life, by obtaining what I have solemnly been wishing for. And those years, would be yet increased, by that delightful and healthy climate.[35]

Early in 1818 trouble began with the Indians in Florida, and the Seminole War was the result. General Andrew Jackson in February began to make preparations for his Florida campaign and on March 9 as he neared the border took command of eight hundred regulars and nine hundred Georgia militia. John Houstoun McIntosh, who held the rank of general, was with the latter, and after the capture of St. Mark's, Florida, and the Seminole War, which lasted only a few weeks, the Georgia troops were disbanded, and General McIntosh and his Indian brigade were dismissed on April 24. McIntosh returned to his plantation, Refuge. He had been home barely two weeks when he wrote on May 5 to John Quincy Adams, secretary of state. Correspondence between Adams and the Chevalier Louis de Onis, Spanish minister to Washington, had been going on since the previous October on the proposed ceding of Florida to the United States. One of the terms of the treaty stipulated that "no grants subsequent to August 11, 1802 [were] to be valid."[36] As McIntosh was to be affected by that proviso he wrote to the Secretary of State: "I am one of those persons," he began, "who took up Lands in that Province, subsequent to the year 1802 . . . ." After a lengthy

---

35. Miscellaneous Letters, September, October 1817, relating to John Houstoun McIntosh. National Archives.
36. *American State Papers . . . Public Lands* (Washington, D. C., 1860), VI, 55.

remonstrance, he concluded that "it must be acknowledged, that an insurrection of a handful of men as we were, should not have taken place, had not that Gentleman [General Mathews] been sent among us. And after being assured by his Instruction that all private property should be secured to its owners, in the event of a change of Government, in favour of the U. States; after risking all we possessed to bring this change about; and after too, the clemency and forbearance of the Spanish Government, on not confiscating our property, for taking arms against their authorities, are we now to be treated as traitors, and made outcasts, at the very hour, and by the very instrument, with which you make us your fellow Citizens? Forbid Heaven! forbid it Justice! forbid it Mr. Monroe!"[37]

While the treaty with Spain was pending, McIntosh, fearful that he and some of the property owners of East Florida were to be deprived of their land when Florida was finally ceded to the United States, wrote again to Secretary Adams on February 25, 1819. "Many persons of East Florida," he began, "are much alarmed, at your insisting, in your correspondence with Don Louis de Onis, on all grants, subsequent to the year 1802, being annulled—I am satisfied for my own part, that Mr Munroe, will not ententionally bring to ruin, a number of individuals, whose only political crime, has been, an attachment to his Government and Administration." "My object on the liberty I now take of addressing you," he concluded, "is to inform you, that there is a well grounded expectation, that should the U. States get possession of the Province, either by arms or cession, that the Spaniards will endeavour to carry off with them, the records of the Country."[38]

McIntosh had reason to be apprehensive, as in the years to come he was to lose two thousand acres of land in Florida. The Treaty of 1819 between the United States and Spain for the purchase of Florida, dragged along between diplomats until 1821, when it was finally consummated on July 10 of that year. Seven years later congress passed a supplementary act on May 23, 1828,

---

37. Miscellaneous Letters, April, May, 1818, relating to John Houstoun McIntosh. National Archives.
38. Miscellaneous Letters, February, 1819, relating to John Houstoun McIntosh. National Archives.

"providing for the settlement and confirmation of private claims in Florida," when a committee was appointed to investigate all claims.[39] The committee took two years to complete its work, which seems to have been done thoroughly, and in January, 1830, Samuel Delucenna Ingham, Secretary of the Treasury, sent the comprehensive report to the president of the senate, John C. Calhoun. John Houstoun McIntosh was listed as having two claims: one, a royal grant of eight hundred acres, Mulberry Grove, on the St. John's River, conveyed by the Spanish governor in 1805 to Timothy Hollingsworth, and sold by him to McIntosh on May 2 of the same year, and which was confirmed by the committee;[40] and the other, two thousand acres on the Miami River, which was rejected. The committee reported that the claim was "as good as a Spanish title can be made," and if there had been no conflicting British claim there would be no hesitancy in confirming it, "but as there appeared to be, the recommendation was to reject it." The original grant was made in 1770 after Florida had been ceded by Spain to the British in 1763, to William Thomas Jones by the British governor. Some years later Jones removed to Georgia, and when in 1783 Spain and Great Britain made a second trade, and Spanish rule was again over "Pasqua Florida," Governor Quesada conveyed the Jones grant to John McQueen on November 5, 1795.[41] John Houstoun McIntosh bought the land from McQueen in 1798. The Jones heirs had disputed the claim which was revealed when the federal committee made its investigation and gave its final report that the McIntosh claim should be unconfirmed. Thus John Houstoun McIntosh lost his claim in 1830 while many of his East Florida friends kept their lands through confirmation by the committee.

8

To revert to the time when McIntosh had begun to recover from his impoverished state after the East Florida revolution,

---

39. *American State Papers . . . Public Lands* (Washington, D. C., 1860), 55.
40. *Ibid.*, 67.
41. *Ibid.*, 119. Photostatic copies of the letters of John Houstoun McIntosh, together with others quoted in the foregoing pages, have been presented by the author to the Georgia Society of the Colonial Dames of America. They are known as the Houstoun Collection and are in Hodgson Hall, Savannah.

he found another interest through the advice of a friend in a neighboring county. Between the years 1816 and 1826, Georgia was enjoying great prosperity from a cotton boom, and at the same time a new industry had become popular with planters on the Georgia seacoast. In 1806 Thomas Spalding (1774-1851), of Sapelo Island, friend and contemporary of John Houstoun McIntosh, began his experimentation in the sugar industry. By the time McIntosh had acquired his extensive acres in Camden County Spalding not only had achieved proficiency in the science of planting and making sugar, but he also had experimented in the construction of tabby building, and his result was known as "the Spalding method." McIntosh had retrieved some of his lost fortune from his cotton crops on Refuge plantation. Induced by his friend, Thomas Spalding, McIntosh turned his talents to the sugar industry. After having cleared his land and planted sugar cane at New Canaan, he built a large sugar house after the Spalding pattern. On the suggestion of Spalding, who the previous year had visited Louisiana and had seen the horizontal mills propelled by steam, McIntosh installed the horizontal mill in his sugar house, with the use of animal power, and thereby, according to Spalding, had the first horizontal mill ever worked by cattle power.[42] It was at Marianna that he spent the remainder of his days.

John Houstoun McIntosh lived to be nearly sixty-three years old. His remains and those of his wife, who survived him by eleven years, lie in a small enclosed burial ground not far from the ruins of his Marianna home.[43] The inscriptions are carved on large flat marble slabs:

Sacred
to the memory of
John Houstoun McIntosh
who was born in McIntosh County
Georgia
1st. of May 1773
and died the 9th. of Feb. 1836
How loved, how valued avails
thee not

---

42. Coulter, ed., *Georgia's Disputed Ruins*, 146.
43. In November, 1928, the author visited the site of Marianna and copied the inscriptions.

> To whom related or by whom begot
> A heap of dust remains thee
> 'Tis all thou art and all the proud shall be.
>
> Sacred
> to the memory of
> Eliza
> relict of
> John Houstoun McIntosh
> who gently breathed out her soul
> and passed from this life to a better
> Sept. 20, 1847
> in the 78th year of her age.[44]

Of all the immediate descendants of Sir Patrick Houstoun, Baronet, it remained for John Houstoun McIntosh, the son of his only daughter, to provide the most spectacular episode in a dramatic career that involved international issues with five nations: Great Britain, Spain, Russia,[45] France, and the United States.

---

44. The children of the John Houstoun McIntoshes were: John Houstoun McIntosh, Jr., who first married Mary Higbee, by whom he had issue, second, Charlotte Higbee; George, who did not marry; Catherine, who first married Henry Sadler, and had issue, second, the Reverend Mr. Elliott, and had issue; and Eliza Bayard, who was the second wife of General Duncan Lamont Clinch, by whom she had several children. (Houstoun Family Tree).
45. In 1813, President Madison accepted the Czar of Russia's offer to mediate on the question of a friendly alliance with Florida, Russia, and Spain.
    For the complete story of East Florida and its relationship to the countries mentioned above see Fuller, *The Purchase of Florida, Its History and Diplomacy*, 182-212.

Bibliography

PRIMARY SOURCES

Georgia:

Chatham County Court House, Clerk's Office, Savannah:
  Judgments, Box 7.
  Minutes of the Superior Court, 1792.
  Superior Court Minutes, Book G.

Department of Archives and History, Atlanta:
  Executive Minutes, 1789-90; 1791-92.
  House Journal, 1784-86.
  Governor and Council Minutes, January-May, 1789.
  Receipt Book.
  Senate Journal of 1791; 1791-1793.
  State Officers' Appointments, 1754-1827.

Hodgson Hall, Library of the Georgia Historical Society, Savannah:
  Bethesda Manuscript Letter Book.
  Miscellaneous Papers, 1784-1799, Box 3.

Office of the Secretary of State, Atlanta:
  Commissions Book.

Health Department, City of Savannah:
  Mortuary Records.

DEEDS, GRANTS, WILLS AND ADMINISTRATIONS

Chatham County Court House, Savannah, Georgia.
Habersham County Court House, Clarkesville, Georgia.
Liberty County Court House, Hinesville, Georgia.
Department of Archives and History, Atlanta, Georgia.
Office of the Secretary of State, Atlanta, Georgia.
Ordinary's Office, Chatham County Court House, Savannah, Georgia.
Mrs. Samuel C. Lawrence, Charleston, West Virginia.

MISCELLANEOUS

Two Documents, Legal, of John Houstoun, owned by Miss Mary Benjamin of New York City.

George McIntosh, *The Case of George M'Intosh, Esquire, A Member of the late Council and Convention of the State of Georgia; with*

[391]

The Proceedings thereon in the Hon. the Assembly and Council of that State. Audi alteram Partem! Printed in the Year MDCCLXXVII. (A copy is in the Library of Congress, Washington, D. C. Photostatic copy in Hodgson Hall, Savannah.)

New Jersey:

Records of Mercer County Surrogate's Court, Trenton.

New York City:

Minutes of the Common Council, 1806, 1808, 1813.
Record of Baptisms and Marriages, (Collegiate) Reformed Protestant Dutch Church.
Record of Burials of Woodlawn Cemetery.
Register of Burials of Trinity Church.
Records of the Surrogate's Court.
Records of St. Andrew's Society of the State of New York (Courtesy of Mr. Robert Graham, Recording Secretary).

Pennsylvania:

Historical Society of Pennsylvania, Philadelphia: Anthony Wayne Collection; Emmett Collection; Dreer Collection; Gratz Collection; Old Congress Convention Collection, Case 1, Box 7.
Calendar of Franklin Papers in the American Philosophical Society, Philadelphia.

South Carolina:

South Carolina Historical Society, Charleston: Henry Laurens Letter Book.

Washington, D. C.:

War Department, Adjutant-General's Office: Muster Role of the Historical Department.
Department of Interior: General Land Office and Veterans' Administration Records.
National Archives, Records of the State Department:
    Miscellaneous Letters, September, October, 1817; April, May, 1818; February, 1819, relating to John Houstoun McIntosh.
    Territorial Papers, Florida, January-December, 1812; February 1813-December 1817.

Bibliography

FOREIGN

England:

British Museum, London: Sloane MSS, Public Records Office, Historical Department, Lyon-King-at-Arms, London.

Scotland:

Inverness Records, and others, in the County of Inverness and Shire of Elgin, through Millar and Bryce, Searchers of Records, Edinburgh.
Graduates Lists, University of Edinburgh.
Minumenta of the University of Glasgow, published by the Maitland Club.
Records of St. Andrews University.

Jamaica:

Kingston Burials Copy Register, Spanish Town.

BIBLES

Jonathan Bryan, owned by the heirs of Mrs. Willoughby Sharpe of New York, lineal descendants.
Sir George Houstoun, Baronet; Colonel James Johnston, Jr., owned by the heirs of Mrs. Macartan Campbell Kollock of Atlanta and Habersham County, Georgia, lineal descendants.

LETTERS

Mackay-McQueen-Cowper Collection, owned by The Georgia Society of the Colonial Dames of America. Deposited in Hodgson Hall, Savannah.
Miscellaneous letters owned by Miss Susan Marion Kollock of Atlanta.

FAMILY PAPERS

Bayard, James R., of Long Island, owned by Mrs. Marie Bayard Collins of New York.
Demeré's Diary, Raymond, owned by Mr. Edward Houstoun Demeré of Atlanta and San Francisco, lineal descendant.
Houstoun, owned by the heirs of Mrs. Macartan Campbell Kollock of Atlanta, lineal descendants.
Houstoun, owned by James Patrick Houstoun, Jr., of Houston, Texas, lineal descendant.
Bryan, owned by Mrs. Samuel C. Lawrence of Charleston, West Virginia, lineal descendants.
Woodruff, owned by Miss Edith D. Johnston of Savannah, collateral descendant.

SECONDARY WORKS

Adams, Charles Francis, ed., *The Works of John Adams, with a Life of the Author, Notes and Illustrations*, 10 volumes. Boston: Little, Brown and Company, 1850-1856.

Adams, James Truslow, ed.-in-chief, *Dictionary of American History*, 5 volumes. New York: Charles Scribner's Sons, 1940.

Agnew, J. L. and Lee, F. D., *Historical Record of Savannah*. Savannah: J. H. Estill, 1869.

American State Papers, Documents of the Congress of the United States in Relation to Public Lands. Washington, D. C.: Gales and Wheaton, 1860.

Andrews, Charles M., *Guide to the Materials for American History to 1783 in the Public Record Office of Great Britain*. Washington, D. C., 1912.

Anderson, Mary Savage; Barrow, Elfrida DeRenne; Screven, Elizabeth Mackay; and Waring, Martha Gallaudet, *Georgia: A Pageant of Years*. Richmond: Garrett & Massey, Inc., 1933.

Armes, William Dallam, ed., *Autobiography of Joseph LeConte*. Boston and New York: Appleton & Company, 1903.

Bailey, L. H., *Standard Cyclopaedia of Horticulture*. New York: The Macmillan Company, 1915.

Barrow, Elfrida DeRenne, and Bell, Laura Palmer, *Anchored Yesterdays*. Savannah: The Review Printing and Publishing Company, 1923.

Bassett, Victor H., *A Medical Biography*. Reprinted from the Bulletin of the Georgia Medical Society, Savannah, Vol. 1, October, December, 1935, and January, 1936. (Pamphlet.)

Beveridge, Abner J., *The Life of John Marshall*, 4 volumes. Boston and New York: Houghton Mifflin Company, 1916.

Blair, Ruth, compiler, *Georgia Official and Statistical Register*. Atlanta: Stein Printing Company, 1929.

Bloom, Sol, *The Story of the Constitution*. Washington, D. C.: United States Sesquicentennial Commission, 1937.

Boyd, Thomas, *Mad Anthony Wayne*. New York: Charles Scribner's Sons, 1929.

Brevard, Caroline Mays, *A History of Florida . . . .*, a posthumus work in 2 volumes. Edited by James Alexander Robertson. Deland, Florida: Florida State Historical Society, 1924.

Bryan, John Stewart, *Joseph Bryan: His Times. His Family. His Friends. A Memoir*. Privately printed. Richmond, Virginia, 1935.

Bibliography

Bulloch, Joseph Gaston Baillie, *A History of the Families of Bayard, Houstoun of Georgia and the Descent of the Bolton Families of Assheton, Byron, and Hutton.* Washington, D. C.: James H. Dony, 1919.

Burnett, Edmund C., ed., *Letters of the Members of the Continental Congress.* Washington, D. C.: Carnegie Institution, 1928.

Burroughs, W. Berrien, "Sketch of William Houstoun," in *Men of Mark in Georgia.* Atlanta: A. B. Caldwell, 1907-1912.

Candler, Allen D., ed., *Colonial Records of the State of Georgia.* Atlanta: Franklin Printing and Publishing Company, 1906-1916, I, II, IV, VII, VIII, IX, XIII, XIV, XV, XVI, XVIII, XXI, XXII, XXIII, XXIV, XXVI.

Revolutionary Records of the State of Georgia. Atlanta: Franklin Turner Company, 1908, I, II, III.

Caughey, John Walton, *McGillivray of the Creeks.* Norman: University of Oklahoma Press, 1938.

Chapman, A. W., *Flora of the Southen States.* New York: Iverson, Phinney & Company, 1866.

Clarke, William Bordley, *Early and Historic Freemasonry in Georgia 1733/34-1800.* Savannah, Georgia, 1925.

Clizbee, Azalea, compiler, *Catalogue of the Wymberley Jones DeRenne Georgia Library 1700-1924.* Privately printed, 1931.

Collections of the Georgia Historical Society. Privately printed for the Society, Savannah, 1840-1916; "Letters of Joseph Clay, Merchant of Savannah, 1776-1793 . . . .," Vol. VIII (1813).
"Letters from General Oglethorpe to the Trustees of the Colony and Others, from October, 1735 to August, 1744 . . . .," Vol. III (1873).
"Letters of Governor James Wright," Vol. III (1873).
"Letters of James Habersham, 1756-1775," Vol. VI (1904).
Thomas Spalding, "A Sketch of the Life of General James Oglethorpe," Vol. I (1840).

Colonial Records of the State of Georgia, The. 16 unpublished volumes in the State Archives, Atlanta. Typed copies in Hodgson Hall, the Georgia Historical Society Library, Savannah.

Cobb, T. R. R., ed., *A Digest of the Statute Laws of the State of Georgia* . . . . Athens, Georgia, 1851.

Corse, Carita Doggett, *The Key to the Golden Isles of Georgia.* Chapel Hill: University of North Carolina Press, 1931.

Coulter, E. M., ed., *Georgia's Disputed Ruins;* Marmaduke H. Floyd,

"Certain Tabby Ruins on the Georgia Coast." Chapel Hill: University of North Carolina Press, 1937 .
——*Thomas Spalding of Sapelo*. Baton Rouge, Louisiana: Louisiana State University Press, 1940.
——*Short History of Georgia, A.* Chapel Hill: University of North Carolina Press, 1933.
Columbian Lyre or Specimens of Transatlantic Poetry. Glasgow, Scotland: Richard Griffin & Company, 1928.
Crane, Verner W., *The Southern Frontier, 1670-1732.* Durham, North Carolina: Duke University Press, 1928.
Crawfurd, George, *The History of the Shire of Renfrew .... Brought from the earliest accounts to the year MDCCX.* Paisley, Scotland.
DeBrahm, John Gerar William, *History of the Province of Georgia with Maps of Original Surveys 1751-1771.* Savannah, Georgia, 1849.
Dictionary of National Biography (British), Leslie Stephen and Sidney Lee, eds., New York and London, 1908.
Douglas, Edward M., *Boundaries, Areas, Geographic Centers and Altitudes of the United States and the Several States . . . .*, a Geological Survey Bulletin. Washington, D. C.: Government Printing Office, 1930.
Duncan, Alexander McCrie, compiler, *Roll of Officers and Members of the Georgia Hussars.* Savannah, Georgia, 1907.
Documentary History of the Constitution of the United States of America. Washington, D. C.: Government Printing Office, 1894.
Earl of Egmont, ed., *Diary of the First Earl of Egmont, Viscount Percival*, 3 volumes. London: Historical Manuscript Commission, 1923.
Elliott, Stephen, *A Sketch Book of the Botany of South Carolina and Georgia.* Charleston: J. B. Schenck, 1821.
Encyclopedia Americana, The. New York and Chicago: American Corporation, 1940.
Encyclopedia Brittanica, ninth edition, 27 volumes. Chicago: The Werner Company, 1891-1894; eleventh edition, 31 volumes. Cambridge and New York: University Press, 1910; fourteenth edition, 30 volumes. New York and Chicago: American Corporation, 1940.
Ettinger, Amos Aschbacher, *James Edward Oglethorpe, Imperialist, Idealist.* Oxford, England: Clarendon Press, 1935.
Ferrand, Max, ed., *United States Constitutional Convention, 1787.*

Records of the Federal Convention, 4 volumes. New Haven: Yale University Press, 1927.
Fielding, Mantle, *Dictionary of American Painters, Sculptors and Engravers*. Philadelphia: Mantle Fielding, 1926.
Ford, Worthington Chauncey, *The Writings of George Washington*, 2 volumes. New York: G. P. Putnam's Sons, 1890.
Fosdick, Lucien J., *The French Blood in America*. New York and London: Fleming H. Revel Company, 1906.
Fuller, Hubert Bruce, *The Purchase of Florida, Its History and Diplomacy*. Cleveland: The Burrows Company, 1906.
Gamble, Thomas, "History of the Municipal Government of Savannah from 1790-1911," in Thomas Gamble, compiler, *Report of Hon. Herman Myers, Mayor*. Savannah, 1900.
——*Savannah Duels and Duelists 1733-1877*. Savannah: Review Publishing and Printing Company, 1923.
Gardner, Alexander, *Archaeological and Historical Collections Relating to the County of Renfrewshire*. Paisley, Scotland, 1885.
Georgia Society of the Colonial Dames of America, The, compiler, *Some Early Epitaphs in Georgia*. Durham, North Carolina: Seaman Printery, 1924.
Grice, Warren, "Nathaniel Pendleton, Georgia's First United States Judge," *Report of the Forty-second Annual Session of the Georgia Bar Association*. Macon, Georgia, 1923.
——"Joseph Clay, Junior," in *Report of the Forty-second Annual Session of the Georgia Bar Association*. Macon, Georgia, 1925.
Hamilton, George, *A History of the House of Hamilton*. Edinburgh: T. Skinner & Son, Ltd., 1933.
Hamilton, William, compiler, *Description of the Sheriffdoms of Lanark and Renfrew*. Glasgow: John Dillon & John Fullerton, 1831.
Hardee, Charles Seton Henry, *Reminiscences and Recollections of Old Savannah*. Privately printed, 1929.
Harlow, Alfin F., *Old Bowery Days: The Chronicles of a Famous Street*. New York: D. Appleton and Company, 1931.
Harris, D. D., Thaddeus Mason, *Biographical Memorials of James Oglethorpe, Founder of the Colony of Georgia in North America*. Printed for the author from the German translation of the Reverend John Martin Bolzius. Boston, 1841.
Hartridge, Walter Charlton, ed., *The Letters of Don Juan McQueen*

to His Family. Columbia, South Carolina: Bostwick and Thornley, 1943.

Heitman, Francis B., *Historical Register of Officers of the Continental Army During the War of the Revolution.* Washington, D. C., 1893.

Henderson, Archibald, *Washington's Southern Tour.* Boston and New York: Houghton Mifflin Company, 1923.

Heyward, Duncan Clinch, *Seed from Madagascar.* Chapel Hill: University of North Carolina Press, 1937.

Hill, Roscoe R., ed., *Journals of the Continental Congress, 1774-1780* .... Vols. 32-34, 1936, 1937.

House, Homer D., *Wild Flowers.* New York: The Macmillan Company, 1934.

Hull, Augustus Longstreet, *A Sketch of the University of Georgia.* Atlanta: Foote and Davies Company, 1894.

James, Marquis, *The Life of Andrew Jackson* (first edition). Indianapolis: Bobbs-Merrill Company, 1938.

Jenkins, Charles Francis, *Button Gwinnett, Signer of the Declaration of Independence.* Garden City, New York: Doubleday, Page & Company, 1926.

Johnston, Elizabeth Lichtenstein, *Recollections of a Georgia Loyalist.* New York: M. F. Mansfield & Company, 1901.

Jones, C. C., Jr., *Biographical Sketches of the Delegates from Georgia to the Continental Congress.* Boston: Houghton Mifflin Company, 1891.

———*Biographical Sketch of the Honorable John Habersham of Georgia.* Privately printed. Cambridge, 1896.

———"The Dead Towns of Georgia," in *Collections of the Georgia Historical Society,* IV. Savannah, 1878.

———*History of Georgia, The,* 2 volumes. Boston: Houghton Mifflin Company, 1883.

Journals of the Continental Congress, Edited from the Original Records of the Library of Congress, Chief Division of Manuscripts. Washington, D. C.: Government Printing Office. Worthington Chauncey Ford, ed., Volumes I through XV, 1904-1909; Gailard Hunt, ed., Volumes XVI through XXVII, 1910-1928; Roscoe R. Hill, ed., Volumes XXXII through XXXIV, 1936, 1937.

Kimber, Edward, *A Relation or Journal of a Late Expedition to the Gates of St. Augustine on Florida Conducted by The Hon. James Oglethorpe With a Detachment of His Regiment et. from*

Georgia; Sidney A. Kimber, ed. Reprinted from the Original Edition, London, 1744; Biographical Notes, Charles E. Goodspeed. Boston, 1935.

LaFar, Mabel Freeman and Wilson, Caroline Price, *Abstract of Wills Chatham County, Georgia, 1773-1817.* National Genealogical Society, Washington, D. C., 1936.

——"Henry Holcombe (1762-1824) . . . ." Reprint from *The Georgia Historical Quarterly* XXXVIII, No. 3 (September, 1944).

Lamar, Joseph R., *The Bench and Bar of Georgia During the Eighteenth Century, Annual Address Before the Thirtieth Annual Session of the Bar Association, Warm Springs, Georgia, May Twenty-ninth, 1913.* Reprinted from the Annual Report.

Lossing, Benson Johnson, *Harper's Encyclopedia of United States History.* New York: Harper & Brothers, 1901.

Lovell, Caroline Couper, *The Golden Isles of Georgia.* Boston: Little, Brown and Company, 1932.

M'Call, Hugh, *History of Georgia,* 2 volumes. Savannah: W. T. Williams, 1816.

Mackenzie, George Norbury, *Colonial Families in the United States.* New York and Chicago: The Grafton Press, 1940.

Maclean, John Patterson, *An Historical Account of the Settlements of Scotch Highlanders in America to the Peace of 1783, Together With Notices of Highlander Regiments and Biographical Sketches.* Glasgow, Scotland: Helman-Taylor, 1900.

Marshall, John, *The Life of George Washington,* 5 volumes and atlas. New York: William H. Wise & Company, 1925.

Mathews, F. Schuyler, *Field Book of American Wild Flowers.* New York: G. P. Putnam's Sons, 1902.

Miller, Stephen S., *Bench and Bar of Georgia . . . .,* 2 volumes. Philadelphia: J. P. Lippincott Company, 1858.

——*Memoir of Gen. David Blackshear . . . .,* Philadelphia: J. P. Lippincott Company, 1858.

Minutes of the Union Society Being an Abstract of Existing Records from 1750-1858. Savannah: John M. Cooper Company, 1860.

McCain, James Ross, *Georgia as a Proprietary Province.* Boston: Richard G. Badger, 1917.

McCrady, Edward, *The History of South Carolina in the Revolution, 1750-1780: 1780-1783,* 4 volumes. New York: The Macmillan Company, 1902.

McElreath, Walter M., *A Treatise on the Constitution of Georgia . . . .* Atlanta: The Harrison Company, 1912.

Paul, Sir James Balfour, *The Scots Peerage*, 9 volumes. Edinburgh, 1904-1914.

Pierce, William, *Sketches of Characters in the Convention*. (In the Library of Congress).

Porcher, Frances Peyre, *Resources of the Southern Fields and Forests*. Charleston, South Carolina: Porcher, Walker, Evans and Cogswell, 1869.

Redding, Mrs. J. H., *Life and Times of Jonathan Bryan, 1708-1788*. Savannah: The Morning News Print, 1901.

Register of the Georgia Society of the Colonial Dames of America, The. Baltimore: Waverly Press, Inc., 1937.

Rhode Island General Assembly, *The Remains of General Nathanael Greene* . . . . Providence, Rhode Island: Freeman, 1903.

Rochefoucauld-Liancourt, Duc de la, *Travels Through the United States of America* . . ., English Translation. R. Phillips, London, 1799.

Sabine, Lorenzo, *Loyalists of the American Revolution*. Boston: Little, Brown and Company, 1864.

Sachse, Julius F., *Washington's Masonic Correspondence*. Philadelphia: Julius F. Sachse, Masonic Temple, 1915.

Salley, A. S., ed., *Register of St. Philip's Parish, Charles Town, South Carolina, 1720-1758*. Charleston, South Carolina: Walker, Evans & Cogswell Company, 1904.

Semple, William, *The History of the Shire of Renfrew . . . Brought from the earliest Account to the year MDCCX by Mr. George Crawfurd: And continued to the Present Period*. Paisley, Scotland: Printed and Sold by Alex. Wier, Bookseller near the Cross, and by the Author, MDCCLXXXII.

South Carolina Historical and Genealogical Magazine, XVII, No. 1 (January, 1917).

Stevens, William Bacon, *A History of Georgia*, 2 volumes. Philadelphia: E. H. Butler, 1859.

Stack, Frederick William, *Wild Flowers Every Child Should Know*. New York: Doubleday, Page and Company, 1909.

Stoddard, John L., *History of the Independent Presbyterian Church and Sunday School*. Savannah, 1882.

Thomas, William Sturgis, *Members of the Society of the Cincinnati, Original, Hereditary and Honorary*. New York: Tobine A. Wright, Inc., 1929.

United States Constitution Sesquicentennial Commission, *Loan Exhibition of Portraits of the Signers and Deputies of the Conven-*

tion of 1787 and Signers of the Declaration of Independence . . . . Washington, D. C., 1938.

Unpublished Colonial Records of Georgia, "Letter Books of the Trustees, Department of Archives and History, Atlanta, Georgia.

Van Doren, Mark, ed., *The Travels of William Bartram*. (Reprint). New York: The George Macy Companies, Inc., 1928.

Vincent, John Martin, *Aids to Historical Research*. New York: D. Appleton-Century Company, 1934.

Waddell, Alfred Moore, *A History of New Hanover County*. Privately printed, Wilmington, North Carolina, 1909.

Wallace, David Duncan, *The Life of Henry Laurens*. New York: G. P. Putnam's Sons, 1915.

Warren, Charles, *The Supreme Court in the United States*. Boston: Little, Brown and Company, 1923.

Washington's Diary, May to September, 1787. Original in the Library of Congress.

Watkins, Robert and George, eds., *A Digest of the Laws of the State of Georgia . . . to the Year 1789*. Philadelphia: R. Aitken.

White, Henry Clay, *Abraham Baldwin*. Athens: The McGregor Company, 1926.

White, Reverend George, *Statistics of the State of Georgia*. Savannah: W. Thorne Williams, 1849.

——*Historical Collections of Georgia*. New York: Pudney & Russell, 1854.

Wilson, Adelaide, *Historic and Picturesque Savannah*. Boston: The Boston Photogravure Company, 1889.

NEWSPAPERS

Atlanta:
Atlanta Journal
Sunday American

Charles Town and Charleston:
City Gazette of the State of South Carolina
The South-Carolina Gazette
The South-Carolina Gazette and Daily Advertiser

New Orleans:
Louisiana Courier

New York:
New York Gazette and General Advertiser

New York Herald
New York Post
New York Spectator
The New York Times

Savannah:
The American Patriot
Columbian Museum & *Savannah Advertiser*
Columbian Museum & *Savannah Daily Gazette*
The Gazette of the State of Georgia
Georgia Gazette
The Georgian
The Republican; and Savannah Evening Ledger
Savannah Morning News

Magazines

Agricultural History (July, 1938).
De Halve, Vol. II.
The Georgia Historical Quarterly, Vols. I, III, IX, X, XIV, XVI, XX, XXII.
Harper's New Monthly Magazine, Vol. LXX.

Manuscripts

Marie E. Reddy, "Some Notes on Cherokee Hill," 1936; in the files of the Savannah Historical Research Association.

Albert Berry Saye, "Georgia's Delegates to the Federal Convention of 1787. Who They Were and What They Did." Thesis in the University of Georgia Library, Athens.

Maps

Henry Poppell's Map of North America, 1733, showing where the Keowee River was designated as the Isundiga or Savannah River (Library of Congress).

Map of the Altamaha River, section showing Sterling Bluff (Hodgson Hall, Georgia Historical Society Library, Savannah).

Plat showing John Houstoun's plantation at White Bluff (Chatham County Courthouse, Savannah).

St. Simon's Island, Georgia, Chandler's Historical Map, in *The Georgia Historical Quarterly*, I, No. 4 (December, 1917).

Scrap Books

Gamble, Thomas, Thomas Gamble Collection (Public Library, Savannah).

Johnston, Edith D., Book of Newspaper Clippings.

Appendix

HOUSTOUN DESCENDANTS

The publication of this book is made possible through the generosity and the interest of the many descendants of Sir Patrick and Lady Houstoun to whom I appealed.

EDITH DUNCAN JOHNSTON.

Those who responded are:

Anderson, Berrien Palmer, Mr. (RG)* San Rafael, California
Anderson, Berrien Palmer, Jr., Mr. (RG), San Rafael, California
Anderson, Berrien Palmer, III (RG), San Rafael, California
Anderson, Clarence Gordon, Mr. (RG), White Bluff, Savannah, Georgia
Anderson, Jessie, Miss (RG), Savannah, Georgia
Bartholomew, George P., Mrs. (Mary de Caradeuc) (AG), Essex Falls, New Jersey
Bartholomew, Mary Shotter (AG), Essex Falls, New Jersey
Bartholomew, Marjorie (AG), Essex Falls, New Jersey
Benz, Patrick Houstoun (PG), Tampa, Florida
Burnham Caperton, Mrs. (Sophy Mason) (AG), Richmond, Kentucky
Burnham, Katherine Phelps (AG), Richmond, Kentucky
Butterfield, Lydia McLean Anderson, Mrs. (RG), Albany, Georgia (deceased)
Chaffee, John B., Mrs. (Marion Hall) (AG), Providence, Rhode Island
Charlton, John Felder, Mr. (AG), Fort Lauderdale, Florida
Charlton, John Felder, Jr., Mr. (AG), Fort Lauderdale, Florida

---

* The capittal letters after each name indicate from which ancestors the person is descended, viz: A, Ann Priscilla, Mrs. George McIntosh; W. William Houstoun; PG, Sir Patrick Houstoun, Eighth Baronet, the son of Sir George; AG, Ann Marion, Mrs. James Johnston, Jr., the daughter of Sir George Houstoun, Bart.; RG, Robert James Mossman Houstoun, the son of Sir George. There are no descendants on the list of Jean, Mrs. George Whitefield Woodruff, the daughter of Sir George Houstoun, Bart., although an effort was made to locate them.

Chisholm, Frank Anderson, Mr. (RG), Savannah, Georgia
Chisholm, Diana Barnard (RG), Savannah, Georgia
Chisholm, Marjorie Hanford (RG), Savannah, Georgia
Chisholm, Hathaley Houstoun (RG), Savannah, Georgia
Chisholm, Frank Miller, Mr. (RG), White Bluff, Savannah, Georgia
Clinch, Duncan Lamont, Mr., (A), Chicago, Illinois
Cochran, Avery Madison, U.S.A., Colonel (W), Morrow, Ohio
Cole, Bayard McIntosh, Mr. (A), Marietta, Georgia
Davis, Platt Walker, Jr., Mrs. (Janet Houstoun) (PG), Houston, Texas
Davis, Platt Walker, III (PG), Houston, Texas
Davis, Richard Houstoun, Mr. (PG), Houston, Texas
de Caradeuc, St. Julian Raoul, Dr. (AG), Savannah, Georgia
de Caradeuc, Achille, Mr. (AG), Jacksonville, Forida
Demere, Raymond McAllister, Mr. (PG), Turner's Rock, Savannah, Georgia
Demere, Raymond McAllister, Jr., Mr. (PG), San Mateo, California
Demere, Raymond McAllister, III (PG), San Mateo, California
Demere, Robert Houstoun, Mr. (PG), Savannah, Georgia
Demere, Robert Houstoun, Jr. (PG), Savannah, Georgia
Demere, Charles Clapp, Mr. (PG), Turner's Rock, Savannah, Georgia
Demere, Edward Houstoun, Jr., Mr. (PG), San Francisco, California
Demere, Patrick Houstoun (PG), San Francisco, California
Demere, Thomas Ashley (PG), San Mateo, California
Eckel, Frederick Lewis, Jr., Mrs. (Helen Hopkins Charlton) (AG), Owego, New York
Eckel, Frederick Lewis, III (AG), Owego, New York
Farr, Sharon, Mrs. (Janet Johnston) (AG), Chevy Chase, Maryland
Farr, Gavin Malloy (AG), Chevy Chase, Maryland
Farr, Janet Marion (AG), Chevy Chase, Maryland
Farr, Sharon, Jr. (AG), Chevy Chase, Maryland
Farr, Sheila Ladd (AG), Chevy Chase, Maryland
Farrington, S. Kipp, Jr., Mrs. (Sara Houstoun Chisholm) (RG), New York City

Appendix

Gibson, Carlos L., Mrs. (Florence Corona Anderson) (RG), Washington, D. C.
Glenn, Robert Strudwick, Mrs. (Caroline Campbell Myers) (RG), Savannah, Georgia
Griffin, George C., Mrs. (Eugenia Johnston) (AG), Atlanta, Georgia
Griffin, Randolph Page, Mr. (AG), Atlanta, Georgia
Griffin, Clayton Houstoun, Mr. (AG), Atlanta, Georgia
Hall, Charles Lacey, Mrs. (Eleanor Dallas Johnston) (AG), Washington, D. C.
Hall, Lacey, Miss (AG), Washington, D. C.
Halliday, William T., Jr., Mrs. (Claudia Kelly) (PG), Birmingham, Alabama
Halliday, Claudia Houstoun (PG), Birmingham, Alabama
Halliday, Jean (PG), Birmingham, Alabama
Halliday, Patricia Swan (PG), Birmingham, Alabama
Heyward, Bayard Clinch, Mr. (A), Habersham County, Georgia (Deceased)
Heyward, Edward Barnwell, Mr. (A), Habersham County, Georgia
Heyward, Katherine Bayard, Miss (A), Columbia, South Carolina
Hind, Morgan, Jr. (RG), San Rafael, California
Houstoun, James Patrick, Jr., Mr. (PG), Houston, Texas
Houstoun, James Patrick, III (PG), Houston, Texas
Houstoun, William Gano, Mr. (PG), Houston, Texas
Kingman, Ralph Wilcox, Mrs. (Katharine Mortimer Cochran) (W), Homestead, Florida
Lakusta, Boris, Mrs. (Mary Gayley Anderson) (RG), San Rafael, California
Lakusta, Alexis (RG), San Rafael, California
Lakusta, Boris, Jr. (RG), San Rafael, California
Johnston, James Houstoun, Jr., Dr. (AG), Habersham County, Georgia
Johnston, James Houstoun, III, Mr. (AG), Atlanta, Georgia
Johnston, Delia Bryan Page (AG), Atlanta, Georgia
Johnston, Elinor Page (AG), Atlanta, Georgia
Johnston, James Marion, Jr., Mr. (AG), Chevy Chase, Maryland
Johnston, Eleanor, Miss (AG), Chevy Chase, Maryland
Johnston, James Marion, III (AG), Chevy Chase, Maryland

Johnston, Francis Newlands, Mr. (AG), Chevy Chase, Maryland
Johnston, Andrew (AG), Chevy Chase, Maryland
Johnston, Nancy, Miss (AG), Chevy Chase, Maryland
Johnston, Robert (AG), Chevy Chase, Maryland
Johnston, Sandia, Miss (AG), Chevy Chase, Maryland
Johnston, William Bernard, Dr. (AG), Reno, Nevada (Deceased)
Johnstone, Claudia Houstoun, Miss (PG & AG), Augusta, Georgia
Kelly, Jane V. Sullivan, Mrs. (RG), Birmingham, Alabama
Kollock, George Jones, Mr. (AG), Atlanta, Georgia
Kollock, Mary Louise, Miss (AG), Atlanta, Georgia
Kollock, Susan Marion, Miss (AG), Atlanta, Georgia
Lane, Mills Bee, Jr., Mrs. (Anne Waring) (AG), Atlanta, Georgia
Lane, Anita (AG), Atlanta, Georgia
Lane, Mills Bee, IV (AG), Atlanta, Georgia
Lindsay, John H., Mrs. (Sarah Houstoun) (PG), Houston, Texas
Madeira, Edward Livingston, Mr. (RG), New York City
Mason, Lucius Randolph, Mrs. (Sophy Carr Johnston) (AG), New York City
Miller, Alfred C., Mrs. (Anna Dummett Cochran) (W), Homestead, Florida
Miner, Howard Dwight, Mrs. (Louisa Belle Kollock) (AG), Indianapolis, Indiana (Deceased)
Miner, Howard Dwight, Jr., Mr. (AG), Indianapolis, Indiana
Miner, Louisa Marian, Miss (AG), Indianapolis, Indiana
Miner, Macartan Kollock, Mr. (AG), Indianapolis, Indiana
Myers, J. F. C., Mrs. (Caroline McD. Anderson) (RG), Savannah, Georgia
Myers, John Anderson, Mr. (RG), Savannah, Georgia
Myers, John Anderson, Jr., Mr. (RG), Princeton, New Jersey
Monroe, John Fisher, Mrs. (Lucia Berrien Stearnes) (A), Vienna, Georgia
Molyneux, Edmund, Mr. (AG), Cloverdale, British Columbia, Canada
Molyneux, Alfred Ernest, Mr. (AG), Cloverdale, British Columbia, Canada
Molyneux, William Edmund, Mr. (AG), Cloverdale, British Columbia, Canada
McCall, Guyton B., Mrs. (Jane Houstoun Kollock) (AG), Atlanta, Georgia

Appendix

McIntosh, Richard Hill, Mr. (A), Birmingham, Alabama
Pell, Charles Weider, Mrs. (Jane MacDonald Charlton) (AG), Davis, West Virginia
Pell, Charles Weider, Jr. (AG), Davis, West Virginia
Pell, John Charlton (AG), Davis, West Virginia
Raney, George P., Mrs. (Claudia Houstoun) (PG), Tampa, Florida
Roberts, M. Hines, Mrs. (Delia Page Johnston) (AG), Atlanta, Georgia
Schley, Cooper Myers, Mr. (RG), Charleston, West Virginia
Schley, Cooper Myers, Jr. (RG), Charleston, West Virginia
Schley, Margaret Christian (RG), Savannah, Georgia
Schley, Richard Larcombe, Jr., Dr. (RG), Savannah, Georgia
Schley, Richard Larcombe, Mrs. (Carolyn Myers) (RG), Savannah, Georgia
Stetson, Frederic M., Mrs. (Alice Waring) (AG), Savannah, Georgia
Stetson, Frank Waring (AG), Savannah, Georgia
Thomas, Gerald, Jr., Mrs. (Elizabeth Alston Anderson) (RG), San Rafael, California
Thomas, Nancy Beveridge (RG), San Rafael, California
Trist, Mary Helen, Miss (AG), Washington, D. C.
Walker, James T., Mrs. (Elizabeth Myers) (RG), Yonkers, New York
Walker, Caroline Anderson (RG), Yonkers, New York
Walker, Emily Crabtree (RG), Yonkers, New York
Wall, Patrick Houstoun, Mr. (A), Tampa, Florida
Waring, Antonio Johnston, Dr. (AG), Savannah, Georgia
Waring, Antonio Johnston, Jr., Dr. (AG), Savannah, Georgia
Waring, George Houstoun, Mr. (AG), Grand Rapids, Michigan
Waring, Evangeline, Miss (AG), Grand Rapids, Michigan
Waring, Mai Johnston, Miss (AG), Grand Rapids, Michigan (Deceased)
Waring, James Johnston, Dr. (AG), Denver, Colorado
Waring, Anne, Miss (AG), Denver, Colorado
Waring, Ruth Porter, Miss (AG), Denver, Colorado
Waring, Joseph Frederick, Mr. (AG), Hudson, Ohio
Waring, Minna Alston, Miss (AG), Savannah, Georgia
White, Mae McIntosh, Mrs. (A), Birmingham, Alabama
White, Ann Kirke (A), Birmingham, Alabama

White, Richard McIntosh (A), Birmingham, Alabama
Whitman, George A., Mrs. (Marion Houstoun Johnston) (AG), Washington, D. C.

In Memory of
Lineal Descendants
Contributions Were Sent From

Mrs. Edward deClifford Chisholm, of New York City, for her husband (RG).
Mrs. S. Kipp Farrington, Jr., of New York City, for her father, Edward deClifford Chisholm.
Mr. John Felder Charlton, of Fort Lauderdale, Florida, for his aunt, Ella Molyneux Johnstone (AG); and for his cousin, Robert Tyler Waller, Jr. (AG).
Mrs. Edward Houstoun Demere, of Atlanta, Georgia, for her husband (PG).
Mrs. James Patrick Houstoun, of Houston, Texas, for her husband (PG).
Mrs. J. P. S. Houstoun, of Jacksonville, Florida, for her husband (PG).

Usolicited Donation

Mr. Olin T. McIntosh of Savannah, Georgia, lineal descendant of John McIntosh Mohr.

Index

Aberdeen, Scotland, 339.
Abercorn, town, 73.
Acadia, 334.
Acts of legislature, defense of province, public roads, ferries, 74; for working roads, 76; attainder and disqualifying, 122; Savannah incorporation, 275; for Chatham Academy, 281; health officer in Savannah, 308.
Adams, President John, appoints George Woodruff, 161; writes of Georgia delegates, 202; pamphlet on *Thoughts of Government*, 213; on McIntosh committee, 364; writes Bulloch, 208.
Adams, President John Quincy, cedes Creek lands to Georgia, 251, n. 134; correspondence on Florida, 386.
Adams, Nathaniel, 145.
Adams, Samuel, meets Georgia delegation, 202.
Africans, Relief and Protection of Aged, 179.
Agricultural Society of Georgia, 174.
"Agreement of Members to Secrecy," 205.
Alamacani Island, 368.
Albany, New York, 334.
Albermarle, Duke of, 11.
Aldermanic rules, 182, 183.
Alexander, William, "Lord Stirling," 334.
Amatis, Paul, 27.
Ambrose, John, 27.
Amelia Island, 369, 379, 383.
American Antiquarian Society, 132, n. 3; 198, n. 18.
American Philosophical Society, 238, n. 109.
Anderson, Clifford Wayne, 315.
Anderson, George, 313.
Anderson, Mr., surveyor, 344.
Andrew, Benjamin, 240, 319.
Annapolis Convention, 330.
Anti-Duelling Association, 177.
Antigua, Island of, 195, 350.
Anniversary of Court Day, 196, n. 10.
Arts, Manufactories and Commerce, Society for . . ., 71.
Armistead, Captain George, 312.
Articles of Confederation and Perpetual Union, 218, 265, 272, n. 166, 328.
Assembly, provincial, 61 ff; membership, 109 ff.
Assembly, General (see also legislature), fails of quorum, 342; ratifies Beaufort report, 271; "struggles in," 320; fails to vote expenses, 322; report on credentials, 322; non-attendance, 243 ff.
Association, 1775, 136, 137, 348.
Associates of . . . Dr. Bray, 21.
Atlanta Art Association, 161, n. 82.
Athens, 323.
Aury, Louis de, 383.
Augusta, meeting Indian chiefs, 328; "White House" incident, 123 ff; Assembly meets in, 126, 242; hospital in church, 299; captured by British, 299; highway to, 306; garrison, 314; seat of government, 233.

Bailey, Doctor Liberty Hyde, 19, n. 26.
Baillie, Eliza, 311, 316.
Baillie, George, 294.
Baillie, Harriet Louisa, legacy from uncle, 287, 316.
Baillie, Mrs. Johanna Houstoun, 311, 315.
Baillie, Mrs. Jourdina Crooke, 294.
Baillie, Robert, 22, 347, 348, 355, 365.
Baillies, Scotch settlers, 43.
Baillie, Thomas, 22.
Baker, Sir William, Kt., 110.
Baldwin, Abraham, Trustee of college, 322; deputy Federal Convention, 330; in constant attendance, 330; signs Constitution, 332; attends Pierce's funeral, 338.
Baldwin de Bigres, 1.
Banks:
   Planters (q. v.), 166; Bank of the State of Georgia, 191; Marine and Fire Insurance, 176; Merchants National, 176, n. 124; United States, 176.
Banks, Sir Joseph, manuscripts of Doctor Houstoun, 20 and n. 28.
Baptist Church, 177, 184.
Bard, Peter, 306.
Barck, Miss Dorothy C., 336, n. 41.
Bargeny, Lord, 2, 3.
Barnard, "Tim," 175.
Bartram, William, 268.
Bassett, Doctor Victor H., 336, n. 42.
Battle of:
   Antossee, Alabama, 382; Bloody Marsh, 50; Falkirk, 340; Flodden, 2; Lexington, 119.
Bath, England, 129 and n. 58.

[409]

Bayard, Ann (Mrs. Nicholas Serle), 336.
Bayard, Annetje Loockermans (Mrs. Samuel), 333.
Bayard, Ann Stuyvesant (Mrs. Samuel), sister Peter Stuyvesant, 333; emigrates to America, 333.
Bayard, Catherine Van Brugh Livingston (Mrs. Nicholas), 333, 335, 367.
Bayard Eliza (Mrs. John Houstoun McIntosh), baptismal record, 335, 367; goes to Savannah, 367; marriage, 367.
Bayard, Elizabeth Reinders (Mrs. Nicholas), 333.
Bayard, Mrs. Esther (Mrs. Nicholas Serle), 337, n. 42.
Bayard homestead, 341, n. 52.
Bayard, Judeth Verlet (Mrs. Nicholas), 333.
Bayard knight, 333.
Bayard, Margaret Van Cortlandt (Mrs. Samuel), 333.
Bayard, Mary (Mrs. William Houstoun), baptimisal record, 335; marriage, 333.
Bayard, Nicholas, I, residence, 335, 367; secretary province, 333; member Royal Council, 333; mayor, 333; marriage, 333.
Bayard, Nicholas, II, 333.
Bayard, Nicholas, III, 333, 340.
Bayard, Doctor Nicholas Serle, 336 and n. 42.
Bayard, Nicholas (early), 333.
Bayard residence, 335 and n. 41.
Bayard, Samuel, II, 333 ff.
Bayard, Samuel, III, Bayard, Annetje Loockermans (Mrs. Samuel), 333.
Beaufort Convention, 266 ff.
Beckwith, Reverend S. Carey, 161, n. 83.
Bedon, Elizabeth, school teacher, 344.
Belcher, William, 213.
Bell, Andrew, 31.
Benbridge, Henry, artist, 50.
Bennet, Andrew, Secretary St. Andrews University, 11, n. 6.
Bethesda, 151 ff, 232, 282.
Bethesda Crisis, 1791, 153 ff.
Beverly, James, 104.
Bewlie, 35.
Bisset, Alexander, 280.
Black, James v. Seyburn, Edward, 197.
Blackshear, General David, letters from Floyd, 160; from McIntosh, 382.
Blair, Miss Ruth, 290, n. 209.
Bloody Marsh, Battle of, 50.
Bloodworth, 330.
Board of Trade, 75.
Boehaave, Herman, Physician of Europe, 10, 19.
Bolivar, Simon, 383.
Bolton, John, 166, 183.

Bolton, Robert, 144, n. 37, 344.
Bolzius, Reverend John Martin, describes Thanksgiving, 50.
Bond, Mrs. Henry A., Edenton, North Carolina, 206, n. 36.
Bond, S. M., 175.
Bonaventure Cemetery, 120, 115, n. 22.
Boog, James, 382.
Boote, William R., Inspector General, 176.
Borlam McIntoshes, 346.
Bosomworth, Mary, St. Catherine's grant, 166.
Bosomworth Papers, 56.
Bosomworth, Reverend Thomas, controversary on, 56; letter to General Assembly, 57 and n. 34; on eviction, 79.
Boston, rice from Savannah, 190.
Boudon, David, limner, 142 and n. 31.
Bourquin, Henry, 110, n. 11; 118.
Bowen, Commodore Oliver, commands naval forces, 215; Florida campaign, 217; insulting letter to Houstoun, 220; goes north, death, 220; petition refused, 220, n. 70.
Bowly, Molly, opposite church, 134.
Box, Philip, opposes Houstoun, 114 ff; candidate for alderman, 181.
Box, Stephens's story, 41 ff.
Brampton, 234.
Brigham, Doctor Clarence S., 132, n. 3, 198, n. 18.
British, reach Georgia, 1812, 167; protection against invasion, 167; advance delayed, 219; take Savannah, 123; evacuate city, 237; war ships in river, 296, n. 14.
Brown, Andrew, 311.
Brown, George, 134.
Brown, Mrs. Harriet Thompson Houstoun, applies for bounty lands, 315; second marriage, 311; death, 315.
Brown, Lieutenant Colonel Thomas, British officer, 123.
Brown, Sarah, 283.
Brownson, Nathan, speaker, 271; trustee of college, 322.
Brunswick, Georgia, 292.
Bruce, James v. Carner, Samuel, 197.
Bryan Bible, 209, n. 45.
Bryan's Cowpen, 289.
Bryan, Hannah (Mrs. John Houstoun), q. v., birth, parents, baptism, 209.
Bryan James, signs deed, 209; arrested, 224; back in Georgia, 236; oath as treasurer, 236.
Bryan, Jonathan, council member, 70; fortifications commissioner, 75; reprimanded, 78; peace commissioner, 94;

Index

arrested, 119; vice president of Georgia, 208; plantation and children, 224; arrested and imprisoned, 224; on prison ship, 226; stayed until war over, 229; writes from Long Island, 236; back in Georgia, 236; record at council meetings, 236; death, 273; befriends McIntosh, 364; elected Provincial Congress, 207; sent to Charlestown, 210.

Bryan, Mrs. Jonathan (Mary Williamson), marriage, 209; at Purrysburg, 228; at Brampton with daughters, 229; death, 235.

Bryan, Joseph, 288, 289.

Bryan, Josiah, 345.

Bryan, William, signs deed, 209; in the army, 224; house seat rejected, 319.

Brydie, Doctor, 195, 293.

Buchan, Earl of, 340.

"Bulloch," 175.

Bulloch, Archibald, of Skidaway, fined, 134; Houstoun's client, 197; call for meeting, 198; elected to Continental Congress, 199; leaves for Philadelphia, 201; dress in Congress, 202; entertains two Adamses, 203; follows Zubly, 205; signs Agreement, 205; elected to Provincial Congress, 207; elected President of Georgia, 208, 351; elected Continental Congress, did not go, 208; dispatches committee to South Carolina, 210; receives copy Declaration, 211; writes Houstoun, 296; death, 213, 351.

Bulloch, Noble W. J., 179.

Bulloch, William B., president State Rights party, 177; mayor, 181.

Burke, Thomas, 181.

Burnett, Adjutant General Frank C., 299, n. 22.

Burr, Aaron, 274, n. 168.

Burrington, Thomas, on Mungo Graham affair, 81 and n. 32; on committee, 113.

Butler, James, 211.

Butler, Shem, 211.

Butler, Pierce, Beaufort Convention delegate, 265; personal history, 266.

Butler, William, 94.

Calhoun, John C., 388.

Campbell, Colonel Archibald, commands Savannah, 225; detached to Augusta, 224.

Campbell, Commodore, Hugh George, 369.

Campbell, Maria (Mrs. Lemuel Kollock), 172, n. 115.

Candler Hospital, Warren A., 184, n. 145.

Candler's Revolutionary Records of Georgia, errors in, 198, n. 17; 223, n. 74.

Capers, Reverend Dr., 177.

Carteret, Lord, retains share of plantation, 86.

Carteret, Mr., tells of Houstoun, 48.

Caswell, Governor Richard, 221, 251.

Cathcart, Eleanor, 6.

Cathead Creek, 92, 126.

Causton, Thomas, keeper of stores in Georgia, 24; loan to Scottish settlers, 24; accused of selling rum, 27; takes Houstoun into custody, 36, ff; sent to England, 38.

Cecil, Leonard, 144, n. 37; vestryman, 264; hospital commissioner, 308.

Chapman, James, 254.

Chapman, J. Y., 179.

Charles I, 262.

Charles II, 1, 86.

Charles Town, South Carolina, Scottish settlers land at, 24; comments on Georgia, 24; residents threaten Indian traders, 58; John Houstoun in, 210; taken by British, 300.

Charter, Georgia, 64.

Chase, Samuel, 203, 204, 205.

Chatham Academy, act for establishment, etc., 281 ff; awards, 283.

Chatham Light Dragoons, 314.

Cherokee Hill, 307; army united at, 234.

Cherry Street, Hanover Square, 338.

Chinaberry trees, 182.

Christ Church, Savannah, rectors, 54, 55, n. 30, 135, 155, 282, 102, 135, 148, n. 46; wardens and vestrymen, 155, 164; pews for sale, 164; legislature meets in 237; election wardens and vestrymen, 275; bell rings for meeting, 276; burying ground, 153, n. 56; Whitefield memorial service, 345; Jay Treaty meeting, 284.

Christie, Thomas, bailiff, 35, 64; accused of selling rum, 27; Houstoun's debt to, 37; revenge on Houstoun, 37, 42.

Church, first in colony, 55 and n. 30.

Church of England, 56, 344, 294.

Cincinnati, Society of, 305; Institution Society, 305; Georgia delegates, 305 and n. 31.

Clark, Lieutenant Colonel Elijah, 249.

Clarke, Sir Alured, British commander in Georgia, 300 ff.

Clarke, Archibald, 283.

Clarkson, Major Mathew, 232.

Clay, Joseph, member Constitutional Convention, 212; delegate from Chatham, 240; presents commission to Houstoun, 257; suspended, 257; letter on records episode, 261; vestrymen, 264; boundary commissioner, 265; judge for election, 275; alderman, 276; on committee to meet President, 278; administers oath, 279; letter from Laurens, 297; deputy paymaster general, 297; hears from Houstoun, 298; hospital commissioner, 308; elected to Congress, 320; trustee of college, 322; letter to Coppinger, 320.

Clay, Joseph, Jr., trustee Chatham Academy, 281, 293; also of Bethesda, 151.

Clifton, William, council member, 65, 70; fortifications commissioner, 75; peace commissioner, 94; attorney general, 81, n. 32.

Clinch, General Duncan, 342 and n. 57; 390, n. 44.

Clinton, Sir Henry, 225, 228, 303.

Clymer, Daniel, of Philadelphia, 121; letter from Houstoun, 121, n. 37.

Cochran, Doctor John, of Kingston, 18; has effects of Doctor Houstoun, 18.

Coddington, Deputy Commissary Purchaser, 298.

Coffee Bluff, 240, 101.

Collins, Mrs. Marie Bayard, 280, n. 184; 318, n. 3.

Colonial Dames House, Savannah, 173, 116.

Colony of Georgia, 14, 60, 61.

Columbian Museum & Savannah Advertiser, 1796, withdrawn from public, 163, n. 87.

Commerce in Georgia, 94.

Common Council of Trustees, 14, 41, 17, 64.

Commons House of Assembly (See Georgia Legislature).

Company of Apothecarys, 16, n. 15.

Confederation Congress, 264.

Confiscated Estates, 126.

Constitutional Convention, 330 ff.

Constitution, Georgia's, 212; fiftieth article, 262; 1789 convention, 274; 1777, 320, 232.

Continental Congress, 135, 201, 218, 204, 322, 236.

Cook, Andrew, 355.

Cope, George L., 314.

Coppinger, Governor Cornelius, 320, 379, n. 25.

Cornwallis, Lord Charles, 301, 303.

Corse, Mrs. Carita Doggett, 341, n. 54.

Cortez of Spain, 377.

Cosgrove, James, 344.

Cottage, Oglethorpe's Frederica home, 47, n. 13.

Cottage, The, McQueen home, letter from, 170, n. 111.

Cotton culture in Georgia, 175, n. 119; 389.

Coulter, E. Merton, letter to, 125, n. 51.

Council, Executive, formed, 214; attends fire, 215; gives governor powers, 216; moves to Augusta, 223; adjourns to Savannah, 242; decision on Count d'Estaing's claim, 247; Creeks attend, 249; instructs Clark, 249; receives records, 261; releases McIntosh, 355.

Council of Safety, formation of, 125, 136, 201; special session on Wright's arrest, 207; committee reports on defenses, 210; Houstoun attends, July, 1776, 211 and n. 47.

Counties:
Bryan, 179; Burke, 53, 158, 244; Camden, 179, 381; Chatham, 179, 238, 244; Cherokee, 315; Effingham, 244; Franklin, 245, 247; Glyn, 158; Houston, 290, n. 207; Laurens, 382; Liberty, 143, 244; McIntosh, 179, 184, 287; Richmond, 221, 243, 244; Wayne, 316; Wilkes, 221, 244; St. David's, 347.

Courts of Georgia, 196, n. 10.

Couper, James Hamilton, 316.

Cowper, Basil, Loyalist, 121 and n. 39; serves with Houstoun, 137, 286.

Cowper, Mary Anne and Margaret, letters, 170, 286.

Cranston, Reverend Walter, 311.

Crawford, William H., Secretary of Treasury, 384.

Croker, Mrs., 211.

Cronin, Timothy, 343.

Crooke, Clement, 294.

Crooke, Mrs. Heriot Cunningham, Philip Box story, 114.

Crooke, Robert, 294.

Crooke residence, 294 and n. 8.

Crooke, Richard Cunningham, 345; parents, 294; clerk for council, 294.

Crown takes over Georgia, 64.

Cruger, Colonel John Harris, British officer, at Ninety-six, 123.

Cunningham's, Mrs., boarding house, 64.

Cunningham, Robert, 294.

Cuthbert, Alfred D., 181.

Cuthbert, George, 73.

Cuthbert, Doctor James, 293.

Cuthbert, John A., 314.

Cuthbert, Seth John, in legislature, 321; trustee Chatham Academy, 281; elected to legislature, 321.

Cuthberts, Scottish settlers, 43.

Cuyler, Mrs., meeting at, 136.

Cuyler, Jeremiah, house, 136, n. 15.

Cuyler, Captain Telemon, 197.

Cuyler, Telemon Cruger, 197, n. 15.

Dame Priscilla Houstoun (see Lady Houstoun), 98, n. 9; 108, 347.

Dana, Francis, 325.

Dane, Nathan, 329.
"Daniel," 175.
Darien, named by Dunbar, 44; Houstoun plantation in, 287, 288, n. 199.
"Dark work," 41.
Dartmouth, Earl of, 119.
Dearborn, Henry, Secretary of War, 312.
Deane-Lee Feud, 230.
deBrahm, John Gerar William, surveyor-general, 65 and n. 11.
Declaration of Independence, 177; copy received in Savannah, 211, n. 47.
Dedimus potestatem, 260.
Definitive Treaty of peace, 245.
de Houstoun, Sir Finley, 1.
Demere, Captain Raymond, Frederica plantation, 46, 47, 347, 355, 357.
Demere, Edward Houstoun, Jr., 121, n. 36.
Demere, Major Raymond, diary, 121 and n. 36; 297.
Demere, Raymond McAllister, 30, n. 18.
de Padvinan, Hugo, 1.
Deputies Federal Convention, failed to sign, 332, n. 36.
DeVeaux, James, legislator, 73, 319.
Deveaux, Peter, letter on records episode, 261, 181.
Digby, Earl of, 15.
Disqualifying Act, British, 122, 304.
Dobree, Elisha, 31.
Douglas, David, speaker of the House, 73.
Dowers, Elizabeth Catherine, 189, n. 160.
Dowers, Elizabeth Vergereau Woodruff, (Mrs. John), 189, n. 160, 170.
Dowers, John II, 189, n. 160.
Drawing, portraits, miniatures, 185.
Drayton, Stephen v. Gwinnett, Button, 197.
Drayton, William H., 213, n. 51.
Duane, James, 364.
DuBois, Sir Charles, 15.
Dunbar, Captain George, friend of Patrick Houstoun, 26; takes letter to Peter Gordon, 26; sister, Priscilla, 43; settler of Joseph's Town, 1733, 43; convoys settlers, 43; commissioner to recruit Highlanders, 43; names Darien, 44; grant, 45; building house at Frederica, 44; brother William, heir, 45; Frederica plantation, 46; lieutenant in Oglethorpe's regiment, 50; letter from Provoso, 52; sent on Indian mission, 57; executor, 97.
Dunbar, James, Priscilla's father, 44.
Dunbar, Janet, Priscilla's mother, 44.
Dunbar, Priscilla, sister of George (see Lady Houstoun), 43; sails for Georgia, 43; parents, 44; baptism, 44; marriage, 45.

Dunbar, William, brother of George, 45.
Duncan, William, president hospital, 184, n. 145.

Earl of Egmont (see also Percival), clears up Houstoun error, 42; on Darien and Dunbar, 44; records Houstoun marriage, 45.
Early, Governor Stephen, 167.
Ebenezer, 73; legislature meets there, 237.
East Florida, campaigns, 217, 348, 359, 368, 374, 383; proclamation to inhabitants, 374; General Pinckney's part, 375; McIntosh-Panton story, 348; inhabitants want annexation, 368, 371; planters meet, form republic, 374; victory at Amelia, 369; constitution, 370, 375; Pinckney and U. S. Troops, 374; inhabitants keep grants, 388.
Edenton, North Carolina, on post road, 206, n. 36.
Edinburgh, Scotland, 339, 309.
Eighteenth Amendment, 179.
Elbert, Colonel Samuel, Florida campaign, 219; withdraws troops, 219; trustee Chatham Academy, 281; second in Georgia Battalion, 299; officer Cincinnati, 305; elected to Congress, 321; governor, 326; writes Houstoun, 329.
Elbert, Samuel, Jr., 217, 281, 283.
Ellington, Reverend Edward, 148, n. 46.
Elliott, Mr., 84.
Ellis, Henry, second governor of Georgia, arrives in colony, 68; returns to England, 69.
Elizabethtown, New Jersey, 338.
Episcopal Missionary Society, 191.
Eppinger, John, 181.
Estaing, Charles Hector Theodat, Count d', claim in Georgia, 247; grant in Franklin County, 247.
Evans, John J., 181.
Everard, Sir Richard, "conspirator," 40, n. 10.
Ewen, William, 137, n. 18; Vernonberg petition, 110, n. 11.
Exchange, City, 199, 177, 183, 311.
Executive Council (see Council).

Fahm, Mr., 145.
Fallowfield, 27.
Fallowfield, John, 27.
Falligant, Judge Raiford, 30, n. 18.
Federal Point, 342, n. 56.
Female Orphan Asylum, 185.
Fencibles, Savannah, 176.
Fenton, Mark, 117, 195.
Fernandina, Florida, 369.

Few, William, committee to notify governor, 243; elected to Congress, 320; trustee of college, 322; leaves for Philadelphia, 323; on Grand Committee, 329; deputy Federal Convention, 330; funeral, 388.
Filiature, for silk culture, 73; legislature meets there, 238; academy held there, 282; club meetings, 145, 156, 154.
Findley, Alexander, 344.
Finhalloway swamp, 291.
Fires, Savannah, 1778, 215; 1796, 162.
First Continental Battalion, 352, 299.
First Georgia Regiment, 167.
First Presbyterian Church, 178.
Fort George Island, Florida, 341, 368, 381.
Fortifications, Georgia, plan for, 75.
Floyd, General John, 169.
Floyd, Mr. and Mrs. M. H., memorial to Doctor Houstoun, 20, n. 32.
Floyd, Marmaduke Hamilton, 341, n. 54; 291, n. 2.
Floyd, Mrs. Marmaduke H., 381, n. 30; 305, n. 31.
Flora of the Southern States, 19, n. 27.
Florida, Apalachacola, 368; St. Marks, 249.
Foreste, Antoine Reire Charles, Sieur de la, vice consul of France, 246; Congress certifies him, 247; must be in Georgia for recognition, 247.
Foley, Lieutenant, 312, ff.
Ford, Henry, 25, n. 6.
Forts:
  Augusta, 299; Hawkins, 290; Jackson, 167, n. 104; Oglethorpe, 167; Tonyn, 217, 299; Wayne, 167; Howe, 298.
Foulis, John, merchant, 133.
Franklin, Benjamin, 238, n. 109.
Franklin College, 323.
Franks, Major David S., 232.
Frazer, Doctor George, 293; Houstoun partner, 293; death, 295.
Free Masons, 29.
French Academy of Science, 10.
French and Indian Wars, 70; victory, news in Savannah, 70.
Frederica, Stephens "box," 41; Patrick Houstoun there, 41; boat communication, 53; home of Dunbars, 46; description of, 46; Oglethorpe's home in, 47 and n. 3.
Frink, Reverend Samuel, 245.
Fuller, Elizabeth (Mrs. Alexander McQueen), 173.
Fuller, Thomas, 174.

Gadsden, General Christopher, signs agreement, 205; duel with Howe, 219, n. 66.

Galvez, Don J., 324.
Gardner, John, 179.
Gaston, William, 181.
George, II, 95, 166.
George III, 95.
Georgia Batallion, 211.
Georgia Continental Establishment, 305.
Georgia Gazette, 100, n. 1.
Georgia Hussars, 314.
Georgia Infirmary, 180.
Georgia, State of, melancholy situation, 210; in 1776, 210; constitutional convention, 212 and n. 49; adolescent, 217; war with Florida, 222; South Carolinians settling in, 94; Great Seal, 264, 323; in bad repute in Congress, 327; loop hole on negligence, 328 ff; adopts tax levy, 328, n. 27; clashes with South Carolina, 269; ratifies Constitution, 332; first state constitution, 213.
Georgia, Royal Province, beginnings of, 64 ff; strides in government, 108.
Gibbons, Mr., 319.
Gibbons, John, 240.
Gibbons, Thomas, 277.
Gibbons, William, 151, 243, 257, 261, 275, 279, 281, 283, 321 323.
Glasgow Scotland 22; University of, 23.
Glen, John, 199, 304.
Golf Club, 163.
Goshen, town of, 73.
Gordon, Peter, 26, 28.
Gould, James, 27.
Governor and Council (see Royal Council).
Governor's fee (1784), 253, n. 143.
Graham, Ann, portrait, 125, n. 51.
Graham, Elena (Nelly), engagement to Sir Patrick Houstoun, sixth baronet 124 ff.
Graham family, 125.
Graham, Frances Crooke, (Mrs. John), 124, 294.
Graham, Lieutenant Governor, witness to commission, 80; biography 124 ff; 125, n. 51; estate to Greene, 321.
"Graham, Mrs.," 83.
Graham, Mungo, petition, 79; petition for lot, 80, n. 31; involves Patrick Houstoun, 79 ff.
Graham, Patrick, president of colony, 65, 76; president Royal Council, 65; death, 67; president upper house, 67; Mungo Graham's assertion, 79.
Grant, Andrew, emigrates to Georgia, 22; writes joint letter, 25.
Great Britain and Spain, 368 ff.
Greene, General Nathanael, appointed assistant justice, resigns, 263; receives

welcome, 320; given Mulberry Grove, 321, n. 160.
Greene, Nathanael, Jr., 171, n. 113.
Green, James, 306.
Green, John, 116.
Grimke, Colonel John Faucheraud, 233.
Gronau, Reverend Israel Christian, teacher at Ebenezer, 54, n. 28.
Gronovius, Johan Frederic, dedicated plant to Houstoun, 18, 19.
Groover, William, 94.
Guerry, William, 324.
Guerard, Governor, 264.
Gwinnett, Button, 346; arrested, 119; buys St. Catherine's, 166; elected Continental Congress, 208; speaker assembly, 213; on committee draft state constitution, 213; elected state president, 213; commissions officers, 214; duel with McIntosh, 214; neighbor of McIntosh, 351; "unravels mystery to McIntosh," 351; Signer, 351; feud with McIntosh, 352; letter from Hancock, 352; orders McIntosh arrested, 352; goes to southward, 353; Button Gwinnett v. Stephen Drayton, 197.

"Habersham," 175.
Habersham, James, member and secretary Royal Council, 65; sent to Augusta, 68; letter to Shipley, 71; fortifications commissioner, 75; Mungo Graham affair, 81 ff; peace commissioner, 94; acting governor, 68, 241; assignee, 135; rejects Jones election, 241.
Habersham, James, Jr., 134, 345; elected speaker, 238, 243; vestryman, 155, 264; trustee Chatham Academy, 281; on treaty resolution, 284; in Hunt Club, 140; trustee college, 322; residence, 1780, 166, n. 98; in Solomon's Lodge, 308.
Habersham, Major John, 345; president of house, 244; warden Christ Church, 264; Beaufort Convention delegate, 266; personal history, 265; trustee Chatham Academy, 281, 282; commands Georgia Battalion, 299; officer Cincinnati, 305; in Hunt Club, 141.
Habersham, Colonel Joseph, 151; assistant justice, resigns, 263; vestryman, 264; alderman, 276; on committee to meet President, 278; commissioner for market, 306; in Solomon's Lodge, 308; hospital commissioner, 308; in Hunt Club, 140; Bethesda Trustee, president Union society, 151, 156; Houstoun executor, 159; elected to Congress, 321; arbitor

for McIntosh, 367; mayor, 282; elected to provincial congress, 207.
Hagart-Spiers, A. A., 4, 11.
Halifax, town, 73, 111.
Hall, Lyman, elected to Continental Congress, 201, 208; attended previously, 201; elected governor, 240; proclamation, 242; signs agents' commission, 264; address from Cincinnati, 305; letter on credentials, 322; signs Indian treaty, 328.
Hamilton, Alexander, 274, n. 168; 330.
Hamilton, Lady Anna, marriage, 2, 3; Stewart descent, 3; frightened and death, 4; memorial to, 5 and n. 16.
Hamilton, history of, 3, n. 5.
Hamilton, James, Earl of Arran, accompanied James V on matrimonial expedition to France, 3.
Hamilton, Sir John, First Lord of Bergany, 2; governor of realm, tutor to Queen, 3.
Hancock, John, letter from Georgia delegates, 199; President of Congress, 199, 352; signs Agreement, 205; letter with Declaration, 211; letter to Governor on McIntosh, 352; recommends apprehending McIntosh, 352; letter from Treutlen, 364.
Hand, Edward, 325.
Handley, Captain George, 273.
Hartridge, Mrs. Agnes, owner of map, 47, n. 10.
Harding, Captain, 215.
Hardwick, town of, 89.
Harrington Hall, 47.
Harris Francis, council member, 65; prepares address to governor, 74; fortifications commissioner, 75; peace commissioner, 94; Vernonburg petition, 110, n. 11; colonel Light Infantry, 122.
Hartridge, Walter C., 355, n. 147; 295, n. 10.
Haupt, George, receives prize, 283.
Havana, 320, 325, 368.
Hawkins, Thomas, 34; inquired on "box," 41; Frederica plantation, 46.
Hayes (or Hazes), Doctor, 195, 293.
Heard, Stephen, 321.
Heathcote, George, 15.
Helventine, Mr., 343.
"Henry," 330.
Henry, Patrick, 119, n. 30.
Herbert, Reverend Henry, D. D., 21.
Hewes, Joseph, 206.
Heyward, Thomas, 278.
Higbee, Charlotte, 340, n. 44.
Higbee, Mary, 390, n. 44.
Higgenson, Stephen, of Massachusetts, 328.

High Museum of Art, Atlanta, 161, n. 82.
Highlanders of Scotland, 44.
Hill, John, 252.
Holidays in Georgia, 29.
Holcombe, Reverend Henry, D. D., 184.
Holland Society of New York, 336, n. 41.
Hollingsworth, Timothy, 388.
Holmes, John, 317, 343.
Hooe, Mary Elizabeth (Mrs. William Patrick Johnston), 189, n. 160.
Hopewell, Georgia, 266.
Hopkey, Sophy, 30.
Horsby, William, 319.
Hortein, Patrick (see Houstoun).
Horton, Lieutenant, recommends abolishment of forfeitures, 39; reports on Houstoun, 39.
Houstein (See Patrick Houstoun), 51, n. 21.
Houstonboro, 252.
Houston, Archibald, 332.
Houston, Margaret, 332.
Houston, William Churchill, 332.
Houstoun, General Sam, genealogy of, 7, n.
Houstoun, Ann, Lady (Mrs. George), advertises furniture, 162; director orphanage, 185; receives legacy, 185; last visit to Oaklands, 189; buys pew, 189; returns home, 189; portrait, 186; death and burial, 190; will and epitaph, 190.
Houstoun, Mrs. Anne D., of Johnstone Castle, 60, n. 38.
Houstoun, Ann Marion (Mrs. James Johnston, q. v.), birth, 138; letter from, 186; marriage, 163; legacy from uncle, 286.
Houstoun, Ann Priscilla (Mrs. George McIntosh, q. v.), birth, 60; marriage, 346; education, 344; mother's legacy.
Houstoun Bible, 140, 153, 161.
Houstoun Castle, description of, 4 and n. 11; sold, 6, 22, 60.
Houstoun, Catherine Priscilla Ann, 340.
Houstoun, Chapel of, Scotland, tombs and effigies, 5; torn down, 6.
Houstoun children, 50, 52, 58, 136, 138, 139, 140, 142, 144, 149.
Houstoun and Company, 133.
Houstoun coat-of-arms, 6, 192.
Houstoun, Dame Priscilla (Lady Houstoun), 108, 98, n. 9.
Houstoun, Doctor, relative of botanist, 18.
Houstoun, Eliza (daughter of Doctor James), 310, 315.
Houstoun, Edward, 30, n. 18.
Houstoun, Elizabeth Bayard (Mrs. Duncan Clinch), 341, 342.
Houstoun, Eliza McQueen (marriage to Raymond Demere), 30, n. 18.

Houstoun Family Tree, 161, n. 82.
Houstoun and Fraser, 307.
Houstoun, George, of Paisely, 60.
Houstoun, George, First of Johnstone, 2.
Houstoun, Sir George, seventh baronet, birth, 52; epitaph, 52, n. 24; Hardwick lot, 59; age, 94; career, 131; brother's companionship, 131; land deed, 131; military commission, 132; attorney, 132; plantations, 132, 143, 156; leading merchant, 132; member Council of Safety, 136; advertises, 133, 135, 140, 148, 156; marriage, 135 and n. 11; fines, 134; own business, 135; signs association, 135; brother's executor, 141; children, 136, 138, 139, 140, 142, 144, 158; Loyalist, 137; Retreat, 138; road commissioner, 138; on watch, 138; on banishment list, 139; emerced, 139; restored, 139; in Hunt Club, 140 ff; hospital commissioner, 141, 308; closes business, 142; buys rice, 143; pilotage commissioner, 143; negroes, 143, 158; title, handicap, 144; officer Union Society, 144, ff; justice of peace, 145; officer Solomon's Lodge, 145, ff; address to Washington, 147; Bible preserved, 148; commons commissioner, 149; visits north, letter from, 150; officer Bethesda, 151, ff; officer St. Andrew's, 154 ff; church warden, 155, 264; rejects city warden election, 144; plantation for sale, 156; failing health, 156; death and obituary, 157 and n. 76; will, 157; nephew's guardian, 366 ff; files bill of complaint, 366; McIntosh's administrator, 365.
Houstoun, George, Jr., 161 and n. 83.
Houstoun inscription, 4.
Houstoun, Harriet Thompson, adopted by uncle, 283; shares estate, 287; letter from Carolside, 309; marriage to Proctor, 311; marriage to Brown, 311; applies for bounty lands, 315.
Houstoun, James, emigrates to Georgia, 22; legislator, 73; deputy registrar, reports as, 108.
Houstoun, Doctor James, birth (date unknown), 53; age, 94; property, 292; petitions for land, 291; in legislature with brothers, 118, 292; on committees, 292; medical training, 292 ff; partner, 293; Sunbury lot, 295; plans for service, 297; marriage, 294; acts for friend, 295 ff; writes Bulloch, 295; leaves for Philadelphia, 121, 297; home with letter from Laurens, 297; attached to hospital department, 298; in Hunt Club, 141; writes Clay, 298; on Continental

Index

pay roll, 299; in Charles Town, paroled, 300; arrested in Savannah, 300; correspondence on, 301; on British disqualifying act, 304; applies for land bounty, awarded, 305; original member Cincinnati, 305; on rules committee for, 305; delegate for, 305; elected to legislature, 306; justice of peace, 306; commissioner for market, 306; roads commissioner, 306; pay for services, 306; Colerain, 307 and n. 35; other property, advertises for settlement, 307; member Solomon's Lodge, 146, 307; health officer, 308; Academy trustee, 308; wife's death, 308; goes to Scotland, 309; death, 283, 309; children, 310 and n. 43; will and executors, 310; plantations, 310; Patrick's legacy to, 310.

Houstoun, Mrs. James, 293; marriage, 294; Obituary, 309.

Houstoun, James Edmund, 310 and n. 43; marriage, 310; children, 311, n. 44; death, 311; applies for bounty lands, 315.

Houstoun, Mrs. James, second marriage, 311.

Houstoun, James Edmund, Jr., 311, n. 44.

Houstoun, James Patrick, Jr., 4, n. 11.

Houstoun, Jane, 310, n. 43.

Houstoun, Jean (Mrs. Woodruff, q. v.), birth, 136; marriage, 160.

Houstoun, Johanna (Mrs. George Baillie), legacy from uncle, 286; marriage, 311.

Houstoun, Sir John, second baronet, 6, 23.

Houstoun, Sir John, third baronet, 6, 23.

Houstoun, Sir John, fourth baronet, 6, 23.

Houstoun, Sir John, knight, obtained charter of barons of Houstoun, 2; wife, Agnes Hopepringle, 2.

Houstoun, Sir John, knight, wife, Margaret Stirling, 2.

Houstoun, Sir John, knight, wife, Ann Campbell, 2.

Houstoun, John (son of James E.), 311, n. 44.

Houstoun, Governor John, birth (date unknown), 52; age, 94; witness, 131; mother's executor, 136; epitome of life, 193; loyalty, 193; legal education, 194; oath of supremacy, 194; White Bluff lots, 195; plantation and slaves, 195; small pox at plantation, 195; appears before Royal Council, 196; sentries stationed, 196; counselor and clients, 197; alive to politics, 197; call for meeting, 198; estimate of him, 198; appointed to draft resolutions, 199; elected to provincial congress, 199, 201; elected to Continental Congress, 199; leaves for Philadelphia, 201; Adams's description of, 202; entertains two Adamses, 203; feeble speech, 204; Zubly myth exploded, 204; signs Agreement, 205; committees in Congress, 206; journey south, 206; arrives home, 207; elected provincial congress, 207; attends Council of Safety, 207; elected to Continental Congress, did not go, 208; message from Adams, 208; marriage, 209; sent to South Carolina, 210; continues law practice, 211; on Declaration committee, 211; at state convention, 213; elected executive council, 214; elected governor, 214; conveys reports, 215; given dictator powers, 216; writes Laurens, 216; Florida campaign, 216, 217 ff; out-generaled, 217; at Fort Tonyn, 217; not censured, 220; hiding at Retreat, 223; escapes to Augusta, 223; leaves important papers, 223; term ends, 223; hunted by British, 223; hears from Walton, 225; writes Laurens about Bryans, 226; "refugee in South Carolina," 229, 254; letter about Laurens, 231; letter from Langworthy, 232; part of army, 233; confidential officer, 233; joins wife, 234; on British Disqualifying Act, 234; called back to Georgia, 236; council wants reports, 236; joins legislature at Ebenezer, 237; committee work, 238, 239, 242, 254; appointed to wait on General Wayne, 239; Vernonburg property for sale, 240; living at White Bluff, 240; Chatham County delegate, 240; elected speaker, 240; resigns for Jones, 241; on committee for Assembly place, 238; elected governor, 243; address, 243; meets council, 244; signs grants in new counties, 245, 253; signs d'Estaing's claim, 247; Indian "Talks," 247; authorized for Indian presents, 247; negotiation with McGillivray, 247; official connection ends, 250; directed to write governors, 251; proclamation on Georgia lands, 251; letter to Caswell, 251; term ends, 253; trouble on house election, 253; town house and description, 254, 255; part in county's feud, 257; rejects chief justiceship, 257; letters in newspapers on, 258; letter on records episode, 261; vestryman, 264; on boundary commission, 264, 265; Beaufort Convention, 265 ff; leaves by boat, 266; lone stand, 268; minority report, 269, 271; Rutledge's counsel, 272; Bryan's executor, 273; loses application for Federal office, 274; nomination for governor, loses, 275; alderman, 276; jjustice of peace, 275; first Savannah mayor, 276; takes oath, 276; declines re-election, 277; on committee to meet President, 278; judge of superior court, 278; presented honorarium, 279; plantation matters, 279, 280; portrait, 280, 281, n. 184; resigns judgeship, 281; president academy, service, 281, 282 ff; distributes premiums for, 282; retires to private life, 283; adopts niece, 283; on treaty committee, 284; failing health, 285; sells White Bluff lots, 285; death, 285; obituary, 285; Cowper letter on, 286, n. 193; will and legacies, 286; manumits slaves, 286; property, 287; resting place unknown, 197; county and streets named for, 290; estimates of, 290; writes Franklin, 238, n. 109; fees, 253, n. 143; salary, 281, n. 185; brother's executor, 310; prepares bill for citizenship restoration, 139; watch from William, 318; trustee for college, 322; signs brother's credentials, 323; absent from council, 352; bondsman for McIntosh, 360.

Houstoun, Mrs. John (Hannah Bryan, q. v.), at Purrysburg, 224; joins husband at Round O, 234; hears of mother's death, 235; father's death, 273; shares husband's estate, 287; dower, 287; plantations and occupation, 289; sells house, 288; death and burial, 289.

Houstoun, Sir Ludowick, wife, Margaret Maxwell, death, 2.

Houstoun, Maria Church (Mrs. John Ripley Madison), 340, 342.

Houstoun, Mary Williamson, 311, n. 44; 315.

Houstoun, Mossman, in Scotland, 309; ensign, 311; manager assemblies, 311; recorder, 311; captain U. S. A., 311; advertisers for recruits, 312; Sandwich incident, 312 ff; to New Orleans, 314; lawyer, 314; captain, Hussars, 314; makes map, 314; appointed major, 314; aide to governor, 314; made lieutenant colonel, 314; in Philadelphia, 315; legacy from sister, 315; in hospital, 315; death, 315; broken romance, 315.

Houstoun, Sir Patrick, first baronet, created baronet, 1, 2, 23; marriage, 2; children, 5; death, 23.

Houstoun, Sir Patrick, fifth baronet, founder of American family, 1; emigrates to Georgia, 24; Georgia grant, 22; birth and parents, 22; at Glasgow University, 23; characteristics, 23; site of grant, 24; joint letter of protest, 25; letter to Peter Gordon, 25; sells rum, 27; joins Solomon's Lodge, 30; lot for store, 26; grant near Savannah, 30; letter on Indian trade, 32; letter to Oglethorpe on loan, 32; needs more servants, 34; invited to Colonel Stephens's, 35; taken into custody, 37, ff; reported "good inhabitant," 35; dissatisfied, 39; killing off cattle, 40; involved in Thomas Stephens's plot, 40; reports on Parker, 41; Stephens's good neighbor, tells of "box," 41; in Frederica, 46; Christie's report, 42; visits to "Southward Settlements," 43; marriage, 44; complains on promises, 45; bounty of corn, 45; letter from Verelst' on Trustees' approval, 45; Carteret's report on, 48; confidential errand, 48; writes for servants, 49; miniature, 50; commissary, 50; in New York, 52; military service, 51; statement on children, 53; position under President and Assistant, 53; letter on packets sent, 53; makes wine, 56; friendship with Oglethorpe, 55; signs Bosomworth papers, 56; witnesses Indian signatures, 57; carries Bosomworth's letter, 57; permanently at Rosdue, 57; signs petition on grievances, 58; on Indian stragglers, 58; letter about son, Patrick, 60; represents Vernonburg, 62; obtains title, 64; family portraits, 64, n. 8; on Royal Council, 65; register of grants, 65 ff, 85; takes oath, president of Council, 67; sent to Augusta, 68; acting governor, 69; receives prize, 71; attendance at council, 70; grant re-conveyed, 71; prepares address to governor, 74; fortifications commissioner, 75; surveyor for roads, 75; president Upper House, 77 ff; delivers messages, 76; Mungo Graham story, 79 ff; takes oath as register, 88; collects quit rents, 88, 90; work on, 91; leases island, 91; petitions more land, 92; acres, 93; peace commissioner, 94; signs proclamation, 95; attends last meeting, 95; memorial read, 90; death, 96; will, 97; interment, 97; epitaph, remains removed, 97.

Houstoun, Sir Patrick, sixth baronet, birth, 50; Hardwick lot, 59; goes to Scotland, 59; returns to Georgia, 107; age, 59, 94; appointed father's successor, 98; title, 107; salary and commission, 107; reports, 107, 108; signature, 108; grants, 127; knowledge of colony needs, 108;

Index

elected to legislature, 109, 117; on committees, 110, 111, 118, 117; Vernonberg petition, 110; opposed by Box, 114 ff; defeated, 117; declines taking seat, 117; justice of peace, 117; Cathead plantation, 346; loses speaker election, 118; meets Governor Wright, 118; political uncertainty, 118; absence from legislature, 119; arrested and pays fine, 119; living in Darien, 120; conduct equivocal, 120; proscribed by both houses, 122; involved with George McIntosh, 120, 348; goes to Philadelphia, 121; writes to Clymer, 121; not on Loyalists' list, 122; on Patriots' list, 121, 125; military commission, 122; British messenger, 123; restored to Royal favor, 124; engagement to Nelly Graham, 124 ff; Loyalist, 125; adjusts affairs, 128; property confiscated, emerced, 126; property, 127; pays emercement, 127; letter to South Carolina governor, 127; leaves Georgia, 128; goes to Bath, England, 129; death and burial, 129; will, 128; obituary, 129; estate advertised, 149.

Houstoun, Sir Patrick, eighth baronet, parents, 173; birth, 136; claims title, 175; profession and marriage, 173; wife's parents, 173, 174; her death and funeral, 174; joins Agricultural Society, 174 ff; member "Fencibles," 176; bank director, 176; party politics, 176; receiver tax returns, 175; city treasurer, 176; with State Rights party, 176; on standing committees, 178; president Temperance Society, 178; trustee Georgia Infirmary, 179; president of, 180; travels and letters, 180; house, 180; officer Anti-Duelling Association, 177; property owner, 180; administrator brother's estate, 184; death, 191; pays cousin's expenses, 315; children, 174, note.

Houstoun, Mrs. Patrick (wife of eighth baronet), 173, 174.

Houstoun, Sir Patrick, Knight, wife, Maria Colquhoun, 2.

Houstoun, Sir Patrick, Knight, rescued prince, 2; wife, Janet Cunningham, 2.

Houstoun, Sir Peter, Knight, at Battle of Flodden, wife, Helen Shaw, 2.

Houstoun, Priscilla, Lady (Priscilla Dunbar, q. v.), will, 94; executors, 104; plantation life, 99; characteristics, 99; sons, 99; advertises property, 100; town house, 100; conveys property to sons, 101; sells Rosdue and Coffee Bluff, 101; epitaph, 97; death and burial, 102; will and legacies, 102; property for sale, 104; house for sale, 136.

Houstoun, Priscilla (Sir Patrick's daughter), birth, 142; miniature, 142; visits Oaklands, 187; returns home, 189; letter from niece, 187; garden at Retreat, 190; death and will, 191; legacy from uncle, 286; pays cousin's expenses, 315.

Houstoun, Rachael Moodie, 142, n. 3; 57, 153, 367.

Houstoun residence, 100.

Houstoun, Robert James Mossman, birth, 142; alderman, 181; resigns, 183; marriage, 183; secretary meeting, 183; death, 184; residence and property, 184.

Houstoun, Mrs. R. J. M., marriage and death, 183.

Houstoun silver, 160, n. 80.

Houston Street, 335, n. 41.

Houstoun, Sarah Ann Moodie, 183.

Houstoun, William, of Carthagena, 18.

Houstoun, Doctor William, botanist, 9, 10; birth, 9; death, 9, 18; at St. Andrews, 10; at Leyden, 10; doctor of medicine, 10, 11 and n. 6; French Academy of Science and Fellow Royal Society, 10; service South Sea Company, 11, 12, 16; in employ Sir Hans Sloane, 11; in Jamaica, 11; letters to Sloane, 12, 13; in London, 14; agreement with Trustees, 15; memorial to, 20, n. 32; conveyance to Panama, 17; ill in Kingston, 18; manuscripts in Jamaica, 19, 20; petitions Trustee for kinsman, 22; poem to Houstonia, 19, n. 26.

Houstoun, William, delegate, birth, 60; age, 94; witness, 131; buys Cathead acres, 127; Chatham delegate, 240; on committee, 319; in Hunt Club, 141; education, 317; home with brothers, 317; in brother's office, 317; law work, 317; guardians, 317; goes to London, 317; at Inner Temple, 317; visits Paris, 318; returns home, 318; gift to John, 318; for Patriots' cause, 318; buys brother's confiscated estate, 318; elected to legislature, 319; admission questioned, 319, ff.; bounty grant, 318; on Greene welcome, 320; applies for law practice, 318; elected to Congress, 321, ff.; voted in legislature, 321; no credentials sent, 322; trustee of college, 322; resigns from, 323; leaves for Philadelphia, 323; arrives after adjournment, 323; presented, 323; on committees, 324, 325, 330; news of brother's death, 324; his resolution carried, 324; on committee for Lafayette, 324; characteristics and appearance, 325; carries sword to Congress, 325; writes to Elbert, 326, 329; pay in arrears, 329; on Grand Committee, 330; deputy Federal Convention, 330; arrival in Philadelphia, 330; motions and vote, 330, 331; loses resolution, 331; enters debate, 331; leaves Philadelphia, 331; marriage, 333; goes to Savannah, 337, 367; councilor at Supreme Court, 339; portrait, 340 and n.; children 340; legacy from brother, 286, 340; illness and death, 341; interment and removal, 341; descendants, 342.

Houstoun, Mrs. William (Mary Bayard), 334; baptism, 335; marriage, 335; attends Washington reception, 338; children, 340; visits sister, 341; death and burial, 341, 368; epitaph, 341 and n. 54.

Houstown, Sir P. (Houstoun),

Howe, General Robert, succeeds Lee, 214; Florida campaign, 217, 298; raised to major general, 218; criticisms of him, 222; loses caste in Georgia, honored in North Carolina, 219, 220; loses Savannah, 222; retreats to South Carolina, 222; duel with Gadsden, 299, n. 66.

Howe, Lord William, 297, n. 17.

Hugh, Sir, son of Reginald, benefactor to Monks, 1.

Hugo de Padvinan, 1.

Hume, James, 294; Loyalist, 295; Governor Wright's nephew, 295; council takes house, 296; member Royal Council, 297; visit from Houstoun, 309; Houstoun's executor, 310; place, Carolside, 188, 309.

Hume, Mr., 28.

Hunter, James, commanding Savannah Fencibles, 176.

Hunting Club, 140 ff.

Huntingdon, Selina, Countess of, 151 ff.

Hussars, Chatham, 314; Georgia, 314.

Iconography of church, 55.
Independence Day, 176.
Independent Presbyterian Church, 178.
Indian affairs, 1782, 221.
Indian trade in Georgia, diverted to South Carolina, 31; conference in Savannah, 31, 324; South Carolina's jealousy of, 58.
Indians, Chickasaw, 31; sign Malatche papers, 57; Augusta meeting, 68; "Talks," 71; grievances to Council, 69; Creeks, Upper and Lower, 72, 79, 222; "Grand Conference," 71; title to lands, 81; brutal acts, 221; Cherokees, 239, 247, 248, 251; lands ceded by Adams, 251; relinquish lands, 265; Oconee lands, 247; Indian Nations, 57.

Indigo, 132, 365.
Ingham, Samuel Delucenna, secretary of treasury, 388.
Inverness, Scotland, home of Dunbars, 44; parish registry on births, 45, 60.
Irvine, Doctor John, assignee, 135, 155.
Islands:
    Cumberland, 381; Green, 73, 114; Hutchinson's, 95, 269, 143 and n. 33; May, 184; Ossabaw, 53; Sapelo, 53, 197, 222, 287; Skidaway, 73, 114, 288; St. Catherine's, 53, 166; Tybee, 112; lazaretto on, 112; small pox on, 195; repairs to lighthouse, 144; Wilmington, 73, 114, 288.
Isle of Hope, Parker's home, 101.
"Itinerant Observer," writes of Frederica, 46.

Jack, Colonel, 215.
"Jackson," 175.
Jackson, General Andrew, 386; president, 176.
Jacksonboro, 234 and n. 99.
Jackson, General James, given keys of Savannah, 237; grant, 253; letter on records' episode, 261; "Nineteenth," 307; Bethesda trustee, 151; on Greene welcome, 320; on legislative committee, 243, 320; Florida campaign, 386.
Jail, condition of, 54.
Jamaica, 342, 350.
Jamaica, Institute of, 20, n. 29.
James River planters, 142, n. 31.
Jay, John, president of Congress, 232; chief justice, 284, 324; marriage, 338; Treaty, 284.
Jay, William, 176.
Jefferson, President Thomas, 119, n. 30; 312.
Jenkins, Charles Francis, gift from, 208, n. 39; writes on Georgia's Constitutional Convention, 228, n. 83; 280, n. 182.
Jenkins, Edward, sold rum, 27.
Johnson, Reverend John, Bethesda story, 151, ff.
Johnson, Mrs. Robert C. (Margaret McIntosh), 336.
Johnson, Robert C., 336.
Johnson, Samuel, of North Carolina, 206; Hermitage, 206.
Johnson, William Samuel, 330.
Johnston, Doctor Andrew, 163; on committees, 111; physician, 293; in Georgia, 293.
Johnston, Mrs. Andrew (Bellamy Roche), 163.

Index

Johnston, Andrew, Jr., 345.
Johnston, Ann Moodie (Mrs. W. R. Waring), care of brothers and sisters, letter to grandmother, 186; letter to Aunt Priscilla, 187; marriage, 187, n. 184.
Johnston, Bellamy Roche, 187, 189, n. 160.
Johnston, David v. Jones, Joseph, 197.
Johnston, Eliza Herriot, 188, n. 155, 189.
Johnston, Eugenia Marion, 256, n. 149.
Johnston Family Bible, 163, n. 88.
Johnston, George Houstoun, 189, n. 160.
Johnston, James (son of Lewis), 345.
Johnston, James (ship's mate), 349 and n. 8.
Johnston, James, Founder Georgia Gazette, 100, n. 1.
Johnston, Colonel James, Jr., birth and parents, 163; marriage, 163; present, 160; secretary St. Andrew's and Golf Club, 163; alderman, 163; vestryman, 163; chairman church subscriptions, 163; senior warden, 164; commissioner bank subscriptions, 164; letters for and against his election, 165; elected state senator, 166; president Planters Bank, 166; planter, St. Catherine's, 166; property of heirs, 167; War of 1812, 167; lieutenant colonel, 167; writes governor, 167-169; president Union Society, 169; visit abroad, 187; returns home, 189; death and obituary, 190; buys Houstoun home, 288 and n. 202; legacy from Houstoun, 159; executor, 159.
Johnston, Mrs. James, Jr. (Ann Marion Houstoun, q. v.), marriage, 163; death, 186.
Johnston, Jane Priscilla, 188, n. 155; 189, n. 159.
Johnston, Doctor Lewis, legislator, 73, 110; treasurer, council, 121; provost marshall, 240; physician, 293.
Johnston, James Marion, Jr., 160, n. 80.
Johnston, Louisa Caroline, 188, n. 155; 189, n. 156.
Johnston, Mary Helen, 189, n. 160.
Johnston, Matthew, 163.
Johnston, James Robertson, 189, 160.
Johnston, Priscilla Augusta, 189, n. 158.
Johnston and Robertson, cotton shipment, 163.
Johnston and Simpson, Charles Town merchants, 104.
Johnston, Susan Marion, 189, n. 160; 288, n. 202.
Johnston, Doctor **William Martin**, **345**; Savannah physician, 293.
Johnston, Doctor William Patrick, 189, n. 160.
Johnstone Castle, 10.

Jones, Doctor George, 151, 279.
Jones, George Noble, 305, n. 31.
Jones, Colonel Noble, 63; council member, 65; fortifications commissioner, 75; peace commissioner, 94; signs proclamation, 95; Vernonburg petition, 110, n. 11; physician, 293; house, 294.
Jones, Doctor Noble Wimberly, 73; legislator, 118; Vernonberg petition, 110, n. 11; friend of Houstoun, 197; call for meeting, 198; elected to Continental Congress, 199, 201; did not attend, 201; elected to provincial congress, 207; speaker of house, 213, 214, 241; physician, 293; appoints William Houstoun, 242; state business in Charles Town, 251; writes Houstoun on caveat, 252; on committee to meet President, 278; presides at Jay treaty meeting, 284; officer Union Society, 145.
Jones, Thomas, letter to Verelst on Stephens, 40; report on conspirators, 48.
Jones, William Thomas, 388.
Joseph's Town, 43.
Journal, legislature, missing, 220, n. 70.

Kellet, Alexander, council member, 65, 74; provost marshall, 65; prepares address to governor, 74.
Kelsell, Darling and Munro, 132.
Kensington, 183.
Kimber, Edward, 51.
Kimber, Reverend Isaac, 51.
Kilkenny, Ireland, 174.
Kinderlen, Governor, of Florida, 373.
King's Council (see Royal Council).
Kingsley, Captain Zephaniah, 381.
Kingston, Jamaica, 11, 17, 18, n. 24.
Kiowee River, 251, 265, 268; source, 270, n. 163.
Knox, William, 70; fortifications commissioner, 75; peace commissioner, 94; signs proclamation, 95; London agent, 110; letter to Wright, 318.
Kollock, Augusta Johnston (Mrs. W. E. Eppes), 191.
Kollock, George Jones, 189, n. 160; 288, n. 202.
Kollock, Mrs. George Jones, 189, n. 160.
Kollock, Doctor Lemuel, 172, n. 115.
Kollock, Mrs. Macartan Campbell, 189, n. 163; 131, n. 1.
Kollock, Doctor Phineas Miller, 189, n. 160.
Kollock, Miss Susan Marion, 30, n. 18; 187, n. 154, n. 191, n. 169; 185, n. 149; 189, n. 160; 309, n. 38.
Lafayette, Marie Jean Paul Joseph Roche Yves Gilbert du Montier, Marquis de,

121, 177; received by committee, 324; visits Washington, 324.

Lafitte, Peter S., 128, n. 57.
Laird of Cocklaw, Parish of Beath, Fifeshire, Scotland, 134.
Land grants, requirements, 21, 22, n. 1; forfeitures forgiven, 40; re-conveyance of, 89.
Land lottery, 176.
Langdon, John, of New Hampshire, 203.
Langworthy, Edward, secretary, 213, n. 52; 344; letter to Houstoun, 232; elected to Congress, 232; secretary of convention, 214; teacher, 232.
Lawrence, Alexander A., Jr., 274, n. 167.
Law, Reverend Joseph S., 179.
Lawrence, Mrs. S. C., 209, n. 44; 289, n. 203.
Lazaretto, 112 and n. 16.
Laurens, Henry, merchant of Charles Town, 194; goes to England, 194; sympathies, 194; letters from Governor Houstoun, 222, 229; President Continental Congress, 229; resigns, 226, and n. 79; 232; tries to help Bryans, 227; embarrassed before Congress, 229; mission to Holland, 232; and capture, 232; imprisoned in London, 232; letter to Clay, 297; befriends McIntosh, 364.
LeConte, 118, 239.
LeConte, John, 143.
LeConte, Joseph, 143.
LeConte, William, 143.
Lee, 330.
Lee, General Charles, commander Southern Department, 210; asked to report to Congress, 210; expedition to Florida, 217.
Legislature, Georgia, branches, 67; organization, 72; representatives, 73; elect speaker, 73; organizes, 74, 292; differences in branches, 74 ff; Mungo Graham affair, 79 ff.
Leslie, General Alexander, 300.
Lewden, Mr., 145.
Lewis, Josiah, 213.
Leyden, University of, 10.
Liberty Pole erected, 200; error in Jones's *History*, 198, n. 18; 211.
Lincoln, General Benjamin, replaces Howe, 220; establishes headquarters, 225; sends Rutledge on mission, 272; joined by Pulaski, 300; surrenders Charles Town, 300.
Lindsay, Reverend Benjamin, rector Christ Church, 232; tutor, Bethesda, 282.
Linnaeus (Karl von Linne), 18; dedicates plant to Houstoun, 19.

Little, William, agent Indian affairs, 68; causes Reynold's unpopularity, 68.
Little Tallassee, 249.
Livermore, 329.
Livingston, Catherine Van Brugh (Mrs. Philip), 334.
Livingston, Kiliaen Van Rensselaer (Mrs. Robert), 334.
Livingston, Mary, 334.
Livingston, Mary Alexander (Mrs. Peter Van Brugh), 334.
Livingston, Mary Tong (Mrs. Robert), 334.
Livingston, Peter Van Brugh, 333, 334.
Livingston, Philip, Signer, 334.
Livingston, Philip, 334.
Livingston, Robert, 334 ff.
Livingston, Governor William, 338.
Lloyd, Edward, alderman, 276, 285.
Lofetin, Stephen (alias John Brown), 312.
London, 21, 39, 71.
Lopez, Don Jose, 369.
Lords Proprietors, South Carolina, 86; surrender American plantation, 87.
Lords of His Majesty's Privy Council, 64.
Louisville (named capital), 256.
Louisiana, 324.
Lower House (see legislature, Georgia).
Lowton, Reverend Timothy, 135; estate, 155.
Loyalists, leave Savannah, 296, n. 14; in Florida, 368.
Lucas Theater, 255, n. 149.
Lucena, James, 291.
Lynch, Thomas, signs Agreement, 205.
Lyon-King-at-Arms, 64, n. 8; 141.

McAllister, George Washington, 314.
McAllister, Matthew, alderman, 276.
McAllister, Matthew Hall, 177.
McBane, Highlander, 17.
M'Corrie, Andrew v. Moore, James, 197.
McCormick, Robert, 240.
McCradie & Company, 367.
McRae, James, bought Houstoun Castle, 6.
McGillivray, Alexander, letter on Indian lands, 247; birth and education, 248; negotiations with Spaniards, 248, 249; leader of mother's people, 248; letter to McLatchey, 249; signs treaty with U. S., 251, n. 134.
McGillivray, Lachlan, 137.
McGregor, Gregor, 383.
McIntosh, lieutenant colonel, 305.
McIntosh burial ground, 341, n. 54.
McIntosh, Catherine (Mrs. Henry Sadler), 390, n. 44.
McIntosh, Ensign, 313.
McIntosh, George, partner of Houstoun, 120; birth, 346; education and profes-

Index 423

sion, 346; marriage, 346; elected to assembly, 346; signs Articles of Association, 348; ships rice to Houstoun, 355; 1776 disaster, 347; Panton-rice story, 348 ff; justice of peace, 349; delivers statement to Bulloch, 351; domestic life, 351; absent from council, 352; sufferer from McIntosh-Gwinnett duel, 352; refuses to sign Gwinnett commission, 352; ill, 352; arrested and jailed, 353; declares innocence, 354; released on bond, 355; writes Panton, 361; affidavits on, 355, 357, 358; asks for hearing, 360; writes from Darien, 362; writes pamphlet, 363; health suffers, 364; goes to Congress, acquitted, 364; children, 364; dies intestate, 364; leaves property, 365; effects on plantation, 365; Houstouns and Baillie administrators, 365.

McIntosh, Mrs. George (Ann Priscilla Houstoun q. v.), mother's legacy, 102; living at Rice Hope, 351; death, 351; children, 351.

McIntosh, George, Jr., 390, n. 44.

McIntosh, John (brother of George), 346, 347.

McIntosh, Major General John, 359, n. 17.

McIntosh, John Houstoun, birth, 347; Stuart legacy, 101; pays cousin's expenses, 315; marriage, 367; significant Florida figure, 366; uncles, 366; guardians, 366; enquires father's estate, 366; case against McIntoshes, 366 ff; "awards," 367; father's Crown grant, 367; planter, 368, 389; leader in East Florida, 368; elected Director, 369; writes to Troup, 369; letters to Government officials, 370, 376, 378, 384, 386, 387; humiliated and ruined, 372; waits on Pinckney, 375; presents memorial, 376, ff; correspondence with Pinckney, 376; marked man, 379; challenged by Spaniard, 379; goes to Washington, 380; tries to retrieve property, 381; sells Fort George, 381; house at Marianna, 381 and n. 30; writes Blackshear, 382; general in Jackson's troops, 386; returns to Refuge, 382; writes about his grants, 386; loses land in Florida, 387; more about claims, 388; turns to sugar industry, 389; dies at Marianna, 389; epitaph, 389; children, 390, n. 44.

McIntosh, Mrs. John Houstoun (Eliza Bayard), marriage, 367; lives at Fort George, 341, 381; dies at Marianna, 389; epitaph, 389.

McIntosh, John Houstoun, Jr., 390, n. 44.

McIntosh, General Lachlan, 346; colonel Georgia Battalion, 211; sent to South Carolina, 210; duel with Gwinnett, 214; serves with distinction, 266; ordered to join Lincoln, 233; on boundary commission, 204, 265; on committee to meet President, 278; presides at Jay meeting, 284; in Augusta, 365; president Cincinnati, 305; president St. Andrew's, 154; Indian commissioner, 327; family vault, 337; commands First Continental Battalion, 299; brigadier general, 299; bondsman for brother, 360; hears of his death, 365; secures brother's effects, 365; prisoner in Charles Town, 365; nephew's administrator, bill filed against, 366 ff; personal history, 266; elected to house, 323.

McIntosh, Mary, 368.

McIntosh, Roderick, 349, 363.

McIntosh, William, 346, 349, 363; owns Oglethorpe's home, 47, n. 13; petitions for administration, 366; bill filed against, 366 ff; asks for Houstoun's report, 236.

Madrid, Court of, 324.

McKenzie, Jean (Mrs. Thomas Moodie), 134.

McLean, Andrew, 121, n. 38.

McMullin, Edward J., 280, n. 184.

McQueen, Alexander, birth and parents, 173; guardian, 174; business, 174; marriage, 173; summer home, 174.

McQueen, Mrs. Alexander (Elizabeth Fuller), father, 173; marriage, 173; death, 174.

McQueen, Eliza, 286.

McQueen, Eliza (Mrs. Patrick Houstoun), marriage, 174; death, 174.

McQueen, Eliza (Mrs. Robert Mackay), 170.

McQueen, John, birthplace and residence, 173; legislator, 174.

McQueen, John (second), 174; Fort George home, 368.

McQueen, Mrs. John (Ann Dalton), birthplace, 173; goes abroad, 174.

McQueen, Sarah (Mrs. Robert J. M. Houstoun), 183.

M'Guire, James, had McCrae's estate, 6; son demolished Houstoun castle, 6.

MacDonnell, Judge Alexander R., 154, n. 58.

Mackay, Captain Hugh, 43.

Mackay, James, council member, 70; reprimanded, 78; peace commissioner, 94.

Mackay, Patrick, witness to commission, 80.

Mackay, Robert, letter on Graham-Houstoun engagement, 124, 294, n. 7.

Mackays, Scottish settlers, 43.

Mackbane, Archibald, 34, 44.

Madeira, 16, 17.

Madison, President, James, 368 ff.
Madison, Commander John Ripley, 342.
Madison, Mrs. John Ripley (Maria Church Houstoun), 342; death, 342.
Madison, John Ripley, Jr., 342, n. 56.
Madison, Sarah Jane Dummett (Mrs. John Ripley, Jr.), 342, n. 56.
Madrid, Court of, 324.
Malatche papers, 57.
Malbone, Mary (Mrs. Robert Mackay), 124.
Manning, Reverend James, 325, 329.
Marbois, Francois de Barbe, 324.
Martin, Clement, council member, 73; death, 121.
Martin, John, 134; council's secretary, 361; governor, 238; officer in regiment, 214.
Mary, Queen of Scots, 3, 334.
Martyn, Benjamin, Trustee's secretary, 17; letter from Hawkins, 34.
Marshall, James, 166.
Marshall, John, 119, n. 30.
Marshall, W. P., 175.
Mason's Bible, 148.
Masons jewel, 146, 157.
Massais, Captain, 373.
Massachusetts Bay incident, 137.
Mathews, Governor George, 368 ff.
Maxwell, Thomas, 237, 238.
Maxwell, William, 319.
Mendenhall, Thomas, 181.
Middleton, Ann (Mrs. James Bryan), 289.
Middleton, David, 289.
Midway (Medway) District, 73.
Militia, colonial, organization, muster, 63.
Millar and Bryce, Scottish researchers, 44, n. 5; 64, n. 8.
Milledge, John, on committee, 345; 110, n. 11; Bethesda trustee, 151.
Milledgeville, 167.
Miller, H. P., 341, 53.
Miller, John, assistant clerk University of Edinburg, 60, n. 39.
Miller, Philip, horticulturist, 15; attorney for Houstoun, 16 and n. 8; Houstoun's seeds in Chelsea Garden, 20.
Miller, Robert, successor to Houstoun, 18; arrival in Jamaica, 18.
Milton, Captain John, conveys records, 223, n. 74; officer Cincinnati, 305.
Miniatures, Patrick and Priscilla, 50; Priscilla and Robert, 142.
Minis, Isaac, receives prize, 283.
Minis, Philip, 272, 365.
Minis, Philip v. Condon, Benjamin, clients of Houstoun, 197.
Missing document, 366, n. 14.
Mitchell, Governor David B., 370, 314.
Mohr, John McIntosh, 345.

Molyneux, Edmund, 189, n. 160.
Monroe, James, secretary of state, 370, ff.
Montaigut, David, 145.
Moodie, Ann (see Ann, Lady Houstoun), birth, 190; marriage, 135.
Moodie, John, witness to will, 128, n. 57.
Moodie, Rachel, 187.
Moodie, Thomas, deputy secretary, 101; home and marriage, 133; signs proclamation, 134.
Moore, Elizabeth, 367.
Moore, Philip, 367.
Morales, Colonel, 383.
Moravian Seminary, 188, n. 155.
Morel, Bryan M., 175.
Morel, John, Bethesda trustee, 151.
Morel, Mrs. John (Mary Bryan), at Purrysburg, 224.
Morel, Peter Henry, 145.
Morris, Mr., 374.
Morris, Captain, 298.
Mossman, James, house, 114; ardent Loyalist, 295; residence, 300; vestryman, 264; Houstoun executor, 159, 310; arbitor for McIntosh, 367.
Mossman, Mrs. James (Elizabeth Crooke), Philip Box story, 114 ff, 294.
Moultrie, General William, 228.
Mount Vernon, 324, 338.
Muir, Reverend George, 4, n. 11; 5, n. 16.
Muirhead, J. S., secretary Glasgow University, 23, n. 3; 60, n. 39.
Murphey, Daniel, superintendent Indian affairs, 238.
Mulryne, John, on committee, 113; involved in Box incident, 114; harbors Wright, 120.
Musgrove, Mrs. (Mary Bosomworth), 26.

Nanan, New Providence, 316.
Nassau, 312.
Navigation, Savannah River, 270.
Negroes, 110, 182, 183; leasing, 49; Lady Houstoun's servants, 102.
Netherclift, Thomas, 132, 319.
Netherlands, 3, 333.
Newburgh, New York, 305.
Newburyport, Massachusetts, 344.
New Hampshire, 328.
New Hope, South Carolina, 286.
New Jersey, College of, 334; Washington's headquarters in, 340.
Newton, Sir Isaac, 11.
New York, 237, 322, 338.
New York Historical Society, 335, n. 41.
"Nightly Club," in Stephens's journal, 38; members, gentry, 38; matters grew hot, 39, 154.

Index

425

Ninety-six, South Carolina, 123.
Noel, John Young, chairman treaty resolution, 284; solicitor for McIntosh, 367.
Non-intercourse Act, 369.
Normandy, 1.
Norris, Reverend Mr., "conspirator," 40.
North Britain, Scottish settlers sailed from, 24.
North Carolina, governor of, 251.
Northern Division, Houstoun's home in, 53.
Nullification Party, 177.

Oath of abjuration, 292.
Oglethorpe Bible, 148.
Oglethorpe, James Edward, founder of Georgia, 9, 14: donation to Trustees Garden, 15; letter from Dr. Houstoun, 17; birthday observed, 29; letter from Patrick Houstoun, 32; writes to Trustees about it, 33; Thanksgiving proclamation, 50; his regiments, 51; health at Frederica, 47; in battle, 50; expedition to St. Augustine, 51; leaves Georgia, 52; Frederica home, 47, n. 13.
Old burial ground, 183, 190, 192.
Oaklands, New Jersey, 185 and n. 149.
O'Bryan, William, on committee, 238 and n. 109; delegate from Chatham, 238, 240; presents commission to Houstoun, 257; suspended, 257; letter on records episode, 261; vestryman, 264, 238, n. 109; hospital commissioner, 308, 137.
O'Daniel, Owen, 90
O'Neill, Arturo, Governor of Pensacola, 250.
Onis, Chevalier Louis de, 386, 387.
Osborn, pirate, 350.
Osborne, Henry, 278, n. 177.
Ottolenghe, Joseph, in charge of silk culture, 66, 71, 73.

Paisley, Scotland, 1, 22, 60.
Panton, Thomas, 349 ff.
Panton, William, store-keeper, 249; McIntosh rice story, 348 ff; letter from McIntosh, 361.
Pape, Miss Nina, 310, n. 43.
Papillon, Miss Cecily Gertrude, Graham descendant, 125, n. 51.
Paris, 245.
Parker, Henry, 40; alliance with Everard, etc., 40; in room with Houstoun, 41; president of colony, 61, 81; daughter, 101; home, 101.
Parker, Sir Hyde, raids White Bluff, 224; arrests Bryans, 224.
Parker, Mrs., mantau maker, 134.
Park and Tree Commission, 182, n. 140.

Parishes:
St. Andrew's, 117, 291, 345, 347; Christ Church, 114, 292; St. Davids, 101, 127, 131; St. George's, 53, 111, 127; St. John's, 201, 222; St. Paul's, 110, 127, 341; St. Philips's, 127, 195; St. Patrick's, 127; St. Thomas's, 127; St. Matthews, 291; St. James, 292.
Parrish, Lydia A. (Mrs. Maxfield), map of St. Simon's, 47, n. 10; research on Tannants, 294, n. 8.
Parsons, Theophilus, of Boston, 328.
Patterson, General, 303.
Peace celebrations, 70, 169.
Peace commissioners in Paris, 232.
Peare, James, Jr., 257.
Pearson, Mary Priscilla Woodruff (Mrs. Charles), 161, n. 82.
Pendleton, Nathaniel, Federal judge, 274; Hamilton's second, 274, n. 168; appointed deputy Federal Convention, 330.
Pensacola, Spanish governors of, 248, 373, 388.
Percival, John, Lord Viscount, Earl of Egmont, Trustees President, 21; records on forfeitures, 39.
Peter, the Great, 10.
Pettit, 330.
Petitions for land, 89.
Petre, Lord, 15.
Philadelphia, 1776 excitement, 201, 207.
Philips, Steven, 215.
Pickens, General Andrew, Beaufort convention delegate, 265; personal history, 265.
Pierce, William, Deputy Federal convention, 330; grows weary, leaves, 330; joins Baldwin, 332; takes copy to Georgia, 332; death, 337; candidate for governor, 275; comment on Houstoun, 325.
Pink House, 166, n. 98.
Pinckney, General Charles Cotesworth, Beaufort convention delegate, 265; personal history, 265, 330.
Pinckney, General Thomas, 374, 378.
Pilotage Commissioners, 143.
Plantations:
Bewlie, Stephens's, 35; Colerain, 307; Brampton, Bryan's, 229; Houstoun graves there, 310; Constitution Hill, 367; Cathead, 119, 288; Federal Point, 342, n. 56; Harrington Hall, Demere's, 47; Marianna, J. H. McIntosh's, 381 and n. 30; Nineteenth, General Jackson's, 307; Ockstead, Causton's, 381; New Canaan, McIntosh's, 382, 389; Refuge, 367; Retreat, George Houstoun's, 138, 240; Rice Hope, George Mc-

Intosh's, 346; Rosdue, Patrick Houstoun's, 30, 35; various spellings of, 30, n. 18; well cultivated, 49; description of, 30, 59; Lady Houstoun's, 101; John Houstoun's, 240, 285; Windy Hill, 280; Gibbon's, 343; Cedar Grove, 184; Morengo, 311.

Planters Bank, incorporated, 166; location, 166, n. 98.

Poppell, Henry, map, 268.

Pooler, Robert, 177.

Portress, John, 343.

Potter tract, 307.

Powell, James Edward, Council member, 70; sent to Augusta, 68; fortifications commissioner, 75; peace commissioner, 94; signs proclamation, 95; on committees, 110, n. 11; pay as councilman, 253.

Presbyterian meeting house, 136.

President and Assistants, against Bosomworths, 56; grievances report, 81.

Preston, H., 154.

Preston, Reverend Willard, 179.

Prevost, Colonel Augustin, enters Savannah, 222; begins march to South Carolina, 228; at Port Royal, 228.

Pride of India trees, 182 and n. 140.

Pritchard, James v. Butler, James, 317.

Portsmouth, England, 24.

Proclamation, King's death, 94; read, 96.

Proctor, Doctor George V., 311.

Provincial Assembly, first, 62; qualifications of representatives, 61; members' grievances, 63.

Provincial Congress, first, 136; meeting in 1775, 201; election of delegates, 208.

Provoso, John, letter to Dunbar, 52.

Purvis, Lieutenant Colonel Arthur, 311, n. 46.

Pulaski, General Casimir, joins General Lincoln, 300.

Purrysburg, South Carolina, Houstoun visits Bryans, 224; family there, 228; General Lincoln's headquarters, 225; General Moultrie there, 228; Washington there, 278.

Quebec, fall of, 70.

Quesada, Governor, 388.

Quit rents, 85 ff., 89.

Rae, Colonel Robert, 299.

Records of Chatham County, 263, n. 155.

Rees, David, 253.

Reformed Dutch Church, 335.

Regiment, Oglethorpe's, 47, 51.

Rehm, Frederick, delegate from Chatham County, 240.

Reid's Bluff, 298.

Rendon, Don Francis, 324.

Renfrewshire, 1, n. 1; 22.

Republic of East Florida, 370 ff.

Republic of Mexico, 383.

Resources of the Southern Fields and Forests, 19, n. 27.

Revington's New York Gazette, 229.

Reynolds, John, Royal Governor, arrival in Georgia, 65; letter from Savannah, 66; meeting for Indians, 68; recalled to England, 68; addresses Assembly, 66.

Rhode Island, 124.

Richmond and Lennox, Duke of, 15.

Rivers:
Altamaha, 44, 184, 269, 291, 298; Chatooga, 267; Crooked, 51; Flint, 290; Great Ogeechee, 25, 73, 76, 92, 359; Isundiga, 268; Little Ogeechee, 30, 73, 156; Midway, 295; Mississippi, 248, 324; Newport, 92, 295; Savannah, 31, 167, 267, 268; Sapelo, 348; Satilla, 217; St. Mary's, 217; Tugaloo, 251, 267; Turtle, 101; Vernon, 30, 41, 62, 138; Pon Pon, 234, n. 99; 240; Oconee, 323; Forest, 101.

Robarts, Joseph W., 179.

Robertson, James (partner), 163.

Robertson, Archibald, 339.

Robertson, Attorney General James, 301; correspondence on Houstoun, 301 ff.

Robertson, William H., 182, n. 140.

Robinson, Pickering, council member, 65.

Rochefoucauld-Liancourt D'estissae, Francois Alexandre Frederic, Duke de la, 285.

Rollins, John F., 341, n. 54.

Rosses, 100.

Ross, Hugh, 101.

Ross, John, 104.

Ross, Professor, 27.

Ross, Thomas, executor, 101; wife, 101.

Ross, William, witness to will, 104.

Round O, 231; Houstouns there, description of, 134.

Royal Council, formation, 64; members, 65; members oath, 66; first meeting, 66; receives Indians, 71; petitions on grants, 89, 92; meetings monotonous, 92; proclamation on King's death, 95.

Royal Governors (see Reynolds, Ellis, Wright).

Royal legislature (see legislature, Georgia).

Rum in Georgia, lack of, hardship, 27; Houstoun sold, 27.

Russell, William, council member, 65.

Russia, 390 and n. 45.

Index

427

Rutledge, Edward, signs Agreement, 205; Houstoun's counsel, personal history, 272.

St. Andrew's, University of, 60 and n. 39.
St. Andrew's Society, 154 ff.
St. Augustine, 272, 350.
St. Bartholomew, massacre of, 333.
St. Christopher's (St. Kitts), 294.
St. George Island, Florida, McIntosh home on, 341; burials on, 341, n. 54.
St. John's River, Florida, 348, 369.
St. Mary's, Geogria, 336, n. 42, 342.
St. Paul's Church, Augusta, 299.
St. Philips Church, South Carolina, 161 and n. 83.
St. Simon's Island, Houstoun's lands on, 47, n. 10; description of, 47, 316.
Savannah: buzzing community, 28; demonstration for governor, 65; Reynold's letter on, 65; healthy, 94; news of King's death, 95; guard house, 110; captured by British, 126, 138, 222; in 1812, 167; peace celebration, 1815, 169; first census, 182; population 1809, 182; trees, 182; storm, 1804, 182; anti-British, 194; celebration for Declaration, 211; fires, 162, 215; inhabitants commended, 215; British enter city, 22; Washington's visit, 147, 278; incorporated a city, 275; description, 1790, 275; meeting on Jay Treaty, 284; resolutions to President, 284; market, 306; seamen's hospital, 308; assemblies, 311, 345; wardens, 144; population, 1790, 275; schools, customs, transportation, 345; entertainments, 345; inhabitants and Bulloch's death, 213; aroused over McIntosh arrest, 353.
Savannah Poor House and Hospital, 183; situation, 184.
Seagrove, James, 337, 381.
Scarbrough, William, buys Planters Bank, 166, n. 98.
Schools, Savannah, 343, 344.
Schuyler, Adomiah, 334.
Scotch Highlanders, 43, 291.
Screven, Mrs. Franklin Buchanan, 124, n. 47; 173, n. 116; 209, n. 45; 224, n. 76.
Screven, Doctor James Proctor, 288, n. 202.
Screven, Major John, 181 and n. 133.
Scringer, Mr., house, 153 and n. 56.
Seamen's hospital, 308.
Seminole War, 386.
Seneca River, 270, n. 163.
Seymour, James, 344.
Sharp, Mrs. Willoughby, 224, n. 76.
Shaw, Helen, 2.

Sherman, General William T., 180, n. 131.
Sheftal, Moses, 181.
Sheuber, Justus H., alderman, 276.
Shipley, William, secretary arts and commerce, 71.
Ships:
    Assienta, 13; Anne, Georgia colonists' ship, 17; Betsy and Nancy, 358; Brig, Ann, 195; brigantine Georgia, delegates sail on, 201; Firefly, 312; Jenny, sloop, 337; Malaparte incident, 313; Prince of Wales, Dunbar's ship, 43; Race Horse, 359; Sandwich incident, 312; Planter, 129; Port Mahon, 65; St. Andrew, 350; Lynx, 342.
Silk culture, 71.
Simpson, Attorney General James, 303.
Simpson, John, on committees, 110, n. 11; 114; John Simpson v. Robert Bremer, 197.
Simpson, William, lot on Bay street, 111.
Sinclare, Houstoun's servant, 34.
Sketch Book of the Botany of South Carolina and Georgia, 19, n. 26.
Sloane, Sir Hans, birth, 11; physician to nobility, 11; travels, 11; member Royal Society, 11; College of Surgeons, 11; created baronet, 11; death, 11, n. 8; collection of books, etc., 11, n. 8; negotiations with Dr. Houstoun, 15; donation to Trustees Garden, 15; recommends Houstoun's successor, 18; gift of garden, 16.
Slavery, prohibited in Georgia, 49.
Smallpox, Houstoun's plantation, 195.
Smith, Reverend Haddon, rector Christ Church, 102, 135.
Smith, James, 179.
Smith, John, of Medway, 113.
Smith, Lawrence, artist, 185.
Smith, Richard, 202.
Smith, Melancton, 329.
Smith, Meriwether, 229.
Social Customs, colonial, 345.
Society for the Propogation of the Gospel in Foreign Parts, 21, 54.
Society for the Propogation of Christian Knowledge, 21.
Sola bills, 33.
Solana, Don Manuel, 379.
Solomon's Lodge of Free Masons, 29, 145 ff; 157, 307.
South Carolina, Dr. Houstoun sails to, 13; colony founded, 86; sends military aid, 216; clashes with Georgia, 58; invading Georgia's rights, 31; aroused over boundary, 265; sends claim to congress, 271; provincial assembly, 31; claims source

of Savannah River, 267; repudiation of Lords Proprietors, 267; clashes in, 328.
South Carolinians, comments of Savannah, 24; visit Georgia, 195.
Southern Department, 325.
South Sea Company, Houstoun surgeon of, 11, 17; Snow lost, 13.
Southward settlements, 43.
Spain and Great Britain, 368, ff; 384.
Spanish campaign, preparation, 51; invasion, 50.
Spalding, Charles, 311, n. 44.
Spalding pattern, 389.
Spalding, James, 363.
Spalding, Thomas, 47, n. 13; experiments in sugar, 389; advises McIntosh, 389; licensed by Houstoun, 197.
Spencer, John Basil, 145.
Spencer, William, 110, n. 11.
Spiers, Alexander, Barony of Houstoun alienated to, 6.
Squares:
Chippawa, 177; Columbia, 182; Ellis, 276; Johnson, 182; Reynolds, 66, 166; St. James, 181; Market, 162.
Stamp Act, news in Georgia, 112; repeal, 113.
Standard Cyclopedia of Horticulture, 19, n. 27.
State House, Philadelphia, 204.
"Stephanian Scheme, A," 40.
Stephens, Thomas, plot to redress malcontents, 40.
Stephens, William, Trustees secretary in Georgia, invites Houstoun to dinner, 35 ff; letter to Oglethorpe about Causton, 38; keeps eyes on malcontents, 39; box story, 41; death, 61; report on Houstoun, 48.
Stephens, William, of Chatham County, letter on records episode, 261; warden, Christ Church, 264; commissioner for market, 306; in Hunt Club, 140; Bethesda trustee, 151, 153; Houstoun's executor, 159.
Steven, William (or Stevens), 279.
Stewart, Captain, 349.
Stewart, Daniel, shipmaster, father of Ann, 101.
"Stiles," 175.
Stiles, Miss Margaret Couper, 316, n. 52.
Stiles, Samuel, 359.
St. Julian, Mr., 16, 17.
Stirk, Samuel, letter on records episode, 261; vestryman, 264; alderman, 276.
Stirling Bluff, site of settlers' grant, 25.
Stirling, Hugh, emigrates to Georgia, 22; site of grant, 24; writes joint letter, 25.

Stith, William, chief justice, 263.
Stokes, Attorney General Anthony, 317.
Storr, Mrs., 187.
Stuarts, 100.
Stuart, Ann (or Stewart), witness to will, 98; left legacy, 101; wife of Hugh Ross, 101; legacy from Lady Houstoun, 101.
Stuart, Gilbert, 316, and n. 52.
Stuyvesant, Judith Bayard (Mrs. Peter), 333.
Stuyvesant, Peter, Dutch governor, 333; marries, 333.
Sugar industry, 389 ff.
Sully, Thomas, 186.
Sunbury, Georgia, Savannah's rival, port, 295; King's square, 295; sick there, 298; Houstoun brothers meet there, 298.
Supreme Court of the United States, The, 339.
Surgeons mates, 292.
Surinam, 348 ff.
Sutcliffe, John, 304.
Symmes, 330.

Tabby buildings, 46, 167.
Tannant, Edward, 294.
Tannant, Eliza Crooke (see Mrs. James Houstoun), 345, 294 and n. 8.
"Tallasee and Fat Kings," 248, 249.
Tailfer, Doctor Patrick, comes to Georgia, 22; site of grant, 24; writes joint letter, 25; distasteful to Oglethorpe, 39.
Tattnall, Josiah, Sr., involved in Philip Box incident, 115 and n. 22; council member, 121.
Tattnall, Josiah, Jr., 151.
Taverns:
Brown's Coffee House, 154, 308; Coffeehouse, 38, 143, 145; Alexander Crieghton's, 154, 345; Liberty, 345; Lucy Tondee's House, 238; Tondee's, 136, 200, 345, 348; Liberty Pole, protest meeting at, 198, n. 18.
Telfair, Alexander, planter, 175.
Telfair, Edward, on committee with Houstoun, 242; governor, and Houstoun affair, 256 ff; denounced and praised, 263; on boundary commission, 248, 264; again governor, 275; proclamation on Savannah election, 275; issues Houstoun's commission, 319, 257; on Greene welcome, 320; elected to Congress, 321.
Temperance Society, Savannah, 178.
Thanksgiving in Georgia, 50, 70.
Theater, plays at, 170, 171.
Thickness, P., early colonist, 28.
Thomas, Major Jonathan, 311.
Tobago Island, 350, 359.

Index

Tomo-chi-chi, Mico of the Yamacraws, gives land for Savannah, 31.
Tonyn, Governor Patrick, signs permit to British officers, 350; letter on McIntosh, 352.
Transportation, colonial, 344.
Treaty of Amity, Commerce, and Navigation, 284.
Treaty with Spain, 387, 388.
Trenton, New Jersey, 185, 324.
Treutlen, John Adam, elected governor, 214; alleged murder, 214; orders McIntosh produced, 360; furious over pamphlet, 364; writes Hancock, 364.
Troup, Governor George McIntosh, 369.
Trustees for Establishing the Colony of Georgia in America, 14, 25; common council of, 14; loan to Houstoun, 33; surrender charter, 64.
Trustees Garden, development in Savannah, 14; description of, 15, 20, n. 32; financial assistance for, 15; Doctor Houstoun's memorial at, 20; Declaration read at, 211.
Tuckerman, Henry, 186.
Turkey Camp, 288, n. 199.
Turner, Emily Green (Mrs. Robert Tyler Waller), 189, n. 160.
Turner, Joseph, Bethesda tutor, 282.

Union Society, 144, 156, 157.
Union and States Rights Party, 176.
University of St. Andrews, 60 and 39.
University of Edinburgh, 60 and n. 30.
United States Bank, 176.
United States Congress, debate on Laurens's affair, 229; peace proclamation, 245; ratifies Beaufort report, 271; Indian controversy, 326; clamor in, 327; recommends McIntosh arrest, 353; his case before, discharges him, 364; provides for Florida claim, 388.
United States Military Academy, 311, n. 46.
"Up-counties" and "low-counties" feud, 256.
Upper House, organizes, 72 ff.
Utrecht, Holland, 333.

Vallence, Captain, 348.
Van Brugh, Johannes Pieterse, 334.
Van Cortlandt, Olaff Stevense, 333.
Van Rensselaer, Killian, 334.
Van Sweeten, "Experiments in Animal Respiration," 10.
Vendue House, 104, 126.
Verelst, Harman, Trustee's accountant, 53; letters from Houstoun on his marriage, 45; on packets sent, 53; on wine, 55.

Vernonburg, history of, 62, 110; road to, 75; district, 73; Houstoun's property advertised, 240.
Veterans Administration, 315.
Village, The, 316.
Virginia, Governor of, 251.
Virginia Museum of Art, 142, n. 42.

Waldburger, Jacob, Bethesda trustee, 151.
Wade, Hazekiah, 243.
"Wallace," 175.
Wallace, Sir William, 340.
Wallace, James, 312.
Wallace, John, 144, n. 37.
Walton, George, call for meeting, 198; elected Continental Congress, 208; prisoner at Savannah, writes Houstoun, 225; letter on records episode, 261; elected judge, 283; appointed deputy Federal Convention, 330.
War of 1812, 167; peace, 1815, 169.
Ward, Esther, 337, n. 42.
Ward, Peter, 337, n. 42.
Waring, Miss Minna A., 160, n. 80.
Waring, Doctor William Richard, 191, 187, n. 154.
Washington, General George, army in New Jersey, 121, 230; visit to Georgia, 147, 278; aide-de-camp, Pinckney, 265; entertained by Heyward, 278; Savannah visit, 278 ff.; founder of Cincinnati, 305; Lafayette's visit to, 324; records Georgia deputies, 330; inauguration, 338; escorts Mrs. Washington, 338; box from Buchan, 340; portrait by Robertson, 340; 150th anniversary, 338, n. 46.
Washington, Mrs. George, 338.
Washington reception guests, 338.
Watch, town, 138.
Waters, "Mr.", 112.
Watson, Charles, 110, n. 11.
Watts, Robert,
Wayne, General Anthony, marches into Savannah, 237; letter on Indian "Talk," 239; asked to influence northern merchants, 273.
Wayne, Richard, writes cousin, 273.
Wells, George, 213.
Wereat, John, 139; president of council, 233; befriends McIntosh, 364.
Wesley, Reverend John, mentions Houstoun's plantation, 30; trial in Georgia, 30, 38.
West Florida, 368.
West India Company, 333, 368.
West Indies, 237.
Westerly, Long Island, 341, n. 52.
"West, Mr." of Liberty County, 319.

Weynant, Major Morrison V. R., 335, n. 41.
White Bluff, road to, 75; plantations there, 195; small pox at, 195; Houstoun's hiding place, 223; raiding party there, 223; resort, 140.
"White House," (Augusta) story, 123 ff. and n. 43.
White, Samuel, of Massachusetts, 112.
Whitefield, Reverend George, missionary in Savannah, 54; application for college lands, 110; Bethesda, 151; memorial service for, 345.
Whitefield, James, Bethesda trustee, 151.
Whitefield, Thomas W., 311.
Wilkinson, John, 323.
Williams, Richard F., 180.
Williams, Thomas F., of Connecticut, 364.
Williams, William, 30.
Williamson, Mary Anne (Mrs. James Edmund Houstoun), 310.
Williamson, Colonel Macajah, joins Houstoun, 217; at Fort Tonyn, 217, 219.
Williamson, Richard F., 314.
Williamston, North Carolina, 206.
Wilson, John B., 290, n. 208.
Wilson, Mrs. Millar, 341, n. 54.
Wood, Joseph, 213.
Woodlands, 190, n. 167.
Woodruff, Aaron Dickerson, 160.
Woodruff, Aaron Dickerson, Jr., 185, n. 149.
Woodruff, Elias, 160.
Woodruff, Reverend George Houstoun, 161, n. 82.
Woodruff Family Papers, 161.
Woodruff, George Whitefield, marriage, 160; ancestry and birth, 161; children, 161, n. 82; leaves Savannah, 185; death and property, 191; obituary, 191; buys Houstoun home, 288; heirs, 191.
Woodruff, Mrs. George W. (Jean Houstoun), birth, 136; marriage, 160; death and heirs, 192.
Woodruff, Joseph, delegate from Chatham, 240.
Woodruff, Mary Joline (Mrs. Elias), 160.
Worcester, Massachusetts, 198, n. 18.
Wright, Sir James, royal governor, arrives in Georgia, 69; news of King's death, 95; appoints Sir Patrick Houstoun, Jr., 107; absent from province, 118; returns, 118; house needs repair, 118; letters to Dartmouth, 119; arrested, breaks parole, 120, 207; asked for day of prayer, 137; proclamation, 195; strives to hold Georgia, 199; rejects Jones's election, election, 241; letter on Houstoun, 318.
Wylly, Alexander, speaker of house, 294; Stamp Act letter, 112, 315.
Wylly, Mrs. Alexander (Susannah Crooke), 294, 315.
Wylly, Alexander Campbell, 315.
Wylly, Mrs. Alexander Campbell (Margaret Armstrong), 315.
Wylly, Mrs. Mary, 289.
Wylly, Richard, 367; commissioned major, 214; letter on records' episode, 261; vestryman, 264; judge for election, 275; debt paid to, 289.
Wylly, Susannah Campbell, broken engagement, 315; parents, 315; portrait, 316; death and burial, 316.

Yamacraw, 31, 111, 288, 337, 296, n. 14.
Yellow fever epidemic, 337, n. 42.
Yonge, Henry, surveyor, 65; legislator, 73.
Young, Dr. Charles, physician at Rosdue, 211, 293.
Young, Jane, 294 and n. 8.
Young, Thomas, Scotsman, involved in box incident, 114.
Young, William, legislator, 117; speaker, 118.

Zespedes, Governor Vizenke Manuel de, 249.
Zouberbuhler, Reverend Bartholomew, 55, n. 30, 97.
Zubly, Reverend, John Joachim, sermon, 136; legislator, 118; elected to Continental Congress, 201; leaves for Philadelphia, 201; debate with Chase, 203; leaves Congress, 205; banished from Georgia, 205; accused of correspondence with Wright, 205; baptizes Bryan child, 209, death, 205; Yamacraw property, 205.

www.ingramcontent.com/pod-product-compliance
Lightning Source LLC
Chambersburg PA
CBHW011720220426
43664CB00023B/2890